# DELACROIX

# DELACROIX

RENÉ HUYGHE

*Member of the Académie Française*

*56 colour plates, 405 black and white illustrations*

HARRY N. ABRAMS, INC. *Publishers*

*To the most faithful of Delacroix's friends after his death,*

*the Comtesse de Waresquiel,*

*Madame Raymond Escholier, née Léouzon-le-Duc, and*

*Monsieur Raymond Escholier, who for forty years has worked so that*

*the glory of Delacroix should stand revealed at his Centenary*

Library of Congress Catalog Card Number: 63-19565

Translated from the French by Jonathan Griffin



Printed and bound in France by Intergraphic

# CONTENTS

# I THIS WAS A MAN

'Ah, how I would like to come back in a hundred years, to find out what they think of me!'

DELACROIX[1]

pl 34 'MY TOMB WILL BE in the cemetery of Père-Lachaise, on the height, in a position somewhat apart. No emblem, nor bust, nor statue will be placed on it. My tomb will be copied with the utmost accuracy from the Antique, or Vignola, or Palladio. . . .'

On the height . . . in a position somewhat apart. . . .

This haughty and solitary image, by which Delacroix, rejecting the affectations of romanticism, himself decided what should be his face after death, occurs in the opening lines of his will.

The constantly increasing frailty of his body, undermined by illness and finally by haemorrhages, had made it clear that the end of his adventure as man and artist was at hand. Ten days after writing these lines Delacroix died—it was 13 August 1863—at seven in the morning of a heavy summer day, after a long night of
pl 32 agony during which he could only clasp the hand of his faithful servant Jenny.
He died in the provincial, old-fashioned calm of his house at the corner of the
pl 19 Place Furstenberg. Its windows opened on the garden flanked by the studio he had had built. This garden was continued beyond the party wall, by another. It was surrounded by old buildings, not very high, in which, as evening fell, he could watch the lights coming on. Both house and garden were on land which had belonged till recently to the ancient abbey of Saint-Germain-des-Prés. The bells of its church had just rung the morning Angelus.

On Monday, 17 August, which was the day after the *Fête Impériale*, the neighbourhood was roused by a concourse of friends, officials and onlookers; these, as noon approached, assembled in the small square, usually silent and deserted, in front of the house porch, now transformed into a mortuary chapel. Soon the procession moved off towards the nearby church of Saint-Germain-des-Prés. Here huge black hangings festooned the romanesque columns, leaving still visible the paintings of Flandrin, which seemed a flat contradiction of the dead man's work. And indeed the Institut inexorably hemmed him in, for the pall bearers were Nieuwerkerke (Superintendant of the Beaux-Arts), Jouffroy the sculptor (at that time President of the Académie des Beaux-Arts), Gisors the architect and

Flandrin himself, while a delegation of green-coated academicians followed.

'Who are they burying?' asked the passers-by. 'Monsieur Delacroix . . . you know, the artist. The gentleman from the Institut. The one you used to see going by in the morning, buttoned up tightly in his overcoat, and wearing his huge stock. . . . He didn't look very strong, poor man. He would be on his way to paint that chapel in Saint-Sulpice, the one that was closed for such a long time while he was working there, and was re-opened two years ago. . . .'

There was the grinding of the wheels as the hearse moved forwards, the clacking of the hooves of the black horses on the roadway; and the shuffling of the cortège stood out against a silence soon mitigated by low voices—and by the slow tramp of the four companies from the Garde Nationale sent to pay tribute to a Commander of the Légion d'Honneur. Soon there would be several speeches. It was hot.

Next day the press spoke of a 'considerable attendance' and of a 'respectful crowd', but in *Le Temps*, a few days later, Théodore Pelloquet made this bitter correction: 'The procession which accompanied the illustrious departed to his last dwelling-place was not very numerous.' Some people had been shocked by the absence of any carriage, or of any representative of the Imperial court.

Two years before this, on the 21 July 1861, the Chapel of the Holy Angels in Saint-Sulpice had been unveiled. For nearly four consecutive years Delacroix had devoted himself to it, and for its sake he had moved back to the Left Bank where his youth had been spent, that he might be near his place of work. He had submitted himself to the strictest time-table in order to finish the enormous task, and the only interruptions had been when his strained health broke down or when he stole off to his country place at Champrosay: even from there he often came pls 24, 25 up in the early morning, as he had long been accustomed to do, to put in a day's work.

Already in 1853, at Christmas, when he was engaged on the decoration of the Hôtel de Ville, he had written in his *Journal:* 'I told Rémusat how I'm always called at dawn, and that even at this time of year I hurry off to my work through frost and snow with the greatest pleasure and enthusiasm.'

Baudelaire[2] confirms this: 'In the last days of his life all the things that are usually called pleasure had disappeared; they had all been replaced by a single bitter, exacting and terrible one—work, which had become not merely a passion but might well be called a frenzy.'

## *Attitude to Society*

He did also—without enthusiasm but with the discipline of a man of the world— pls 10, 12 conform to the rites of social life. He was fully aware of the situation of which, later, Manet was also to be a victim: the unpleasant position of being considered a revolutionary, or even a maniac bent on destroying the most sacred traditions, when in reality—in the case of both men—a bourgeois upbringing and an innate love of correctness made them long for public acceptance. A man lives in society, in a definite circle whose rules he knows and observes; anyone who engages in a vain struggle against them and wastes his energy on this must be crazy. The best guarantee of the liberty that is essential—the freedom of the inner life and of the creative activity in which it expresses itself—is surely the neutrality of other people, which is got by refraining from offending them. Delacroix had also discovered that, if life is a struggle in which all one's forces must be thrown on to the side where one's *raison d'être* is involved, the wise man will calculate and economize those forces; he will then see that titles, honours and high position establish recognition for one's work—establish it on foundations which, though morally brittle, do in fact stand. To provoke other people gratuitously by seeming not to conform to their values, to attempt to impose one's work on them by its virtue alone (which they will not yet be able to perceive), would be naïve and Quixotic—especially at a time when to cause scandal had not yet become a sort of conformism. Delacroix consented to look as if he were playing the game of the others, that he might be able to impose on them his own.

It was not vanity but policy that made Delacroix accelerate his victory over the sheeplike public, offering himself eight times as a candidate for membership of
pl 8 the Académie des Beaux-Arts—which outrageously rejected him again and
again, from 1837 to 1854, and is now so proud to count him as one of its members.

Similarly when, thanks to his friendships in Bonapartist circles (and partic-
pl 21 ularly to his cousin and mistress Madame de Forget), the accession of the Prince-
President opened for him the way to official favours, he did not feel obliged to despise these: he tried to obtain 'an honourable situation'; he became a member of the municipal commission; for a moment there was talk of making him a senator and he put up no resistance—far from it; he even, in 1849, applied for such important posts as that of Director of the Musée du Louvre, or of the Gobelins factory, and later, in 1855, he considered the Directorship of the Beaux-Arts. But he gave up when he saw that the intrigues would absorb him, and that his peace of mind would suffer more from these than it could gain from their success. In September 1849 he had written to Madame de Forget: 'I have examined and re-examined myself and quite definitely do not find in me the stuff of a Director. I have lost my sleep ever since that idiotic idea came into my head. . . . So please let it drop, once and for all.'

Apart from this fit of ambition which in 1849 nearly entangled him, Delacroix also took constant care to make a good impression in the various official or society circles on which the progress of his career might depend. This was surely better than if he had indulged in those untimely and spectacular anti-social gestures by which the Impressionists nearly succeeded in obstructing the development of their art through depriving themselves of any State commission. It was thanks to the official commissions which resulted from his wise policy—carried out at no excessive cost—that Delacroix was able to display his genius as a great decorative painter and was, paradoxically, made free of the walls and ceilings of the Chambre des Députés, the Luxembourg, the Hôtel de Ville and the Louvre, not to speak of the churches; and yet he never for a moment modified the principles of his art, but continued to shock the conventional.

This diplomatic façade of his must not be allowed to deceive us: he himself was not taken in by the men and women whom he met, and behind that exquisite cold courtesy of his, which protected him from fools while seeming to make concessions to them, he was judging them; he was judging life. After one
pl 23 dinner-party he commented on the hostess, Madame Villot, that she had 'plunged

into fashionable life, which gives her no society except that of the most futile and boring people.'[3] He was no less bitterly lucid in his views of official circles: on the 17 April 1854, returning from the Elysée, to which he had been invited by Napoleon III, he noted: 'Profound boredom at the very thought of attending this grind. I brought away with me the usual feeling of bitterness and contempt for myself at being mixed up with all these worthless people.'

Those who failed to see beyond the aspect of him which he revealed to others in society could not praise too highly his ease of manner and his charm. This purely external appearance, which was all that many of his contemporaries saw of him, has been well depicted by Arsène Houssaye in his *Confessions*:[4]

'Eugène Delacroix was the gayest, most stimulating, most luminous guest one could possibly have. Just as being an artist did not prevent him from being a man of the world, being a man of the world did not prevent him from being an artist.... He talked of everything like a man who has travelled... through all the worlds of the imagination. There is no great poet from Homer to Byron with whose works he was not familiar, no philosopher in whose card castles he had not lived, no artist whose studio he had not been through.... His mind was so subtle that it understood everything at the first phrase. If this was boring, he would interrupt; but if the man was a good talker, he let him go on, for he loved eloquence for eloquence's sake.... He knew everything and knew how to forget —which is the summit of knowledge.... He was by turns severe like art itself and gay like wit itself.... Eugène Delacroix was no less delightful as a host than as a guest, his table was exquisite; and around it, dressed in black, would be seated a whole Olympus of the demi-gods of art: painters, poets, and musicians.'

Théophile Gautier also spoke of the seductive charm of the personality which Delacroix displayed to satisfy other people, but was more keenly aware of the real being beyond it, who by this means assured his autonomy, and whose strange secret presence now and then filtered through. It is in his *History of Romanticism* that he has left us this famous and striking portrait:

I, page 57

'His pale olive complexion, his thick dark hair which remained so to the end of his life, his fierce eyes with their feline expression, shielded by long lashes whose points curved back, his subtle, thin, slightly wrinkled lips over the magnificent teeth and under the shadow of the slight moustache, his powerful chin with its robust width emphasizing its stubbornness, these composed a face possessed of a wild, strange, exotic, almost disquieting beauty. It suggested some Indian Maharajah who, after being perfectly educated at Calcutta as a gentleman, has come, dressed in European clothes, to inspect the civilization of Paris. Those nervous, sensitive, mobile features of his scintillated with wit, genius and passion.' And Gautier adds:

'No-one was more attractive than he, when he was willing to take the trouble. He could soften the fierceness of his expression with a beautifully urbane smile.... He was easy, velvety and winning, like one of those tigers whose supple, formidable grace he excelled at rendering, and in the drawing-rooms everybody used to say: "What a pity so charming a man should paint such pictures!"'

The portrait painted by Arsène Houssaye in his *Confessions*[5] is less well known (and, it must be admitted, deservedly so), but is worth quoting for the confirmation it supplies from a later period in the master's life:

'What a strange charm there was in that face with its broken lines! There was in it something of the rebel angel who has redeemed his soul by the greatness of his genius. . . . His hair, still black, still thick, shows the persistence of his youth; those deep eyes, with their shading lashes and lids, defy the rays of the sun; the subtle nose, so firmly in its place, has nostrils that quiver with impatience; the mouth is disdainful, yet kindness is revealed there. The cheeks are furrowed by the passions of art. The soul is withdrawn, yet ready at the slightest shock to explode like thunder.'

pl 9 There is, then, both the façade of Delacroix, the man of the world, member of the Institut, the Commander of the Légion d'Honneur, phlegmatic, master of himself to the point of impassivity, sometimes impenetrable, at others brilliant, and the inner Delacroix, secret, walled up, but revealed every now and then by the scintillating glance filtering through from behind close quivering eyelids, by a contraction of the strong, hard jaws, by a certain swift tremor of the muscles which his nervous system has electrified. Taciturn, laconic, with thin sealed lips, economical of words (which would tire the weak throat from which he suffered), he would sometimes, after the initial reticence, let loose a spate of speech, which gave expression to his tumultuous thought, and left him exhausted.

Was this conventional person, in whom a disquieting stranger emerged only in flashes, really the leader of the romantics, as public opinion has delighted to depict him? Here was no red waistcoat, such as that which spread over the excellent Gautier's growing paunch: instead, a strictly buttoned-up frock-coat fitting tightly over the slender chest. This—with the head rising proudly upon a silk cravat whose ample knots were often, in addition, covered by the thick scarf indispensable to a man so vulnerable to the cold, and the walk, nervous yet with a thoroughbred precision in its movements,—made up an elegant appearance (though he did not, as is often imagined, seem frail).

An unpublished manuscript in my possession, which is contemporary and is signed A.S. (standing perhaps for Alfred Sensier?) warns us against any such misconception:

'He looked tall, his shoulders were not narrow. . . . He did not suggest, when one saw him, a person who was cossetted or convalescent. . . . He was thin, and yet his bone structure was strong and well proportioned. . . . A highly nervous genius, native courage, full of passions under a sheath of reserve, needing only the spark of some sympathetic or stimulating word to set it going with confidence and abandon.' Such is the portrait drawn by this objective witness. The chief impression Delacroix made was that of an aristocrat, accustomed to self-control and able to keep his distance. When he was already getting on in years, he could fascinate his young cousin Riesener, who later became Madame Lauwick: at a reception at the Tuileries, to which she was taken by her father, she met her illustrious relative and was so dazzled by him that she hardly noticed the Emperor. It is true that Delacroix, dressed in his green uniform and wearing a sword, offered her his arm. She remembered also the refinement of his way of speaking, such that he even slurred the 'r's as, in his childhood, he had heard men of fashion under the Directoire do—and, later, Englishmen.

To get an even better idea of how unsuited Delacroix was to the part of the revolutionary leader, for which people cast him, opposite Ingres as leader of the classicists, we need only consider the actual meeting between the two men, of which the memoirs of Maxime du Camp have preserved for us a precious record:[6]

'A banker who was imperfectly aware of the quarrels dividing the French School of painting had had the unfortunate idea of gathering several artists at his table, including Ingres and Delacroix. Delacroix was received politely, Ingres treated with honour. The short, untidy, intolerant little man, for whom world history stopped short at Raphael, with his narrow, stubborn face and awkward speech, legs too short, stomach excessive and hands too large, had a high opinion of his own importance and was conscious of being a master. Wherever he was he dominated, did not ask anyone's name and saw in those about him nothing but admirers. They sat down at table; towards the middle of the meal Ingres began to show signs of impatience—he had just learned that Delacroix was among the guests. . . . He, the orthodox *par excellence*, to be sitting at the same table as that heretic, that renegade, and partaking of the same meal! He was disturbed and rolled his eyes furiously. Delacroix, upon whom his glance had fallen several times, had adopted the stiff expression usual with him when he did not feel at ease. Ingres tried to contain himself, but could not. After dinner, taking with him a full cup of coffee, he abruptly approached Eugène Delacroix, who was standing in front of the fireplace, and said to him: "Monsieur! drawing is honesty! Monsieur! drawing is honour!" As he spoke he jerked so much that he upset the cup of coffee over his shirt and waistcoat. "That's too much!" he exclaimed, and then, seizing his hat, announced: "I am going; I will not stay here any longer to be insulted!" People crowded round him and tried to calm him down, to persuade him to stay: in vain. When he had nearly reached the door, he turned: "Yes, Monsieur, it is honour! Yes, Monsieur, it is honesty!" Delacroix had remained impassive.'

Where is the romantic's lack of restraint?

It was there, hidden under the impassivity acquired through long discipline. The clear-sighted observers have noted it; they could see the dualism in Delacroix's personality—that artificial correctness of his, closely controlled in proportion to the violence of the seething within. But he reserved this violence for other uses than vain demonstrations: his work lay waiting. Chesneau says perceptively:

'Under an acquired courtesy, the result of training and of social necessity, he had trouble in hiding an acuteness of sensibility, a sensual ardour, a vehemence of passion which kindled his eyes to flame.'

And Baudelaire has summed up, in a single lightning phrase:

'A volcanic crater artistically concealed beneath bouquets of flowers.'[7]

Not only did his personal appearance betray his dual nature, not only did the assumed and conventional coldness, which was the first thing one met with, imperfectly conceal the flames of the furnace within, but the same contrasts were confirmed by the way he received people in his studio.

Various people, among them Piron and Baudelaire, have described the studio at 54 (now 58) rue Notre-Dame-de-Lorette which he occupied for so many years—
from 1845[8] until December 1857 when he moved to his last studio at 6 Place pl 17
Furstenberg. It was difficult to get in, for the place was fiercely guarded by his
servant Jenny, who was well aware of the value of her master's time and peace of pl 32
mind. The very first impression was one of surprise: in contrast to the equatorial

temperature imposed by his threatened health, the severe, almost glacial, look of the room showed the same desire for sobriety, for spareness, as did his dress and manner. Here is Baudelaire's description:

'The eye was first struck by a sober solemnity and by the austerity characteristic of the old school. . . . Here were no rusty suits of armour, no Malayan creeses, no ancient Gothic ironmongery, no jewellery, no tinsel, no bric-a-brac.'[9]

In 1852, in an article in *L'Illustration*, A. J. Du Pays expressed the same astonishment:

'If one's imagination had dreamed, in advance, of a whole world of rich spoils, costumes, armour, curiosities of every kind from the Orient and the Middle Ages, it was mistaken. The walls are covered with paintings and sketches, and one is somewhat surprised to see, among these paintings, a copy by the artist himself from Raphael.'

In point of fact there were four of these, as the catalogue of the sale after Delacroix's death bears witness,—in particular, a copy of the Child Jesus from *La Belle Jardinière*, which fetched one of the highest prices of all: 5,000 francs.
pl 13 The engraving accompanying the *Illustration* article shows some utilitarianly simple tables and chairs, the indispensable stove with an enormously long pipe, the pictures either stacked in piles or crowding the walls, and a few plaster casts, all in the cold light from the window, unmitigated by any curtain.

Here Delacroix, circumspect and reserved, awaited the visitor. Niggardly of his time and of his words, he was slow to involve himself in conversation. On this too, Gautier supplies definite testimony:[10]

'He always began by intending to keep silence, or at most to interject a few words into the conversation; for already he had the beginnings of that throat infection which killed him in the end, though he fought it off for a long time by a carefully thought out and resolutely maintained régime. But very soon he would be yielding to temptation and developing, in the most expressive language, the cleverest and—surprisingly enough—the wisest ideas.'

To this well known testimony I cannot resist adding another, which has passed unnoticed since it lies in the files of a provincial paper, the *Union de l'Ouest;* here Victor Pavie, a member of the romantic circle, wrote, a few months after the master's death, 9 March 1864:

'It was in a frock coat that this dyed-in-the-wool romantic painted, with that nervous wrist of his moving so swiftly, tautened by the impatient summons of his brush. . . . It was in his accents, his gestures, the play of his voice and the lively and unexpected colour of his phrases that his conversation, though sparing of metaphor and using a small vocabulary, sparkled. . . . I can still see, darting from those veiled eyes of his, the twin flashes which used to set his palette on fire. . . .'

So we have a double Delacroix,—the one half-turned towards the world of people and offering it an exquisite but distant politeness, and the other, that of his self-communing and of his deep recesses, preserving and even heightening the insatiable ardours which had produced the fever of his youth. This fever did not abate: it consumed him more and more, but he closed over it. At first projected outwards, it gradually withdrew and folded in upon itself, as the result of wounds of which little is known. One day in 1844, in the presence of his pupil and collaborator from Toulouse, Louis de Planet, who has recorded this in his

*Souvenirs*,[11] he allowed himself a moment of abandon: after mentioning the strange suicide of Gros, and that of Léopold Robert, in spite of what seemed to be success all along the line, Delacroix added: 'Well, everyone has his troubles, his struggles. . . . It's a very sad thing, humanity, and defies imagination.' As he said this, Planet adds rather naïvely, 'He looked very gloomy and I could see the moment coming when I should have to cheer him up.'

## *Friendship—Love—Family*

To Delacroix human relationships had brought disillusion. Friendship, in the first place. He had given himself up to it as an adolescent, with an incredible fervour which comes out in many passages of his letters to Soulier, Pierret and Guillemardet—those companions of his youth with whom he had regularly fore-gathered on New Year's Eve. Year by year, from 1817 onwards, in wash drawings (in many of which the fire of punch seems to set the shadows dancing), he gave permanence to the memory of these gatherings, young hearts beating together in affectionate companionship. On the 6 November 1818, when he was twenty, he wrote to J. B. Pierret: pl 16

'The tears come into my eyes when I think of my isolation and, at the same time, of all those acquaintances who have showed some fondness for me. I am not happy, not really happy, except when I am with a friend. The hours that I must pass with him are my treasure, the only one that endures in my memory: they are my luxuries and my real wealth.'

Nearly ten years later, he began a letter (dated 'Tours, September', of which only the second part, written a few weeks later on 20 October, has been printed by Joubin[12]) with these lines:

'The joy I feel when somebody hands me a letter that has just come can only be compared to the most charming emotions of the most charming of passions.'

But with the passing of years the chilling experience of disappointments, disenchantments and disagreements (often kept alive by the jealous and exclusive devotion of Jenny Le Guillou), accumulated, until nothing was left but old habits, and an apparent cordiality masked an irremediable coldness—with occasional, nostalgic moments of affection that only made the loss of illusions more painfully clear. While he often took a melancoly pleasure in reminiscing with his friends, he confesses in his *Journal* on 2 May 1853:

'I am isolated now among these old friends! There are any amount of things they simply cannot forgive me—first and foremost the advantages fortune gives me over them.'

And in the same year, on 14 December, after coming home from a dinner through the frost and under 'a wonderful moon', he comments sadly:

'Could it really be the same Pierret I was walking arm in arm with? What fire there used to be in our friendship! How much ice there is now!'

But he had too much self-control to let the extent of his disillusion be seen. It was possible, at the time of his death, for Baudelaire to suggest:

'It was as if Delacroix had reserved the whole of that virile and deep sensibility of his for the austere experience of friendship. . . . While he did not like to be disturbed for the sake of trifles, he could show himself helpful, courageous and warm-hearted when it was a question of something important. Those who knew him well had many occasions to appreciate his truly English loyalty, punctiliousness and reliability in his relations with others. While he was exacting towards other people, he was no less severe towards himself.'

Loss of illusions! Perhaps that was what emerged most clearly from his experience. Driven by his insatiable aspirations, he had hurled himself into life like a cannon ball. Everything conspired to slow him down, rein him in and disappoint him in his thirst for the absolute. And since there was nothing he hated more than mediocrity, he withdrew. On his advanced positions he maintained a thin curtain of politeness to protect his withdrawal into himself. There he lurked like a wounded beast in its lair.

But love: surely there was that, at least? As an adolescent he had rushed to meet it, with the same fervour that he brought to everything. His ardour was kindled almost at random and quickly felt itself deceived. Disenchantment again! In a series of youthful letters of his, recently discovered by M. Alfred Dupont,[13] we can see him at the age of seventeen pacing up and down under a girl's window until he arouses the suspicion of an Austrian sentry—for this was when Paris was occupied by the Allies. Two years later, in 1817, he fell in love with a young
pl 66 English girl, Elisabeth Salter: he did not have far to go to find her, for she was
pl 4 living under the same roof, that of his sister, Madame de Verninac, at 114 rue de l'Université, where she worked as a maid. . . . His passion flared up: he speaks of it ecstatically in his letters; those which he wrote to her in English turned up a few years ago and would be worth publishing.

In 1822 came the turn of Julie, '*la Cara*',[14] occasion of a dramatic conflict with his friend, Soulier, whose mistress she was. 'What a division! Oh, heaven, the madness of it!' Then came his liaison, which lasted nearly fifteen years, with
pl 22 Madame Dalton,[15] for whom in 1825 he painted *Tam O'Shanter*. She, indeed, was a Frenchwoman, but married to an Englishman; and his attachment to her seems to have been a deep one. It involved a fresh conflict with Soulier, who early in 1830 conceived a 'passing infatuation' for her, thus taking his revenge for what had happened before: in another still unpublished series of letters, which reveals this hitherto unknown drama, Delacroix exclaims that Soulier has 'treated as a pastime without consequence something that occupied my heart and imagination almost exclusively', and he reproaches his friend 'with having given a bitter taste for ever to a sentiment that was my only happiness in the midst of the insipid life I live. . . .' 'I find the world as it is too insupportable,' he confessed in another letter from this series, so long unknown to the historians of Delacroix.

pl 20 Then there was his affair with Marie-Elisabeth Montchablon, the wife of Ingres' pupil Clément Boulanger (and later of Cavé, Chef de Division of the Beaux-Arts). She was herself a painter who had received the Salon medal and was well thought of among the romantic painters, and also the author of a book to which Delacroix wrote a preface. Much that has been written about their relationship needs correction. She went with Delacroix to Belgium in September 1839, and left him there, but this episode by no means ended their friendship.[16]

Possessed, like all creatures of high breeding, of an extreme sensibility and modesty, Delacroix made no parade of his love affairs. But in the part of his *Journal* written when he was very young, especially at a time when preparatory work for the *Massacre at Chios* caused a procession of lovely girls through his studio, there are many notes revealing the temptations and opportunities presented by his models. The result has been a wrong idea of the importance of love in his life: it has often been considered merely ancillary, on the ground that at nineteen he fell in love with his sister's maid, and also because a false interpretation has sometimes been given to his trusting and grateful affection for his servant Jenny,[17] whom he sadly described as 'the only human being whose heart is mine without reserve'. A touching picture of his relations with her occurs in a well known passage from Baudelaire's *Art Romantique*:

'One day, it was a Sunday, I saw Delacroix in the Louvre with that old servant of his who worked for him and looked after him devotedly for thirty years; and the elegant, subtle, learned man was taking the trouble to point out and explain the mysteries of Assyrian sculpture to the excellent woman—who indeed was listening attentively.'[18]

The fact is that Delacroix, hard pressed by his passion for work, by his weakening health and—a factor not to be forgotten in spite of his discretion about it—by his financial situation, which for a long time was almost desperate, soon began to keep his distance from absorbing liaisons. A letter, also unpublished, written on 1 May 1830 to his nephew, Charles de Verninac, sums up the situa- pl 27
tion lucidly and ironically:

'A woman is only a woman, always basically very like the next one. . . . This delicious passion . . . can destroy a man in the nicest possible way: the lover's life, especially when one's in love with two or three women, more or less absorbs all one's faculties, and in this situation nothing is so essential as that income of 20,000 a year which I expect from my fairy godmother—the ungrateful hussy.'

He shied away from marriage, being too intent on keeping complete liberty in order to devote himself to his work. Here too Baudelaire is the clearest witness:[19]

'Delacroix had made painting into his only muse, his only mistress, his sole and sufficient passion. Certainly women had meant much to him in the tumultuous times of his youth . . . but long before his death he had excluded them from his life. . . . He considered a woman as an *objet d'art*, delightful and stimulating but—if one allowed her on to the threshold of one's heart—a disobedient and troubling kind of *objet d'art*, one that would gluttonously devour a man's time and strength. . . .'

In writing this, Baudelaire was simply echoing conversations he had had with the painter, who himself wrote, in his article on Prud'hon:[20]

'Painting, according to Michelangelo, is a jealous mistress: she requires the whole of a man.'

In Prud'hon's tragic old age Delacroix found the confirmation of his fears:

'Poor Prud'hon experienced the truth of this and paid for it, for it cost him his peace of mind during almost all his life.'

And yet, although Delacroix was reluctant to engage in adventures and preferred them to be transient ones—indeed in 1830, for instance, he described himself
as 'on the spree with Mérimée, Beyle' and others—this did not prevent him from pls 175, 177

dreaming of finding a woman who would be the right companion for him. Already in 1823 he noted:[21]

'Now I think of it, the severest wound life inflicts is this inevitable solitude to which our hearts are condemned. A wife who is one's equal is the greatest of all blessings. I would rather she were my superior in every way than the reverse.'

Although he is fond of including in his letters and notebooks sceptical, disillusioned and even caustic remarks about women, in the Voltairean tradition which was so dear to him, he sometimes allowed his writing to betray a feeling of regret for a life in which his heart might have had full play. It is enough to refer to an entry in his *Journal* on 29 May 1853, a brief confession which seems to go very
pls 23, 15 deep. He mentions the wife of his friend Villot, keeper of the Louvre, who was now his neighbour at Champrosay and with whom his relations had in recent years become decidedly cold; he has been 'reflecting deeply about her qualities, how devoted she is in her own way, the affection she has for me, and which I return', and then he adds: 'There are people who are born united: the thought of her always delights me and moves me.'

In this way Delacroix sometimes, when alone, confessed to himself the repressed impulses of his heart.

Already on 26 April 1824 he wrote down in his diary a heartfelt comment which contains one of his essential longings: 'I wish I could identify my soul with another person's.' It was a desire which, in spite of the hopes and illusions of his youth, he only managed to fulfil in friendship, and only expected to satisfy through painting—yet perhaps he hoped that one day he might have the luck to
pl 21 slake it by some great love affair. His liaison with his cousin, the Baronne de Forget (daughter of General de Lavalette, who had made a famous escape from imprisonment), remained practically unknown until Raymond Escholier wrote a book about it.[22] To this book there is little to add. But it seems worth noting that an unpublished letter to his nephew, Charles de Verninac, proves that Delacroix was already paying court to *la bonne cousine* by 1 May 1830; apparently this did not lead to a liaison until 1834, for it was from that date that Madame de Forget instructed her executor, de Féligonde, to destroy her correspondence with her cousin.[23] There are many signs suggesting that by 1839-40 Delacroix was already somewhat disillusioned. And in 1846 all he could express to his '*consolatrice*' was his '*tendresse la plus vive*'. And yet he had found in her a human being in close harmony with him. When Abel Hermant, who knew her in her old age (shortly before her death, which took place as late as 1886), describes her as 'affable and cold, grave, almost austere, secret'[24] this might almost be a sketch of Delacroix himself. Their closeness rendered his disillusion the more deep—indeed irremediable.

To find the causes of this would be to penetrate Delacroix's innermost thoughts on the meaning of life. One factor in it, certainly, was his disappointment at discovering that a human being so close to him—perhaps the closest of all—was nonetheless a stranger to his chief preoccupations: her perpetual flurry of social activity, her submission to the futile rules of society (to what Delacroix once described to Soulier as '*les sottes obligations du monde*') and her perpetual attempts to steer her cousin's and lover's career towards an official success (which partly explains, as we have seen, the ambitions to which he gave way for a time just before 1850)—all this doubtless contributed, along with certain infidelities, to the renewal of his scepticism about human affections.

Two anecdotes, current in Delacroix's family, throw light on the sad ending of this love affair. The first tells of a day when Madame de Forget had climbed the steep and narrow staircase from the courtyard to his rooms in the Place Furstenberg and had rung the door bell, but he, to avoid meeting her, escaped through his garden and through the covered passage leading from it to the street. The second tells of her last visit to him when he was dying. The rumour had spread that his death was approaching, and on about 10 August when one of his colleagues in the Institut, sent by the Académie des Beaux-Arts, came to enquire, Delacroix refused to receive him and, according to Silvestre, muttered 'with inexpressible melancholy' that 'I have been bored enough, insulted enough, made to suffer enough by those people, my God!' One might have thought that a visit from his beloved cousin would bring him some compensating comfort; and indeed she also rushed to see him, but with a fashionable woman's desire to be always smartly dressed she had got herself up in an enormous and unmanageable crinoline, so that she had great trouble in getting through the narrow door of the room in which Delacroix would soon be lying dead. From his bed he greeted her with a weary and disillusioned gesture that expressed the irremediable exhaustion of body and soul. Perhaps he then recalled how one day he had jotted on a sheet of paper [published in the supplement to his *Journal*]:[25] 'Women are only interested in amusements and dress...', and on another page:[26]

'"Give them", says Lord Byron, "sweets and a mirror and they will be perfectly happy"; it is true, frills and furbelows are their element; they have a horror of serious people and of anything that is serious.'

Yet we must on no account think of Delacroix as a misogynist: even though he felt he could not confide the burden of his soul to women, at least he sought in them one of the enchantments of his life. Arsène Houssaye, in his *Confessions*,[27] gives us valuable evidence of this:

'He was full of tenderness . . . he adored women: he never painted them without giving them the superb attitudes of goddesses. As early as 1836, when I saw him at the house of the Princess Belgiojoso, he could not keep away from the ladies' corner. . . . He used to say that a woman has the best eye for an artist's geinus.'

Did not Delacroix endorse this judgment when, late in life, he wrote in his *Journal* on 2 July 1855: 'The society of women has always an infinite charm, in spite of my retirement'?

But what about family attachments? It was to these, apparently, that Delacroix remained most faithful. But here also deep wounds were inflicted on him—by death. In 1855, in a letter dated 15 October, he could write to his cousin Lamey:

'You are mother, aunt and sister to me, and what makes me very happy is that I, too, remind you of those who have been dear to you. . . .

It is possible that this implacable series of amputations which Delacroix suffered so early in life permanently injured his sensibility, so that it withdrew into itself

and ceased to be trusting and expansive. The sadness that came from this cause is expressed in a letter of 20 November 1847 to George Sand, when his aunt,
pl 26 Madame Riesener, had just died:

'As the human beings necessary to our existence disappear one by one they take with them, each, a world of feelings which cannot be revived with anyone else. . . .'

pl 3 Think of it! As early as 1805 he lost his father, after watching, as a child, his impressive career as a *Préfet,* first at Marseilles, then at Bordeaux where he died.
pl 5 Then, in 1807, the younger of his two brothers, Henri, on whom, as an officer in the Napoleonic wars, all his childhood dreams of glory concentrated, was killed at the battle of Friedland. In 1814, 3 September, came the death of his mother, who as a widow had moved to Paris (rue de l'Université): it was on the anniversary of her death that Delacroix in 1822 began to keep his *Journal,*[28] seeking refuge in this solitary self-communion and transferring to it his centre of gravity, as though already to cease exposing himself to the assaults of the outer world. He was not destined to marry, or to have children; but he watched closely over the entry into adult life—just after his own—of his nephew Charles de Verninac, only two years younger than himself, and looked after him like a younger brother, almost like a son. In 1829 he saw him off to America in the Foreign Service and then, five years later, learned that he had died in New York of yellow fever caught at Vera Cruz. ('In him', as Rivet says, 'he lost any direct future he might have had' —'*tout avenir direct*'.) The portrait Delacroix had painted of his nephew hung above his bed until he died.[29]

pl 4 What remained to him? His sister, Madame de Verninac, in whose house he had lived for some time after his parents' death, had died in 1827. Quarrels over their inheritance, which had been disastrously mismanaged, had somewhat spoilt their relationship. Delacroix then found himself almost without any private income, and for a long time afterwards money troubles caused him far more suffering than his discreet silence allows to appear. The extravagances of his nephew Charles, whose debts he felt obliged to settle, did not help matters.

pl 6 There remained his elder brother, Charles, the general, with whom he often went to stay at his place at Le Louroux in Touraine. But here was another cause of sadness: he saw his elder brother enslaved by an unsuitable marriage which, indeed, gave Balzac the material for *Un Ménage de garçon.* 'He, so open, so loyal, marked out by his character to take his place in the front rank of those who deserve esteem, lives surrounded by coarse people, by scum', wrote Delacroix, early on in his *Journal,* on 13 September 1823. But he was deeply grieved by his death at the end of 1845.

While life thus, by its disillusionments, repressed again and again Delacroix's enthusiasms, the weaknesses of his health were also busy restricting the circle of his possible activities. This failure of his body was to be another of the causes throwing him back upon the solitude of his work and of his *Journal.* From the very first entries in the *Journal* we can see Delacroix undermined by a fever that again and again exhausted him: I shall recur to it in order to estimate the effects it had on his character and sensibility. A letter dated 16 March 1830 from his unpublished correspondence with his nephew Charles de Verninac discloses the accident which had happened to him in the preceding December, after his return from Valmont, where his cousins the Batailles had a country house with the remains of an ancient Gothic abbey in its grounds. He had been spending his holiday there, as he often did.

'A few days after my return, the horse drawing the cabriolet fell and I received a severe cut just above one eye. Luckily the scar is now hidden under the eyebrow. But I still have a nervous trouble in my eyes, which has bothered me ever since. I have been ill almost continuously, sometimes confined to bed, so that work has suffered considerably.'

In 1835 came the first attacks of that laryngitis, no doubt tubercular, which slowly undermined and finally killed him. By about 1842 this had become 'a kind of mucous fever, which has caused the perpetual bronchial irritation I am suffering from at present'—as he was to write to George Sand later. Year after year he had pl 29
a series of illnesses. In 1841, on 17 February, he complains of 'such earache that I was unable to write and did not know what I was doing.' On 20 April he tells George Sand: 'I feel thoroughly unwell and my throat is bad.' A little later: 'My headache started again yesterday evening.' On 25 June: 'I have been very unwell all this time.' In September he goes to Trouville because of his eyes and of 'what my doctor calls atony'. In 1842 he was four-and-a-half months without working: he had no strength, and his voice had gone—on 28 March he warned Lassalle-Bordes that if his assistants came to see him at his studio he would only be able to communicate with them by notes; and Lassalle-Bordes comments: 'When his nerves let him down, he fell into a prostration that was painful to see.' Such was the record of a few months from the time of his full maturity. Three years later the Faculty ordered him to go to the Pyrenees 'at once', to take a cure at Les Eaux-Bonnes.

## *Mirage and Solitude*

And so, at the age of about forty-five, Delacroix had either lost those dearest to him or given up his illuisons about them. To regain intensity in life, he had only himself to fall back on, and he could only find a reason for existence in his art; and since his physique now gave him no more than a failing help, he had to count almost exclusively on his moral energy to drive his work to completion. Faith in his work had to be sought almost entirely within himself, for with very few exceptions his paintings encountered nothing but hostility and denigration. In the eyes of the public he was the destroyer of tradition—of which he saw himself as the true continuer and reviver. To get some idea of the violence of the abuse heaped on him as an artist, we should remember how his old enemy Ingres, at that time universally accepted as the head of the French School, had the windows in the Louvre opened after Delacroix had gone out, exclaiming that he left behind him a smell of sulphur. Later Delacroix would speak of 'that mass of the stupid, who, incapable of making any judgment of their own, are always ready to fall back on that of hatred.' This description, which occurs in his article on Prud'hon (published in November 1846 in the *Revue des Deux Mondes*), was in part a bitter reflection on his own situation.

At the age of forty-four, at the time when usually a man feels that he is at the height of his development and of his mastery of life, Delacroix could write to George Sand (on 8 July 1842):

'Decidedly I have the spleen, *ma pauvre amie*. One of my friends tells me that he too went through this sort of critical age. Luckily, he has assured me, it was a matter of a few years before he reached the haven of indifference. . . . The prospect is not exactly cheerful, and I am really in a sad state. . . . The weather is atrocious for the nerves.'

What is left to a man when the joys of life flee before him in this way, changing into disappointing mirages, and when his afflictions set upon him from all directions? Faith in humanity and its future, the inspiration of so many minds in the nineteenth century? Delacroix's lucid outlook could not share in the generous illusions of those whom he calls in his *Journal* for 22 May 1853 the 'high priests of the religion of unlimited progress'. The unrestrained enthusiasm and hopefulness characteristic of his time left him ice cold. The entry in the *Journal* on 22 March 1850 tells us what he really thought:

'Contrary to these baroque ideas of continual progress, which Saint-Simon and others have made fashionable, humanity is muddling along at random, whatever people may say. Perfection is in one place while there is barbarism in another.' The people of our own time, who have recovered from many of the illusions of the nineteenth century as the result of increased experience, will be inclined to sympathise with Delacroix when he wrote:

'This so-called modern progress in our political system is . . . nothing but a stage in evolution, a chance happening at this particular moment in time, and we are just as liable to embrace despotism tomorrow with all the fury that we have employed in breaking from restraints.'

Liberty? The progressive achievement of liberties? Delacroix had been too well schooled in turning away from outward successes not to look for this also in his inner life. The 1848 Revolution, which let loose such a flood of illusions, made him write to George Sand, on 28 May, that:

'This liberty bought by battles is not really liberty—which consists in coming and going in peace, pursuing one's thoughts,' and so on. . . .

His own conviction was this:

'People are always talking of liberty, it is the cherished aim of all revolutions, but they don't tell us what this liberty is. . . . Political liberty is the great phrase used, in fact, to justify the sacrifice of the most real liberty there is—that of the mind, that of the soul.'

This recalls his advice to Villot:

'To find the elements you will need, look only in yourself.'

It has to be admitted that subsequent social developments and the political struggles and revolutions which led men to hope for a collective and authoritarian happiness opposed to individualism, are not calculated to discredit in our eyes Delacroix's historical perceptiveness.

As for the extension of material well-being which might result from the progress of scientific discovery, Delacroix was no less sceptical about that. The *Journal* for 22 May 1853 gives voice to this scepticism:

'Man is making progress in all directions: he is mastering matter, there can be no question, but he is not learning to control himself. By all means build railways and telegraphs, cross the continents and the oceans in a twinkling of an eye, but also steer the passions as you steer your aircraft! Above all, abolish the evil passions, which have not lost their detestable power over men's hearts in spite of the liberal and brotherly maxims of our time. This is the problem of progress, and even of true happiness.'

Happiness, Delacroix felt, is not manufactured by machines: it is a question of balance and expansion within.

Circumstances may, of course, get in its way, but it has its roots in the human personality and can be resolved only by the individual's dialogue with himself. Will the means placed at man's disposal to increase his power over the outside world take control of the effects produced on the inner world of each person by this increase of powers, of appetites and, doubtless, of satieties? Will not the harmony between outward experience and that inner experience which is the basis of moral health be distended till it breaks?

'Improvement of this kind, increasing luxury and apparent well-being, has exercised a pernicious influence on the health and physique of the new generations and is, in general, bringing about a moral decadence.'

The thesis advanced by the biologist Alexis Carrel, long after Delacroix, was the same. In our own day its weight has become formidable.

Delacroix's penetrating mind discerned consequences of which his contemporaries had no inkling, and we who know what has happened in the century since his death can only be struck by his clear-sightedness. To begin with, he spoke of mass production as 'exploitation by a grasping machine and leaving the greater part of its product in the impure, atheistic hands of the speculators': has anyone described the danger of capitalism more relentlessly? How would the people react to it? The workers, said Delacroix, would lose their solidarity with the nation: 'They will not go on fighting to defend the property of machines.' And the peasants? They 'used to get their living from the land—painfully, I agree, but with the feeling that their energy and perseverance were well employed.' What would they do henceforth? 'They rush to the towns, and there they find only disappointments; they complete there the perversion of those feelings of dignity produced by a love for one's work, and the more our machines feed them the more they will degrade themselves.' The new environment would contribute to this social neurasthenia: 'Towns will have to be built proportionate to this unemployed and disinherited crowd. . . . Huge barracks will have to be built for them, in which they will be lodged pell-mell.'[30] People of a later time were to use the phrase 'the concentration camp world'. . . .

In Baudelaire it is possible to follow the development of these ideas, which he got from Delacroix. He may well have been thinking of himself and of the collision between his early illusions and the tart scepticism of the great painter when he wrote:

'The talker who abandoned himself to childish Utopian enthusiasms in front of M. Delacroix was very soon subjected to his bitter laugh with its burden of sarcastic pity; and if, in his presence, one imprudently brought out that great illusion of modern times, the monster balloon of perfectibility and unlimited progress, he would be quick to ask: "Where then are your Phidiases? Where are your Raphaels?" '[31]

In these lines published by Baudelaire in *L'Opinion Nationale* at the time of Delacroix's death in 1863, it is perhaps right to see a recollection of some such interview as that recorded in the *Journal* between Delacroix and Baudelaire himself on 5 February 1849:

'He [Baudelaire] jumped to the subject of Proudhon, whom he admires and calls the idol of the people. His views seem to me as modern and progressive as could be.'

Knowing what Delacroix's ideas were, one cannot share the optimism of Crepet, who thought he could see in these lines an expression of approval. . . .

Did Delacroix, envisaging the future of humanity with so little enthusiasm, rest his hopes on a different future? Was it on faith that he based his reason for living? Did he justify his existence by that? Did he believe in a future life and find consolation in it? Did he find in religion a compensation for present disappointments? Here also Delacroix met with a closed door. Through his family and upbringing he was a child of that rational, sceptical eighteenth century which had attempted to substitute the lights of reason for those of heaven. To him death, that inevitable end, could only be a passage 'from something to nothing',[32] into 'night, fearful night',[33] to that 'cruel nothingness' of which he spoke in April 1863, four months before his death, in a letter to his oldest friend, Soulier. On his deathbed, he is said to have refused the aid of a religion from which he had detached himself. When the doctor mentioned the last rites in his hearing, he muttered: 'You hear what he said . . . why this play-acting?' With his accustomed honesty, he refused to yield to those who pressed him to save appearances.

Materialism? How far he was from that! For there is the wonderful phrase in the *Journal*, written less than a year before his death, which reveals to us his deep faith in a principle of spiritual ascent—the reason for living and the justifying hope for mankind. On 12 October 1862 he wrote:

'God is within us: the inner presence that causes us to admire the beautiful, that makes us joyful when we have done well and consoles us for not sharing in the happiness of the wicked.'

Far removed though he was from the religion of his fathers, he discerned a germ of perfectibility—the only one—within himself, deep down in himself, deep down in every man: the quest for improvement.[34] On to the desert of dull grey dust the lightning had fallen, and a fire had blazed up. It is as though we were already listening to Van Gogh's affirmation:[35]

'There is something within me, what then is it? . . . I feel in me a fire which I cannot put out—which, on the contrary, I must revive even though I do not know to what this will lead me.'

It was in himself and not in any religion learned from others that he found the intimate revelation: that everything, even what seems to have neither meaning nor direction, and to exist for an instant only to vanish, is justified. Faintly, deep down within a man, an irresistible aspiration knocks and pushes: if he knows how to listen, if his ear is sharp enough to catch it, it will prompt in him a need to rise towards some pole, which is not anywhere round about him, not in front of him, not behind, but is above him, and he cannot be aware of it unless he will raise his head and look at it. A strange force of attraction opens a way to escape from the dismal boredom of reality and its endless circling, on condition that a man heaves himself up towards the possible, towards what can be created, towards what we call 'something better'. Is not this what Van Gogh also meant when, brush in hand, he meditated on Gustave Doré's *Ronde des Prisonniers*,[36]—the idiotic, stupid tramping between four enclosing and stifling walls, and at the same time, up above, the free air and the light?

Was Delacroix an unbeliever, or a man touched by faith? This has been often debated, but for him the question lay elsewhere, outside these alternatives. Perhaps he would have adopted as his own two of the *Fusées* written with such incisive power by his young admirer and friend Baudelaire. One of them says: 'God is the only being who does not even need to exist in order to reign'; the other: 'What is created by the mind is more alive than matter.'[37] The reign of God through the creative action of mind. . . . What does the mind create, what does it conceive in order to create it? The Beautiful, the Good—those two immemorial summonses to surpass oneself, which a man can hear, but only in himself, through that strange instinct which drives him to seek the truly human quality. And of what consequence, then, is the daily experience of 'man . . . that ignoble and horrible animal'—so described by Delacroix to George Sand, in a letter of 21 November 1844?

The pyramid, at its base, is made up of a blind crowd, which tramps about and tramps itself down with its own weight; and yet, out of its mass it extracts, stage by stage, those who make the effort to rise and, finally, to establish its highest point: the hero, the saint ('Give me', Baudelaire prayed, 'the strength to do my duty every day and so to become a hero and a saint'[38]) and—Delacroix adds—the genius.

As he knew from harsh experience, 'Truth is revealed only to the genius, and the genius is always alone.'[39] What significance, then, has the nausea produced by the sordid or painful details of life? Is that where a man should look for the vocation which should govern his living? 'Satisfied with little—I mean, with little of what gives the crowd its pleasure—but aspiring, on the contrary, to the highest through inner contemplation,' Delacroix faced the battle of solitude.

Delacroix lived in the world of men, looked at them, looked about him, and what he found was mediocrity, disillusion, bitterness. He submitted to the law of solitude. In 1824 (he was only twenty-six) he remarked in his *Journal*, on 14 May:

'The poet who lives in solitude but produces a great deal is the man who enjoys those treasures which we carry in our hearts, and which steal away from us when we give ourselves to others. For when a man surrenders himself entirely to his soul, it unfolds itself completely to him, and it is then that this capricious creature grants him the greatest happiness of all . . . I mean that of expressing the soul in innumerable different ways, of revealing it to others, of learning to know oneself, and of continually painting oneself in one's works . . . of going out towards all the souls capable of understanding your own, and then your painting becomes a place where the souls of all men gather.'

Thirty years later he was still faithful to this conviction:[40] 'Great and delicious sensation of peace and solitude, of the deep happiness this yields.' And yet he added: 'No-one is more sociable than I.... I think my nervous, irritable constitution is at the bottom of this strange longing for solitude which seems so strongly opposed to the friendly disposition I carry to such almost absurd lengths.'

But if fate and his stern efforts have set a man upon a mountain where isolation increases with height, he will still be familiar—this time in himself, in his body and his instincts—with that misery of the human condition from which he would shake himself free. And always he must again struggle to heave himself out of his own reality, to break the bonds in which Michelangelo's *Slaves* writhe for ever, to extract himself from his own heavy matrix.

'Is there any being that is more of a *slave* than man? His weakness and his needs make him dependent on the elements and his fellow men. And external matters are the least of his troubles. The passions he finds within him are the cruellest tyrants he has to fight, and it may be added that to resist them is to resist his very nature.'[41]

He did reach the top of the pyramid, the loneliest point and the most dangerous. There vertigo lies in wait on every side: the vertigo of being alone, of having renounced the animal strength of being borne up by the crowd; but also the vertigo of pride; and also that of one's responsibility towards others, towards everyone, which one discovers then and must take up, sometimes in spite of them, sometimes against them. And then, isolated certainly, but by deliberate separation from men and from all the commonest attachments to them, the elect will at last feel his reason for living—and will communicate it to them, never having served them better than when he seemed to be breaking the bond of solidarity with them. When, on 16 January 1860, three years before his death, Delacroix mentioned Michelangelo and commented: 'He felt compelled to appeal to men's imaginations even when he avoided their company,' he was surely thinking of himself.

Solitude cuts a man off, but it enriches and strengthens him; it severs many bonds we are sorry to see parted, but it allows us to strike root in the essential. Delacroix's *Journal* has this, as early as 31 March 1824: 'The things one experiences when alone with oneself are much stronger and more virgin'; and a good deal later he confided this to his friend Baron Rivet:[42]

'One tries to enjoy everything and fails to enjoy oneself. When you don't enjoy yourself, it is as if you were someone else. Hardly ever, except in solitude, can one really enjoy oneself.'

But what does he mean by 'enjoying oneself'? Not, certainly, the cultivation of a jealous isolation, but a recovery of the real through oneself—'that is to say, to let outside objects strike us in the complete relationship there is between them and our own nature.' For this one must return to nature. Loosening the bonds of society, friendship or passion which had threatened to tie him to other people, and escaping behind an affable politeness, Delacroix contrived for himself frequent periods of withdrawal, in which he could return to his silent dialogue with things. Since there is no getting away from having a body, he sought to immerse his own in a living contact with the natural life of plants, animals and the elements. When he was very young, he went often to Valmont, a place steeped in romanticism through its abbey ruins, or else accompanied the Verninacs to their place at Boixe, which caused the ruin of the family fortunes. Later he found wooded countrysides in the Berry, when he went to stay with George Sand at Nohant, or again, at Dieppe, the fickle, catlike sea. And then, from June 1844 onwards, he had his own small house at Champrosay—the secret of which he told only to a few intimate friends. There he lived alone—so Baron Rivet reports in the precious text unearthed by Raymond Escholier—dividing his time between his studio (which he had set up in a modest way in a farmer's house) and walks by the banks of the Seine or in the Forest of Senart, and choosing 'most often a sunny corner by the herbaceous border in a simple country garden.'

pls 152, 153

pl 267

By that time he had cut all the lines which tie a man to the episodic, to the accidental in which others delight, and which entangle him with countless knots. Delacroix had gone back to his roots. He walked on the earth, he bewitched his eyes with the harmonies between flowers, he drank the sunshine through his skin, he plunged in among the shadows of the forest and the mystery of its deep slow forces, he would listen now to a bird's song, and now would sniff the scent of plants, of crushed leaves or the freshly dug loam. And in these things, in these direct, fresh and piercing impressions of the world, of himself and of life revealed, he found once more the youth which he thought had vanished.

'Came home at about ten; the rain made all the fresh green things smell delicious; the stars brilliant, and, above all, that fragrance! From near Gilbert's kitchen garden as far as Quantinet, a scent from the time of my youth—so piercing and so delicious that there is nothing to which I can compare it. I walked that way, to and fro, five or six times: I could not tear myself away. . . .'

The dazzled young man of this note was fifty-five: he made it on Sunday, 29 May 1853. Five years later, on 12 August 1858, when he was already sixty:

'Went out into the country at six o'clock in the morning . . . brought home a great bunch of water lilies and bull-rushes; I spent nearly an hour paddling about on the slippery clay banks of the river and hugely enjoyed capturing those poor flowers.'

A few weeks earlier, on 14 July, he had been at Plombières:

'I made some enchanting discoveries; rocks and woods and, above of all, water —water of which one can't grow tired. One feels a continual longing to plunge into it, to be a bird, to be a tree with roots steeped in it. . . .'

But was this all? Simply to renounce human company, become absorbed in oneself, be no more than an Aeolian harp, return to the breast of mother Nature? No: the water in which Delacroix longed to plunge once more suggested to him the Baptist—it was truly a lustral water that would wash him clean from the mud in which human beings gradually sink, which sticks to one's skin and dries on it, stifling it with an impenetrable coating, with the carapace formed by conventions and habits, by meannesses and insignificant actions, by false human contacts limited to endless repetition of commonplaces, by mediocre desires, shabby preoccupations and the many worries with which everyone is obsessed. On

2 August, again at Plombières, just after exclaiming: 'I can't tear myself away from all this: the grandeur and charm of it!' he observed: 'And no-one near me was paying attention to it. I kept meeting groups of people: the men were talking only about money; I was struck by this.' He, at these times, felt washed clean, alone and naked to himself. 'You should look into yourself and not round about yourself.' For it was to himself, and into himself, that he was led back by that contact with the life of things—that life which all his senses drank in, but which then reawakened deep down in him its own echo.

The experience showed him that he must look for himself not in confrontations with other people and the compromises which these involved, but in a pure intransigent creative activity in which he would be his whole self, magnified by the beauty of the means of expression. Instead of seeking the common measure with the mass of people, he would find himself, would realise himself completely, and would then bring and reveal to others the irreducible essence, throwing his work at them as a gift that would make no concessions and would withhold nothing. This conviction that nothing really worthwhile even for others—indeed, above all for others—can be achieved by associating with them and their mediocre appetites, but only by taking oneself in hand and shaping oneself into an example of excellence that will excite others to emulate and share it, establishes Delacroix as an aristocrat. He does not believe in the virtue of the crowd, but only in what stands out from it. He believes that mediocrity is the natural condition of man, and that excellence is only to be found in man at the uttermost heights to which his efforts sometimes enable him to rise. He does not appreciate the virtue of the mean, but only that of an exacting *élite*—and of those who separate even from this in order to surpass it. 'I look in vain for truth in the masses, I find it, when I find it, only in individuals.

'If light is to arise out of the shadows, God must kindle in them a sun.'[43] Popular language recognizes this kind of aspiration when, sometimes, it praises a man by saying: '*C'est un seigneur!*' Paul Jamot was fond of saying of Delacroix: 'He is a prince.'

Delacroix's principal claim to be remembered by posterity may well be not only the order and brilliance of the paintings he bequeathed it, but also the greatness of the soul which found expression in them. Certainly his quality as a human being prevents him even now from occupying, in the minds of most people, the position which is his due. He is not easy of access, as were Victor Hugo and even Voltaire on account of an element of mediocrity in their characters, a mediocrity in which most people are at home and can contemplate themselves admiringly, amplified by an *écho sonore*. Delacroix was not one of them. In death he rests 'high up, in a place somewhat apart'—as he had desired his tomb to be. He disturbs some people profoundly by the despotic bonds by which he draws their souls to his, while others wander about his greatness, obscurely aware of it and resentful of it for being, though splendid, still too foreign to their nature. In him they seek in vain the familiarity which makes the excellent Corot so much beloved: Delacroix permits no familiarity, only intimacy.

## *The Supreme Duty: Creation*

Delacroix did not bequeath his work to everyone, only to some. 'What the public cannot find in it,' he says in his will, 'artists will understand.' Artists—and poets. . . .

While he devoted all his strength to his painting, he knew that he must first shape the self to put into it. Therefore he plunged into himself and, deep down there, listened to the dark forces throbbing like arteries; he allowed them to take shape, to condense in his head into images, vague at first, but imperious, irresistible, whose logic escaped him though their power drew him on; he placed himself at their service, he projected them outside him and made into visions; these also arose at first like confused clouds, but then condensed, massed and organized themselves under the pressure of his relentless lucidity, and so became pictures, in which he could read himself as though in some dark mirror and offer himself to others to read, in order to bring to them the revelations they held sleeping within themselves.

In his work he became free from the moods of indecision, disgust and weariness produced by the life of action, which does its best to mould us into something other than our true nature. He was moved, indeed carried away, by a faint call which grew definite when he concentrated on it his sharp hearing, and to which, when he had heard it, even though he did not yet understand it fully, he could not choose but give the voice and music of his art. It was then that he raised that song of his, perhaps without ever altogether knowing what he had put into it and what it would convey. Into it he put his whole self, conscious and unconscious; in it he pursued and realized himself without deviation or misunderstanding; in it he transmitted the substance of himself which, without this transposition into an enduring image, would have vanished along with his earthly life. He did more than transmit it, he completed it—forced it to become something more than it had been, the fulfilment of what it could be and ought to be.

And so he came to feel that there was one duty only in his life: work—creation—the adventure which led on and on, grew more and more definite, drew closer to its aims and, over the years, from picture to picture, sometimes attained them. From time to time, all of a sudden, an important part of his vision would become incarnate, with no room for any retouching or addition; but immediately other potentialities would appear, impatient to take their turn, and from problem to problem, in a single continuous sweep, a destiny evolved, and came to fruition.

To his work, therefore, he transferred all his enthusiasms, all his love. On 30 November 1853 he confesses in his *Journal*:

'I go to my work as other men rush to their mistress, and when I leave it I take with me into the solitude of my home, or into the midst of the distractions I go in search of, a delightful memory that has little resemblance to the lover's uneasy pleasure.'

In painting he found forgetfulness and consolation for the inanities of life. He copied out a saying of Voltaire's about work: 'It becomes in the long run the greatest of pleasures and takes the place of all the illusions one has lost.'[44] His 'Consuelo', his *consolatrice*, was not now Madame de Forget, or any woman: it was his task and his work. To his old friend Soulier[45] he writes:

'I have not even the common distractions of ordinary people to divert me. As I am usually ill, I have given these up entirely, and I often spend my evenings by my fireside. My illusions drop away, one after the other, and only one remains —or rather, it isn't an illusion, it is a real pleasure, it is the only one without any mixture of the bitterness of regret: I mean work. But indeed this is my only passion. May it last longer than all the others!'

It was also his only protection against the reality whose measure he had taken. This time it is to George Sand that he writes, on 24 November 1853:

'We shall work on till our death throes: what else in the world is there to do, except perhaps get drunk, when the moment comes at which reality has ceased to measure up to one's dream?'

This surely is the key to that paradoxical and desperate boredom which would descend on him suddenly and with crushing force when he separated himself from his easel. He had placed his whole reason for living and all his hopes so resolutely in his work, that when he was exhausted and allowed himself some relaxation, he groped and could find nothing to lay hold of. At such times he would let himself go and give way to despair. Fortunately, painting did not let him go. Even in 1843, on 20 November, his pupil Planet noted:

'He has the impression that, the older he gets, the more his brain seethes with ideas for painting.' And indeed Delacroix was to die muttering sadly: 'I had in my head enough for forty years more. . . .'

In this way Delacroix moved on into the withdrawal of his last years, and there can, I think, be no more evocative image of the culmination of his life than the description given by Odilon Redon of how, one night in 1859, he watched and followed him with silent admiration:

'He walked through the dark streets of Paris alone, with his head bowed, treading the pavement like a cat; a notice containing the word "pictures" attracted his attention; he went up to it, read it and moved off again with his dream. On through the streets he walked until he reached the house in the rue de La Rochefoucauld where he no longer lived.'

Was this absent-mindedness, an imperfectly erased habit? Or a pilgrimage in honour of the woman he had loved most, his cousin, Mme. de Forget, who lived near there and had refused to follow him, at his request, to the Left Bank?

'He returned quietly with his thoughts to the rue de Furstenberg, that silent street where he now lived.'

Let us leave him there, on the threshold of the house in which he was destined to die—and which, at the beginning of this chapter, we watched him leave, a few years later, for the final dwelling-place where the fleeting episode of his life would be buried.

More and more irresistibly over many years he had taken the most intimate and intense part of himself elsewhere—into his work. He is there still, shining with inextinguishable fires, and it is there that we must look for him and live his real destiny with him. In this, as in many other things, Baudelaire understood him better than anyone: 'He knew passion and the supernatural only through his enforced intercourse with the dream world,' and the dreams in which he found himself, and in which we in turn find him as he truly was, are his pictures.

# NOTES ON THE PLATES TO CHAPTER I

Delacroix was born near Paris on 26 April 1798 (7th Floréal, year VI), in an eighteenth-century house taking up two sides of a courtyard (pl 1) which gave on to a small garden (pl 2). This was at Charenton-Saint-Maurice, very close to the banks of the Seine. *Birth*

1 *29-31 Grande Rue, Charenton-Saint-Maurice; the house where Eugène Delacroix was born.*

2 *The courtyard from the garden.*

Delacroix came from that upper bourgeoisie whose rise had already been effected by the *Ancien Régime*, and whose supremacy the Revolution would establish. His father—who became a minister, an ambassador and a *Préfet*—and his mother (pl 3)—who came from a family of great cabinet-makers—had one daughter (pl 4) and two sons (pls 5, 6), both of whom took up soldiering under the Empire: the third son, born much later, was Eugène. *Family*

3 *Charles Delacroix and Victoire Oeben, c. 1804. Medallions by Chinard. Petit Palais, Paris.*

4 *Henriette de Verninac, 1799, by Jacques Louis David. Louvre, Paris.*

5 *Henri Delacroix by H. F. Riesener. Private collection.*

6 *Charles Delacroix by his brother Eugène. Private collection.*

7 *Portrait by Delacroix, thought to be of his sister on her deathbed. On the reverse, the painting has the title 'La Morte, 1857', in an unidentified hand. Henriette de Verninac, to whom this portrait bears some resemblance, died aged forty-seven in 1827. This earlier date corresponds more exactly to the technique of the painting.*

Starting life with relatives in high places—for instance his cousin the eminent lawyer Berryer (pls 11, 12)—Delacroix contrived to become a perfect man of the world (pl 9), admitted into the most exclusive of the Salons (pls 10, 12). He took pains to attend official functions (pl 8) in order to counterbalance the reputation of being a revolutionary which his art gave him. *Delacroix in society*

*8 Eugène Delacroix as a member of the Institut (Académie des Beaux-Arts), 1858, by François-Joseph Heim. Louvre, Paris.*

*9 Eugène Delacroix by Eugène Giraud. Bibliothèque Nationale, Paris.*

*10 Eugène Delacroix at a musical evening (with Musset, Mérimée, Auber, Gounod), c. 1850, by Eugène Lami. Formerly Jean-Louis Vaudoyer Collection.*

*11 Pierre-Antoine Berryer (1790-1868). Lithograph by Delpech.*

*12 Delacroix, Musset and Berryer at a soirée, by Eugène Lami. Private Collection.*

*Delacroix in his studio*

Though he was considered a wild romantic, the place of work Delacroix arranged for himself was a somewhat bare and severe studio (adorned with casts of classical sculpture) which his frail health made him keep overheated. Such was his studio in the rue Notre-Dame-de-Lorette (pl 13), where he worked from 1845 to 1857.

*13 Delacroix's studio, 54, rue Notre-Dame-de-Lorette. Engraving in 'L'Illustration' 1852. Bibliothèque Nationale, Paris.*

*14 Paint cabinet belonging to Delacroix, from his studio.*

*Friends*

Friendship occupied a large place in Delacroix's life, and the companions of his youth (pls 16, 46, 94) remained very dear to him. He was on friendly terms, also, with certain critics and art historians—among these Villot (pl 15), whose learning he found valuable, although later there came a coolness between them.

*15 Frédéric Villot by Delacroix, 1832. National Museum, Prague.*

*16 Félix Guillemardet by Delacroix, c. 1827. Louvre, Paris.*

*His home in old age*

At the beginning of 1858 Delacroix moved to rooms near Saint-Sulpice, in the Place Furstenberg with its country town atmosphere (pl 19). The rooms give on to a garden (pl 18). Here he had his studio till his death. He decorated the outer wall with casts of classical sculpture (pl 17).

*17 Delacroix's studio, 6 rue Furstenberg.*

*18 Delacroix's studio from the garden. The stairway on the right, leading to the house, was formerly protected by a roof.*

*19 Place Furstenberg today.*

*Women*

Delacroix was both greatly attracted by women and careful to keep them at a distance in the interests of his work. After various youthful love affairs (pls 66, 67), he had two long liaisons, one with Madame Dalton (pl 22), the other with his cousin Madame de Forget (pl 21). He seems also to have had a tender attachment to Madame Villot (pl 23); and a brief escapade with Madame Boulanger (pl 20) led to a lasting friendship.

*20 Elisabeth Boulanger (later Madame Cavé) by Ingres. Private collection.*

*21 Joséphine de Lavalette, Baronne de Forget. Medallion by David d'Angers, 1847.*

*22 Aimée Dalton by Delacroix, 1831. Private collection.*

*23 Pauline Villot in Moorish costume, by Delacroix, 1833. Private collection.*

*The country house*

The Villots opened Delacroix's eyes to the charm of Champrosay, and in 1844 he went to live there, in a house which he first rented, then bought in 1858 (pl 25). With its outlook over a garden and over deep country to the horizon (pl 24) and its nearness to the Forest of Senart it confirmed the painter in his passion for nature.

*24 Delacroix's house and garden at Champrosay.*

*25 The entrance to the house at Champrosay.*

*Family affection*

Delacroix's emotional nature found stability, and often consolation, in his near relatives: on his mother's side, particularly, in the Rieseners (pl 26). His affection for his cousin Léon Riesener (pl 28), who, like his father, was a painter, remained constant. He was attached to his nephew Charles de Verninac (pl 27) as to a younger brother, and was shattered by his early death.

*26 Madame Henri Riesener by Delacroix, 1835. Private collection, Paris.*

*27 Charles de Verninac by Delacroix, c. 1830. Private collection.*

*28 Léon Riesener by Delacroix, 1834. Louvre, Paris.*

*Intimate friends*

George Sand (pl 29) and, through her, Chopin (pl 172) became close friends of Delacroix, who often stayed with them at Nohant (pl XXIX). For a long time a friend of his youth, Pierret (pl 132), and Pierret's wife (pl 30), helped him with his bachelor housekeeping; and it was they who found for him Jenny Le Guillou (pl 32), his housekeeper, whose influence over him increased until his death.

*29 George Sand by Delacroix, 1834. Private collection.*

*30 Madame Pierret by Delacroix. Private collection.*

*31 Claire Pierret by Delacroix, c. 1821. Wildenstein & Co., London.*

*32 Jenny Le Guillou by Delacroix, c. 1840. Louvre, Paris.*

*The end of a life*

With the years Delacroix withdrew more and more into a lonely life devoted to creative work. The haughtiness, almost coldness (pl 33), with which he defended himself against the importunate is reflected even in the tomb he designed for himself (pl 34).

*33 Delacroix. Photograph by Pierre Petit, 1862. Bibliothèque Nationale, Paris.*

*34 Delacroix's tomb in the cemetery of Père-Lachaise, Paris.*

1

2

3

4

5

6

7

8

9

10

11

12

13

14

15

16

17

18

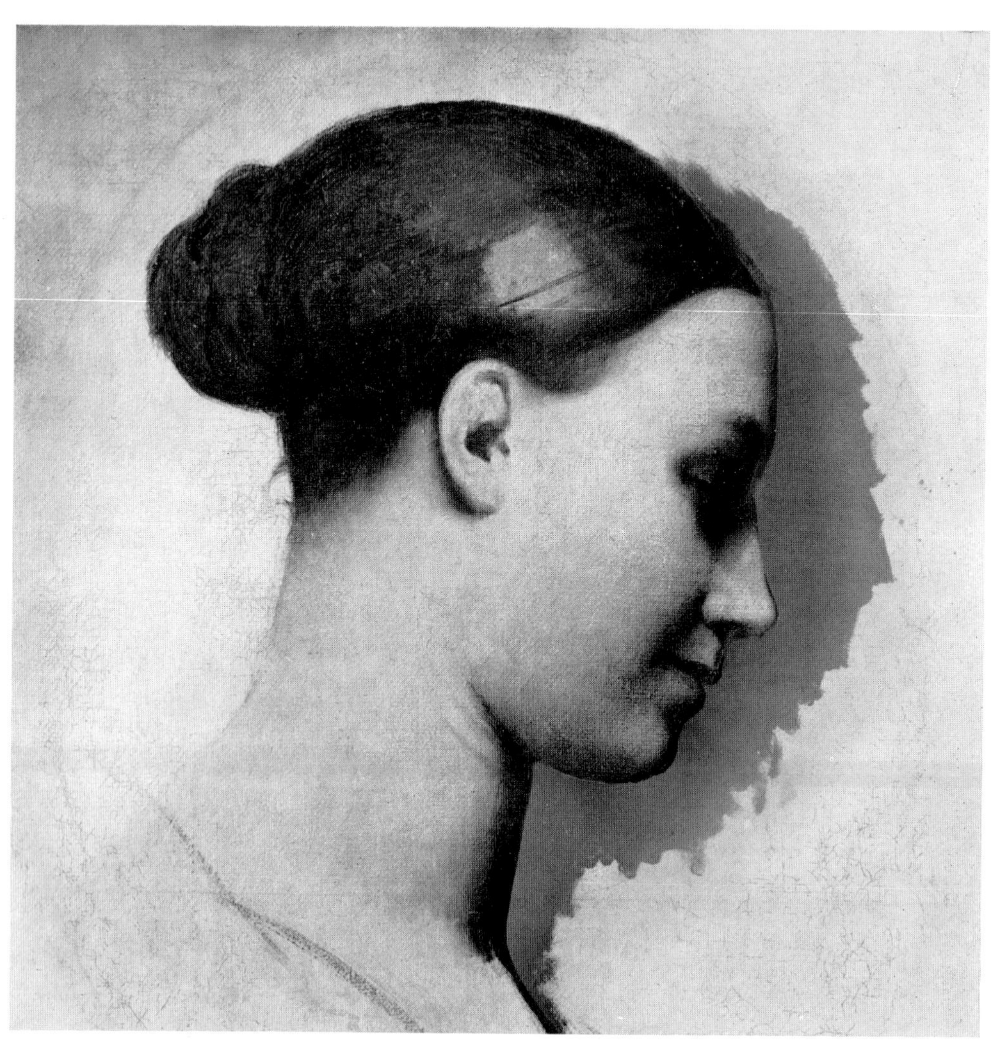

20

21

22

23

24

25

26

27

28

29

30

31

32

33

34

# II STARTING POINTS

How does a man become a man? He appears on the scene, he enters into time, and is there for a few decades. At the moment of his birth he is already in part determined by his situation and temperament, by the many tendencies due to his heredity, all of them preparing to develop simultaneously and to combine or conflict within his moral and physical system. But living involves also facing up to circumstances, measuring up to the weight of other people, things and events, and being launched out into an adventure that will constitute the second element of determinism in a life. Up against the first and inner determinism and the second and outer one, the principle of unity which moulds the Self will carry out its decisive action. It will tend towards a state of balance without which the whole would go to pieces—a balance between the inner forces in all their impatience for deployment (sometimes to one another's detriment), but also that necessary balance between the man's personality, as it grows more and more pronounced, and the world surrounding and assailing it.

To arrive at this balance is hard enough; but in addition, no sooner is it reached than it is endangered—by its projection in time, by the perpetual novelty of fate. Each human being moves forward like a tight-rope walker, along the swaying wire which has to be traversed from end to end, and on which every fresh step, if it is to avoid a fall, requires the simultaneous effort of the whole body: at each moment the hard-won, perpetually menaced success has to be renewed. Such efforts, simply not to fall! But progress cannot be confined to putting one foot before the other, while merely staying upright and avoiding a fall. Progress means also an advance towards some goal, and drawing nearer to it. To live is not simply to last, passively, by adapting oneself to new events within us and outside. Certainly the other animals confine themselves to that—to keeping alive as long as possible; but man, in so far as he is more than an animal, expects something else of life—he is a creator, his business is to build himself and his work. He drives himself and it onwards towards that completion in which he hopes to find more of what he aspires to be.

While fate and determinism have provided him with—and imposed on him—the complex and tumultuous raw material for his impatient hands to mould, he can only win through to freedom in so far as he insists on extracting from that raw material something that does not yet exist, something into which he desires to be changed. He feels within him a shadowy longing to surpass the giver, to go beyond what has been provided by fate and, in so doing, to assert a certain power—the power to bring something new. He wants not merely to choose, but to improve; and it is here that he finds that field of liberty into which he desperately aspires to enter.

Sometimes it is in action—upon things, upon other people, upon himself—that a man looks for his success; sometimes it is in a body of work detached from himself, on which he relies to carry and perpetuate his imprint, the thing he has to say, and then he becomes a writer or an artist.

It is in the complex relationships between what a man receives and what he wills—relationships, in other words, between the past and present on the one hand and, on the other, the future towards which he strives—that a human career works itself out: it is no good trying to shut it up inside that network of fatalities which some historians are too exclusively concerned with detecting; and it is equally vain to try to find the whole of it in a hypothetical independence. The reality is not a sterile contradiction between determinism and liberty: it is life, and this consists in reducing the former to a starting-point—which is, unhappily, inescapable—and fashioning the latter into the ideal destination of the road on which a man sets out and makes more or less headway. It would be impossible to study an artist and his work if one were not permeated by the awareness that both of them are subject to this two-way attraction, and that they deserve our interest in so far, only, as they escape from determinism and attain freedom. Similarly, to understand the development of a human life, it is first essential to assess the constraints that define it historically, so that one may then follow its liberating ascent towards the point where it will at last feel itself to be a conscience in control of itself, able to decide where it is going.

And then, one day, death comes. The hard struggle to carry that ceaselessly maintained balance further and further onwards and upwards is at an end. For some people this end is a fresh beginning: the living man is succeeded by a defined thing, a memory, an example, a lived adventure that will influence the adventures still to be lived—a body of work. In the barrel of a firearm, the explosion of the powder, its smoke, light and din, are let loose: this violent pressure is powerless against the walls that hold it in, but it drives the projectile out to the escape it seeks; and when the explosion is over, it is the projectile that now continues gliding forwards—to strike other men.

## *Hereditary Factors*

When on 26 April 1798 (7 Floréal, year VI), Eugène Delacroix was born in the
house at Charenton-Saint-Maurice, at the gates of Paris, which still—precar- pl 1
iously—exists (and which it is to be hoped will be preserved out of public respect
for his memory), his father was absent, being at that time Ambassador of the
French Republic '*près celle Batave*' and detained abroad by his duties. The
spacious bourgeois house, with its sober late eighteenth-century style, presents to
the street a single storey lit by a row of ten windows, above which there rises a
steep tiled roof. On the other side there is a paved courtyard and beyond this a pl 2
garden. The way in from the street is through a large iron gate, flanked by a
small doorway for those on foot.

All this expresses perfectly the world from which Delacroix came—that of the bourgeoisie which, in its tenacious climb to power, had begun by imitating the manners and culture of the aristocracy, then rose to association with it in subordinate but indispensable posts, and at length leapt forward to attack it, arousing against it the revolution of the people and taking its place. For a moment, indeed, the bourgeoisie had almost been itself swept away by the flood it had let loose; but after Thermidor it recovered the reins: the Directoire was the prelude to its irresistible rise in the nineteenth century.

Eugène's grandfather, Claude Delacroix, had been factor to the Counts of Belval in his native Argonne. His eldest son, Charles Delacroix de Contault, the painter's father, after beginning his career as a teacher at the Rodez, became secretary to Turgot, and followed him from Limoges to Paris. 'He was so placed', Delacroix notes in his *Journal*,[1] 'that everything had to go through him . . . his waiting-room was filled with the eminent, great ladies and people of all ranks in quest of favours.' In 1779 he retired from his position as principal private secretary *(premier commis à la Marine et au Contrôle Général)*, but he threw himself wholeheartedly into the Revolution. As representative for the Marne in the Convention, he voted for the King's death. (His son, to whom his memory was dear, seems to have pondered deeply over this. In a school notebook dating from 1814,[2] the property of the Malvy-Verninac family, he copied out a passage from Menée de la Touche in defence of regicides: 'Are they responsible for the decision which their conscience, whether enlightened or not, has dictated to them?' It is clear that he had in mind his father's case.) When the bourgeoisie judged that the disorder was becoming too dangerous and began taking measures to re-establish order to its own advantage, Delacroix's father joined in this movement: he became a member of the *Conseil des Anciens* and then, in 1795, Minister for Foreign Affairs for a year and a half, until on 16 July 1797 he was replaced by Talleyrand and sent as Minister to Holland. He gave, very naturally, his allegiance to the Empire, and for two years, from 1800 to 1803, he was *Préfet* at Marseille. He ended his days as *Préfet* at Bordeaux, dying there on 26 August, 1805.

But was he really the painter's father? The question has been much debated, and there have been various hypotheses as to who 'supplied his place'. One decisive document forms part of the evidence—the brochure which the military surgeon Ange Imbert Delonnes (1747-1818), published in December 1797 'by order of the Government', with the title: 'The operation for *sarcocèle* performed on 27 Fructidor, year V, upon Citizen Charles Delacroix.'[3] Delonnes, who had been a *médecin consultant* and later became Inspector General of the Health Services, had been an accepted specialist in tumours of the testicles ever since the publication, in 1785, of his *Cure radicale de l'Hydrocèle.* In the 1799 and 1812 reprints of this brochure the curious may study two plates showing the growth after its removal.[4]

One of the six health officers who witnessed the operation was Ferdinand Guillemardet, a friend of the patient and also his colleague, for he was Ambassador of the Republic at Madrid (and, as such, had his portrait painted by Goya). He was also a witness at the registration of Eugène's birth, and André Joubin (in conversation with me towards the end of his life) maintained that he was the real father—but he died before he had time to set forth evidence. Let us not be too hasty: it is at least certain that Charles Delacroix's physical condition, up to the operation which took place seven months before the painter's birth, had deprived him of 'all the advantages of virility'. This is definite. Eugène Delacroix was perfectly aware of it, to judge from the fact—which Joubin revealed—that the unimpeachable brochure was in his library as Piron, his residuary legatee, inherited it. It has been suggested that, in putting back the date of his birth by a year, as he often did, Delacroix may have been moved by a desire to make it look more legitimate.[5] The thought of the terrible operation in which his 'worthy father showed a wonderful courage'—it lasted two hours and a half, with four intervals—was no stranger to his mind: he wrote with veneration of how his 'admirable and noble father',[6] after entertaining the doctors to a lunch before the operation, summoned up, in the last interval, the strength to say, calmly: 'My friends, that makes four acts of your operation, may the fifth not turn it into a tragedy.' This admiring passage is Delacroix's only allusion to the matter.

What more did he know? Was he aware of the rumour which, according to Théophile Silvestre, to Maxime du Camp and to Madame Jaubert (friend of the famous lawyer Berryer, himself a cousin of Delacroix's), was current in his pl 11 lifetime, that his real father was Talleyrand? Among the notes found in his notebooks and published by Joubin as a supplement to the *Journal*,[7] there is one describing certain features in the character of the Prince of Benevente—his 'circumspection', and his 'prudent reticence' in particular. It would be hard to draw any conclusion from this. That Talleyrand took an interest in the career of Charles Delacroix, who in 1797 was fifty-seven and therefore thirteen years older than he, working first to have him made Minister of Foreign Affairs and then to move him out of France and take his place in the Government—and perhaps elsewhere—is well known. That the painter's features have hardly any resemblance to those of Charles Delacroix, or indeed to his mother's, whereas pl 3 his distant bearing, the proud and aristocratic set of his head, his 'constrained smile', his 'yellowish pallor'[8] and his whole cast of features irresistibly suggest the illustrious diplomat, is obvious to anyone who compares their portraits. Delacroix's low and emphatic eyebrows, his deep-set eyes with their heavy eyelids, his pl 36 tight-lipped, disdainful mouth, his firm rounded chin, and even the way this was embedded in collar and high cravat—all this insists on the comparison. Lacour-Gayet, a strong partisan of the hypothesis, rightly draws attention to the portrait pl 37 of Talleyrand painted by Ary Scheffer in 1828, in which the likeness is disconcerting. Some have objected that, in David's *Coronation of Napoleon I*, the great statesman's profile gives us a pointed and upturned nose not repeated in the pl 35 leonine muzzle of his supposed son; but the argument can be turned the other way, for the young Delacroix of about thirty-five, as he appears in a sketch he did of himself at the time of his Moroccan journey, or again in Gigoux's lithograph, has a similar nose, and in both cases the nose put on flesh with the years. Paul Jamot, one of Delacroix's fervent admirers, recalling 'the charm and lofty distinction of his manners . . . the strange authority which emanated from his whole appearance', ranked him in the category of 'princes'. He was unmistakably an aristocrat, the fires of his intelligence masked by a sometimes haughty chilliness. This would be easy to explain if, in fact, the blood of the Talleyrand-Périgord family had flowed in Delacroix's veins, as it did in those of the Duke de Morny, who would thus have been his nephew.

Though his descent was aristocratic, the section of society from which Delacroix came was that upper middle class, or bourgeoisie, which at the end of the eighteenth century made its bid for the position of ruling class. The career of Charles Delacroix is typical of this stubborn rise, whose rapidity explains that tang of the *parvenu*, excessively in evidence in the 'high society' of the early nineteenth century and faithfully recorded by Balzac. It certainly hung about Ingres, who came of humble stock in the Midi and was soon strutting around with all the pompous solemnity of a middle class that has arrived too quickly at the top. In complete contrast, Eugène Delacroix maintained with sovereign ease the style of that refined eighteenth-century society whose luxury the bourgeoisie aspired to take over, though often unable to do more than ape its manners. For this peculiar position of his (in the world of letters there was a similar contrast between Vigny and Balzac) the mysterious heredity so credibly attributed to him would provide an explanation.

But what of his mother's side? She was considerably younger than her husband, being only twenty against his thirty-seven at the time of their marriage in 1778—a difference of age quite usual at that time. She was forty when Eugène, her fourth
pl 6 child, was born. His birth came long after that of Charles, who was nineteen
pl 4 years older than he, of Henriette, who was born in 1780 and married in the year
pl 5 of his birth, and of Henri, his elder by fourteen years. Through his mother, Eugène Delacroix was connected with a line of artists; for she was one of the daughters of Jean-François Oeben, the famous cabinet-maker to Louis XV and a protégé of Madame de Pompadour; and he, coming from Germany to Paris, had there married Françoise Marguerite Van der Cruse, the daughter of another well established cabinet-maker, this time from Flanders, whose name had been gallicised into Delacroix or, more usually, Lacroix,[9] as is shown by the maker's sign on his works. Thus the painter had received from his legal father a name which, curiously enough, was already that of his grandmother on his mother's side. Her sister, Marie Marguerite, was also a Delacroix-Oeben, since she married Simon, her brother-in-law. Delacroix's grandfather, Oeben, died in Paris in 1763, leaving behind him, with his widow, an unfinished masterpiece, the *bureau de Louis XV*, now one of the treasure of the Louvre. Both of them fell to the care of Jean-Henri Riesener, likewise from Germany: he was born in 1734 at Glatbeck near Essen, his father being employed in the chancellery of the Prince-Elector of Cologne, and in 1769 he finished the famous desk, the fruit of eight years' work—by which time he had for two years been married to his master's widow. He took Oeben's place in the *Cour des Vétérans*, within the Arsenal, becoming in 1774 '*ébéniste du mobilier de la Couronne*' by the favour of the future Queen Marie-Antoinette, then Dauphine. He may well have known his wife's youngest grandson, for he died only in 1806 (after remarrying).

Is there anything, other than its anecdotal interest, to justify spending time on this genealogy? Without doubt there is. It was through his connections on his mother's side that Delacroix was steered towards the arts, in particular towards painting. Of his mother, Baron Rivet remarked that 'coming of a family of artists, she was well fitted, by her natural distinction, to entertain for her husband'.[10] She too had, from childhood, been immersed in the aristocratic eighteenth-century society whose imprint was so strong on Delacroix. And he, indeed, 'spoke of his mother invariably with a tender and pious admiration'. She died at the age of fifty-six, in 1814, when Eugène was just sixteen; and we know from his *Journal* how severe was the blow to him.

Both through her and through the Rieseners, Delacroix was introduced, even as a child, into the studios of painters. Indeed, evidence preserved by Madame Escholier (née Léouzon-le-Duc, a direct descendent of the Rieseners), and examined by Mlle. Geneviève Vieillefond in her thesis for the École du Louvre (1952), reveals that Delacroix used to go, during the holidays, to draw in the studio of his uncle. Born in 1767, Henri-François Riesener, the son of the great cabinet-maker, was himself a painter, a pupil first of Vincent and then of David. Introduced into the Imperial circle by his wife, Félicité, who had been a lady-in-waiting to Josephine, and whose father was Pierre Longrois, 'keeper' of the furniture in the château de la Muette, he had become a portrait painter of repute: his subjects included the Emperor, General Ordener, Marshal Bessières and Eugène de Beauharnais—to whom, indeed, Delacroix's two brothers and their cousin Bataille had been aides-de-camp. On the fall of the Empire he went to live in Russia for seven years, after which he returned to Paris and lived on there until his death in 1828. Faithful as he was to the neo-classical ideals, his painting cannot have had much influence on that of his half-sister's son, whose real career, indeed, began during his absence; but his own son, Léon, who was also a painter, bears witness that it was in his studio that Delacroix *'fut pris du goût de la peinture'*. It was his uncle Henri who sent Delacroix as a pupil to Guérin, and who, as early as 1813, when he was still at school, introduced him to Baron Gérard, later appointed official painter to Louis XVIII on Talleyrand's recommendation. The salon of Baron Gérard was held in high repute and in due course Delacroix became a frequent visitor, meeting there many people who were important to his intellectual life as well as to his career. Talleyrand, Talma, Mlle. Mars, Balzac, Mérimée and Stendhal were among those he saw there, and it was there that he acquired the valuable support of Thiers. In a note, recovered for us by Piron, he says:

pl 36

pl 28

'Gérard's salon was one of the most curious things of that time. The man himself was unusual. One went to visit him Italian fashion, that is to say at midnight, and often our host would come to life and charm us with his reminiscences.'[11]

In his cousin, Léon Riesener, who was ten years younger than he, Delacroix evidently found and encouraged a turn of mind that was like his own. At the age of fifteen, in 1823, Léon became a pupil of Gros. The new generation had turned its back decisively on the academic conception of art.

## *Between the Latin and the Germanic*

Through his mother Delacroix acquired not only contact with a circle of people that encouraged his vocation as an artist, but also the German heredity that may well be one of the keys to his complex nature. The deplorable political use made of the idea of race during the last few decades has inclined us to place a taboo on it—and so to fall into an opposite excess. Knowledge of the family from which a person comes can help us to discern the interweaving of his nature, not only throwing light on the circle of people that has exercized its social pressure on him and the constraints that have moulded his initial form, but also by exploring his heredity. When the first cry comes from the new-born child, it is already different from that of any other: it contains the still primitive sketch of a human character. Even before experience of life has begun to mould him, each individual is already the confluence and the consequence of biological forces that will leave their mark both on his physical appearance and on his moral nature. How complex they are! They include both the individual legacies of his relatives for several generations and the tendencies of the races from which he issues. Of what slow fashioning by geography and history, by climate, scenery and events, are these the product? Just as they are often to be recognized at the first glance in unmistakeable physical features, so also they come out in a definite predisposition that will constantly influence the man's relation to his own inner problems and to those set him by the outside world. A particular approach governs the way in which he faces up to them, seizes them and conceives them.

The historian of art knows this better than anyone, accustomed as he is to discern, at the first glance, the school—indeed the moment in the growth of the school—of which a picture is the product. Through all the oscillations of taste that characterize its phases the destiny of a school throws up certain elements that are constant and easily recognizable: they are the features of a face—that of the race which the school represents.

But this idea of race needs to be clarified. It includes a confused mixture of hereditary temperaments and material and psychological influences, the play of which drives constantly in one direction, together with social and cultural forms perpetuated by tradition and education. Great indeed is the subtlety required to analyze all these accurately! But no matter: the result, the quotient, is there.

In Delacroix a French and Germanic ancestry converged. At the same time the principal problem of romanticism at the beginning of the nineteenth century was to open French tradition, which had become exclusively and jealously Latinized, to the revelation of the Anglo-Saxon and Germanic cultures and to their very different ways of thinking and feeling. When this is remembered, it is easy to see how Delacroix, in whom hereditary tendencies from both these worlds met, was predestined to realize the synthesis for which his time was waiting.

It is of course right, when approaching the work of one of the greatest French painters, to bear constantly in mind the share of the timeless in the achievements of a genius; but this does not relieve us of the need to follow up the ways by which he comes to those achievements, and raises himself to a plane where the details of the access to it are forgotten. However universal the result, it was obtained by starting from determined data. These survive, transfigured, in the substance of the man's work.

To put the problem another way: a strong personality can only fulfil itself by conferring unity—which the work will reflect—upon tendencies that are diverse, tumultuous and often conflicting. It is their association and fusion that are important: the unity that emerges and is independent of them has neither sense nor value unless one measures what has fed it. We must therefore separate by analysis the constituent factors, which the final success in its synthesis makes us forget, but of which it is nonetheless the product.

It is rare for a great man to be able to bring into the world elements totally unknown before him; but those that are supplied to him he transforms, by the way in which he forces them to combine and to enrich one another: by so doing he gives them a new appearance which could not even have been imagined before and seems a discovery; it is, in fact, a creation—his creation.

This was precisely the rôle of Delacroix. France in his time was torn between the idea she formed of herself, through her classical traditions, and the enrichments she felt fitted to receive; indeed she felt that she must make these her own, on pain of ceasing to renew herself and of declining and drying up.

These enrichments lay all around her, within reach, in the literature and art of those neighbouring peoples who, for a long time neglected and despised by her, had been gradually revealing themselves to her during the eighteenth century, until with the destruction of the Empire they broke in. These were England and Germany. The genius of each of them seemed irreconcilable with the French genius; and yet for a century, though their full importance was not realized, they had been gradually infiltrating, and romanticism was about to assume the mission of recognizing and extolling them. But it could not see how to do this except at the cost of a renunciation of the French past.

Minds that are all of one piece and therefore simple can usually see in the complexity of their time no more than a pretext for antagonisms and conflicts: a man must be either of the past or of the future, therefore either a classic or a romantic. But in this way, the dilemma is a sterile one. Mediocre people in every period allow themselves to become shut up in it, taking up doctrinaire positions and unable to think in terms of anything but intransigence and hatred. The outstanding mind is sensitive to the contributions of both sides, it dreams of making them work together towards a wider conception that will include both of them, smash the confining dilemma and flow out to a fresh horizon. Such was Delacroix's task.

The endlessly resumed discussion of whether he was really romantic or classical can only be futile, for his originality consisted precisely in putting a stop to the contradiction in which those of his time were becoming bogged down, and in making it possible to move onwards by opening up an unknown path. The seeming incompatibility between the two cultures, the Latin and the Germanic, had been increased by the conflict, and it had to be surmounted if there was to be any progress. Both of them had, so to speak, a 'freedom of the city' in France, and it was of long standing: the Middle Ages had instinctively brought them into close union, in conformity with the natural genius, already well established, of the French people. That the style which, in the thirteenth century, attained

I SELF-PORTRAIT
*1835-7 Oil on canvas. 26 x 21 (065 x 054)*
*Louvre, Paris*

true classicism, was given the name of 'Gothic' is itself an index of how far, later on, people saw in it aspirations that are typically Germanic.

It cannot be too strongly stressed that France is destined, by her position in Europe and in history, to be the mediator between the Mediterranean civilization and that of the Nordic plains from the Baltic to the Channel. While the former was the heir to Antiquity, the latter gathered up that whole series of nomadic invasions from the East, one of whose waves brought the Gallic people. Their confluence and association produced Europe. No nation was more fitted to bring them to fusion than France, whose contrasting strains came from both sources, and whose culture was worked out through a continuous competition between borrowings from the South and from the North. To this mixture France owed the brilliant success of her civilization and art in the Middle Ages; but later she went back on her own genius, confined it to its classical bases and attempted, in succession to Renaissance Italy, to subdue Europe to a unilateral, exclusively Latin hegemony. Napoleon, in his efforts to go one better than the rationalism of the *siècle des lumières* (itself enlightened with too crude a light by the Encyclopaedists) brought Europe for a moment into subjection but in the end provoked it to rebellion, arousing in it the determination to lay claim to centuries-old national resources—which in their turn soon imposed their domination. This was the conflict which Delacroix seemed ordained, by his mixed origins, to transcend.

The bourgeoisie, of which (as we have seen) on the father's side he was the product, had adopted unquestioned the traditions and culture of the aristocracy. But it had already, in the eighteenth century, from Montesquieu to Voltaire, looked to England for a political example by which it might hope to realize its desire—a monarchy giving way before the rise of social forces and ceding to the middle classes the government of the country. Cultural influence from England had inevitably followed the political, and had prepared the way for that of Germany. But the Revolution, the Directoire and the Empire produced a stiffening of the Latin disciplines, symbolized by the 'revolutionary' religion of the Goddess Reason. Ancient Rome was considered the right and proper inspiration for every republic and the regulative model for manners and the arts. Under the Empire, education became essentially the teaching of the humanities, and was brought within the rigid mould where it still is. In it Delacroix was brought up.

When Madame Delacroix settled in Paris after the death of her husband, she arranged to send her youngest son to the Lycée Impérial, afterwards the Lycée Louis-le-Grand.[12] He wrote later: 'I know the ancients—that is to say, I have learned to put them above everything.' In 1813 he won prizes for Latin and Greek translation, and in 1814 for Greek translation. And throughout his life he remained a faithful admirer of the great men of Antiquity: of Homer, 'the source', who, however, mingled with the sublimity natural to him the imperfec-

II DANTE AND VIRGIL IN THE INFERNO
*1822 Oil on canvas. 74 x 97 (189 x 246)*
*Louvre, Paris*

tions of a primitive; of Virgil, the purist, the most perfect; of Horace, whom Delacroix described (in a letter of October 1818 to his friend Guillemardet) as 'the greatest physician of the soul', and in whom he found, as he grew older, the moral quality which—even more firm and poignant—he admired in Marcus Aurelius. In another letter (written in the same month, to Pierret) he says: 'The reading of the Ancients tempers us afresh and renews our sensibility; they are so true, so pure, and pierce through into our real thoughts. . . .'

To this basis he added the principal French classics: Corneille, whom, however, he though unequal; Racine 'the summit of perfection'; then Molière, who had the courage to be simple; Boileau, with his capacity for 'true thoughts and right ways of putting things'; Montesquieu, whose mind he loved for its lucidity and sobriety; and lastly Voltaire, that thinking-master of the eighteenth-century bourgeoisie, whom he would quote untiringly in his *Journal*, whose books would travel with him to Dieppe and to Champrosay, and whom he came to value far above Jean-Jacques Rousseau.

Among his contemporaries, he read Chateaubriand, and later, with many reservations, Balzac and George Sand (a friend of long standing, whose carelessness and exaggeration of style he nonetheless found painful) and Sainte-Beuve who, together with the *Revue des Deux Mondes* and, sometimes, the *Revue Britannique*, must have introduced him at least at second hand to many writers. It would be hard to imagine sources more in conformity with the tradition and spirit of his own class. It is easy to see how contradictory Delacroix was bound to appear to many who visited him: they found his conformity with the ideas of his class reassuring, but were disturbed by the opposite and seemingly irreconcilable tendencies which showed, provocatively, in his art.

A few years ago, in the Château de Croze (near Brive), where Delacroix had so often stayed, Madame Malvy (née Verninac) discovered a series of school notebooks, which by a happy chance had survived at the back of a bookcase (and which have been made available to me by her kindness and that of Maître Rheims). In them one can follow, as though looking over the shoulder of the child Dela- pls 39-41
croix, the interests which stirred in him during his schooldays. He describes himself as 'Eugène Delacroix, a good boy', 'in spite of what jealous people say'. They often express an acute longing for the holidays: in the *classe de troisième, première année d'humanités* under the severe rule of M. Quénon, he notes, already in March, that 'the holidays are getting near'; and when term begins again, on 26 October 1812, and it is his second year in the same class and under the same master—he remarks sadly: 'Alas, the holidays are over, but they will come again'—and adds: '*Bien pensé*'. Nonetheless he worked hard at his Greek and Latin authors. It was they who laid down in him the material for future pictures, such as that of the *Death of Marcus Aurelius*, who makes his appearance here in a composition, as also does a list of the episodes in the life of Achilles, which he was to treat later in decorating one of the cupolas of the Library of the Chambre. His literary interests were already much wider than one would have imagined. Voltaire is in evidence, naturally, but already in 1812 there are references to Montaigne, to Rabelais (whom he quotes) and even to Cervantes, Camoëns and 'Torquato Tasso, born at Ferrara'. Two years later, when he has reached the *seconde classe*, he has clearly developed, for he mentions Bernardin

de Saint-Pierre's *Paul et Virginie*, Chateaubriand's *Atala*, Tasso again, and now Ossian, whom the enthusiasts for the Nordic literature were to set against Homer.

This interest in literature was accompanied by an interest in painting: what a quantity of illustrious names already figure in his notebooks! They are drawn not only from the Italian Renaissance—Raphael, Michelangelo, Titian and Correggio—but also from the seventeenth century—Dominichino, Guercino, Guido Reni—and Spain is represented by Murillo, Flanders by Rubens and Van Dyck, while the greatest share falls to France, from Jean Cousin and the great classics, Vouet, Poussin, Le Sueur, Le Brun and Mignard, down to Jouvenet, Carl Van Loo and Vernet, and finally to the masters of the contemporary neo-classical School, 'Guérin, Girodet, Régnault'. His knowledge was already fanning out wide.

Yet the pre-romantic tendency already makes itself felt. At the age of fourteen he transcribes a poem about the Lake of Geneva, on which the longed-for storms are rising:

*Du haut de ce rocher qui porte aux cieux sa tête*
*Entendez-vous tonner et mugir la tempête?...*
*L'air gronde, le soleil a voilé son flambeau*
*Et le lac courroucé n'est qu'un vaste tombeau....*

pl 42 One finds also, in these notebooks, the dawning of his taste for the legendary Middle Ages—in phrases where he describes a novel in which a 'bold colonel' penetrates into a ruined castle with 'Gothic stairways where ghosts were often seen by the superstitious.' In these 'barbarous times . . . the belief in spectres and phantoms died hard.'

Dimly though these literary explorations reflect the new departures from convention, the many drawings in the school notebooks venture much more firmly out on to the road later taken by Delacroix's fervent inspiration. We find soldiers, battles, horsemen and the wounded—subjects he chooses from contem-
pl 40 porary life—even a sketch of a gunner firing his cannon which shows that he has discovered Géricault. His taste for the Middle Ages is confirmed by drawings of horsemen in armour—cheek by jowl, indeed, with figures and busts from Antiquity. Generals of the Empire shake down with eighteenth-century officers in cocked hats. One or two oriental figures foreshadow a later predilection. The cursive quality of his drawing, transcribing directly as it does the impulses of the nervous system, is even more revealing than the choice of subjects, and considerably so. The first sketches express a violence that is something quite new, piercing through the inevitable influence of David: now we come upon a dishevelled head in profile, now upon a tense nude, now upon a draped and bowed form foreshadowing Rodin's sketches, while other drawings exhibit some powerful strokes which suggest Géricault, or a wiry deployment of virtuosity with many flourishes. Greedy to be at life and consume it, the irrepressible and frenetic power which was soon to be amplified in his painting is already there, turning its back on the Latin wisdom and setting up claims against the prevailing taste for the constant and the definitive. It is connected with that other hereditary strain in him, with the blood of his Rhineland grandfather and Flemish grandmother, which had planted deep in him the inarticulate aspirations of the Germanic world. These were by nature irrational, resisting any attempt to tie them down

or elucidate them by logic, insatiable in their longing for a tumultuously exalted emotional life, they drew upon the organic instincts and had much more in common with the subconscious than with ideas. They were there in Delacroix, ready to collide with his traditionally Latin education, which was necessarily opposed to the expression, or even recognition of them.

Though his mother had bequeathed them to him, she was busy binding him to the world in which she had been brought up. It was a world whose relative autonomy kept the sense of its origins alive. Although her father Oeben and her father-in-law Riesener, in making their great contributions to the French art of cabinet-making, had so far assimilated the qualities of the Louis XV and Louis XVI styles as to become eminently representative of these, they had still not been absorbed by the world of the Parisian craftsmen. Under the *Ancien Régime* the Guilds were watchful and did not encourage the intrusion of foreigners: these therefore were forced to remain grouped together and to find some legal device that would authorize them to settle. As is well known, in the seventeenth century and even in the eighteenth, a certain strain of Nordic realism was introduced into the French School of painting and was maintained there, thanks in part to the persistence of a colony of people from the Northern countries, grouped in the district round about Saint-Germain-des-Prés. This was outside the boundaries of the Paris of that time and therefore outside the jurisdiction of the *maîtrises*: there they had their own chapel and even held professional meetings; and the pictures expressive of this tendency could be exhibited at the Saint-Germain fair. The Le Nain brothers, and later Watteau, were in close touch with this Flemish circle. It was rather the same with the furniture-making art in the middle of the eighteenth century: the German colony of furniture-makers was very large and had established itself likewise in a district, the Faubourg Saint-Antoine. And in fact the Cistercian nuns, who owned large church properties, procured for them the right to establish themselves in independence of the guild regulations. Sometimes the King granted them his franchise: this was the case with Oeben, and later with Riesener (who had inherited Oeben's rights by marrying the latter's widow): both men, as purveyors to the Crown, obtained their franchise from the King. It has been calculated that in ten years Riesener received from the treasury the equivalent of four hundred million francs at the old value; but with the Revolution this prosperity turned to ruin.

So Delacroix had in his own nature the deep need, in which France also stood, to make the two opposing streams that had met at her origin co-exist and marry—one of them consisting of the Germanic peoples, in the wide sense that includes Celts, Burgundians and Franks, and the other of the colonizers from the Mediterranean who imposed on the country the structures of their thinking. At the beginning of the nineteenth century the problem was particularly acute: it was becoming a conflict that was tearing both literature and the arts in two. Delacroix could feel this dualism as a live thing deep down in him, and all who knew him have stressed how clearly it made itself felt: it caused in him the juxtaposition of a thought and behaviour completely in control and subordinate to reflection, and a tormented, volcanic, 'sulphurous' temperament. It could lead to only two reactions: either to yield to it, allow it to develop with all its conflicting consequences and succumb to its unbalance, or with a firm hand to master it more and more, reducing its initial antinomy and drawing from this the elements of a complex and generous wealth; either to be a plaything of chance, torn to pieces by it, or to become an outstanding person who would extract from its contradictory energies a greater propulsive force. By choosing the second and sticking to it inflexibly, Delacroix acquired not only an intrinsic greatness but also a position as arbiter, which enabled him to dominate and resolve the conflict in which his period was exhausting itself. In so doing, he worked the transition from a past of which he was the culmination to a future of which he was the awakening.

## *New Times*

The tough alloy which Delacroix was destined to make was to be smelted in the fire of events. His inherited temperament carried potentialities only: these were to be made real by reacting to the pressures of life. Our vital impulse can only press towards the future, which, by the conditions it imposes, gives it its rhythm. The conditions in which Delacroix found himself plunged were those of one of the great moments of history.

The transition from the classical period, permeated by Latin reason, to the new period, stirred by the deep and shadowy forces of sensibility, was the expression of an even more far-reaching revolution. I have written of this elsewhere in such detail that there would be no point in going over it again.[13] To put it briefly: the old agrarian civilization, which had dominated unchallenged for centuries, indeed millennia, had begun to decline and its decline was marked by increasingly violent subsidences, which first cracked, then brought down the most lasting structures. A new era, tentatively begun by the eighteenth century, in England first, with its discovery of mass production, was soon governed by a hitherto unknown principle—energy, bringing with it the doom of the stability aimed at and achieved till then. Force, with its propulsive dynamism, was more and more completely to take the place of the motionless security of slowly won and perfected forms; change became more and more rapid, intensity grew to be a new ideal supplanting that of quality and of its patient polishing; emotion and shock were soon to be valued more than reflection and certainty.

With the French Revolution, the end of the eighteenth century made the elimination of the old monarchic organization of things irremediable, and the nineteenth century opened the struggle between the proletariat and bourgeois capitalism. Of this shock France was the initiator, but its waves went out until they unsettled the whole of Europe. This made France the centre of the new events; and yet she was at the same time the most firmly established trustee of the rural civilization of the past. And so, paradoxically, while a revolution in 1789 brought her heritage crashing down and appealed to a renovating future, to a future already open to progress, still she clung hard to Antiquity and to the Roman Republic. By a similar and parallel paradox, art, or at any rate the theory of art, became reluctant to appeal to anything but the motionless forms of classical sculpture, to an ideal laid down ever since the time of the ancient Greeks, and laid down for ever, in the cult of ideal beauty; yet at the same time the inspiration of this art was irresistibly attracted by tense and violent subjects, by subjects of cruel and ferocious energy. David, the great master of the period, the recognized head of the French School, shows Brutus, inflexible in his despair, receiving the bodies of his sons beheaded at his orders; from his *Thermopylae* and his *Horaces* to his Napoleonic soldiers, he is obsessed with the theme of men taking impulsive oaths to conquer or to die; death exalts him, whether it be that of Socrates or of Marat.

The whole of his School followed close on his heels, so that Le Barbier was provoked into exclaiming that the Salon—though more or less monopolized by the neo-classicists—was 'no more than a vast cemetery', 'a scene of frightful butchery'. We should think of this before we talk lightly of the Davidian frigidity, which indeed is only apparent. In reality the new School and its leader were obsessed with violent arts and passions, but wanted these petrified within a plastic order. Thus France was entering upon the nineteenth century with a burden of insoluble contradictions, which she left to that century to resolve. They were surely analogous to those that dwelt within Delacroix, harrassed as he was between the disciplines demanded by his classical taste and the dark, voracious violences of his heart.

For indeed that energy, that new power quivering within him, to which he would in time try to give free expression, worked in him as a consuming thirst; but the traditions of the teaching he had received confronted him with the rigid obstacle of forms consecrated by a painstakingly acquired perfection. Among the practitioners of this were his uncle Riesener whom, before his departure in 1815, he saw painting portraits in the style of David with careful, finical brushwork; Guérin, to whom his uncle introduced him long before he became his pupil on 1 October 1815;[14] and Gérard, who very soon admitted him to his salon and encouraged him at the start of his career.

Guérin has certainly a strong influence on him, for he made his acquaintance very early. On 25 August 1813, before he had left school, he wrote to one of his school friends, Jules Allard:

'I went this morning to see M. Guérin and say goodbye to him. . . . I am sorry I cannot study with him this year. But when I have left this school of ours, I mean to go to him for a time, so as to have at least a small amateur talent.' What followed is well known: when—very soon—the fall of the Empire deprived him of any hope of an official career (his family was not in favour at the Restoration—he was the son of a regicide and related to General de Lavalette, who had been condemned to death at the same time as Marshal Ney and had made his escape in memorable circumstances), Delacroix threw himself into painting, regarding it no longer as an amateur distraction but as a possible profession. The passion for art had been strong in him for several years, for when he was nine or ten, according to Théophile Silvestre, he had gone into the Louvre 'on one of his free days', and 'the sight of those pictures decided his vocation; when he left the Museum, he was a painter.'

His chosen master, Guérin, did not merely inculcate in him the formulae of the School of David: he too had in him, deep down, the secret violence that lurks under David's coldness. Guérin was an awakener of talents. In his studio Delacroix met not only Champmartin and Ary Scheffer, but also an older student, Géricault, who returned there from time to time. Géricault, in his youth, had been Delacroix's neighbour in the rue de l'Université, and indeed had gone to the Lycée Louis-le-Grand in the same year as he, in 1806; but he was seven years older and was in the *4ème* when the younger boy, though more precocious, was only in the *7ème*, so that they did not really get to know each other until Géricault, already made famous by his successes between 1812 and 1814, returned to his former master to draw from the nude. Guérin's studio was considered the one with the best tone.

'Guérin', says Etex, 'had managed to gather round him the pupils from the best families, who made it a point of honour to be above the Bohemianism and slovenliness affected by the students at the École des Beaux-Arts.'

He made a deep impression on his disciples, as we see from the *Souvenirs littéraires* of Maxime du Camp, who says that Delacroix 'never mentioned Pierre Guérin to me . . . except in terms of affection and respect and, speaking of Géricault, he told me: "His death is a great misfortune for me."'

pl 50 In Géricault, as is well known, Delacroix admired, among many other things, an elegance or—to use an expression that was then becoming current—a dandyism which he himself was proud to imitate. But most of all, the two painters—who soon became friends in spite of the awe the younger one always expressed for the elder—were drawn together by another and much more important characteristic they had in common: they were the first to give open expression to that poetry of energy, of impatient force, which romanticism was to take as one of its starting points. Géricault arrived at this through an implacable power of restraint, through will-power repressing and stilling impetuosity; but the younger man did so by giving full freedom to its insatiable wildness: it is possible that both of them learned the lesson—a secret and repressed one—from their common master. Géricault's early drawings—those, for instance, which fill a certain notebook now in the Louvre (analyzed with penetration by Raymond Regamey[15]), show that his master, far from teaching him the elaborately acquired softness and the melting forms often characteristic of his own painting, brought out in him the feeling for harsh simplifications and positive effects of light. One need only examine those pictures in which Guérin resisted the demands of the public with its taste for
pl 49 insipidity—for instance his *Return of Marcus Sextus* (painted in 1799) or his *Clytemnestra* (1817): their intensely tragic subjects, all concerned with death, the taut rigidity of the attitudes and the sinister violence of the silhouettes confess the explosive ardour smouldering under that apparent coldness. For the explosion to take place, there was need for the forms to be unfrozen, for the petrified lesson of the marbles to be rejected in favour of that of the Venetian and Flemish painters, and for a return to be made to fluid expressiveness by means of the modulation of light, sinuousness of line and vibrant colour.

In Géricault the seething inner tumult was rising, like lava in a volcano just before the eruption, but the outward firmness, learned in the studio, was further reinforced. It needed Delacroix to take the decisive step, to let the flames blaze out and the smoke roll through the free air.

Where did Delacroix find the impetus that alone could give him the courage to let loose forces which Géricault was still repressing? First and foremost, let us not forget, in the Louvre, marvellously enriched by the spoils of Napoleon's conquests. Here he experienced the revelation of the paintings of Rubens from Antwerp and of the Titians and Tintorettos brought from that city of Venice which he would always long to see and never see. Velázquez and his Spanish pupils also impressed him powerfully, as we know from the copy he made of a pl 55 picture by Carreño da Miranda. This copy is mentioned several times in the *Journal* for 1824. So powerful was the impression that the small picture known as the *Self-portrait in the costume of Hamlet*, which has reached the Louvre pl 56 from the Paul Jamot Collection,[16] is almost a pastiche.

Apart from these old masters, his bolder contemporaries, as he himself tells us, opened for him the new road on which he was impatient to set out. 'I already preferred Prud'hon and Gros to Guérin and Girodet', he confessed in the biographical note which he drew up for Piron. And in fact Gros, who was one of pl 48 David's pupils and clearly his favourite one, had had the courage to unchain the energy repressed within neo-classicism. Deep down in himself David knew perfectly well that this disciple of his was not rejecting him: on the contrary, he could hear in the work of Gros the voice he himself had refused to give to the secret violence he kept firmly gagged within him. He even praised, as Delestre records, 'the new, the unexpected look of the work Gros has done'; he rejoiced in it as a proof of the fertility of his teaching. The contradiction between David and Gros, which has sometimes been stressed, lies only in the means of expression. The tendency of both artists was to make painting more intense, more powerful, but David remained stuck in his doctrinaire vetoes, while Gros, who was already bolder, saw a way out that could be learned from Rubens—for whom indeed, as is well known, the painter of the *Sabine Women* had an unbounded pls 59, 60 admiration.[17] Both artists obeyed the drive of that energy which, we have seen, was the law governing development at that time; and both of them were leading towards Delacroix: all that was left was for him to cut the knot of extreme constricting discipline with which Géricault had tied up an extreme aspiration to violence. If we wish to understand the deep-seated logic that was then guiding the French School towards its destiny, it is here that we must look for it, not allowing ourselves to be shut in by divisions into opposed categories which mask reality by their very respect for its superficial appearance.

Delacroix recognized in Gros the example he was waiting for, and Gros felt in Delacroix the coming fusion of what he had tried to do. In 1822, whereas Guérin advised his former pupil not to exhibit his *Dante and Virgil in the Inferno* II, page 58 (to which, at Gérard's request, Thiers had devoted a sensational article setting Delacroix well and truly on the way to glory), Gros was on the side of the enthusiasts.

The development of iconography is always revealing, for the choice of images provides an unconscious symbolism that confesses a hidden course of the sensibility of a man or period. In the early nineteenth century the appearance of the horse as a theme, with its frenetic movements, its nervous prancing, its galloping

III THE MASSACRE AT CHIOS
*1824 Oil on canvas. 164 x 139 (417 x 354)*
*Louvre, Paris*

and leaping and the waving of its mane, was not the least of the signs of the time
made visible in painting. David, quite early, had brought it on to the scene,
in the shape of Potocki's magnificent courser, and he had shown Bonaparte's
pl 61 horse gambolling in the snows of the Saint Bernard. But it was left to Gros to
revive Rubens' enthusiasm and give the sensitive beast free range. The classical
painters had dedicated themselves to the celebration of the human form and its
serene poses; but now the preference was to go to the animal with the shining,
quivering coat, the hooves that strike sparks, the foaming mouth, the eye whose
gleams came straight from the nerves. Delestre, the biographer and pupil of
Gros, laid bare the true reason for the sudden attractiveness of the horse to
painters:[18]

'Man', he writes, 'distinguishes himself as such by displaying the power of his reason: he can control himself and wisely repress a useless excitement. The horse's instinct, on the contrary, allows it to be carried away by passion.'

To be carried away by passion—this was indeed the new aspiration, of which
the horse became the visible sign. Delacroix recognized that it was Gros who
pls 53, 54 used it with the greatest eloquence: 'Géricault was best at rendering the strength
of horses, but he never managed to paint an Arab horse as Gros did . . . he
hasn't the impetuosity and lightness of Gros,' who has 'rendered better than
pl 62 anyone . . . the movement and the soul of a horse, its eye, its coat and the brilliance of the gleams that pass over it.'[19] Géricault, a rider whose love of horses was
to cost him his life, could make the animal rear, but could not refrain from subjecting it to the law imposed by the firm, unyielding hand, which mastered it
and restrained its leaping: the whole of him was in both the impulse and the
pl 58 restraint. Delacroix, in water-colours that date from his early twenties, went
back to the example of Gros: he invented slender, bewildered animals which he
pl 65 shows breaking into an uncontrollable gallop, or terrified by lightning, or (if need
be) spurred on by the devil—the very horses whose infernal cavalcade was to be
heard in the music of Berlioz.

## *Fever*

What goad was required to make the energy which had been latent and tied down in David, contained by a furious effort in Géricault and burning its way outwards in Gros, take its free course in Delacroix? Quivering nerves, certainly, and Delacroix lived on his. But there was, in addition, the stimulus of fever. Even when he was still a boy, there were signs of this menace to his health; and it was not long before there began that disintegration which, causing cracks even in a robust constitution, allows the electricity of the nerves to transgress the protecting boundaries. Delacroix himself has told us (in a statement reported by Piron and amplified by Alexandre Dumas) of the trials which seemed determined to harrass him from the very first:

IV STUDY FOR THE MASSACRE AT CHIOS
*1824 Water-colour. 13 x 12 (034 x 030)*
*Louvre, Paris*

'In succession I was nearly burnt in my bed, nearly drowned in the port of Marseilles, poisoned by verdigris, hanged by the neck with a real rope and almost choked by a bunch of grapes.'

But these external accidents were not all: he was also threatened from within. Though it was not till he was about forty that his health took its decisive turn for the worse, the illness had smouldered in him for a long time. In January 1835 he admits to an alarming attack of what would develop into the 'very serious throat infection', probably tubercular, that killed him in the end in spite of all the treatments he underwent and the precautions he constantly took. For a long time his health had been undermined: even as a boy he had had accesses of fever which profoundly affected his temperament and sensibility, as well as his behaviour. The *Journal*, begun on 3 September 1822, is soon telling us of his physical sufferings: by 22 October he is complaining of his 'slightness of build . . . I am nearly always ill, I cannot talk for long . . .'—and this when he was only twenty-four! Two years later, on 27 February 1824, he notes: 'My health is bad, as capricious as my imagination.' His correspondence even suggests that the first attacks of his illness go back several years further: in a letter to his brother, the general, on 20 September 1820, he pinpoints the beginning of it. He had left his brother's place at Le Louroux to go and stay with his sister in the forest of Boixe in Angoumois. The sun was hot, and there was 'a long halt'; but, he adds, 'the heat of the day became too great, and I went to have a rest in the inn: stupidly I caught a chill, which degenerated almost immediately into a slight fever. I reached Châtellerault really ill. . . .' He was forced to stay in the inn there for several days, waiting for the diligence, whose timetable was erratic. The fever went on for nearly a month, according to the correspondence:

'It still has hold of me, and is making me as thin as a match and about as strong as a bit of tinder. . . . It was a slow fever, and attacked me every day, no appetite, perpetual boredom and disgust with life, and such weakness that I would faint when I got up out of my chair.'

In spite of quinine and other treatment, it pursued him to Souillac, where a month later he was with his brother-in-law Verninac. We can see a foreshadowing of what was to become the very rhythm of his life: 'The beginnings of the fever,' he complains to Soulier on 22 October 1820, 'gliding through my nerves, began to set the blood in my veins oscillating between icy cold and devouring heat.' Back in Paris, he still could not throw off his illness: 'The fever', he tells his sister on 6 December, 'has got its roots in my bones and never misses its time.' It was to be, from then onwards, the intermittent but indefatigable companion of his life. It worked on his sensibility: 'I am always possessed by a slight fever, which makes me liable to be more emotional,' he confesses in the *Journal* on 12 April 1824. It explains those singular alternations of exhaustion and boredom with an exaltation that inflamed his genius and drove it onwards. It even became one of the components of his idea of art, for he spoke later of the 'need to have fever' in order to over-excite the imagination and go beyond oneself.

This going beyond the normal was a new element in art. Delacroix admitted it and cultivated it as a major resource of inspiration, revealing unknown possibilities in us. In this too, Delacroix was a forerunner of the modern school. In

*Fig 1* STUDY OF HORSES. Pen drawing. Cabinet des Dessins, Louvre, Paris.

his *Souvenirs littéraires* the critic Maxime du Camp, who did not understand Delacroix completely but was on friendly terms with him, has caught the painter at a moment when he was in this abnormal condition which, perhaps owing to the accident of bad health, he was one of the first to use as a means to creative activity. It was in the studio in the rue Notre-Dame-de-Lorette, where he worked for thirteen years, from 1845 to 1857. In that 'overheated studio, where he was always afraid of the cold, where he wore a woollen surcoat and kept his neck swathed in an enormous cravat because of his weak throat, and where he lived in a stifling atmosphere, he gave himself up too much to himself and did not put up enough resistance to that inner wildness, the fever of work.'

Again the word 'fever', the right word for the quivering energy which gripped the painter.

'I was lying on a sofa, watching him work. Neither of us spoke, and he had forgotten I was there. He was painting a small picture, a *Fantasia* . . . Delacroix was extremely animated, he was breathing noisily; his brush took on an astonishing agility. The hand of the horseman in the picture became bigger and bigger . . . and acquired such proportions that I exclaimed: "But my dear master, what are you doing?" Delacroix gave a startled cry, as if I had woken him abruptly. He said to me: "It's too hot in here, I am going mad." Then he took his palette knife and with a single stroke removed the hand. He had a wild look; mechanically he applied a few scumbling strokes to the foreground, as if to calm himself down. "It will soon be dark," he said, "shall we go out?" And a few moments later we were walking along side by side in silence. . . .'

It was then, in the street (night had fallen, it was in the winter), that Delacroix muttered: 'They say work is a rapture; no, it is an intoxication, as I know very well.' How Delacroix lives again in this surprisingly little known passage!

In this way the contradictory tendencies, Latin and Germanic, in Delacroix's ancestry were defined and deployed by the conflict between the mental rules received by him from his classical and Cartesian education, and the unexpected rhythm produced in him by his state of health and his fevered sensibility, which led him into that unquiet and exhausting zone where reason abdicates its control and gives place to unforeseen revelations. For the second time destiny helped Delacroix to cross the gap between the past, whose heritage he upheld, and the future, whose doors he broke down with reverberating blows.

The task laid on him was to settle the strife between the confused powers jostling within him and the efforts of his will to dominate them and to give them a fresh unity. Being physically too weak for active life, he transposed the battle into the world of images, projecting on it, as though on a screen, the inner tumult which he undertook to surmount. In that world he endowed the tormenting forces with a face; he watched their growth and—spectator as well as creator—gave direction and final resolution to their conflict.

## *The Child of his Time*

If instinct made Delacroix, burdened as he was by a drama within him, shift from the plane of ordinary life to that of imaginative creation, the very age in which he lived, together with the whole generation of the romantics, was pushing him in this direction, which was indeed the only issue from the crisis whose playthings and actors he and his contemporaries were. What his heredity had placed in him and his physical condition had developed was to be also imposed on him by historical circumstances, for there was a strange harmony between the various fatalities acting on him.

Delacroix was thrown into the battle of romanticism. This movement, it is often said, was born of the *maladie du siècle*. What does that mean? The revelation of energy which, as we have stressed, was to become the new principle of society, in the field of practical matters as well as in the aspirations of men's minds, had been favoured by events. At the end of the eighteenth century society had been suddenly struck and carried away by a storm of forces, hitherto ignored or repressed and now suddenly liberated. The Revolution, after the pause during which the Directoire had attempted to recover breath, had handed on its radical brutality and violent paroxysms to the Empire. War—and above

V GREECE EXPIRING ON THE RUINS OF MISSOLONGHI
*1827 Oil on canvas. 82 x 58 (209 x 147)*
*Musée des Beaux-Arts, Bordeaux*

all the Napoleonic wars, for in Napoleon there arose the new genius to fit the new course of events—had spread an intoxication and a frenzy of action over the whole of Europe. Battle ranged over the continent like a hurricane; the flame and thunder of artillery burst out everywhere on an unprecedented scale; no place was safe from the charges of the cavalry, now the lord of battles. Energy, that new power, was revealing itself to the world with the sudden violence of a squall. Literature and the fine arts echoed this impatience of all restraint. 'Arise, longed for tempests,' cried Chateaubriand, and Germany was already answering: *'Sturm und Drang!'*

The young, from Géricault onwards, had been brought up in an atmosphere of enthusiasm for war and for its epic expansion. Delacroix's first years had been fed on tales of those battles in which his two brothers had ridden gallantly out—in gaudy, gleaming uniforms, one of them to death, the other to the Empire's fall, which condemned him to frustration. After this prodigious interlude, it seemed that everything was working together to re-establish the former order, but the Restoration had worse in store: behind the bright curtain of the repatriated *émigrés*, the rise of the bourgeoisie, of its materialism. Some might see in the Restoration a return to the past after a convulsion which had been surmounted and annulled. In reality the new order was a more stifling one: it committed the future; for the motley but exalted ideal which had raised the men of the Revolution, and then those of the Empire, above themselves, it had substituted a positive idea of life which dissipated what were now looked on as dreams and took account of nothing but concrete realities. This harsh awakening filled the *enfants du siècle* with despair, and their spokesman, Musset, in his *Confessions* had expressed better than anyone its cruelty and the misery it caused in the souls of a frustrated young generation. The 'terrible wind making all the trees shudder' had given place, he said to:

'A deep silence.... In the gloomy forest of the old Europe everything had trembled, then silence came instead.... The whole sickness of the present time comes from two causes, and the people that has passed through '93 and through 1814 bears in its heart two wounds: what was, no longer is; what will be, is not yet. Look nowhere else for the secret of our troubles.... There formed, from that time on, two camps: on one side, the exalted, suffering spirits, all the expansive souls, who had need of the infinite, bowed their heads, weeping.... On the other side, the men of flesh remained standing, inflexible, satisfied with definite amusements and untroubled by any cares except that of counting their money. There was only a sobbing and a burst of laughter: the one coming from the soul, the other from the body.'

The new men had decided to believe only in hard facts, to study nothing else and to base on them the 'positive' attitude of mind. But these facts brought only an overwhelming disappointment to the hearts that had begun to throb—and to set the drums throbbing—for something quite different, which had suddenly

VI THE EXECUTION OF THE DOGE MARINO FALIERO
*1827 Oil on canvas. 57 x 45 (145 x 115)*
*The Wallace Collection, London*

vanished like smoke. But it could be recreated by the imagination, which therefore became, for these young men, the last recourse and, as Delacroix put it, 'the queen of faculties'. It alone made possible an escape from the hard facts. To these, more and more, by dint of meditating on the scattered elements rescued from the past by memory or brought by hearsay from distant and unknown lands, it opposed constructions of its own, in which desire played a greater part than did reality. It alone could provide the food capable of satisfying the appetites aroused by the revolutionary adventure and the Napoleonic epic—appetites apparently forbidden by the crash of the 'impetuous centaur' to the ground when the horse had been struck down. In the imagination romanticism was to seek its supreme resource, caught as it was between the empty shells of the dead traditions and the crushing fact of growing materialism. Delacroix was to establish the reign of the imagination in between a rejection of academic frigidity and a refusal of the dead weight of realism.

This man, who had learned to find delight for his spirit in the reading of the classics, now turned to the examination of new and very different books, in which the rising trouble in men's minds was beginning to inspire the hymn to the imaginary. Their very source was inevitably other than, indeed opposed to, that of the older writers: they could not derive from the old culture with its self-satisfaction and satiety, but only from those which it had disdainfully pushed aside, and whose contribution was to express instincts to which an answer, not yet in existence, would be sought. To begin with, there was the culture of Great Britain. It had been discovered, discreetly, in eighteenth-century France, and Voltaire himself, little gifted though he was to understand it at all profoundly, had turned to it with curiosity. Here Delacroix found Shakespeare, who to his classical judgment might well seem 'confused in the midst of sublime things left incomplete', but who extracted from the emotional side of him expressions of unbounded 'admiration' and even 'exaltation'. He found also writers who were more or less his contemporaries: Sir Walter Scott, an inexhaustible source of thrilling stories; and one very close to him and his own problems—Byron. But there was also German culture, then becoming known in France, especially since the publication of Madame de Staël's influential book in 1810; and here Delacroix opened his mind to Goethe and to Schiller.

Delacroix became aware very early of English literature, which had penetrated into France a considerable time before: Shakespeare began to be known there in about 1745-48, even before the great twenty-volume edition by Le Tourneur, which was published between 1776 and 1782. It has been shown that between 1760 and the Revolution about three hundred books from across the Channel were translated into French. The emigration, by sending abroad a hundred and fifty thousand French people who till then had chosen to keep their intellectual curiosity shut up in their own country, had transformed even the most obstinate of them, and at the fall of the Empire their return home produced a great effect. Delécluze, in his *Souvenirs de soixante années*, gives a date to this literary renewal: 'Walter Scott and Byron invaded France in 1816.' And indeed there were twenty complete editions of Byron between 1818 and 1847; there were two productions of *Marino Faliero*, one at the Comédie Française, the other at the Porte Saint-Martin, and its theme inspired the picture which Delacroix sent to the VI, page 74

Salon in 1827. But he was by no means the first person to transfer Byron's
themes into painting: in this, as in other things, Géricault precedes him, for he
began in 1819-20 his series of lithographs on the *Giaour* and *Lara*, and in 1823
followed them up with the *Bride of Abydos*. These poems, and the works of
Sir Walter Scott haunted Delacroix to the end of his life. Robaut[20] reckons that
more than fifteen of his pictures were inspired by the *Giaour*: the episode of the
pl 204 battle with the Pasha alone made its appearance at the Salon in 1827, and was
206 repeated in 1835 and 1856, each time thought out and handled afresh. In 1824
Delacroix was already reading *Childe Harold*: on 16 May he writes in the *Journal*:
'Discussed *Childe Harold* with my aunt'—meaning Madame Riesener, with
whom he was staying at Frépillon. A few days earlier, on 11 May, he noted: 'To
fire yourself for ever, remember certain passages of Byron', and added (referring
to the *Bride of Abydos*): 'I feel these things as painting can render them.'

Delacroix could read English literature in the original, for already by 1816 he
was learning the language. In that year one of his school friends, Horace Raisson,
who later collaborated with Balzac, had introduced him to Edouard Soulier
(in 1827 Delacroix put the portraits of the two side by side in a lithograph,
Robaut no. 192). Soulier, brought up in England by his father who was an
*émigré*, had already travelled a good deal; he gave English lessons—in particular
to the poet Andrieux of the Académie Française, the man who, when consulted
by Balzac's parents on his first attempt at writing (a play about Cromwell)
strongly advised that he should busy himself with anything rather than literature.
He worked at the *Hôtel des Domaines Extraordinaires*, where Raisson himself
was employed, but was not on the established staff: his room was on the upper
floor of the building in the Place Vendôme, and he was secretary to the Intendant,
the Marquis de Maisonfort, whom he later followed to Italy when he became
French Minister at Florence. He had learned water-colour painting, then a
peculiarly British technique, from Copley Fielding, who was a friend of his, and
he transmitted its secrets to Delacroix at the same time as those of 'that fair
tongue' in which the painter was 'so desiderous to be readily instructed' that in
December 1818 he took the trouble to write a whole letter in it. Even in 1817 he
pl 67 had already hammered out with the dictionary a 'miserable letter' which, 'however
66 clumsy, will ring true' and had sent it to Elisabeth Salter. Foreign languages
indeed seem to have been associated with his early love affairs: even in 1814 there
is a mention, in one of his school notebooks, of a 'pretty guirll' (*sic*) next to the
exclamation '*O cara troppo fanciulla*', and to these incoherences: '*les perfides
attraits que j'adore . . . Beauté . . . volage, volage!*' It was not long before he
pl 125 got to know the British painters: in 1816-17, at the Louvre, he met Bonington, a
young pupil of Gros. Through Soulier he made the acquaintance not only
of Copley Fielding but of his brothers, Newton and Thalès: with Thalès he
became so friendly that in 1823 he shared the studio which the young
pl 124 Englishman had rented on the attic floor of 20 rue Jacob. In 1825 Delacroix set out for England and stayed there for a few months.

Germany also was very much in his mind. German literature and philosophy were beginning to be widely known in France. In 1801 Charles Villers had published, at Metz, his *Philosophie de Kant*, while at Amsterdam there appeared Kinker's essay in French on the *Critique of Pure Reason*. Again it was the *émigrés* who ensured that a hitherto disdained culture should penetrate into France. In 1802, the year when de Gerando (who had married an Alsacian woman who was well up in German philosophy) was writing a *Mémoire sur Kant*, Destutt de Tracy read to the Institut a paper on Kinker's book, which made a great impression on Maine de Biran. Many thinkers now turned towards Germany—among them Ampère, Cuvier and, of the younger men, Guizot and Cousin, whose lectures Delacroix later attended, though only six years his junior. 'When I left school', he recalled on 4 October 1855, 'I wanted . . . to know everything; I went to lectures; I thought I would become a philosopher with pl 47 Cousin, another poet who was trying to be a *savant*.' Cousin, who from the age of twenty had been pushed by his master Royer-Collard, took his place when he went into politics, and in 1815 became *Maître de Conférences* on Philosophy at the *École Normale*, besides teaching at the Sorbonne. In 1817 he expounded the work of the Scottish philosophers, superceding the philosophy of Condillac, which was the basis of the psychology then accepted in France; and from 1819 he devoted himself to Kant. Delacroix, in a letter of 16 November 1818 to his friend Pierret, says that he hopes 'this year again to be present at the beginning of Cousin's course of lectures.'

Above all, there had been Madame de Staël's famous book *De l'Allemagne*, published in 1810 and banned by Napoleon. In his *Journal* for 26 January 1824 Delacroix tells us that, as he was thinking of writing 'a sort of memorandum on painting' (the idea later developed into his sketch for a dictionary of the Fine Arts) he had been consulting the works of the authoress of *Corinne*: 'I find in Madame de Staël exactly my own way of developing my ideas on painting. This art, like music, is *above thought*'; and he adds: 'Hence their advantage over literature, through vagueness.' In this note we can see Delacroix cheerfully crossing the frontier of the traditional rationalism, with his mind wide open to the revelations offered by German thought. In the *Œuvres littéraires*,[21] among the *Impressions* and *Méditations* taken from the papers published by Piron, there is to be found a long dissertation on Kant: it proves that Delacroix had initiated himself into Kant's theory of aesthetics, and that he was not ignorant of the theories which Madame de Staël had undertaken to popularize. Delacroix understands that to the Germans the basis of art was not 'imitation of nature': on the contrary, 'Man has in his soul innate sentiments, which real objects would never satisfy, and it is to these sentiments that the imagination of the painter and the poet is able to give form and life. What does the first of the arts, music, imitate?'

In this way there was emerging in Delacroix a new idea, quite different from the one long accepted by the Latin tradition—the idea that the purpose of painting is not to imitate either nature or a model prescribed by the canons of ideal beauty. Its mission is to express the deep life of our soul, and from its very 'vagueness' it draws a superior power, that of reaching, beyond clear-cut and distinct thought, the zone which we now call the subconscious. Painting thus becomes close to music.

These new convictions, soon to be the basis of Delacroix's philosophy and the justification of his painting, were not to be found by him in the teaching he had had. In himself, then? Perhaps; but he was surely helped by the increasing acceptance of a new mental world, foreign to the Latin tradition and founded on Germanic philosophy—of which he obtained glimpses very early, and which awakened, deep down in him, aspirations placed there, no doubt, by his heredity. Before he left school he knew something of German philosophy: and he often again heard talk of it in the salons he visited—in Gérard's, for instance, where the eminent Germans who passed through Paris were always received, among them Humboldt, that close friend of Goethe. He came on it again in the conversation of Heine, whom he frequently met with George Sand and Chopin and who, in his *Salon de 1831*, had given currency to the idea that art derives more from the soul than from nature. He found also that it was much in the minds of some of his old friends such as the Lyonnais painter Chenavard who, as he tells us in his *Journal* (September 1854) discussed Leibnitz and Kant with him. Delacroix was, it must be admitted, apt to sense in it the tedium of 'what is beyond our range'.

But in Goethe, who was more of a literary artist and less of a metaphysician, he found, presented more attractively and more accessibly, those basic ideas which set him free from the Latin limitations and answered his own instincts. In particular he read and re-read, as the supplement to the *Journal* shows,[22] Blaze de Bury's introduction to the translation of *Faust*. What struck him was the idea that, side by side with the explicit language of words expressing ideas, man has at his disposal 'the symbolic language of his inner contemplation', whose go-between is the image. Delacroix copied out a passage from Goethe:

'I should like to renounce words and, like plastic nature, speak only in images. This fig-tree, this snake . . . the man who could decipher its real meaning would eventually be able to do without all spoken or written language.'

In this way: 'The soul tells, by drawing, a part of its essential being, and these are in fact the deepest secrets of creation.'

The purpose of painting consists, then, not in the description of realistic appearances, any more than in that of intelligible ideas which words can explain: it is to reveal, by the expressive and suggestive power of its phantasms an inner world, the world which the artist secretly contains. Such was the conviction forming gradually in Delacroix.

As he became aware of this inner, personal vision and had recourse to it more and more, he used to express it the word 'ideal', and used it in what, for philosophy, was a German sense. The French had been accustomed to talk of the ideal, of ideal beauty, but in the Platonic sense, meaning whatever is close to the perfect and absolute type, to the Idea. Delacroix (and this proves that he was influenced by German thought) meant by 'ideal' that which is mental, therefore subjective, stained by the individual's own way of seeing and feeling. He makes this clear in a fragment which attacks the very basis of objectivity:[23]

'A fact is almost nothing, since it passes. All that remains of it is the idea; really it only exists in the idea, because this gives it a colour and represents it by tingeing it in its own way and according to the mood of the moment. . . . A fact does not really exist because thought gives it a second life by colouring it, by *idealizing* it.'

His underlining the word shows clearly to what extent for him it signifies subjectivity—quite contrary to the classical usage, which takes 'ideal' to mean an absolute. Not only his thought but the words he chooses to express it echo German philosophy.

## *Liberation of the Personality*

That, then, was how Delacroix's mind was shaped. Unknown forces awoke in him at every fresh shock from the outside. He listened with enchantment to the confused, sonorous hubbub, which was like that of a great orchestra tuning up, with an increasing multitude of incoherent sounds, before it launches out into the playing of the expected symphony: already, by their particular timbres, one can distinguish the main groups of instruments, which will soon unite but are still confusedly clashing. A classical education inculcating the taste for lucid, co-ordinated and self-mastering thought; a British contribution encouraging poetic feeling and heightening the power of enjoyment and suffering; a German contribution driving him to the expression of secret aspirations too vehement to fit in with the traditional rationalism: all these—logic and lucidity, ardour and passion, subjectivism and suggestion—had to be brought to life and associated in a fertile co-operation, in order to extract from this a painting.

But around what rallying centre can tendencies so various, each referring to a different culture, be grouped? There is no rule broad enough to include them. The only common ground that can be assigned to them is the actual place where they meet and develop—that is to say, the personality whose wealth and torment they are. If the individual, with his own way of feeling and expressing this, and with the ecstasy he derives from the diversity that divides him, can become the subject of art; and if art is no longer obliged to respect and apply the theories accepted by the collectivity but, on the contrary, to adapt the rules to the personal independence stifled by those theories and to place them at its service—then the problem would be solved.

Towards this solution the Western world and its art had been moving for several centuries. The craftsman, who confined himself to placing his individual gifts at the service of an iconography imposed by society and of a technique elaborated by corporate effort, had been succeeded in the Renaissance by the artist, asserting himself as an exceptional being; but the artist still put himself wholly at the service of a universal beauty. Very soon, however, there appeared, side by side with the notion of principles that must be observed, the idea of an artist's 'manner', the style proper to each artist. With Giorgione painting began to advocate a world which is not the one we are in, nor the one our reason can conceive by elaborating its perfection, but another world—the world a man lives within himself, like a dream or a vision which he means to reveal. While the processes of thought tend necessarily to universality, those of feeling assert themselves in their particularities, and art will be a means of transcribing and communicating them. In the eighteenth century reason, though still triumphant, was more critical, indeed sceptical, than affirmative, and the men of that century began to think that opposite the identity of the rational forms there stood the relativity of the feelings—whose importance in the field of the arts was already stressed by the Abbé du Bos in 1719. Art became more and more bound up with sensibility, as was indicated by the very term 'aesthetic',[24] adopted by Baumgarten as the title for the *Traité* which he published in 1750 and 1758.

When Delacroix came on the scene, this emergent contradiction had become critical: must art base itself, first and foremost, on conformity and established truths, or, on the contrary, on invention and originality? The Latin culture championed by Italy and France opted for the former solution; Germany and England voted for the second. And in France, although the disciplines founded on dogmas desperately closed their ranks, the problem had now been raised. It was raised at the very heart of the neo-classical School from which Delacroix as a student received both his intransigent professions of faith and his hidden doubts.

Delacroix could perceive these in his master Guérin, himself a disciple of Regnault. Nothing, it might be thought, could be more Davidian than his art. But David, we must not forget, himself used to tell his pupils that he intended to prepare them 'through your nature and not against your nature'. Delécluze, who was a pupil of his before devoting himself to criticism, has stated that David 'recognized that a master must not seek to transmit his own manner, but that his duty is to cultivate and develop the salient qualities of his pupils.' Guérin went even further in this direction. With him it was rather as it was with the excellent Gustave Moreau, whose studio inspired both Rouault and Matisse, as well as other Fauves. From Guérin's studio there came many romantics: to Géricault and to Delacroix we may add Sigalon and d'Orsel. The truth is, the painters of David's School were often tormented by the new ideas, but their temptation was stifled by their inability to invent a new and free technique. Here again Delécluze was clear-sighted, when, discussing Guérin, he noted that his 'picturesque execution . . . is devoid of suddenness and energy.' To express the new uneasiness there was needed a fresh grammar and vocabulary. It was Delacroix's task as a painter to forge this. His predecessors had failed to do so, not even perceiving its pressing necessity.

The case of Girodet is even more striking than that of Guérin. All the ferments of romanticism were present in him; Chateaubriand, Ossian, moonlight nudged at him, trying to inspire him. But his style remained icy and froze all these aspirations—and this although ever since he left David's studio he had been haunted by the problem of personal originality as the creator of new things. Hardly had he reached Rome, the proud possessor of his Grand Prix, when he wrote to his tutor, Trioson:

'As soon as I came into the presence of the productions of the princes of painting, I felt the *need to be myself*, to *become original*; I have done everything to this end, and I hope I have succeeded in making *something new*'.

What is more, a passage written by Girodet supplied Delacroix with the basis for a fruitful train of thought. On 27 April 1817, Girodet had read, at a meeting of the four Académies, some 'considerations on originality in relation to the arts of design', and these were published a few days later in the *Moniteur* (besides eventually finding a place in his *Œuvres*). The problems of that official painter corresponded too closely to those agitating Delacroix at the start of his career for him not to be deeply influenced by them; and in fact he took the trouble to recopy the passages that came closest to what he was seeking, in a notebook which dates from the same year.

Girodet, that pupil of David, arraigned the dogma of ideal beauty with which traditional painters had fettered themselves: to it he opposed a recognition of the relativity of the beautiful—which Delacroix, much later, was to reaffirm in two articles, *Questions sur le Beau* and *Des variations du Beau*, published in 1854 and 1857 in the *Revue des Deux Mondes*.

'How', wrote Girodet in a passage which Delacroix copied out, 'can the artist, driven as he is by curiosity into remote regions, and seeing as he does in each one of the peoples of the world the different and peculiar idea it has of the beautiful . . . remain a firm adherent to the healthy doctrine of absolute beauty?'

This was to raise afresh the problem indicated a century earlier by du Bos, and to deduce from it the validity of the future solution—that the artist has the right to be original, and feels the need of this.

'The artist, who is only a part of the great whole, has but one soul and limited senses organized in a certain way; he has only one way of feeling and being struck by things.'

That 'quality of absolute particularity', which manifests itself in 'the independence resulting from the artist's own impulse', and that 'rapid instinct preceding reflection' gave him 'the faculty of freely seizing upon the objects of imitation offered him by nature, so as to subject nature to the power of his genius, and to co-ordinate them with his own conceptions.' Here, surely, are the basic ideas later taken up again so frequently by Delacroix in his notes.

Girodet recognized that the great painters of the past made use of this faculty: 'All men of originality have stamped their works with an unique and particular character, the Schools and systems notwithstanding.' Here is a disciple of David urging a young man to rise in insurrection against the discipline of rules. Delacroix, unquestionably, quivered in response to this unexpected call whose reverberation must have astounded the dome of the Institut:

'If this character is an inflexible one, then from the struggle between the artist and his time it is the artist who emerges victorious—and genius, that irresistible torrent, carries away with it the conspiring crowd of false principles and absurd systems.'

It was in vain that Girodet uttered a few prudent reserves, and warned artists against 'imitation originality', against the danger of falling into 'continual torment' and of 'merely giving birth to extravagant conceptions for themselves alone'—this did not prevent Delacroix from responding. He felt in himself that 'imperious need to listen only to his own inspirations without regard to the established rules'; he saw himself at the centre of the 'concentric circles, the remotest of which touches those regions of deep darkness in which the monsters have their birth.' Girodet could hardly have known Goya's etching to which, just twenty years before, the artist had appended the inscription: 'The sleep of Reason produces monsters'; but Delacroix may well have been familiar with it already through Guillemardet's father. Certainly he was well aware that

VII STILL LIFE WITH LOBSTERS
*1827 Oil on canvas. 31 x 42 (080 x 106)*
*Louvre, Paris*

he relied, and always would rely on the Latin heritage: the day would come when he would declare that 'reason must be a party to all our swervings'. Surely he was then dimly remembering Girodet's warning: 'But there are still limits, even in delirium.'

In this text, of which he stressed the passages that struck him the most, that lodged themselves in his memory and gave direction to his thinking, Delacroix found both the forward impulse (for it spoke of 'times when people look for a liberator to come to their rescue') and the precise limit that would guard him against excess: 'A fertile imagination governed by an enlightened judgment.' Delacroix was to take up the opening definition and make it his own: 'To be original is, above all, to preserve the true character of nature by co-ordinating it with our conceptions.'

In those two large pages of notes Delacroix had written down his future *credo*: one of the last of the Davidians, one of the masters of the School of which he himself was a disciple and with which he perhaps had not yet the courage to break completely, had given him the framework within which he would be able to reconcile his innate respect for rational control and for the masterpieces of the past with his growing thirst to venture into new fields.

Delacroix knew what he wanted, and how he wanted to achieve it. Armed with what he had inherited from the past, with impulses received from the present and with strange inspirations within demanding expression, he could now undertake his life's work.

VIII BARON SCHWITER
*c.1827 Oil on canvas. 86 x 56 (218 x 143)*
*The National Gallery, London*

# NOTES ON THE PLATES TO CHAPTER II

*Talleyrand's son?*

That Delacroix's aristocratic bearing and the set of his head resemble Talleyrand's, whose natural son he may have been, is incontestable. The resemblance between them at different ages is even more remarkable: in each of them the nose is at first sharp and slightly turned up (pls 35 and 36), but becomes straighter and thicker with age (pls 37 and 38).

*35* JACQUES-LOUIS DAVID: *The Coronation of Napoleon I (detail of Talleyrand), 1804. Louvre, Paris.*

*36* HENRI-FRANÇOIS RIESENER: *Portrait of Delacroix, c. 1814. Private collection.*

*37* ARY SCHEFFER: *Portrait of Talleyrand, 1828. Musée Condé, Chantilly.*

*38 Delacroix. Photograph by Legé and Bergeron, 1862. Bibliothèque Nationale, Paris.*

*Schoolboy drawings*

In Delacroix's unpublished school notebooks some of his distinctive characteristics soon make their appearance: his nervous drawing, for instance, in the flourishes (pl 39), the liveliness with which he applies a wash (pl 40), the fascination with warlike subjects implanted in him by the epic days of the Empire, and even the conflicting attraction of classical and romantic themes (pl 42).

*39-42 Pages from Delacroix's school exercise books, c. 1812. 39, 40, 42: Malvy-Verninac Collection. 41: Bibliothèque de l'Institut d'Art et d'Archaeologie, Paris.*

*The old masters*

Delacroix studied the masters, all of them, from Holbein, the sharp realist (pl 44), to Raphael, the devotee of ideal beauty (pl 43), not neglecting, either, those who at the time were still regarded as 'gothic', such as Cranach (pl 45).

*43 Sketch after Raphael's 'Balthazar Castiglione'. Cabinet des Dessins, Louvre, Paris.*

*44 Sketch after Holbein's 'Duke of Norfolk'. Private collection, Switzerland.*

*45 Sketch after Cranach's 'Man in Armour'. Cabinet des Dessins, Louvre, Paris.*

*From the life*

Delacroix was equally interested in the life of everyday, which he caught in bold sketches: he followed his friend Leblond through the stages of a sneeze (pl 46), and got into trouble, as Constantin Guys was to do, for sketching the audience at lectures he attended at the Sorbonne and the College de France (pl 47).

46 *Frédéric Leblond. Cabinet des Dessins, Louvre, Paris.*

47 *Students at a lecture. Cabinet des Dessins, Louvre, Paris.*

*Direct influences* Having gone as a pupil to Guérin, whose Davidian sense of drama impressed him (pl 49), he looked about for examples of a more free technique: this he found in the sketches of Gérard, a family friend who helped him at the start of his career (pl 51), but above all in Gros, that unconscious romantic (pl 48), and in the expressive power of Géricault, an older pupil of Guérin (pl 50).

48 ANTOINE-JEAN GROS: *Napoleon visiting the Victims of the Plague at Jaffa, 1804. Louvre, Paris.*

49 PIERRE-NARCISSE GUÉRIN: *Return of Marcus Sextus, 1799. Louvre, Paris.*

50 THÉODORE GÉRICAULT: *Portrait of Eugène Delacroix, c. 1818. Musée des Beaux-Arts, Rouen.*

51 FRANÇOIS GÉRARD: *Portrait of Madame Le Cerf. Louvre, Paris.*

*The example of Géricault* Delacroix, like Gros and Géricault, found in the horse an incarnation of vital ardour; but his tendency was to stress not so much, like Géricault, its powerful forms (pl 53) as its nervous, quivering movement—though of this also he could sometimes find examples in the elder pupil, especially in his sketches (pl 54). The Turk on the rearing horse in Delacroix's 1824 *Massacre at Chios* (pls 52 and III), is clearly reminiscent of Géricault's 1812 *Officier de Chasseurs.*

52 *The Massacre at Chios, 1824 (detail). Louvre, Paris.*

53 GÉRICAULT: *Five Horses in a Stable. Louvre, Paris.*

54 GÉRICAULT: *Officier de Chasseurs. Study for large painting exhibited at the Salon, 1812. Louvre, Paris.*

*The lesson of Velázquez* The nineteenth century discovered Spanish painting and its bold techniques. Through Carreño da Miranda, of whom he copied a picture (pl 55), Delacroix was led to his master Velázquez. The lesson bore fruit, and his so-called *Self-portrait in the costume of Hamlet* (pl 56) shows what his imagination and execution gained from it.

55 *Charles II of Spain (after a painting by Carreño da Miranda, then believed to be a Velázquez), 1824. P. Fabius Collection, Paris.*

56 *Self-portrait in the costume of Hamlet, 1821. Louvre, Paris. Now at the Place Furstenburg studio.*

*Horses* The horse was to be the preferred animal of the nineteenth century. Its energy, freedom of movement and swift nervous responses were right for the new period that saw the release of the ardours of romanticism and the beginnings of modern speed. Napoleon's use of it transformed military tactics. Its galloping ran through painting, and through music from Chopin to Berlioz and Liszt. In succession to Géricault (pl 63), Gros (pl 62) and even—earlier—David (pl 61), Delacroix was to be the finest interpreter of its vitality (pls 57, 58, 65).

But in a century in which the life of the soul was the main interest of art, the attraction of the horse lay chiefly in its expressive eye, traversed by moods of frenzy and melancholy. Already David had been struck by this (pls 59, 60) and, for all the coldness of his technique, was the first, since Rubens, to open this path to Delacroix (pl 64).

57 *Frightened Horse emerging from the Water, 1828. Bibliothèque Nationale, Paris.*

58 *Study of Horses. Musée d'Art Moderne, Paris.*

59, 60 DAVID: *The Rape of the Sabine Women, 1799 (details). Louvre, Paris.*

61 DAVID: *Bonaparte crossing the Saint Bernard Pass. Musée National, Malmaison.*

62 GROS: *Murat at the battle of Aboukir. Sketch for painting now at Versailles. Institute of Arts, Detroit.*

63 GÉRICAULT: *The Race of Riderless Horses on the Corso in Rome, 1817. Louvre, Paris.*

64 *The Battle of Taillebourg, 1837 (detail). Musée de Versailles, Galerie des Batailles.*

65 *White Horse frightened by a Storm, 1824. Museum of Fine Arts, Budapest.*

*Letter to Elisabeth Salter*

A notebook of Delacroix's now in the Louvre, contains manuscript notes (pl 67), one of which seems to be the draft of the letter he wrote in English to Elisabeth Salter (pl 66), who was maid to his sister, Henriette de Verninac, and with whom he fell in love. He mentions her in a letter of December 1817 to Pierret, and at the end of that month he is more definite:

'This evening, leaning heavily on the dictionary, I wrote a wretched letter that will tell her what she needs to know. I don't understand it too well, and God knows if anyone else will; my soul was in suspense and pulled by the ear in one direction, in the other by the wish to say things that have some common sense in them.'

Meanwhile Delacroix went down to the kitchen and had just begun to make love to the maid, when the unexpected return of his sister sent him back to his room; and there, he adds, 'with my head full of what has happened between us, I shall copy out, warm and fair, my barbarous and tormented letter'—and he signs it: Yorick.

66 *Portrait of Elisabeth Salter, c. 1817. Private collection.*

67 *Two pages from one of Delacroix's notebooks (Carnet 9156, pp. 22, 23). Cabinet des Dessins, Louvre, Paris.*

35

36

37

38

Cahier de corrigés, De la classe De 3ème
Première année d'humanités, au Lycée Impérial
M. Guénon professeur le 6 Mars an 1812.
Eugène De Lacroix né le floréal
De la république française (27 avril 1798).

39

40

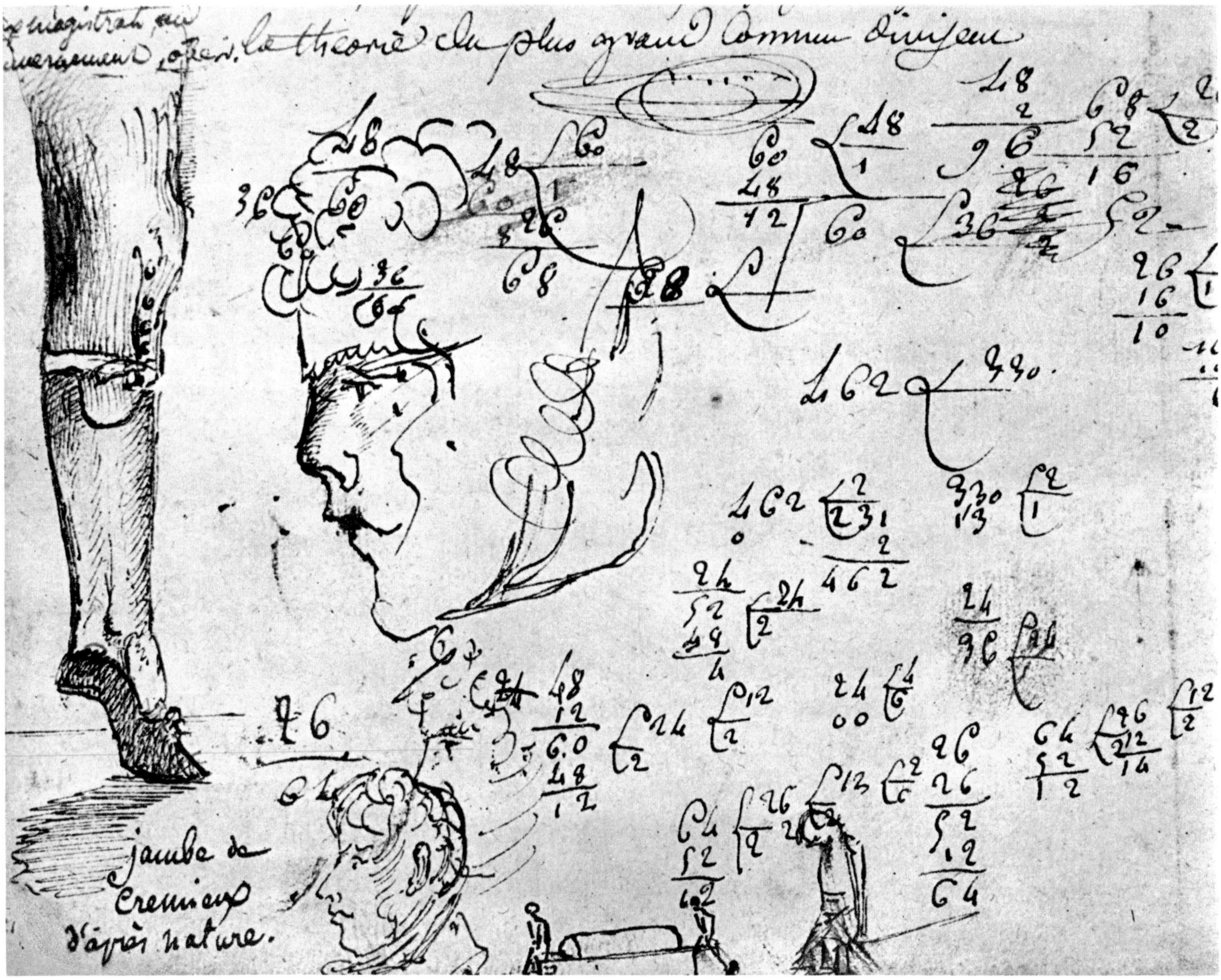
la théorie du plus grand commun diviseur
jambe de Cremieux d'après nature.

41

Cahier de brouillons
Delacroix

Eugène Delacroix

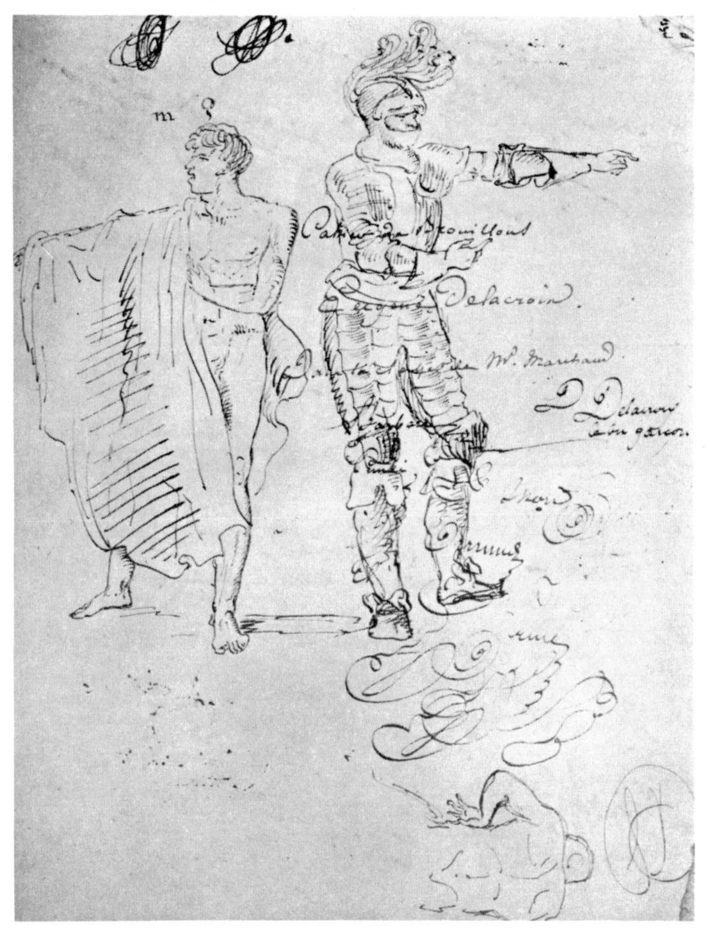

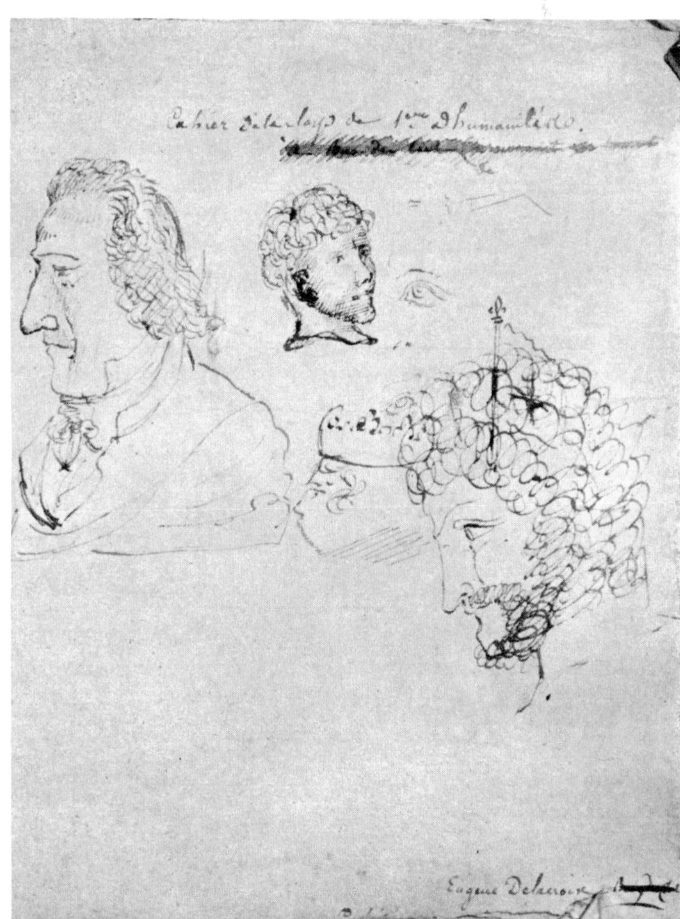

42

43

44

45

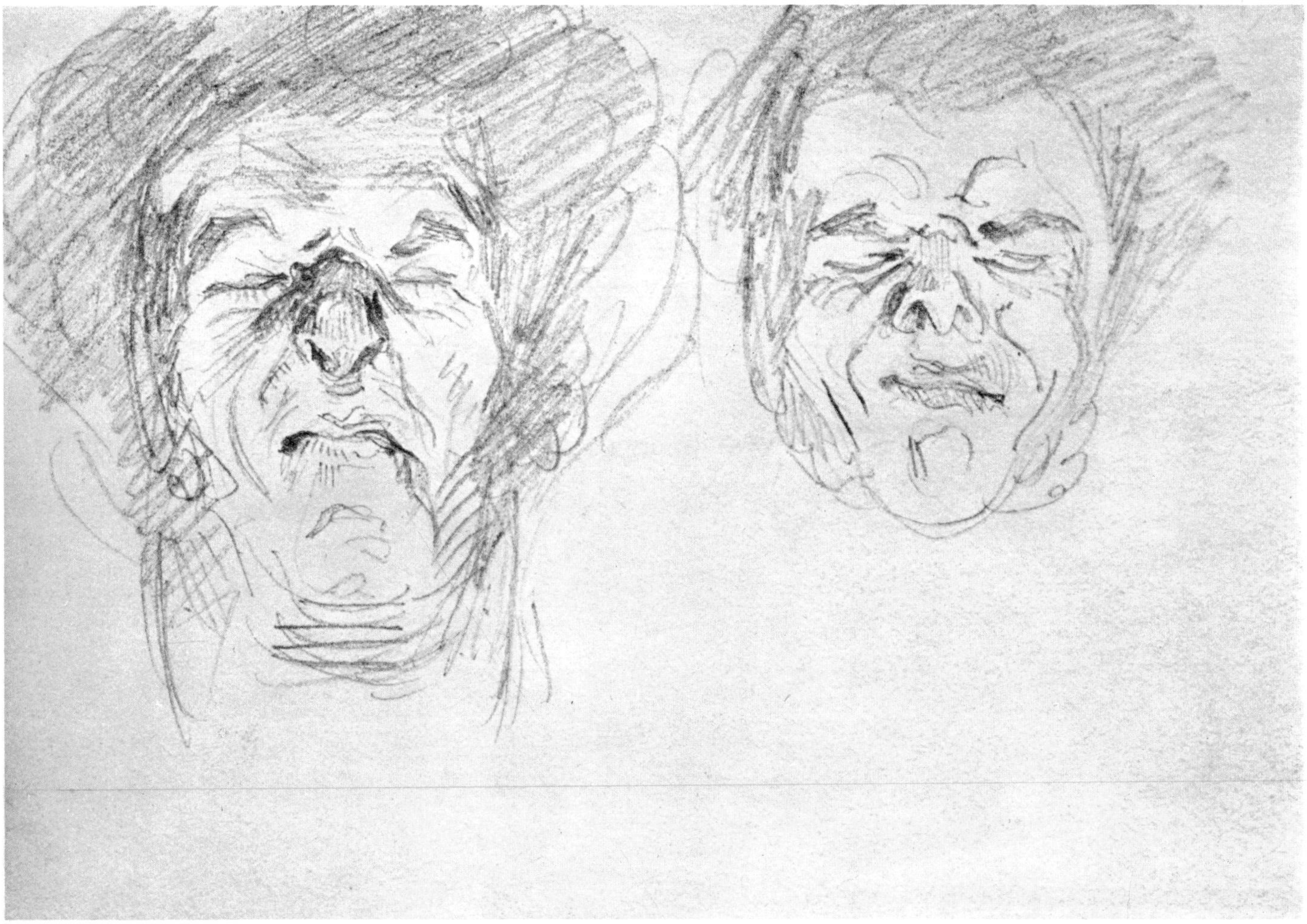

46

47

48

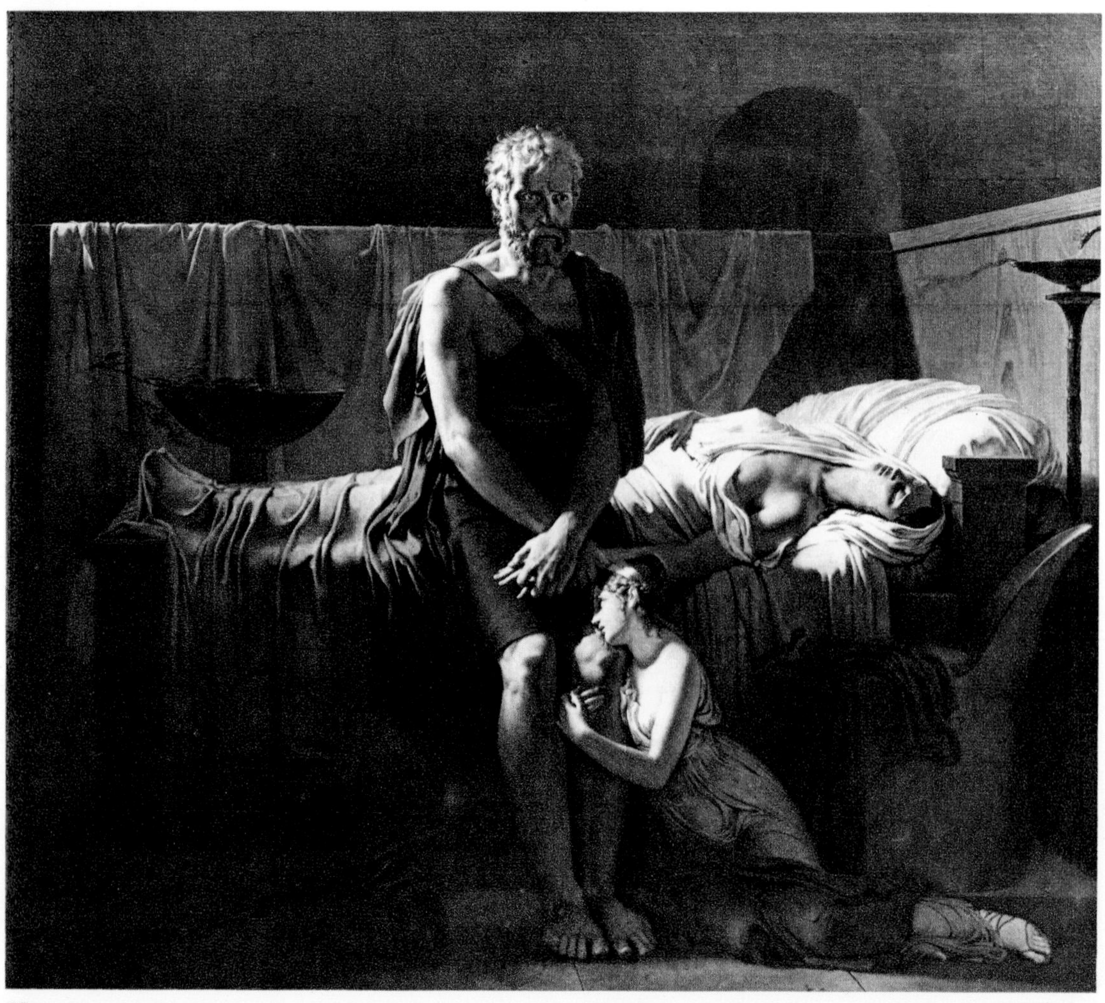

49

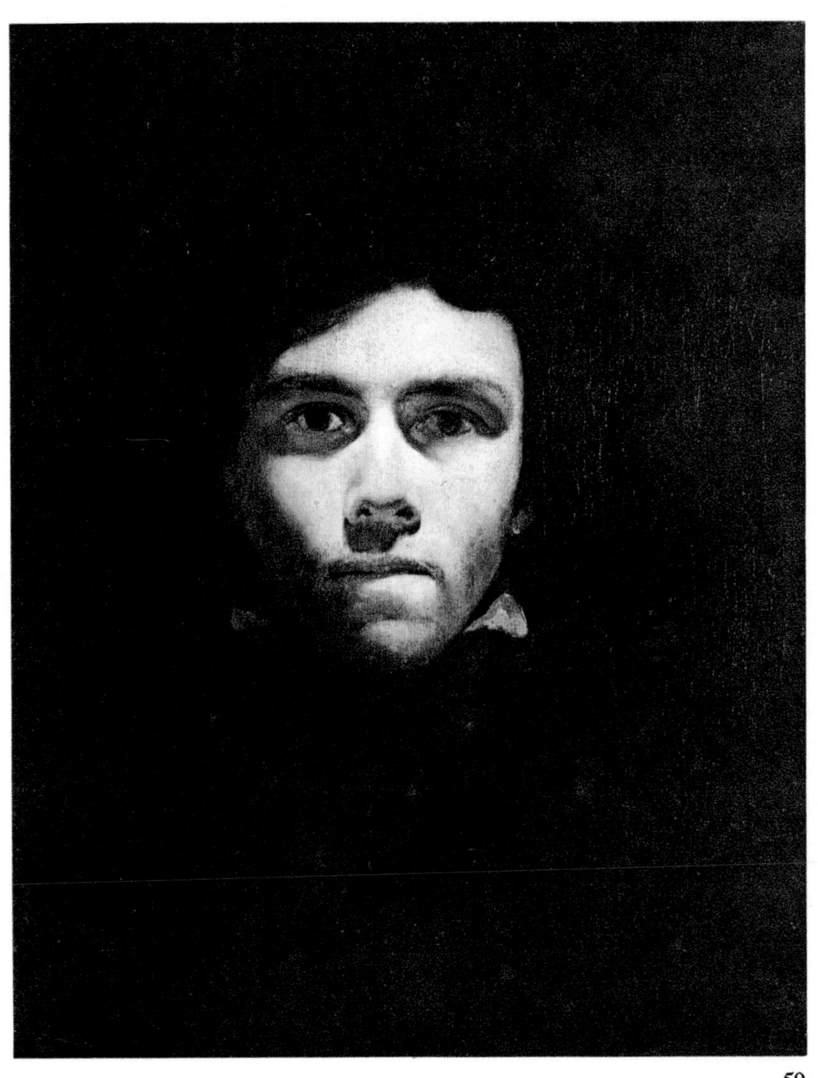

50

51

52

53

54

55

56

57

58

59

60

BONAPARTE
KAROLVS . MAGNVS

62

63

64

65

66

molest Which may be wrought with a hammer and Which cannot use one's hand, or had But one hand mandatary that Come to a benefice. I not see you and you forget it absolutely. Often I have expected you and you have continued my advertissements. I conceive you are Wearied to see me in Stairs to the face of the Whole house, and I confess it's not please me much. Yet, if we Could understand we Could find the means to have even any Swift moments. I not have lost memory of this happy evening When the all babblers and troublesome Were removed. You not remember probably last friday; But I have that present to my mind and I resume better for the want of so Welcome occasion. Often When I go near the Kitchen I hear your a lot of Laughing, and I laugh in no Wise. You ask me perhaps What matter it it to me. I answer With only Such is my temper. that Caprice and my fantastical humour. I frame great many purposes to See you easily but needless. If Was the fine season, I Could hope With you much happiness; But We are far of. One Say M-L has lost her process and She Will appeal: its perhaps Shall prolong her residence in Paris. & I Cannot Call again to my mind that fortunate friday, Without a start of pleasure. the security of our ... added are over to the delight of your view. O my ...

and, since had been Cooled so deliciously. If my mouth Could be so nimble to pronounce your language as to savour so great sweetness, I not should be so Wearied When I endeavour to speak or to Write you. Pardon me if I Call again to your memory the happiness Which you have granted me. not regardless that, yet are so rare the Delights of Life. I beg you a favour: not refuse me. When M-L. Will be go South and When also I glimpse you Make me Known of that. Some times you shall Say it to me on the Stairs: or if it not may be, you Will have Complaisance, to Say — You have Some thing to tell me: and I shall You will not omit, you will Know What it signifies. I amuse you. tell me Sunday a thing Which interest me. You laugh at it and you prepare to amuse me With trifflings. You are cruel person Which play affecting the another. Nevertheless not be angry at it: I am a pitiful Englishman and I bet I have told in this Write a multitude of impertinence. It must therefore pardon me in consideration of my good intentions. thought of me I will go out this evening. Neither Come a few ... I hope god Will remove ours enemies. I beg him for that. My Whisker not String more.

67

# III BEGINNING OF A CAREER

DELACROIX HAD NOT YET come face to face with life: at the death of his mother in 1814 he was only sixteen, and he continued to live in the family house, together with his sister Henriette, and with his brother-in-law Raymond de Verninac who, before he retired, had been Ambassador to the Sublime Porte in 1795, *Préfet* of Lyons in 1800 and 1801, then Minister Plenipotentiary in Switzerland. Delacroix's closest companion was the son they had had in 1800, his nephew Charles, whose premature death in 1834 was a terrible blow to him. It is often said that Delacroix lived not only with but on his brother-in-law; but a book of accounts, which has been preserved in the family, shows that the young orphan was already in 1814, and still in 1820, paying not only for his laundry but for his food, as well as his incidental expenses such as having his watch repaired, church collections, etc. His contribution was fixed at a hundred francs a month. In this way he learned the value of money very early on, before the fearful money troubles which were to ruin his family—and which he overcame only gradually, by desperately hard work. But, as his cousin, Léon Riesener, records (in his notes published by Escholier), Delacroix 'reduced to nothing when he was about twenty, but sustained by the most lovable wisdom and moderation, contrived to combine extreme poverty with perfect dignity.' He also sometimes went short in order to pay the debts of his adored nephew—and in addition to buy back the
pl 4 portrait of his sister by David, which the young man sold on two separate occasions. (This portrait, later donated to the Louvre by M. de Bestegui, remained the principal adornment of Delacroix's rooms to the end of his life.)

When people deplore the difficult material circumstances endured by certain great artists of the nineteenth century, such as Millet, they never think of Delacroix, whose proud reserve forbad him to complain. But he needed courage to pass through some very hard years, and an echo of this does sometimes make itself heard in his letters to his intimate friends. 'One must try to be a pauper and fume as little as possible,' he wrote to Soulier as late as 28 January 1829.

Delacroix's mother, after a long widowhood, left at her death little more than the forest property of Axe, near Mansle in the Angoumois. This had been acquired from the La Rochefoucaulds, partly, it seems, in settlement of debts to Delacroix's father; but these were enough to buy only part of the property and the balance had to be found. When Madame Delacroix died, the creditors closed in, a law-suit began and the whole inheritance was gradually engulfed: in addition, its management by the Verninacs proved uneconomic. From 1818 to 1820 Delacroix went regularly to spend his holiday months at the *maison des gardes*, where his sister's family lived. The financial débâcle was complicated by a quarrel between her and her elder brother.

This conflict may have played a part in deciding Delacroix to leave the rue de l'Université in 1820 and settle at 22, rue de la Planche (now rue de Varenne), where he stayed until 1823. His brother-in-law's death in 1822 brought him close to his sister again, and she in turn sought refuge with him. This did not last very long: Henriette resumed her independence, rendered precarious by the ruin of the family, and was forced to become a lady-in-waiting, just as Eugène was obliged to take the decision to earn his living with his brush. He had planned, in collaboration with his friend Soulier, to earn money by colouring drawings of machines with water colours, but a certain fantasy in the execution prevented him from finding a regular source of income in this work. Nor did a few lithographs and caricatures published in *Le Miroir* and in *Le Nain Jaune* provide a more lasting solution, but in the summer of 1819 he obtained, through a friend, his first commission for a picture—the *Virgin* which is still in the church at Orce- pls 69, 71
mont near Rambouillet. Two years later Géricault came to his help by handing over to him a similar commission, which he himself had had from the Count de Forbin, for a *Virgin of the Sacred Heart*, intended for a convent at Nantes; pls 72, 73
it is now at Ajaccio. This brought in 1,500 francs, and gave Delacroix a breathing-space. It was then that he undertook his *Dante and Virgil in the Inferno*, which in 1822 was exhibited at the Salon and made a great sensation. II, page 58
The State bought it for 1,200 francs. From then onwards Delacroix could hope to live by his art: he decided to devote himself to it with all his strength, and his story now became chiefly that of his works.

## *Early Decisions—Géricault and the 'Dante and Virgil in the Inferno'*

The natural tendencies of Delacroix's temperament were already revealed in those school notebooks preserved by the Malvy-Verninac family, which start in pls 39-42
1811. In them the taste for arabesques and flourishes, which he multiplies at the least excuse into whirlwinds of nervous energy and complicated knots, shows that what he will look for in drawing will be not so much the chance of delimiting (and so defining) by an outline his idea of a form, as of a free, lively and swift deployment of movement or gesture. This impulsiveness—and also in his case weakening health—would lighten the rein usually applied by full physical development to the flow of nervous impulses, which aspires to project itself in the darting movements of the hand. Even in the very first sketches that accompany these volutes he tries to catch the stir, the leaping movement of a man or a horse. Very soon he is instinctively finding the strokes, hatchings, whipping and waving lines, curves and expressive loosenings whose resources the genius of Rembrandt had explored. Soon also he tries his hand at adding a wash, so that the drawing melts into space. From 1812 to 1814 we can follow the progression that leads the young student from the still uncertain, slightly tremulous strokes of his first attempts to flourishes that are already almost masterly. In 1813 and 1814 he

*Fig 2* A MAN OF LETTERS IN MEDITATION, 1821. Lithograph after a drawing by Delacroix.

won prizes for drawings. Two engravings are dated by Robaut from 1814: one is an etching, the copper for which was supplied by the bottom of a saucepan; not surprisingly, it contains a charging horseman, but there is also in it a caricature—a monkey disguised as an *Incroyable*.[1]

pl 74

It is indeed noteworthy that Delacroix's first works, starting in 1815-16, were engravings, etchings or lithographs (which the new pupil at the École des Beaux-Arts published chiefly in *Le Miroir*). The lithograph process, invented in 1796 by Senefelder a Bavarian, had just been brought to France by de Lasteyrie, who in 1814 had set up the first lithograph printing shop in that country. Stone lends itself better than copper to freedom of drawing and Delacroix was quick to see what the new technique could give him. His *English Troops*, *Travelling Actors*, and the *Trapeze Artist of Coblentz* show a beginner's awkwardness: the tremulousness of the schoolboy's first sketches reappears in them. His models, in this *genre* in which the British artists had long been ahead, were Rowlandson and Gillray; they taught him to sketch an attitude or a mimicking gesture, to 'catch it from the life' and, at the same time, to exaggerate the chief feature or quality—another factor that helped him to overstep the cult of form as taught at the École.

pls 75, 76

fig 3

He received a far stronger impetus from the discovery of Goya and his engravings. These he must have come to know very early on through one of the great friends of his youth, Félix Guillemardet, whose father, as Ambassador of

*Fig 3* SKETCH AFTER GOYA'S 'LOVE AND DEATH', Caprichos. Pen drawing. Cabinet des Dessins, Louvre, Paris.

the Directoire to Spain, had sat to Goya for a famous portrait. While Delacroix left more than forty sheets of drawings after Rowlandson, there are a dozen others after Goya. His *Journal* tells us that on 19 March 1824 he was looking in his studio at works by the Spanish master in the company of Edouard Bertin (the future editor of the *Journal des Débats* and at that time a painter), and that he was thinking of doing some 'caricatures in the style of Goya'. Delacroix's drawings prove that he studied Goya's *Caprichos*—probably as early as 1819, if not in 1818. Michel Florisoone has shown in a penetrating analysis[2] that, in addition to the two copies known to have been in France (the one acquired by Vivant-Denon in 1809 and the one Fontaney acquired in about 1830), the *Caprichos*, which were published in 1799 in Madrid, must have been brought back by Guillemardet, who would doubtless have highly valued their revolutionary satire. The volume which Delacroix possessed in 1830—he showed it to George Sand and to Musset (who also derived from it much inspiration)—must have come from Guillemardet. The shock of Goya's genius confirmed in him something of which he had already had glimpses through the English artists—that drawing, by turning away from form to place itself at the service of expression, that is to say of life, can, by cursive freedom and the atmosphere produced by wash, convey the fugitive intensity of impressions.

pls 77, 78

But it took more than this to liberate Delacroix from the hold the School had over him. He had learnt there to revere plastic architecture—the architecture of the human body as taught in the drawing schools (he himself left some beautiful examples of this), and that of composition as practised in the drawing competitions (at which he never managed to obtain an official award). The pl 68 *Roman Matrons*, which he sent in for one of these in 1818, and the *Jesus before Pilate* of 1819 derive from the type established by seventeenth-century classicism and reaffirmed by the neo-classicists: in these pictures the depth is cut out by a succession of planes, of which the foreground is reserved for the figures and the others are marked by architectural screens; the surface is organized through the intersection of the horizontals and verticals formed by this scenery, in the manner of Sébastien Bourdon, except in the cases where the whole is divided by an ascending diagonal according to the seventeenth-century scheme familiar alike to Rubens and to Vignon. Lethière, who won the Prix de Rome in 1784, was still using this arrangement in his *Death of Virginia*, shown at the 1830 Salon. Although Delacroix applied it faithfully to his *Jesus before Pilate* in 1819, he did, in the same year, use aquatint in an *Interior* (Robaut no. 39) which stresses the fantastic silhouetting of shadows against strong lights as taught by Goya.

But in his pictures he still did not dare to infringe the official teaching:
pl 71 the *Virgin of the Harvest* at Orcemont, with its pyramidal composition, sinuous modelling and colour established by clear tones, looks like a pastiche of Raphael. Delacroix was stretched between the two poles that were pulling him in opposite directions: the wash in his 1818 *Roman Matrons* serves only to accentuate the regularity of the contours or to mould the masses, and yet, already in 1817, in his
pl 94 *New Year's Eve*, he allows himself to modulate the shadows, to make them clash, zig-zag and stretch, to set the silhouettes dancing to the flames in the manner of the *Caprichos*.

He had to make the choice: Goya, or Raphael? All his impatient sensibility drew him close to Goya, but the way of thinking he had been taught made him admire Raphael. For the Orcemont *Virgin* did he not, according to Chesneau,[3]
pl 70 make a copy of the Christ Child in the *Belle Jardinière*? It was sent for restoration to Haro who was the supplier of painting materials not only to Delacroix but to Ingres, and there Ingres saw and admired it; when he found out whom it was by, he exclaimed: 'The miserable creature! And he paints the pictures he does!' But Delacroix was perfectly sincere: in 1830, the year of *Hernani*, he contributed an article on the Urbino master to the *Revue de Paris*, in which he said:

'People have a blind need for novelty, which at once makes them cold towards the really beautiful pictures. . . . The sublimity of his [Raphael's] talent . . . a soul that converses with the gods manifests itself on earth. . . . He is never banal. . . . His spirit spreads over everything, along with life and movement, the most perfect order, a bewitching harmony. . . .'

Would M. Ingres have judged or spoken differently?

In the next year, 1821, Delacroix achieved a little more freedom for his *Virgin of the Sacred Heart*. Without turning his back on the example of the Italian Renaissance, he now had recourse to the seventeenth-century masters—already, as we have seen, mentioned in his 1812 school notebooks. Their more baroque quality lent itself better to effects of movement and drama: from them he borrows the huge figures in the foreground, the ascending impulse which mingles the figures together, and the rolling clouds.

But clearly he had not found his way. On 21 February 1821 in the letter to Soulier which speaks of the fever already attacking him, he complains: 'No torch has come to throw, in an instant, a vivid light on the path I have to follow.'

And yet he had already received the decisive impetus. It came from the very artist who had handed over to him the commission for this large picture—from Géricault, his elder and friend, of whom he stood in awe. 'Although he gave me the most friendly welcome, the difference of our ages and my admiration for him put me in the position of a respectful pupil,' he confided to Piron.[4] In his studio 'near the Ternes', Géricault showed him the unfinished *Méduse*— pl 79 and even asked him to sit for the exhausted man with the drooping hand in the foreground. The revelation of this picture went straight to Delacroix's heart: 'The impression it made on me was so vivid that, when I left, I ran like a madman all the way back to the rue de la Planche.'[5] This was in 1818 or 1819.

Thanks to Géricault, Delacroix was now to find the way to unite the tendencies that were tearing him apart: from him he would learn how to set himself free for that art of intensity, of frenzy even, which his sensibility was demanding, without thereby breaking with the classical tradition of form. Perhaps indeed this conjunction of tendencies is the essence of Géricault himself: he too had been nourished from the classical sources and therefore dared not infringe the principle of form and contour—so much so that he could only think of painting as sculptural; yet at the same time he was stirred by the rising wind of energy in his own temperament and in his period. To prove how sculptural his idea of painting was at this time, we need only refer to the evidence of his friend Montfort, who depicts him, during the painting of the *Radeau*, as 'looking perfectly pl 81 calm', although his inner tension was revealed by a 'slight heightening of colour in his face'. In front of the picture itself, Montfort exclaims: 'How it seems to jut out of the canvas, especially in the parts still only sketched in! . . . It was like a fragment of sculpture in the preliminary stage.' As for the intensity, this was hidden and contained in the picture, just as it was in the appearance of the artist who, as he painted, 'did not move . . . either his body or his arms about.' The tension was present in the subject, in the drama that tormented the figures—but also in the style of the picture, in which the violence of the muscles and the brutal contrasts of light and shade seem all the more wild for being caught and petrified in the human form. Two equal powers, each brought to the extreme of violence, firmness of contour on the one hand and, on the other, the inherent frenzy, neutralize their opposing pressures. The same applies to the men and animals, the horsemen and horses, which in other pictures by Géricault set the discipline of will power and an animal impetuousness against one another, to result in a terrible stillness.

Here Delacroix recognized the two powers that were beginning to do battle in him: he had felt himself incapable of choosing between them, and now he marvelled at seeing them thus composed and balanced. A way out had been opened before him: he plunged along it, and the result was *Dante and Virgil in the Inferno*, painted in two-and-a-half months, in time for the 1822 Salon, which opened on 24 April. The picture stems directly from the *Radeau*. There is also a picture of 1821 that prepared for it—the *Naufragés abandonnés* (Robaut no. 1473), in which we find repeated the huge wave, the poor people kindled by hope, and the handkerchief fluttered towards a distant sail. In the *Dante and Virgil in the Inferno*—in which it has been claimed that Géricault himself lent a

*Fig 4* SELF-PORTRAIT AS A YOUNG MAN, 1823.
Pencil drawing.
Cabinet des Dessins, Louvre, Paris.

hand—the influence is less direct. Delacroix had understood that a tragic theme, the paroxysm of a situation that confounds a man's whole being, can give free course to the intensity which, he felt, was the very sap of art: in this picture the damned 'are all those who inhabit the empire of tears'. He found in them an echo to his own torment. At about the same time he confessed, in a passage quoted by Piron:[6] 'Really to live in my way, that is to say through the feelings and the heart, I am obliged to seek my enjoyments in painting and to seize them from there.' But, while Géricault looked for drama in contemporary reality, Delacroix turned towards the inner world: he drew his subject and inspiration from a situation already imagined by a poet. Very soon he would be writing in his *Journal* (11 April 1824):

'And so, to find a subject, what one should do is to open some book that can give inspiration, and to let oneself be guided by its mood . . . and the same with engravings. Dante, Lamartine, Byron, Michelangelo.'

To gain a clear idea of Delacroix's position, let us compare three pictures
pl 80 whose connection is obviously close: Girodet's *Scene from the Deluge*, sent to
the Salon in 1806, but again exhibited at the 1814 Salon (at which Géricault
pl 82 showed his *Wounded Cuirassier*), the *Radeau de la Méduse* (Salon, 1819) and the
II, page 58 *Dante and Virgil in the Inferno* (Salon, 1822). There is continuity here, but also development. All three pictures show man face to face with the power that is stronger than he and crushes him—symbolized by the fury of the elements, especially of water. Girodet takes his theme from the most firmly anchored tradition, Géricault from contemporary life, and Delacroix from a poem. Girodet places the accent almost entirely on the anatomy of the bodies; Géricault still gives this an essential place, though at the same time he foreshadows Courbet with his blue-green and translucent wave; Delacroix remains faithful to the idea of a composition of naked or draped bodies, but he plunges these into an atmosphere that is all shadows and stifling mists and seems on the point of dissolving them. In the first two the composition is still plastic—it is produced by the propagation of a movement that passes from limb to limb; in the third picture it

is beginning to aim at a musical effect for the whole, into which everything seems to melt and unite, like the voices in a choir. The details are still superb, and the light moulds them in relief—and yet they no longer trace lines of geometrical construction but rather rhythms: the damned, clinging to the boat and trying to heave themselves up or falling back into the water, sketch an undulating, curling movement which stresses that of the dancing wave. This is something quite different: light and colours are no longer used to define form, they come together to create an incantatory chant, in which the oppressive sadness of the cold grey and blue tones is torn by the painful cry of the reds, just as the heavy, livid mist shutting off the space beyond is rent by the ruddy glow from the infernal city in flames. pl 90

Delacroix started from Géricault, but was already moving away from him: he found in him the bridge enabling him to cross the obstacle, but the road on which it set him was to take him a different way. This accounts for his ambiguous attitude towards Géricault. It was largely made up of grief for his premature death—which prompted, on 27 January 1824, this cry: 'Poor Géricault, I shall think of you very often! I imagine your soul will sometimes come and hover about my work. . . .' But with this fervour there mingled a certain reserve, traces of which Piron indicated when he remarked that Delacroix, in his writings 'makes little mention of Géricault; this may be because, to his way of thinking, Géricault, in spite of all the great qualities by which he shone, was still not a man of genius.'[7] The observation is of capital importance, coming from one of Delacroix's intimate friends, the one who became executor of his will. And what is the criticism? 'That in him fertility and boldness of imagination do not come up to his power of execution.'

Between what Géricault offered him and what he sought in Géricault there was, in fact, a vitally important gap. True, Géricault had injected into painting the energy which fascinates the modern world, 'the vigour, the daring'[8] which Delacroix admired in him; but in this he was only developing what Delacroix had postulated and demanded, and still not spiriting away what had paralysed Delacroix. In point of fact, Géricault went on thinking and constructing his pictures architecturally, out of elements taken from reality, copied from the model and intelligently combined. In this way, like David before him and Ingres after him, he painted by covering the canvas gradually with successive pieces, as stones are assembled to fulfil the plan conceived by a master builder. On this Montfort and Gigoux are positive: he transferred his design, squared up, to the canvas and then, using the model (kept always before his eyes), filled his 'well-defined tracing' with the energetic rendering of what he saw, and so progressed methodically 'small square by small square'.

Delacroix's idea of art was not compatible with this 'complete subservience to what the model gave him',[9] any more than with such methodical elaboration by juxtaposition. Delacroix was looking for something different: he wished to

IX WOMAN WITH A PARROT
*1827 Oil on canvas. 10 x 15 (025 x 039)*
*Musée des Beaux-Arts, Lyons*

give an outward appearance to the confused, lived world that set his nerves, heart and soul quivering—a world which he experienced before he could see it
pls 85, 87 and, above all, conceive it. In his first sketches, therefore, he projected a confused and seething cloud, still indistinct but loaded with pressing potentialities. This cloud he gradually shaped and defined by a sort of groping and attrition, extracting
pl 91 ing from it the image which he would now have to make intelligible, explicit and communicative. It is the way in which the sculptor's thumb works, starting with a formless lump of clay. Villot, in the preface to the catalogue of the 1865 sale, records Delacroix as explicitly contrasting this technique, in which 'everything must be sacrificed to the whole', with the traditional piece by piece technique. 'However unfinished a picture may be, everything must have its relative importance; a picture that is not far advanced is a picture seen through a more or less thick gauze, but it is a picture, let us not forget.' It was the opposite method to Géricault's.

## *Liberation through the Old Masters and Gros*

For the present Delacroix was only twenty-four: he was still untried. Where could he find, in painting, examples of the mobile, synthesizing technique that he sought, of an all-embracing vision proceeding from the whole to the details, in absolute contradiction to the dry method that starts from outlines and reaches the whole by a juxtaposition of parts? Certainly not in Géricault, whose influence was still holding him back, bogging him down in the opposite opinion, as this entry in the *Journal* for 7 April 1824 still shows: 'The first and most important thing in painting is the outlines. . . . If they are there, the painting is firm and finished.'

He found the example that would set him free from this dogma which was hindering his progress, first and foremost, in the museums. It was there in the Venetian painters: at that time, perched on his ladder, he was copying Veronese's *Marriage at Cana*; and in 1824 he also copied Giorgione's *Concert Champêtre*—and was to keep the resulting picture by him to his death. In Giorgione he found that enveloping magic which is produced by an overall musicality of colour. In Velázquez he discovered the technique of expression by patches of colour, in which the touches of the brush had more to do with sensory impressions than with intelligible form and a modelling worked out by reason; and he had closely studied Velázquez, had himself copied work by him, and had bought a copy by Géricault of one of his pictures. On 19 March 1826 he records 'an excellent day' spent at the Louvre, and the painters he mentions with many exclamation marks are—alongside Poussin—Rubens, Titian and Velázquez. Even two years before this the *Journal* had shown the direction in which he was moving:[10] 'Ah! what would be strange and really beautiful would be to unite the styles of

X HENRI DE VERNINAC
*c.1827 Oil on canvas. 24 x 20 (061 x 050)*
*Collection: Mr and Mrs Arthur Sachs, Paris*

Michelangelo and Velázquez.' For Michelangelo he might just as well have put Géricault. 'Giorgione has a great deal of that,' he says, meaning atmosphere combined with plastic firmness. . . .

In practice what would be needed was a less dry technique, one that would allow the movement of the brush free play in a fluid medium and that would transpose into painting the dynamic and cursive style already characteristic of his drawings. The danger of fixity, of petrification, would be spirited away when colour enabled the brush-stroke to run freely, like a wind ruffling the surface of a stream. Velázquez had confined himself to transmuting form into patches of colour and so giving it a vibrant quality: this was already a great deal. But there was a master who possessed the secret of conveying the quivering agility of life itself—Rubens. pl 84

'Fury and zest in brushwork cannot go further,' wrote Delacroix on 9 July 1850, after contemplating the *Christ in Judgment* at Brussels. Here the very aim of art was reached: 'The imagination receives a shock, which is renewed every time one sets eyes on the picture,' for it has 'a movement, a variety and, at the same time, an incomparable unity.'

But even in the contemporary school of painting there was one living painter —a pupil of David, and indeed his favourite pupil—who, also a fanatical admirer of Rubens, had likewise found in him the revelation of a differing kind of art. This painter was Gros. Delacroix was introduced to him by Géricault who, as Piron tells us,[11] 'admired Gros and, like preachers in the pulpit who would raise their birettas every time they pronounced the name of Christ, never mentioned him without expressing enthusiasm and respect'; and Géricault, though he 'had not the impetuosity and lightness of Gros', had shown Delacroix the way he himself had not managed to take. Gros had by instinct laid that way open, though without realizing all the consequences of his initiative. He remained timid, uncertain, crushed by the responsibility of being the heir-apparent of the School: indeed his torments of indecision ended in a lamentable suicide. But Delacroix was there, ready to bring out all the fruitful consequences latent in his art.

Gros had, indeed, divined that in Delacroix was the continuation of his own work. When Guérin was advising his pupil not to exhibit *Dante and Virgil in the Inferno* at the Salon, the enthusiastic Gros had paid for the framing. His secret wish—though Delacroix did not guess it till much later—seems to have been to take Delacroix as his pupil and groom him for the Prix de Rome. He could feel the young artist's closeness to Rubens: of the *Dante and Virgil*, he 'finally told me, after praising its merits in detail, that it was "chastened Rubens"'. Coming from him, who worshipped Rubens (describing as 'most sublime' a Rubens that he had seen at Genoa on his way to Rome in 1793) and yet had been brought up in the severe school of David—this was the highest possible praise. Delacroix received permission from the master to go to his studio and see his 'famous pictures of the Empire', which the new régime would not allow to be exhibited. He spent four hours there. Perhaps it was these four hours that at last showed him his true path.

There is a mystery about Gros. How did that modest artist from Toulouse come to invent—a quarter of a century before Delacroix, and at a time when neo-classicism was challenged only by the dreams of Prud'hon and the glimmers

of pre-romantic moonlight—that lightning style of drawing which prepared the way for, indeed already fulfilled, the *volte-face* of the French School? One cannot help seeing here the obscure working of that incessant drive towards the transition from the static to the dynamic, from a world set within forms to a world carried away by energy. There had been a prelude to this in the eighteenth century, in Fragonard. In the hands of Gros, and of Delacroix after him, the pen became the recorder of a seismograph of the nerves. And even before Delacroix, Gros perceived that the ardent theme in which the required impetuosity
pl 92 could be expressed was inevitably the horse. In his sketch for his *Bucephalus vanquished by Alexander*, for instance, he invented the type of composition—till then little known—in which two forms carried away by the same action (in this case, the rearing horse and the man who will get the better of it), seem to rise in one whirlwind, like flames that intertwine as they rise. This bold scheme was to
pl 93 be the one used in the pictures Delacroix would later paint of wild beasts fighting and of horsemen battling with lions.

Gros also perceived the essential importance colour was to have in the art
pl 48 to come, through its direct action on the senses and the nerves. In his *Victims of the Plague at Jaffa*, Girodet singled out for praise '*cette teinte éclatante*' and '*ta palette brûlante*', which reminded him of Veronese and Titian. And Guérin, praising the same picture, listed its outstanding qualities as 'expressiveness, energy, colour and impact'—a perfect definition of the new resources towards which the art was moving and which Delacroix was to conquer for it.

Even in the matter of the genesis of the work of art and the process of its creation, Gros anticipated Delacroix and went beyond the stage at which Géricault would stop. To him the impression and impact of a picture must come from the whole. Therefore the general *élan* must never be broken. Delestre reports him as saying:[12]

'It is essential to proceed as a whole, by movement, lines, light and shade, by total effect. You cannot apply yourself to a part without looking at the whole. . . . Carry each part onwards simultaneously, so that if by any chance your labours were interrupted there would be a homogeneity in each fraction, whatever stage the work had reached.'

It is as if those words were spoken by Delacroix himself, whose paintings always, at every stage, formed a whole because the process of finishing them was only an increasing definition of their details.

Gros's very temperament—that quivering, excessive sensibility of his, and a gloomy turn of mind that lent itself as easily to the expression of dramatic tensions as it did to that of physical energy—brought him very close to Delacroix.

All these things helped to make him praise the *Dante and Virgil* without reserve. And encouragement came to Delacroix from many other sources: the purchase of the picture by the State and its exhibition in the autumn at the Luxembourg; also the unconcealed approval of another painter of the School, Baron Gérard, as well as that of a young critic who was a frequent guest of his, Adolphe Thiers. A recent arrival in Paris from Marseilles, Thiers sounded an enthusiastic fanfare in the *Constitutionnel*: 'I do not think I can be wrong', he wrote, 'in saying that M. Delacroix is gifted with genius.' He went on to add: 'The opinion I am here expressing about him is shared by one of the greatest masters of the School.' His enthusiasm has been attributed to the covert protection extended by Talleyrand to his natural son. But the facts are more simple: the master to whom Thiers refers is obviously Gérard himself, on whose relations with the Delacroix family we have already remarked. The proof of this is given by Delacroix in the notes he left for Piron, where he says that he had still not thanked his advocate, even after a second article, praising the *Massacre at Chios*, had appeared: 'I did not even know to whom I was indebted for such kindness. Gérard invited me to Auteuil, and there at last I saw that unknown friend.'[13] It is clear from this that it was the well-known portrait painter Gérard who introduced Delacroix to Thiers after having first 'revealed' him to the critic.

## *The 'Massacre at Chios': the East: M. Auguste: Farewell to Géricault*

With such support, all he had to do was to go on and make progress. At the next Salon, that of 1824, a second masterpiece, *The Massacre at Chios*, showed that Delacroix had succeeded in emerging from the closed circle in which a too strict adherence to what he had learned from Géricault might easily have imprisoned him. With confidence, his boldness increased: the picture is considerably larger than its predecessor—164 in. high by 139 in. wide, as against 74 in. by 97 in.; and in it his art at last becomes entirely personal, as does his technique. III, page 67

What made him choose this theme? As always, a fascination with the human tragedy—with the instincts and passions seething at the centre of a man's nature, and with the terrible blows they strike at his deep-seated longing for happiness. Appetites clamour for their satisfaction, and meet with obstacles or victims in 'other people': there is voracity—but also despair. The realization of this was already present, terrifyingly, in the vision of Dante guided by Virgil among the wandering shades and the eternal fires, while frantic waves tossed the boat and the damned clung to it, torn by their passions, convulsive, biting the wooden gunwale and almost capsizing the boat as they tried, in tumultuous confusion, to reach an impossible safety.

But would not the human tragedy be given greater force if it were brought into the field of real events and removed from that symbolic one in which Dante's work had placed it? The examples of Gros and Géricault were there to show —with the *Jaffa* and the *Eylau*, the *Wounded Cuirassier* and the *Méduse*—that tragedy has far more impact when we find it in the life that surrounds us. Dumas revealed in 1864 that Delacroix had once confided to him: 'It was from the *Victims of the Plague at Jaffa* that the initial idea of my *Massacre* came to me. pl 48 I didn't completely clean Gros's palette; only you mustn't breathe a word of this. . . .' But Delacroix was in a difficulty that did not trouble his two predecessors: in their time real events were heroic and epic and they had only to plunge into them to find episodes in which the sublime was mingled with the everyday; but such events were receding and had become, for his generation, a thing of the past. The great catastrophes had come to an end, and Europe now dreamed of nothing but comfort. Already Géricault, after 1814, had been forced to fall back on newspapers stories: the *Radeau de la Méduse* was one of these, and the

*Assassination of Fualdès* and the *Slave Trade* were other subjects of the same kind, left unfinished because of his sudden death.

Yet war and its tumults never cease. It was now blazing up throughout the Near East where, beginning in 1821, the Greeks were struggling to regain their liberty and coming up against the ferocity of the Turks. The real event was there to hand. And by its remoteness, by taking place at the far end of the Mediterranean where the Asiatic world begins, it appealed to the imagination as well as being rooted in reality. Beyond the immediacy of the theme, Delacroix was able to pursue that way of escape, which the eighteenth century with its 'chinoiserie' had already entered, towards an oriental world whose difference from the one known to us was enough to allow of the cultivation of dreams and illusions.

The poetic impetus which Delacroix was apt to find in literature was also present. Delacroix had filled his sails with the breath of Dante: he now offered them to that of Byron, the poet of violent feelings and bold actions—with whom contemporaries found it so natural to associate him that in 1830 Tony Johannot placed their two profiles together on a medallion designed as an illustration for Nodier's *Histoire d'un roi de Bohême.* Byron's *The Giaour, The Bride of Abydos, The Corsair* and *Lara,* from which Delacroix derived such lasting inspiration, had appeared in 1813 and 1814, and on 24 July 1823 the poet had chartered a brig, the *Hercules,* to take him from Genoa to Greece where he met his premature death on 19 April 1824 at Missolonghi.

The truth was, Delacroix had long been attracted by the East. The paintings of the School of David celebrating the Egyptian campaign had brought the exotic costumes of the Turks into the visual repertoire of the artists. The sketches in Delacroix's school notebooks reflect this. And in 1817 two of his earliest lithographs showed the Persian Ambassador and his favourite wife in their sumptuous trappings. These were the prelude to a water-colour painted in 1821, *La Favorite,* in which the theme of the harem, with all the charm of luxurious costume and a mysterious half-light, makes a first tentative appearance in preparation for the *Women of Algiers.* A small picture dating from the same year shows a *Turkish Horseman Firing.* At about the same time, following in the footsteps of Bellini and Rembrandt, who had watched the East arrive in the
pls 100, 101 harbours of Venice and Amsterdam, Delacroix studied and made copies of Persian miniatures. At the very moment when he was doing the preparatory work for the *Dante and Virgil in the Inferno,* his obsession with the idea of the East was growing more conscious, and on 15 September 1821 he told Soulier that he was thinking of sending to the Salon a picture 'whose subject I shall take from the recent wars between the Turks and Greeks.' In thus taking a theme from the events of his day he perceived 'a chance of distinguishing oneself'. Having never seen the Mediterranean light, he asked his friend to send him a few water-colours of Naples, where he was then staying. Delacroix began to familiarize himself with the picturesque costumes of the combatants on both sides by making a few sketches of episodes from the Greek war. In 1822 and, still more, in 1823,
pl 102 various studies in oils show the development of his quest: with enchantment he discovered the lively colours of the clothes of the Suliots, of the Palikares wearing the *fustanella*—and even of the Hindus, since there arrived from Calcutta a model whom he was able to paint several times.

*Fig* 5 Géricault: LE RADEAU DE LA MÉDUSE

*It goes without saying that, in this diagram and in those that follow, the object has been merely to stress certain lines of force suggested by the painter with particular insistence. Such drawings must never be taken literally: they are not, and cannot be, strict or exclusive of other elements in the painting, but aim only at making the intended composition or main point more legible.*

He had met with a guide, who had an effect on the whole course of his work. This was M. Auguste. His name, it is true, is less well known than that of Gros or Géricault, but his influence went very deep. Born in 1789, he was nine years older than Delacroix, and so was more or less contemporary with Géricault—who, though only two years younger than he, always treated him with respect as an elder. Delacroix must have come to know Auguste, who lived at 11 rue des Martyrs, through Géricault, whose studio was at number 13. The impression made on Delacroix was evidently great, for there is an aquatint of a hunt, dated 1816 by Robaut,[14] the design of which is taken from an original by Auguste. What is more, in the 1933 exhibition 'Eugène Delacroix au Maroc'[15] which included works by Auguste, it became clear—and to Joubin first of all—that Auguste's horses must have impressed Delacroix even more than those of Géricault. They have an elegance and a leaping nervous quality foreshadowed occasionally by Carle Vernet. In the 1816 aquatint by Delacroix this is seen in the impetus of the horse jumping the hedge and the vigour of the one that is already gathering speed to catch up with the hounds. pl 99

Just as Delacroix was a descendant of the great cabinet-makers of the eighteenth century, Jules-Robert Auguste came of a line of famous goldsmiths. Having started as a sculptor and won the Prix de Rome, he had set out for Italy in 1811, but had gone much further afield, opening the way for the orientalists to come. He had travelled all over the Mediterranean, discovering not only Dalmatia and Greece (where he had made drawings of the Parthenon friezes) but also Asia Minor, Syria and Egypt. Spoils of these travels, in the shape of quantities of Greek, Persian and even Indian costumes, jewellery and other objects, had accumulated in his studio, side by side with medieval weapons, copies of the great masters and paintings by the English artists. This Pandora's

*Fig 6* THE MASSACRE AT CHIOS
Both this and the painting on the opposite page are based on the same arrangement—a divided pyramid, or M.

box, whose lid Delacroix lifted with bewitched delight, contained all the enchantments that were to intoxicate his romantic heart—the East, the Middle Ages and even English painting, since Auguste, who returned from the East in 1820, had in 1822 made a pastel copy (doubtless at the Royal Academy) of Constable's
pl 109 *View of the Stour near Dedham*.

Though distant in manner (and it was here no doubt that Delacroix acquired his idea of Dandyism), Auguste was extremely affable to the young artists brought to see him by Géricault, whom he met in 1816. Those who were attracted by his somewhat mysterious reputation included not only Delacroix, but also Bonington, who in turn brought Fielding. Many of the celebrities of the time were constant guests at his table, and here Delacroix met such friends as Poterlet, Mérimée (whom he met also at Baron Gérard's), Stendhal and Balzac. Auguste carried kindness to the extent of lending pieces from his collection—a kindness that Delacroix was able to return later on, thanks to the objects he himself brought back from Morocco.[16] Many of these borrowings were occasioned by the work on the *Massacre at Chios*, whose progress Auguste came to watch. 'He is delighted with my painting; his praises have given me new life,' writes Delacroix on 7 July 1824. The relations between the two painters ceased only with the elder one's death in 1850, and the younger one kept several of his pastels and drawings.

Though attention was drawn to M. Auguste in 1910 by Charles Saunier's articles in the *Gazette des Beaux-Arts*, his style did not begin to be really known until the 'Delacroix au Maroc' exhibition of 1933. It then became clear that his works might well have been the occasion of some false attributions, even by the best qualified experts.[15]

M. Auguste not only revealed to Delacroix certain authentic aspects of the Orient: he also helped him to link up again with the eighteenth-century tradition of painting, with which the School of David had broken. He was one of the first, perhaps the first, to rehabilitate Watteau (he owned the justly contested half of the *Enseigne de Gersaint*, which passed through the Michel Lévy Collection), Pater, Lancret and Chardin (whose *House of Cards*, now in the Louvre, belonged to him). There are even certain aspects of Delacroix's burning sensuality as these were later to burst out in his *Sardanapalus*—in particular, the contrast between the frail-looking luminous flesh of the fair women and the dark skin of the coloured people with its blueish lights—which already make their appearance in this precursor of his. Sometimes, indeed, Auguste seems to be foretelling, through Delacroix, Baudelaire's troubled dreams of women who are damned. His *Eastern Woman crouching on a Rush Mat*—the figure is close to a still life with a guitar and a water jug—is very like Delacroix's pastel, *Seated Algerian Women* in the Louvre, and seems quite ready to take its place with the *Women of Algiers*. Another pastel, *Les deux amies*, of a fair woman and a dark woman with their arms about each other on a sumptuously oriental couch, seems to be waiting for a description by Baudelaire.

XI, page 123

pl 98

Delacroix's first thought for his picture for the 1824 Salon was of a *Botzaris surprising the Turkish Camp.*[18] But in May 1823, after much hesitation, he noted: 'I have decided to do for the Salon some scene from the massacre at Chios.' This atrocious slaughter, in the course of which the Turks devastated the peaceful island, leaving behind them 20,000 dead as reprisals for the losses they themselves had suffered in Tripoli, had taken place in April 1822.

From January 1824 onwards the *Journal* allows us to follow the hard struggle into which Delacroix now threw himself: it involved long bouts of painting from the model, interrupted now and then by delightful moments of relaxation when some lovely girl was available, such as Émilie Robert who sat for the figure of the captive girl.

One of the earliest chalk sketches,[19] though it already places the principal figures and assigns to them, more or less, the part they would eventually play, shows clearly how far Delacroix still was from the spirit of his picture—which was to be the spirit of his art, at last revealed. In this drawing, the actors in the drama still, as in the classical tradition, occupy a sort of proscenium: they are massed in a foreground, behind which the outline of a mountain establishes a landscape background. There is as yet no hint of that limitless, mysterious space which, in the end, Delacroix would open out, renouncing the closed volume in order to deploy the poetry of a distant horizon. What is more, the human figures still obey the old static law: they are composed in two groups, which are arranged to fit in with two great lateral verticals framing them, and two diagonals that, after crossing in the middle of the picture, go right up to the top, while their other ends are at the lower angles. Each figure is firmly planted,

pl 106

XI THE DEATH OF SARDANAPALUS
*1827 Oil on canvas. 145 x 195 (395 x 495)*
*Louvre, Paris*

motionless and defined by its outline. Delacroix is still, here, under the influence of Géricault and his plastic research. 'What a sublime model!' he exclaimed as he made his copy of the *Radeau*. On 7 April 1824, he was still saying: 'The first and most important thing in painting is the outlines. . . . If they are there, the painting is firm and finished.'

figs 5, 6 But the composition also is Géricault's: the arrangement in an M, whose legs, vertical at first, were soon to be set farther apart and become sloping, is the same as that of the *Radeau*. In this there are two masses joined together: the peak of the one at the left is the mast supporting the sail, while that of the right-hand one is the man waving a rag with his outstretched arm; the points of these pyramids lean away from each other, and their outer sides go down to the lower angles of the picture, while the inner sides intersect.

When, on 7 May 1824, the *Journal* notes that 'it must contain that fine black, that felicitous darkness, and limbs done in the way I know how . . .', it makes one straight away think—as no doubt he was thinking—of the *Radeau*: of those anatomical pieces powerfully defined and bathed in a gloomy, almost Caravaggesque light, in that almost monochrome element where lights and shadows conflict. This suits the funereal mood of the tragic event in which are displayed 'all shades of physical pain and moral anguish: the ravages of sickness and the terrors of death'. But who is describing the picture in this way, and what picture? It is Charles Clément describing the *Méduse*.

## *The Gunpowder: Discovery of English Painting*

Would Delacroix then never succeed more than he had done in the *Dante and Virgil* in shaking off the influence of the elder painter? One might well wonder. And yet, at the very moment when he was noting down the thoughts that seem to encourage such a doubt, there came from his pen the spark that set fire to the powder—that lit up, for Delacroix himself, his own revelation: 'My picture is acquiring a torsion, an energetic movement which I absolutely must complete. . . .' From that moment everything was changed: the dynamic supplanted the static; all that remained was to consolidate the victory of light-colour over shade-modelling.

But that was to take place only in the last days of his work on the *Massacre at Chios*, the great canvas he had begun to paint on 12 January 1824 (at his lodgings at 118 rue de Grenelle Saint-Germain). For the moment, movement was more and more lost in composition, and from the drawings to the water-
IV, page 69 colour and then to the canvas one can follow the rising strength of the whirlwind eventually let loose. On the left there is a subsidence: this group of figures, at

XII STUDY OF FEMALE NUDE
FOR THE DEATH OF SARDANAPALUS
*1827 Pastel. 16 x 11 (040 x 027)*
*Louvre, Paris*

first the higher of the two, with two motionless sentinels at the top, falls in upon itself in the despair caused by renunciation and death, and the soldier, who still in the water-colour stood out from it, accepts this levelling down and gives place to two Turkish warriors who are mingled with the mass. But on the right, by an inverse and balancing movement, everything is raised higher, along with the rearing horse of the Turk with the turban. Certainly Géricault is not forgotten. In that horse rearing and neighing and foaming at the mouth, pl 52
one remembers and recognizes the movement, the inflamed eye and the upflung foreleg of the horse ridden by the *Officier de Chasseurs*—especially in the pl 54
sketch, where it too faced left. In Delacroix's group everything is leaping and hurling itself forwards, as the desperate young man is doing—is twisting and breaking, like the captive girl, whose movement is tearing from her what clothes she has left, and as, above all, the Turk at the top of the group is doing (he seems to be tying himself into a knot in his effort to grasp his sword, which is itself curved). There are some preparatory drawings that throw a good deal of light on Delacroix's search for his solution—as for instance that pen draw- pl 107
ing[20] in which the convulsive, rapid stroke seems to create a nest of writhing serpents.

Although, on 20 May, Delacroix notes that he has 'plumbed the problem', he soon had to face it all over again. As regards the composition, he had found the life which it was his aim to kindle and project—he had found it in a composition in which the movement seems to pass from one figure to the next like an electric current, or rather like a wave raising and swirling the water's pliable form. But life does not reside merely in the figures of a painting: it is in everything, in them but also around them, in the air, in the light (which plays over them)—above all, in the colour, from which there emanates an irrepressible vibration that will communicate itself to the sensibility of the onlooker. Delacroix was discovering the magnetic power of colour: that discovery was dawning in him, to which Baudelaire was to give explicit expression in a passage that no doubt echoes the conversations between the two men:

'Just as a dream takes place in an atmosphere of its own so a conception that becomes a composition needs to move in a coloured medium peculiar to it. There is clearly a particular tone, given to some one part of the picture, which becomes the key and governs the others.'[21]

In this case it was to be that harmony of red and blue, condensed in the girdle and dress of the dead woman with the child, on the right: red and blue, blood red and livid.

Just as, to achieve the design, Delacroix had had to emerge from the firm outline and discover the moving arabesque, so also to achieve the colour he was forced to abolish the accentuated modellings that dull the tone: here once more he would have to free himself from Géricault. Where could he find the necessary impetus? It was supplied to him by British painting. Delacroix had already heard talk of this at the house of M. Auguste and had been able to examine his host's copies of Constable, and indeed of Haydon. Soulier had put him in touch with the group of British water-colour landscape painters who had come to Paris—above all, with the four Fielding brothers; and it will not be forgotten that in October 1823 he had begun to share the small studio

occupied by Thalès Fielding at 20 (now 52) rue Jacob. In this also his friend-
pl 134 ship with Géricault had been of help to him; for the painter of *The Derby at Epsom* had seen Constable's *Hay Wain* in London when it was exhibited in 1821 and had (as Delacroix wrote much later, in a letter of 31 December 1858 to Silvestre) 'returned quite overwhelmed by one of the great landscapes which he went over to see'. Delacroix had already had a foretaste of Constable when, visiting his old fellow-student Régnier, he had seen and (in November 1823) 'seen again a sketch by Constable' which drew from him (in his *Journal* on 9 November) the exclamation 'admirable and incredible thing'.

From that moment his sketched-out picture was to take a new direction. In the same week that brought him so lively an impression of the novelty of Constable's sketch, he had 'settled the composition of Chios'; but as the painting drew near to completion, this was all thrown open to question afresh by the violent disturbance produced in him by that style of painting so new to him. It so happened that the French dealer Arrowsmith who had visited the great English landscape painter in January and persuaded him to send some pictures over, revealed to the public three masterly works of his in the early days of June.
pl 110 These were, it seems, the *Hay Wain* (which had made such an impression on Géricault), the *View of Hampstead Heath* (perhaps the one now in the Louvre) and the *Canal in England* (which H. Isherwood Kay[22] is no doubt right in identi-
pl 109 fying as the *View of the Stour near Dedham*, now in the Huntington Collection). These pictures were to be hung in the Salon (as numbers 358 to 360), at the same time as the *Massacre at Chios*. Delacroix was able to profit by them, for the opening of the Salon had just been postponed for a few months, until 25 August. 'That man Constable has done me a world of good,' he noted on the evening of the day when he first saw them. And he went back to see them again on 25 June.

The story has been told again and again of how Delacroix—whose *Massacre at Chios* had been accepted after some resistance by the jury of the Salon, of which Gérard, Girodet and Gros were members—was overwhelmed when, during the hanging of the pictures, he saw the Constables. It is said that, harrassed by self-doubt, he asked permission to have his picture back, and that in the Salle des Caryatides, on the ground floor of the Louvre, he transformed it, in the course of four days' frantic hard work. The anecdote possesses a symbolic value, rather than strict accuracy. Michel Florisoone[23] has gone into the question with caution and clear-sightedness. He remarks that two different facts have obviously been jumbled together. Villot, in an article that appeared in 1856 in the *Revue Universelle des Arts*, tells of a rehandling of the picture at a late stage under the influence of Constable; but this, according to him, took place in the studio, while the picture was still not quite finished. Independently of this, that great critic Théophile Silvestre reported certain remarks which he heard Delacroix make: in his *Artistes Vivants*, which also appeared in 1856, he says that the painter was allowed to take the picture at the last moment into the Salle des Antiques, but he speaks only of retouchings. It seems clear that these are two distinct episodes; and this fits in with Chenavard's statement that Delacroix revised his picture twice. Villot mixed the whole story up again much later, in the preface he wrote for the sale of his property on 11 February 1865.

However this may be, certainly Delacroix's painting—and with it the main stream of French painting—took a new course as the result of contact with the British innovators, whose influence, as even their compatriots admit, was much less strongly felt and much less discussed in their own country than in France. Constable, in his *Correspondence*, has told of his delight at the effect produced by his pictures in Paris: 'They have caused a stir,' he wrote on 7 July, when they were still in Arrowsmith's gallery.

## *The Way lies Open*

The *Massacre at Chios*, as Villot has stressed, brought with it a break in Delacroix's development. It is the end of his first manner, of what Villot calls his 'academic' manner; and in it there begins the 'second style, a mixture of Venetian, Flemish and English ways of painting'; this last had been revealed not only by Constable, but by Lawrence as well, who also exhibited at the 1824 Salon. Through them, Villot continues, 'methods that were infinitely better fitted to express his thought were suddenly revealed.' It could not be better put: I would merely add that the pictures by Bonington, which he had already seen in about 1816-17 at the Louvre, also played their part. Both artists and public were dimly aware that this was happening: but the traditionalists began to rise in resistance, Gros was worried, and the critics let fly. In spite of this, Delacroix was awarded his second-class medal by the jury, and the State bought the picture for the considerable sum of 6,000 francs, four times the price he had received for his *Dante and Virgil in the Inferno*.

Delacroix was freeing himself from the past that had been clogging him, and was beginning to see clearly what it was he was seeking in art and how he could achieve it. True, the picture is still heavy with reminiscences: there floats over it a general resemblance to the *Victims of the Plague at Jaffa*, as Delacroix recognized; also, in accordance with an inveterate habit which he had acquired from traditional painting and from which he was never completely to shake loose, he had arranged the figures in a principal plane, as though down stage in the theatre. For centuries—and largely because of the classical perspective taught ever since the Renaissance—a picture had been presented as if it were a regular box with parallel sides, open in front, in order that all the lines of recession should converge at a central point—just like a stage. This applies to van Eyck, to Vermeer, to Raphael and to Velázquez. Depth was indicated—even in the landscape, and indeed there most of all—by means of parallel planes, like flats. In this picture Delacroix has not yet escaped from this schema: the isolation of the foreground plane, which even becomes a dark, compact silhouette in the cases of the Turk with the gun and of the horse's forelegs, is still as arbitrary as in a picture by Géricault.

Yet something has happened: what is it? A comparison between the preparatory water-colour and the finished picture, as we have it after the final drastic revisions, supplies the clearest possible answer. The landscape background, pl 108
which was to have closed the scene in, has been replaced by a vista, by a void. To use Wölfflin's now accepted phraseology for distinguishing between the classic and the baroque, closed space has been succeeded by open space. The vision is

no longer the prisoner of a perspective network that leads it towards a single, logically established point: it is thrown into space, like a handful of grain. And there it scatters over the plain, traversing a confusion of sheets of light and shade; it spreads out widely like bands of sea and land dying into each other; it floats and unrolls like the smoke of conflagrations and like clouds. In this picture the discovery of a new space—space without limit or centre, space without structure or organization, space that is light, space that is infinite—demands our recognition.

Up to that time, traditional art had been based on form—that is to say, on what was by definition finished, finite. It may be said that in Delacroix's painting form was safeguarded: were we not struck by the strong, categorical isolation of it, by the way it was affirmed in the architectural masses of the composition, derived as these were from the geometrical scheme of firmly based pyramids? Yet here too the principle of dissolution had been introduced—this time by the brush-work. Constable, who himself was permeated by what could be learnt from the Dutch painters, from Koninck and Ruysdaël,[24] had shown Delacroix the 'dream quality' that, in place of the defined 'ideas', could be derived from an expansion of space, by revealing in it a quivering of light rather than a plane that could be divided into sections. But Delacroix's experiments in this direction owed much more to his friends the water-colour painters and to the portrait painter Lawrence.

Discussing the final retouching of the *Massacre at Chios*, Villot, with his enthusiasm for pictorial *cuisine*, was careful to note that Delacroix 'thickens the lights, introduces rich half-tones', makes his colours 'sparkle' by replacing oil with varnish, and avails himself of 'frequent scumbling'. All these devices combined to break up the block constituted by the form and to make this participate in space—even dissolve in it— instead of separating the two by the determinant means of local tone, outline and modelling. The scumbles produce passages that join the tones and melt them together, while the other devices break up the plane limited by the form, by filling it with scintillations and bursts of light. The local tone, so decisive as a means of establishing the autonomy of a figure or an object, is broken up—either by means of stripes (which are so frequent in Oriental dress, and of which Delacroix became enamoured long before Matisse), or by decomposing both the colour (now analyzed into its complex shades) and the touch (now chopped up in a way that was later to become a habitual technique and to be known as *flochetage*). As Villot says:

'Instead of laying on the colour, brilliant and pure, in one precise place, he interlaces the tones, breaks them up and, making the brush behave like a shuttle, seeks to produce a tissue whose many-coloured threads constantly cross and interrupt one another.'

Later on, Delacroix was to give his painting 'the shaggy look of a tapestry seen from the back'. He had not reached that stage: he had as yet scarcely an inkling of this new resource, but he had noticed how Constable repudiated 'uniform colour'. Twenty years later, after he had gone to live in his house at Champrosay, he made the point explicit: 'Constable says that the superiority of the green of his fields is due to its being made up of a multitude of different greens (juxtaposed not mixed).'[25]

Unquestionably Delacroix thus prepared the way for the experiments of the Impressionists, and even for those of their more systematic successors, as Signac claimed in his well-known essay: *De Delacroix au néo-impressionisme.* But it should be admitted that there was an element of coincidence in this. Delacroix's own experiments started off in a different direction: the truth of light, which became the creed of the Impressionists, was not really of very much importance in his eyes. For him it was only an instrument: light, through its brilliance and through the exaltation it communicates to colours, was the mistress of intensity within a picture's optical system, so that light and colours, by their governing and determining action, could serve to amplify and suggest a different intensity—a moral intensity, whose nucleus and definition lay in the subject it treated.

Through its overall diffusion light works against the abstract fragmentation produced by a form: it turns the picture into a new, autonomous world, distinct from the one we are in and observing, and inhabited by an immaterial though visible reality of its own, which strikes us at the first glance. With it there appears, as a definite element, an atmosphere, and painting, instead of bringing into play the intellect with its analysis of the forms and their details, catches up in a single undivided revelation the sense of sight and the sensibility that prolongs it. It no longer provokes reflection, but sets us dreaming: 'Silent power that at first speaks only to the eyes, then invades and seizes hold of all the faculties of the soul.' (*Journal*, 8 May 1824.) Constable was certainly already conscious of this difference, for in 1824, the year when the *Massacre at Chios* was painted and exhibited, he said of the traditional painters of the French School:

'The truth is, they study (and they are very laborious students) pictures only; ... they make painful studies of individual articles, leaves, rocks, stones, etc. singly; so that they look cut out, without belonging to the whole.'

A whole is what a work of art should be, before all else, for it should offer us 'the unity that comes from some creative power whose source is indefinable'.[26]

Delacroix was beginning to understand that this was what was lacking in Géricault—in whose work he later noted a 'constant absence of unity'.[27] He found this both in composition and in the individual figures, especially in the horses. 'Each detail adds itself to the others, but forms only a loosely-knit whole.' He quoted his old friend, the Lyons painter Chenavard, who at Dieppe had said to him 'that he did not regard Géricault as a master, because he does not possess *l'ensemble*: this is his own criterion of a master.' To achieve unity was Delacroix's principal ambition.[28]

Why? Because, by its very nature, painting offers itself to the eye of the beholder all at once, to be taken in at a glance. Because, also, without this it cannot attain its aim—which is to communicate to the onlooker the sensuous and human wealth of which the artist must make it first a part and then the trustee. Late in life, comparing his own pictures with those of Géricault, Delacroix in a mood of heart-searching examined his own *Entombment of Christ* with this result: 'The whole inspires an emotion that astonishes even me. One cannot tear oneself away, and there is not a detail that sticks out, asking to be admired or distracting attention.' In 1824 Delacroix had not yet reached this supreme degree of skill: his *Massacre at Chios* still includes passages where he is delight-

*Fig 7* PAGE FROM A SKETCHBOOK. Pen drawing. Cabinet des Dessins, Louvre, Paris.

ing in his technical virtuosity for its own sake (as, for instance, in the still life in the foreground), or is trying out his powers of expression. 'Oh, smile of a dying man. . . . The gaze of the mother! The despairing embrace. . .', he wrote on 8 May 1824. Yet even to this list he could not help adding the warning: 'It must all hold together!'

Henceforth Delacroix was free from the constraints that had hindered his advance. Among the masters around him—past and present, French and foreign—he had found those who had helped him to forge his own means of expression. His career lay open before him—and through a gate that was already triumphal.

## NOTES ON THE PLATES TO CHAPTER III

*At the feet of Raphael*

In his entries for the competitions at the École des Beaux-Arts (pl 68), Delacroix submitted himself to the classical mould. His first commissioned picture was a homage to Raphael: both the preparatory drawings and the picture showed that he had taken as his model *La Belle Jardinière*, of which he made a copy at that time (pls 69-71).

68 *Roman Matrons giving up their Jewels for their Country, 1818. Cabinet des Dessins, Louvre, Paris.*

69 *Studies for the 'Virgin of the Harvest' for the church at Orcemont, near Rambouillet, 1819. Cabinet des Dessins, Louvre, Paris.*

70 RAPHAEL: *La Belle Jardinière, Louvre, Paris.*

71 *Virgin of the Harvest, 1819. Church at Orcemont, near Rambouillet, Seine-et-Oise.*

*Learning from the Italian seventeenth century*

Already in his second commissioned picture (pls 72, 73) Delacroix was more definitely returning—through Géricault, who had got him the commission—to the seventeenth century, whose productions, whether Italian or French, he always valued. Here it is Guercino who springs to mind.

72 *Virgin of the Sacred Heart, c. 1821. Ajaccio Cathedral.*

73 *Study for the 'Virgin of the Sacred Heart', 1821. Cabinet des Dessins, Louvre, Paris.*

*The lesson of the engravings*

Delacroix's first known work—dating from 1814—is an etching on the bottom of a copper saucepan (pl 74). Engravings widened his visual repertoire: he copied the English caricaturists, especially Rowlandson (pls 75, 76) and learned from them how to accentuate character by drawing, while Goya taught him how *chiaroscuro* produces effects of drama and even of fantasy (pls 77, 78).

74 *Engraving on the bottom of a copper saucepan, 1814. Bibliothèque Nationale, Paris.*

75 *'The Ridiculous Kiss', c. 1818-20. Sketch after Rowlandson. Musée des Beaux-Arts, Orléans.*

76 *Studies of heads after Rowlandson, c. 1818-20. Cabinet des Dessins, Louvre, Paris.*

77 FRANCISCO GOYA: *Que se la llevaron! (And so they kidnapped her!) Caprichos.*

78 *Sketch by Delacroix, c. 1818-24, after Goya's engraving: 'Que se la llevaron!' (And so they kidnapped her!) Caprichos. Cabinet des Dessins, Louvre, Paris.*

*The first masterpiece* *Dante and Virgil in the Inferno* (pls 86 and II) emphasizes both Delacroix's sources and his originality. While he remains faithful to sculptural drawing of form (and especially of anatomy) by definite outlines, as is proved by some of the preparatory studies (pls 85, 87) he is already moving away from the neo-classical painters and the exclusive preponderance they gave to drawing (pl 80).

He harks back to the Italian *Quattrocento* (pl 89); but Rubens—to whom he will attach himself more and more (pl 84)—is now teaching him intensity of movement (pl 88) and of expression (pl 91). Géricault, whose *Radeau de la Méduse* (pls 79 and 81) is here his direct inspiration (pl 83), has encouraged him to attempt a more compelling atmosphere by giving more and more importance to the landscape background (pl 90), and to accentuate this atmosphere by the liberties and violent contrasts of his techniques (pl 82).

79 THÉODORE GÉRICAULT: *Study for 'Le Radeau de la Méduse', 1818. Louvre, Paris.*

80 A.-L. GIRODET: *Scene from the Deluge (detail), Salon of 1806. Louvre, Paris.*

81 GÉRICAULT: *Le Radeau de la Méduse, 1818. Louvre, Paris.*

82 GÉRICAULT: *The Wounded Cuirassier, 1814. Louvre, Paris.*

83 *Two sketches after Géricault's 'Radeau de la Méduse', c. 1820. Cabinet des Dessins, Louvre, Paris.*

84 *Studies of heads after a hunting picture by Rubens. Cabinet des Dessins, Louvre, Paris.*

85 *Preliminary sketch for 'Dante and Virgil in the Inferno', c. 1821. Cabinet des Dessins, Louvre, Paris.*

86 *Dante and Virgil in the Inferno, 1822. Louvre, Paris.*

87 *Study of a boatman for 'Dante and Virgil in the Inferno'. Louvre, Paris.*

88 *Studies of the damned for 'Dante and Virgil in the Inferno', 1822. Cabinet des Dessins, Louvre, Paris.*

89 *Study for Dante. Cabinet des Dessins, Louvre, Paris.*

90 *The Infernal City in Flames, 1822. (Background to the 'Dante and Virgil'.) Cabinet des Dessins, Louvre, Paris.*

91 *Heads of Dante and Virgil, 1822. Cabinet des Dessins, Louvre, Paris.*

*The impelling force of Gros*

More even than Géricault who remained faithful to 'sculptural' disciplines, Gros (pl 92) revealed to Delacroix that the art of painting—or of drawing—includes a liberating dynamism, whose means of action are a liveliness in the handling and a directness in the touch (pl 93).

92 ANTOINE-JEAN GROS: *Sketch for 'Bucephalus vanquished by Alexander', 1798. Private collection.*

93 *Horse attacked by a Tiger, c. 1825. Cabinet des Dessins, Louvre, Paris.*

*Light and shade; mastery of wash*

Very early on, and especially in certain private notes (pl 94), Delacroix discovered in wash, with its play on simple contrasts of values, a more directly painterly technique, and one that he was to develop later through the practice of water-colour painting.

94 *Delacroix and his friends on New Year's Eve, 1817. Cabinet des Dessins, Louvre, Paris.*

*From drawing forms to drawing impressions*

In the early years whose climax was the *Dante and Virgil*, Delacroix completed not only his apprenticeship, but also the development which took him from linear vision (pl 96) completed by modelling (pl 95) to a notation by means of lights and reflections (pl 97).

95 *Head of a Man. Cabinet des Dessins, Louvre, Paris.*

96 *Self-portrait at about twenty years of age. Cabinet des Dessins, Louvre, Paris.*

97 *Drawing of a horse. Cabinet des Dessins, Louvre, Paris.*

*Influence of an older artist*

Jules-Robert Auguste fills a marginal but notable place in nineteenth-century painting. As a great traveller and an enthusiast for the Middle Ages he exerted a quite novel influence on artists such as Géricault who were rather younger than he; and he did much to interest Delacroix in the East and to inform him about it (pls 98, 99).

98 JULES-ROBERT AUGUSTE: *Eastern Woman crouching on a Rush Mat. Formerly Ch. Saunier Collection.*

99 AUGUSTE: *Study of Arab Horses. Maurice Perret-Carnot Collection, France.*

*Discovery of the East*

Long before he went to Morocco, Delacroix tried to find out about the East: he discovered its ancient civilizations—Egypt (pl 103), Assyria, whose monuments were coming again to light; and he became fascinated by Islam, which he began, very early on, to study through Persian miniatures, rugs, etc. (pls 100, 101). Then he tried his hand at depicting—on the living model, such as Count Palatiano—Oriental clothes lent him by, among others, M. Auguste (pl 102).

100 *Study after Persian miniatures, with colour notes. Cabinet des Dessins, Louvre, Paris.*

101 *Study after Persian miniatures, with colour notes. Cabinet des Dessins, Louvre, Paris.*

102 *Sketch for 'Count Palatiano'. Louvre, Paris.*

103 *Studies of Egyptian Art. Cabinet des Dessins, Louvre, Paris.*

*Preludes to 'Chios'* Delacroix was determined that in the *Massacre at Chios,* which was suggested to him by the war then raging between the Greeks and the Turks, local colour should clothe genuine human feelings: an orphan girl weeping among graves (pl 105) would give him the theme of the human face wild with grief (pl 104).

104 *Orphan Girl in the Graveyard, 1823. Louvre, Paris.*

105 *Orphan Girl weeping in the Graveyard, 1823. Formerly Haro Collection*

*Union of contraries* The preparatory drawings for the *Massacre at Chios* show that in Delacroix two possibilities lived side by side: whirling, unbridled life in all its ardour, rendered by a baroque type of drawing (pl 107); but also a thoughtful order, establishing the composition firmly (pls 106, 106a).

106, 106a *Preliminary drawings for the 'Massacre at Chios', 1824. Louvre, Paris.*

107 *Preliminary drawing for the 'Massacre at Chios', 1824. Louvre, Paris.*

*Landscape's contribution* It remained for Delacroix to give to his compositions—now that he was assured of their having both form and dramatic life—the limitless environment of natural scenery, light and air (pls 108 and III). The revelation of this came to him from the British landscape painters with their great originality—and especially from Constable, whose works were just then becoming known in France (pls 109, 110).

108 *The Massacre at Chios, 1824 (detail). Louvre, Paris.*

109 JOHN CONSTABLE: *View of the Stour near Dedham. The Henry E. Huntington Library and Art Gallery, California.*

110 CONSTABLE: *The Hay Wain (detail). The National Gallery, London.*

111 *The Massacre at Chios, 1824 (detail). Louvre, Paris.*

68

69

73

74

75

76

77

78

79

80

82

83

84

85

86

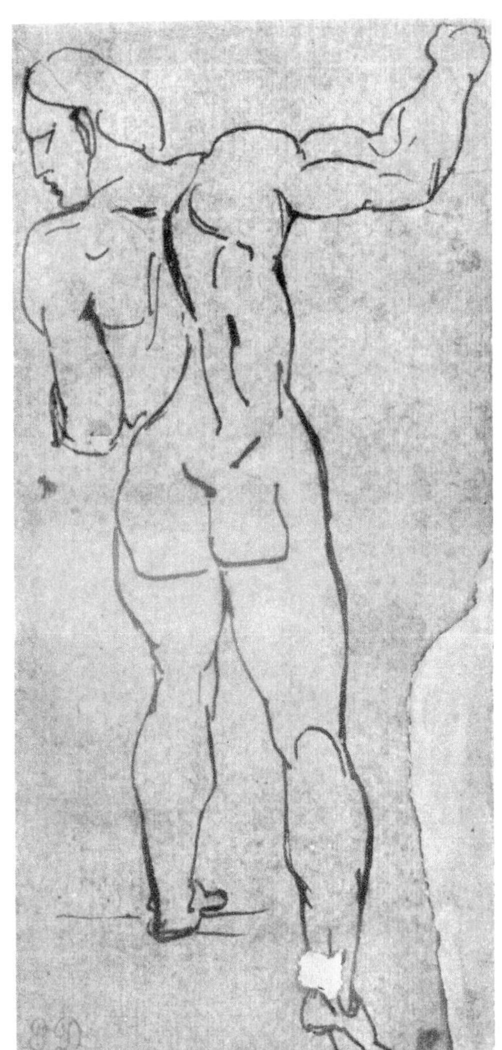

87

88

89

91

92

93

94

95

96

97

98

99

100

101

102

103

104

105

106

106 a

107

108

109

# IV IMPETUS AND RELAPSE

THOUGH DELACROIX, in achieving his liberation in 1824, owed much to the example of others, he owed most to the inner vocation which had steered him in their direction.

The temperament of Delacroix was, in fact, quite different from that of the muscular and sporting Géricault. His health was precarious, he was impatient, he lived on his nerves. That vital force which it was his aim to translate into painting—the aim that made him Géricault's successor, and made him feel himself his brother—could not issue in a cold tenacity of effort: it was vibrant and impulsive, incompatible with even a tense immobility. All his resources threw themselves into the initial impetus, at the cost of soon relapsing and causing, by his speedy exhaustion, those crises of emptiness and ennui which came to him so frequently. This natural predisposition was accentuated in him by the weakness of his health, undermined as it was by a fever that both increased his over-excitement and exhausted his resistance. For example, like Géricault, he felt that the horse was a predestined subject—but how differently he felt it! The solid, sturdy animal to which the older artist devoted such long study, was of no interest to him: he was attracted by the prancing and leaping creature with its lightning releases of energy. Those of Gros and Vernet in painting, and the Arab horse in reality, were what inspired him.

## *Temperament and Theory of Art*

All this emerges clearly from the first years of the *Journal.* Here are some of the sparks that came from his pen while he was working at the *Massacre at Chios.* On 25 April 1824: 'To let oneself get hot . . . to enter into the subject with fire. . . .' On 1 May: 'I was in a delirium of composition this morning. . . .' On 7 May: 'If I am not agitated like a snake in the hand of the pythoness, I am cold. . . . Everything good that I have done has been done in this way. . . .' On 11 May he thinks with dread of his death, when he will no longer be 'stirred by thoughts and emotions and desires for poetry and every kind of generous expansiveness. . . .'

But as soon as the flame had burst forth, the ash collapsed. 'There are moments of sadness and boredom which have all that is needed to test one harshly. . . . As soon as inspiration isn't there, I am bored,' he confesses, only a week after an ecstatic entry. There are plenty of such admissions of exhaustion as this: 'The whole day out of sorts, an insipid melancholy . . .' (18 April), or again: 'Tired and feeling unwell all day' (2 May). So he goes on from release to collapse, jerkily, chaotically. At the age of fifty-six[1] he would still be noting that he works 'with frenzy . . . unable to detach myself.' But each of these fiery bouts, when he gives so much of himself and goes out to his very limits and beyond, leaves him empty, and he remains so until he can recharge himself with the electricity that will leap out and exhaust itself in another flash. Later, when he had collaborators such as Lassalle-Bordes, they too remarked on these alternations by which, after letting himself be carried away by his daemon, he sank into a dull exhaustion.

Delacroix's constitution, mental and physical, was the basis of his genius: it was the source of his greatest happiness, but also of his misery. He felt that he must exploit it: in response to life he quivered with intensity and violence, more than anyone else and in a different way. That unique taste, which sometimes filled his mouth like some burning and dazzlingly bright pimento, demanded that he should get it into his art and, through his art, into the beholder. 'Why am I not a poet!' he exlaims on 25 April 1824: 'But at least let me experience as much as possible in each of my pictures what I want to convey into the souls of others.' To experience. . . to transmit . . .—is that not what poetry does? 'How I would like to be a poet!' he repeats several times. But indeed he was one, with the paintbrush.

Already his view of art was making itself clear. As early as 1822 he could see it.[2] The painter, he says, 'sees forms from nature outside him': this by itself would be nothing, but in addition 'he meditates within himself', and 'what the soul finds inwardly moving in those objects which only strike the senses' becomes the field of the creative artist, his mission. It can 'be embodied through writing', but at the cost of a sacrifice, of 'altering and changing its essence'. Painting, which, like music, addresses itself more directly to the senses and so appears to be 'more material' art, is, on the contrary, able to avoid denaturing that essence, for in it 'justice is done honestly to what is finite and to what is infinite', to the visible that is set down, and to the invisible that is suggested. 'That is what is miraculous about it.' Painting succeeds in building 'a sort of mysterious bridge between the souls of the persons in the picture and that of the spectator.' Indeed, Delacroix's conception of his art was so clear that, by the beginning of 1824, he was already able to think of writing 'a kind of memorandum on painting'.[3] This was the germ of his dictionary of the Fine Arts, which he was to start and leave unfinished, and of his articles on the theory of art.

What he meant to communicate—the substance of his art—existed in that tumultuous, passionate, quivering response of his to certain sights, certain subjects, certain ideas and—why not?—certain books he read. This response was entirely his own—indeed one may say that it was what defined his innermost individuality. It was this that he had to make clear and make others feel. He said as much on 14 May 1826, in a well-known passage:

'You can add one more soul to those that have seen nature in a way that is their own . . . . The novelty is in the spirit that creates, and not in the nature that is painted.'

Such, at least, is the lesson of the great masters: 'They painted their soul when they painted things, and your soul is asking you to give it its turn. . . .'

But the transmission must be made effective; and this required a technique that could communicate from one nervous system to another, from one soul to another, what the artist had experienced in his own individual way. It was enough to be oneself, forcibly and with simplicity. 'If you cultivate your soul, it will find its way to the light and will display itself. It will make for itself a language. . . .'

To 'cultivate one's soul', but also to 'make a language for it',—the old problem of subject and form is here both set and solved. The soul seethes and rises to ecstasy: the language it demands must be fashioned for it. The experiment of the *Massacre at Chios* had been conclusive: far from trying to define and condense inspiration in the excessively finished and chiselled words that forms are, the artist must cultivate the rapidity, the fluidity and continuity that can catch and convey the breath of the inner life in all its fugitive vigour; he must also acquire a brilliance that will strike the onlooker and facilitate access to his work by an expressive mimicry in the touch, a vivacity and musicality in the colour, a sparkling and fine shading in the light. Of all this Delacroix saw hints in the British School of painting.

This made him wish, more and more definitely, to go and study on the spot a school to which he already owed so much and from which he expected to learn even more. He was also attracted by the civilization of England—by what his many British or anglicized friends in Paris, from the Fieldings to Soulier, had made him think he would find in it.

## *Visit to England—'Pure Painting'*

On 24 May 1825, less than a year after the first showing of the *Massacre at Chios*, Delacroix left his new studio at 14 rue d'Assas, and, like Géricault but a few years later, started for England, going via Calais and Dover. A decisive importance is usually, and quite rightly, attached to Delacroix's later journey to Morocco; but this should not lead us to undervalue his visit to England. In the three months he devoted to it—from May to August—he was to establish his pictorial language.

It was inevitable that a man so varied and unstable in his impressions should have made some rather contradictory judgements on England. Sometimes he reacted with enthusiasm, sometimes with a foreigner's chauvinistic mistrust. In spite of being occasionally lonely, bored and even disappointed, he spent most of the time in a whirl of excitements. The Fieldings, particularly Thalès Field-
pl 118 ing, had made many preparations for him and had found him somewhere to live.
pl 117 Delacroix visited Etty (whose *Storm* may have given him the initial idea for his many treatments of *Christ on the Lake of Genesareth*) and Lawrence; he was disappointed to miss Constable and Turner, who were out of London, but he saw their pictures; and he visited assiduously the public and private picture galleries,

rediscovering in them masters already known to him—but of whom he now saw examples chosen from a less classical point of view than the French and closer to his own aspirations. He also went to see various old friends, especially painters—English ones such as Bonington, and French ones such as Lami, Poterlet, Isabey and Henri Monnier: London was at that time much frequented by young painters of the French School, and it is easy to imagine the enthusiasm with which this circle initiated itself into the new resources offered to their eyes, hands and palettes.

Delacroix found other pleasures; he was soon lodged with Elmore, a horse-dealer to whom he had an introduction from M. Auguste, and both the painter and horseman in him found plenty of outlets. He became friendly with an English nobleman, a friend of Elmore's, who introduced him to the delights of 'yachting' (he describes himself as '*fou de la marine*'). 'Their music', he writes, 'is atrocious', but in the theatre he saw a version of *Faust*, which he was to remember when he did his series of lithographs on that subject. Above all, as he wrote to Pierret on 27 June, 'words fail me to express my admiration for the genius of Shakespeare.' pls 115, 116

He was struck by the manners of the English, among whom the *canaille* had, he observed, 'a sort of savagery and fierceness', while society affected 'the noblest' politeness—indeed the dandyism towards which Delacroix was already predisposed, and which was to play such a part in his whole idea of life. None-theless, having had the experience, he returned home without too much regret, convinced of the excellence of French ways, for as he summed it up to Pierret on 1 August: 'decidedly there is something sad and uncouth in all this, which does not fit in with what we have in France.'

After his return, Bonington spent some time in his studio, and this prolonged the effect on him of the British technique of painting. Much later—in a letter of 30 November 1861 to Thoré—Delacroix described 'the lightness of execution which, especially in the water-colour medium, seems to turn his pictures into diamonds, by which the eye is flattered and enchanted, independently of any subject and anything they may represent.' This last phrase implies the idea of 'pure painting', apart from subject and realism; and in fact Delacroix was never closer to this than at that time, when he cultivated colour and touch for their own sakes. By bringing into play more and more dazzling notes, he increased his mastery of them and his ability to subject them to the service of that art of expression and suggestion which was still his basic dogma.

Maxime du Camp, in his *Souvenirs littéraires*, tells of having seen him 'one evening near a table on which there was a basket filled with skeins of wool. He kept picking up the skeins, grouping them, placing them across one another, separating them shade by shade, and producing extraordinary effects of colour. I heard him say: "The most beautiful pictures I have seen are certain Persian carpets."'

Here I cannot resist quoting a similar anecdote about the all too short-lived painter Emile Deroy, told by Théodore de Banville in his *Souvenirs*.[4] Deroy was possibly the man who first revealed the genius of Delacroix (of whom he was a fanatical admirer) to Baudelaire. It was he, in any case, who painted the copy of the *Women of Algiers* which for a long time adorned the poet's room.

Banville tells us how he watched Deroy, in the Luxembourg gardens, 'waving in the air, sometimes slowly, sometimes with a quick jerky movement, a whole lot of bits of stuff of different colours, some vivid and some soft, attached to a string; every now and then he would stop, apparently savouring an indescribable pleasure.' Although Delacroix—and the British painters as well—had showed him that colour ought to be 'dazzling and rich' Deroy thought, in this also like Delacroix, that this should be only the beginning, and taught that colour must also be 'varied, lovingly united to thought, and completely transfigured according to the nature of the subject treated.'

This led him to say, with Delacroix, and with Baudelaire who repeated the remark, that 'a picture, when seen from so far off that the onlooker could not tell what subject it represented, should be already able, through its highly musical qualities, to put the onlooker's soul into the mood desired by the painter.'

It may be that Delacroix's expressive power was so intense only because it was based on this constantly deepened experience of the possible combinations of colour apart from any representation or signification. This optical science—which was at the origin of Impressionism, certainly, but was used by the Impressionists with a quite different intention—made Delacroix master of the keyboard to which he was to entrust his music. He loved colour in two ways, which he was unable to dissociate: as 'pure' colour, simply deploying its own resources; but also as a means of expression and suggestion. After experimenting in pure colour under the influence of the British painters, he went on, though without ever turning his back on this, to subordinate it to the second conception.

In the then unpublished article by Rivet, quoted by Piron,[5] there is a striking demonstration of this point. Rivet tells how Delacroix's *Sardanapalus*, which was 'gloomily energetic' in the sketch, became something quite different under the influence of the fair girl, the 'half naked slave throwing herself on her master's bed.' Carried away by the splendour of that flesh, 'whose sensuous quality aroused him to an ecstasy of enthusiasm . . . he lost the general tone of the picture. . . . The whole scene took on a different effect from the one it was designed to express.'

Bewitchment with the beauty of pure colour had irresistibly carried him away. But in his later work he refused to yield to such deviations from the discipline of expression. Reflecting upon this later on, Delacroix described how he had developed:

'Nowadays my palette is not what it used to be. My palette is perhaps less brilliant, but it no longer goes astray. It is an instrument that plays only what I want to make it play.'[6]

He had doubtless not forgotten that giddy fit of joy in colour, that transport into which the powers of the palette had carried him away in the case of his *Sardanapalus*, and had come, in his later days, to fear such excesses. In point of fact, immediately after painting that picture, he began a phase—perhaps it should be called a crisis—of *chiaroscuro*. Then, as though sobered by this, he emerged into his final conception of musical colour, of which the chief duty is to set the onlooker's sensibility quivering in unison with the emotion the artist has put into his picture. From that time on, he was faithful to the conviction thus described by du Camp: 'His theory was this: in a picture, it is the colour that must dominate because it is the colour that gives the first impression.' This method is a musical one. Delacroix created symphonies rather than pictures: his *Entry of the Crusaders into Constantinople* is a symphony in blue major, XXVII, page 283 while his *Dante and Virgil in the Inferno* is a symphony in green minor with a II, page 58 red key signature. . . .' But in order to obtain such a full possession of the suggestive powers of colour, a thorough knowledge of its nature and possible combinations—of, so to speak, its grammar—was essential. It seems clear that Delacroix could not have passed from the art of plastic expression which he had learned from Géricault to the art of chromatic expression which was to be that of his maturity without this mediating period, during which he explored the possibilities of colour and made its means his own.

Bonington seemed to him the most dazzling master, indeed a living condensation, of this new body of knowledge, which he felt to be one of the foundations of the British School of painting. He went so far as to imitate him, and some of pls 122, 123 Delacroix's water-colours impress us as answering variations upon a theme by Bonington. He made copies of pictures by him: his lithograph *The Message*[7] is a transposition of a water-colour by his friend. His *Marino Faliero*—which he VI, page 74 finished in 1826 and sent to the 1827 Salon, and which, according to Lassalle-Bordes, was one of his favourites, if not the favourite, among his own pictures—shows clearly how far the two artists were engaged in the same experiments. The Scala dei Giganti in Delacroix's picture is also found in a *Doges' Palace* pl 119 attributed to Bonington, but more probably by a French hand.[8] Delacroix's *Marino Faliero*, when exhibited in England after the Salon, received a welcome there which confirms his affinities with British art. It is now in the Wallace Collection.

Delacroix's pursuit of the colour *matière* in its full intensity and value was carried so far that a sudden immobility seemed to descend upon his painting: the lines now submitted to a sharp geometry, to which the calligraphic fineness of the brushwork corresponded, and the wild impetus held its breath so that the whole effort might be devoted to this jeweller's work, through which Delacroix was to master chromaticism. Between the pure white of the Scala dei Giganti and the black of the open doorway, the iridescent scale stretches from the icy cold of an incisive green and a few pale blues, through all the variations of gold from a pale yellow to deep copper colours, till it reaches the most flamelike reds and oranges.

At this period Delacroix gave himself free play in his effort to combine colours into the most unexpected and delightful relationships; and a voluptuous treatment of the nude went with this extreme delight in colour. This is evident in his series of *Odalisques*, the most dazzling of which is the *Woman with a* IX, page 113 *Parrot* in the Lyons Museum: she lies back nonchalantly among the stuffs and pl 130 cushions, whose yellows, blues, greens and bright or wine-dark reds surpass in splendour the plumage of the bird. His *Duke of Orleans showing his Mistress to the Duke of Burgundy* is definitely an erotic picture strengthened by historical association, and Bonington would not have been ashamed of it.

Delacroix was never to go further with the fireworks of the palette than at this time. One need only mention his *Pierret in Turkish Costume* (1825), with its pl 132 interplay of the violets of the belt and table cover and the dark green of the tunic; his *Count Palatiano* dressed as a palikare, painted in the following year; or

pl 131 again his *Baroilhet the Singer in Turkish Costume*, with its sumptuous carmines standing out against a green background that grows lighter towards the top till it
VII, page 83 becomes a celestial blue. In his *Still Life with Lobsters* (exhibited at the 1827 Salon, and now in the Louvre) the reds of the crustaceans and the pheasant set up a relation of contrast with the greens of the feathers and the lizard, and this relation is interwoven in the tartan stripes of the game bag, while in the landscape background the red worn by the hunters stands out against the greens and dark blue of the plain, just as the brass of a horn sounds in the depths of the woods.

Delacroix transfered these valuable experiments even into large-scale painting,
pl 341 if we may judge by the sketch (1826) which is all that survives of his *Emperor Justinian composing the Institutes*—a huge canvas almost four metres high, destroyed in 1871 in the burning of the Conseil d'État. Théophile Gautier singled out its 'brocades starry with precious stones, the Asiatic wealth of Constantinople'. And in fact it is known that Delacroix, in order to gain documentation for the picture, made copies of plates illustrating Byzantine art.

In order to give his colour an increased translucency and brilliance, Delacroix at this time had recourse to certain purely technical refinements: in particular, he made use of copal varnish, derived from the hard, limpid resin of a tree that is found chiefly in Madagascar. Though Delacroix later put these experiments in their proper place, he never lost interest in them, and in 1858 he was still wondering[9] if the secret of van Eyck's translucent, enamel-like paint might not lie in grinding the colours with varnish, 'which would make it possible to keep the colours fresh'—the oil being added only at the moment of painting.

Delacroix placed fluidity of touch at the service of chromatic and calligraphic intensity. The drawing is not only sharp, but mordant, impulsive and incisive.
pl 65 Already in 1824 his water-colour of the *Horse frightened by a Storm*, with the leaping, whirling whiteness of the horse harmonizing with the jagged lightning, was an astonishing example of this. The same movements, intensified till they have the violence of spasms, are displayed and multiplied in the frantic battles between horses which he painted in 1825. Then, in the *Ballad of Tam O'Shanter*, which was inspired by Burns' poem and was painted for his beloved Mme. Dalton, his unchecked rush seems to tear into strips and carry away with it the mists lingering on the plain under the moonlight, so that the whole countryside is leaping and gliding, as swiftly as the painter's brush, in that fantastic ride, that panic flight. The same rushing and tearing is to be found in the
pl 133 lithograph of the *Flight of the Smuggler* (1826), which was designed as an illustration of a ballad by Bétourné.

These furious clinches and these frantic leapings combined together in 1827 in a treatment of certain Hellenic themes reminiscent of Chios and of Byron: they are to be found at the heart of the battles between the *Giaour and the Pasha* and
pls 136, 138 of the *Scenes from the Present War between the Turks and Greeks.*

Delacroix needed a flowing technique, not only to carry a picture through with a speed that would not allow his impetus to flag, but also to communicate to the eye a physical impression of mobility, of an indefinite transition unhindered by the firmness of any fixed delimitation—in a word, to ensure that the total effect, on which he relied for the emotional shock, should not be impaired by the breaking up of the interest into localized, more or less autonomous fragments.

Against the dryness that made the academic School lifeless, he set a liquid handling which surprised his contemporaries. It was well described by Henry de La Madelène:[10]

'No one has ever had a livelier hand for pinning down by rapid strokes the fiery conceptions of genius. His burning brush seems to fly over the canvas, and the composition emerges all at once, without hesitation, without any cooling off, palpitating like life itself. Light, perspective, depth and movement—it is all there in those hurried touches whose certainty leaves one gasping.'

This was true of the oil paintings; but it was in water-colour painting—learned from Soulier and studied with those close companions Fielding and Bonington—that this 'liquid technique' had its origin. Water-colour painting, indeed, both pls 127, 128 in its material bases and in the resulting appearance, makes use of the qualities of water—of its quivering mobility, its responsiveness to the least breath, its translucence and its sparkling brilliance. Just as we talk of the 'water' of a diamond, it would be tempting to introduce this word into studio terminology in order to describe the oil painting of the British painters and the style which they, especially Lawrence, inspired Delacroix to explore at this period.

The renewal of his technique is not, however, exclusively due to England. Through him it was possible for the French tradition to rediscover its eighteenth-century antecedents, which had become despised and forgotten since the reaction of David and his pupils against them. What Delacroix did, in short, was simply to adorn with a new and fresher brilliance a technique of painting discovered by the Venetians, developed by Rubens and adopted and refined by the French School from Watteau to Fragonard. 'Flanders and Venice are united here,' he himself remarked in front of one of M. de Morny's Watteaus.[11] 'Admirable execution,' was again his later judgment.[12] Hanging in his studio, he had—and kept to the end of his life—what he thought was a Watteau; it was in fact a copy of the *Assassins Maudits* in the Hermitage; he left it to Baron Schwiter whose portrait by him, now in the National Gallery, London, VIII, page 84 is the most magnificent example of what Delacroix learned from the art of Lawrence.

## *The Inner Man and the Spleen*

Delacroix's pictorial language, which always required the flashes, the promptitude and the abandon of a nervous system that is creative only when it is over-excited, was now subjected more and more to the service of a soul that could only find and listen to itself in the periods when it was withdrawn into itself; but at those moments what it found was exhaustion and despair. One consequence of this temperament—which would nowadays be called cyclothymic—was that Delacroix emerged from himself only to flash like lightning, either in words or with the brush, and went back into himself only to stumble, exhausted,

XIII LIBERTY LEADING THE PEOPLE
*1830 Oil on canvas. 102 x 128 (260 x 325)*
*Louvre, Paris*

against the walls of a dull cell. As he admitted on 13 June 1824, 'As soon as inspiration isn't there, I am bored.' He rose and took fire only to fall back the more heavily. Of this basic dualism within him he became fully aware, and it made his life a desperate struggle to reconcile its opposing terms.

If we come upon him during the hours when he is withdrawn, meditating, alone with himself, it is a quite different Delacroix that we find from the one of whom nothing could be seen or heard but the crackling blaze of his achievement—a Delacroix prematurely convinced of the vanity of human existence. Let us look over his shoulder and read his notes. Up to the beginning of 1824, when he nerved himself to undertake the *Massacre at Chios*, the *Journal* is absorbed by youthful love affairs and somewhat copybook moralizings; but on 25 January in that year there comes the first knocking at the door of solitude: 'I kept telling myself that one of the sad things about this wretched life of ours was the duty of being ceaselessly face to face with oneself.' Each person has his 'leaden coat to drag about', and what can other people do for him? It would not be surprising if Géricault's inexorable illness and tragic death had supplied the shock that brought him up against real heart-searching. He began to re-read letters from his friends, male and female, and he felt the swift passing of the happy moments. 'Ordinary, ignorant people are indeed happy,' he exclaimed—but what of the man who thinks and feels? 'I am a man. What is this I? What is a *man*?' A feeling of the vanity of the world and the difficulty of communicating with anyone laid hold of him.

Again and again he was to say: 'One is forced back to solitude.' He was discovering solitude—it was bound to catch him and close over him. True, 'the things one experiences when alone with oneself are much stronger and more virgin.' He hoped that this would bring him liberation from futile activities, 'inner satisfaction . . . calm', and even health. Such were his thoughts in 1824, the year in which the *Massacre at Chios* presented to the world such a spectacle of passionate ardour.

Solitude made possible for him what he called, in his letters to Soulier, 'my only passion . . . work'. There he could experience that fever of creative activity which, for him, was a saving ecstasy. But work itself, though for a moment it deadened him to other things, could not conceal from him the irremediable fugitiveness of life. Life can be intense but how fragile it is! Not only do the minutes fly away, but their savour goes with them. We are hurried along by 'blind destiny', and what is left to us? 'An infinite desire for what we never obtain; an emptiness that we can never fill'[13]—hence 'an extreme itch to produce in whatever way we can, to struggle as much as possible against time, which hurries us away.' And at the end, what? There is the dawning of 'a kind of philosophic calm which prepares us for suffering and raises us above trifles.' It is the only hope; for, apart from that, all he can see is 'the emptiness of life, the uselessness of our desires and our regrets.'

XIV LIBERTY LEADING THE PEOPLE (detail)
*1830 Oil on canvas.*
*Louvre, Paris*

'Boredom, emptiness', he says again on 9 August 1855—a terrible litany. For, he says of solitude, 'There is none, or almost none, heavier than mine.'

But for a long period the *Journal* is not there to help us to follow this inward debate. It was interrupted on 5 October of that same year, and not resumed till 1847.[14]

But Delacroix's confessions continue: they are before our eyes in his paintings. In them his disillusioned meditation is pursued, and is embodied. Side by side with the feverish pictures, filled with the leaping of frantic horses, or with the flowering of bouquets of burning colours by a hand that rushes on half-unconsciously, there is a whole other series in which though certainly the fireworks of imagination and brushwork are not extinguished, the deep and secret voice makes itself heard.

Can it not, in fact, be heard already in the *Massacre at Chios*? Let us go back to that page in the *Journal* on which, on 25 April 1824, Delacroix offers us the key to the secret. To describe it he even uses the word 'allegory': it might be more exact to say that he hopes to make of painting a whole series of symbols of his soul. But he also, immediately, reveals the content of the allegory he was seeking: 'blind Destiny dragging away all the suppliants who would, at the last moment, try in vain by their cries and prayers to arrest its inflexible arm.' To illustrate this vision of life, all he needs to do is to look about him for some exemplary event, and to find it in the life of his own time. A few days later the *Journal* indicates that work on the *Massacre at Chios* has begun. He now knew what it was he wished to say 'to the eyes', but also that his visible creation must 'win and seize hold of all the faculties of the soul ... of the hearts that will receive it'. His task was now marked out. 'No more *Don Quixotes*[15] and things of the kind, which are unworthy of you. Go in deep.' On this condition alone would he be able at length to say, when looking at his own pictures: 'That is what I have always felt inside me!'

*Chios*, therefore, marks the crucial moment when Delacroix discovered not only his supple, vibrant, warm, pictorial language, but also himself, and when he threw himself at the heart of human existence, feeling to the full its intensity but also its precariousness—the disproportion between its aspirations and its achievements.

The human drama—it was already in his *Tasso*, of 1823. The poet is seen in his prison cell, in that prison which Delacroix was able to suggest, and which Van Gogh, later, cried out against in heart-rending terms:[16]

'There is something inside of me, what can it be? ... And circumstances often prevent men from doing things, prisoner in I do not know what horrible, horrible, most horrible cage.... One cannot always tell what it is that keeps us shut in, confines us, seems to bury us; nevertheless one feels certain barriers, certain gates, certain walls.... And one asks, "My God! is it for ever, is it for all eternity?" '

So I imagine Tasso is meditating also, in the prison which life is to the poet.

What are the other people in the picture? Madmen or warders—for one of them can be seen cracking his whip menacingly. Essentially, Sartre in his *Huis Clos* added nothing to this.

But there is another symbol expressed in Delacroix's *Tasso*, and the painter was already referring to it in 1819 when he wrote to Pierret:

'What tears of rage and indignation he must have shed when he saw that... they were accusing him of madness and impotence! How often he must have beaten his head against the bars when he thought of the baseness of human beings! . . .'

Such is the picture, taken from Byron, which he interrupted in order to devote himself to the *Massacre at Chios*. In the following year he took it up again, in a new version; then again in 1826, in a water-colour; and again in pl 146 1827, in a quite different composition. The theme haunted him during these years between *Chios* and *Sardanapalus*, and it does, in fact, connect the two pictures; for this man, closed in over his own grief, leaning on his elbow, deep in thought, apparently renouncing everything except meditation on the horror or indifference of life, is Tasso, certainly, but is also Sardanapalus, the subject of Delacroix's next large-scale painting, the next blow he intended to strike at the Salon.

While the attitude of Tasso, bowed in disillusion, makes us think of that of Sardanapalus, it also suggests the attitude which, in certain preparatory studies, Delacroix gave to his *Christ in the Garden of Gethsemane*, exhibited at the 1827 Salon. He too leans his exhausted head on his elbow, in hopeless renunciation—and even lies on the ground in the absolute nakedness of his moral agony. In the large definitive picture, eventually hung in the Church of Saint-Paul-and-Saint-Louis, the gesture of limitless detachment with which he refuses even the consolation of the angels is a parallel, on the divine plane, to the fierce drawing back of Sardanapalus as—looking downwards not up to heaven—he abandons to destruction everything in which he had found pleasure. Delacroix, in his pictures, had gone after the same enchantment—women with thrilling flesh and dishevelled hair, horses neighing and rearing, all the splendours of texture and of colour.

## *The Renunciation of 'Sardanapalus'*

XI, page 123 With his *Death of Sardanapalus* Delacroix delivered himself over to the public and the majority gave him the response which his disillusioned philosophy must have foreseen—sarcasm and fierce philistine criticism. He became, more than ever, Tasso—silent and alone in the middle of a taunting circle; he became that *Albatross*, mentioned by Baudelaire, later, as '*exilé sur le sol au milieu des huées*'.[17]

The 1827 Salon included twelve pictures by Delacroix—two of them added when it was decided in 1828 to prolong the exhibition. One of these two was the *Sardanapalus*. A thirteenth picture was refused—the portrait of *Baron Schwiter*, that evocation of the dandy and reflection of the influence of Lawrence. (There was a portrait of a woman by Lawrence in this Salon, in which Bonington also exhibited.) The other pictures included *Marino Faliero*; *Count Palatiano*; *Still Life with Lobsters*; *Milton and his Daughters* and *Faust in his Study*. These represent his debt to England; but two large-scale pictures—*Christ in the Garden of Gethsemane* (116 in. by 143 in.) and *The Death of Sarda-*

*napalus* (145 in. by 195 in.)—were there to bear witness not only to the development of his technique but also to that of his thinking and his poetic feeling.

For the *Sardanapalus*—while it gathers up and adopts all the new mastery that has enriched Delacroix's technique, and while its very subject is a fresh homage to English literature, especially to Byron[18]—is also perhaps the first complete statement of what was stirring Delacroix at the deepest level and seeking for expression in form and colour. Up to then it would have been possible—mistakenly—to believe that there was no more than a deviation, perhaps tradition reasserting itself. But this time the break was clean: it was, as Delacroix himself put it, 'an Asiatic feat of arms against David's Spartiate pastiche'—in fact, a revolution. The jury drew back, hesitated; the public and the critics cried 'Scandal!' One of these, A. Jal, though usually favourable to Delacroix, agreed that 'he has been carried away beyond all limits'. The painter even came in for a severe rebuke from the director of the Beaux-Arts, Sosthène de La Rochefoucauld, and has left us an amused account of this. Invited to one of the director's evening receptions, he put on 'my best coat and best white cravat. . . . I really imagined the man was going to offer me the Croix d'Honneur'; but instead he 'came over to me and gave me a proper scolding'.

Delacroix himself vacillated, face to face with his own boldness. He felt 'an abominable impression' when at the private view he saw that 'damned painting hanging beside the work of the others'; these are his words in his letter to Soulier of 6 February. A month later he went back on this: 'Some people say it is a complete catastrophe, that the *Death of Sardanapalus* is the death of the romantic.' But is it, he asks himself 'a real fiasco'? (Later he was to use the expression 'my retreat from Moscow'.) 'I am not at all sure. . . . This picture has qualities and defects, and . . . if there are things that I could wish improved, there are a good many others that I think myself happy to have done.' The picture was to disappear for nearly a century as though it had been ostracized: it went back to his studio, was not exhibited either at the 1855 Exposition Universelle or at his posthumous exhibition in 1864, but was acquired in 1921 by the Louvre from Baron Vitta,[19] that great enthusiast for Delacroix, who had been keeping it jealously along with other treasures. It met, even then, with a divided reception, and there was no lack of picture lovers who felt obliged to make a grimace of doubt in front of this still contested masterpiece, although it was in fact the most decisive and complete affirmation of Delacroix's genius as a painter. He himself was aware of this, deep down, as he showed when he described this 'massacre number two' as 'one of the finest feathers in his cap'.

The vast picture, like the large-scale canvases of Rubens (to whom Delacroix here draws closer than ever), suggests an enormous cornucopia. From it there rolls a tumultuous treasure of jewels and human figures. The wave breaks and dies at the feet of the king, who is himself an incarnation of the Death which he is awaiting, and which awaits him, doubtless within the golden ewer that is being held out to him.

Everything Delacroix had loved, everything he had dreamed of, everything in which he had taken unrestrained delight, is in that cascade: one can almost smel the heady perfumes of it, mingled with the smell of blood rising in heavily curling puffs like the smoke from the fire that is just taking hold. There is the body of

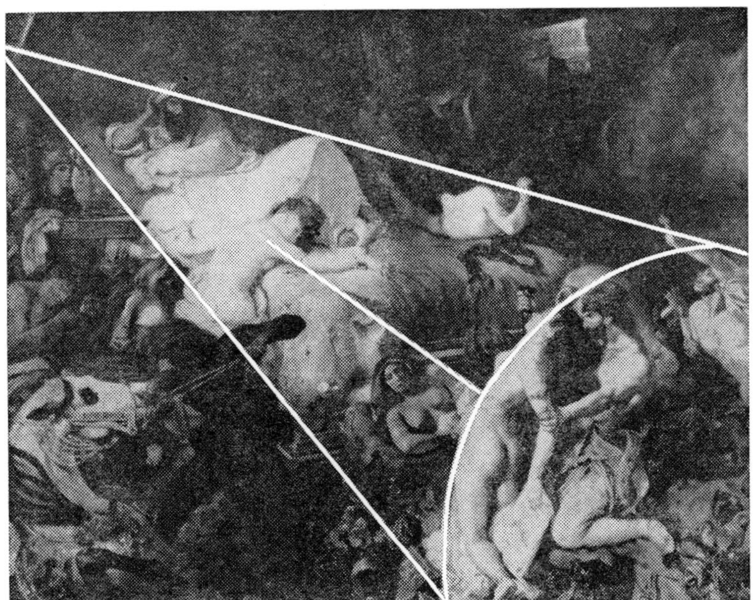

*Fig 8* THE DEATH OF SARDANAPALUS. The diagonal composition is strengthened by the converging lines, which seem to draw the whole painting towards Sardanapalus and the upper left-hand corner.

the woman, with its curves as lissom as her wavy hair and its flesh as bright as a fruit made of light itself. The *Odalisques* that Delacroix had depicted lying on voluptuous couches are now rolling on the bed of Death and their beauty exhales a sudden fragrance like flowers cut down. One of them draws herself up in a
XII, page 124 spasm as her throat is cut, another stretches out towards the piece of stuff which will strangle her, another is already gasping in the death agony, and the most moving and tender of them all—she was, as we know, a Greek and was called Myrrha—is already abandoning herself, with arms, hair and body submissively offered, to imminent annihilation. In the sketch she was dark, but became fair in the picture that she might seem even more frail and ephemeral. Then also there are the horses rearing nervously, their eyes almost human and their manes
pl 140 carefully braided like a woman's hair, as Delacroix loved to paint them—but this time in convulsions of despair as the steel stabs into them and sets the red blood flowing over the white of their coats. Never have necklaces of precious stones,
pl 142 carved vases and glittering goldsmiths' work been piled up with such wealth and such greedy relish; never has colour been so resplendent, uniting in one floral sheaf luminous whites, sparkling golds, pinks and reds and splashes of orange that quiver with silvery gleams and reverberate against patches of green. But already the smoke is rising with its heavy and bitter folds that will soon stifle the whole scene in their unbreathable darkness. The trajectory of youth has here reached its zenith: it is fire still, but already soot: it is at the brief moment of suspense when it flashes and spreads out before starting on that other curve which will bring it falling back into night and the abyss.

Here Delacroix brings together all the spells by which he had been bewitched: the poems of the English lyric poets, especially Byron, the marvels of the Orient sparkling fierily like a precious stone, and the nostalgia for the past—for this is a fabulous Orient, more especially since the discovery of the ruins of Khorsabad and Nineveh did not take place until fifteen years later (in 1842). Never will imagination fly further into the fairyland of forgotten times and exotic worlds. In this sense the *Sardanapalus* is perhaps Delacroix's most romantic picture.

It is so in its composition also—if romanticism may be regarded as a fresh incarnation of the baroque genius. The *Dante and Virgil* had been built up by means of a pyramidal mass arranged in the foreground, clearly settled on its base (even though this seems to sway with the motion of the waves and the spasms of the damned), and with a definite axis. The *Massacre at Chios*, following up the *Radeau de la Méduse*, retained this method of presentation in a plane, but in it the pyramid, split at the top as though by the stroke of an axe, became two, with two points hurled apart on either side of the central breach. But now, in the *Sardanapalus*, there is a type of composition absolutely unrelated to these predecessors—one that appears also in the 1827 version of the *Tasso in the Madhouse*, in contrast to the earlier versions painted in 1824 and (more strikingly) 1825, in which the triangular grouping still made itself felt. For an arrangement of the picture-space as an elevation, almost an architectural one, using the elements placed side by side or on top of one another, Delacroix now substitutes an impulsive binding together of parts that are melted into a single movement sweeping across the whole canvas. The great diagonal, of which Rubens, that master of the baroque, had produced the most resounding examples, is reborn.

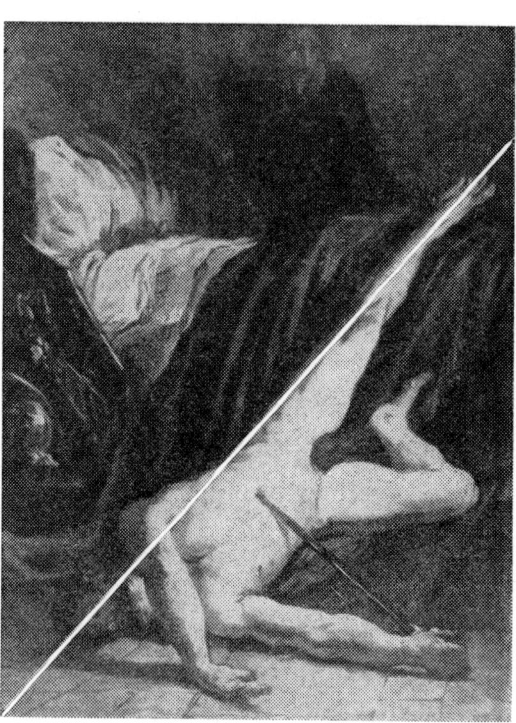

*Fig 9* DEATH OF CATO
The diagonal line cutting across the picture, typical of baroque composition, shows the influence of David.

This was something that Delacroix had as yet scarcely tried explicitly, except in his *Death of Cato* (1824). And there it was still a studio device, almost Davidian—a repetition of a rigid formula exemplified by David himself in such paintings as the *Death of Hector*[20] (which also appeared at the 1824 Salon). The diagonal divided the picture into two, but was not yet the expression of a breathless ascent, of an assault upon one of the upper corners of the canvas, carrying the whole of the picture with it. *Marino Faliero*, *Justinian* and *Christ in Gethsemane* contained forestastes of this, but not until *Sardanapalus*

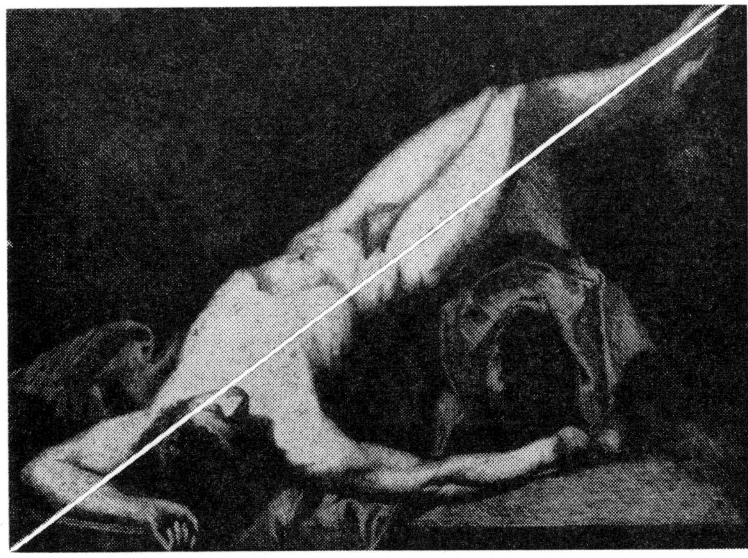

*Fig 10* David: THE DEATH OF HECTOR. David, who had studied Rubens, sometimes made use of the diagonal composition which was revived by Delacroix.

does it emerge decisively. Here the composition no longer draws a line: it submits to a movement that carries everything away. The whole of that mass of living and dying creatures, of human beings and horses, is caught like a shoal of fish in a net, which hauls them in, tightening, towards the fisherman. Just as the fish fight to escape, so each part of the whole is still free to respond to its own life in defiance of order; and yet an irresistible force commands the whole mass and, though still respecting its tumult, unifies it in a final convergence.

There is here no base to suggest stability, nothing to rest on: the bottom of the frame seems to cut through the living flesh of this agglomeration. Nor are the contents of the picture arranged on a single plane, the picture plane: the multitude drain away not only upwards but into an imagined depth. Instead of geometrical perspective converging towards its vanishing point, there is an irresistible displacement towards a pole of attraction whose unshakeable fixity has an effect of fatality and fascination. And there, in fact, it is, like a spider at the heart of the threads she has stretched out in which her victims are struggling convulsively: the icy stare of Sardanapalus.

Does the subject matter of the new picture bring safely to shore the deep meaning, so that it gradually emerges and makes its mark? Let us see what Delacroix says of it in the catalogue of the Salon:

'He is besieged in his palace by the insurgents. . . . Reclining on a superb bed on top of a huge pyre, Sardanapalus orders the eunuchs and palace officers to cut the throats of his women and his pages, and even of his favourite horses and dogs; none of the objects that have contributed to his pleasures must survive him. . . .'

*Sardanapalus* is indeed a festival coming to an end, a tumult of life falling into nothingness, a glory turning into night: there can be no doubt that in this theme Delacroix was seeking an echo of his own fate, no doubt that one should read in it a farewell to youth, to his insatiable aspirations, his unruly pleasures, his many vainly seething dreams—and an invocation to a silence that must succeed the tumult. And in fact Delacroix's painting now entered into a phase of less prodigality and greater concentration. He had come to the point where the centrifugal movement governing him turned back and he was now concerned not so much to project himself to the periphery of his being and to throw the tentacles of his curiosity and desires out in all directions, as to go down deep into himself and to find there his centre and his heart—and also his true balance. He could feel this turn of the tide coming, and could note its signs.

A writer, who was also a poet, succeeded in understanding this better than any critic. Maurice Barrès, in *Le Mystère en pleine lumière*,[21] rightly perceived that 'the duty of constant effort and advance' was 'one of the ideas that always carried him onwards'. He says further: 'The world of dreams, of luxury and romance is only a first stage. It is essential to get out of the great romantic bazaar.' This, he says, is 'already' the meaning of 'the great stare of Sardanapalus, looking out across the heaped up splendours, beyond and forwards.'

This return to the inner man—and it was something he could not refrain from expressing in the instinctive, therefore symbolic, language of painting—set Delacroix face to face with his own cold thinking, which could only be despairing: in its most secret recesses his mind had the same calm, implacable, frozen outlook as his Sardanapalus. As soon as he ceased to allow the quivering agitation of his nerves to carry him away and to delight him, he looked at himself and at life with that illusionless stare. Again and again his *Journal* returns to the same thought: 'A kind of philosophic calm which prepares us for suffering. . . . To witness the spectacle of the world through this ridiculous window. . . . Will all this, then, be annihilated? . . . An emptiness that cannot be filled. . . . To embrace the skeleton. . . .' Are not these the fragmentary phrases that we would hear from Sardanapalus himself, were he not so detatched from everything as to disdain even to murmur his secret?

If anyone is inclined to think that this is merely a literary interpretation, he has only to compare the *Sardanapalus* with the other pictures painted by Delacroix in that period, and he will soon recognize that all these works are inhabited by the same thoughts. It is as though one heard them spoken aloud by his *Tasso* and his *Christ in Gethsemane*, and they are to be read in the mute, impressive gaze of his *Greece Expiring on the Ruins of Missolonghi*. All these pictures V, page 73 were exhibited in 1827. The last mentioned was inspired by the events of the time: after the *Chios* massacre there had come the heroic end of Missolonghi which, besieged by the Turks since 1821 and the scene of Byron's death in 1824, was buried under its own ruins in April 1826.

The *Greece Expiring* was exhibited in London in 1828, together with the *Marino Faliero*. How revealing is the contrast between the two! The one dis- VI, page 74 plays all the exuberant fanfares of the sheer joy of painting, of invention in colour; the other a cold and nocturnal harmony—that livid flesh close to death, that huge mantle with its icy night blue, that light which is rendered lunar by the 'smoke of battle darkening the sky'—just as the smoke of another fire invaded the *Sardanapalus*.

XV THE MURDER OF THE BISHOP OF LIÈGE
*1829 Oil on canvas. 35 x 47 (090 x 118)*
*Louvre, Paris*

It may well be said that the *Sardanapalus* led him on until by the very excesses of his palette, he offered his most vibrant homage to Rubens: now, by a kind of reaction, he moved back in the direction of cold tones, *chiaroscuro*, black and white. The time had come for the lithographs and the theme of Faust.

## *Faust and the Sadness of Fate*

A different Delacroix was at work, if not revealing himself, at least finding, in his turn, the right to expression: the disillusioned Delacroix, the man who could hear, beyond the fairyland of life which he was so well fitted to enjoy without reserve, the sad voice of Fate. In the inexhaustible theme of Faust he could see, repeated, the mixture of temptations, questionings and moods of despair which he himself felt. A letter written to his publisher, Motte, in October 1827, proves that he had then been working at this theme 'for the last two years'. One of the first of the eighteen plates that were to be published in 1829 shows
pl 148 Faust standing motionless in a despair which is the same as that of the *Greece Expiring*. 'Poor empty skull,' he is thinking, 'what are you trying to say to me with your hideous grimace?' This question is inscribed as a caption, and Delacroix would soon recur to it for Hamlet. The next plate—*Faust and Wagner*—carries with it an equally despairing text: 'Happy the man who can keep the hope of remaining afloat on this ocean of horrors! . . . The spirit spreads its wings in vain; the body, alas, has none to give it.' Then Delacroix was caught up by Goethe's drama, and took from it a passage here and there: he found there human thought face to face with its enigmas and the human heart face to face with its desires, both of them slipping into misfortune and evil because they seek appeasement and cannot have it. 'Fire! Help! Hell is kindling. . . .' The devil, fanning the flames of these temptations and flashing the light of love in his deceptive mirror, leads Faust on to the seduction and degradation of Gretchen (Marguerite) and causes the death of Valentine. But 'we are still a long way from the
pl 135 end of our run. . . .' Faust and Mephistopheles, at the Witches' Sabbath, ride on the burning horses that have always haunted Delacroix's imagination and galloped through his dreams. 'On! On!' and there comes the end of Gretchen. Goethe put into her mouth the complaint that one might well give to the favourites of Sardanapalus: 'And yet I am still so young! So young! And to die so soon!' 'Dawn is lightening on the horizon', but it is only another threat. It is indeed true: 'Happy the man who can keep the hope of remaining afloat on this ocean of horrors.'

Goethe was right when he told Eckermann that in his *Faust* Delacroix had 'found exactly his proper food'. Apart from his well-known praise of Delacroix's illustrations—they had, he said, 'surpassed my own pictures of the scenes I myself wrote'—there are several phrases in which Goethe puts

XVI BOISSY D'ANGLAS AT THE CONVENTION
*1831 Oil on canvas. 31 x 41 (079 x 104)*
*Musée des Beaux-Arts, Bordeaux*

*Fig 11* STUDY FOR HAMLET. Pen drawing. Cabinet des Dessins, Louvre, Paris.

his finger on what must have appealed most deeply to Delacroix at that time:

'The picture of a spirit like our own which has suffered all the griefs that torment humanity, and experienced all the agitations that disturb it, has shared all its hatreds and has enjoyed all the delights to which it aspires. . . .'

But he also observed with penetration that Delacroix 'in this dark work' had 'assimilated all the gloom inherent in its original conception.'

The dark smoke that, in the *Sardanapalus*, rose together with Death to obscure the lavish, still living and breathing splendours, seems in fact to spread gradually over the whole of Delacroix's painting, which till then had glowed like a border of flowers. It has, of course, been shown that chance played a considerable part in bringing Delacroix into touch with Goethe's masterpiece. At any rate, in 1824, he spent an evening with his friend Pierret, looking over the engravings done by Peter Cornelius on this theme in 1810; and in the following year (as he writes, again to Pierret) he had seen in London a performance of 'Goethe's *Faust*, but in an arrangement. . .'—possibly Marlowe's play. He had been struck by the sets: 'Effect cannot be carried further on the stage.' It seems very likely that some of the scenes haunted his imagination, especially the church scene, from which, eventually, he made a lithograph and several pictures: 'The church is represented, with the priest chanting and the organ in the distance. . . .'

The triumphantly successful performances of Shakespeare at the Odéon in September 1827 kindled the enthusiasm of all the young romantics in Paris: they certainly helped to fix Delacroix's attention on that drama of the soul tortured by its own perplexities which German literature had brought forcibly on to the stage with *Faust*, and English literature with *Hamlet*. It was natural that the meditation of the Prince of Denmark on Yorick's skull should follow, in Delacroix's work, the meditation of Faust; and in fact he treated it in a lithograph in 1828. This was only the prelude to the series of lithographs executed in 1834, though not published till 1843.

In spite of the part played by chance in drawing his attention to it, Delacroix concentrated on Goethe's play and found nourishment in it only because he found there an echo and an answer to his own problems. On all the joys that formed the web of earthly life, seeming to be its expression and its very object, Delacroix now bent the cold gaze of his meditation and it rendered them remote. The failure of his *Sardanapalus* was no doubt a factor, but the picture itself had been a manifestation of this tendency. The dreams which the imagination depicts and by which it is haunted, are the outward sign of movements already troubling the depths. It was surely no mere chance that, in one and the same year (1826), Delacroix conceived two major pictures that seem to echo one another: in the *Sardanapalus*, the king looks down from the height of his disillusioned ambition with a gaze of contemptuous farewell at all the splendours in which he had seemed to find the enchantment of living; in the *Christ in the Garden of Gethsemane*, we see a Christ who has likewise reached the ultimate weariness and, with a gesture of exhaustion, rejects the angels who are weeping with despair, and refuses to look at them. '*Mais le ciel reste noir et Dieu ne répond pas*' ('But heaven remains dark and from God no answer comes')—we pass readily from the picture to Vigny's poem[22] which, though it was written much later (in 1844), was perhaps inspired by it. (It is, in fact, much more likely that the poet was struck by this picture—which had been much talked of in Paris and was so close to his own feeling—than, as has been suggested, by Mantegna's painting, which he saw in London in 1839.) Delacroix made several studies for this scene. The angels disappeared, and nothing was left but night, desertion, the treachery of human beings—and the agony of the soul.

Faust is suspended between the domain of the devil drawing him down, the domain on which the gaze of Sardanapalus was fixed, and the domain of God beckoning him upwards—the domain from which the angels came in their effort to console Christ, but in vain:

*Il regarde longtemps, longtemps cherche sans voir.*
*Comme un marbre de deuil tout le ciel était noir.*

(He gazed for a long time, for a long time sought, unseeing.
Like mourning marble the whole heaven was dark.)

Delacroix's *Greece Expiring* likewise stumbles and falls into the ruins where the fire is now mere ashes.

In all this Delacroix was expressing the moral crisis he was going through. He was awakened from the ecstatic delight which he had allowed to carry him at its own sweet will. His letters to his close friends are revealing. One written to Soulier on 21 April 1826 begins: 'My dear friend, I am overwhelmed with sadness and boredom. . . .' In May he explains: 'Age brings with it changes in one's character. In some people'—and he evidently counts himself as one of these—'what it brings is misanthropy and melancholy, painting everything in gloomy tones.' And he speaks of 'accesses of moral suffering'. Physically, also, he was in a bad way: so emaciated that afterwards, early in February 1828, he told Soulier: 'I am not now so thin. Apparently I was close to death.' In a notebook published by Piron[23] he mentions, as having contributed to this decline in his health, the excessive social activity in which he had earlier indulged:

'I managed to work very hard all day and then, in the evening, I put on silk stockings and stayed at parties till two or three in the morning—at amusements which I leave to your imagination. I wonder again however, with a delicate enough constitution, I was able to sustain all this exertion. . . . In such cases a great deal must be credited to the resources of youth, to its ceaseless tendency to repair the damage, and I kept young for a very long time.'

But he began to feel tired, and on 26 April 1828 he announced to Soulier that he was reforming his way of life:

'The few evening parties to which I go out of habit to be bored and seek distraction end by exhausting me physically. . . . The imagination—when, as a culminating misfortune, this fatal gift is added to the rest—completes a man's ruin and torments the wretched soul till it is broken in pieces. The love of glory—a lying passion, a ridiculous will-o'-the-wisp that always leads us straight to the abyss of melancholy and vanity. Not to speak of love itself which causes keener sufferings but does bring a few really refreshing moments.'

The indulgence in this last phrase was due to Madame Dalton, '*la belle*', who had been his mistress since 1825 and was to remain so till 1839, when he helped her to go to Algeria. The same note is heard in a letter to Pierret on 27 October 1828:

'I no longer find the same charm in things. Alas, there is a prism of enchantment that gradually loses its colours. This roseate veil is beginning to come damnably apart in front of me and I find little enjoyment in what used to stir my imagination. Even that is growing icy, and all it can do now is to torment me on the silliest occasions. Devil take us, it is all idiotic, you, me, him, us, everyone. . . . '

It is as though one were listening to the melancholy thoughts of 'my old friend Sardanapalus', as Delacroix called him.

## *Chiaroscuro—Rembrandt—The Middle Ages*

The pictures painted by him in these years—he was still not quite thirty—reflect the darkening of his life. Murder, battles, individual or collective assassination, death in all its aspects, shadow, night, the Middle Ages with the mystery of Gothic buildings—these are the themes on which his inspiration at that time rang the changes. Never had the wild beast instincts of the human animal so insistently obsessed him. Christ, in his pictures, moves on from the moral agony of Gethsemane to physical agony: three pictures whose theme is the

XVII A PAGE FROM THE MOROCCAN SKETCHBOOK
*Meknes, 1 April 1832 Water-colour. 8 x 5 (019 x 012)*
*Louvre, Paris*

Crucifixion and the Deposition are dated by Robaut from the beginning of 1829.

As he went down into the inner shadows, he developed his technique for the expression of this funereal and discouraged mood. Though the scenes depicted by him were always violent episodes from human or wild life, the violence at their centre now became enveloped in a gloomy veil: this diminishes the importance of the story and a heavy swathe of melancholy, within which the tragedy rages confusedly, rises up like a mist over a swamp. In earlier pictures form had seemed to him the essential means of expression, and had obliged him to stress the human figures, amplify their dimensions, bring out the individuality of the protagonists and display in these the familiar anatomical elements so dear
pl 216 to the classical tradition: The *Natchez* (1824), inspired by Chateaubriand, is a striking example. But now he was completely freed from this academic scruple, and permitted himself a style of drawing that was mobile rather than defined, relying chiefly on the resonances of colour to communicate his original feeling. He arrived at an art of synthesis rather than analysis, of magical effect rather than of rational exposition: in this consists that transformation of his style which disturbed his contemporaries, soured their initial benevolence and aroused them first to resistance, very soon to anger.

More and more he sought to create a general atmosphere, an *ambiance* as we now like to say, or, in his own better phrase, the 'music of the picture'. His attention was concentrated on anything that would break the isolation and particularity of forms, bodies and objects, anything that would bind them together and bathe them in a collective, unanimous presence, anything that would mingle and associate them, anything that would make the passage from the discontinuous to the continuous. His preoccupation was—by any movement that would connect actions and lines in a single uninterrupted propagation of the impetus, by whatever exchange relationships could be produced between colours through the harmony of their tones and through the reflected lights, or even, simply by the wake left by the brush—to establish a psychological, plastic and chromatic dominant. It was inevitable that at this time he should discover
pls 150, 151 the resources of *chiaroscuro*, the only means capable of giving a kind of fluid consistency to the area cut out by the frame. This became so important to him that, though the pure enchantments of the palette were still fresh to him, he even began to sacrifice colour to the density of the shadow in which it was plung-
XV, page 179 ed. In his interiors, from the *Murder of the Bishop of Liège* to the *Boissy*
XVI, page 180 *d'Anglas*, and in his exteriors from the *Battle of Poitiers* to the *Battle of Nancy*, he went in quest of a global space—either a vast hall with its far end lost in the shadows, or a huge plain filled with twilight. Instead of detaching or stressing the main episodes in the scene he traced out a collective confusion with a mass of figures seething tumultuously within it.

The imperative nature of this urge cannot be better shown than by following his successive rehandlings of a single subject. The first version of the *Bishop*

XVIII SEATED ARAB
*1832 Water-colour. 8 x 11 (019 x 027)*
*Louvre, Paris*

*of Liège*, dating from 1827, defines the scene as it was to be treated in the great picture painted in 1829 and exhibited at the 1831 Salon; but in this first version Delacroix concentrates the interest on the principal group that fills the picture, leaving practically no place for the *décor*, which is barely indicated: the whole composition is centred on that main group. Two years later the action is no longer important, only atmosphere: the same people are there, but now separated and pushed back into the depth of the picture, indeed almost lost in the crowd of onlookers and in the immensity of a hall that recedes into infinity with a tunnel-like perspective, into shadows accented by torches. The diagonal type of composition is taken up again from the *Sardanapalus*, but here, instead of clearly dividing the picture surface by a transverse line, the diagonal tunnels through and out into depths beyond.

This was the fulfilment of what Delacroix had begun in the sketch for the *Sardanapalus*. In that picture, it will be remembered, he had been deflected into a sudden return towards splendour of detail: the fair slave had seduced him, making him forget the total effect in which he had feared to lose her, and in this sense the *Sardanapalus* was a step backwards from the way he had taken, or a magnificent splash of foam against a rock that for a moment breaks and stops the onrush. But now, in the *Bishop of Liège*, it flowed on; and two years later the *Boissy d'Anglas at the Convention*, also exhibited at the 1831 Salon, confirmed the choice Delacroix had made. In the two pictures the subjects are similar and terrible. In the first, in accordance with the story as told by Sir Walter Scott in *Quentin Durward*, Guillaume de la Marck, the Wild Boar of the Ardennes, has the throat of his adversary the Bishop of Liège cut with a butcher's knife during an orgy to celebrate victory. In the second, the howling crowd, which has broken all restraint, advances with the freshly severed and dripping head of the Deputy Féraud on the point of a pike, and the President of the Convention, Boissy d'Anglas, stands firm, though horrified, and accepts the loathesome encounter. The arrangement in both is the same: the architectural background recedes to one side into a depth that is rendered limitless by the half-light, relieved only by the light that strikes across it from the windows and by the flash of the bayonets. In both pictures there is the same almost wholly indistinct seething of the crowd in confused eddies. This is pierced in the *Boissy d'Anglas* by the loud note of the tricolour flag, like a cry that stands out from a rumour of voices—just as, in the *Bishop of Liège*, the darkness is torn by the light, or rather the lightning, of the white cloth. Théophile Gautier found the right words to describe the dizzy confusion of the *Murder of the Bishop of Liège*: 'Who would ever have thought that anyone could paint the clamour of a crowd, could paint *tumult*? *Movement*, yes; but this not enormously large picture howls, shouts and blasphemes.' Théophile Silvestre was almost as happy in his description of the *Boissy d'Anglas*: 'The mob pours in like an angry river. . . walls, stairways and galleries crack and totter,' and he feels able to claim that 'Delacroix has reached the ultimate limit of the fantastic and of the terrible.'

What produced this new mastery of total effect by means of *chiaroscuro* to which, provisionally, Delacroix sacrificed colour? Sustained work at lithography, especially for the *Faust* series, must have had much to do with it. From the stone and from the lithographic crayon he had learned to subdue the line, making it lose its clarity of outline, expand into the area of shade and add to this a vibrant intensity.

But it must also have been at this time that he really discovered Rembrandt. Mentions of Rembrandt occur, for the most part, later in his *Journal*, where they increase in frequency. On 28 April 1853 he says that he 'admires the Rembrandts excessively'. At the end of 1847 he describes having been greatly struck by the 'expressiveness' that he finds 'in the vagueness of that dream-world'; and in 1851, on 6 June, after the reopening of the restored galleries in the Louvre, he even utters what he calls a 'blasphemy that might almost make the hair of all the men of the School stand on end'—that one day, perhaps, people will 'discover . . . that Rembrandt is a much greater painter than Raphael.' Rembrandt was, he thought, 'more naturally a painter', and his 'elevation' consisted 'in his mysterious conception of the subject'. Rembrandt and Delacroix had in common the disciplined power to make 'sacrifices', so as to concentrate interest on the essential and to 'augment the power of expression'. Rubens also attained this, but 'by means of certain exaggerations'; Rembrandt, on the contrary, did so through 'the vagueness which he extends in a striking manner over the secondary parts.' Delacroix was pursuing the same aim, but he wished 'the artifice not to be felt at all, and the interest nonetheless to be marked as it should be.' He was in favour of sacrifices, 'but they must be infinitely more delicate than they are in Rembrandt's style, if they are to answer to my desire.'

Here Delacroix is taking up the distance he intends to keep, and making clear his own position in relation to the two great masters whom he admires. But there were times when even his reservations were swept away: on 29 July 1854, after comparing Rembrandt with Titian and Poussin, he added: 'In Rembrandt —and this is perfection—the background and the figures are one. The interest is everywhere: you make no division, any more than you do in a beautiful view offered you by nature, where everything combines to enchant you.' This is what Delacroix was seeking to do, and succeeded in doing, from the *Bishop of Liège* onwards. He had himself found the effects which he was to describe later (25 January 1857)—effects that 'carry... into the imagination that emotion, that disturbance' which Rembrandt makes 'the soul experience' through 'vagueness, magic, expressive drawing'.

That his intense concern with Rembrandt goes back to an earlier date than this, we know from a letter of his to Poterlet, which shows that in 1827 he was interested in a copy of Rembrandt by his friend, 'a real masterpiece'; and he was in touch with Samuel William Reynolds, the English specialist in mezzotint engraving, about a plate after the Amsterdam master. The main effect of his *Bishop of Liège* can only have been inspired by Rembrandt. 'As for the white cloth,' wrote Chesneau,[24] 'it was, according to him, the crucial point of the picture, Austerlitz or Waterloo.' He had great difficulty in carrying it out, and went back to it several times. He must then have looked for help, as he was accustomed to do, to the masters, and above all to the one who could best guide him in this adventure.[25]

Up to this time Delacroix had not yielded to the wild enthusiasm of the romantics for the Middle Ages. But now, clearly, he felt a new sympathy for

Gothic architecture, which had often shocked the classicist who survived in him. For while the classical monuments, with their distinct lines and planes, satisfy the search for formal harmony, those of the Middle Ages are, above all, designed to impose a state of feeling. They do so by the spellbinding hold they establish, simultaneously and confusedly, over all the senses. They create an atmosphere rather than a volume, by the breaking up of the planes, by the half-light, with all its variations, eating into and absorbing the lines. Delacroix came to feel that this was the ideal setting for his pictures, in which a single feeling must spread throughout like the clouds of incense under the pointed arches, and make itself heard like the rumbling of the organ. It was a setting governed by that 'vagueness' which he valued so highly in Rembrandt—working as a whole upon our sensibility before intellectual analysis could have time to distinguish and separate the constituent elements. The effect which he could extract from Gothic architecture was shown by him in another picture painted in 1831, though not exhibited till the 1834 Salon: his *Melmoth*, sometimes, but XXIII, page 251 wrongly called, *L'Amende Honorable*. This time the subject was taken from Maturin's '*roman noir*', and the scene is supposed to take place in a Dominican convent in Madrid. Delacroix wrote to Pierret from Valmont, on 30 September 1831, that it was the great hall in the Palais de Justice at Rouen that had pl 158 given him the setting for this picture, which he was finding 'quite inspiring'. Villot recorded, similarly, that 'for the vaulting' in his *Bishop of Liège*, Delacroix used sketches 'made in the Palais de Justice at Rouen'.[26] On his way to Valmont to visit his cousin Bataille, he broke his journey at Rouen to see his aunt Riesener. And it was at Valmont, near Fécamp, that, when still a child, he had first discovered the Gothic and its emotional power. The place has been admirably kept up by the Béraldi family, who inherited it, so that it is possible to revive, in one's imagination, Delacroix's early visits to the ruins of the church near the house. He was already at Valmont in 1813, when he was fifteen; and it was from Valmont that he visited Rouen for the first time, at the beginning of 1814. The buildings there disturbed the convictions he had acquired at school:

'Some of the churches—and especially the cathedral,' he wrote to Félix Louvet on 10 January, 'have caused me some surprise by the boldness of their fine Gothic vaults and the prodigious height of their towers, loaded outside as well as inside with innumerable ornaments or arabesques, with which our fathers liked to be lavish, but which were certainly inferior to the noble simplicity of Greek and Roman architecture.'

An early shock, this, which stirred his latent romanticism. . . . And indeed he used the word, together with '*romanesque*', in reference to his cousins' house, 'a former Benedictine abbey'. His imagination did not take long to burst into flames, and to exaggerate the length of the corridors ('great corridors of which one could hardly see the end'), and the picturesqueness of the little narrow pl 156 stairways; and it delighted, above all, in the 'old half-ruined church' with the tombs of the lords of Estouteville, from whose Gothic carvings, according to Riesener, he took casts. In 1829, when he resumed the habit of going to stay at Valmont, he recognized that these were 'very fine in style'. He admired also the 'huge windows . . . with their dark stained glass'—to which he later added one of his own design by grouping together fragments. He could feel a new pl 154 thrill rising in him: 'All these things inspired in me a multitude of wholly romantic ideas. . . . At night the wind whistled through the cracks in the vaulting, and the owls that lived in the church awakened us.' He loved most of all to 'walk alone, dreaming, among the ruins of that silent church, whose echoing walls repeated the sound of my footsteps.' Riesener describes the look of the ruins at night, when they went there to take casts of the tombs:

'The water was freezing. The roof of the church let the light through. The rays of the moon came in and sparkled among the dew-covered foliage growing in the nave. We amused each other by throwing vast shadows on the colonnades of the aisles.'

It was then, surely, that Delacroix's first great revelation of romantic feeling occured: the breath of the countryside brought by the wind over the great trees of the park and the waves of the nearby sea (whose fury he sometimes watched and wondered at), the ancient, timeworn walls in their moving stand against ruin and the rampant assaults of the vegetation, the night and, in its shadowy mystery, the recumbent stone effigies, the cry of the owls and the soft shimmering of the moonlight—all these spells united to disturb his soul with emotions towards which, in common with that time of fermentation, it already aspired. At the moment which now concerns us—the second half of 1831—he again found[27] in
pls 152, 153 that 'abode of peace and forgetfulness of the whole world' the charms that had bewitched him as an adolescent, and his spirit, 'wandering at its own sweet will . . . creates palaces and enchantments. . . .'

Nothing could have been more natural than that he should allow his thoughts to turn to the Middle Ages, for the whole of the taste of that time was steering him in that direction. In 1829 he had been commissioned to do lithographs to illustrate Mme. Amable Tastu's *Chroniques de France*. He went back to Sir Walter Scott—to *Quentin Durward* (as a water-colour of the Princesse de Croy shows, as well as the *Bishop of Liège*), to *The Bride of Lammermoor*, to *Ivanhoe*. . . . In 1828, in his *Alchemist's Study*, he brings together Faust's philtres, his interest in the supernatural, owls perched on Gothic chairs and the *chiaroscuro* of Rembrandt's etchings of philosophers. The same small window, heavily barred, dispenses its miserly light to his *Tasso's Cell* (1827), to his
pls 159, 160 *Marguerite in Prison* (1827), to his *Alchemist* (1828), to his *Front de Bœuf* (litho-
162 graph, 1829) and to his *Louis XI* (also 1829), an illustration for Béranger's *Chansons*.

Commissions, which reflected the contemporary interest, made him continue to study and explore the Middle Ages. Hardly had he finished painting his *Richelieu celebrating Mass* for the Duke of Orleans in 1828 (a picture destroyed
pls 163, 164 in the burning of the Palais Royal in 1848 and surviving only in sketches) than Sosthène de La Rochefoucauld, thinking better of the dark resolutions he had expressed at the time of the uproar over the *Sardanapalus*, commissioned
pl 165 from him a *Battle of Nancy*. This was painted in 1831 and exhibited in the 1834 Salon. Early in 1829 the Duchess of Berry imposed on him a similar theme, the *Battle of Poitiers*. He completed the picture in 1830, but the Duchess, forgetful of her undertakings, never took delivery of it, to the great annoyance of the painter.

## *Global Effect—The 'Music of the Picture'*

Delacroix was clarifying the idea that had been haunting him—the idea of a 'global picture', in which everything—scenes of tumult and confusion, lines, colours and light—works together to create the total effect, and the attention, steered away from particular objects or details, is carried along as though by a wave. He now keeps the eye away from the temptation to analyze, and tries to create a complete spell in which the sensibility, as though hypnotized, will let itself be dominated by a 'silent power' that 'seizes all the faculties of the soul.' Painting must no longer be an addition of parts, but a single whole, revealed at the first glance and then penetrated as one would penetrate some new atmosphere filled with scents, murmurs and song.

The themes best suited to such an art are those in which there is a collective, unanimous movement. This is why, in that period when Delacroix was becoming aware of the art towards which he was moving, he had recourse to episodes of large-scale, concerted action involving multitudes of people swayed by whirling eddies that toss or mingle the individual figures. The crowd in the *Boissy d'Anglas* flows and tumbles from the tribunes at the back towards the foreground, like a torrent in which gleams, flashes, faces arise fleetingly—flecks of foam on an indivisible advancing wave. When this reaches the foreground, it comes up against the impetus which, starting from the lower left-hand corner, was rising in the direction of the right-hand tribune, to flourish at him, defiantly, the severed head. The perspective of the wall, losing itself in the shadows of the whole, seems to be there merely to stress with a parallel the direction of this spurting movement, which has just struck and broken against the inflexible vertical of the President, reinforced by all the weight of those heavy flags, hanging down with no breath of air to stir them. Similarly, in the *Battle of Nancy*, two armies are colliding, like opposed lances, and Duke Charles the Bold, although his death is the principal subject, is there only as the consequence of the shock between those two masses: it is almost as if he were already ejected from the picture.[28]

For the *Battle of Poitiers* Delacroix, as his sketch shows, at first thought of a kind of rough sea of living creatures, the more distant part of which would melt into the vast expanse of the plain: its colliding waves, whipped up by contrary winds, are perceptible only in the foreground, where the movements of weapons, banners and charging or falling warriors form a terrible, seething surf. The final picture gives organization to this tumult, gives it a centre, which is illuminated, and is framed by the sides of a lozenge of soldiers facing in four directions. This centre—the rock against which the assaults converge—is the block formed by the king, his son and the dead horse. From every direction, like the ripples sent chasing across cornfields by the wind, the charges of the assailants are seen converging; they are materialized in the main fighting in the foreground; in the distance, beyond the king, routed cavalry are dispersing, with a tempestuous waving of manes.

In both pictures, the *Poitiers* and the *Nancy*, the process of creation was similar: when the movements of the whole had been established and distributed in space, then only did Delacroix stress and make more intelligible the main elements (by geometricizing certain lines, marked by a lance or a pole, and by articulating certain masses, where the interest and significance are concentrated). In his fear that the details might escape and create a diversion, he first and foremost sought the enveloping element that would contain that undivided mass; and he plunged the human collectivity, which he obtained by his handling of crowds, into the material, organic collectivity of nature. In both these battle pictures he raises the horizon as high as he can, so that nothing may stand out against it or above it, but everything be drowned in a single element where each episode will be no more than an eddy.

In the interiors this global, dominating atmosphere is supplied by the *chiaroscuro*; in the open air scenes by the vastness of the plain—to which everything is made to belong, so that hand-to-hand combats and the most frantic struggles
pl 166 create no more than a confused seething. Between the sketch for the *Battle of Nancy* and the finished picture, Delacroix had the idea of an implacable horizon line, which nothing new could pierce or disturb. For the *Battle of Poitiers* he started with this idea, and returned, in the finished picture, to a tumult of spear-heads, lances and flags which, ruffling and breaking the surface, make the violence of the combat more sharply felt. This enabled him to make the head of John the Good emerge alone in the midst of them, so that it seems like the head of a shipwrecked sailor struggling desperately against the waves that will stifle him and drag him down.

The two battle pictures express essentially different situations by means of the different positions they assign to the protagonists. John the Good is refusing to go under and is desperately sustaining the assault: expressively, he is keeping afloat, though not at the centre but carried towards the left by the thrust pushing him backwards. Charles the Bold is beaten: the picture catches him at the final moment when he is about to be struck from the world of the living. In both pictures there is a great lance: the one defending John the Good seems to support and raise him, while the one turned against Duke Charles is overwhelming him, thrusting him down the slope he will never remount, hurling him into annihilation.

Delacroix is, by now, truly a master of expressive power: he controls and uses it like the conductor of an orchestra, and I doubt whether there is any, among the earlier masters, who was able in the art of painting to bring together so much fury, *brio* and authority.

What is more, Delacroix was completely conscious of the resources he was now able to bring into action with such ease. A well-known passage, written by him in his *Journal* a few years later,[29] proves this. In it his whole doctrine is expressed:

'If, to a composition that is already interesting by virtue of the choice of subject, you add an arrangement of lines that reinforces the impression, a *chiaroscuro* that arrests the imagination, and colour that fits the character of the work, you have solved a far more difficult problem and you rise superior: the result is harmony with all its combinations adapted to a single song, it is a musical tendency.'[30]

At this stage painting has gone beyond the means of action of rational thought —its precise but limiting frameworks are broken: something vaster, yet also more intimate, has been attained and possessed. Thus painting really comes close to music. On 16 October 1857 Delacroix explained, in the *Journal*, his conception of the power of music:

'Superiority of music, absence of reasoning (not of logic) . . . the enchantment this art produces in me; it seems that one's intellectual part has no share in this pleasure. This is what makes the pedants rank music lower than other arts.'

What is music but an atmosphere of sound organized by means of rhythms? Similarly, a picture is a luminous atmosphere organized through relations of lines and colours. The dualism and balance which music establishes between its construction and its expressiveness have their exact parellel in painting. But to understand this and master it there was need of a man gifted both for music and for painting. This was the case with Delacroix. George Sand, comparing him with Chopin in her *Impressions et Souvenirs*, remarked that Chopin was 'a musician, nothing but a musician. His thought can only come out in music. He has plenty of wit, subtlety, irony, but he cannot understand painting and sculpture at all.' In contrast, 'Delacroix, who is more varied in his gifts, appreciates music; he knows it when he hears it, and he understands it; his taste is sure and exquisite.' When Delacroix was explaining reflected light to Chopin, he made use with perfect naturalness of references to the world of sound, and 'established a comparison between the tones in painting and the notes in music'. And Chopin listened, 'his eyes wide with astonishment'.

Delacroix's vocation for music showed itself when he was a child.[31] One of his notes for Piron says: 'I had, very early on, a pronounced taste for drawing and for music', and he tells how at Bordeaux, where his father was *Préfet*, he attracted the attention of the old cathedral organist, who was giving his sister lessons and had been a friend of Mozart. While playing in the drawing-room, the young Delacroix accompanied 'the choir with basses and ornaments of my own, whose rightness he admired' and in which he recognized 'real aptitude for music'. The *violon d'Ingres* has become a current French expression for a master's second talent: Delacroix's violin would have done just as well. Chesneau[31] used the expression, 'the ardour of a vocation' in speaking of Delacroix's attachment to music. In 1824, when at work on the *Massacre at Chios* Delacroix 'took pleasure in playing over' on his favourite instrument 'the melodies of *Figaro, Tancredi* and *Don Giovanni*, which he had heard the night before.' He had also studied the piano, as the entry in his *Journal* on 12 October 1822 tells us, and the guitar: in his unpublished school notebooks I have found mention of the guitar lessons he was taking at that time, and he was later fond of playing on this instrument in the intervals of painting.

It is indeed clear from his *Journal* that he was fascinated by music, all his life long, and pursued it all over the place in concerts and in private receptions. Far from separating the two arts, he tried always to associate them: in particular he found a fresh impetus for his painting in listening to the singing and the organ

XIX THE ROOMS OF THE COUNT DE MORNAY

*c. 1832 Oil on canvas. 16 x 13 (041 x 032)*

*Louvre, Paris*

in the churches where he was working. He tried to get permission—first at the church of Saint-Denis-du-Saint-Sacrement, when he was painting his *Christ in Gethsemane*, and later at Saint-Sulpice when he was decorating the Chapel of the Holy Angels, to work on Sundays and so be able to enjoy the music of the services. But this did not go smoothly: 'The Emperor, the Empress and Monseigneur', he writes rather bitterly on 3 August 1854, 'are conspiring to prevent a poor painter like me from committing the sacrilege of liberating, on Sundays as on other days, the ideas he extracts from his brain for the glory of God. . . .' His assistant, Andrieu, has told how—in one of those gusts of youthfulness that still blew across his usually melancholy nature—he had dressed up a dummy in his own clothes and placed it behind the grill closing the chapel, in order to arouse the Sunday anger of the beadle and provoke him to break in—much to the poor man's embarrassment afterwards.

Moreau remembered a visit in August 1856 with Delacroix to the 'Saint-Sulpice frescoes which were still wearing their jacket of planks'; and Delacroix 'took pleasure in showing me the magnificent angel in the Heliodorus picture, striking with his avenging rod the profaner of the temple. This had only just been finished, and the master attributed its exceptional success to the indefinable state of mind into which he had been plunged by the sound of the organ playing the *Dies Irae*. And 'in support of this remark' Delacroix told him that, at the church of Saint-Denis-du-Saint-Sacrement, the 'grief-stricken attitude of Saint Mary Magdalene, who has fainted' was full of the echoes of the '*chants religieux du mois de Marie*'. And in fact the *Journal* for 30 August 1855 shows us Delacroix at Saint-Sulpice, 'inspired by the music and the singing in the church. . . . This music puts me into a state of exaltation that is favourable to painting.'

Music also made him more receptive to the pictures of other painters. He listened to music while he was looking at Prud'hon's work in the church of Saint-Philippe-du-Roule, and 'the emotional side of his painting seemed to free itself and come to me on the wings of the music.' Thirty years earlier, on 4 March 1824, he had described music as '*la volupté de l'imagination*'.

In the phase under discussion—when, having already been freed from subservience to form and outline by his discovery of colour and light, he was at last arriving at the idea of a painting as a piece of music (*ut musica*, no longer *ut poesis*)—his preoccupation with this idea emerged, as was inevitable, even in his choice of subjects. This, as was natural, was closely bound up with a preoccupation with *chiaroscuro*. In 1830 he painted his *Gluck at the Piano*, in pastel and
pl 169 water-colour,[33] of which Villot made an engraving: in the shadowy room the light is concentrated on the instrument, on the composer playing his *Armide* and on the listener, the two being lit by reflected light from the 'supposed score, the pages of which are blank'. Next year he took up the same theme again, adapting it—in a picture exhibited later at the 1833 Salon—to *The Emperor*

XX WOMEN OF ALGIERS (detail)
*1834 Oil on canvas.*
*Louvre, Paris*

*Charles V*, who is shown in a monk's habit, playing the organ, while another monk, close by him, listens. In 1832 came his *Paganini*, a bony and demoniac marionette drawing magical sounds from the night of the picture. Here again, according to his pupil Lassalle-Bordes, he was conscious of the closeness of the two arts. It was by 'practising like Paganini' for an hour every day 'nothing but scales' that he had acquired 'his astonishing technique. . . . We too have to practise.' The multitude of Delacroix's drawings bear witness to the experience he gained by this incessant and laborious training: Robaut has listed 6,629 drawings and 1,525 pastels, water-colours or wash drawings, as against the 853 pictures—to say nothing of some sixty sketch books. This is how it was possible for him to acquire his almost instinctive possession of the means of transferring vision to paper or canvas—that 'great rightness of hand' through which 'vision could be rendered with ease.' pl 168

With his subjects drawn from the 'dark past and abysm of time', the mysteries of shadow, the suggestive power of music and the great indistinct storm clouds—never before had Delacroix been so strongly drawn to the problem of expressing the ineffable, for which painting seemed to him ideally fitted. A great part of him was fascinated by this miraculous power of conjuring up and conveying emotionally what cannot be expressed in words. Yet his nature was too complex and rich for him to abandon himself to this entirely. Strengthened by a solid classicist education, the Latin was still there in him: he meant to go beyond it but not to give it up, and he refused to allow himself an abdication of order and lucidity.

In the very years when his enchantment with the unknown was at its strongest, one can feel that the bone structure of reason is still firm in him, under the half-light that conceals it. In 1830, when he was working on the *Battle of Poitiers* and still thinking of the *Battle of Nancy*, and when he had not yet begun the *Boissy d'Anglas*, which brought him nearer than ever to Rembrandt, political events suggested to him a theme that would make him break new ground.

## *Return of the Latin: the 'Liberty'*

*Liberty Leading the People*, or *28 July 1830*, later exhibited at the 1831 Salon, was bought for 3,000 francs by the new government, which in March had honoured the painter with the Légion d'Honneur. This picture—afterwards considered too subversive and several times relegated to obscurity—made a vivid impression on the public. Stepping over the remains of the barricade, on the roadway covered with dead and wounded, the Republic advances with her breast bare and a Phrygian cap on her dark dishevelled hair; between a street-arab and one of the insurgents (whose face is clearly modelled on the painter's own) she raises the new tricolour flag against a sky in which the sunshine is beginning to pierce through the smoke of the gunpowder. XIII, page 169

Delacroix's enthusiasm for the Revolution was certainly not unreserved. By nature an ingrained aristocrat and by education an upper-class bourgeois, he was only moderately smitten by the outburst of popular fury: Alexandre Dumas has even stated that while Delacroix enjoyed seeing the three colours flying again, associated as they had been with the glories of the Empire, he reacted to the explosion of the people's anger with caution and even alarm. Later he moved further and further away from his unconsidered enthusiasm and from the threatened dictatorship of the blind masses. At the time of the 1848 Revolution he confided to Soulier, on 8 May of that year, the loss of his illusions: 'I have buried the man I used to be, along with his hopes and his dreams of the future, and now I walk quite calmly past his grave as if it were that of a stranger.'

But in 1830 he was still vibrating in response to many illusions that had not yet been disappointed.

He felt also, at that time, that he was associated with a renewal of art and the human spirit which could only find its place by joining forces with liberty in public life. He knew very well that, by the side of this and of its insurrection, his own place of honour was marked out. Not content with donning, in December 1830 (in company with Villot), the uniform of the Garde Nationale (displaying, incidentally, a sartorial concern that had more to do with dandyism than with fanatical patriotism), he also, in January 1831, joined the *Société Libre de Peinture et de Sculpture*, drafted its petition and presented it to the Minister. In this he asked that the Administration should exercise control over the jury ('accessible as it is to a *clique* spirit') and should hold 'a kind of balance between the rival claims'—that is to say, should put an end to the intransigent dictatorship of the 'so-called classicists'. A change was taking place in France: the past, which had been brought back by the Restoration, was again being effaced by the future on the march. Delacroix could see the deeper meaning of the revolution that lay behind the rising: he was aware that this was a violent manifestation of a change in men's minds which could not be repressed, and that it was helping to clear away the obstacles obstructing the emergence of the new truths. It was therefore working for him, and he associated himself closely in its action.

Delacroix's *Liberty* follows in direct line his *Greece Expiring*, painted four years earlier. The general basis of the two is similar: a huge figure both real and symbolic, standing on bloodstained fragments of ruin mingled with dead bodies, conforms to the firm rhythm of a pyramidal architecture. Even the type of woman is the same—the dark haired, straight-nosed woman with the great dark eyes, full-curved lips and a face solidly drawn and modelled like some head from Antiquity. The type had made its appearance in the *Massacre at Chios* with the young dead mother and the despairing wife; and it was to reappear in the *Women of Algiers*, in the one who wears a rose in her hair and holds a narghile. It was inspired, no doubt, by one of his favourite models, perhaps by Émilie Robert, '*la mia carina Emilia*', who shared with Hélène and Laure his attention as a painter and his attentions as a man at the time when he was painting the *Chios*. This sculptural woman brings gravity alike to grief, to action and to voluptuous nonchalance. But she also recalls Delacroix to his concern with the human body, with the beauty of its volumes and movements, with its individual presence—and with the language of forms.

Both in the *Greece Expiring* and in the *Liberty*, the chief part is played by one central figure occupying at least two-thirds of the picture. It is strongly detached from the rest by outline and relief, and is inscribed in a primarily geometrical composition. All this seems like a resurgence of principles learned from Géricault and, beyond him, from the classical School: and indeed this was still present and basic in Delacroix, in spite of his increasingly bold forays in the direction of the baroque liberties of style, whose object was the contrary one of movement and fusion.

His contemporaries seem to have been aware of this, and the more moderate among them, who had been frightened by the master's increasing originality, hailed in these two pictures a reassuring return to calm and to those norms which Delacroix seemed to have rejected or forgotten. In the *Journal des Débats* the severe Delécluze conceded that the *Liberty*, 'a painting full of vitality', gave evidence, especially in its colour, of 'a rare talent which fully recalls the manner of Jouvenet'. Let us not be too quick to smile at this: the observation is a pertinent one, and it will be possible one day to see the extent to which Delacroix's painting is the natural successor to the great French artists of the seventeenth and eighteenth centuries, especially from the moment when these managed to receive what Rubens had to teach. But first, justice will have to be done to these undervalued artists.

The truth is, the *Liberty* does mark a moment of suspense, like the crest at which the two opposing slopes meet. At first sight the picture seems classical: in its construction it uses a grouping of half-naked or draped anatomical elements, organized in accordance with a triangle fitting within the limits of the frame. The apex of this falls on the axis of the picture; the bodies lying on the ground form its base; one of its ascending sides is stressed by the rifle held by Delacroix, then by the arm brandishing a sabre, then by the pole of the flag—they form an almost continuous line; the other by the leg and white shoulder belt of the street-arab, then by the left arm of Liberty and then by her right arm; the acute angle between this arm and the flagpole is the apex of the construction.

But it does not take long to see that this sort of jutting pediment is not as stable as it at first seems. It is pushed upwards by an irresistible movement which rises until it finds freedom in the floating veils of the standard. It is also carried to the right by the twist of the figure of Liberty, as though she were pressed upwards and round by the wounded man who heaves himself tensely up towards her. This is confirmed by the musket she carries in her left hand, and its imperiously pointing bayonet—and again by what seems like a wind of enthusiasm pushing everybody upwards and to that side in an impatient longing to cross the obstacle and to advance. In fact the whole picture is filled with two connected drives. The first of these rises in a crescendo which, starting from the bodies on the ground, struggles painfully up with the wounded man, then climbs passionately and ends by bursting out triumphantly in the clothes worn by Liberty, in her body and in her raised arm brandishing the flag. This first impetus transforms the static pyramid into an eruption of the whole mass, and it is accompanied, almost in the musical sense, by the development of the colour, which is heavy, opaque, livid and cold in the lower part, then grows gradually lighter and warmer, from the blue of the wounded man, through the subdued yellow of the dress, to the burning fanfare of the flag. But it is also completed by the second movement—by a general projection forwards, so that the crowd comes out of the confused depths of the picture to take possession of it, like a wave leaping over a dyke, as the figure of Liberty symbolically steps over the barricade. The picture seems on the point of spurting out over the onlooker, propelled forwards like Rembrandt's *Night Watch*.

The composition, then, is both architectural and dynamic. But it is also psychological: the geometrical framework seems to be merely the support, or rather the springboard, guiding and assisting the accelerating impetus that carries everything in the picture area. This impetus, likewise, simply mimes and expresses the moral meaning of the picture: life—proud, impulsive and creative—marching gradually from vanquished and lifeless remains, sucking upwards with it the impatient efforts of men and hurling these into an opening of brightness in which, like its outward and visible sign, colour bursts out. Rarely had there been seen a picture in which the various resources which art can bring into play had been so completely reconciled, associated and made to reinforce one another; rarely had there been seen such a combining and balancing of the conflicting forces—here complementary—of the classical legacy and the romantic discovery. Even allegory, beloved of the classicists, and the lyricism of action by which the romantics were carried away, were here joined together in bold and surprising ways, together with the realism that would soon be devoted to the observation of contemporary life and to the idea of 'modernity'.[34]

From time to time a work of art contrives to bring together and express all the ideas that mean most to the spirit of a particular time and give it its meaning. This is certainly the case with Delacroix's *Liberty Leading the People*, in which the clamour of a generation on the march becomes a joyous and unanimous hymn.

There is plenty of other evidence of the conflict that was now being waged, with Delacroix's mind as its battleground. Even while, in the line of pictures that goes from the *Sardanapalus* to the *Boissy d'Anglas*, he was indulging in the most unbridled orgy of romanticism he ever allowed himself, he showed how his academic education and tastes were still alive in him and impatient to express themselves also. There were his sketches for the *Four Seasons* with which he was to have decorated Talma's dining-room.[35] These, full of memories of a tradition that runs from the Fontainebleau School to Prud'hon, were the prelude to the Valmont frescoes, which he painted in 1834—through which they led on to the long series of large-scale decorative paintings.

In 1831 an open competition was held for the three historical paintings which were to adorn the debating chamber of the Chambre des Députés. Delacroix presented not only his sketch for the *Boissy d'Anglas*, in which he gave himself up to all the new delights that were tempting him, but also that for his *Mirabeau*
pl 183 *protesting at the dismissal of the États Généraux by the Marquis de Dreux-Brézé*. In this the composition—though it does consist of two opposing forces (the protesting movement of the deputies led by the energetic Mirabeau, and the cold stillness of the representative of Louis XVI)—seems an extreme example of the classical rules: the purely architectural setting imposes a rhythm with its vertical columns, while the horizontal lines of its cornices are guided smoothly by the perspective towards their meeting point at the corner of the hall where an empty space separates the protagonists. The clever, balanced arrangement, the exact rectilineal coldness of the principal lines, and even the way in which the heads are placed at the same level like caryatids—all this seems to exclude any

idea of breaking with the rules. The pictures seems a complement or counterpart to the *Boissy d'Anglas*—to its tumult, breathless fury, shadows and spasmodic bursts of light and colour.

Delacroix, at the age of thirty, was clearly divided between the conflicting inclinations of his temperament and of his education. He was still hesitating before choosing between them.

# NOTES ON THE PLATES TO CHAPTER IV

*The English feeling for nature* When, in 1825, Delacroix was confronted with the English landscape, for which he had been prepared by his study of Constable, Bonington and the Fieldings, he developed in response a free and fluid vision and technique (pl 112); it contained the beginnings of Impressionism, and was especially favoured by the water-colour medium. At one blow he was free from the discipline and constraint of form.

*112 Landscape near London, 1825, with the River Thames, the dome of Saint Paul's Cathedral on the left and Greenwich on the right. Cabinet des Dessins, Louvre, Paris.*

*113 English Landscape, 1825. Cabinet des Dessins, Louvre, Paris.*

*Life in England* Delacroix was a curious observer of English society, of its traditionalism (pl 114) and—prepared for this by Géricault—of its love of horses (pls 115, 116). Since he lodged with the trainer Elmore, to whom M. Auguste had recommended him, he had at his disposal a stableful of models.

*114 'A Doctor of Civil Law' at the University of Oxford. Cabinet des Dessins, Louvre, Paris.*

*115 Studies of horses, c. 1825-30. Cabinet des Dessins, Louvre, Paris.*

*116 Studies of horses, c. 1824-5. Cabinet des Dessins, Louvre, Paris.*

*British painting* During his visit to England the pictures of the British masters made a deep impression on him. It is not, for instance, hard to trace in Delacroix's *Christ on the Lake of Genesareth* (pl 117), painted some thirty years later, a reminiscence of Etty's *Storm* (pl 118).

*117 Christ on the Lake of Genesareth, 1853. Walters Art Gallery, Baltimore.*

*118* WILLIAM ETTY: *The Storm. City Art Gallery, Manchester.*

*Friendship with Bonington* Delacroix's friendship with Bonington (pl 125), who had come to Paris fifteen years earlier and had studied with Gros, both prepared him for and continued the impressions he received in England. In Paris, before the visit to England,

Delacroix shared Thalès Fielding's attic studio in the rue Jacob and has left a water-colour impression of the view from it (pl 124). There he already lived in an English circle. Of them all, he preferred Bonington. He painted him at work (pl 126); and sometimes he made what amount to replicas of his paintings, both in subject and in treatment (pls 122, 123). It was from a picture by a follower of Bonington (pl 119) that he copied the historical setting (pl 121) for the *Execution of the Doge Marino Faliero* (pls 120 and VI).

*119* RICHARD PARKES BONINGTON *(School of): The Doges' Palace. The National Gallery of Canada, Ottawa.*

*120 The Execution of the Doge Marino Faliero, 1827. The Wallace Collection, London.*

*121 First sketches for 'Marino Faliero'. Cabinet des Dessins, Louvre.*

*122 François I and his Mistress, 1826-7. The Fogg Art Museum, Cambridge, Mass.*

*123* BONINGTON: *François I and Marguerite of Navarre. The Wallace Collection, London.*

*124 View from the studio of Thalès Fielding, 20 rue Jacob. Dr. Fritz Nathan and Dr. Peter Nathan Collection, Zurich.*

*125* J. D. HARDING: *Portrait of Bonington. Lithograph after a picture by Margaret Carpenter. Author's collection.*

*126 Bonington, c. 1825. Private collection.*

*Water-colour technique*

Painting in water-colour (pl 127) and gouache (pl 128) now held no secrets for Delacroix: it helped to give him a decisiveness and lightness of technique that enabled his art to move ahead swiftly along the new paths of which he dreamed.

*127 Interior of a Farmhouse. Cabinet des Dessins, Louvre, Paris.*

*128 Seated Woman reading. Cabinet des Dessins, Louvre, Paris.*

*Period of sensuality*

It was round about 1825 that Delacroix's painting came to its highest degree of refinement—perhaps also to its most acute sensuality, and this even in the choice of subjects: this was the period of so many of his voluptuously reclining Odalisques, whose luminous flesh gleams in the half-light of the harems (pl 129) or, as in *Woman with a Parrot* (pls 130 and IX), is married with the most dazzling brilliance of palette.

*129 Odalisque. Fitzwilliam Museum, Cambridge.*

*130 Drawing for 'Woman with a Parrot'. Musée des Beaux-Arts, Lyons.*

*Oriental clothes*

The fantastic costumes in which Delacroix, following Watteau, dressed his friends for their portraits were Eastern: they gave him an excuse for indulging in chromatic splendours. To this end his friend Pierret (pl 132) and the singer Baroilhet (pl 131), a great lover of painting, both turned Turk.

*131 Baroilhet the Singer in Turkish Costume, 1825. Louvre Paris. Now at the Place Furstenberg studio.*

*132 Pierret in Turkish Costume, 1825. Private collection.*

*The horse in all its ardour*

The ardour that produced both the chromatic intensity and the lively sensuality of Delacroix's work at this time gave his horses a swiftness and mettle such as had already struck Géricault at the races in England (pl 134). Delacroix used these thoroughbreds in his lithographs (pl 133), even including them as an element of the fantasy in his *Faust* series (pl 135).

*133 The Flight of the Smuggler, 1826. Lithograph.*

134 THÉODORE GÉRICAULT: *The Derby at Epsom, 1821. Louvre, Paris.*

*135 Faust and Mephistopheles (illustration to Goethe's 'Faust'). Library of the École des Beaux-Arts, Paris.*

*The East: fresh source of intensity*

The East, with its light, colour and magic, gave Delacroix the setting in which his intense visions could expand: again and again after the *Massacre at Chios* he returned to it, in his episodes featuring Greeks and Turks, in which the splendour of the clothes and the thoroughbred liveliness of the arab horses (pls 137, 139) are enhanced by the frenzy of the fighting (pl 136). Till the end of his life (pl 138) he kept coming back to these subjects.

*136 Scenes from the Present War between the Turks and Greeks, 1827. Oskar Reinhart Collection, Winterthur.*

*137 Young Turk fondling his Horse, 1825-6. City Art Gallery, Luxembourg.*

*138 Scenes from the War between the Turks and Greeks, 1856. Formerly Rothschild Collection.*

*139 Moorish Horseman. Cabinet des Dessins, Louvre, Paris.*

*Sardanapalus: fire and ash*

The *Death of Sardanapalus* (1827) marks the climax of this phase of exaltation and prepares for its supersession. The desperate satiety of the beaten potentate (pl 141) is a renunciation of all those splendours—of jewels (pl 142), quivering steeds (pl 140) and voluptuous bodies (pl 143), all immolated in the death-spasm (pls XI, XII).

*140 The Death of Sardanapalus, 1827 (detail). Louvre, Paris.*

*141 Studies for the 'Death of Sardanapalus'. Louvre, Paris.*

*142 Study of still-life for the 'Death of Sardanapalus'. Louvre, Paris.*

*143 Two nude studies for the 'Death of Sardanapalus', c. 1827. Cabinet des Dessins, Louvre, Paris.*

*Heritage of David's tragic feeling*

In these transitional years the vein of melancholy and of the wilfully macabre in Delacroix became increasingly important: his *Death of Cato* (pl 144) painted in 1824, shows clearly its origin in the tragic feeling of David and his school: it goes back to the subject, and even to the diagonal composition, of David's *Hector* (pl 145)—a picture much in the public eye just then, for, though painted in 1778, it was shown afresh at the 1824 Salon, two years before its painter died in exile at Brussels.

*144 Death of Cato, 1824. Musée Fabre, Montpellier.*

*145* JACQUES-LOUIS DAVID: *The Death of Hector. Engraving by Jules David. Author's collection.*

*Inner despair*

The tragic tension of David's subjects, which came of the sensibility of the time when the Revolution and the Empire were imminent, prepared Delacroix to become aware of a sadness inherent in his own temperament—a sadness that was more nearly of the true romantic kind. It emerged in his *Tasso* of 1824 and 1825, that incarnation of the neglected and wretched genius, as well as in the despairing posture of his *Sardanapalus* and in the later *Tasso*, painted in the same year, 1827 (pls 146, 147).

*146 Tasso in the Madhouse, 1827. Oskar Reinhart Collection, Winterthur.*

*147 Study for Tasso, 1824. Cabinet des Dessins, Louvre, Paris.*

*Faust*

In Goethe's *Faust*, which he illustrated in a series of lithographs published in 1829, Delacroix found his own disillusioned musing on human vanities philosophically developed (pl 148). He followed Faust through his adventure in Satanism, which lent itself so well to romantic art (pl 149).

*148 Faust in his Study, 1827. Lithograph.*

*149 Faust and Mephistopheles in the Harz Mountains, 1827. Lithograph.*

*Chiaroscuro*

The sombre musing that led Delacroix from Tasso to Faust called for a new way of looking at things—one dominated by Rembrandtesque half-lights and glooms (pl 151). These too became a permanent part of Delacroix's art: his *M. Bruyas* (pl XLII) still has the despairing sadness of his *Tasso* and his *Faust*, and is set in an interior with strong *chiaroscuro* (pl 150).

*150 M. Bruyas in his Study. Formerly Choiseul Collection.*

*151 Renaissance Scene. Formerly (1934) Pearl White Collection.*

*The Middle Ages*

The Middle Ages, especially when imagined as they then were, through their ruins, fitted in well with these dark meditations. Delacroix was interested in medieval architecture (pl 156), sculpture (pl 155) and stained glass (pl 154). He studied the ruins at Valmont when he stayed there (pls 152, 153), and visited Rouen, where the great hall of the Palais de Justice (pl 158) suggested to him, even in 1855, the setting for such pictures as his *Foscari* (pl 157)—where the old man's pose resembles that of *Bruyas,* painted two years earlier.

*152 Ruins of the Abbey of Valmont, 1831. Private collection.*

*153 Delacroix painting the Ruins of Valmont, c. 1831. Louvre, Paris.*

*154 Study of stained glass windows. Cabinet des Dessins, Louvre, Paris.*

*155 Studies of Gothic sculpture. Cabinet des Dessins, Louvre, Paris.*

*156 Drawing of medieval staircase. Cabinet des Dessins, Louvre, Paris.*

*157 The Two Foscari. 1855. Musée Condé, Chantilly.*

*158 The Great Hall in the Palais de Justice at Rouen. A contemporary lithograph.*

*The imprisoned life* *Chiaroscuro* and the Middle Ages, which Delacroix's imagination found so tempting, especially after 1827, lent themselves well to lithographs inspired by Goethe (pl 161) or Sir Walter Scott (pl 160). They derive all their tragic intensity from the theme of being shut up in a cell with thick walls and a narrow iron-barred window (pls 159, 162).

*159 Faust and Marguerite in Prison, 1827. Lithograph.*

*160 Front de Bœuf and the Witch, 1829 (Ivanhoe). Lithograph.*

*161 Marguerite at the Spinning Wheel, 1827. Lithograph.*

*162 Louis XI, 1829. Illustration for Beranger's 'Chansons'. Engraving by Pourvoyer.*

*Transition* The *Cardinal Richelieu celebrating Mass,* which is known only from sketches, shows how, in 1828, Delacroix was still divided between his love for wealth of colour and his love for indoor effects in which the sumptuous is wrapped in half-light and shadows (pls 163, 164).

*163 Preparatory study for 'Cardinal Richelieu celebrating Mass', 1828.*

*164 Sketches of Louis XIII costumes for 'Cardinal Richelieu'. Louvre, Paris.*

*The funereal and macabre* With his *Battle of Nancy,* Delacroix's tendency towards gloom gains the upper hand: the battle becomes funereal, stifled by the snow, by the twilight, by the overcast sky and by the horizon which became more crushing as Delacroix moved from the sketch (pl 166) to the final picture (pl 165).

*165 The Death of Charles the Bold at the Battle of Nancy, 1831. Nancy.*

*166 Sketch for the 'Battle of Nancy', 1828. Ny Carlsberg Glyptothek, Copenhagen.*

*Music* Delacroix's initiation into *chiaroscuro* during the years 1827-30 helped him to become more aware of those enveloping atmospheric effects of which painting is capable: these he associated closely with the atmospheric effects created by music, to which he often referred at the time.

*167 L'amoureuse au piano, 1843. Formerly Jean-Louis Vaudoyer Collection.*

*168 Portrait of Paganini, 1832. The Phillips Collection, Washington.*

*169 Gluck at the Piano, c. 1830. Engraving by Villot after Delacroix.*

*Liberty Leading the People*

In 1830 the figure of *Liberty* striding upwards from death towards life, from sombre masses towards colour and light, in a picture that combines a regular pyramidal composition with a violent spontaneity of drawing, sums up well the complex and contradictory pulls between which Delacroix was divided (pl XIII).

*170 Study for 'Liberty Leading the People', 1830. Cabinet des Dessins, Louvre, Paris.*

*171 Study for 'Liberty'. Cabinet des Dessins, Louvre, Paris.*

112

113

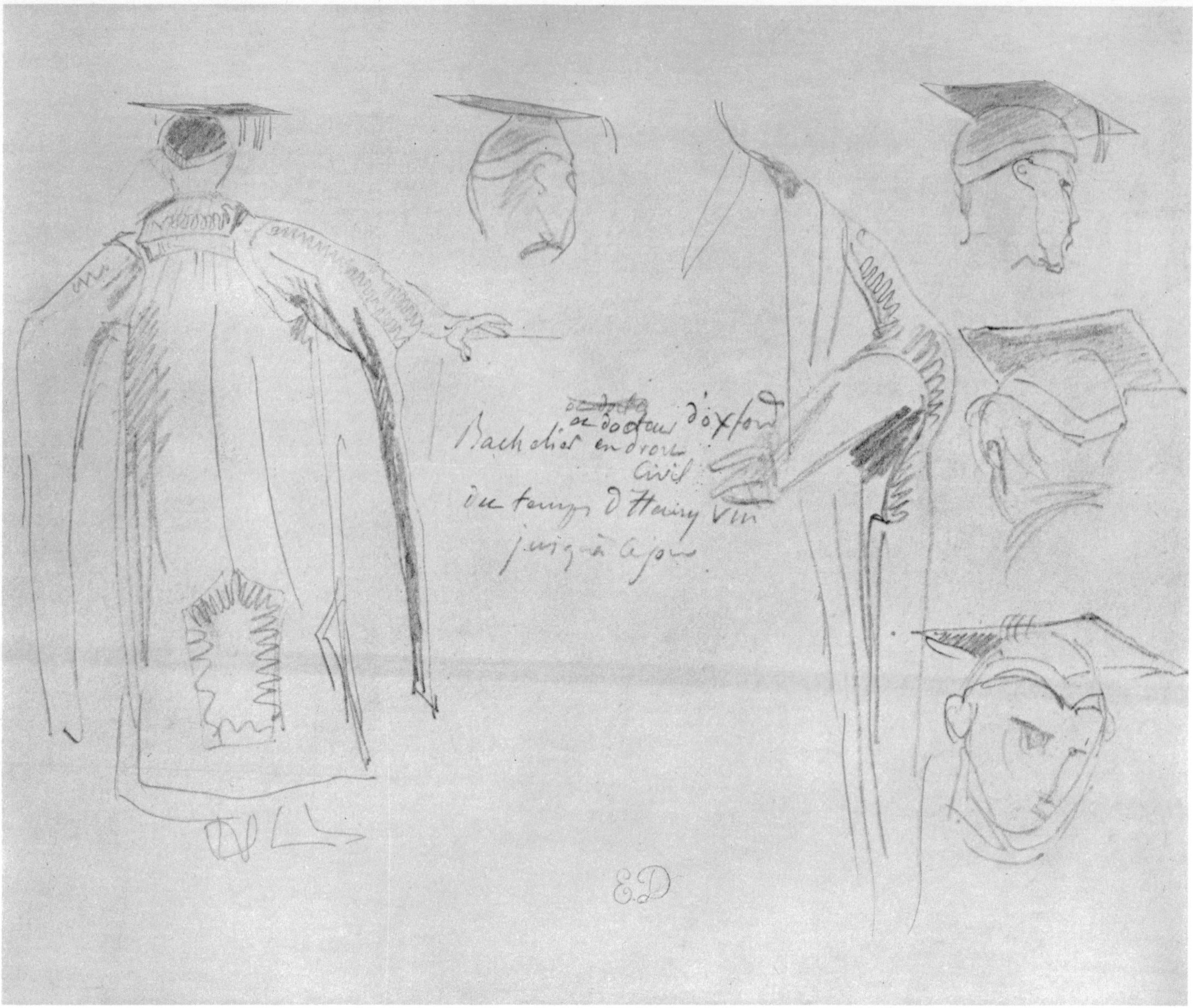

114

115

116

117

118

119

120

121

122

123

124

125

126

127

128

129

130

131

132

133

134

135

136

137

138

139

140

141

142

143

144

145

146

147

148

149

150

151

152

153

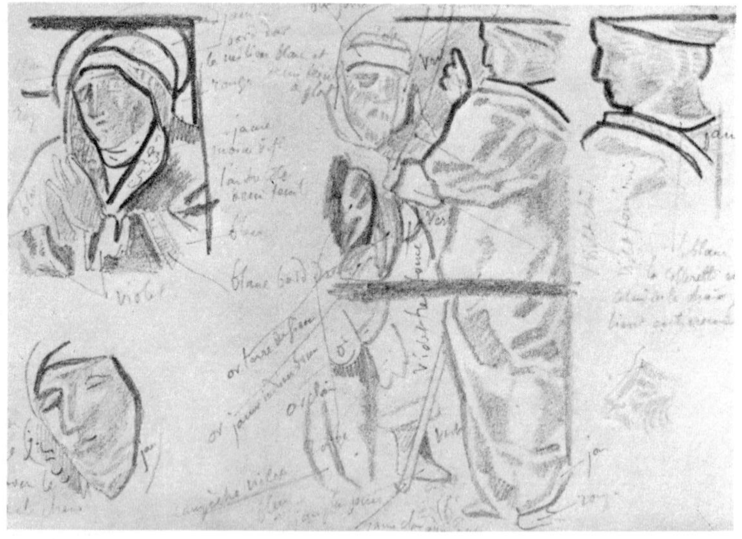

154

155

156

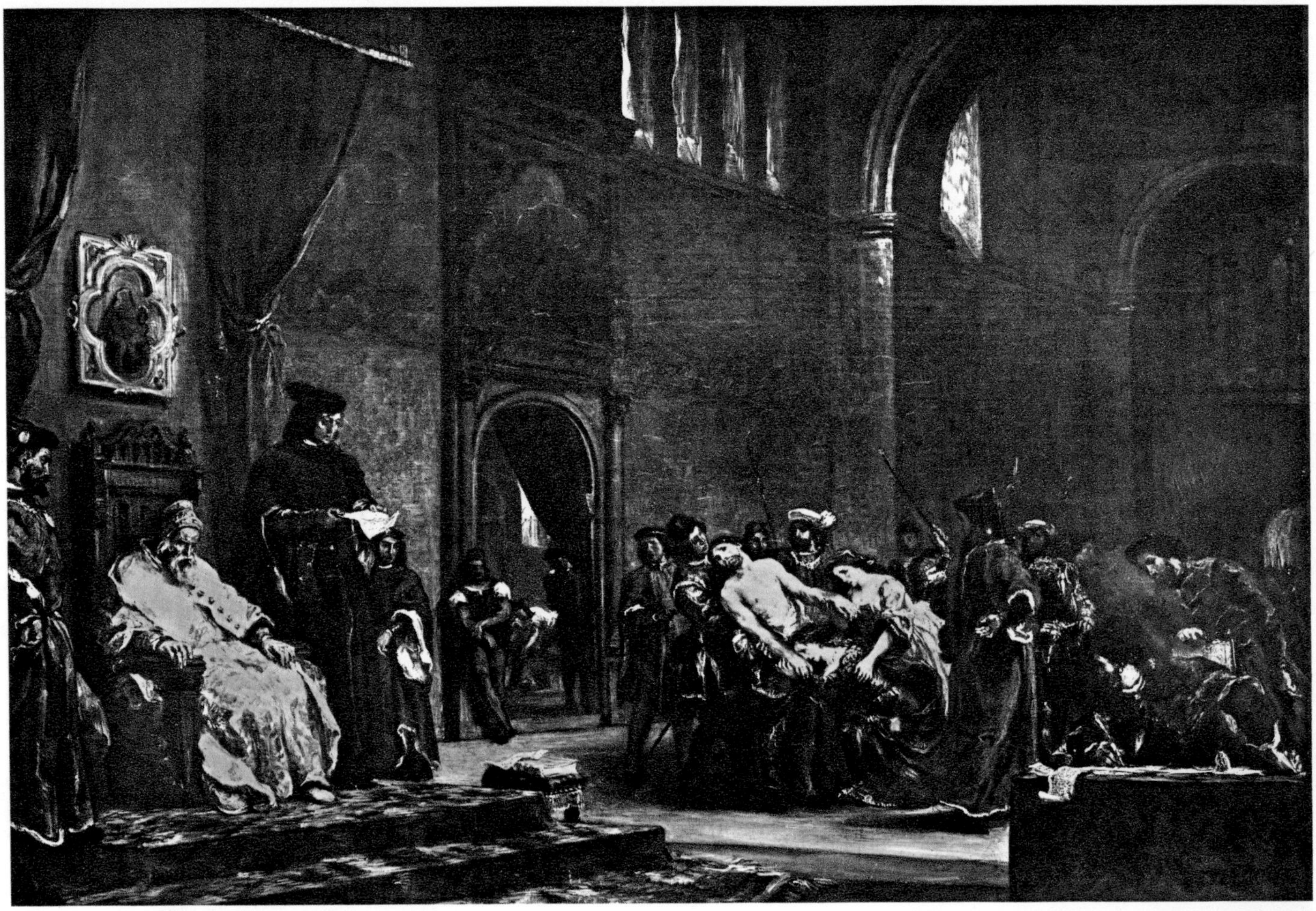

157

158

159

161

160

162

163

164

165

166

167

168

169

170

171

# V DANDYISM IN FRANCE

'What, then, is this passion which has become a doctrine and has won adepts with a dominant influence—this unwritten institution which has formed so haughty a caste?'

BAUDELAIRE[1]

DELACROIX HAD REACHED the mid-point of his life. He had apparently not made up his mind to accept one, and reject the other, of the two opposing attitudes whose conflict filled the first half of the century—classicism and romanticism. The public did not hesitate to do so: it made Ingres the champion of the classicists and Delacroix the leader of the insurgents besieging the ancient fortress. The caricature by Bertall, which appeared in 1849 in the *Journal pour rire* forcibly expresses the antinomy in which the two artists were being imprisoned. It shows the 'duel to the death between M. Ingres, the Thiers of line, and M. Delacroix, the Proudhon of colour'. In front of an architectural background formed by the Institut, the two combatants, dressed for a tournament, are charging each other on heavily caparisoned steeds. Ingres is brandishing, as the symbol of drawing, a pen-case, and Delacroix a paint brush, symbol of colour. 'No hope of quarter being given,' says the caption. And again: 'If M. Ingres wins, colour will have to be proscribed all along the line'; but on a pot of paint, perched on Delacroix's saddle, we read: 'Line is a colour.' And a streamer from the mouth of Ingres proclaims: 'Rubens is a red.' Reactionaries versus revolutionaries, draftsmen versus colourists, classicists versus romantics—contemporary opinion was determined to reduce everything to this simplification.

And yet the writers on Ingres have shown how at first he appeared as the leader of a new clan, in which there was an early glimmer of romanticism, and it is certain that his taste for oriental things and for the Middle Ages, together with his mannered drawing and his precious and violent harmonies, did not exactly mark him out to be the faithful successor of David. Equally, the writers on Delacroix have said again and again how irritated he was by a classification which did not correspond at all to his real tastes. He hated to be saluted as a flag of romanticism, and his retort was: 'I am a pure classicist.' Nor did he consent to be treated as a pendant to Victor Hugo. The poet, on his side,[2] far from regarding Delacroix as his *alter ego* and as the leader of the new school, accused him of betraying it and of not understanding its real attitude.

'The young chief of the movement in painting,' he said, 'had not the same boldness in words as he had in pictures. He tried, by the concessions he made in conversation, to disarm the enemies raised up against him by the originality of his admirable talent. A revolutionary in his studio, he was a conservative in the drawing-rooms, disavowed the literary insurrection and preferred tragedy to drama.'

This, as Delacroix's private notes in his *Journal* amply prove, was not precaution or affectation, but a reflection of his innermost doctrine—of the duality of tendencies which he was always seeking to bridge, since he refused to condemn one of them in the name of the other. Charles Rivet[3] has recorded Delacroix's own opinion:

'I found myself, and still find myself, in a strange situation. Most of those who have taken my side were, in general, merely taking their own . . . and using me as a flag. They have enlisted me, whether I would or no, in the romantic coterie.'

## *The Cult of Personality in French Tradition*

Delacroix felt that he belonged to a different family; and, if we are to understand his position, the importance of this group, which was underestimated in the nineteenth century, must now be stressed. By what name should it be called? It was not classical, although it reacted against disordered exuberances and favoured the strict disciplines imposed by reason and will. Nor was it romantic, although it considered that the source of all creative activity lay in an inspired richness and in a generous flow of sensibility. It might best be called Dandyism, provided that the word is given its full range and is not restricted in the usual way, to mere elegance of dress and behaviour. Barbey d'Aurevilly, though he has a true craftsman's approach to the subject, called Dandyism[4] 'this vague thing which nobody has ever been able to define.' He himself did not recoil before the task of defining it, for in the next year—the year of the meeting between Delacroix and Baudelaire, both of whom were adherents of the new aesthetic and ethical point of view—he published at Caen his *Du Dandysme et de Georges Brummel.* The book went into three more editions, the first two of them in 1862 and 1879 with important new matter.

What had chiefly struck the public in Brummel, d'Orsay and a few other devotees, was a meticulous refinement of social elegance. But this was only a superficial prelude to the movement which developed later, and which thought out a doctrine of moral behaviour whose effect on certain lofty spirits was profound.[5] With them there appears what André Ferran has felicitously called '*le Dandysme intérieur*' (inward Dandyism)—of which he regards Baudelaire as an adherent. Delacroix should be taken as an earlier example of it. This alone would enable us to understand the impossibility of fitting him in to the limits of either romanticism or classicism, and the position he occupies on one of the dominant lines of the nineteenth century.

Barbey d'Aurevilly—who, born, in 1808, came between the generation of Delacroix, born in 1798, and Baudelaire, born in 1821—hastened to clarify this dangerous confusion. 'Those minds that see things only from their petty aspect', he wrote, 'have imagined that Dandyism was, above all, the art of dress. Most certainly it is that, among other things, but it is much more.' In fact, 'Dandyism is a whole way of living, and is not attained merely by its materially visible side.' Neither Delacroix nor Baudelaire repudiated that side, but for them, with the correctness of behaviour it implied, it was only an outward accompaniment to an ideal of man and life. 'The reality of Dandyism', Barbey explains, 'is human, social, spiritual.' In it may be found Delacroix's true nature; in it the apparent inconsistencies of his character are reconciled. Self-domination in daily life is shown by a scrupulous respect for the conventions; in the inner life it is expressed by a clear submission to the rules of reason—but at the same time it never bars recourse to the flowing springs of the individual, to the affirmation of what is distinctive in his sensibility and to the cultivation of even its most passionate expression. In these conditions, there is no longer a contradiction between classicism and romanticism: there are the two complementary aspects of a personality determined to explore itself to the full, to experience both its impetus and its power of control. Dandyism brings the two together in a true, rejuvenated and renewed humanism based on the cult of the individual, both of his private qualities and of his collective obligations. It makes the most of the original treasures of the self, yet at the same time raises it, by a voluntary discipline and a strict acceptance of the structures of thought, until it has an exemplary and universal value.

Baudelaire wrote of this in *Le peintre de la vie moderne.* He says there that the basis of Dandyism is the individualism brought in by the nineteenth century: 'It is a kind of cult of one's self';[6] but he shows, nonetheless, that this cult is not an indulgence but a discipline. It is a self-discipline freely conceived and accepted by the self.

'It will be seen', Baudelaire adds, 'that in certain aspects Dandyism verges on religion and on Stoicism. All the complicated material requirements to which they [the Dandies] submit, from an irreproachable dress at every hour of the day and night to their engagement in dangerous sports, are merely a gymnastic calculated to strengthen the will and to discipline the soul.'

But in saying this Baudelaire was reflecting Delacroix's own thinking, with which he had been familiar since 1845. And Delacroix himself noted, at Dieppe on 13 September 1852: 'To feel you have done the right thing raises you in your own eyes. You can then enjoy, in default of any other reason for pleasure, this first of pleasures: to be satisfied with oneself.'

Such an attitude had roots that went far back in French tradition and culture: but clearly it was conceived only under the revealing impulse which came from England, whence the movement acquired its name and its outward behaviour. Both through his solid classical culture and through his early initiation into English ways, Delacroix was at the confluence of the two streams.

Dandyism, as it developed in France, would in fact have been no more than a superficial phenomenon of distinction and good form, had it not, by an elegant process of adjustment, adopted what was a long-standing tendency in that country of moralists and psychologists: a disposition to give major importance to the inner life, to a knowledge based not so much on the collective beliefs supplied from outside as on personal self-examination, on introspection, and to find in the self the primary reality. Already, at the moment of emergence from the Middle Ages, Montaigne had laid down the fundamental principles in two celebrated sentences in his *Essays*. One of them is: 'I have no other object than to depict myself'; but this statement, which might lead to egoism and mere withdrawal into oneself, was corrected by the other, which gives it its full application: 'Each man carries in him the whole shape of the human condition.'

To turn towards one's most private qualities, to seek reality in subjective experience and yet to find there the basis for truths of the widest application and to reveal these to other people, was a programme to which French thinking was always inclined. Descartes took as his starting-point the rejection of the assertions generally taught, and would only trust, as an ultimate certitude, the experience of the consciousness of his own existence: he knew of no other method by which to try, in spite of that rejection, to found a body of universal truths. Pascal also—whom the schools often contrast with him—was acclaimed as a master by the apostles of Dandyism. In his 1862 Preface, Barbey remarks:

'If Dandyism had existed in his time, Pascal, who was a Dandy in the way one can be in France, would have been able to write its history before he entered Port-Royal.'

He, like Descartes, plunges deep into himself to find other truths which, in his case, are more apt to interest and move the people of our own time: there he found himself face to face with man the chimera, the monster, chaos and prodigy and the field of contradiction; he came upon the terror of being face to face both with oneself and with the infinite—but also, far more than in the logic of dogma, had the reassurance of their reality. 'It is the heart, not the reason, that feels God.' By this lucid, thought-out, inner affirmation, a man wins his nobility and his dignity. Baudelaire spoke, later, of the 'best evidence we can give of our dignity'.[7] Through it man—so small, so puny by the scale of the world—will attain greatness, that greatness of which Delacroix constantly thought, remembering the advice he had inherited from Stendhal, 'not to neglect anything that can make you great'. He too invoked dignity—'*la dignité, le respect de son caractère*'.[8] The individual, when he considers himself in his precarious unity as a thinking being, feels crushed. He hears that 'eternal complaint against the boredom and the emptiness' of which Delacroix was so painfully aware.[9] And yet, at the same time, in that small share of energy determined to assert itself in its own way, he experiences his true greatness.

Another representative of the inner Dandyism, in which in the nineteenth century man's long train of thinking about himself had resulted, was Alfred de Vigny. There is a note of his which says:

'Destiny and man as I conceive them: destiny carrying him away like the sea, and he great because he oustrips it or great because he resists it.'[10]

On the one hand, man sees himself launched, like the ship's boat of Byron's *Don Juan*, on a limitless ocean whose plaything he is—and its depths are his own and its waves his passions. The image occurs also in Baudelaire:[11]

*Et mon âme dansait, dansait, vieille gabarre*
*Sans mâts, sur une mer monstrueuse et sans bords.*

On the other hand man, condemned to that boat, finds there his assets—lucidity and energy, both of them drawn from the resources of his own self. On 8 November 1854, Delacroix was savouring 'with happiness' the 'feeling of freedom and of being in possession of oneself, which must be the only good to which I am justified in aspiring.'

Willpower is the guarantee of this; and he copies out from Maine de Biran—who helped so much to give the nineteenth century the real consciousness of the self—these sentences:[12] 'It is essential that the will should preside over what we are: that is stoicism, and no other system fits our nature so well.' Thus arose and developed that essentially French train of thought: in the knowledge and cultivation of the self it found, equally, the wealth of a sensory experience deeply felt, the wealth of a reflective experience, implacably clear-sighted, and the wealth of a will inflexibly exerted and determined to lead the whole man on to his fullest and highest potentialities. In this light it is easy to understand how Barbey could say that he saw in Dandyism 'an act of utmost individual power. . . the ability to be oneself.'

At the end of this trajectory we find Apollinaire, who, in his *Musicien de Saint-Merry*, cries: 'I sing of the possibilities of myself beyond the world of the stars.' And in fact the creative artist, while remaining faithful to the rules of control and self-mastery that have been the making of the real classics, can nonetheless attain the innovating aim of romanticism, which excludes sterile repetition and the mere use of the rules, seeking instead the adventure of doing what has not yet been done; as Baudelaire claimed:

*Plonger au fond du gouffre, Enfer ou Ciel, qu'importe!*
*Au fond de l'Inconnu pour trouver du* nouveau.[13]

(To drown in the abyss—heaven or hell, who cares?
Through the unknown we'll find the *new*.[14])

Apollinaire also, abandoning to the past 'those who were the perfection of order', invites us to launch out to the winning of

*De vastes et d'étranges domaines*
*Où le mystère en fleur s'offre à qui veut le cueillir.*

(Vast, strange domains where mystery in flower
Offers itself to any who will pluck it.)

But it was not till the twentieth century that to place oneself thus finally 'outside order' became the accepted thing. Delacroix and Dandyism would not go so far. Though they sought in the self 'new fires, and colours never seen before', this did not make them willing to sacrifice control.

Instead, Delacroix remained attached to the classical tradition on which he had been brought up. At Strasbourg, on 25 August 1859, he could still copy out with enjoyment Boileau's preface to his 1701 edition:

'What is a new, brilliant, extraordinary thought? It is not, as the ignorant are ready to believe, a thought that no-one has ever had, or should have had:

it is, on the contrary, a thought that must have occurred to everyone and that somebody takes it into his head to express for the first time.'

It is tempting to compare this observation, borrowed from the most weighty Aristarchus of all, with the one made by Delacroix when still in the fire of his youth:[15]

'The novelty is in the spirit that creates, and not in the nature that is painted. . . . You should know that there is always something new to say, show it to the others in what they have undervalued. Convince them that they have never before heard tell of the nightingale and of the appearance of the vast sea, of each of the things their gross senses are only able to feel when someone has taken the trouble of first feeling it for them. . . . Nature has stored up in the great imaginations that are to come more new things to say about her creations than she has created things.'

Delacroix, then, is situated paradoxically half-way between Boileau and Apollinaire, at the climactic moment of Dandyism in the middle of the nineteenth century, the moment when it seemed possible to reconcile and balance the tendencies inherited from the past and those that were quivering with impatience for the future.

And yet Delacroix was a disciple of Voltaire. He mentions him seventy times in the *Journal*—much more often than Shakespeare, and much more often than Byron! He took Voltaire's works with him to Dieppe in 1855, and to Champrosay in 1860. He thought of his dictionary of the Fine Arts (which remained a sketch) as a continuation of the *Dictionnaire philosophique*. And even Jean-Jacques Rousseau offended him; he was shocked by what he called the 'lack of reasoning that one notices in turgid authors, alongside their great qualities.'[16] True, he was not insensible of the 'feeling for vague impressions and for melancholy' that he found in Rousseau, but he condemned 'the falsity, bad taste, absence of real logic', the preferring of emotion and effect to truth, and the resulting blind confidence in spontaneity. It was in Voltaire that he found —and copied out to make it his own—this passage (from the *Questions encyclopédiques*): 'The rarest thing is to combine reason with enthusiasm. . . . Controlled enthusiasm is the property of the great poets.'[17] Even in Voltaire he recognized an echo of the kind of balance he was trying to achieve, and from Voltaire he transcribes his own programme of creative work, with its alternation of the two contrary powers: first 'reason holds the pencil', then 'the imagination warms up, and enthusiasm goes into action: it is a steed carried along upon its course. But the course is the one mapped out.' Delacroix approves: 'Everything he says is excellent,' he comments.

And he approves of Voltaire again when, comparing enthusiasm to wine, he warns against the excess of it—which some may well think a good description of romanticism: for 'it can excite such tumult in the blood vessels and such violent vibrations in the nerves, that reason is completely destroyed.' Neither Voltaire nor Delacroix would accept this excess. On 6 April 1856, in his *Journal*, Delacroix contrasted 'French dispositions' with 'Nordic dispositions' from Edgar Allan Poe to the Germans: 'These people take pleasure only in what is outside or beyond nature: the rest of us cannot let ourselves be so unbalanced and *reason must be a party to all our wanderings*.'

To Delacroix the first requirement of creative work was to explore and express the self in its full sincerity, but this self was not, as Rousseau thought, made up of nothing but our spontaneous impulses—it included also that cold and lucid gaze at the world, which is just as much a part of us for all that it curbs us. While, through his enthusiasm, Delacroix opened the way to modern art, to its limitless revelation of the unknown and of the potentialities we carry in us, his 'classicism' was equally a foreshadowing of that icy thought of Paul Valéry's: 'The spontaneous, even when it is excellent, even when it is seductive, never seems to me to be enough mine.'[18] For a man's individuality is also, and just as much, defined by perfect self possession. For this reason Delacroix always attached the utmost importance to the composition in a painting—'that wise and firm labour on this elevated and volcanic land.'

This equilibrium which Delacroix contrived to maintain between two tendencies treated as contrary by the men of his own time and again separated by those who came after, is his Dandyism. The self is the basis of life, the source of all creative activity; but it manifests itself both as the feeling of our affective personality and as our individual power to know ourselves and to go where we think we must. To attain this fullness involves the cultivation both of the imagination, which responds to what is welling up in the depths of us, and the reason, which gives it embodiment. 'It is the uniting of these two faculties, imagination and reason, that makes exceptional men.'[19]

This programme was revealed to him in his youth, and he remained faithful to it when he grew old. On 27 February 1824 he wrote, full of hope: 'I am acquiring reason without losing the emotion excited by the beautiful'; and on 9 October 1849, worried at seeing that 'a certain vividness of impression' was diminishing with age, he wrote: 'Perhaps the very great men, and I fully believe this, are those who, at an age when their intelligence has its full power, have kept a part of that impetuous impressionability which is characteristic of youth.'

The self as sensibility, the self as lucidity, the self as will-power—these were the three conceptions of self which the nineteenth century brought to the fore equally, and which Delacroix, like all the Dandies, intended to assume equally. But the first two terms can only be reconciled under the arbitration and direction of the third. No complete culture is possible in an individual unless, to the resources of emotion and to those of reason, there is added an acceptance of that energy which will imprint a discipline on the former and impart an intensity to the latter.

Until just before the nineteenth century, the self had had its analysts but not, as yet, its heroes. What was needed for this was that the collapse of the great collective illusions should divert the tense and excessive energies which first the Revolution and then the Empire had aroused, into the individual and the secrecy of the inner life. This harsh transposition, which explains the rise of Dandyism, can also be followed in Stendhal.

Born in 1780, eighteen years before Delacroix, he took part, first as a sub-lieutenant of the Dragoons and then as *Commissaire des Guerres*, in the epic adventure. It led him from Milan to Russia. Stendhal experienced the ecstasy of action and domination: he admired Napoleon both as a surpassing individual and as an animator of huge masses of men. After Waterloo he saw all this fervour deprived of any general object, withdrawing into the hearts of individuals and there awakening measureless and stormy longings. 'For many years there had been perhaps not a single hour when Julien had not told himself that Bonaparte, an obscure lieutenant without fortune, had made himself master of the world with his sword.' An Empire, a phase of history, had been forced to reduce itself to the scale of a personal destiny. Passion was no longer a passive self-abandon to dark forces: it was now in alliance with the individual's positive energy, either in the form of love or in that of ambition. If love, it was the nineteenth century Don Juan from Byron to Stendhal and Barbey d'Aurevilly, forcing women to yield to his will; if ambition, then it was society that must yield to an individual's display of force, and the coveted sign of this complete yielding would be glory. 'When a man wants a thing vividly and constantly,' said Stendhal, 'he succeeds.'

This ecstasy of the will-power, enabling the individual to assert and spread himself, appears as a feature shared by a number of great minds of the period—those precisely, who in one way or another are connected with the line of Dandyism. Positive energy in the individual, as one can see again and again in Stendhal, is at one and the same time intoxicating and violent like a passion, and lucid and self-controlled like cold reason. In it there takes place the junction and reconciliation of two opposing tendencies which had, till then, been cultivated with resentful exclusivity by the classicists and the romantics. It was also the final resort of the Dandy. 'The world belongs to energy,' said Tocqueville. And when, in his *Les Déracinés*, Barrès, one of the last of these representatives of the cult of the self, described Napoleon as 'a method placed at the service of a passion', he put his finger on the essential source of Napoleon's prestige with the young men of that time. He was, in fact, both a 'soul on fire' (to use an expression of Barbey's) and an ice-cold, calculating head, upheld by an inflexible will.

Transpose this programme into the field of art, and you have defined Delacroix. But Stendhal's ideal was the same, and was also that of Balzac and his heroes. Listen to Balzac describing Louis Lambert's will: 'a contraction of the inner being, capable of gathering, concentrating and then projecting itself into another being.' It is as though one were following the process of creation as Delacroix conceived it, when the artist first imagines and then communicates. There is hardly any difference between this and the ideal of Mérimée, who hid beneath irony and sarcasm a passionate sensibility to which he gave play in his imaginative stories. Or that of Barbey d'Aurevilly, who saw the will in action as the essential weapon of the self in its effort to appease its passions and to heave itself up to greatness. He said of it in his enthusiasm, 'energy, even in the evil passions, always excites in us astonishment and a kind of admiration.'

At the beginning of the nineteenth century there appeared, also, a philosophy of the self in which the chief place was reserved for the will: this was the philosophy of Maine de Biran. Delacroix was aware of it. He had attended, as we know, the lectures of Victor Cousin, who was strongly influenced by Maine de Biran and considered him 'the greatest metaphysician to have contributed to the honour of France since Malebranche.' Maine de Biran had been administrator of the Dordogne when Delacroix's father was about to become *Préfet* of the Gironde; he was a fellow member of the Conseil des Cinq-Cents; in 1806 he became *Sous-Préfet* of Bergerac, and later he was its deputy till his death in 1824, by which time he was a *Conseiller d'État*. He belonged, therefore, to the circle from which Delacroix had come, and his ideas must have been frequently mentioned in the drawing-rooms he frequented. Both men were firm believers in keeping a private diary. And we know that Delacroix had studied his philosophy, at least through the medium of Sainte-Beuve: this is proved by the long extracts copied out by him in 1857 from the *Moniteur* article, as resumed in the *Causeries du Lundi*.

To Maine de Biran the essential problem was, in conformity with the French tradition, that of the consciousness of our own being, the '*sens intime*'; but he regarded this self, apprehended by an effort of introspection, as essentially an active force, brought into play against the resistances opposed to it, beginning with the body. The self is only known immediately as an acting force. 'The immediate feeling of the force . . . is none other than that of our very existence, from which the feeling of activity is inseparable. . . . Each individual person knows himself, *certissima scientia et clamante conscientia*, as a force that acts and operates throught the will.' Such a philosophy is part of the romantic movement, in the sense that, like that movement, it takes its place at the culmination of the evolution leading to individualism, to awareness of life through the self; but it distinguishes itself from romanticism, just as Delacroix and French Dandyism did, by its rejection of abandonment to unchecked effusiveness. This effusiveness, so dear to the German innovators, abolishes the will and self-direction in the dilemma of either being swept away by the innate, torrential flow of passion or dissolved in absorbing communion with the forces of nature. Either of these results was deeply repugnant to Dandyism, which protected itself against both of them by associating the self and energy closely together, by regarding the former in accordance with Maine de Biran, as 'the immediate feeling of force', and combining the two together under the significant name of '*la force-moi*' or '*la puissance-moi*'. This was the essentially French attitude. It was to have its influence on post-romantic German philosophy. In that of Schopenhauer—who, indeed, was a contemporary of Delacroix—the will is the primary source of all activity, the body being only its 'objectivity'. A more distant influence of these ideas was to appear in Nietzsche, when he exalted the will to power.

## *The British Contribution*

Thus Delacroix took his place in the direct line of French thinking; but he was also one of those who showed themselves most ready to absorb the English example, without which there would have been no French Dandyism. In fact, at the beginning of the nineteenth century, Dandyism made its appearance as an exclusively English creation, and its prestige in France was one aspect of that anglomania which flourished there in the eighteenth century, and reached its climax early in the nineteenth. In 1815 Delacroix had seen British troops of occupation encamped on the Champs-Élysées, and had even made the *Troupes Anglaises* the subject of one of his first lithographs, in 1816—an extremely caustic picture, inspired by the satirical style of Rowlandson and Gillray. His friendships with the sons of French *émigrés* and with Englishmen, and then his visit to England in 1825, had a strong, but different, effect on him. It is hardly necessary to recall how enchanted he was by both English poetry and English painting during his formative years—how his example and constant inspiration was Byron, the most lyrical and elevated embodiment of English Dandyism.

Anyone who undertakes to study the sources of English Dandyism—which the French *émigrés* brought back with them from London and used as a protection against the rising tide of bourgeois vulgarity, must recognize the part played in it by a French influence that dates from much further back. (It is rather the same with tennis and golf, which came to France from England only after having crossed the Channel in the other direction much earlier.)

Barbey d'Aurevilly identified as the originators of the Dandyist movement 'the courtiers of Charles II who drank from French champagne glasses a lotus bloom that produced forgetfulness of their country's sombre and religious customs.' In self-defence against the Puritanism which, at their return home, threatened to bend them to its stifling rule, these men appealed to the example of the French libertines; and these had already made use of scepticism and a cult of the free personality in order to resist the Catholic, anti-Protestant, anti-individualist wave which was seeking to repress the independence won in the sixteenth century. Barbey was justified in ranking Pascal with Méré and the Duke de Roannes as a precursor of Dandyism; and again he was perspicacious in picking out Lauzun, on account of his 'originality' and of his mixture of '*honnête homme*' and '*homme singulier*', as a 'Dandy before Dandyism'. Under the Régence the unbridled, noisy and provocative reaction against the restraints imposed by Louis XIV took a form not unlike the opposition of the English court aristocracy to the Roundheads. And now, at the beginning of the nineteenth century, the aristocrats, whether of birth or of intellectual power, defended themselves in the same way against the bourgeois conventionality which, first with the Revolution and then with the Empire, had settled a heavy cloak over France.

Dandyism proper took shape in England in about 1810, crossed to France as early as 1813 (according to Lady Morgan[20]), and triumphed in the person of d'Orsay—who was born in 1801 and was therefore Delacroix's contemporary. To a large extent it merely drifted into social life and produced the 'fashionable'; the definition of Dandy in the 1835 edition of the *Dictionnaire de l'Académie* is: 'Word taken from the English, designating, in France, a fop obsessed with dress, a man with an affected appearance.' And indeed Delacroix was not insensitive to this external aspect: not only did he dress, all his life long, with the strictest and most sober elegance, but he boasted of having been one of those who introduced English fashions of dress to Paris. Baudelaire, in the article published after the painter's death, tells us how he 'used to confess that in his youth he had given himself up with pleasure to the more material vanities of Dandyism and used to tell with a smile, yet not without a certain vainglory, that, together with his friend Bonington, he had worked hard to introduce the taste for English styles of shoes and clothes among young men of elegance.'[21]

Yet what he admired in the English was a conception of a man's conduct as a whole. In Bonington he valued his 'British *sang-froid*' which, he said, was 'imperturbable' yet 'did not deprive him of any of the qualities that make life agreeable'. This was the human example he tried to resemble. In addition, before Bonington's, the influence of M. Auguste had made itself felt. Mérimée, who also came under it, described his 'real affability' but also his refusal of 'extreme intimacy' and his 'somewhat cold expression, whose correctness indeed forbade any familiarity' even after long acquaintance. Delacroix to some extent modelled himself on this. Rivet depicts him at their first meeting, which was probably at the house of Baron Gérard, as 'thin, delicate, with a rather cold and reserved countenance, but with a simplicity that did not exclude elegance.' Nothing, here, of the romantic dauber. 'His aim apparently was to avoid being confused with those heroes of the studio, those dishevelled Raphaels who think they can attain originality by eccentricity.' Baudelaire wrote of his manner with admiration, saying that 'he also derived from himself, that is to say from his genius and the consciousness of his genius—far more than from his long experience of society—an assurance, a politeness which, like a prism, admitted every colour, from the most cordial affability to the most irreproachable insolence. He possessed a good twenty different ways of saying *"mon cher monsieur"*, which to a practised ear represented a singular scale of feeling.'[22] This might just as well be a description of Talleyrand, of whom it is also recorded that he could ascend and descend all the scales of politeness when he had guests to dinner and was presenting a dish for their pleasure. Baudelaire's conclusion was: 'Eugène Delacroix, although he was a man of genius, or because he was a man of genius, had in him much of the Dandy.'[23]

Delacroix would have been the first to agree. On 11 September 1841 he wrote jestingly to George Sand from Trouville that his doctor had diagnosed atony, and that this must be interpreted as lack of *tonus*—'of tone not of *bon ton*, please; a Dandy of my standing has provided himself with plenty of this, and it is by this that Hippolytus is known in Greece.' A Dandy he certainly was, and he said so clearly—but chiefly in his refusal to believe that one could deserve the name, 'as many unthinking people seem to believe', by 'an immoderate taste for dress and material elegance'. And it was Barbey d'Aurevilly who laid it down that 'to the perfect Dandy these things are only a symbol of the aristocratic superiority of his spirit.'

The term 'aristocrat' is, it is true, as equivocal as the term 'Dandy'. Its value has been considerably debased since 1789, for it has become the symbol of a class and of the ill-founded pretension to surpass other men. But etymologically the word applies only to a justified pretension: it signifies the pre-eminence of the better, the superior man. It implies a rejection of the flattery of the masses, with all the affected vulgarity and demagogic appeal that goes with it, and a belief that it is the duty of anyone capable of doing so to set an example to the masses, to keep before them a perpetual inspiration to rise through being exacting towards oneself. This does not exclude, but rather, demands, that 'absolute simplicity' in which Barbey saw 'the best way of distinguishing oneself'. It was in this sense that Delacroix was both a Dandy and an aristocrat.

By this moral application, the French type of Dandyism became distinguished from the English, which usually covered up emptiness under a perfect observation of social ritual. French Dandyism, on the contrary, sought in sobriety and dignity the discipline that is the means to inner intensity. It aimed at deserving both the respect of other people and self-respect. In this Baudelaire owed a great deal to Delacroix, and Banville's portrait of the former in his *Souvenirs* applies perfectly to the latter: 'He dressed like Brummel . . . with a perfectly correct English elegance uncommon at that time among the romantics; he had and displayed the highest degree of self-respect.'

## *Intensity balanced by Discipline*

This respect implied an obligation to develop 'in oneself something greater than what is visible', to use an expression of Barbey's.[24] If, as Philarète Chasles asserted, the English dandy, 'from the age of fifteen to the age of sixty' never 'experienced an emotion',[25] the French Dandy regarded his own outward conventionality, in all its refinement, as simply a way to the more complete mastery and possession of an inner life developed in secret. This he pursued by cultivating both originality, which vindicates the self, and intensity, which is its force. Delacroix, uniting as he did outward coldness and inner fire, is a perfect model of the Dandy; he might have said, like Baudelaire: 'You think me cold and do not see that I am imposing on myself an artificial calm.'[26] This impassivity, as it attained undisputed dominance, produced in France the Parnassiens: on that day romanticism was dead. But in Delacroix romanticism had only been submitted to a rule: it was still intact in all its seething life and the exaltation it demanded of the sensory faculties. All those who knew the artist were struck by this. Madame Ancelot detected, behind all his 'grace, restraint and reserve', a genius composed of 'impulsiveness, fire and inspiration.'[27] Gautier similarly, in his *Histoire du Romantisme*, saw Delacroix as 'more alive than anyone to the fever of his time . . . an uneasy, tumultuous, lyrical, disordered, paroxysm-ridden genius', but all this behind the 'coldness' he affected. Delacroix cannot be understood without this mixture. In his imagination, as in the hand that held the paint-brush, there was the 'frenzy' of which he still spoke at the age of fifty-six[28]—and to which the 'daily frenzy' invoked by Baudelaire corresponds.[29] And this frenzy must be reinforced by every means. Baudelaire went so far as to say:[30] 'It is essential to be always intoxicated. Everything lies in that. It is the one and only thing,'—meaning to go to the utmost limits of oneself, and to extract from oneself, as from an instrument played with a violence that almost breaks the strings, the most strident, startling and unexpected notes. But this reflection also was one which Delacroix had expressed more than once.[31] 'How comes it that, in a half-intoxicated state, certain men—and I am one of them—acquire a lucidity of vision far greater, in many cases, than they have when they are calm?' And on another day[32] he adds: 'Happy are those who, like Voltaire

XXI WOMEN OF ALGIERS
*1834 Oil on canvas. 71 x 90 (180 x 229)*
*Louvre, Paris*

and other great men, have been able to reach this inspired condition while drinking water and eating moderately.' Delacroix never consented to join 'the people who make themselves drunk on opium and hashish, who arrive at exalted states of mind that are frightening, who have perceptions that are totally unknown to the man of *sang-froid*, etc.' He left all that to Baudelaire, or to De Quincey, though not disdaining the glass of wine which, on an empty stomach, whips up the nerves.

While a torrent must have a slope and water flowing down it, there must also be banks to canalize and prevent the water from losing itself in the ground. Although the British Dandies were merely examples of fruitless elegance, luckily there was also Byron. No-one could go further than he in exalting the inner fire, and yet, as Mérimée observed:[33] 'He had that faculty which distinguishes the poet—I mean that in the midst of the most impetuous stirrings of passion, he could observe himself and make a study of himself which he was later able to use.' There is no such thing as valid creative work unless the stream of molten lava finds a solid mould to cool it and give it shape. The forces of expansion and of firmness must be balanced.

Baudelaire, who understood Delacroix so well and recognized in him many of the things to which he himself aspired, stressed this complementary dualism, which he found in Mérimée as well: 'It was', he said in his *L'Art romantique*, 'the same apparent, slightly affected coldness, the same cloak of ice covering a shrinking sensibility and an ardent passion for the good and the beautiful.'[34]

Baudelaire also found another plane on which this complementary dualism could be identified, when his imagination showed him that the complete man keeps the gift of childhood—which experiences things intensely, 'sees everything as new . . . is always drunk'[35]—and so remains in touch with the gifts of inspiration, yet is able to add to these the virtues of maturity, its possession of 'virile senses and an analytical mind'. But in saying this he was surely passing on to us, once more, an echo of things he had heard Delacroix himself say.[36] And it was Delacroix to whom Baudelaire pointed as the best example of this achievement, which several generations had dreamed of, since he had 'immense passion together with a formidable willpower', but was also 'coldly determined to seek the means of expressing passion in the most clearly visible way.'[37]

Thus Dandyism proposed a type of human being who would pursue a single, tense and complete equilibrium, in his day to day behaviour as in his idea of art, in which he would combine romanticism and classicism, and in his morality, according to which a man's value would depend both on his inner wealth and on his firmness of will. Not only was Delacroix an incarnation of this type, but he included among his friends almost all those of his time who have left this image behind them—such as M. Auguste and Géricault among his elders, Stendhal and Mérimée among his companions of his own age, and Baudelaire among the younger men whom he deeply influenced. There were exceptions: with Vigny,

XXII WOMEN OF ALGIERS
*1849 Oil on canvas. 35 x 44 (084 x 111)*
*Musée Fabre, Montpellier*

his contemporary, and with Barbey d'Aurevilly who was Baudelaire's, he was hardly acquainted, if at all. All these men, whether painters or writers, applied this same concept of life and art to their techniques of expression; and they all, in varying degrees, came under the English influence. Delacroix is, as it were, the point at which they join.

M. Auguste had impressed him in his youth, and he continued to see him
during a good quarter of a century, for the *Journal* still mentions an exchange of
visits in 1849 and M. Auguste died in 1850. It is a sad glimpse that we catch
of 'the poor man sitting in his dusty armchair, alone in the middle of that great
dark glory-hole.' One wonders if this vision had not something to do with the
*Michelangelo* which Delacroix painted only two years later. pl 180

Géricault, as we know from Silvestre, attracted Delacroix 'by his politeness and elegance', but was also, as the *Journal* tells us, regarded by him as 'the greatest artist of our time'. And what, in fact, did Delacroix find in his painting if not the combination of a bitter, apparently unbridled violence with a constant, exaltation of the technical mastery which controls and overpowers that brute force? And what in his technique if not, similarly, an enclosing outline, imprisoning the impulsive force of the muscles?

As for Mérimée, another faithful friend of M. Auguste, Delacroix saw him pl 175
regularly until about 1840. The memories they shared were indeed many—
meetings at the houses of Gérard, the Misses Clarke, of Madame Ancelot,[38] and
other meetings also at many 'small dinner parties *en famille* and with a few other
original spirits' such as Musset and Vieil-Castel: exquisite supper-parties rather
than dinners, often held at the Café Anglais, and lacking neither dazzling
conversation, nor gastronomic refinements, nor the presence of ladies of easy
virtue and of *petits rats de l'Opéra*. This was the last refuge of the spirit, according to 'poor Beyle' as Delacroix used to call him. But the three men must have pl 177
felt drawn together much more by the deep similarities of their minds, characters and styles, which, as both Silvestre and Baudelaire noted, came out even in
their ways of talking. Baudelaire discerned in them their blend of the 'perfect pl 176
gentleman without prejudices or passions' and 'the enlightened man' formed
'by the eighteenth century and by Voltaire much more than by Rousseau'[39]—the
type of mind that can compass both a free imagination and a controlled lucidity.
Of Delacroix, Baudelaire remarks that like Stendhal 'he was terrified of being
taken in'. He adds that 'A man to whom he could be more legitimately compared,
as regards outward appearance and manners, would be Monsieur Mérimée.'[40]

These men were peers and recognized this in each other. It should be emphasized, in passing, that Delacroix's keen vision had discerned the real value of Stendhal at a time when it was still grossly undervalued. In the biographical notes he entrusted to Piron, he said of Stendhal: 'I regard him as the writer who has perhaps the most distinction, with the best French style it is possible to use in speaking: I mean, among moderns.'

Vigny, on the other hand, is not mentioned by Delacroix either in his *Journal* or in his letters; their paths did not cross. And yet he surely read Vigny's poems when they appeared in the *Revue des Deux Mondes*. I can almost prove this: when Delacroix wrote in his *Journal* that 'man spends his life in the convulsions of uneasiness and in the lethargy of ennui', there is clearly a reminiscence of the splendid lines by Vigny that appeared, with his *Mont des Oliviers*, in the *Revue des Deux Mondes* on June 1844, in which he depicts man as suspended:

*Entre l'ennui du calme et des paisibles joies...*
*Entre la léthargie et les convulsions.*

Also, as we have seen, it seems very likely that Vigny, when he wrote that poem, had in mind Delacroix's picture of *Christ in Gethsemane*, the hanging of which in the church of Saint-Paul-and-Saint-Louis in 1827, after its exhibition at the Salon of that year, had made a considerable stir.

## *Dignity in Face of Destiny*

Vigny was the man whose thought seems nearest to that of Delacroix. Never had Stoicism and Dandyism been more closely associated. It would be interesting to trace the parallel between them—as also with their common inspiration in art and common master in Dandyism, Byron.[41] Even to touch on it brings us into that private recess where the soul of the Dandy—with its heightened sensations, dominant lucidity and clinching will—comes at last into the proudest solitude. This solitude in relation to human beings is like that of the great wild beasts. It is the way the lion keeps apart from the horde, though feeling that he is its leader. The image comes in Byron's *Manfred*: 'The lion is alone, and so am I.'

Vigny echoes Byron in his *Journal d'un poète*: 'The lion walks alone in the desert. So let the poet walk always.' Delacroix, who had already, in 1824,[42] spoken of the 'poet who lives in solitude' copied out, a quarter of a century later, this sentence from Balzac: 'Solitude is habitable only by the man of genius.'[43]

To this solitude in relation to human beings, enclosed by destiny and chosen by wisdom, is added the more frightening solitude in relation to nature. The sense of brotherhood and communion with nature felt by the romantic artist, the continual echo of his own heart which he believes he hears there, the *Einfühlung* on which the Germans were to found a theory of aesthetics, is unknown to the Dandy: his cold, lucid gaze dissipates these illusions. 'Nature', wrote Delacroix, 'does not bother about man, or his works, or in any way about his passage over the earth.'[44]

On the contrary, he writes, 'Man must be resolved to do constant violence to nature; and, on its side, nature is not behindhand . . . but seems impatient to shake off the masterpieces of man's imagination and hand.' The face which the world shows to mankind is an unfriendly and terrible one: 'Nature echoes our sad moods: the murmuring of the winds and sea, the long night with its terrors and its silence, the sunset with its melancholy, and solitude wherever one comes upon it—these arouse black thoughts, apprehensions of annihilation and destruction.'[45] Is this merely a mask over the face of God? Unfortunately, while 'all nature carries a burden and seems waiting to be relieved', and 'the whole world seems to be waiting for some kind of clear happiness . . . the Being of Beings scarcely ever shows to his creatures any but the angry side of his countenance.' Vigny sums this up towards the end of his *Mont des Oliviers*: *'La Terre, sans clartés, sans astre, et sans aurore. . . .'* He too had an intense feeling of how nature pursues her way without any point in common with that of man. In *La Maison du berger* he speaks of *'tout un monde fatal, écrasant et glacé'* (a whole world ruled by fate, crushing, ice-cold), and of how the heart, weighed down by this, 'drags along, struggling, like a wounded eagle'. If nature could speak, it would only be to say:

*Je roule avec dédain, sans voir et sans entendre,*
*A côté des fourmis les populations.*

(I neither look nor listen, but drive on,
Disdainfully, the swarm of men and ants.)

Delacroix also reflected on the common fate of human beings and ants, when he was at Champrosay.[46] 'We are shut up all together, animals, men and vegetation, in this great box, the world.' And man is not much more developed, is a 'mass of ignorance and brutality'. 'What is there about us that could interest the providence that has placed us in this strange world—to adorn it, so they tell me?' As for God, 'If man is his favourite among his works, why abandon him to hunger, filth, massacre and all the terrors of a hazardous life? . . . How can the God who will not allow the soul of a foolish Patagonian to be lost concern Himself so little about his passage over this earth?'[47]

Vigny would reply: 'only with a cold silence, the eternal silence of the divinity'—the silence which he described in his *Mont des Oliviers* where Christ calls upon his Father. . . . And Delacroix returned on 15 March 1853 to the thoughts he had in his youth, when 'saddened by the spectacle of which we are witnesses, and in which we are ourselves the actors and the victims', he had exlaimed: 'How can this world, which is so beautiful, include so much horror! The stars seem to lean from heaven over those peaceful dwelling-places, but the passions that inhabit them, the vices and the wars are merely lulled to sleep, or are awake and watching in the shadows. . . .'

What, then, is the attitude of the man who is conscious of being thus deserted, yet conscious also of his dignity? Vigny gives the answer: 'The just man will oppose disdain to absence.' He will listen to what the wolf can teach him: 'Suffer and die without a word.' But Byron had cited, besides the wolf that 'dies in silence', the camel, that 'labours with the heaviest load' and had said:

*If they,*
*Things of ignoble or of savage mood,*
*Endure and shrink not, we, of nobler clay,*
*May temper it to bear—it is but for a day.*

XXIII MELMOTH (INTERIOR OF A DOMINICAN CONVENT)
*1831 Oil on canvas. 51 x 64 (130 x 163)*
*Philadelphia Museum of Art, W.P. Wilstach Collection*

Delacroix was not far removed from these two men and he wrote to Villot, on 26 September 1840, about the intellect and the heart:

'Even though one suffers a great deal in both of these, it is to rise the better above the vulgarity and the thousand necessities of human life. . . . Look only in yourself, to find the elements you need.'

In this silence into which he withdraws, and in the ensuing solitude, a man arrives at the ultimate confrontation with the self. To this he must henceforth devote his strength and his cares, finding in his dignity supreme reason for living. Even if the world answers the anguished appeal of the human race with an unbroken silence and besets it with 'that universal conspiracy of matter, eternally acting against the products of the inventions of genius', a man has at least always the consolation of admiring his own constancy, or of enjoying greatly and steadily the variety of fruits that have emanated from him.[48]

To resign oneself to the need of standing firm in face of destiny, to create relentlessly the best that is latent in one's soul, to answer life's refusals with gifts in the shape of one's works—such was the conclusion Delacroix brought to the train of thinking which Byron had started. Manfred, with the same inflexible pride, had relied entirely on himself: [49]

*'There is no power. . . can exorcise*
*From out the unbounded spirit the quick sense*
*Of its own sins, wrongs, sufferance, and revenge*
*Upon itself, there is no future pang*
*Can deal that justice on the self condemn'd*
*He deals on his own soul.'*

And he concluded:

*'Away! I'll die as I have lived—alone.*

This first, pre-eminently Byronic Dandyism came to an end with Delacroix and Vigny. Baudelaire,[50] who was full of it and had learned it from Delacroix, in time began to take a different direction, the one also taken by Barbey d'Aurevilly. From the Promethean Dandyism—still faithful to the rationalism of the *siècle des lumières* and ending in a stoic resignation in face of the silence of the Creation—these men passed on to a Christian Dandyism. This, in the case of Baudelaire, was sometimes coloured with supernaturalism or even mysticism, as the result of a new influence, that of Joseph de Maistre. 'De Maistre and Edgar Poe have taught me to think', said Baudelaire, [51]thus indicating clearly the influences which, in his case, followed that of Delacroix, dominant in the years immediately after 1845.

Going back to the beginning of the movement, we have to recognize the great shadow of Chateaubriand. He too had been strongly impressed by England and its Dandyism during the emigration in 1795; but he remained attached to the Christian faith and immune from the influence of Byron. When Baudelaire, on

XXIV THE BATTLE OF TAILLEBOURG (Sketch)
*1837 Oil on canvas. 21 x 26 (053 x 066)*
*Louvre, Paris*

the cover of his *Paradis artificiels*, announces as 'in the press' a book on *La famille des dandies: ou Chateaubriand, de Custine, Paul de Molènes, Barbey d'Aurevilly*, his view of the line of descent is clear. In 1860, in a letter dated 3 December to Calonne, he announces his intention of 'treating Chateaubriand from a new point of view, as the father of Dandyism.' From then onwards, to the 'tragedy of which each man is the hero', and which is still the substance of Dandyism, there is added an 'eternal confidant, namely God'.[52] This brings us to a new chapter of Dandyism, which is not the one whose pages Delacroix turned even though, through Baudelaire, his influence was still powerfully felt.

This cultivation of the Self and of its resources, which are different in each person and therefore unique, the pursuit of the gift one can make to other people by embodying it in works of art matured by the mind, was the aim Delacroix had adopted for his life: it helped him to face his lucid and sad view of the human condition. Coming from the studios of the classicist painters and drawing away from these, he had at first been seduced by all the new impulses, greedy for life, which he had felt quivering within him. But his very conception of life had soon shown him the danger of too exclusive an abandonment to a delight which had at first intoxicated him, hurling him into a headlong ride through the land of passions, of tragedy and of the imagination. To convey his conception into the soul of the onlooker, he had worked out a technique of fusions, of exchanges of light, colour and atmosphere. And now approaching maturity awakened in him the compensating concern for form, structure and composition. In one and the same year, with the sketch for his *Boissy d'Anglas* and that for his *Mirabeau and Dreux-Brézé*, he appeared to launch out simultaneously in the pl 183 two directions: it was as though he was still swaying, undecided, between the romantic escape and classical obedience. But the human position he had adopted demanded that he should reconcile these in a wider synthesis, which would harmonize with that of his moral life.

An unexpected event, his journey to Morocco, was to bring the determining shock. This set him free from what threatened to be an *impasse*; it enabled him to discover the new vision for which his art was waiting.

# NOTES ON THE PLATES TO CHAPTER V

*The inner man* Chopin, with whom Delacroix was on terms of warmest friendship and admiration, was to him the type of the complete man who conceals behind a refined distinction of manner a soul on fire with inspiration, yet governed by intelligence (pl 172).

*172 Frédéric Chopin, 1838. Louvre, Paris.*

*The Dandy* Delacroix lived in the circle of the Dandies, who took pride not only in an elegance that was inspired by English models, but also in a sensibility responsive to all the emotions of art. Baron Schwiter, with whom he became friendly early on, was a typical member of this group of young romantic painters fascinated by England (pls 173, VIII).

*173 Baron Schwiter, c. 1827 (detail). The National Gallery, London.*

*The balanced man* Dignity of manners and of character, intensity of feeling, lucidity of thought and self-mastery were equally important to Delacroix (pl 174).

*174 Self-portrait, 1842. Uffizi Gallery, Florence.*

*Spiritual friendships* Delacroix kept up close relations with certain famous writers who, like him, valued what may be called a cold and controlled intensity: among those of his own age, Stendhal (pl 177) and Mérimée (pl 175), and among younger men Baudelaire (pl 176).

175 ROCHARD: *Prosper Mérimée, 1853. Musée Carnavalet, Paris.*

*176 Photograph of Charles Baudelaire by Étienne Carjat, c. 1863. Bibliothèque Nationale, Paris.*

*177 Stendhal (Henri Beyle) in a contemporary engraving.*

*Constancy of character* Throughout his life Delacroix exhibited a rare mixture of an ardent temperament always on the *qui vive*—which made people compare him to a wild beast—with the discipline of good manners (pls 178, 179).

*178 Daguerreotype of Eugène Delacroix, 1842. Bibliothèque Nationale, Paris.*

*179 Photograph of Eugène Delacroix by Nadar, 1861. Bibliothèque Nationale, Paris.*

*The depths of the inner being*

Behind that benevolent yet chilly manner of his, Delacroix concealed a soul tormented by all the problems of the human predicament and inclined towards the darkest melancholy. He embodied it in his paintings of *Christ in the Garden of Gethsemane,* which he repeated several times (pl 181, 182, 336), and in that of Michelangelo crushed by the loneliness of creative work (pl 180).

180 *Michelangelo in his Studio, 1850. Musée Fabre, Montpellier.*

181 *Study for 'Christ in the Garden of Gethsemane', for the Church of Saint-Paul-and-Saint-Louis, 1826-7. Cabinet des Dessins, Louvre, Paris.*

182 *Sketch for 'Christ in the Garden of Gethsemane'.*

*Violence and coldness*

The dualism of Delacroix's character, which brought together impulsiveness and coldness, explains the dualism of his art. Though recognized as a leader of romanticism, he was driven to go beyond romanticism and to achieve an art that was lucid and ordered—that is to say, classical. For the competition held to decide who should decorate the Chamber in the Palais-Bourbon, he painted in 1831 not only his vigorous and indeed violent *Boissy d'Anglas* (pl XVI), but also his balanced and rectilinear *Mirabeau* (pls 183, 184).

183 *Mirabeau and the Marquis of Dreux-Brézé, 1831. Ny Carlsberg Glyptothek, Copenhagen.*

184 *Sketches for Mirabeau, c. 1831. Cabinet des Dessins, Louvre, Paris.*

172

173

174

175

176

177

178

179

180

181

182

183

184

# VI BLAZE OF NOON

DELACROIX SET SAIL for Morocco on 11 January 1832 with M. de Mornay. It was the beginning of the most overwhelming experience of his life. The journey seems to have been decided upon at the beginning of December 1831, for on 8 December he wrote to Villot: 'I shall probably be off to Morocco next week. You may laugh, but it is quite true, and I am in a whirl.' What he expected was that the journey would bring him the revelation of a completely strange world of which, like all the romantics, he had often dreamed—the East, a 'different' world in which he would find the shock of the new and the absence of the old traditions which had become stifling. What he found, in fact, was a true understanding of those traditions, a complete renewal of them. The obstacle that was still holding him up, the impossibility (as it seemed at that time) of uniting romanticism and classicism, was about to vanish, and a fresh, surprising reality would show him their natural union.

## *Morocco: Renewal of Sensation*

The historians of Delacroix have already suggested that he was brought into
pl 185 contact with M. de Mornay through theatrical circles—and, in particular,
186 through M. de Mornay's mistress, Mlle. Mars. A valuable and as yet unpublished series of letters of hers to Randouin, *Sous-Préfet* of Dunkirk, which runs from 3 February to 31 March 1832, supplies confirmation of this: I have been able to consult it through the kindness of M. Alfred Dupont, who has since published the passage I quote.[1] Mlle. Mars, then fifty-three years of age, writes to her young lover after an evening party she had just given:

'He left on 1 January at three in the morning. . . . We had had our usual New Year's Eve gathering, joined by his travelling companion, Eugène La Croix (*sic*), a young painter who has talent, wit, social graces and, they say, an excellent character—which is not to be despised when people have to spend four or five months together.'

She discloses that it was Duponchel, the director of the Opéra, who had suggested Delacroix to take the place of Isabey, the first choice: Isabey had declined the offer because he had already been to Morocco. 'When I heard this, I asked Duponchel to look about among his artist friends for someone who might welcome such a journey.' The choice fell on Delacroix, perhaps on the recommendation of Armand Bertin. A small historical point is thus cleared up.

Charles de Mornay, who had been a Gentleman of the Bedchamber to Charles X, had just been charged by the new French government with an embassy to Muley Abd-er-Rhaman, the Sultan of Morocco, of whom France was now a neighbour, having launched out into the Algerian adventure a bare two years before. The journey started badly, with snow at Lyons and Avignon, high winds and rain at Marseilles. From Toulon the crossing took thirteen days, in the course of which Delacroix caught enchanting glimpses of the 'delightful coasts' of Minorca, Majorca and Malaga, 'the kingdom of Granada'—his first sight of Spain. Unfortunately, fear of cholera made quarantine more severe than usual, and, although they touched at Algeciras, they could only look at the Spaniards from a distance: even so, Delacroix was already struck by the 'picturesqueness' of the houses and the beggars. 'The whole of Goya was there, palpitating all about me,' he wrote to Pierret on 24 January; but, he added, 'this did not last long', for on that same day he was 'at last before Tangier'. Here the travellers were welcomed by Amin Bias, the Sultan's Minister for Foreign Affairs and Finance, of whom Delacroix painted a water-colour portrait. 'You can imagine', he says, still in the letter to Pierret, 'my pleasure in seeing for the first time those whom I had come so far to see.' The next day he explored the town: 'I am quite overwhelmed by what I have seen. . . . I am like a man dreaming, who sees things he is afraid to see escape him.' There were receptions, 'black, yellow, green *marabouts*', soldiers and 'the oddest military fanfares'—and, in addition, the Jewish women, who were 'admirable . . . pearls of Eden!'

pl 187

pl 189

This man whose habit was to escape into the dreams of his imagination and to let these carry him into the 'elsewhere' of the past or of distant places, suddenly saw this hitherto inaccessible elsewhere rushing at him like a boomerang and becoming concrete actuality. He had been used to leaving reality for dreams: now, before his eyes, the dreams were crowding into reality. Delacroix was at first disturbed, thrown off his bearings: an intensity normally sought only in the inner life cannot be restored to sensations with impunity. What was more, there was nothing Delacroix found more repugnant than realism: to his way of thinking, the outside world was there to provide a vocabulary, a visible and communicable form, for what the artist carried confusedly within him; it must never impose itself on him and become the substance of his work. 'It is from the cruel reality of objects that I am trying to escape when I take refuge in the sphere of artistic creation,' he had stated; and again: 'A man with a soul needs, to fill it, something other than external objects, which are nothing to the soul—something other than that which attracts the common run of men and is not worth the shadow of a feeling.'[2]

And indeed Delacroix's fear that, in the dialogue between self and nature, between the inner and the outer world, the first would succumb to the pressure of the second, never really left him. In 1853 he still comes back to it:[3] 'The model draws everything to it and there is nothing left of the painter.' And in Morocco reality fell upon him: in his letter to Pierret from Tangier on 29 February 1832 there is a sentence that reveals his panic in face of something that imposes itself

pl 191

on him too imperiously; he speaks of 'the living, emphatic sublime which fills the streets here and assassinates you with its reality.' He was delighted, yet the very wildness of his delight caused in him a sort of terror, since it was invading him from outside and threatening to disturb his own reality.

At the same time he was discovering that sensations can, in their novelty, become a source of poetry, when they are no longer a reminder of what is already known and a return to a sterile inventory, but set the whole nervous system in an uproar and strike it like the strings of an instrument, drawing from it a melody. He took 'rides in the country round about'[4] and found that the sensations he received had a strength he had long forgotten. 'In the midst of natural scenery of such vigour, I am experiencing sensations like those I had in childhood. Perhaps a confused memory of the southern sunshine, which I saw when I was a small child, is awakening in me.' It seems possible that at the moment when he was in danger of being drawn by romanticism into the closed and narrow realm of the imaginary, these first days in Morocco showed Delacroix that sensations, far from neutralizing an artist, can supply him with a new intensity. Always, in his painting, he had recourse to exact details—to an ornamental hem on a dress, to a sparkling earring—but on condition that they should be striking and that, by being so, they should give that authenticity to the vision born of the spirit, give it credibility (as Paul Bourget was to say later, discussing the novel); on this condition realistic details, instead of dispersing the vision by their contrast with it, make its presence more strongly felt.

But in real life this presence is soon dulled, and this is another weakness in sensations—which, though they have an essential part to play in art, cannot be its basis. In Morocco Delacroix experienced the truth of this also; already on 20 March, after being shut up in Meknes for several days, he was aware of it and wrote to Pierret: 'I am finding that sensations wear out in the long run, and the picturesque assaults your eyes so strongly at every step that in the end one becomes insensitive to it.' Art needs to be nourished by deeper realities, more fully inherent in the artist himself. Morocco would, in fact, confirm these in him and even reveal them to him, for he had not always been aware of them till then.

Apart from the picturesqueness, which at first delighted him but became dulled by habit, the sensations flooding in on him helped him, by their very visual intensity, to grasp more firmly the conception of art towards which he felt attracted—and at the same time to eliminate what remained of the domination exercised over him by the prevailing aesthetic of the French School of painting:
pl 199 that of form. In Morocco the eye no longer had time to take its bearings, to mix with what it perceived a memory of the forms that had been learned, to impose upon fact the established accumulation of thought and, with it, a conventional design. The eye was struck instantaneously by shocks so violent and direct that, in a revelation that anticipated Impressionism, they reduced themselves to a single experience of light and of patches of colour: if, sometimes, they reconstituted form, it was only through the accident of something opaque standing out against the brightness. The light in Morocco was so dazzling that Delacroix at first thought his sight would not stand it; on 8 February he mentioned this uneasiness to Pierret: 'The only thing is, I am rather worried about my

*Fig 12* TWO SQUATTING ARABS. Pen drawing. Cabinet des Dessins, Louvre, Paris.

eyes. . . . Although the sun has not reached its full strength, its brightness and the reflections from the houses, which are all of them whitewashed, tire me excessively.'

The notes he took at the time (and which André Joubin did well to place in the deplorable gap in the *Journal* from 1824 to 1847) show clearly that perceptions of colour and light were of primary importance to Delacroix at that time. The journey to Morocco reinforced and justified them, and from then onwards his interest in them was to increase constantly: it is this that makes him the decisive forerunner of Impressionism. On the first day after his arrival he noted, at the end of an alley, 'men sitting under a kind of arch, standing out in brown against a piece of sky'. . . a 'yellow caftan', another that was 'dark blue', another 'canary yellow', and again 'green sleeves', a material that was 'amaranth purple' or 'scarlet', and 'a red band . . . and bridle'. Nature was simply a symphony of tones: on 29 January 'the sea a deep fig-like blue-green, the hedges yellow on top because of the bamboos, green at the bottom because of the aloes'. Sometimes it makes him giddy—as did, on 8 March at Alcassar-el-Kebir, 'standards . . . designs on varied grounds, red, blue, green, yellow, white; others with foot-soldiers in striped clothes. . . .' Surely no artist before had noted tones with such acuteness.

Colour felt in this way is no longer a means of clothing form, of defining volumes, helping to isolate them in space; on the contrary, it is part of space; it emanates from and returns to the light which fills it. It is the vibration of that light, and is inseparable from it. Already on 26 January at Tangier he was associating them together in depicting an interior: 'The pasha's alcove had a ceiling with radiating ribs, etc.; the anti-chamber small painted sections.' Another note, on 1 April, says: 'Vivid rose colour of the figure against the white wall,' and again: 'Reached the market-place, looked back along the dark alley. fig 12 Crouching Moslems vividly lit.' He was struck again and again by white—the white of a whitewashed wall, of a marble, of a tile, of a piece of cloth or of 'the almond trees in blossom'. It drove him wild with delight when he reached pls 195, 196 Meknes on 15 March: 'Patches of white over the whole hill. Shapes of all sorts, white always dominant.' Shade was no longer a dark atmosphere hiding, as in Rembrandt, the mystery of things, or containing, as in the *Boissy d'Anglas*, their seething and menacing horror: it entered into a clashing dialogue with the light, answering it and sending it hurtling back. On 21 February Delacroix xxv, page 273 saw the Jewish wedding: 'White sleeves, background of shadow.' But often, through reflected gleams, this rough dialogue became a harmony, a conspiracy: 'The shadows full of reflections, white in the shadows.' The two effects combine: 'Cast shadow full of reflections and standing out against the wall, bright yellow reflected light.' And on the first page of the notebook,[5] dated 2 March, we find: 'Men in bright light at the side. Shadow of white objects filled with blue reflections. Red of the saddles and turban, almost black.'

At the start, then, this born colourist drank deep of the combinations of colours unknown to him and unforeseen. They were those which Islam had spread from Persia to Spain. Delacroix spent some twenty days at Meknes, waiting to be received by the Sultan, guarded 'like a prisoner' and 'living in a Moorish palace adorned with tiles and mosaics.' He experienced delights which were still as fresh as ever, a century later, for Matisse and for modern art.

## *A True Romanticism*

There seems to be a real and important contrast between the West and the East (at least in so far as the West knew the East, during many centuries—and that was chiefly the part influenced by Persia). The West, in its Mediterranean civilization, developed the transcription of the visible through forms: it strove to give things definition through modelling and outline, to separate them from the surrounding medium, and to find the beautiful in harmonious proportions between them. Colour, of which it was far from being unaware, was to the Western mind chiefly a supplementary means of distinguishing the forms from their parts or one another. But Eastern art, especially that of distant Iran (first transcribed through Byzantine intermediaries and then spread by Islam), assigned itself an opposite aim: it sought not so much to satisfy the intellect's need for clarity as to produce sensations that would be agreeable both through their intensity and their combination; the material of objects and the light in which it was bathed heightened one another by sparkling brilliance, and colour was the sumptuous path of their exchanges.

In consequence, Eastern art, instead of striving to distinguish and analyze, plays upon variations of intensity and develops an overall feeling of a complex but simultaneous experience: its end product is a state of sensibility in the onlooker. The result is that, when art passes from the visible to the mental, that of the West tends towards an intellectual play of ideas, things also being distinct, clearly defined, coherent and logically articulated; while that of the East tends towards absorption in an experience—and, in its highest manifestations, is directed not so much towards reasoned thinking as towards spiritual revelation.

It will be objected that, in the West, medieval art had much the same aims and used much the same means; but this art, precisely, was filled with the lessons of the East, since the Christian faith had its origin there, and since the prestige of Byzantium and the traffic of the pilgrimages and crusades kept Eastern influence alive. This indeed was one of the reasons why classicism repudiated the Middle Ages, in its desire to go back to the pure heritage of Antiquity. It was also one of the reasons why romanticism, in its revolt against what had come to seem a dry intellectualism, instinctively had recourse to the maligned Middle Ages—and to an East which had been reduced to the picturesqueness of 'chinoiserie'. It was this double appeal that had attracted Delacroix to romanticism in spite of his profound reserves: he felt that here was a means of getting in touch with the soul and setting it in motion, of achieving a total perception of the self and the world. And this, as we have seen, very soon produced in him—in spite of the influence of Géricault—a reaction away from form isolated and defined by outline, and brought out in him his contrary vocation for colour and *chiaroscuro.* The content of classical and traditional painting was found by reflection, that of the painting which Delacroix desired and was to achieve was experienced and was imposed by emotion.

But romanticism exaggerated and falsified emotion: it soon strayed away from the sincerity, the 'naïveté' so often invoked by Delacroix: it cultivated effect, and effect easily slid into adulteration: it often became artificial. And Delacroix loathed this impurity, this suspect magniloquence. Although with all the force of his instinct he rejected the abstract limits and conventions of classicism, he could feel how far the true classicists—those of the past—possessed, over the romantics, the crushing superiority of probity, clarity and balance, the high virtues of art. This, as we have seen, had made him hesitate and refuse to choose one or the other of two styles, each of which both attracted him and drove him into the opposite camp.

In Morocco he discovered that he had been shut up in an artificial and absurd dilemma: in reality things were much simpler and more natural. Intensity—which romanticism championed against regularity and order, but sought in violence, tumult, darkness and a frantic chaos of passions—was part and parcel of real life; and life flourished in colour and light: why indeed should life find its fulfilment only in the vehemence of the morbid and not in the strength of health? Why should that energy which Géricault already had made his object be necessarily gloomy? Could it not burst forth in the life-giving splendour of nature? Was it not this that Rubens, Gros and Géricault—Delacroix's guides and gods—had celebrated when, in their pictures of horses, they had exalted the free action of animal force?

And indeed 'the wildest imaginations of Gros and Rubens' seemed to him almost insignificant beside a spectacle which he witnessed in his first week at Tangier—those horses fighting on the sea-shore. He noted it down on 29 January and wrote to Pierret about it on 8 February. Later, in 1834, it inspired a picture of the *Encounter between Moorish Horsemen*—and again, as late as

1860, his *Arab Horses fighting in a Stable.* Strangely enough, by some presentiment, he had already in 1825 groped for this theme in his *Horses Fighting.*[6] The frantic life he had dreamed of during his feverish youth was now before his eyes. The pawing horses, their prodigious discharges of nervous energy and fury which threw them and their riders (when they had riders) into violent conflict: the men at full stretch in an action where din and speed were unrestrained and the flash of bright clothes mingled with that of the guns; the wild beasts with their concentration and fusion of animal power at its maximum: all this Delacroix had imagined—as also feminine voluptuousness—in the light of the East, and had foreseen it in his pictures of Greek horsemen, of the fights be-
pls 204, 206 tween the Giaour and the Pasha, and of his Odalisques. But now he saw it with his own eyes in its proper setting.

He had only to combine under the Moroccan sunshine his impressions of horses fighting, of Rubens, of the wild beasts he had studied with Barye in the Jardin des Plantes or at the Saint Cloud fair, to realize those symphonies of energy and ardour, his pictures of lion hunts, tiger hunts and animals fighting. The heart was already in him, but now the warm red blood that had still been lacking was supplied to him by Morocco.

He found it not only in the animals he saw but in the men and scenery, as he travelled further on into that new country. On 5 March the embassy had started on its journey to Meknes, where the Sultan had decided to receive it. They had hoped, for a moment, that the reception would take place in the then impenetrable Marrakesh. '*C'est furieusement l'Afrique à présent.*' A succession of escorts was sent by the various pashas: 'disorder, dust, din'. And there were many parades in their honour: 'Masses of people . . . music . . . endless shooting', 'the horses in the dust. The sun behind them. Arms stretching back in violent gesture.' Among the 'thousands of shots let off in our faces' there was no lack of 'random bullets whistling in the midst of the rejoicings.' All this
pl 207 gave him the theme for the *Arab Fantasias*, which he painted in 1832 (Mont-
208 pellier) and 1833 (Frankfurt, Städelsches Kunstinstitut) and for his *Moroccan Military Exercises* of 1847.

At Meknes on 15 March they were met by music and flags and deafening shots. After the tedious wait in the residence assigned to them they had their audience with the Sultan on 22 March, in the open air. Delacroix noted that the Sultan had a 'considerable resemblance to Louis-Philippe', though 'younger' and with a 'thick beard'.

On 5 April they began the journey back. And from Tangier Delacroix was
pl 202 able to go to Spain: on 16 May, after the usual quarantine, he landed at Cadiz,
200 and went to Seville. At every step he stumbled upon Murillo, Zurbarán and
Goya. But on 28 May he took ship again for Morocco. He left Tangier again
pl 190 on 10 June and, after brief calls at Oran (18 June) and Algiers (25 to 28 June) reached the quarantine station at Toulon on 5 July. Here he had a long and uncomfortable wait; but it gave him the leisure to put his sketches and impressions in order and to set down his principal memories in a series of eighteen water-colours. These Delacroix presented, as a token of well-merited gratitude, to M. de Mornay who had proved throughout a charming travelling companion.

Throughout the journey, as described in the notes he jotted down and the descriptions he sent to his friends, we meet with the scenes that were later to become pictures: 'The picturesque abounds here. At every step there are, ready made, pictures that would make the fortune and glory of twenty generations of painters.'[7] On 21 February it is the Jewish wedding, on 12 March the River Sebou, on 15 March the walls of Meknes—before which Delacroix was to depict his *Sultan of Morocco* and, later still, when the haze of memory and dream pls 223, 224
had risen about them, the *Disciples and Holy Women raising the Body of Saint Stephen*, painted in 1853. pl 226 On 23 March he saw 'men playing draughts' and on 30 March the Sultan sent those 'Jewish musicians from Mogador' who recur in the 1847 picture. Nor should we forget, among the subjects that were to nourish his art for the rest of his life, the women of Algiers. pl 212

It was indeed a harvest and sometimes it required considerable boldness to gather it in. At Meknes, in particular, 'the dress and appearance of a Christian', he reported to Pierret on 2 April, 'is so antipathetic to these people that one has always to be escorted by soldiers'—who were joined by 'a huge band of onlookers who are not sparing with such insults as dog, infidel, *caracco*, etc., and who jostle to get near me and pull faces at me from close to.' More than this, it was 'impossible to draw openly from nature, even a hovel'. As for going up on to the roof terrace, this 'exposes you to be stoned or shot at', since the women liked to spend their time on the roof-tops and 'the jealousy of the Moors is extreme'.

At Alcassar-el-Kebir on 8 June, Abu, the general escorting him, only just managed to save him from a furious Moor ('my alarm; we run for it; the sabre was already drawn'). Delacroix concludes: 'It needs all my curiosity to brave the curiosity of this scum';[8] but curiosity he certainly possessed: he was all eyes, he engraved what he saw in his memory and in his heart, and he took the risk of making many rapid sketches and furtive water-colours.

He soon saw that he had come upon more than a repertory of subjects. On his return he was no longer the same man. He said as much on 30 August in a letter to Villot, who was then at Champrosay:[9] now, he writes, Paris 'bores me profoundly: men and things appear to me in a quite different light since my journey.' He had gone outside our civilization, its routines and its discussions of sterile ideas. He had come face to face with life in its primitive truth and nakedness, and by this light he was forced to revise all his former convictions. He suddenly realized that he had escaped from the futile dilemma in which he had thought he was shut up. If, as romanticism postulates, real life was ardour and paroxysm, at least it was not so in the negative and unbalanced way currently imagined: at the same time, classicism, for all its powerful restraining action, was not the elimination of life—it too was life and part of the lesson of life.

XXV JEWISH WEDDING IN MOROCCO
*c. 1839 Oil on canvas. 41 x 55 (105 x 140)*
*Louvre, Paris*

Delacroix wrote on 29 February, also to Villot: 'If at any time you have a few months to spare, come to Barbary, you will find there the naturalness which is always disguised in our part of the world, and you will feel there the precious and rare influence of the sunshine, which gives a penetrating life to everything.'

The sun, Delacroix found, chases away the smoky shadows of romanticism, while naturalness has no need of the restricted rules of classicism. The 'penetrating life' of which he spoke was not only intensity freely put forth, but also a balanced harmony: these two aspects, usually treated as opposed, are both of them properties of life and are quite naturally united in it. But to find them one must go to the source. The peoples of North Africa 'are closer to nature in pl 210 a thousand ways: their clothes, the shape of their shoes. And so beauty is a part of all that they do.' Whereas we, who have perhaps not yet reached 'the end of what an advanced civilization can produce'. . . . 'we in our corsets, tight shoes and ridiculous casings are pitiable.'[10] Already Delacroix was beginning to move apart from Baudelaire, who was never to make the pilgrimage to the source and who, hostile to the natural, always took an extreme delight in modernism, in what he called '*la modernité*'[11]—which, in his case, always had something uneasy and tainted about it. Yet Baudelaire, although he considered that 'almost all our originality comes from the stamp which time imprints on our sensations',[12] was well aware, like Delacroix, that there was another kind of beauty. 'Modernity is the transitory, the fugitive, the contingent, one half of art' (that half which woos the eternal baroque)—but, he added, 'the other half is the eternal and immutable'[13] (to which the classicists laid claim). Delacroix, XIII, page 169 who had just painted his *Liberty Leading the People*, in which he himself (in a top hat) figured among the insurrectionists of 1830, might have gone with the poet in accepting this dualism, had he not had the eternal values revealed to him, living in the present day on the soil of Africa. To Théodore Gudin, the marine painter, who had gone to Morocco before him, he confided: 'I am really sorry, now, for those artists who have some imagination but are prevented from ever having any idea of the marvels of grace and beauty of those virgin and sublime natural scenes'[14]—scenes which had, he felt, not only grace but nobility. pl 211 And in describing the costume of the country to Duponchel, he remarked: 'It has an overwhelming quality of beauty and nobility.' Beauty, associated with grace and nobility, leads us away from the 'expressionist' and romantic arts, which associate beauty with intensity alone: it is surely the kind of beauty that we usually seek in classical Antiquity. But Delacroix found it in Morocco, found it as his heart had already told him it should be—very different from the beauty on which the followers of David had tried to impose a pedantic caricature.

XXVI THE SHIPWRECK OF DON JUAN
*1840 Oil on canvas. 53 x 77 (135 x 196)*
*Louvre, Paris*

The beautiful abounded there; but, as Delacroix wrote to Villot on 29 February, 'not the beautiful of which the fashionable pictures are so proud. The heroes of David and company would cut a poor figure, with their pink limbs, beside these children of the sun: but on the other hand—or so I like to think—the costume of the ancient world is better worn there.' He had felt this obscurely since he landed: a note made on 4 February records his first shock of pleasure at the Gelapia (as he spells it, phonetically), the costume of the people, of the merchants and the children. 'I remember this Gelapia', he wrote, 'a costume precisely like one from the ancient world, in a small picture in the museum: hood, etc. The cap is the Phrygian cap.' And on 2 April at Meknes he observed 'the cloaks, the togas and a thousand details that belong absolutely to Antiquity.'

But there was more than the costume: the way of life called forth the same ideas. 'Habit and ancient custom govern everything', and this gives to the people 'a majesty which we lack even in the gravest circumstances.'[15] Thus Delacroix felt that he had before his eyes the true world of Antiquity, still existing in natural surroundings. He wondered anxiously (in a letter to Pierret of 29 February) whether, when he came home, he would be able to recapture 'the living, striking sublime that walks the streets here', and he adds: 'Imagine, my friend, what it is to see, lying in the sun, walking the streets or mending shoes, men of consular type, each one a Cato or a Brutus and not even lacking the disdainful air which the masters of the world should have. . . . I tell you you will never be able to believe what I shall bring back, because it will fall far short of the truth and nobility to be found here. Antiquity has nothing more beautiful'—and 'all in white like the senators of Rome and the Panathenaic procession of Athens.'[16] The circle was closing: Delacroix had found once more the steps that lead up to the Acropolis.

Later, in 1845, when the American painter Catlin brought some of his Red Indians to Paris, Delacroix again experienced the same emotion: before his eyes the natural man recovered his first nobility, and again he thought of the Greeks and Romans. fig 13

At the end of a letter of 4 June to Auguste Jal[17] Delacroix makes the direct comparison between what he saw in Morocco and Greek art. He repeats that 'the beautiful fills the streets' and, since his correspondent was already familiar with Algiers, goes on to say:

'Here there is something even simpler and more primitive; the Turkish admixture is less; the Romans and the Greeks are at my door: I have had a good laugh at the expense of David's Greeks, apart, of course, from his sublime technique. I know them now; the marbles are the truth itself, but one must know how to read what they have to say, and our poor moderns have seen in them no more than hieroglyphs. If the school of painting persists in always setting the families of Priam and Atreus as subjects for the poor nurslings of the Muses, I am convinced . . . that it would be infinitely better for them to be sent as cabin boys to Barbary on the first ship, rather than to go on wearying the classic soil of Rome. Rome is no longer in Rome.'

The revelation experienced by Delacroix was all the more solid and durable because it confirmed in him something he had already felt. He had already

*Fig 13* SKETCHES OF IOWA INDIANS. Pen drawing. Cabinet des Dessins, Louvre, Paris.

suspected that the Antiquity championed by the School of David was the result of a misunderstanding. He had discovered this in 1824, when studying antique coins. It was then that, by a decision that was involuntarily symbolic, he gave Baron Schwiter one of his most romantic water-colours, the *White*
pl 65 *Horse frightened by a Storm*, in exchange for a set of impressions of coins. He then began drawing them again and again, first using the method of the official School—that is to say, outline; then he saw that this was wrong, and that this rendering of form by isolating it was, in plastic terms, nonsense. The result, a year later, was six sheets of lithographs, completed in the same year by two wood engravings. Some of these were drawn from pieces in the collection of the Duke of Blacas. Another lithograph reproduced one of the Parthenon metopes which Delacroix studied at the British Museum—*Theseus vanquishing*
pl 273 *the Centaur Eurytos*.

Delacroix looked for confirmation of his discovery in the masterpieces of Greek sculpture. Silvestre, with his usual penetration, detected here 'a key to his work, the principle of which, indeed, far from varying, was simply strengthened as time passed. It was the principle which, ten years after his journey to Morocco, Delacroix expounded in the *Revue des Deux Mondes* (1 February 1846), in an article on Prud'hon—in whom he saw the 'naïve', that is to say spontaneous, criticism of neo-classicism and of its 'strange hatred for the resources of the picturesque in painting.' Chesneau had already seen what light these observations throw on the lithographs. 'The true spirit of Antiquity', Delacroix used to say often and forcibly, 'does not consist in giving each isolated figure the appearance of a statue, for the real characteristic of Antiquity is the skilful amplitude of the forms combined with the feeling of life.' But this feeling of life disappears in the 'isolation of the figures' when they are cut off by line: Prud'hon saved himself from this by remaining 'first and foremost "a painter"—that is to say that, upon a field to which he is chiefly concerned to give depth, he arranges groups surrounded by air and light.' Art cannot safely stray from the path of life; and this vanishes when the forms cease to belong to a shared place—that is, 'the air and light', in which they move freely and share in the atmosphere.

Thus Morocco showed Delacroix, in the crucible of reality, all the various elements which, when taken over by doctrinaires, are divided between opposing Schools. He had found contact with life, in which all these things were recognized and harmonious. He was now sure of himself.

Even his romanticism found support in his short experience of Spain. There also, it is true, he observed 'affinities with the Moors . . . the devil's own sunshine'. But night came into its own, with all its mystery and power which the African sun had threatened to disperse. 'Midnight strikes at the Franciscans', he noted at Cadiz on 18 May; 'singular feeling in this strange country. This moonlight. . . . These white towers in the moon's rays.' And five days later: 'Alcala. Night. The moon on the melancholy water. The croaking of the frogs. The Moorish Gothic chapel . . . near the aqueduct.' And even in the morning, going into the cathedral of Seville, he again finds and delights in the 'magnificent obscurity', and a medley of emotions—'the music, etc.!'. The 'etc.' refers, no doubt, to flights of imagination and a tentative love affair: '*la signora Maria Josefa* . . . evening with M. Williams. M. D. melancolica. Guitar. On the way back, the soldier playing the guitar in front of the guardroom.' And there was Mme. Ford. 'She corrected the music and I was beside her.' But she proved 'coquettish': 'I tried all day in vain to find her; I wandered about the streets like a Spanish lover.' That is all we are likely to know of it, and no doubt there was not much more to know; but Spain added to the bright sunshine and sparkle of Morocco a half-light, a fragrance and the beginning of a dream, and of all this nothing was lost. Soon, at the 1834 Salon, the *Women of Algiers* was to show the public how these various new acquisitions XXI, page 245
could be amalgamated into a poetry that belongs to Delacroix alone.

After his return he stayed in Paris until he paid a brief visit to the Rivets at Mantes in April 1834. This period brought a number of events that were to prove important in his life. In November 1834 at Buloz's request he began his portrait of George Sand, dressed as a man: their friendship began more or less as a love affair, but very soon settled into a frank and firm comradeship. Through her he met Chopin, another close friend. About this time also he became the lover of his cousin Mme. de Forget. And, at this time or a little later, on the recommendation of Pierret's wife, whose servant she had been, Jenny Le Guillou came to him as housekeeper—the beginning of what was perhaps his closest link with a simple human being. In July 1834 Charles de Verninac, his beloved nephew, died in New York.

The fruits of his experience in Morocco were revealed to the public at the 1834 Salon. At the previous Salon Delacroix, in the *Rooms of the Count de* XIX, page 195
*Mornay*, seemed to be recapitulating—before starting out on a new phase—his

astounding mastery of realism, and this is perhaps even more evident in the sketch now in the Louvre. Some of his exhibits at the 1834 Salon continue the earlier period dominated by English literature and Rembrandtesque *chiaroscuro*: the jury rejected the *Hermit of Copmanhurst* from *Ivanhoe* but accepted *Melmoth*, (*Interior of a Dominican Convent*) inspired by Maturin's *roman noir*, and the *Battle of Nancy*. But there were also the *Street in Meknes* and the *Women of Algiers*; and there would have been the *Encounter between Moorish Horsemen*,[18] had the jury not refused it. This was also the time of the two *Fantasias*. In the three pictures last mentioned it is possible to observe Delacroix finding his new balance. The *Encounter* (1833), with its composition which rises like a whirl of dust lifted by the storm, is a furious battle scene of a pure, baroque impetuousness. It belongs to the line of the *Fighting Horsemen* of 1825 in the Moreau-Nélaton collection at the Louvre, and of the various pictures of the *Giaour and the Pasha*. Indeed, the group of frenzied animals is practically copied from an earlier *Horses Fighting*,[19] a prelude to the Giaour pictures.

The *Fantasia* of 1833[20]—Delacroix in his Moroccan notes refers to it as '*Courses de poudre*'—concentrates on furious movement but is organized with greater mastery; the horsemen rush at full speed in the picture plane, from right to left along a horizontal, with a slight trajectory-like curve, and the inclination of the horses' necks and the gun makes a succession of diagonals; the rectilinear movement is stressed by the distant horizon. In the *Military Exercises* of 1832[21] this contrast is marked: the horsemen gallop foreward in the picture plane (from left to right this time), but their unity is broken up: the main group dashes with mad speed along a line which is continued, behind, by the flowing cloak and is projected, before, by the parallel gun barrels. The horses' heads seem, by their varied inclinations, to break up the forwards movement into successive phases. The impulse suddenly comes up against a vertical, which bends under the shock: it is formed by the first rearing horse, whose rider, thrown backwards, helps to check its movement and pin it down, an effect continued and stressed by the gun barrel that is raised in the air and thrown backwards. The effect is like the sideways view of a strong-bow, with the arrow in position cutting across the curved but resistant upright. The whole of Delacroix's art is formulated here, stretched as it was between the two extremes—the irresistible violence of the movement and the implacable mastery of the wrist that reins it in at will; a horizontal darting forward and a vertical that is bent with the strain of checking this. The dynamic and the static, the romantic and the classic—all is here, in what is almost a symbolic collision resulting in a equilibrium. In these three pictures, all painted at the same period, the career of Delacroix is resumed—at first hurled forwards in a frantic rush, but then taken in hand and directed by firm, ordering thought.

## *The Women of Algiers*

And now, in the full possession of his art, Delacroix could give himself up to the poetry that was in him, resulting in the *Women of Algiers*. There have been
pl 217 many accounts of how the picture was conceived and of the experience on

which it was based. Until that moment Delacroix had failed to find other than Jewish women as models—such as, on 10 February, Dititia 'dressed as an Algerian woman'. It was difficult for a Christian to enter an Arab house and for a man to penetrate into a harem; but Porrel, the harbour engineer, obtained this favour from a *chaouch* in the harbour administration, whose house, it seems, was in the rue Duquesne, Algiers. When Delacroix emerged from a dark passage into the reserved quarters and, with his eyes dazzled by the sudden light, saw (in Cournault's words[22]) 'in the midst of that heap of silk and gold' the 'lovely human gazelles . . . now tame' (the words here are Mornay's) he became 'exalted to the point of fever, which was calmed with difficulty by sorbets and fruit.' Cournault speaks of 'moments of fascination and strange happiness'. The woman, he says, was 'very pretty, and M. Porrel told me that Delacroix seemed as though intoxicated by what he saw.' He reports Delacroix's exclamations: 'It's beautiful! It is as if in the time of Homer!'—again the theme of Antiquity rediscovered, but at the same time the women in their nonchalant beauty seemed like fragrant flowers in some secret hot-house, langorous among the splendour of gold-framed mirrors in the half-light, of all the marvellous stuffs they had embroidered, of painted furniture and of coloured tiles, like music perceived by the eye. Here Delacroix found the secret dream a reality: the woman withdrawn to devote herself to her original mission—the work of her house, the love of her man, the education of her child: 'This', he said, 'is woman as I understand her, not thrown into the life of the world, but withdrawn at its heart, as its most secret, delicious and moving fulfilment.'

Delacroix hastily recorded his 'sensations' in his notebooks with his water-colour brush. Morîm Bensoltane sat for the woman on the left who is leaning on her elbow and for the one crouching in the centre, Zohra Bensoltane for the one on the right. There were also Bahya and Zohra Tarboudji and Khadoûdja. These names, noted down by Delacroix and rediscovered by Georges Marçais, prove that the women were not Jewish, but were genuine Moslem women of Turkish stock. Thus Delacroix was not the victim of a confusion or of trickery, as Loti was later in the case of his *Les Désenchantées*. Besides sketching the Turkish slippers, dresses and scarves, Delacroix took several examples back with him. (These he left to Cournault.[23]) Delacroix notes in pencil that the striped blouse is 'cherry-coloured' or 'soft violet', the trousers 'deep green' or '*vert fleur d'or*', or again 'red-dyed silk', while a scarf is soft blue, green, yellow and gold. He remarks that an arm can shade from 'lilac violet' to 'violet lake'. Elie Lambert has shown that Delacroix probably found further documentation in a house of a more welcoming sort in what he calls the 'rue Casrine'—probably 'Kossair'—which may explain the lithograph, not published till 1865[24] in the *Gazette des Beaux-Arts*, in which the model boldly displays her naked breast.

What was he going to do with these meticulous notes? On 29 February he wrote anxiously: 'I even feel certain that the considerable quantity of information I shall be bringing back from here will be of only moderate use to me. Far away from the country where I found it, it will be like trees torn up from their native soil.' This might indeed have happened, if the information had stayed in Delacroix's memory like dried plants in a herbarium. But the inner work was done on them: the trees that had been pulled up were soon replanted in soil that was Delacroix's own. Sensations that had been external and heterogeneous put forth fresh roots: they took on the character of the medium to which they had been transferred, of Delacroix's sensibility; the objective passed over into the subjective. Claudel perceived the secret of this process of transmutation when he studied a painting by another visionary, Rembrandt:[25]

'The famous portrait of Burgomaster Six which, as you know, shows a man leaning on a window-sill reading. It seems to me an image of the painter, who belongs at one and the same time to two worlds, the inner and the outer, and makes use of reality to decipher the spells.'

The artist has then to convey to other people this transmutation in words found in the book of life. Baudelaire has said the same thing:

*. . . Le monde*
*Hier, demain, toujours, nous fait voir notre image.*

(The world
Past, present and to come shows us our image.)

The pretty models observed by Delacroix came together, in his mind, with memories that lay waiting for them—with the *Odalisques* of Bonington or Auguste, on which he had fed his imagination before translating them into his early pictures of oriental women: such pictures as his 1827 lithograph of the 'favourite slave of the Persian ambassador', his copies of Persian miniatures, his 1821 *La Favorite*, and his pictures of women of 'mixed blood', a series which began in 1821[26] with the Montpellier picture and continued with *Aline the Mulatto* (painted twice in 1824 at the moment of the *Massacre at Chios*), and with *Aspasie the Moorish girl* (painted three times in 1826,[27] when he was also painting his series of voluptuous small pictures of odalisques in preparation for the seductive victims in the *Sardanapalus*).

In this way two worlds that were made for one another—the one he carried within him waiting for the other that would recognize itself there—were married and became one. The reality already chosen by Delacroix according to the affinities he found in it with his own nature now passed over into imagination and became united with what Delacroix called the 'ideal' within him. Reality, which 'assassinated' him with its beauty at the first shock, became art when it was sufficiently integrated with his inner dream to give this the right embodiment. A selection took place, allowing to survive only 'that which the soul finds genuinely moving in objects which strike the senses.'[28]

Baudelaire, who was so strangely close to Delacroix, was able to clothe this dream in words:[29]

*Sur de profonds coussins tout imprégnés d'odeur*
*. . . Que nos rideaux fermés nous séparent du monde.*

(On deep sweet-smelling cushions let me lie
. . . and our drawn curtains shut us from the world.)

*Les plus rares fleurs*
*Mêlent leurs odeurs*
*Aux vagues senteurs de l'ambre,*
*Les riches plafonds,*
*Les miroirs profonds,*
*La splendeur orientale,*
*Tout y parlerait*
*A l'âme en secret*
*Sa douce langue natale.*[30]

(The rarest flowers
mingle their scents
with the vague fragrance of amber.
The rich ceilings,
the deep mirrors,
the oriental splendour,
all in that place would
speak to the soul, in secret,
its gentle native tongue.)

The real world had evoked in the artist's soul memories of its native tongue—or rather an exchange had taken place: the real world borrowed from Delacroix his soul, which took from the real world, in return, an embodiment. From the real world or from the memory of it, which Delacroix had already transmuted and made his own?

In point of fact, the woman leaning forwards, on the right of the *Women of Algiers*—the one whose dark hair is lit by a rose bloom—is no longer Zohra Bensoltane: though she has kept the precise attitude sketched in a water-colour in the Louvre,[31] her profile is taken from earlier pictures—we have seen it already in the *Massacre at Chios* (1824), in the *Greece Expiring* (1827), in the *Liberty Leading the People* (1830) and it recurs in another picture of 1824, the *Natchez*. The half-closed eyes, the parted lips and the profile of which Delacroix was so fond, reappear in the *Women of Algiers* and linger there, like some flower floating on a stream and checked for an instant by a branch. After this they disappear.

XX, page 196

pls 213, 214, 215, 216

This absorption in the dream world continued its work in Delacroix throughout his life. The effect was like that of a stone falling through the water in a deep pool: we follow it with our eyes, but gradually it loses its form, quivers and takes on more and more of the colour of the water. So the sights seen by Delacroix were assimilated by this sensibility: memory did its slow work on them, analogous to the imagination, gradually transforming them. Does not memory pre-

XXVII THE ENTRY OF THE CRUSADERS INTO CONSTANTINOPLE
*1840 Oil on canvas. 161 x 196 (410 x 498)*
*Louvre, Paris*

sent to the past the same distorting mirror that imagination presents to the future, and are they not the two aspects of a single function, through which our inner truth colours and adopts the external truth supplied by the senses? This too has been expressed by Baudelaire in his poem *La Voix*:[32]

*Deux voix me parlaient . . .*

One, the voice of reality, said,

*La terre est un gâteau plein de douceur . . .*

The other:

*Viens! oh! viens voyager dans les rêves,*
*Au delà du possible, au delà du connu!*

(Two voices spoke to me . . .
Earth is a cake full of sweetness. . . .
Come! oh come explore the world of dreams,
Beyond the possible, beyond the known!)

And by that light, 'behind the painted scenes of life', he could 'see strange worlds distinctly.' Claudel, recalling an old Chinese tale, compared the experience to that 'frontier of the two worlds' found by a sage on the mountain and in the mist after having travelled a long way.

By taking up so often a subject already treated in an earlier picture, Delacroix makes it possible to follow step by step this penetration into the other world. The *Women of Algiers*, for instance, remained alive in him. In 1847—to adopt Robaut's data—the picture in the Rouen Museum of the *Jewess of Algiers at her*
pl 218 *Toilet* (which Joubin calls *Interior of a Harem at Oran*, on the basis of a reference in the *Journal* on 26 May 1847) is evidence of the work that had been going on in secret: here the shadow has risen and enfolds the negress facing us who lifts to one side the curtain which, if she let it fall, would hide the scene; and in the interior thus revealed for a moment—and in its shaded light—one of the women is standing, as in a sketch made by Delacroix at Algiers in which the same fan appears. Her head is inclined slightly to one side. Another woman, almost devoured by the *chiaroscuro*, is seen from behind, lying on a bed. In
XXII, page 246 1848[33] Delacroix, before starting on a second version of the *Women of Algiers*, cast his mind back to the 1821 *La Favorite*—to his first movements towards the world of the East, as seen through Greece in her time of danger, and made of this figure a woman of Algiers—sitting, leaning on her elbow among deep cushions and with her head inclined in the same way, close to a great curtain that will at any moment fall and hide her. But what a change this is! Where there had been no more than curiosity exploring the exotic and the picturesque, there is now an entry into another world. Chesneau did well to quote, in connection with it,

XXVIII THE ENTRY OF THE CRUSADERS INTO CONSTANTINOPLE (detail)
*1840 Oil on canvas*
*Louvre, Paris*

Baudelaire's sentence: 'Just as a dream takes place in an atmosphere of its own, so a conception that becomes a composition needs to move in a coloured medium peculiar to it.'[34] In this case yellow and gold and red—'ideas of joy, wealth . . . and love'—make a play against green and light blue tints which join their coolness with the half-light in order to add a piercing, almost painful sharpness and vibrancy.

For Delacroix's colour also evolved as he left the real world more and more XXI, page 245 behind to penetrate further into the dream world. The 1834 *Women of Algiers* was still brilliant, each figure in it playing her part to the full in the joy of encountering, as in an orchestra, the others' timbre, and all combining to make music. In this composition the eye rushes from one harmony to another, finding in each of them some different and unexpected enchantment, and what it retains of the whole is the dazzling impression which may well have come to Delacroix from the Moroccan festivals he saw. And this even though the picture as we see it today is only a pale memory of the original. Renoir has told us how, in his lifetime, he saw it change and grow old and how, one day, he wept to find it as darkened, as different from when he had first come upon it, as he himself was XXII, page 246 from his own youth. The second version of the *Women of Algiers*, that of 1849, was begun in 1848 or thereabouts, and Delacroix says in his *Journal* that he worked on it 'with pleasure' and 'with ardour'. For the first time in one of these new treatments of an old theme, the original composition is repeated faithfully throughout—but it is transmuted: the format is reduced, and the figures are more absorbed into the whole. Everything is concentrated: distracting details are eliminated, the iridescent tiles of the background have disappeared, the colour is unified and subdued. At the same time the verticals and horizontals parallel to the frame are stressed, so that they form a kind of supplementary border which further isolates the composition, creating a closed medium irrevocably separated from the world outside—as the water of an aquarium is retained by the rigidity of the glass walls. The negress on the right has again her original attitude, but she now forms a single block of shade with the dark curtain she is holding up. This, as in the *Interior of a Harem at Oran*, would hide the scene of the picture if allowed to fall, and one feels that this may happen at any moment. We are admitted into another world, closed in on itself and hugging its nucleus of light—for the light is not a continuation of the light surrounding the spectator outside the picture, its source is in the picture, hidden by the curtain. The result is that the light, instead of making the colours blaze and spurt in all directions as in the 1834 picture, now produces a central hearth, the concentrated nucleus of a nebula; it binds together the three women, who are still in the same attitudes, but it also makes the surrounding and enclosing obscurity more strongly felt. The whole scene appears distanced, withdrawn into a different and precarious world, one that may at any moment retire into itself and escape us, extinguished by the closing of a shutter or the falling back of the curtain.

In 1857 Delacroix painted his *Woman of Algiers in her Apartment.*[35] The pl 220 nakedness of the torso, the suggestion of music, the tambourine that has fallen to the ground, the presence of flowers (of which a bouquet fills part of the window) and the landscape vista barred with shadows—all this shows the growing ascendency achieved by the dream world over the real world.

*Fig 14* WOMEN OF ALGIERS 1834 Diagonal lines, some of which are parallel with the slopes of the central pyramid combine with the verticals and horizontals.

The attempt to follow this continuous progress has led us away from the 1834 picture. Returning to it, we must now follow a different and complementary transmutation—not that effected by the sensibility dissolving the initial data supplied by the real world, but that produced by intelligence and lucidity; for these also intervene with their demands and their science, to construct the forms in the picture and the composition articulating them together.

In this picture, which seems in advance dedicated to the trinity invoked by Baudelaire, to *luxe, calme et volupté,*[36] life is no longer broken up into expansive gestures as it was in most of Delacroix's other pictures: it withdraws to enjoy its own density and mild radiation. If a man is himself only in action, a woman finds herself in a quiet blossoming, and this is the theme of the picture. But a still plenitude calls for form (which a liberated energy would disperse). So Delacroix felt how much he would gain in this case from plasticity, and established the sculptural volume of his figures with a firm, delimiting line. A drawing of the subject[37] is done in outline, with the minimum of hatchings to suggest the modelling; and, what is more, it is squared out—showing the rigour of construction at which Delacroix was aiming.

But these were only the elements of a total composition that is established—again according to an alliance of classical and baroque—partly upon the vertical and horizontal axes (which were to triumph finally in the 1849 version) and partly on diagonals. To the left, these diagonals are quite straight: the shadow descends from the picture frame towards the right, and its direction is taken up with almost equal firmness by the edge of the reclining figure (the gold brocaded hazma over the trousers being now indeed stiffly outlined) and is continued by the slope of the cast off slipper. This strong diagonal cutting off the whole of the lower left-hand corner finds its answer in a parallel which cuts off the upper right-hand corner: this is established by the curtain and is carried on, beyond the negress, by a red braiding which reaches to the picture frame. The inverse diagonals, though simply sketched, are nonetheless firmly situated, the top left-hand one by the slope of the mirror, the lower right-hand one by the movement of the negress's right leg. The tiles of the wall and of the floor echo this diagonal framework with their fragmentation into varied polygons, while it is corrected by the verticals and the horizontals, by the pyramidal central figure, even by the central axis—this last suggested by the panel in the background beside the wardrobe with its door ajar. So stability is established in an unstable element; and indeed the general arrangement seems to be schematized by the small tiles of the wall at the side which, similarly, form lozenges inscribed in squares. Calm and intensity, logic and the dream world, equilibrium and subtle transitions, slumbering shadow and luminous colours, cold tones (green, blue and grey) and hot tones (orange, red and brown)—Delacroix seems to have aimed at bringing all these together and mastering them all in a single overriding harmony that would confirm his accomplishment as a mature artist and as a human being.

## *The Sequel to Morocco*

In the important pictures which, at various stages in his later life, Delacroix devoted to his memories of Morocco, the two discoveries he had there encountered in luminous unity are always revived—life expresses its most ephemeral part in an explosion of its force, but expresses also its more durable part through an order that suggests a calm eternity. Before this, the figures in his pictures had been hurled into action: if they were still, this was in an impatience for action or an exhaustion after it, and their positions always expressed their relation with it at that moment. But in Morocco Delacroix came upon a new philosophy of life: a man sitting down no longer had his crossed legs nervously ready to spring up; squatting like the Buddha or nonchalantly lying full length, he was self-exiled from the passing moment—indifferent, and taking no part in the movement, he looked out at the flowing of time from the dream in which he was living. At most there sometimes entered into this stillness a resignation to fate, an abdication which showed, in the expression of his face, as a hopeless melancholy. The gestures were part of an immemorial repetition: they had acquired the patina and nobility of the centuries. The two draped women who have come to the fountain to draw water—Delacroix made a water-colour sketch of them and treated the subject again later—combine with their individual youthfulness the grandeur of extremely ancient traditions, a manifestation of the permanence of the race; the perfect balance of the amphora, which is upright on the shoulder, is associated with that of the arm holding it there with sinuous suppleness. The vivacity of the moment is joined to the recurrence of the centuries. This virtue, which struck Delacroix in the Arabs, he found also in the Jews: in his article on the *Jewish Wedding*, published in the *Magasin Pittoresque* for January 1842, he praised them for 'keeping more of the force of their ancient traditions' and expressed admiration for those 'outward acts which continue the most ancient customs'.

He never forgot the Arab world. Théophile Silvestre, in his *Artistes*

*Vivants*, reports him as saying: 'The men of that strong race will stir in my memory as long as I live; it is in them that I really rediscovered the beauty of Antiquity'—which itself, indeed, is partly based on the same rediscovery of the immemorial through the passing, reduced by it to the role of the accidental. The Arab hunter sitting upright on a rock, with one arm supported on a raised knee while the other leg is tense and almost vertical[38] was to suggest the attitude for *Tasso* in a sketch for a decorative painting for the Library of the Chambre,[39] and then to become, sixteen years later, the monumental *Hercules* leaning against an ancient column and resting at last from his labours, in a tympanum of the Salon de la Paix of the Hôtel de Ville.

Again, the rider bolt upright on a motionless horse in another of his water-colours[40] confirms an attitude whose nobility Delacroix had already invented in his 1829 lithograph of Du Guesclin; but it was also to find fulfilment in the lordly
pl 222 *Moroccan Caïd visiting a Tribe*, painted in 1837 and now in the Nantes Museum. Again on 9 April 1832, on the return journey from Meknes, he saw Mohammed ben Abou receiving an offering of milk from some women near Alcassar-el-Kebir, and in his picture the nearby horse's hooves, its lowered head and the chieftain's majestic bearing produce the solemn effect of an equestrian statue. There is an 1862 variant, in which the scene is absorbed into the misty vastness of the landscape; but before this it received a masterly reaffirmation in the great
pl 223 picture exhibited at the 1845 Salon and now in the Musée des Augustins, Toulouse, the *Sultan of Morocco surrounded by his Court.*

In the studies and first major sketch for this huge picture—it is nearly thirteen feet high—the subject was treated in breadth, and Abd-er-Rhaman, some way back towards the left (like the *Moroccan Caïd*) was the climax of the long line of people following him and all those coming to meet him, who are grouped about de Mornay. Thus placed at the point of convergence of these two ascending movements, which were divided rhythmically by the solemn verticals of figures in ample drapery, he did not even turn to follow the hand pointing towards the object that was being presented to him. His solemn immobility is like some superb petrifaction of the group which Delacroix caught, in an uncertain, snapshot style, in the water-colour from the Mornay sketchbook (wood engraving in *L'Illustration*, 21 September 1844); and this effect is stressed by the sunshade held behind him (as by the flags behind the *Caïd*). But what nobility has been added! In the Nantes picture and the Mornay water-colour the pole was inclined forwards; but here it leans backwards, the effect being to draw the Sultan up to a yet more magnificent height; and the sunshade's rigid cupola, taking the place of the waving flags, joins with the powerful stability of those Babylonian walls which, with their massive towers, close in the space of the background but also give it breadth. In the final picture this effect of grandeur is not only maintained, it is increased by the reversal of the picture's dimensions: Delacroix has cut off the right-hand part of the scene, in which he had thought of placing Mornay in full-dress diplomatic uniform,[41] and now makes the composition a vertical one, so that the Sultan is still more firmly centred and the monumental elevated effect is brought to the maximum.

The classicism that lives and breathes in this still and ceremonial composition is equally evident in the whole conception of the picture and the spirit in which it

*Fig 15* CHESS-PLAYERS IN JERUSALEM After 1830 and the visit to Morocco, Delacroix's composition became more balanced, and verticals and horizontals were brought into play.

is worked out. But later, in the small picture painted in 1862, this dominant quality of authority, reinforced by the Masaccio-like figures of the draped dignitaries and by the heavy, gloomy walls, became dissipated by a return to animation and to a more pictorial effect. Elie Lambert was inspired to end his study of this picture with this quotation from Delacroix's *Journal* (13 January 1857): pl 224

'I prefer to use the word "classical" of works that display a regular order, that satisfy the mind not only by an accurate, stately or vivid depiction of feelings and things, but also by unity, by logical arrangement—in a word, by all those qualities which increase the impression by contributing simplicity. . . .'

This may be placed side by side with Delacroix's criticism of romanticism, when he compares 'those writers who have ideas but cannot reduce them to order' to 'the barbarian generals who led into battle hosts of Persians or Huns, fighting at random, without order, without unity in their efforts and, in consequence, without result.'[42] The painter must be a musician, certainly, but he must also be an architect. It came quite naturally to Delacroix to associate the rhythm of the figures with that of the buildings. In this he was rediscovering one of the major preoccupations of the classicists, particularly those of the French seventeenth century—Poussin, Le Sueur and especially Sébastien Bourdon, who was perhaps the most skilled at dovetailing human structures with those of monuments in a shared network of geometrical lines, the human ones more supple, the architectural ones more solid.

Delacroix's impressions of Morocco had in fact joined and reinforced his memories of the masters. In 1835 the so-called *Chess-players in Jerusalem*—the figures are clearly Moroccan—are embedded in a play of verticals and horizontals formed by the walls and steps, across which the diagonal of the shadow pl 231

XXIX EDUCATION OF THE VIRGIN
*1842 Oil on canvas. 37 x 49 (095 x 125)*
*Private collection, Paris*

falling on the background wall cuts boldly. The *Arabs of Oran,*[43] painted in the same year, are organized about a portico which redoubles the rectangle of the frame. The wash drawing, *Arabs sitting at a Street Corner,* which belongs to the following year, has recourse without reserve to a strict combination of right angles, the curve of the arch and the linear network of the tiling.

In 1838 and 1839 Delacroix went still more deeply into the relationship between living man and the lines imposed by his mind on matter through architecture; but now he did so in order to produce an effect of contrast. In the *Fanatics*
XLV, page 403 *of Tangier* he took up again an episode he had noted down in one of the water-colours of the Mornay sketchbook. With their sharp white cut up by sunshine and shadow, the Arab houses form a close series of strong and dazzling cubes, punctured by rectangular openings: verticals and horizontals combine in a firm chequerwork, which is completed by the bisecting shadows. But this order encounters, to use a phrase of Gautier's, 'an incredible turbulence of movements, a ferocity of brushwork that no-one has surpassed', so that, in its unchanging rigidity, it is merely the banks of a furious torrent laden with a howling crowd of gesticulating human beings. These are the Yassouis, so named after Ben Yssa, their founder. 'Excited by prayer and by their own frenzied cries', the catalogue of the Salon tells us, 'to a state of real intoxication', they spread through the streets with 'a thousand contortions'.

And so a fusion is achieved, thanks to the experience of the life of Morocco, at one and the same time turned to stone under the sunshine and exploding in
XVI, page 180 furious outbursts: in a single picture the crowd of the *Boissy d'Anglas* is hurled
pl 183 between the inflexibly traced walls of the *Mirabeau and Dreux-Brézé*; the two come together, just as the dishevelled fanatic, whose excessive gesticulation seems about to throw his limbs out of joint, is placed next, in this picture, to the monolithic bystander in the burnous with its calm folds.

pl 227 Towards the end of his life, in 1857, Delacroix painted a new version and in this, by what appears to be a regressive tendency (already observed in the case of the *Sultan of Morocco,* and one on which we shall have more to say) he inclines the balance to the side of the frenzy that possesses these religious maniacs. Their procession is bursting out of the town like water from a lock that has overflowed, and, though the long straight crests of the masonry are still there, they are part of a tragic conflict of light and shade and a play of diagonals urging the maddened crowd onwards like a torrent towards a fall. The difference is striking between
pl 228 this and the 1838 picture, in which the element of unbalance seemed to be there only to compensate the calm of the background.

In 1839 Delacroix achieved a similar effect of contrast between the action and
XXV, page 273 its scene—with an even greater structural discipline—in his *Jewish Wedding in Morocco,* an elaboration again of notes taken during the journey. In accordance with the severest traditions handed down by the Renaissance, the picture is enclosed in a cubic space, whose framework is strongly marked by the bands of

XXX BASKET OF FRUIT AND FLOWERS
*1848 Oil on canvas. 41 x 55 (105 x 140)*
*Johnson Collection, Philadelphia*

green bounding the first storey and the two side balconies. Here, paradoxically,
Delacroix works out a kind of lesson in linear perspective of which there is
another example painted in the preceding year in his *Christopher Columbus at
Santa María de La Rabida* (where the scene takes place in a white-walled parlour
whose lines of recession are combined with verticals and horizontals and strict
arcs). His *Columbus on his Return from the New World* somewhat similarly drew pl 229
upon architecture for a sweeping diagonal staircase which reminds one of those
used by Carpaccio and Titian in their pictures of the Presentation of the Virgin pl 230
in the Temple. Delacroix, as is well known, even sought help from stage
designers like Ciceri in getting his main design correct.

But the *Jewish Wedding* goes further than these pictures: not only, like them, does it remind one of classical and Renaissance pictures, but it anticipates modern ones, for its planes, made to stand out against one another by contrasts of colour, seem a prelude to the geometrical constructions of Mondrian: the implacably white wall faces us in the picture plane, striped across the middle by two green horizontals, and divided, below, by the long vertical of a narrow door and above by a window and its shutter. In this cage, with its rectilinear geometry and violent white surfaces, a mass of human beings stirs, quivers, swells and, like a long serpent, comes down at the right and curls leftwards across the foreground. The whole picture expresses the same clash—of white with colour, of the bareness of the courtyard and walls with the bunching of the people, of the abstract rigidity of the framework with the agitation of its inhabitants.

While Delacroix was thus able to bring together through contrast the violence of life in action and the coldness of abstract construction, he had also learned,

*Fig 16* STUDIES for the figures of Agriculture or Commerce in the Salon du Roi. The influence of Delacroix's recent journey to Morocco is very striking here. 1833, Pencil. Cabinet des Dessins, Louvre, Paris.

*Fig 17* DELACROIX in Moroccan costume by Pauline Villot. Pencil. Cabinet des Dessins, Louvre, Paris.

and chiefly in Morocco, the broad harmonies that bind man to the scene in which he lives, whether this is one conceived by him according to the laws of his thinking and built by his hands, or one received by him from nature as his
pl 233 original dwelling-place. In one of his last pictures, the *Horses at the Fountain* (painted in 1862), he brought to their highest development these associated cadences of the human, the animal, the vegetable and stone—in which Poussin also had attained fulfilment when he painted *Eliezar and Rebecca at the Well.*

Man, at his full stature, not only harmonizes with the abstract lines imposed by his mind upon what he builds, but is also in unison with the vastness of nature, of which he is a small fragment. This also Poussin had expressed in his great landscapes with figures; and Delacroix likewise discovered it in Morocco. There the authentic majesty which human forms derive from their natural setting was revealed to him for the first time: he saw them recovering, in that almost virgin country, the elegant and easy grandeur possessed by animals, by horses and the great wild beasts. The Moroccan landscape, with its peaceful and endless mountain ranges and its vast expanses scarcely flecked with green under the calcining sun, appeared to him in all the imposing amplitude of a primal land made for a race that was likewise primitively pure. Many notes in the *Journal* bear witness to the strength of these impressions. On 5 March: 'Wild black mountains on the right, the sun above them. Walking through an undergrowth of dwarf palms, stony soil. . . .' And on 7 April, near Reddat on the return journey: 'Mountains in the distance. Went out in the evening after sunset. Melancholy view of the vast uninhabited plain. Croaking of frogs and cries of other animals. Sound of the Moslems praying at the same time.'

In his *Moroccan and his Child* (1833) the two figures crouching in front of a space wavy with hill crests make two flattened pyramids resembling those of the distant mountains, and the long diagonals of the gun barrels reinforce this rising series of successive angles, as do the broad low tents. Similar lines are found in the *Arab Encampment* of 1839. In his 1836 water-colour of *Arab Actors and Clowns*, and in his canvas on the same theme in the Tours Museum, painted twelve years later, the dancing and singing men form a transitory wave that, like a melody dying away in space, scarcely ruffles the level expanse behind them, which is like a sea whose faint waves are visible only in the foreground. pl 236 pl 235

The *Death of Lara*, painted in 1847, another picture in which the drama in the foreground scarcely ruffles the horizontals of the plane of the cloudy sky and the flattened pyramids of the diagonals, is a confirmation of how strong was Delacroix's impression of the profound harmony between living creatures and things, alike immersed in the life of the whole world.

The same feeling, transferred to an ocean setting, supplied the theme for the *Shipwreck of Don Juan*, which he sent to the 1841 Salon. But it can surely be recognized also in his *Crusaders*, a picture conceived about the same time, in which human conflicts and fury sink, with the peace of exhaustion, into the immensity of the panorama of the Golden Horn, where the smoke from the conflagrations can be seen rising slowly into the calm evening air, like the smoke of bonfires in a twilit landscape. In his *Horsemen on the Bank of the River Sebou* (1841) the horsemen are scarcely distinguished from the endless undulations which, with their alternating shadow and light, exhaust themselves against the weighty cliff of the mountain. In his 1858 picture, the *Banks of the River Sebou*, both the horsemen and the bathers are likewise lost in the windings of the water among the bushes, reeds, swollen heavy trees, rocks and hills. Similarly, in his two pictures of *Ovid among the Scythians* which he painted in 1859 and 1862—taking up the subject used in 1844 in the Library of the Chambre des Députés—the figures are placed in the limitless expanse of a pastoral world. XXVI, page 274 XXVII, page 283 pl 237

In these pictures human activity is no longer something that tears the world in two like a cataclysm: Delacroix finds himself in close harmony with the universal respiration of life and its untiring renewal; and, as he grew older, both his mind and his eyes were to become more familiar with this turn of thought. It was Morocco that had made him aware of it but he would go deeper and deeper into it and draw from it ampler resonances.

Coming at a late stage in a very old civilization, and drinking deep of all its vivifying juices and its philtres, Delacroix had been placed by Fate on the path that led to romanticism, symbolism and *fin de siècle* decadence. The intellectual life of his time offered to him insistently its categories and its conventions, threatening to enclose him in its subtle, artificial dilemmas and is eccentricities of thought and sensuality. But Morocco revealed to him, in a sudden blaze, the value of life in its original, yet already immemorial authenticity. He understood then that all is in each and that nothing that is true is ever contradicted by anything true—that art has room for everything, for both the intoxication of action and the calm of contemplation, for both the firmness of thought and the follies of imagination, for both passion and serenity. It was enough that one's work

XXXI CLIFFS AT ETRETAT
*c. 1843 Water-colour. 8 x 10 (020 x 024)*
*Collection: Claude Roger-Marx, Paris*

should be sincere in its origin and unified in its execution. The conviction which was to make possible the large-scale enterprises he was soon to undertake was already established in him; he stated it at the conclusion of his article, *Questions sur le Beau*:[44]

'It is to the outstanding minds that it is given to unite, through their predilection, those different types of perfection between which the pundits see only gulfs. Before a Senate composed only of great men, disputes of this kind would not last long. . . . These men would soon recognize one another by a mark shared by them all, by their power to express the Beautiful, but to attain it each by different routes. . . .'

In Morocco, face to face with reality, whether that of man or of nature, Delacroix had seen the point at which these routes come together.

XXXII LANDSCAPE IN THE PYRENEES AT SUNSET
*Water-colour. 8 x 11 (020 x 027)*
*Louvre, Paris*

# NOTES ON THE PLATES TO CHAPTER VI

*Departure for Morocco*

In 1832 Count de Mornay (pl 185) was sent by Louis-Philippe as Ambassador Extraordinary to the Sultan of Morocco, who received him at Meknes. (The treaty painfully negotiated on this occasion did not succeed in putting an end to the aid given by Abd-er-Rhaman to the Algerians, and four years later the negotiations had to be resumed by Lieutenant-Colonel Baron de la Rüe.) Mornay looked for a historical painter to take with him, and, on the advice of the famous actress Mademoiselle Mars (pl 186), who was his mistress and was older than he, chose Delacroix. It is with some difficulty that one recognizes, under the traveller's kit (pl 187, 188), the artist-dandy and the eminent man of society, whose elegant apartments had evidently intrigued the eye of Delacroix (cf. pl XIX).

*185 Prince Anatole Demidoff in the Rooms of the Count de Mornay, 1833. Painting now destroyed.*

*186* FRANÇOIS GÉRARD: *Portrait of Mademoiselle Mars. Lithograph by Grevedon.*

*187 The Count de Mornay, from the Moroccan sketchbook. Louvre, Paris.*

*188 Self-portrait in travelling costume, 1832. Louvre, Paris.*

*Coasts of Africa*

Delacroix's first (pl 189) and last (pl 190) images of Africa were, of course, of its coast—more or less mountainous, and crushed beneath a blazing light. His mastery of water-colours enabled him to take these rapid and subtle notes.

*189 The Straits of Gibraltar, 23 January 1832. Louvre, Paris.*

*190 The Algerian Coast, 25 June 1832. Louvre, Paris.*

*Travellers' notes*

Delacroix was to stay at Tangier (pl 191) three times—from 24 January to 5 March, from 12 April to 15 May and from 1 to 10 June. Between the first stay and the second he went to Meknes (pl 194), and his notebooks register the stages of the journey (pls 192, 193) to the holy city. Its walls made a deep impression on him: he returned to them in his 1845 *Sultan of Morocco* (pl 223); before them he saw displayed the oriflammes of the royal procession (pl 195).

191 *View of Tangier, 1 March, 1832. Cabinet des Dessins, Louvre, Paris.*

192 *Page from the Moroccan sketchbook: Tleta dei Rissana, 1832. Cabinet des Dessins, Louvre, Paris.*

193 *Page from the Moroccan sketchbook: Sidi Kassem, 13 March, Zar Hône, 14 March 1832. Cabinet des Dessins, Louvre, Paris.*

194 *Delacroix's room at Meknes, 1832. C binet des Dessins, Louvre, Paris.*

195 *Arrival at Meknes, 15 March 1832. Cabinet des Dessins, Louvre, Paris.*

196 *Meknes, 15 March 1832. Cabinet des Dessins.*

*Discovery of the Arabs*

Delacroix made use of his stay in Morocco to study not only its landscape but its human types, whose attitudes (pl 197) and expressions (pl XVII, 198) he caught both in their landscape setting (pl 199) and in the city.

197 *Young Moroccan dancing. Boymans-van Beuningen Museum, Rotterdam.*

198 *Arab in a Turban. Ernst Rouart Collection.*

199 *Page from the Moroccan sketchbook.*

*In Spain*

After his return (pl 201) from Meknes to Tangier and his second stay here, Delacroix went to Spain, landing at Cadiz (pl 202) and making his way as far as Seville (pl 200).

200 *Street in Seville, May 1832. Louvre, Paris.*

201 *Page from the Moroccan sketchbook: Alcassar-el-Kebir, 9 and 10 April 1832. Cabinet des Dessins, Louvre, Paris.*

202 *Cadiz: Spaniards, a moonlit street. May 1832. Cabinet des Dessins, Louvre, Paris.*

*Continuity*

Though the journey to Morocco enriched Delacroix's vision, it did not break its continuity. This comes out strikingly if, for instance, one follows the theme of fighting horsemen through his various treatments of it. In 1825 it is medieval (pl 203), in 1827 it is already Byronic and oriental (pl 204), and in Morocco it was fed by various wild incidents which his eyes encountered there, and which he used in his later pictures, whether these were recollections of his travels (1833, pl 205) or returns to Greek subjects (1835, pl 206).

203 *Horsemen fighting on the Plain, 1825. Louvre, Paris.*

204 *Combat of the Giaour and the Pasha, 1827. The Art Institute of Chicago.*

205 *Encounter between Moorish Horsemen, c. 1843-6. The Walters Art Gallery, Baltimore.*

206 *Combat of the Giaour and the Pasha, 1835. Private collection.*

*Virile intensity*

Morocco nourished and confirmed Delacroix's innate and constant tendencies. The Arabs, especially those on horseback, led to his *Fantasias* (pls 207, 208) and reinforced his vigour, rapidity of execution and love of nervous intensity.

207 *Arab Fantasia ('Military Exercises'), 1832. Musée Fabre, Montpellier.*

208 *Arab Fantasia ('Courses de Poudre'), 1833. Städelsches Kunstinstitut, Frankfurt.*

*Vision of woman*

The Arab and Jewish women whom he saw encouraged another side of Delacroix's sensibility; graceful (pl 210) or hieratic (pl 209) and dressed in clothes whose forms and colours were new to him, they excited his passionate curiosity, made him take many notes (pl 211).

209 *The Jewish Bride, 21 February 1832. Louvre, Paris.*

210 *Moroccan Woman, 1832. From the Moroccan sketchbook. Musée Condé, Chantilly.*

211 *Three sketches of Arab women, with colour notes, 1835. Louvre, Paris.*

*A recurring face*

Though Delacroix thought that, with the harems, he was entering upon an unknown world, he brought to it and placed in its setting the type of woman he carried within him. Among his *Women of Algiers* (pl 212, cf. pls XX, XXI) we find the face already singled out for praise, from 1824 to 1830, in *The Massacre at Chios* (pls 213, III), in the *Natchez* (pl 216), in the *Greece Expiring* (pls 214, V) and in the *Liberty* (pls 215, XIII).

212 *Women of Algiers, 1834 (detail). Louvre, Paris.*

213 *The Massacre at Chios, 1824 (detail). Louvre, Paris.*

214 *Greece Expiring on the Ruins of Missolonghi, 1827 (detail). Musée des Beaux-Arts, Bordeaux.*

215 *Liberty Leading the People, 1830 (detail). Louvre, Paris.*

216 *The Natchez, 1824 (detail). Lord Walston Collection, Cambridge.*

*A meditation continued*

Just as the strength and ardour of the men and horses of Africa had come, like a tributary, to swell the river of Delacroix's imagination, so the enclosed and dreaming beauty of women moved onwards through his 1834 *Women of Algiers* (pl XXI) and its later versions (1849, pl XXII) or variations (1847, pl 218; 1857, pl 220) until it was absorbed into compositions that are a mingling of the East and Antiquity and even a reminiscence of Watteau (1854, pl 219).

217 *Study for the 'Women of Algiers', 1833. Louvre.*

218 *Interior of a Harem at Oran, 1847. Musée des Beaux-Arts, Rouen.*

*219 Turkish Women bathing, 1854. Hertford Museum, Connecticut.*

*220 Woman of Algiers in her Apartment (Odalisque), 1857.*

*A recurring attitude* Delacroix's ceaselessly enriched continuity becomes apparent when we trace the constancy of an image through his work. The grandeur of a horseman reining in his mount makes its appearance already in 1829 with his *Du Guesclin* (pl 221), clothes itself in the nobility of Arab costume in his *Moroccan Caïd* (1837, pl 222), which is based on a scene witnessed by him at Alcassar-el-Kebir in 1832, and appears yet again in the final versions of his *Sultan of Morocco*, for instance in that of 1862 (pl 224). The huge picture painted in 1845 (pl 223) had given this posture its maximum sculptural fixity.

*221 Du Guesclin at the Château de Pontorson, 1829. Louvre, Paris.*

*222 Moroccan Caïd visiting a Tribe, 1837. Musée des Beaux-Arts, Nantes.*

*223 The Sultan of Morocco surrounded by his Court, 1845. Musée des Augustins, Toulouse.*

*224 Sultan of Morocco, 1862. Vanderbilt Collection, New York.*

*A recurring effect* The massiveness of the walls of Meknes, which shut off the space in the *Sultan of Morocco* (pl 223), recurs in a picture with a medieval setting such as the 1846 *Abduction of Rebecca* (pl LI) and in a religious picture such as the 1853 *Saint Stephen* (pl 226)—of which another version (pl 225), painted in 1862, is set in a landscape clearly derived from the Atlas Mountains.

*225 The Martyrdom of Saint Stephen, 1862. The Barber Institute of Fine Arts, Birmingham.*

*226 Disciples and Holy Women raising the Body of Saint Stephen, 1853. Musée Municipal, Arras.*

*Hymn to life* After his journey to Morocco Delacroix was fully conscious of the two sides of his temperament—which are also the two sides of art, and must complete each other. One of them, bound up with the expression of instinctive forces, exalts life and its ardours: these are to be found raised to the pitch of paroxysm in Delacroix's *Fanatics of Tangier*, painted in 1836-8 (pls XLV, 228), a picture whose starting-point was a water-colour in the 1832 Mornay Album. The theme is taken up again in 1857, in a composition that is even more frankly baroque (pl 227).

*227 The Fanatics of Tangier, 1857. Art Gallery of Toronto.*

*228 The Fanatics of Tangier, 1836-8 (detail). Jerome Hill Collection, New York.*

*The discipline of reason* The other side of Delacroix faced in the direction of thought that imposes order. His journey to Morocco revealed to him true classicism, and so steered him closer to it. His pictures of *Christopher Columbus* (1838-9) are composed on a geometrical frametwork; the *Columbus on his Return from the New World* (pl 229) is even based on a reminiscence of a Renaissance picture, a Titian of which Delacroix had seen an engraving (pl 230). Many of Delacroix's Moroccan pictures submit to this severe discipline of verticals and horizontals (pls 231, 232), which even in 1862 (pl 233) has lost none of its vigour.

229 *Columbus on his Return from the New World, 1839. The Toledo Museum of Art, Ohio.*

230 TITIAN: *Presentation of the Virgin in the Temple. Accademia, Venice.*

231 *Chess-players in Jerusalem, 1835. The National Gallery of Scotland, Edinburgh.*

232 *Arab Women at a Fountain. Louvre, Paris.*

233 *Horses at the Fountain, 1862. Formerly Chester Beatty Collection.*

234 *Head of an Arab woman. Louvre, Paris.*

*Limitlessness of nature*

Delacroix's journey to Morocco not only confirmed his two-fold aspiration towards baroque expression (pl 227) and classical expression (pl 233), both sides of which went on developing as long as he lived: it also amplified that feeling for limitless space, which had made its appearance already in 1824 with the *Massacre at Chios*, under English influence (pl 108), and was still in evidence in 1831 (pl 165) on the eve of the journey. He was never to forget the vast Moroccan horizons (pls 235, 236); he would bring them even into scenes inspired by *Tasso* (pl 237) or by Antiquity (pls 238, LVI), and into some of his last pictures.

235 *Arab Actors and Clowns, 1848. Musée des Beaux-Arts, Tours.*

236 *Arab Actors and Clowns, 1836. Bührle Collection, Zurich.*

237 *Ovid among the Scythians, 1859. The National Gallery, London.*

238 *Erminia and the Shepherds, 1859. Nationalmuseum, Stockholm.*

186

187

188

189

190

191

la rencontre avec l'autre Pacha
musique à cheval
montagnes vertes avec terre jaune dans la distance
l'anecdote des fromages qu'arrangeait le Pacha de Tanger

192

Soleil très ardent. route dans une plaine immense
le 14 mars mercredi Zar Hone
Parti par un beau soleil du matin.
Blanc des étoffes et couleurs très vives

193

194

195

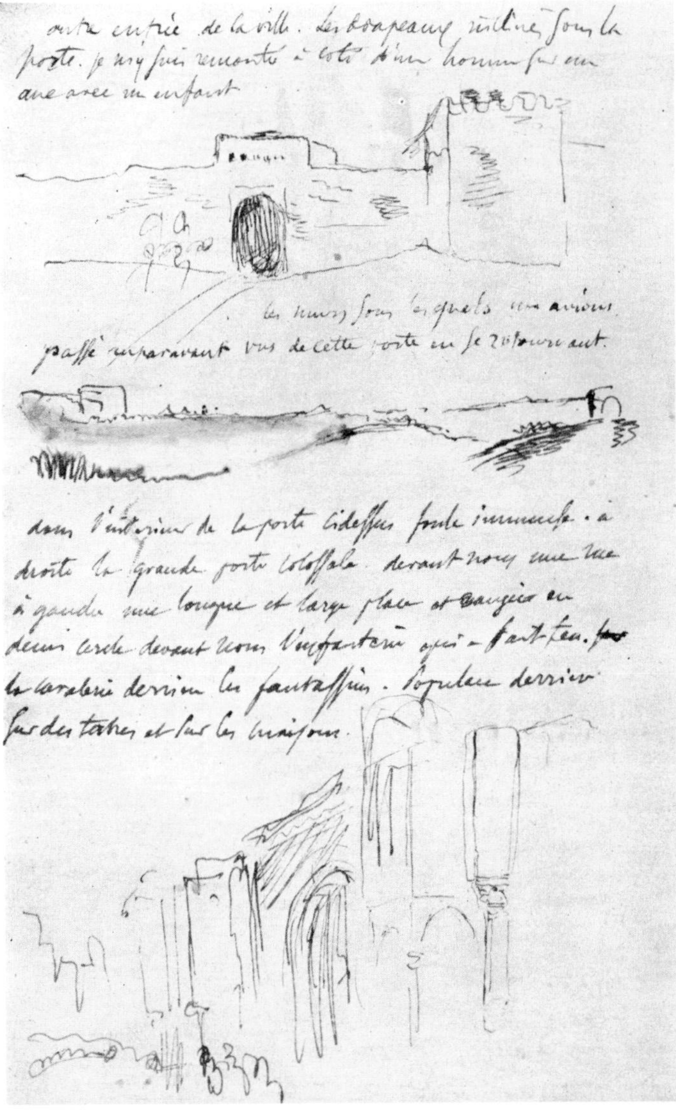

196

197

198

199

200

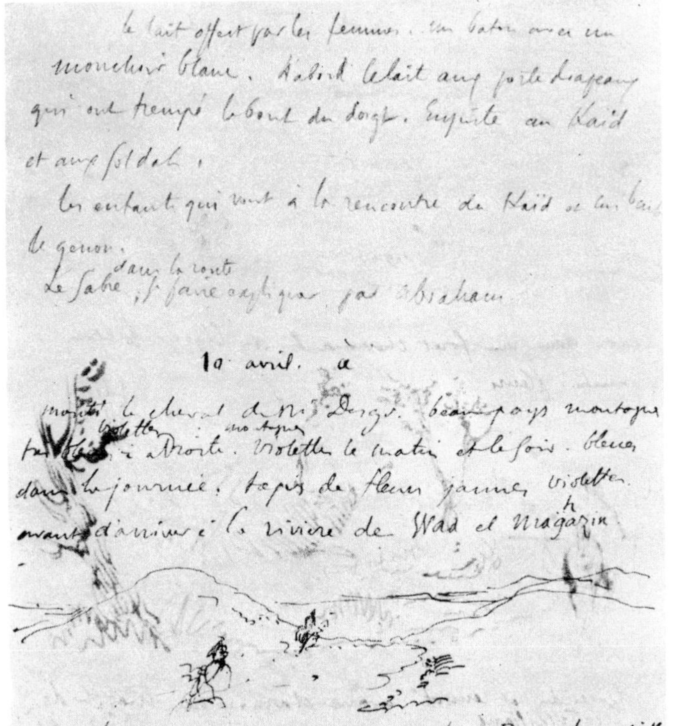

le lait offert par les femmes. un baton avec un mouchoir blanc. Kalid le lait aux porte drapeaux qui ont trempé le bout du doigt. Ensuite au Kaid et aux soldats.

les enfants qui vont à la rencontre du Kaid et lui baisent le genou.

Le sabre dans la route, se fait expliquer par Abraham

10 avril.

monté le cheval de Mr Drummond. beau pays montagnes à droite. violettes le matin et le soir. bleues dans la journée. tapis de fleurs jaunes violettes avant d'arriver à la rivière de Wad el Magazin

passé la rivière et dejeuné dans les mêmes broussailles

entré dans la grande plaine où a été defait D. Sebastien. à droite très belles montagnes bleues. à gauche plaine à perte de vue, tapis de fleurs blanc, jaunes clair, jaune foncé, violets

201

202

203

204

205

206

207

208

209

210

211

212

213

214

215

216

217

218

219

220

221

222

223

224

225

226

227

228

229

230

231

232

233

234

235

236

237

238

# VII THE SEARCH FOR BALANCE

DELACROIX RETURNED FROM MOROCCO aware of the response awakened in him by the true classicism which disdaining routine and restraining rules moves upwards, through the discovery of the higher discipline, to the expression of a balanced, natural life. He had caught sight of the complete art which was now to be his aim, though without renouncing the aspirations and vigour of his per-sonal temperament. For this he would need to renew and enlarge his means of expression, but not deny the sources of his poetry or cease to be faithful to himself.

## *From Passion to Form*

The essential motive power in Delacroix had always been the torment which life sets up in a man by awakening in him appetites which his thinking condemns and tries to check. But thinking also acquires a torment of its own, for aware-ness of life awakens questions that find no answer, and this leads to a growing despair. Delacroix constantly felt the stirring within him of that fundamental uneasiness which the human condition will not let rest, and he continued to draw the substance of his inspirations from his strife with it. Could the moving expression demanded by this be made to fit in with the balance and serene gran-deur revealed to Delacroix by the patriarchal wisdom of a primitive world? Could the corrosive bitterness of a highly developed civilization and the 'new thrills' discovered by it be united with the immemorial traditions and their material force?

Delacroix was to strive with all his will-power towards such a reconciliation. But he was to find it only gradually. Since his return from Morocco coincided with the beginning of the series of commissions for large-scale decorative paint-ings, and since this mural art was more suited than any other to his new aspira-tions, he at first tended to reserve the more classical part of his experiments for the new enterprise. And at the same time, he seemed inclined to reserve the violent twists and turns of his spiritual life for small, more confidential pictures, whether easel paintings or engravings.

pl 239 In the 1835 Salon there appeared his *Prisoner of Chillon*, painted in the year before. When we remember that that was the year his nephew Charles de

Verninac died on the other side of the Atlantic, we shall see how much a subject like this meant to Delacroix. In a stifling, nightmare world of darkness the prisoner, pulling desperately on the chain by which he is tethered, is trying to reach his young brother, who is dying at the foot of the wall opposite. But the space cannot be crossed. Is it possible to imagine a more direct projection of Delacroix's own anguish than this picture with its icy, shadowy harmony?

A painting, the *Entombment of Christ*, and a lithograph, *Clifford finding the* pl 240 *Corpse of his Father on the Battlefield*, dating from the same time, confirm Delacroix's obsession with the enigma of death and pain. So, even more, does the *Hamlet* series.[1] He returns to the theme of Hamlet and Yorick's skull. In the 1828 lithograph of this subject, and again in a final version painted in 1859, a somewhat theatrical procession of monks is visible; but in the 1839 painting pl 242 Delacroix concentrates on Hamlet's intense questioning, setting it in the cemetery of Toulon, which he had had all too long a time to observe during the quarantine that ended his Moroccan journey. 'Alas poor Yorick. . . a fellow of infinite jest; of most excellent fancy... Here hung those lips, that I have kiss'd I know not how oft. Where be your jibes now? your gambols? your songs?'

The scene occurs also in the series of sixteen lithographs which he began in 1834. These were published at Delacroix's own expense in 1843, but only thirteen of them: the complete series did not see the light until 1864. The graveyard scene, which was among the last of them to be executed, in 1843, repeats the composition of the 1839 picture, but in reverse (as is often the case with an engraving of a painting). In the painting the line rises from the lower right-hand corner towards the gravedigger and continues along the arm that holds his spade; reaching the shoulder, it turns at right angles and rises along his other arm, which is holding out the skull to Hamlet; behind Hamlet it is carried on by the hill to the picture-frame. It is the same wedge-like baroque composition that is used so emphatically in the *Battle of Taillebourg* (1837). fig 18

In the *Hamlet* series there is seldom evidence of the preoccupation with balanced lines that makes itself felt in Delacroix's art—but chiefly in the large-scale compositions—after his journey to Morocco. In these lithographs, whose black and white develop all the resources of *chiaroscuro* for the interiors, and of moonlight for the scenes on the Elsinore terrace, the diagonal is always dominant. Moonlight, a ghost, murders, Ophelia's madness and death, gravediggers and open graves (Yorick's and Ophelia's) with Hamlet and Laertes struggling fiercely, and then the final agony—what could be more Shakespearian or more romantic? And yet these lithographs were done between 1834 and 1843 at the height of Delacroix's period of large-scale mural painting and of classicism.

Nor is the effort towards classicism any more evident in a parallel series of seven engravings which—from 1836 to 1843—Delacroix devoted to Goetz von Berlichingen. (Here again there were two editions, in 1843 and 1864.) Delacroix returns to the Middle Ages, with armour, shadowy halls in castles, and combats in which the adversaries are knotted in inextricable fury, as they are in the 1835 version of the *Giaour and the Pasha*, perhaps the wildest treatment of that pl 206 theme. So at this time Byron, Shakespeare and Goethe, the great sources of romantic inspiration, were grouped together in Delacroix's work. His treatment of Goetz on horseback, wounded, is itself a reminiscence—reversed and set in a

*Fig 18* THE BATTLE OF TAILLEBOURG The groups descend from right to left, following a series of points and angles, of which the arm and arrow of the archer on the left form the bisecting line.

deep forest—of the *King Rodrigues* he had painted in a few hours for the famous fancy dress ball given by Alexandre Dumas on 15 March 1832, in the heyday of romanticism. Those days were now well and truly over, especially for Delacroix after what he had seen in Morocco. Having, in these intimate works, confessed his loyalty to the torments of his spiritual life, he now looked for a wider, more universal expression for them: side by side with these picture-confessions, in which there was no sign of any modification of his art, he was to show his real development more clearly in his last large-scale canvases which, strung out between 1837 and 1841, accompany his first mural paintings and act as a kind of transition between these and his easel painting.

The *Battle of Taillebourg*, commissioned for the Galerie des Batailles at Versailles, is like a watershed between the two slopes of Delacroix's work. All the warlike and dramatic fanfares of romanticism are still sounding in this picture: the battling of men and horses, the furious hand-to-hand fights, the bloodshed, the eyes dilated by terror or rage, the standards flapping amid the smoke of the fires, and even the water of the river against the stonework of the quay, recall the cruel themes that haunted Delacroix's youth and reappeared at their wildest
XXIV, page 252 in the 1835 *Giaour and the Pasha*. The sketch for the *Battle of Taillebourg* is dominated, like that for the *Battle of Nancy*, by the vertical of a building and is made up of collective movements of indistinct and seething masses of combatants.
pl 246 There may be, in this case, a reminiscence of Rubens' *Battle of the Amazons*
fig 19 with its whirling movements called forth by the arch of a bridge. But Delacroix gives up the Flemish painter's circling movement: taking up again the composi-
pl 165 tion attempted in the *Battle of Nancy*, he creates an enormous wedge, above the point of which there rises the equestrian figure of the King, 'carried away', as the catalogue of the Salon puts it, 'by his ardour'. His white charger and his blue clothes heightened with silver *fleur de lys* and immaculate ermine make a centre of brightness in the midst of the reds and browns. This wedge, which is destroying the enemy, is also the angle at which the two movements of the attack are

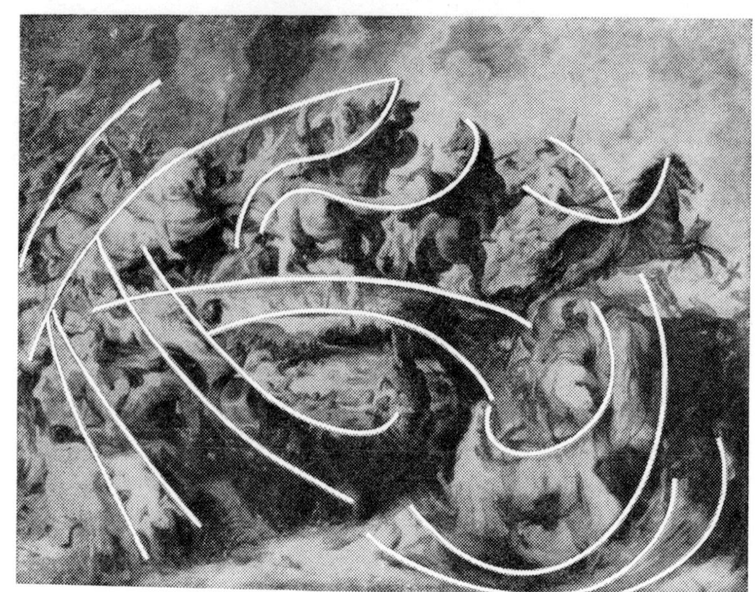

*Fig 19* Rubens: THE BATTLE OF THE AMAZONS
It is from this picture, or rather from the left-hand part, that Delacroix took the basic idea for Taillebourg, in which the ascending impetus of the horsemen and the descending slope of the bank are arranged around the outline of the arch.

converging, the one coming down the slope of the bridge, the other up that of the river bank. The final picture attenuates the curve of the arch and does away with its great diagonal shadow, in order to eliminate lines that might interfere with the general composition in the form of a lance. This is, on the contrary, stressed by the miniature repetitions (or scattered echoes) of it in the various upraised arms. Saint Louis himself, who in the sketch was recoiling under the force of an enemy's attack, here reinforces the dominant angle, by the angle between his forward-leaning body and his forearm, which is raised behind his head and continued by the weapon he is brandishing.

How conscious Delacroix was of these compositional devices can be gauged by studying the way in which, when commissioned to treat the same subject again for a stained glass window in the chapel of Dreux, he adapted himself (in the water-colour from which his pupil Lassalle-Bordes was to make the cartoon) to the attenuated, vertical format imposed on him. The angle between the bridge and the river bank is wide and almost gives place to the vertical produced by the piles of stone. At the point of the angle, where the picture placed the head of an archer whose arrow marked the bisecting horizontal, there is now a horseman who, twisting round on his mount seen from behind, operates the transition from the diagonal that runs from the lower right-hand corner to the diagonal that will run to the upper corner on the same side. For all the animation of the battle and the movement of the principal lines, the figures, both in the cartoon and in the final picture, stand out from the general confusion by virtue of their more pronounced and sculptural mass; the geometrical form of the large regular stones of the bridge and quay is likewise asserted. The spirit of the *Battle of Nancy* is still alive, yet there is now introduced a monumental power not to be found in that picture's snowy, twilight plain. pl 243 fig 20

The 1836 *Saint Sebastian rescued by the Holy Women* is perhaps the first of Delacroix's pictures in which solid volumes are stressed with such authority: the composition is clearly derived from Rubens' *Deposition*, repeating as it does the attitude of the tortured body seated on the ground with one leg in perspec- pl 248 pl 247 tive and the other stretched out; and in it Delacroix displays the new knowledge of anatomy he had gained in working on the walls of the Salon du Roi.

It recurs in 1838, in the *Medea* now in the Lille Museum—so much so that Delécluze, that veteran Aristarchus of classicism, was almost beside himself with delight. Delacroix's usual abandon had reappeared in the sketch for this
pl 250 picture: there the folds of the drapery zig-zag in obedience to a stormy blast, or are stretched tight like the rope of a cracking whip, and the fury of the murderous mother rises and flares like the flame and smoke of a brazier, which are then
pl 251 whirled away by the wind. But in the picture, though the general scheme of the attitude is maintained, it is as though the storm has been suddenly lulled: nothing remains but the pyramid of the three bodies, whose modelling and outline make a firm statement of sculptural solidity. What had been vehemence and disordered projection is now symmetry—between, for instance, the legs of Medea and those of her elder child, or again between this child's thigh and the calves of the younger child, while the axis is marked by the verticality of a long, brightly lit fold which, in the sketch, was twisted.

If one could trace from its beginnings the genesis of an image in the painter's mind, one would have some considerable surprises. Would it, for instance, be rash to suggest that, before painting this picture, Delacroix studied Raphael's *La Belle Jardinière* (in which the movement of the shoulders and left arm is similar,

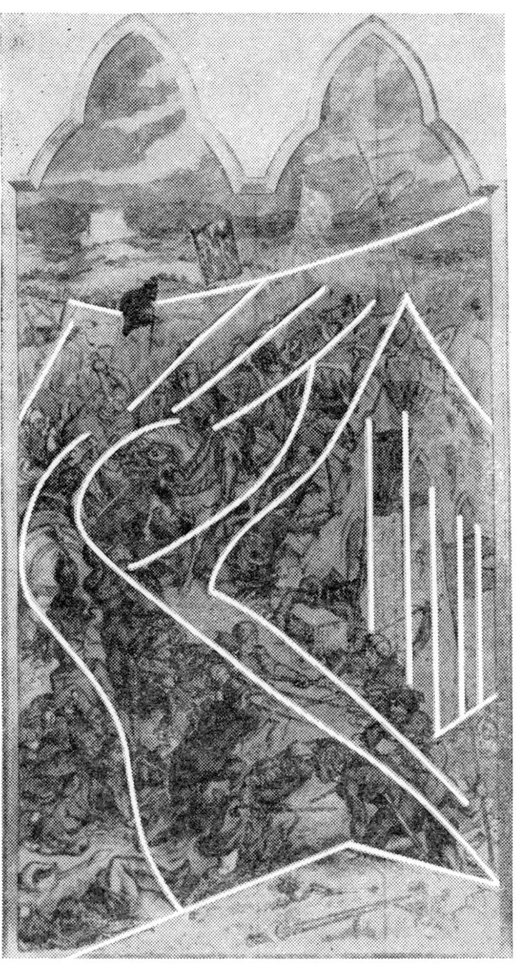

*Fig 20* BATTLE OF TAILLEBOURG (Cartoon for the stained glass window at Dreux).
The composition of the painting is preserved, in principle, but is adapted to the vertical shape, which emphasizes the piers of the bridge and the angle formed by their slopes.

though here reversed) and Andrea del Sarto's *Charity*—both pictures in the pl 249 Louvre? In these two pictures there is a similar pyramidal composition formed of a group of children surmounted by a woman's torso. There is even a possible model for the child on the right with the bent leg. And the *Journal* gives us a clue: on 15 April 1823 Delacroix noted: 'Today I have been greatly admiring Andrea del Sarto's *Charity*. The truth is, this picture moves me more than Raphael's *Holy Family*. . . . How noble and elegant and strong his children are! And the woman—what a head and what hands! If only I had the time to make a copy.'

In contrast, in the 1859 version (National Galerie, Berlin) Delacroix returned pl 252 to his first feeling: the tragic figure in her effort to escape is striding over the rocks with the same vigour as Delacroix's *Liberty Leading the People*;[2] the nervous, sinuous fluttering of her garment stresses the wavelike movement. There is always, in these late treatments by Delacroix of an earlier theme (as we have seen in the case of the Moroccan subjects), a strange return to the *vis romantica*.

## *The 'Justice of Trajan': a Complete Art*

The impressive evidence of this maturing was seen in his *Justice of Trajan*, at pl 260 the 1840 Salon. The subject is taken from Dante: here again there is a mother and the death of a child, but this time the mother is demanding justice. Under the sign of Antiquity, which is emphasized by the archaeological truth of the monuments and costumes and, notably, the ensigns and trumpets, a balance is sought between the ardour of life and the fixity of order. Delacroix made no bones about his return, at this period, to classical sources: about 1838, when making the studies for his *Trajan*, he painted the two versions of *Cleopatra and* pl 257 *the Countryman*, in which—especially in the Salon version—the two figures between them fill the frame with their sculptural monumentality.

Similarly, in 1845, while he was working on the Luxembourg Library and on his *Sultan of Morocco*, he painted the *Death of Marcus Aurelius* which is pl 253 now in the Lyons Museum. Here, as we have seen, he was going back to the subject of a Latin translation to be found in one of his school notebooks, dating from 1811. Rarely did he come so close to Poussin, of whose *Death of Germanicus* pl 254 this picture reminds us—or, perhaps still more, of his *Testament of* pl 255 *Eudamidas*—both by its subject, with its stoic mood, and by its severe, restrained composition.

Also in the 1845 Salon, he exhibited *Sibyl with the Golden Bough*. The theme pl 256 is, of course, the one that inspired Virgil, and Delacroix's model may have been the actress Rachel, the ideal of the classicists. 'The Sibyl at the upper end of the dark forest, displaying the golden bough, prize of the great-hearted favourites of

XXXIII ATTILA FOLLOWED BY BARBARIAN HORDES TRAMPLES ITALY AND THE ARTS (detail)
*1838-47 Oil and wax. 289 x 434 (735 x 1100)*
*Hemicycle in the Library of the Palais Bourbon, Paris*

the gods' reminds us of Poussin, who also was tempted by 'Virgil's golden bough, which none can find or pluck if he is not led by Destiny.' Ingres himself had spoken in almost identical terms of the perfection of certain Greek vases, saying of them: 'That line is what one must achieve. That is the golden bough of Virgil, which no one could pluck without being led by Destiny.' But the most significant thing about Delacroix's picture is not that he was following in the footsteps of Poussin and Ingres. It is, surely, that the golden bough meant the reward that crowns the inspired genius, the reward for the achievement that is not obtained by reflection or by method: it symbolizes, surely, the essential aim of romanticism. What passionate symbol would Delacroix have chosen to suggest this, only a few years earlier? But now he has recourse, for its expression, to this serene, sovereignly calm figure, with her regular features recalling the ideal type of the Renaissance, with her gaze lost in the infinite, with her slow and cadenced movement and her relaxed attitude. Inspiration, which formerly had been only fever and abandon, now seemed to him lovely and meditative like the ancient statues. Formerly it had seemed to need, to make it leap awake, the smell of blood and the electricity of the storm; now it was turned towards the laurel of Antiquity.

pl 260 In the *Trajan*, five years earlier, Delacroix's inspiration was still exalted by the din of trumpets and the sight of war horses; and yet already the will towards balance was affirmed even in the sketch—indeed even more intransigently in this first flight than in the fully worked out picture. The great vertical columns descend rigidly to the bottom of the curve like a reversed arch traced by the foreground figures. In contrast, in the finished picture, there is a recurrence of the
pl 245 angle or wedge arrangement which we encountered in the *Battle of Taillebourg*:
fig 21 at first barely suggested, it came in the end to dominate the composition. A ray of light falls straight from the upper right-hand corner and, gaining impetus from the parallels of the architecture seen in perspective and from those of the horse's legs, follows the bent back of the suppliant and strikes like a whip against the opposite edge of the frame; here, after a brief break, the line rebounds at right angles along the mother's outstretched arm and the small dead body. Yet upon this lightning zig-zag with its baroque character there is superimposed the solid order of the architecture: vertical and horizontal axes are formed by the darkly outlined colums, pilasters and entablatures. The broad pyramid of the principal group is supported against the central column, but also swept by the movement of the rearing war horse and crowned by the group of onlookers on the stone pedestal. The two lower corners of this pyramid coincide with those of the picture but are assaulted by two opposing diagonals, the left-hand one traced by the group demanding justice, the right-hand one by that of the attendants; and the sharp edges of the shadows and lights accentuate this fresh element of symmetry. The whole suggests the composition of some masterpiece of the late Renaissance.

XXXIV ORPHEUS BRINGING CIVILIZATION (detail)
*1838-47 Oil and wax. 289 x 434 (735 x 1100)*
*Hemicycle in the Library of the Palais Bourbon, Paris*

Never, indeed, was Delacroix's temptation to see Italy for himself so strong as now. Already, in 1820, his friend Soulier, who had introduced him to England, had nearly succeeded in drawing him in his own wake, when he went to Italy with the Marquis de Maisonfort, his employer. But in those days Delacroix's dream was rather of 'a clear sky, expressive bodies, a thousand enchantments, in fact Italy with all her seductions' than of the Italian Schools of painting: he kept making 'plans for going and consuming my small income in Tuscany', and, although at that time he was taken 'three or four times a month with a strong desire to emigrate to Italy', the plan came to nothing. He thought of it many times after that, but always without result. Now the desire was stronger than ever: on 15 February 1838 Delacroix told Baron Rivet that he was longing to go to Italy, 'which seems every year to retreat before me, because of the perpetual succession of obstacles which imprison us. . . .' He never went. It is left to us to imagine the shock his art would have received from a revelation to which his whole instinct aspired.

Failing this, he turned in another direction for what he sought, and found it in a more confused and complex form—as is evident from the association, in his Trajan, of the violent gestures, the horse's alarm, the wind-stirred flags and the shrilling trumpets with the Roman masses and immutable calm of the architecture. Only one artist before this had succeeded in reconciling tendencies so divergent: Rubens; Flemish in origin and baroque in training, he had observed the great lesson of the Italians and had managed to digest it in his large-scale compositions, particularly in the series devoted to Marie de Medici. In many of pl 259
these a great diagonal crosses the picture surface, while a strict vertical, usually supplied by the architectural setting, states an axis which generates order and balance. Elie Lambert[3] has suggested that the *Trajan* contains reminiscences of the paintings by Rubens seen by Delacroix at Antwerp: if the two wing pieces of the *Raising of the Cross* are brought close together, the result is to place side by side a Roman horseman and a terrified mother carrying her child, and these may have originated the central scene. Delacroix had recently admired the two great triptychs by Rubens in the cathedral at Antwerp, during his brief visit there with Marie-Elisabeth Boulanger, which took place in September 1839. 'So many different pleasures and emotions of all kinds at the same time', he confessed in a letter of 21 September to Pierret, who was aware of the circumstances, 'is truly a dream that one has only once in a lifetime.'

Delacroix's admiration for Rubens has often been stressed: Rubens was the great master whom he felt to be the closest to him, even though there was all the difference between them that there is between the muscle and the nerve, between a sometimes ostentatious health and a subtle *morbidezza*, between the powerful current of a river and a rushing, foaming torrent. Who can forget Delacroix's passionate invocation to that 'Homer of painting', to whom he went, in his early days, in search of the secret of those drops of water trickling over the flesh of the naiads, in order to spatter with them the damned in the *Dante and Virgil*? II, page 58
And Delacroix always retained a predilection for this painter, in whom 'imagination speaks before all else' and in whom 'the life of the soul' is 'placed at every point.'[4] Although Delacroix recognized in him that irresistible flux of life to which he also intended to give free course, and the power to bend subject, draw-

*Fig 21* THE JUSTICE OF TRAJAN
The lines projected from the corner across the painting derive from Taillebourg, but they are combined with the stability of the central pyramidal mass and the verticals, so dear to classical painters.

ing and colour to a kind of irresistibly eloquent diction, what he valued in Rubens most—and this is certain—was the great master of composition. In the last article he wrote, the one on Charlet, which appeared on 1 July 1862 in the *Revue des Deux Mondes*, Delacroix gives us the key to his devotion. There he speaks of the 'persevering labour' concealed under the apparent ease of the great masters. To achieve this, it is necessary to acquire 'the impetus of an execution without retouchings or afterthoughts' by means of a passionate education of the eye and hand; and indeed, 'without a knowledgeable and calculated preparatory study with a view to the final achievement, this *tour de force* would be impossible'—and Delacroix adds: 'even to Rubens'. For 'it is in the conception of the whole, in the first lineaments of the picture, it is above all in the arrangement of the parts that compose it, that the most powerful of his faculties was exercised; it was there that he really worked.'[5]

So then, in Delacroix, not only are the opposing demands of romanticism and classicism combined, but they now allot between them the field that constitutes each of them. As the *Medea* had just shown, broad arrangements of thought-out and solid lines, together with firmly plastic and distinct forms, would be developed by him in paintings covering large surfaces, whether canvases or wall spaces, while fire, fever of execution, unrestrained sensibility, passion and sheer visual delight would come more naturally in easel painting. But this was not the only distinction: the successive phases of the working out of a picture must lend themselves to a wise assignment of the various gifts deployed by the painter. The picture must be conceived in a deep meditation, in which his individual resources, intellectual and sensual, would bring forth their most precious ingredients. Then gradually mature reflection must be brought into play, to bring order among these elements, in order to combine them and draw from them the maximum effect: it is at this point that the art of composition comes in. The execution—the next stage—has to recover that decision made in the heat: the fire that rose from the soul must now issue from the hand, and can do so only by making use of a hard-won manual experience, so firmly possessed as to appear instinctive and spontaneous. (So also the doctor's or the expert's diagnosis seems to be intuitive when really it is the result of a patiently accumulated and assimilated science.)

And in fact it was in this period of mature thought that Delacroix attained the greatest technical boldness. Villot dated from the *Prisoner of Chillon*—and therefore from the period just after the return from Morocco—'the first symptoms of the third and last phase of his technique.' After trying out extended local tones in the Salon du Roi (where he acquired his first experience as a mural painter), Delacroix adopted a new and quite contrary practice—'*flochetage*', which was to be one of the sources of the Impressionist technique.[6] This divided touch was in great part the fruit of his applying himself to the new task of large-scale decorative painting. This, while it drove him to go further along the classical path, also incited him towards a broken technique in which the vibration of the brushwork and the breaking up of the colours would sustain interest throughout the painted area and animate every inch of it with a subdued life. Thus at the moment when Delacroix, in certain aspects of his art, seemed likely to draw nearer to his former adversaries, the champions of emphasis on form and on drawing, he was to offend them perhaps even more gravely in their visual habits by this unexpected and revolutionary brushwork. Perhaps they scented in this, with a sure instinct, the beginnings of Impressionism, which they would abhor when it came: certainly they rose up in arms, and the jury redoubled its severity, so much so that the most 'Roman' of Delacroix's pictures, his *Trajan*, was very nearly rejected. The critics and public opinion joined together, and it soon became fashionable to speak of the decadence of Delacroix. It took a Théophile Gautier to express enthusiasm at the sight of this prodigious outburst of colour:

'The *Justice of Trajan* is perhaps, as colour, M. E. Delacroix's finest picture, and rarely has painting given to the eyes so brilliant a festival. The leg in its dark red and gold buskin against the rose pink flank of the horse is the freshest bouquet of tones ever picked from a palette, even in Venice.'

This disintegration of the touch favoured an analysis of tones, and in fact went with it. Delacroix's eye perspicaciously discerned the pure colours whose

XXXV HESIOD AND THE MUSE

*1838-47 Oil on canvas. 87 x 115 (221 x 291)*

*Pendentive of the 'Poetry' cupola in the Library of the Palais Bourbon, Paris*

HÉSIODE
ET
LA MUSE

interweaving would re-establish the dominant he sought, and these suggested to him unexampled flights of daring: hitherto he had combined rare and delightful harmonies that enchanted the eye, but now, by breaking up the colours, he quarrelled openly with the customary conventions. Trajan's pink horse excited a storm of indignation—even Gauguin did not seem more shocking to his contemporaries! A critic called Théodore Burette, for instance, condemned the brushwork as a 'coarse-grained tapestry'—though he did add that it was 'after a picture by a master', for he could not remain completely blind to the classicism of the picture; and the witty Alphonse Karr joined in making fun of the rose-pink horse and of Trajan as 'a butcher's boy in a brick-red light'.

Knowledge of the laws of complementary colours and simultaneous contrast, which later served the post-Impressionists as a basis for their technique, was of great use to Delacroix. He was not, in fact, ignorant of the works of Chevreul, with which Seurat, Signac and their followers were to saturate themselves. One of my first tasks at the Louvre was to classify the papers and other documents bequeathed by Moreau-Nélaton, and among them, in one of the files devoted to Delacroix, I came across a notebook written by someone who had attended Chevreul's lectures: this is very probably the document used by Delacroix in order to familiarize himself with discoveries whose applications he would later explore. As we have already seen, he sought these experimentally, by combining threads of various colours.[7] He had also a very complete selection of sealing-wafers and, wetting his finger, he would try innumerable juxtapositions, which he would change rapidly after observing them intently with his eye screwed up. He had also placed on the wall of his studio a triangle of which the principle is to be found in one of his Moroccan notebooks: the tones are set next to one another or in diametrical opposition, so displaying the secret of nearby colours and complementaries; red, yellow and blue occupied the points, while the results of their mixture appeared on the side joining them. This fundamental arrangement has long been used in the school text-books; but to Delacroix it was the demonstration of something he had already discovered intuitively. In 1827, when he was VI, page 74 doing the preparatory work for his *Marino Faliero* and had decided to go and consult Veronese at the Louvre, he had suddenly noticed, just as he was getting into the canary yellow *fiacre* he had ordered, that the shadows were violet. He did not go on to the Louvre but went in again, enriched by an important discovery.

## *The 'Crusaders': the Calm after the Storm*

At the same time as large-scale decorative painting absorbed Delacroix's new longing for the classic sources, the remainder of his romanticism was also finding its voice—the melancholy voice of a farewell. In 1840, for Versailles, he XXVII, page 283 undertook to paint his *Entry of the Crusaders into Constantinople.*

XXXVI DEATH OF OPHELIA
*1844 Oil on canvas. 9 x 12 (022 x 030)*
*Louvre, Paris*

What theme could have provided a better opportunity for bringing together all the old spells, those of the Middle Ages and of the East? The sumptuous city lies vanquished by the warriors of the North and 'Baudoin, Count of Flanders, is advancing', says the catalogue of the 1841 Salon, 'followed by a cortège of horsemen with banners.' The basic situation is not unlike that of the *Trajan*: once again there is a confrontation between a gorgeous company on horseback and a crowd of people on foot or prostrate. But the arrangement is reversed: instead of a scene viewed from the side, the main group is coming towards us, making the same general effect as that of Delacroix's *Liberty Leading the* XIII, page 169 *People*, advancing over the barricades straight at the spectator and almost stepping out of the picture; the pyramidal arrangement is also present. But while *Liberty* is springing upwards towards the sky and the light, the central group of the *Crusaders* seems to be dragged down to the ground, to be sinking into twilight, lassitude and melancholy.

In contrast with the pawing and rearing movement of Trajan's horse, the leading horse here seems to be stumbling over human distress and scenting death; his advance is hesitant, his steps uncertain, and he is lowering his head as though submitting to some imaginary yoke. This is the tragic movement Delacroix had discovered already in 1833, for his figure of *King Rodrigues* returning, blood-stained and exhausted, from the battle on a worn-out horse; and he had used it again with the same funereal significance in his 1838 *Arab at the Tomb*, in which the animal stretches out its neck towards the filled-in grave to which its master has come to pray.

Delacroix's *Crusaders* express relapse, weariness. What a trajectory it was that began its rise with the *Massacre at Chios* to reach its dying fall here! Both III, page 67 pictures have to do with a massacre after the taking of a town, amid the splendour of an Eastern landscape: but in the earlier one the proud Turk is pulling his ardent, foaming steed upwards and backwards, like that of Trajan, and the half-naked woman victim draws back in violent tension—while in the later picture the animal and his master, worn out with fatigue and sated with violence, are bend- XXVIII, page 284 ing under the weight of their melancholy; the lines, seeming now to respond to nothing but weight, sag towards the ground, just as the loosened fair hair of the captive girl abruptly completes the droop of her back and head with a vertical pl 263 fall.

The first sketches show that Delacroix, harking back to the *Massacre at Chios*, had thought of placing one of the Crusaders on the right, on a horse in violent motion, with a human prey thrown across his saddle, one arm raised in a hopeless appeal—like Rubens' *Daughters of Leucippus*. This last leap of energy is eliminated in the final picture: though killing is still going on it is now only in the distance—the storm whose last ripples are dying away. The horsemen stand out sombre against the brightness of the landscape over which the bright light is sleeping—again a reminiscence of the *Massacre at Chios* and a contrast with the *Trajan* (in which the light is a ray striking the main group like a spotlight and isolating it against the setting). In the *Crusaders* even the colour, though one of the richest and most inventive *ensembles* in the whole of Delacroix's output, is subject to this mood of exhaustion: the carmines of the *Trajan* are forgotten, the reds tend towards garnet, shades of violet and purple and a pale rose. The cold tones are awakening, along with the cool evening breeze—deep blue and, above all, violets that degenerate into grey, a grey whose heavy clouds are strangling the azure of the sky. 'Stormy and lugubrious harmony!' was Baudelaire's description.[8]

In that evening light romanticism is aware of its exhaustion, with all its passion, cruelty and sensuality. The standards and pennants, whose red and orange are short-lived flames amid cold nocturnal tones, are scarcely moving and seem about to wrap themselves along their poles: the one or two flamboyant flags have fallen to the ground and are being trampled by the horses in their slow advance. The failing ardours of the conquerors are ringed round and contained as if they were a group of captives. The wide horizon, which reminds us of the impla-
xxvi, page 274 cable expanse on which the barque of *Don Juan* was floating in the 1839 picture, subdues even the proudest heads and displays the indifference of the great sheets of water and the distant mountains. The verticals of the high porphyry and marble portico with its impassive, heavy masses, the regular chequerwork of the paving and the rigid lines of the lances and banner poles set up a severe net-
pl 261 work: in the later version, painted in 1852, this is reinforced at the expense of the human figures lost in their setting. Alone, in the background, the wide street cutting through the city and its white houses forms a rising sinuous line, like a wavering cry that will lose itself in space.

With this great canvas something new makes room for itself in Delacroix's art: though there are still fanfares they sound like a final horn call, a receding farewell. Delacroix, already engaged upon a different enterprise, is here conceding to romanticism its sumptuous funeral. From now on, in fact, a kind of appeasement in balance becomes evident, even in pictures of relatively moderate
xxix, page 291 dimensions like the *Education of the Virgin*. This was painted in 1842, during one of the visits Delacroix paid to Nohant, after he had formed his friendship with George Sand and Chopin. (He admired both the composer and his music, and indeed was more at ease with him than with the novelist.) Through the open window he listened to Chopin filling the summer air with his extraordinary harmonies and, as he wrote to Pierret on 7 June 1842, 'they are one with the song of the nightingale and the scent of the rose bushes.' He loved talking with Chopin about art[9]—that art whose profound laws are the same under all the differences of technique.

During this particular visit, Delacroix on his way back from a walk saw a
pl 266 woman on a farm teaching her grand-daughter to read, and at once painted the *Education of the Virgin*, in which the range of cold colours (which we have already seen in the blues and white of the *Battle of Taillebourg* and, more fully, as part of the purplish harmony of the *Crusaders*) reigns unchecked in the concord between the blue dresses and the deep green shades of the foliage. The horizontal of the ground and nearby water and the verticality of the leafy trees at the right-hand edge steady the figures, which are seen full-face and again form a pyramid. The principle is the same as that adopted for the composition of the *Crusaders* in the year before, with the difference that there the screen formed by the architecture was on the left. The lowered eyes, the timid finger on the open page, the full curves of the foliage, the weight of the summer afternoon and the silence of nature whose slumber is broken only by the small hesitant

voice—never had Delacroix achieved such calm and withdrawal, or come so close to time in the shadow of eternity.

Next year the *Pietà*, commissioned from him for the church of Saint-Denis-du-Saint-Sacrement, brought him face to face with a subject of concentrated tragedy; but he applied to it the same type of composition, and this not only in the great mural painting (140 in. by 187 in.) but also in a drawing, afterwards engraved, and in three later pictures on a small scale.[10] Indeed the arrangement is now stressed: there is a central mass, placed on the axis of the picture and presented full face; and it is enclosed in a framework of verticals and horizontals and treated with pronounced symmetry. The symmetry is complete in the drawing, where the scene is wedged tightly between two rising lines, to which the curtains held up by angels add a curve. In the wall painting there are rocks which, though more irregular, play the same part. The small-scale versions reproduce the symmetrical curve which was at first attained by the curtains. The great crucified gesture of the Virgin, crying out her grief with arms flung wide, emphasizes powerfully this completely regular and firmly centred composition. She, indeed, is borrowed from a Renaissance painter—from Rosso, whose tragic painting in the Louvre was available to Delacroix for study.[11] As for the heavy curve of the body of Christ, with the right hand hanging and the heads looking down on him forming an arch, this was surely an idea he found in Titian's *Entombment*. Thus there were quite a number of classical reminiscences derived from Italy, and it seems clear that the winged figures supporting curtains had the same origin.

pl 269

pl 268

But it is in the mural decorations—on which he was working during this period, and from which these classical intrusions are no more than the backwash—that the fulfilment of Delacroix's new aspirations must be sought.

# NOTES ON THE PLATES TO CHAPTER VII

*The shock of death* The insight into the true classicism which Delacroix had gained in Morocco worked only gradually. In 1834 the early death of his nephew Charles de Verninac (pl 27) aroused in him an obsession which confirmed his romanticism. It is conveyed almost literally in the despair of his *Prisoner of Chillon* (pl 239) and his *Clifford* (pl 240). It appears transposed in his *Crucifixion* (pl 241); and it turns him again towards the meditation of *Hamlet* (pl 242), a theme he now treated several times.

239 *The Prisoner of Chillon, 1834. Louvre, Paris.*

240 *Clifford finding the Corpse of his Father on the Battlefield, 1834. Lithograph.*

241 *Christ Crucified between Thieves, 1835. Musée Municipal des Beaux-Arts, Vannes.*

242 *Hamlet and Horatio in the Graveyard, 1839. Louvre, Paris.*

*Battles* Delacroix's romantic vein always emerges with energy in his battle scenes—in, for instance, the desperate struggles of the *Giaour* (1835, pl 206), in the *Battle of Taillebourg* (1837, pls XXIV and 245), with its echoes of Rubens' *Battle of the Amazons* (pl 246) which Delacroix had studied with care (pl 244). These echoes are to be found in the composition also, which is based on the left half of the Rubens picture: the importance given to it and the subtlety of the variations it has undergone (pl 243) show that Delacroix is giving more and more thought to construction.

243 *Sketch of the Battle of Taillebourg for a stained glass window. Musée Condé, Chantilly.*

244 *Sketch after an engraving (reversed) of the right-hand half of Rubens' 'Battle of the Amazons'. Cabinet des Dessins, Louvre, Paris.*

245 *The Battle of Taillebourg, 1837. Galerie des Batailles, Musée de Versailles.*

246 RUBENS: *The Battle of the Amazons. Alte Pinakothek, Munich.*

Delacroix studied the works of the masters and, having assimilated them, he brought into his own pictures the effects that had most struck him. He often had recourse to Rubens, as in his *Battle of Taillebourg*, or again in the 1836 *Saint Sebastian* (pls 247, 248). But he studied the Italian classical painters also: the pyramidal composition and grouping of Andrea del Sarto's *Charity* (pl 249), which he copied in the Louvre, formed the basis of his 1838 *Medea* (pl 251) with its sculptural volumes. The sketch for this *Medea* displays considerably more of Delacroix's usual unbridled energy (pl 250)—and there is more still in the 1859 version (pl 252).

*Meditation on the masters*

247 RUBENS: *The Deposition. Antwerp Museum.*

248 *Saint Sebastian rescued by the Holy Women, 1836. Church at Nantua.*

249 ANDREA DEL SARTO: *Charity. Louvre, Paris.*

250 *Sketch for 'Medea', 1838. Musée des Beaux-Arts, Lille.*

251 *Medea, 1838. Musée des Beaux-Arts, Lille.*

252 *Medea, 1859. National Galerie, Berlin.*

Delacroix's classical aspirations, which had become more and more pressing since Morocco, took shape in about 1838 with his sculptured *Cleopatra* (pl 257), and in 1845 with his Virgilian *Sibyl with the Golden Bough* (pl 256): it has been plausibly suggested that both these pictures were inspired by the tragic actress Rachel, who successfully championed classicism at that time. Also in 1845, his *Death of Marcus Aurelius* (pl 253) went so far as to repeat poses from Poussin (pl 254) and even Poussin's firmness of composition (pl 255).

*Ripening of classicism*

253 *The Death of Marcus Aurelius, 1845. Musée des Beaux-Arts, Lyons.*

254 NICHOLAS POUSSIN: *Death of Germanicus. Minneapolis Institute of Arts.*

255 POUSSIN: *Testament of Eudamidas. Statens Museum for Kunst, Copenhagen.*

256 *The Sibyl with the Golden Bough, 1845. George Wildenstein Collection, New York.*

257 *Cleopatra and the Countryman, 1838. The William Hayes Ackland Memorial Art Center, Chicago.*

Already in 1840 the *Justice of Trajan* (pl 260), with its Roman subject, its concern for archaeological accuracy and its broad architectural composition, had shown the direction in which Delacroix was moving. Yet he was far from repudiating himself: he clung firmly to his power of pathos (pl 258) and to Rubens (pl 259). The general scheme of the picture was a fresh treatment of

*Trajan*

that balanced combination of diagonals, verticals and horizontals characteristic of the Flemish master's greatest paintings (pl 259).

*258 Page of preparatory sketches for the 'Justice of Trajan'. Cabinet des Dessins, Louvre, Paris.*

*259* RUBENS: *Crowning of Marie de Medici at Saint Denis. Louvre, Paris.*

*260 The Justice of Trajan, 1840. Musée des Beaux-Arts, Rouen.*

*Farewell to frenzy* Exhibited with the *Trajan* at the 1840 Salon, the *Crusaders* (pl XXVII) typifies the watershed to which Delacroix's career had come: the victims of disaster, of whom the long series started with the *Massacre at Chios*, are still there and are as moving as ever (pl 263), but the struggles and rapes are now in the distance (pl 262); the horror of death can be read even in the eyes of the horses (pl XXVIII) and the composition is tied down by a strong framework—which even becomes preponderant in the 1852 version (pl 261).

*261 The Entry of the Crusaders into Constantinople, 1852. Louvre, Paris.*

*262 Preliminary Sketch for the 'Crusaders', 1840. Louvre, Paris.*

*263 The Entry of the Crusaders, 1840 (detail). Louvre, Paris.*

*Restfulness of nature* In 1842, before his discovery of Champrosay, Delacroix stayed at Nohant with George Sand. He had painted her portrait (pl 265) side by side with Chopin (pl 172) in 1838, making her sculptural like his *Cleopatra* (pl 257) and *Sibyl* (pl 256). This double portrait is known from a sketch (pl 264), but later on, no doubt for financial reasons, it was cut in two. At Nohant Delacroix became enchanted by the garden (pl 267), and began to make flower paintings (pl XXX). In this rustic setting he placed his *Education of the Virgin* (pl XXIX), based on a touching scene he had observed at Nohant (pl 266).

*264 Preparatory sketch for the double portrait of Chopin and George Sand, 1838. Louvre, Paris.*

*265 Portrait of George Sand. Ordrupgaard Museum, Copenhagen.*

*266 Mother and Child. Mme D. David Weill Collection, Paris.*

*267 George Sand's garden at Nohant, 1842. Metropolitan Museum, New York.*

*The Pietà* In 1844, in the *Pietà* which he painted for the church of Saint-Denis-du-Saint-Sacrement (pls 268, 269), Delacroix achieved a definitive synthesis of an unbearably intense grief with a perfectly strict composition, whose almost Italian equilibrium (derived from Rosso) is pushed to the point of symmetry.

*268 Study for the 'Pietà' for Saint-Denis-du-Saint-Sacrement. Formerly (1930) Mme Lauwick (née Riesener) Collection.*

*269 Pietà, 1844. Church of Saint-Denis-du-Saint-Sacrement, Paris.*

239

240

242

243

244

245

246

247

248

249

250

251

252

253

254

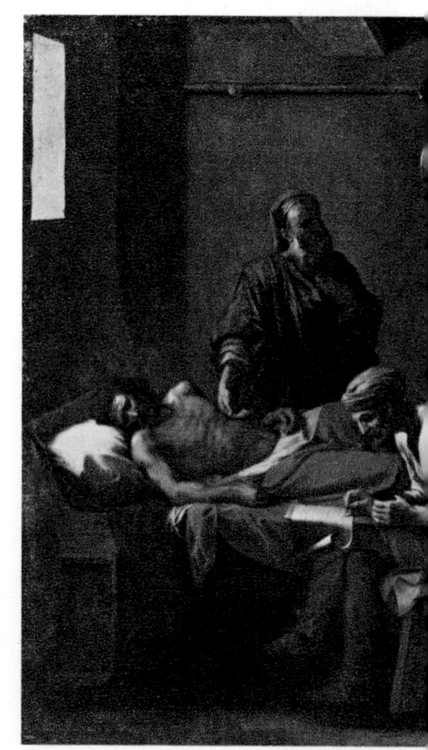

255

256

257

258

259

261

262

264

265

266

267

268

269

# VIII THE GREAT ENTERPRISES

THE GREATEST OF THE FRENCH nineteenth-century painters complained that official ostracism deprived them of the wall spaces on which they could have displayed the full breadth of their inspiration. Delacroix was the exception. No one was more aware than he was of 'all the fire that can normally be expressed only on walls'. But it seemed that, having become the *bête noire* of the Institut and of the jury of its dependent the Salon, he was bound to suffer more than anyone from such systematic rejection. Yet this reprobate, this symbol of the most abominable revolutionary innovations, was picked out to receive commissions from the State. The State bought one of his pictures at every Salon, and ordered from him three pictures for Versailles and its historical series—the *Portrait of Tourville* of 1835, the *Battle of Taillebourg* of 1837 and the *Crusaders* of 1840, while a *Rabelais* was destined for Chinon. Far more important still, the State turned to him for the decoration, first, of the Salon du Roi in the Palais Bourbon in April 1833, then of the Library of the Chambre in August 1838; then of the cupola and hemicycle of the Library in the Luxembourg in April 1840; of the ceiling of the Galerie d'Apollon in the Louvre in March 1850 and of the ceiling of the Salon de la Paix in the Hôtel de Ville in December 1851. Even wall spaces in churches were liberally offered to him—in 1840 in the church of Saint-Denis-du-Saint-Sacrement for his *Pietà*, and, most important of all, in May 1849, the Chapel of the Holy Angels in the church of Saint-Sulpice: this, begun in earnest in 1855, occupied him until July 1861 and gave him the opportunity to achieve what is perhaps his noblest masterpiece.

To what is this favour, so strongly in contradiction with opinion and sometimes so bitterly criticized in the press, to be attributed? Tourneux, in his *Eugène Delacroix devant les contemporains*, has quoted some of these press attacks. For instance, over the first major commission, that for the Salon du Roi, the critic of the *Constitutionnel* gave free rein to his indignation:

'And it is to such a painter that one of the biggest commissions for monumental painting of our time is being entrusted! In this case, really, responsibility is more than engaged: it might be said to have been compromised.'

After the *coup d'état* of 2 December such paradoxical favour might have been explained by Delacroix's acquaintances in Bonapartist circles. But in fact the greater part of this enormous quantity of work was commissioned by the July

Monarchy: the only commissions that came after the accession of the Prince-President were those for the Salon de la Paix, a municipal enterprise, and the Chapel of the Holy Angels, a religious one. Both of these were dependent on LIII, page 465 the Préfecture of the Seine, and Delacroix was a municipal councillor. LIV, page 466 How did the government of Louis-Philippe—a bourgeois *par excellence* and so anxious to please the bourgeoisie—come to be moved by so constant and provocative a boldness? The new régime, it is true, in order to distinguish itself from the reactionary Restoration, had posed as an enlightened Maecenas on the side of romanticism (on the condition that this should be moderate); it saw in this innovating movement a natural affinity with a liberal monarchy that had issued from the Revolution. But there was, above all, the effective presence in power of Thiers.

His star was rising rapidly. From the moment of the Restoration he had rallied to the future king, then Duke of Orleans; he drafted the protest of the journalists against the July Ordinances; and he firmly supported Louis-Philippe during the revolution of 1830, as against Lafayette. He soon became a *Conseiller d'État.* As a Deputy, as Under-Secretary of State for Finance and then, from October 1832, as Minister of the Interior, he was the promoter of the campaign for large-scale public works which the Government started in that year. His transfer to the Ministry of Commerce and Public Works did not remove him from the source of commissions. In 1836 he became *Président du Conseil,* and several times again until in 1840 he went into opposition. From this date until 1850, when the Second Empire brought Delacroix back into official favour, the important commissions were interrupted.

There is even a decisive proof: it is known that in 1837 Thiers had intended to entrust to him the whole of the mural decoration of the Chambre, but that Montalivet, who replaced him at the Interior, divided the work between several artists, leaving Delacroix with the Library only. On 27 October 1838 Delacroix XXXIII, page 335 wrote to Thiers: 'The hand which you have stretched out to me with such gener- XXXIV, page 336 osity was no longer there to help me.' He acknowledged the benevolent part XXXV, page 341 played by Thiers and what it had done for him: 'Out of pure friendship towards me you have offered me one of those decisive opportunities which throw open to an artist a new career, and which must make him great if they do not expose his impotence.'

Thiers had not forgotten that, on the advice of Baron Gérard, he had boldly and openly sided with the youthful Delacroix and his *Dante and Virgil in the Inferno.* The lines he wrote about Delacroix were described later by Baudelaire as 'amazing both in their precocity and in their courage.'[1] Thiers had written:

'. . . . Delacroix has received the gift of genius'; and he added: 'let him advance with assurance, let him devote himself to immense tasks, the indispensable condition of this gift.'

Thiers could not, without going back on what he had said, refuse these 'immense tasks' to his chosen artist. By giving them he was doing homage not only to Delacroix but to his own foresight.

Even in the royal family Delacroix had found support—if not in Louis-Philippe (who had little feeling for his painting in particular, or for art in general, which he crassly regarded as a servant to history), at least in the heir-apparent, the Duke of Orleans, who was inclined by his youthful ardour in the direction of the innovating movements. He had bought the *Hamlet* and presented the *Jewish Wedding* to the Luxembourg. The sale of the Duchess's pictures in January 1853 included Delacroix's *Melmoth*, his *Murder of the Bishop of Liège* and his *Prisoner of Chillon.*

The result was to provide Delacroix, on his return from Morocco, with the opportunity of displaying to the full the new conception of art that he had felt growing clear within him. The amplitude not only of the spaces to be covered but of the subjects to be imagined confronted him with a gigantic task, to which he rose with enthusiasm and authority in spite of his fragile health; and this has ranked him on a level with the Renaissance masters. Théophile Silvestre was right to call him 'the last of the great family.'[2] Le Brun is the only other French painter to have benefited from a similar programme of commissions, but he faced up to it merely with a display of accomplished and often hollow rhetoric. Delacroix remained faithful to his determination to convey a soul through the brush: from violin music—sometimes a concerto—he passed to the full symphony, yet was able unfailingly to measure up to the larger medium.

It is to be hoped that one day the public will have free access to what remains of these great *ensembles* (after the burning of the Hôtel de Ville); the greater XXXVII, page 371 part is in the Chambre des Députés and the Senate. Then only will it be able to gauge the incomparable position that belongs to Delacroix in the history pl 304 of French art. The Apollo ceiling in the Louvre, sublime though it is, cannot give a complete idea of this, since it took its place in an earlier scheme conceived by Le Brun.

From the moment when he was commissioned to paint the Salon du Roi, Delacroix clearly felt that the problem now confronting his art was no longer the same as in the easel painting, in which both modern civilization and his own constantly growing individualism had found the intimate style they required. II, page 58, He had, it is true, yielded to a need to increase the size of his principal pictures: III, page 67 the *Dante and Virgil in the Inferno* (1822), measures 74 in. by 97 in., the *Massacre* XI, page 123 *at Chios* (1824), 164 in. by 139 in., the *Death of Sardanapalus* (1827), 145 in. pl 260 by 195 in., leading on to the *Justice of Trajan* (1840), which measures 193 in. by 106 in.; and after this, as though emulating the scale of his mural paintings, his pl 245 pictures become larger still—the *Battle of Taillebourg* (1837), 183 in. by 214 in. XXVII, page 283 and the *Entry of the Crusaders into Constantinople* (1840), 161 in. by 196 in. Yet these huge pictures merely amplified the entirely personal vision through which he was trying to communicate the imagination of his heart.

But although, in these pictures, Delacroix was treating the individualized impulse on a scale never envisaged before, the official commissions confronted him with a different mission—one that brought him back to a time when art had still been essentially collective. The problem was no longer to make the rays from the magic lantern of the soul legible on a screen and within the area of its frame, but to act within the enveloping volume of an architectural setting, submitting to this and offering the result to the simultaneous gaze of a public moving about within the enclosed space: it was to be effective from a multiplicity of points of view, varying with the changing places of spectators on the move. Towards a picture, space converges as though towards a centre of attraction;

but with an architectural setting—for Delacroix had to deal not only with mural surfaces, limited to a single plane like a picture, but also with ceilings, with cupolas—the painting embraces the space, and it is the visitor who has the impression of having become the centre at which the images assailing him from all directions converge.

In the first of these enterprises, the Salon du Roi, it seems therefore as if Delacroix was renouncing his earlier way of painting in order to submit to the different discipline imposed by the setting. But no sooner had he thus assimilated the conditions of a new problem than he dominated it and, far from yielding to it, subjected it to his demands. His aim, everywhere, was to make of art an instrument of communication between the artist's soul and that of the spectator. Easel painting, like a private letter, was marvellously well adapted to this purpose, and it seemed as if the multiplicity and ringing polyphony of large-scale decorative painting must break this atmosphere of direct confidence; but Delacroix learnt to magnify it to the required scale, and to pass from the insinuating murmur to the full volume of the choir that can fill a great building. Though his medium had changed its scale and therefore its technique, he continued to assign it the same mission; not only to entertain or to feed the gaze as it wanders over the walls, but always to aim at the inner life and at disturbing it. That overall atmosphere of a picture, into which the gaze of the onlooker ventures as into a trap, to be caught and spellbound by the conspiracy of all the resources used, is still, with its power of suggestion, the painter's governing aim; but now it has to be thrown over the spectator like an enormous net from every quarter of space, in order to envelop him in the many meshes of a single direct thought, of a powerfully individualized plastic and chromatic style, of a visual music with a power over the sensibility as imperious as that of organ music.

Far from turning his back on the experiments carried out by Western painters during the last few centuries, Delacroix made use of the methods they had arrived at, but in doing so he rediscovered the magnetic power of the great Byzantine decorative painters. He did study the repertoire of technical solutions offered by the French classical School from the seventeenth century onwards—indeed from the sixteenth century and the School of Fontainebleau—but what he took from them was limited to technique: the means he uses sometimes presuppose what was to be learnt from these sources, but what he aspired to do was utterly different. His intention was not to flatter the gaze by a kind of visual litany including all the resources of the rhetoric of forms: even though there are still traces of this in his vocabulary, his aim was to make them subservient to sensibility, subduing them to a whole whose effect would be to enrich the inner life. Painters like Le Brun, Coypel and Boucher had never bothered to do this: the weakness of their art is that, while they handle the language in masterly fashion, they fail to make it an expression of the soul—indeed do not dream of doing so. Delacroix's bold innovation was to make large-scale decorative painting serve the

XXXVII VIRGIL PRESENTING DANTE TO HOMER
*1845-7 Oil on canvas*
*Cupola of the Library in the Palais du Luxembourg, Paris*

CHE DI LOR SUONA
NELLA TUA VITA
GRAZIA ACQUISTA NEL CIEL

revelation of the soul—the new mission imposed by modern individualism. This brought his aims very close to those of Byzantine painting; but while the Byzantine artists had been subdued to the dictates of a collective soul and its shared faith, Delacroix's painting was to place the same collective means of action at the disposal of a single soul, the artist's own.

## *Sources and Aids*

Delacroix did not consider that the artist should or could start from nothing: his imagination looked for support to the data supplied to it, whether by nature (which speaks to the eyes), by the work of writers (which speaks to the mind) or by the paintings of earlier masters (which address themselves to both). Not that there was any question of repeating or taking over the experiments of others: he must simply profit by them and take the point they had reached as his point of departure, with the chance—given the strength to overcome imitation—of going beyond their achievement. Delacroix looked at and studied the work of
pl 275 his predecessors intensively, but all he sought in it was nourishment and a spur. The consequence is that it is rare to find in him any literal borrowing, but close study often enables us to discover what it is that may have struck him at the beginning—and that still survives beneath the transmutation which started at once.

He studied the outside world, making notes, drawings or water-colours—more words for his vocabulary of images, for he considered nature as a diction-
pl 274 ary. He even used photography, being one of the first to be fascinated by it, well before Degas; he was among the early members of the Société Française de Photographie. (Made public in about 1839, the new technique suddenly acquired an increased popularity in 1847, when Blanquart-Evrard made known the method of photography on paper, invented some years before but not exploited.) Besides sitting for the great photographers of his time, and having himself, as he put it, 'daguerreotyped' in 1842 by the Rieseners at Frépillon, Delacroix often worked from photographs: he copied, above all, the nude studies which were soon distributed, and which were made available to him by Durrier, a friend of Pierret's. Delacroix wrote to Dutilleux on 7 March 1854: 'How sorry I am that so admirable an invention comes so late, I mean as far as I am concerned. . . . It is the palpable demonstration of nature's real design.' This was the source of some of the finest of his nudes.

pl 273 As for the masters, he studied these both at the museums and—often in the evenings by lamplight—at home through the medium of engravings, in which, precisely, the formal side is emphasized. He was doing what so many earlier artists had done, Watteau for instance—meditating over a pose or attitude and consulting the portfolio that contained a mixture of prints and of his own draw-

XXXVIII VIRGIL PRESENTING DANTE TO HOMER (detail)
*1845-7 Oil on canvas*
*Cupola of the Library in the Palais du Luxembourg, Paris*

*Fig 22* PAGE FROM A SKETCHBOOK. Pen drawing. Cabinet des Dessins, Louvre, Paris.

ings. A note sent on 1 December 1838 to the keeper of the *Cabinet des Estampes* in the Bibliothèque Nationale asks that a student's card be given to Auguste Jacquinot; this cousin of Delacroix was no doubt being asked by him to go through the reproductions of paintings for his master's use. Jacquinot was, in fact, one of a group of young people, assistants to Delacroix as well as pupils, whom he had brought together in the studio opened by him in the rue Neuve-Guillemin in that year. It was here that he trained those who were to be his collaborators in the task of decorative painting, which was too great for one man to carry out: there were about thirty of them, and they included Lassalle-Bordes (who, to judge by his later tittle-tattle, does not seem to have deserved the complete confidence Delacroix at first placed in him), de Planet (who came from Toulouse, and whose *Souvenirs* are available), and, from April 1844 onwards, Andrieu (who was to become his most constant and trusted helper). Their names include also Bida, Saint-Marcel, Maurice Sand (the novelist's son) and Valerne (whom Degas admired and painted). The studio was where the rue de Rennes now runs, between the rue du Four and the rue du Vieux-Colombier.

In addition Delacroix sought eagerly for information—this time historical, not plastic—in illustrated books on the Middle Ages, on the East, and on Byzantine art and the art of Antiquity. In 1839 he wanted to know about ancient tripods and asked Villot, the keeper at the Louvre, to look through his archives for engravings—especially in the *Cahiers de figures étrusques* of N. F. Villemin, published at the end of the eighteenth century. He often had recourse to Villot, a man of great learning whom he described as 'embellished with the most varied, the most useless pieces of knowledge.' Clearly they were not always useless, especially when Delacroix was confronted with programmes of decorative painting in which allegory and mythology had a secure traditional place.

But the plastic element was the essential one at this stage, and to acquire it Delacroix went, more than has been realized, to the classical School. Certainly he made constant use of his great favourites, Rubens, his god, and Veronese, of whom he said: 'All that I know I have learnt from him.' But he prized at its true worth the French tradition, beginning with the Renaissance—a fact that has perhaps not been sufficiently stressed. On 6 October 1840, on his way through Rouen, he admired the sculpture of the tombs in the cathedral, especially that of de Brézé: 'In them the merits of Antiquity are united with a modern quality, through the grace of the Renaissance.' This, no doubt, was what touched him in the pictures of the Fontainebleau School, which were clearly the inspiration of his Valmont essays. In January 1832, when he was setting out for Morocco, he wrote (on 8 January) to Pierret that he had 'seen Fontainebleau in passing. Vandalism is having its way there.' Under the pretext of restoration, Alaux (known as 'Le Romain') was busy 'ruining the admirable remains of the paint-
pl 276 ings there . . .' A water-colour, possibly of 1839,[3] is a copy by Delacroix of 'the poet Arion and the philosopher Anaximander' from the frescoes by Niccolo dell' Abbate in the Galerie Henri II.

Delacroix's admiration for Le Sueur, for 'his naïveté and grace', is well known, and, still more, his admiration for Poussin, on whom, in June 1853, he wrote a long study which was published in the *Moniteur Universel.* I have several sheets of studies containing many sketches made by Delacroix after figures and landscapes by the painter whom he considered as 'one of the boldest innovators in the whole history of painting', and whose teaching was subsequently corrupted by Le Brun with his obsession for 'regularity'. But Delacroix had also recourse, much more often than is thought, to painters in whom, though now little appreciated, there survived the great decorative inspiration—such as Guercino in Italy and Jouvenet in France.[4] In fact, just as he condemned the 'second-hand and mechanical' art and 'artificial graces, enervated forms without any accent of nature'[5] of such painters as van Loo or Boucher, he felt that the French decorative painters who combined the influence of Poussin and Rubens had understood how to unite the handling of sculptural forms with a feeling for the whole, which they obtained by the continuity of their brushwork and the fusion of the movements and the light; there lies the true understanding, the true mastery of decoration on a large scale; and Delacroix, while he recognized the necessity of having recourse, in such painting, to the plastic treatment of the human form, was nonetheless determined to keep the suppleness and connectedness of life—not, in this new field, by the establishment of an expressive and unique coloured atmosphere, which is proper to easel painting and difficult to achieve on architectural surfaces, but by a constant and easy alliance of drawing and composition.

## *The Palais Bourbon: the Salon du Roi and the Library*

The series of his monumental paintings began in earnest in 1833 with the Salon du Roi at the Palais Bourbon,[6] a work which took him slightly over three years to carry out and brought him in 30,000 francs; but this was preceded by a few trial flights. The earliest of these is the four paintings intended for Talma's dining-room, apparently commissioned during the summer of 1821.[7] Delacroix had met Talma as well as Mademoiselle Mars in the salon of Baron Gérard. The theme was as traditional as could be—that of the *Seasons*—and so was the style: the sculptural forms of each of the seated allegorical figures were inscribed in an arc of a circle. (Delacroix cannot have foreseen at that time that he would be asked by the Comédie Française, between 1853 and 1855, to paint the portrait of the great tragic actor as Nero, in a purely classical costume and setting.) pl 271 pl 272

These four pictures were the prelude to the essay in fresco painting undertaken by Delacroix in 1834 on the walls of his beloved Valmont. In these paintings, which crown the doors along the front corridor of the first floor, Delacroix was unquestionably getting his hand in for his work at the Chambre des Députés. Here again he painted figures from the pure classical tradition, *Leda, Anachreon, Bacchus*. . . . 'In a few hours', he wrote to Villot on 23 September, 'I have done a small subject in this *genre*, which is somewhat new for me,' and he added that, because of the quick drying, 'the difficulty lies chiefly in finishing and rounding off the forms properly.' Finishing and rounding off the forms, he was back at a problem he had pushed aside ever since his liberation from Géricault's influence and his escape from the authority of the School. In these essays he was practising his scales. The twisting movement of the shoulders (of which a typical example is the negress in the *Women of Algiers*), which had long been one of his means of conveying inner dynamism, and which he was inclined to carry to the point of improbability, is again apparent in the *Bacchus* and, above all, in the *Leda*: but for the most part, in these pictures his firm intention is to submit to the law of frontality of the human form, and to stick to the plane of the wall surface: to stick to the plane and fill up the space by means of the human body and its plastic qualities was precisely the discipline he would need for the great mural paintings. pl 270

In the Salon du Roi the achievement of plasticity seemed to Delacroix the first and fundamental task. The problem he had to solve was indeed a new one, for the surface he had to paint was not regular, like that of a picture. In the huge room, thirty-six feet long, it was not a ceiling that he had to decorate but nine coffers framing a central opening, nor was it the walls, but eight pillars separating bays, and a continuous frieze cut by the archivolts.

Rarely, in any of his work, was Delacroix so frankly sculptural as here. By what we can no longer consider as a paradoxical association, he made use at one and the same time of the examples offered by the classical tradition and by his experience of Morocco: many of his preparatory designs[8] show what were to be allegorical figures draped and dressed in Arab fashion! Wishing to maintain a continuous progression of colour from the lower to the upper part of the *ensemble*, he limited himself, on the large pilasters, to allegorical figures of rivers treated like tall *trompe-l'œil* reliefs by means of a *grisaille* imitating stone. In this he was making use of a definite precedent, remembered from his youth: in 1804 and 1805, as a child, he had watched with curiosity the work on the decoration of the large drawing-room in the former Archbishop's palace at Bordeaux, in which his father had taken up his quarters as *Préfet*. This work was carried fig 16 out by the painter Pierre Lacour, who seems also to have been Delacroix's drawing-master at the Lycée.[9] Lacour's son even claimed that, without this, Delacroix would have remained a stranger to the fine arts; in any case Philippe Burty, no doubt reporting what had been told him by Delacroix, states that 'the decorative paintings done by Pierre Lacour . . . were the first ones to impress him.' It was natural for him to remember this at the moment of undertaking a curiously similar task, for the dining-room of the Bordeaux *préfecture* had likewise broad pilasters between mirrors, and on them Lacour had chosen to imitate stone reliefs in *grisaille.*

Enriched also, as Théophile Silvestre rightly perceived, by his knowledge of
pl 278 the work of Jean Goujon, Delacroix filled and gave life to these elongated surfaces (which he finished in 1835) by endowing his allegorical figures with a wavy twist that, as on the *Fontaine des Innocents*, suggests the 'mobile power and
pls 279, 280 capricious course' of streams. This animation, which communicates to a sculptural figure the movement of muscles in action (sometimes indeed carrying this to excess and producing a strained effect), serves to maintain, along with a classical appearance, that painful intensity which Delacroix, in his pictures, expressed through the drama that was part of the subject.

pl 277 The frieze was not included in the original programme,[10] but became the 'principal part of the whole work'. It contains some sixty figures that have to do with War, Industry, Agriculture and Justice, the allegories of which adorn the ceiling. In them Delacroix has again recourse to violent and contrasting attitudes, twisted torsos, bent or crossed legs and shoulders thrown back to the point of looking strained—embodiments of the painter's inner torment. The only figures at all like them are those of Michelangelo, whose 'wild vigour' and 'powerful gestures and contortions that produce such fine developments of the human form' Delacroix praised in his article on Sigalon's copy of the *Last Judgment* in the *Revue des Deux Mondes* for 1 August 1837. (Another article by him on Michelangelo, published in 1830 in the *Revue de Paris*, likewise spoke of that artist's 'irresistible need to express, at every point, the most extreme and violent feelings' by means of 'the intensely tormented attitude of the body'.) Though to conventional minds this seemed bad drawing and eccentricity, it was in fact dramatic expressiveness.

The always unexpected attitudes of these figures produce an effect of quivering life which, after running through each one of them, communicates itself to the next, so that a kind of chain of magnetism, as through Mesmer's vat, is set up and an uninterrupted impulse passes right round the room. The infinitely varied combination of attitudes, or rather of movements, adapts itself wonderfully to the architecture, with an effective but perpetual renewal: it emphasizes the structure and breathes into it a life which stone cannot possess. What Delacroix says of Michelangelo in his article on Sigalon applies to himself: 'The painter needs forms and contrasts, shadows and lights falling upon full-fleshed bodies in movement.'

pls 281, 282 By contrast there reigns in the ceiling (which was executed first and to which the four angels at the corners make a transition) a calm that is accentuated by the horizontal effect of the large and serene reclining figures.

Thus, in this first attempt in which he confined himself on purpose to the basic problems involved in inscribing human figures within the geometrical forms set by the monument, Delacroix scored a complete success by closely relating dynamic images to static structures. The parts that required a more mechanical ornamentation interested him less, and here he sought help from 'professional decorators' such as Ciceri, head of the paint room at the Opéra. Later also, when he was at work on the Library of the Chambre des Députés, Ciceri helped him to establish the monumental perspective. He and his pupil Boulangé aided Delacroix in other compositions where architecture was important, for instance in the episodes from the life of Christopher Columbus, the *Melmoth* and even the *Trajan*. Dauzats likewise assisted him over the positioning of XXIII, page 251 the setting for the *Two Foscari*. pl 157

Delacroix, now master of his instrument, could pay more attention to the music. And at precisely this moment his protector, Adolphe Thiers, now Minister of the Interior, thought of entrusting to him the rest of the decoration of the Palais Bourbon. Delacroix was already working out a plan that included the Salle des Pas-perdus, the Salle des Commisssions and the Library when, unfortunately, in April 1837, Thiers gave place to Montalivet and Delacroix was allotted the Library only.

Thus reduced, the enterprise was still enormous, and took nearly ten years; it was not finished till December 1847, by which time Delacroix had already been working for two years on the Library of the Senate also. He was able to satisfy 'that need to work on the grand scale which becomes excessive once one has had a taste of it.' The studio set up by him in 1838 provided him with the indispensable assistants.

Early in 1842 he set to work in earnest on the decoration of the Library of the Chambre. Here, in addition to the two huge hemicycles at each end, there were five cupolas, having four pendentives each, to be painted. Of the twenty pls 285-290 pendentives he himself painted five entirely, while he entrusted ten to Lassalle-

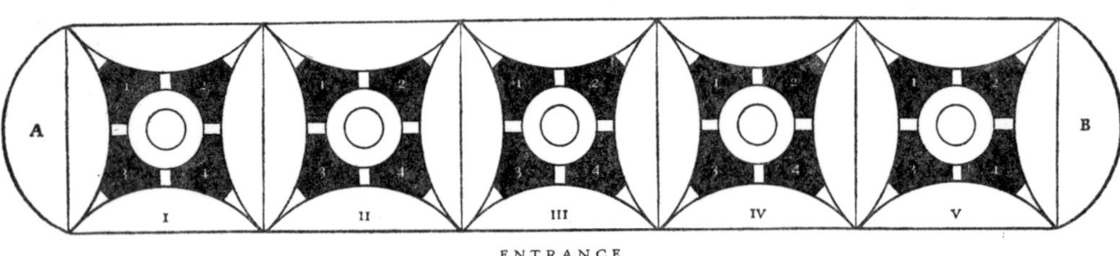


Fig 23 DIAGRAM OF THE FIVE CUPOLAS AND TWO HEMICYCLES OF THE LIBRARY OF THE CHAMBRE DES DÉPUTÉS, PALAIS BOURBON, PARIS

| | A ATTILA B ORPHEUS |
|---|---|
| I POETRY | 1 Education of Achilles, 2 Alexander and the Poems of Homer, 3 Hesiod and the Muse, 4 Ovid among the Scythians |
| II THEOLOGY | 1 Adam and Eve, 2 Tribute Money, 3 Captivity in Babylon, 4 Death of Saint John the Baptist |
| III LEGISLATION | 1 Cicero, 2 Numa and the Nymph Egeria, 3 Demosthenes, 4 Lycurgus consulting the Pythian Oracle |
| IV PHILOSOPHY | 1 Suicide of Seneca, 2 Herodotus questioning the Wise Men, 3 Socrates and his Daemon, 4 Chaldean Shepherds studying the Heavens |
| V NATURAL SCIENCES | 1 Hippocrates, 2 Pliny the Elder, 3 Archimedes, 4 Aristotle |

*Fig 24* STUDY FOR ATTILA in a hemicycle of the Palais Bourbon. Pen drawing. Cabinet des Dessins, Louvre, Paris.

Bordes, four to Planet and one to Léger—keeping, of course, the initial conception and the retouching in his own hands. Since mounted canvas had proved unsatisfactory because of the unevenness of the walls (as became clear when the
xxxiv, page 336 *Orpheus* was being painted), Delacroix turned, in the case of the hemicycles, to a technique of painting on a preparation of wax, retaining the original method for the twenty pendentives only.

This time Delacroix no longer intended to limit himself to a few traditional allegories: his aim was to suggest the history of the human spirit in its effort to master the world, society and itself. First he thought of a panorama that would have brought him down to Dante and to Tasso, but then decided to take his examples solely from Antiquity and the Old and New Testaments. Poetry
pl 286 occupies the first cupola, with the *Education of Achilles, Alexander and the*
xxxv, page 341 *Poems of Homer, Hesiod and the Muse* and *Ovid among the Scythians.* In the
pl 288 second cupola Theology is the subject, with *Adam and Eve*, the *Tribute Money*, the *Captivity in Babylon* and the *Death of Saint John the Baptist.* The theme of the third and central cupola is Legislation, embodied by *Cicero, Numa and the*
pl 289 *Nymph Egeria, Demosthenes* and *Lycurgus.* The next cupola deals with Philosophy, with the *Suicide of Seneca, Herodotus questioning the Wise Men, Socrates and his Daemon* and the *Chaldean Shepherds studying the Heavens.* The last is devoted to
pl 290 the Natural Sciences, with *Hippocrates, Pliny the Elder, Archimedes* and *Aristotle.*

Thus the whole human adventure in its precarious boldness, menaced as it is by its animal bases yet attempting to subject these to the spirit, plays out its destiny between the two poles of the hemicycles, on one of which *Orpheus* taming the wild animals and civilizing men signifies the dawn of civilization, while on the other *Attila* makes felt the weight of the perpetual menace of war and barbarism. (Delacroix had at first thought of the *Crowning of Petrarch* and of the *Phaedon,* where Plato tells of the death of Socrates, in homage to the triumph and the martyrdom of thought in its continual struggle to help man to surmount his own nature.)

It is well established that Delacroix spent long evenings with Villot, questioning him in search of the subjects best fitted to carry out what he intended. Villot himself told Sensier much later[11] that Delacroix came to see him several times when about to start on this work: 'Delacroix, who was extremely meticulous and logical, hesitated for a long time, and there were many consultations between us.'

The Lyonnais painter Chenavard, who was rather more of an intellectual than an artist, can also have been no stranger to a design whose aim was to present a kind of total view of the human enterprise. Chenavard, with whom Delacroix became more and more friendly as the years went by, had known the 'Nazarenes', Cornelius and Overbeck in Rome and, like them, saw art as a vehicle for philosophical thinking—so much so that Théophile Silvestre later described him as 'the gymnosophist'. Intellectual ambitions of this sort were peculiarly a product of the nineteenth century. It believed that the knowledge won by the sciences had made it practically the master of the physical world; having brought to life again the primitive arts and culture, it had begun to look at the origins of human thinking through them; through the development of historical knowledge and method it had begun to survey the whole of human action and creative activity throught the ages; and all this made the men of the nineteenth century believe themselves to be situated at a point where the whole of the past converged and was fulfilled. The explosion of romanticism that took place in about 1840 had enabled men's repressed energies to express themselves, but also to disperse themselves: thought then became colder, more objective, and many dreamed of drawing up a balance sheet of the whole earthly adventure, of putting a line under the sum before entering upon a new era, to which progress seemed to be pointing. On the latter point Delacroix was sceptical, but he was attracted by the amplitude of the programme. Balzac likewise tried to pin down the whole of society in his *Comédie Humaine*; Victor Hugo dreamed of embracing all the generations in the *Légende des Siècles*; Auguste Comte hoped to produce a complete and methodical diagram of knowledge. Vigny, in his *Journal,* observes:

'One of the curious things about our time is the pride shown in its measureless literary pretensions. One man [the reference is to Soumet] calls his book the *Divine Épopée*; another calls his the *Comédie Humaine*.'

The painters were swayed by the same ambitions. The classicists first of all:

XXXIX ROMEO AND JULIET
*1845 Oil on canvas. 24 x 19 (062 x 049)*
*Private collection, Switzerland*

in 1827 Ingres, in his *Apotheosis of Homer*, made a sort of inventory of the human spirit, grouping writers and artists in a pyramid whose apex was their source, the poet of the Iliad. In 1841 Delaroche attacked the same enterprise again in his hemicycle in the École des Beaux-Arts, at the very moment when Delacroix, in the Library of the Chambre des Députés, was breathing into it a real soul. Soon—in 1845—Chassériau depicted *Peace, War and Commerce bringing the peoples together* in the Cour des Comptes, and Papety attempted to show the *Past, the Present and the Future* in another great cyclical series. It was Chenavard, however, whose ambitions were on the largest scale; he was busy working out compositions in which all the systems evolved by human thinking and all the events experienced from generation to generation would combine in a single visual poem. In 1848 he received the commission to paint for the Panthéon a *History of Humanity* on which he had been working for several years already: this was to run from the Creation to the French Revolution, and was to look down on a mosaic floor depicting nothing less than the *Palingénésie sociale*. But the development of ideas under the Empire brought about the abandonment of this programme. It was to have been completed by four large compositions which Gérard would have painted, taking the place of the pendentives of the dome: their themes were to have been the *Age of Religion*, the *Age of Poetry and Art*, the *Age of Philosophy* and the *Age of Science*. These four recur in the scheme adopted by Delacroix, with the addition of *Legislation*. It is natural to compare the three stages into which Auguste Comte (in the course of lectures on 'Positive Philosophy' which he delivered between 1830 and 1842) had divided the march of the human soul in its confrontation with the enigma of the universe—the theological stage, dedicated to the gods, the metaphysical, dedicated to ideas, and the positive, dedicated to scientific laws.

## *The Means and Ends of Painting*

Delacroix, born just before the century opened and maturing when it did, could not remain outside the movement of contemporary thought; but he was far from letting himself be carried away by its excesses. Though attracted by the ambition to make painting measure up to the human mind's effort to extend its grasp fully, there was nothing he disliked so much as 'bookish painters', as '*peintres à idées*', and the last surviving lines written by him—they were jotted down in pencil on 22 June 1863 in a notebook later lost—began with this profession of faith: 'The first merit of a picture is to have been made for the eye.' Here he reaffirmed his taste for pure painting; yet he had not forgotten that reason is the main guide in finding the best means to produce this delight of the eye—'The art of grouping, the art of making the light fall where it should and of painting with liveliness or with sobriety, the art of making sacrifices as well as of commanding a

XL MARPHISA
*1852 Oil on canvas. 32 x 40 (082 x 101)*
*The Walters Art Gallery, Baltimore*

multiplicity of means.' But thought, while it must be constantly present in the artist's work, is not its end, but only the guide to the attainment of that end; and Delacroix returned again and again to the idea—which became widespread long after his time—that painting is made for the sake of being felt and lived, not of being explained. Thus he was able to escape from the dangers that entrapped those who laboured to put forward ideas by means of learned, indeed pedantic allegories and illusions. The figures created by the artist have nothing to do with those that make up the language of deaf mutes: they are not there to be industriously translated, but to be received in a direct emotive shock.

At the very moment when his large scale mural decorations appeared to be competing with the encyclopaedic views of his contemporaries, Delacroix was firmly stating, in an article on Prud'hon published in 1846:[12]

'One finds a mysterious pleasure, I was going to say a pure pleasure and one having greater freedom from all impressions foreign to painting, in the contemplation of those scenes whose subjects have no explanation; in them painting triumphs alone, as music does in a symphony.'

In this he was merely taking up again a reflection on the work of Michelangelo, which he had developed in his 1830 article,[13] where he expressed his doubt whether, in the figures in the Medici Chapel, the great sculptor had 'attached much importance to their meaning' and suggested that 'perhaps he only found one for them after having finished them. . . .' They were, he suggested, chiefly 'conceived as necessary accompaniments to his architecture'; as a sculptor he saw in them 'what sculpture needs . . . forms'. And Delacroix went on to insist:

'Indeed I should have a poor opinion of anyone who, in the presence of these magnificent statues . . . could only think of asking what they mean. Their character is so imposing, and so satisfying to the imagination through the whole they form when taken together, that it does not occur to one to look for some recondite intention in them.'

This was not to deny them a direct significance apprehended by the sensibility.

Delacroix never forgot his perception of the close relationship between painting and music. Already, when at work on the *Massacre at Chios*, he had apostrophized painting in these terms: 'Thou shalt please with a pure and absolute pleasure.'[14] Yet he was aware that it would be folly to make of this too radical and exclusive a doctrine, and that 'one must condemn a sonority that takes the place of the idea' (18 May 1857, and again 13 April 1860). At the same time he added: 'It must be admitted, nonetheless, that there is in certain sonorities, independently of any expressiveness they may have for the soul, a pleasure for the senses. It is the same in painting.'

III, page 66

He was intuitively aware that psychology was a whole and that to divide it up by means of abstract notions was artificial. Painting, he considered, is not—as some people in our own time have claimed, carrying Delacroix's idea to excess by

XLI CHRIST ON THE LAKE OF GENESARETH
*1854 Oil on canvas. 23 x 28 (059 x 072)*
*The Walters Art Gallery, Baltimore*

systematizing it—exclusively for the pleasure of the eyes; but the pleasure of the eyes is its basic condition. This sensual joy is only a prelude: just as a pain, when it reaches the critical intensity, is bound to irradiate and seize hold of the whole nervous system, painting is 'a silent power that at first speaks only to the eyes and then invades and seizes hold of all the faculties of the soul.'[15] In one place he describes listening to a nightingale, to its 'truly unique warbling': it possesses the 'indefinable charm of everything that makes a vivid impression', yet in the end he thought its value lay 'more in the emotions it causes than in itself'. This in 1824: in 1857 he copied out a passage from Voltaire in which the beautiful is described as 'that which must charm the mind and the senses' at the same time—or rather it enchants the senses first and then, by its power of expansion, extends to the soul, setting it also vibrating all through.

The more varied the convergent means employed, the fuller would be the result. 'A musical theme can speak to the imagination when played on a single instrument which has only one way of pleasing the senses, but the joining together of several instruments with different timbres would give the sensation a greater force,' and so make it more likely to reach and disturb the deeper layers of the sensibility. The instruments at the disposal of a painter are all the various means of striking the eyes and rousing emotions through them: form, with its plastic power; colour, through its sensuous resonance; and composition, by combining the two towards a common end. The painter's task is not to conceive an idea and then illustrate it with an image recognizable by its realism: this is the trap into which it is easy for him to fall. Delacroix avoids it by treating the explanatory scheme by which various themes are co-ordinated as merely a supporting framework or, at most, as an intelligent arrangement of the instruments in his orchestra. What matters is the music that is to be played; and this visual music will make its effect first by its sonority and its rhythm, its colour, line and relationships of forms, but then, opening a way through these for itself into our inner life, will produce there a growing emotion. Such is the conception realized in the paintings of the Chambre des Députés.

In these, *form* plays the essential part which Delacroix—having begun by accepting it almost passively from the School and from Géricault and then largely rejected it during his romantic period—had restored to it during the years after his return from Morocco. In 1822 he could describe the figure of Charon
II, page 58 in his *Dante and Virgil* as being treated in the manner of Antiquity: the same
might have been said of the powerfully modelled torso of his *Archimedes*, or
pl 284 again of the *Seneca*, copied from a Roman sculpture. Giotto and Masaccio likewise spring to mind at the sight of the sculptural, almost monolithic grandeur of
pl 283 his *Wise Men*, who stand before Herodotus in solemn robes that remind us of
the Arab *djellabahs*, so similar to the toga. His *Eve* and his *Achilles* are modelled with a firm and precise relief and exact perspective of the limbs that make them into anatomical studies. Delacroix had returned to certain convic-

XLII ALFRED BRUYAS
*1853 Oil on canvas. 46 x 35 (116 x 089)*
*Musée Fabre, Montpellier*

tions of his youth, and could write in August 1842 to his pupil Gaultron: 'Goodbye, dear friend. Persevere in anatomy and strengthen your outlines.'

But now form, to him, is inseparable from the *movement*, conveying life: form is simply the mould that canalizes life and gives it a structure. To Delacroix anatomies are bodies and bodies are gestures, and gesture is the sign of vital intensity and of its human meaning. Where it is almost motionless, this abnormal fixity becomes the age-old solemnity of his *Wise Men* with their concentration of ineffable secrets. So also his *Chaldean Shepherd* is held and, it almost seems, turned to stone by the immensity of the night, while his young companion, sitting behind him, shows the first movement of a curiosity that will soon grow into a similar silent contemplation. In contrast, the abrupt twist of his *Pliny*, turning towards the eruption of Vesuvius and receiving the full shock of pl 290 its blaze and terror, is amplified by the whirlwind of the drapery; and again his *Demosthenes*, so firm and upright in gait, joins the power of his voice to that of the waves by means of the opening gesture of his arms and the tense swelling of his clothes in the wind.

A combination of defined volumes and motive forces sets up the rhythm from which arises the *composition*. This is dominated, in the case of these paintings, by the unusual shape of the surface supplied by the pendentives. Tireless invention enabled Delacroix to find endless new ways of harmonizing his painting with the curves of the base and the horizontal splay of the top. Sometimes, pl 283 as in the *Aristotle* and the *Ovid*, the subject rises in two separate sheaves to right and left, like a flexible V; in other cases, the *Seneca* for instance, stiffer lines open out like the spokes of a fan; in others, again, the masses are arranged along the axis of the more or less triangular surface forming a T with its upper bar curved —the upright and central figure of *Socrates* is articulated upon the two symmetrically outstretched wings of his daemon; and his *Numa*, lying on the bank, pl 289 crowns horizontally the graceful flow of the nymph Egeria's half-naked body, whose foot has just dipped into the water. His *Hesiod*, lying asleep, moves with XXXV, page 341 the curve of the right-hand border, while the Muse fleetingly casts over him her shadow and her breath, like a bird in flight diving from the upper left-hand corner and rising again towards the right.

Often Delacroix was not content simply to fill the given space in this way: he also laid hold of the imaginary depth which his colour was able to suggest there. This is the case with his *Achilles*, who is riding the centaur Chiron out pls 285, 286 towards the background on the left but is shooting his arrow towards the background on the right in the direction indicated by his mentor. Tintoretto alone had practised the art of these trajectories, thrown into space in all directions and complicating its texture. Delacroix—in whom Stendhal had already in 1824 discerned a distant pupil of the great Venetian master—had learnt from him through engravings, as well as from Titian and Veronese, 'examples of vivacity combined with strength'.[16] The most astonishing case is perhaps that of his *Death of Saint John the Baptist*, in which the executioner standing upright by the victim's body (which lies foreshortened and digs far into the depth of the space), is turning round with a sudden movement and presenting, with outstretched arm, the severed head to Salome as she comes down the staircase from the upper right-hand part of the picture. The wall behind counters this with a horizontal.

'In any object', Delacroix stated, 'the first thing to take hold of, in order to render it in drawing, is the contrast of the principal lines. When one makes compositions in full awareness of this, they are such that one could practically reproduce them geometrically on the picture.'[17]

It is by combining these principal lines that a painter arrives at a composition in which their influence is 'immense'.[18] But their work is not simply to distribute the filled areas and the empty ones and the lines that will harmonize them with the divisions of the given surface: they do more than this. As Delacroix shows in a detailed study of two works by Rubens: 'By the way in which the groups are arranged, or rather the one and only group which forms the whole picture, the imagination receives a shock.' The shock results from 'this powerful association'—for 'What does composing mean? It means to associate powerfully'; it comes from the 'bold combination of accessories which augments the impression produced'; and he speaks of 'clouds flying the same direction as a rider carried along by his horse, and the folds of his cloak as it envelops him or flows
pl 293 about his mount. . . .'[19] This could describe his *Attila*.

There are two methods of bringing the lines together—'combining them, contrasting them',[20] but the result is the same: 'the perception of ordered relationships produces the idea of beauty, and an extension of the soul occasioned by their analogy with our nature is the feeling proper to them.'[21] This last observation is not Delacroix's own, but was copied out by him from Senancour's *Obermann*, a book which played a considerable part in the formation of nineteenth-century thought. Delacroix was evidently delighted to find Senancour indicating as the supreme end this convergence of effects in a unity whose result is to move the onlooker's sensibility in the desired direction. As he himself expressed it, 'It is the property of the creative artists, and of them only, to produce in their works the greatest possible unity.'[22] But the commanding relationships established between design, forms and masses could not suffice to produce this unity: there is 'a unity that the lines themselves are not enough to create, in spite of the most ingenious arrangement'.[23] From what does it come? Nature supplies the answer: 'When we look at the objects that surround us, whether in a landscape or in an interior,' we notice that there is between them 'a kind of connection produced by the atmosphere that envelops them and by the varied reflections which make each object, as it were, share in a sort of general harmony.'

This is where *colour* comes in: through it the painter can convey these results of the lighting and can add 'connections' and 'harmonies' invented by him, through the relationships between the tones. This is the discovery made by the modern painters and Delacroix was particularly indignant that it should be slighted by the blind imitators of Greek and Roman art; for certainly it is a technical resource of which Antiquity was ignorant. Delacroix is reported by his cousin Riesener[24] as criticizing the artists of Antiquity for this imperfection:

'In Greek and Roman architecture the painted ornaments, the red, the blue, the yellow and the black, seem to be opposed with the intention of *affirming the divisions of the form* by means of different tones, rather than of enhancing one another by their contrasts and creating harmony.'

It was left to the East to discover 'an infinite variety of nuance' and 'it is the nuance itself that becomes all-important by, so to speak, changing its tone of voice for the harmony required of it. . . .' And Delacroix observes that 'this technique would seem to have reached Europe only with the Moors or at the time of the Crusades. . . .' His journey to Morocco made him feel more certain of this conviction, which was indeed well founded. He applied it in his own work and, instead of trying to accentuate the isolation of the form by enslaving colour to outline, sought in colour a fresh source of relationships that would contribute to the unity of the picture and its total effect. In fact it did more than that. One must, he said, 'admit, whether willingly or no, that colour can add to expression. Contrary to the general opinion, I would say that colour has a much more mysterious and perhaps more powerful effect; it acts, so to speak, without our realizing it',[25] because it acts on our subconscious and awakens instinctive, imperious associations deep down in our sensibility.

Redon remarked that Delacroix, understanding 'that his period was a period of pure expression', created 'expression through colour . . . that colour which might be called moral colour'[26]—the expression of a state of mind in the painter and the cause of an answering state of mind in the onlooker. 'From now on, colour expresses passion and the inner life'—which till then had been the province of landscape. Such a contribution was, in Redon's opinion, 'an outstanding event in the annals of art'; for 'Venice, Parma and Verona looked at colour only in its material aspect. Delacroix alone attains to moral colour, human colour.' Redon illustrates this by an examination of the *Apollo* ceiling, begun pl 304
by Delacroix in 1850 after his work on the Library of the Chambre des Députés. In it Delacroix depicted Apollo surrounded by the gods of Olympus and destroying the serpent Python.

'He paints every detail in its own unique significance. Venus is surrounded with tender blue; in an exquisitely tender grey cloud the cupids fly, fluttering their oriental wings; Ceres has all the poetry of fine landscapes, she is bathed in sunshine. Mercury in his red cloak expresses all the luxury of commerce and of upholstered prosperity. Mars is a terrible purple, his helmet is a biting red, emblem of war. . . . The whole of the subdued part is conveyed not so much by the foaming monster or by the superb body of the reclining nymph . . . as by the indefinable scale of tones, especially those sickly tones that suggest the idea of death.' Thus: 'The attribute that defines each god becomes idle, so much does the colour take over the task of saying everything and of truthful expression.'

In this passage Redon defines perfectly the difference between allegory, whose business is to recall to memory a thought-out convention, and symbol, which produces a direct experience through the sensibility.

What mattered to Delacroix, even more than the expressive power of the parts, was that of the whole. He had therefore to aim at creating a general atmosphere, instead of putting together a mosaic of tones.

## *Form, Colour and Poetry*

Though Delacroix's art found its fulfilment in colour, his interest in colour did not supplant his interest in form. Some of his contemporaries jumped to the conclusion that it did, but they were wrong. Since the journey to Morocco he had attached more and more importance to form and his first great series of mural paintings show this brilliantly; only, his conception of the form was a new one: he regarded drawing as dependent not only on outline but also, and indeed more, on colour. There were people who regarded the two as opposed, and Delacroix was often accused of despising form out of an exclusive passion for colour—erroneously because, although Delacroix raised the questions that led to Impressionism and was the pioneer of its means of expression, he was opposed, in advance, to its conclusions. A similar error was the view, current for a long time, that Delacroix neglected drawing, whereas really his drawing was of a different kind. As Baudelaire was to explain, Delacroix's drawing aimed not so much at establishing immutably a conventional outline as at sending the electricity of life along the outline's conductor wire, carrying the parts with it in the movement of the whole. To Delacroix form was not a sector of space frigidly cut out by an arbitrary frontier, an outline; it was a mass with a centre of gravity —but turned outwards so as to bathe in the luminous medium into which it had been thrown. Delacroix loved Titian's painting so much that, when he was nearly sixty, he exclaimed:[27] 'If one lived a hundred and twenty years, one would prefer Titian to everything.' This was largely because he found in Titian a power to define masses in all their density without any linear artifice, and because this density was chiefly conveyed in his painting by colour.

Outline, when 'evenly and excessively emphasized',[28] does away with relief, because in a rounded object the edge, though inevitably 'the part farthest away from the eye', attracts the eye and seems 'to come forward', setting up a fundamental contradiction. The outline defines the form arbitrarily: it undoes the effect of it by destroying the mass. In reality 'one draws by means of the middles of things as much as by their edges', and 'those painters who are called colourists have a tendency to bring out the relief of things, and the draughtsman to produce a silhouette.' (This was written by Théophile Gautier in *La Presse*, 28 March 1844, evidently after a conversation with Delacroix at the time when he was working in the Chambre des Députés and was full of this idea.) Over ten years earlier, in 1832, Balzac in his *Chef-d'œuvre inconnu* (for which he received a great deal of background information from Delacroix at the time when the two men met most frequently) expresses the same train of thought in other words: 'It is by modelling that one draws—that is to say, detaches things from the medium in which they are'—by means of relief.

Of relief, Delacroix said: 'without this gift, no true artists', adding that it was the 'principal quality of Rubens'.[29] A figure is a total mass and to quote Balzac again, 'a series of roundnesses merge into one another' till together they form a whole. To convey this it is necessary to use what Delacroix called '*le dessin par les boules*'. He referred to 'the drawing of Antiquity in proportionate relief', and recognized it in Daumier's plastic, sculptural vision, as well as in Leonardo da Vinci, of whom he liked to say that 'he has discovered everything!' It was in his lithographs of medallions that he decided most categorically—in conformity with the true lesson of Antiquity—between 'these two kinds of drawing: by means of the middles of things or by outline.' He came down against the latter kind, which it had been a fundamental error of the neo-classicists to prescribe.

His pupil Planet describes how, when working on his *Aristotle*, Delacroix grasped 'the main masses brought out by the light' in the 'figure he intended to establish'. These 'luminous points' must be marked by means of white, and the larger or smaller spaces that stand out and construct the object be described 'by means of ovals'.[30] These were then pulled together by the flowing arabesque of the drawing, which indicated the general connection. The result was to convey the mass of the whole, by starting, so to speak, from its centre of gravity and moving towards its surface, from inside to outside, and from this the figure acquired a kind of expansion into the surrounding space, in which it now bathed naturally instead of being jostled out from it by the outlines.

The consequence of such a method was seen later in Rodin's sculpture and Renoir's painting. But how, in painting, is it possible to obtain a rendering of those basic masses which the sculptor models directly? The painter must, as Delacroix told Planet, 'concentrate his colour by painting these ovoid spaces vigorously and thickly'. Chesneau[31] has explained in rather more detail how Delacroix, in the mural series, began by establishing these masses in *grisaille*; but, 'when modelling a subject in *grisaille*, it is good to imagine by touch the relief of certain strongly lit parts.' As Chesneau explains: 'Small heaps of colour, as it were, must be put at these points, as though to recall the main projections in worn Greek or Roman relief carvings, in which time has done away with the subtleties but the strong parts of the relief and the outstanding planes survive.' The outlines should be established firmly, even 'traced with emphasis', provided they are not laid on thickly. Thus the outline is present no longer in order to define, but only to finish: the paintings in the Palais Bourbon show that Delacroix did not do without it, but in them it is the colour that is responsible for the masses which express the forms. Far from being opposed to these, the colour has the effect of making them more truly felt.

This identification of mass with colour stressed by light on the points of high relief involves a clear statement of the local tone belonging to each volume—which is the opposite of the dispersion that was to take place in Impressionist pictures. In consequence 'the sketch for the picture should show the subject as it would be when the weather is overcast', that is to say in a medium light, which gives the local tone its full play. There is not, really, either light or shade. There is a coloured mass for each object; and the first thing is to determine this tone, 'this true tone... which is what matters in an object and makes it exist.'[32] After this the colours and shades come into play in answer to the surprise effect of the lighting, 'but these are minor incidents'.[33] This can be learnt, above all, from Veronese, who was, moreover, inclined in the direction of this 'simplicity' by the use of tempera: he established 'the local tone from the beginning'.[34] Delacroix often used tempera for the early stages of his work: it made it easier to establish the basic tones, which come out clearer in *demi-teintes*, in which they are not subject to the transforming action of shadows and lights. 'Tempera produces them easily through its neutral evenness.'[35] Afterwards Delacroix would take up the picture again and finish it in oils, a technique much more suited to modulations and variations, since in it the colours are mixed. René Piot tells us, in his notes on information received from Andrieu, that the *Sardanapalus* and the *Women of Algiers*, among other pictures, were produced in this way.[36]

In thus powerfully establishing the masses within the common atmosphere and as its points of concentration, it is important not to let the 'localness' of the colour break the unity of the whole. This involves giving full weight to what binds the whole together, to 'that air, those reflections which form a whole out of objects of the most disparate colours.' The air is the medium in which they are plunged, and the reflections indicate the resulting exchanges. The objects which we see are united 'by a kind of connection produced . . . by the atmosphere which envelops them', but also 'by reflections of all sorts'. In fact, whether in shadow or in half-tones, 'each plane . . . must have its particular reflection'.[37] And Delacroix concludes, in a celebrated axiom, that 'in nature everything is reflection'. Yet he noted that not only 'those painters with little inclination towards effect and colour have paid no attention to this',[38] but 'in many of the great colourists this quality is very often neglected'.

But it is not simply a matter of the purely physical exchanges that take place between one local tone and another through the rebounding of a ray of light from one surface (whose colour it borrows in passing) to another (to which it carries that colour so as to mix it with the original tone): there are others which stem from our own optical and psychological mechanism. A given colour, especially if it is strong, tends to produce the illusion that its surroundings have the complementary colour. As we have already seen, Delacroix had on the walls of his studio a triangular diagram showing these opposed colours; and he told Andrieu, according to Piot, that he had 'discovered the law of contrast' when looking at the orange collar which, on the left of Veronese's *Marriage at Cana*, gives an incomparable power to the nearby greenish-yellow. He observed repeatedly that white linen 'always has green reflections and violet shadows', and he noticed 'that it is the same with the sea',[39] on which 'the shadows that are cast are clearly violet and the reflections always green, just as clearly.'[40] It is as though every colour gives rise, in its neighbourhood, to the complementary which would, in theory, when mixed with it, restore the unity of white. 'The three colours are to be found in everything, in various mixtures.' These secondary effects of colour *in places where it is not*, this remote control exercised by it over definite local tones which it either disturbs or strengthens, or over neutral patches which it animates with a tint not applied to them, helps to produce solidarity between all the parts of a picture.

For these reasons colour is an essential means to the unity of a painting. And Delacroix elevates to the first rank 'the art of binding together the parts of the picture by effect, colour, line, reflections, etc. . . .'[41] For this purpose it is important to reinforce the interaction of the parts, so as to attain that total effect which will move the onlooker deeply; but at the same time there has to be a negative kind of work, chiefly consisting in elimination. What binds the picture together will be more effective if distracting elements are subdued or eliminated—that is to say, everything that diverts the attention and so opposes the final concentration. This is what made Delacroix constantly stress 'the need for sacrifices', for a rejection of everything that does not contribute to the painting's unity. 'Novices . . . want to display everything. . . . The poet does not hesitate to sacrifice the secondary, or to pass it over in silence. The painter's art is that of only drawing attention to what is necessary.'[42]

Thus by a cunning accentuation of everything that helps to forge unity, and by a rejection of everything that breaks it up, a picture sums up its 'poetic aim' in a general effect and makes it immediately felt, as Delacroix said in a passage often quoted:[43]

'There is a type of emotion which is quite peculiar to painting. . . . There is an impression that results from a given arrangement of colour, light, shade, etc. This is what might be called the music of the picture. . . . You go into a cathedral and are too far away from the picture to know what it represents and often you are held by this magic harmony.'

In producing this *quasi*-magnetic effect, colour has indisputably the primacy. As Baudelaire said, in discussing Delacroix's paintings, 'This singular phenomenon depends on the power of the colourist, on the perfect agreement of the tones and on the harmony (pre-established in the painter's brain) between the colour and the subject.'[44] And this is indeed what Delacroix himself had in mind when he said: 'Colour is nothing if it is not right for the picture and if it does not increase the effect the picture has for the imagination.'[45] And so this irrational power which colour has of steering us through spontaneous association towards a certain emotional state, independently of any idea expounded by the subject of the picture, works not only in detail (as Redon shows that it did in the case of the Apollo ceiling), but also, and more movingly, in the whole and in the impression this produces.

This power, discovered instinctively by some of the earlier masters but expounded lucidly and forcibly to many of his contemporaries by Delacroix, figures in a number of passages of various writers from Charles Blanc to Baudelaire.[46] One of the best contemporary studies of Delacroix was by Lady Eglé Charlemont in the *Revue de Paris* for 20 January 1867. She observes that he gave to colour 'not only its importance but paramount importance. He always allowed it the initiative, the privilege of speaking to, seizing hold of and moving the onlooker,' and 'contrived, in each of his compositions, to find a harmony and a general tone for each order of feelings.' She illustrates this with examples, and it is noteworthy that these are all taken from the period which began in about 1838, when Delacroix had reached his greatest mastery, the period of the Library of the Chambre. For instance:

'It is impossible to look at the livid and funereal harmony of his *Shipwreck of Don Juan*, or at the sinister and savage tone of his *Hamlet in the Graveyard*, without being immediately held by an impression of sadness; it is equally impossible to look at the fruit, the golden sheaves, the gay birds sowing the sparkling air with their wings along the frieze of the Conference Room in the Palais Bourbon and on the ceiling of the Library in the Luxembourg, at that limpid, serene, changeless atmosphere in which souls in felicity wander through eternal meadows... without saying to oneself that Delacroix truly enlarged the limits of painting.'

XLIII PEACE RECALLING ABUNDANCE
*1852 Diameter 31 (078)*
*Sketch for the ceiling of the Salon de la Paix at the Hôtel de Ville*
*Musée Carnavalet, Paris*

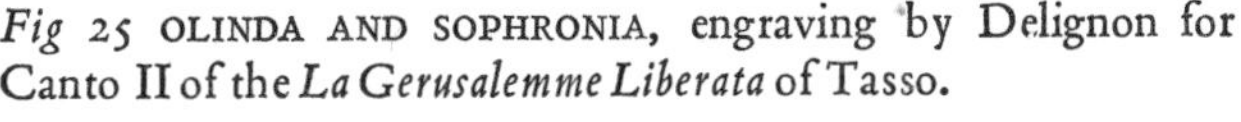

*Fig 25* OLINDA AND SOPHRONIA, engraving by Delignon for Canto II of the *La Gerusalemme Liberata* of Tasso.

*Fig 26* OLINDA AND SOPHRONIA, engraving by Dambrun after C. N. Cochin for Canto II of the *La Gerusalemme Liberata* of Tasso, translated by Baour-Lormian, 1796.

*Delacroix's imagination would often alight on an idea which had come to him several years earlier, but which had affected him deeply. It is occasionally possible to trace the original inspiration. Thus, for 'Olinda and Sophronia' and for 'Daniel in the Lions' Den' (pls 361-362), Delacroix's starting-point was certain illustrations over which he had doubtless day-dreamed when young. It is Baour-Lormian's translation of 'Gerusalemme Liberata' whose influence is most evident in these, as in other scenes inspired by Tasso, such as 'Erminia and the Shepherds' (pl 238). Affinities are apparent in the posture and costume of the figures, in certain details of the architecture, etc. Furthermore, there can be no doubt that Delacroix knew of this work, since his friend Pierret was Baour-Lormian's secretary. However, for the exaggerated height of the pyre and the fast movement of Clorinda on horseback, he must have remembered the engravings from another edition.*

XLIV OLINDA AND SOPHRONIA

*1853-4 Oil on canvas. 39 x 32 (100 x 082)*

*Neue Pinakothek, Munich*

Although Lady Eglé Charlemont modestly lays no claim to be qualified 'to discuss the workings of art' she puts her finger on another example of that law of contrasts, whose infinite resources in the field of line as well as colour Delacroix had perceived:

'Not only', she says, 'did he give each of his works a single harmony, a single impression, but he was also able, within a given picture, to oppose harmony and impression, in order that the two might fortify each other by contrast. This is the method which he took up from Shakespeare and used in a new way in his great composition the *Entry of the Crusaders into Constantinople*, in which the XXVII, page 283 massacre dying down in the foreground lays its 'simultaneously sombre and vigorous, subdued and intense tones' upon the 'gentle landscape with its blue hills winding away into the distance against an unbelievably fresh sky and diving deliciously down into the waves of the Bosphorus.' In fact Delacroix, moving (in a way that was natural to him) from sensuous to spiritual sensibility, extended the law of contrasts from the purely optical field to that of the inner life.

This kind of contrast was applied by him to the ceiling of the Library of the Chambre des Députés. Between the hemicycles at either end comes the series of painted domes. At one end, in the *Attila*, the thick, sulphurous clouds of XXXIII, page 335 death and cruelty, with flames reflected from them, invade the peace of the sky: at the other end, in the *Orpheus*, sunny memories of the Atlas Mountains and XXXIV, page 336 of the Moroccan plain find their way into the Elysian mildness of a landscape where the poet is bringing the enchantment of his words and music to primitive peoples

The painting in each of the cupolas in between sets vibrating a different string of the lyre, using the same evocative power of colour in association with that of lines and masses. There is the freshness in the lively tones of the flowers blossoming among the verdure where the nymph *Egeria* is waiting for Numa—or again in the flowers close to *Hesiod's* head as the Muse in her rose pink radiance inspires him during his sleep. There is the tragic bass added by the accompanying swell of the sea to the voice of Demosthenes. There is the tempest rising from the thick darkness in which Vesuvius is about to bury Pliny. There is the blaze of fire that conveys the anger of the angel driving Adam and Eve into the night. There is the subdued but overwhelming melancholy that lulls the despair of the Hebrews in captivity, where they sit under the tree from which the silent harp is hung. There is the clash between human curiosity, embodied by *Herodotus*, and the impenetrable wall-like mass of the Wise Men—the anxious expectation of those mysterious flashes which may issue from their mouths of shadow.

And, in the *Chaldean Shepherds*, there is the expansion of the human gaze towards the infinite spaces of the night, pierced by the gentle yet lively sparkling of the stars. Anger, cruelty, hope and despair, energy, spiritual illumination, the terrors of the soul and the confrontation with the unfathomable—all those crests and hollows of the human wave are here seen rolling from age to age, conveyed to the eyes and mind by colours, shadows and lights as varied as those of the ocean.

## *The Library of the Luxembourg: the Peace of Nature*

While Delacroix was still working on this enormous task, he had already undertaken a similar one. This he owed, once more, to the good-will of M. Thiers, who on 1 March 1840 again became *Président du Conseil.* In the Luxembourg, Chalgrin's Salle des Séances had proved too small, chiefly because of the political trials, and in 1836 it was decided to enlarge the Palace. The library was to be accommodated in the new part, looking out on the gardens, and several artists had been engaged to decorate it. An unpublished letter of recommendation[47] written on 26 December 1840 by M. Héricart de Thury to the Duke Decazes, *Grand Référendaire*, and advocating an extension of the part allotted to Riesener, shows that the distribution initially planned by Rémusat was as follows: the central cupola for Delacroix, the five coffers of the ceiling on one side for Roqueplan, the five on the other for Riesener, one of the reading-rooms at the end for Louis Boulanger, and the one at the opposite end for Ary Scheffer. Thus pl 294 Delacroix had at his disposal a dome larger than those in the Chambre des Députés—it is 276 in. in diameter and 138 in. high—with a hemicycle joined to it. The work was begun in 1841 and was opened to the public in December of 1846. The fee was 30,000 francs.

In the Chambre, where the series ranged from *Orpheus* causing the dawn of poetry and the arts, to the awakened animal in man ruining, with *Attila*, the fair edifice constructed with such effort, amid such chaotic passions and ordeals; the adventure of the human spirit was left in suspense, on the brink of catastrophe, and the brightness of its opening was doubtfully maintained. In the Senate it is as though Delacroix had determined to push on beyond this melancholy view of life. Beyond it, again referring to Dante, he imagines 'a kind of Elysium in the style of that poet, in which the great men enjoy, as he says, a *serious happiness.*' They wander over 'a smiling plain... where girls are gathering flowers on the banks of a winding stream. . . . '[48] As he said in a letter to Gustave Planche on 9 August 1842, 'It is the moment when Dante... is presented by Virgil to Homer and other great poets.' Dante has passed through the Inferno and now comes to the apotheosis of Homer, but whereas, in treating this theme, Ingres constructed learnedly an immutable pyramid, Delacroix's vision was of palpitating life within a sacred wood—that sacred wood which Puvis de Chavannes later treated again in the Sorbonne fresco, but which here is alive with footsteps, with the murmuring of waters and with the whisper of branches moved by the breeze. Yet Delacroix was even stricter than Ingres in his choice of the elect—less willing than he to include the modern world; for he welcomes into their number, after the men of the heroic era (once more, together with the wild beasts enchanted by the songs of Orpheus) none but the illustrious Greeks and Romans. The Christian world is absent, except for the intrusion of Dante. Confining himself to 'the great men who did not receive the grace of Baptism', Delacroix shows a jealous determination to pay homage exclusively to Antiquity.

Attila has disappeared, and the forces of violence and bloodshed are present only to join in paying homage. There is, for instance, the panther rolling at the feet of Orpheus, of the peace of poetry; and, in the hemicycle dividing the dome from the window which looks over the gardens, we see Alexander making use of 'a gold casket of inestimable value', found among the spoils of the conquered Persians, to enclose the poems of Homer, and only in the distance is there a suggestion of 'a shattered chariot and the field of battle'. According to Villot, it was he, once again, who suggested the general theme to Delacroix, but this time in an instant, for Delacroix 'found me reading Dante's *Inferno*. . . .' pl 296

*Di quel signor dell'altissimo canto*
*Che sopra gli altri come aquila vola.*

The peace of nature, evoked by the Luxembourg paintings, had come to Delacroix as a new experience, after he had been racked more than ever by the storms of the human adventure, depicted by him at the Chambre des Députés. The experience came to him during the visits he made, for the sake of his worsened health, to George Sand at Nohant, to his Riesener cousins at Frépillon, to the Pyrenees to take the waters and, lastly, to Champrosay where in 1844, on Villot's advice, he had taken a small house which he later bought. Morocco had already shown him the contrast between the serene breadth of its plains and mountains and the agitation of human beings; but now the charm of the countryside was fully revealed to him—the freshness of its streams and of its green, the smell of grass and earth, the light and all its delicate shades. On 20 January 1844 he wrote to his pupil, Mme. Rang-Babut: pls 301, 302 pl 300

'I should like now, for my soul's health as well as for my body's, to live a little closer to nature, that is to say to have easier access to the fields, to have air, to eb able to live a life a bit like a peasant's.'

He opened his eyes and, amazed by the sudden calm, discovered that in our organism, driven as it is by our nerves, passion and instincts, there is a part of those instincts that can harmonize with the slow and peaceful rhythm of natural things.

Formerly it had not been these deep respirations that he had heard; even in 1840, at Valmont, he was still revelling in the violence of nature: 'The storms follow one another continually. . . . What rushing sounds of trees, tempest and wind!'[49] Calm, when it arrived, disconcerted him, and on the next day he was writing to George Sand:

'These fine trees and stretches of water throw me into an emotional state that prepares me for something that doesn't come. . . . Imagination is not satisfied. I long, then, for that whirlwind in which one's spirit hasn't the time to see the emptiness, the great darkness we carry inside us.'

He was only just emerging from the period in which—on 15 February 1838—he could say to Rivet: 'My tragic inclinations still dominate me, and the Graces smile on me rarely.' But four years later, writing of Nohant to George Sand, he could confess: 'You know how I love gardens and flowers . . .' and could sing the praises of 'divine nature'. From the tragic and the epic he had moved on to the elegiac.

His discovery of the great peace of natural things appears on the very first page of the notebook in which, on 19 January 1847, he began again to keep the diary interrupted since 1824. He began it, as he says, 'on a happy day': he had been to the Jardin des Plantes, and there, 'as I walked', a 'feeling of happiness increased; it seemed to me that my nature was rising above the vulgarities or petty thoughts or petty worries of the moment.... How necessary it is to shake oneself up from time to time, to stick one's nose out of doors, to try to read in the book of nature.... Certainly the sight of all this makes one better and calmer.'

And he adds that: 'The trees ... were partly responsible for the feeling of pleasure this day has given me.' The secret of this joy was the one that he would never again lose. In 1857, for instance, he makes several notes like the following (12 May, Champrosay): 'I am getting great pleasure from this charming place. It is an inexpressible pleasure to open my window in the morning.' And on 10 August, at Plombières, he wrote: 'Every time I look at a real morning, I blossom out, I feel as if I were enjoying this for the first time and I am bitterly sorry not to enjoy it more often.' In the following year, at the end of July, at the same place: 'I could not resist going down a steep slope to the delicious little stream whose murmur one hears from the road. There I found enchanting things, scattered rocks, woodland paths, clearings and thickets. I drank from the charming stream.'

This man, who had failed to achieve harmony with other human beings or even with himself, had discovered a harmony with things. The mind which had struck roots down into the subterranean world where Dante had seen the damned still shaken and tortured by the convulsions that had made their lives so restless —the mind which still kept Dante company—was now blossoming in answer to the light: the dark sap had fed the flower—that flower which, in the Luxembourg dome, grows beside the stream to which the deer 'is timidly coming to drink', the flower which a girl is about to pick for the sake of its fragrance. It is also the flower of joy whose red is seen between the laurels beside which Mars, with his sword now sheathed, is at last reposing.

Delacroix's plan had already received approval by the middle of 1841, but its execution was constantly slowed by his worsening health: earache and eye trouble were added to the increasing infection of his throat. In spite of this, the dome was almost finished and the whole unveiled at the end of 1846. The canvases of the dome caved in on 5 May 1868, when water came through and threatened to affect the hemicycle also; they were restored by Andrieu, who had already restored the *Dante and Virgil*, the *Massacre at Chios* and the Apollo ceiling. Not that Delacroix failed to concern himself with technical questions of all sorts, in particular the preparation of the wall surface (on this subject he exchanged many letters with the architect de Gisors). Similarly, to make sure that the curve of the ceiling would not produce the illusion of figures falling forwards he had carefully worked things out with the help of a small wooden model.

He studied his predecessors, and takes his place in the line of mural painters who, from Mantegna and Correggio onwards, favoured, when painting domes, a composition in which figures are grouped around the base and leave a central space to which clouds and flying figures give life. In the Luxembourg dome this space is shaped by a wavy line which, rising and falling with the masses of green leaves, marks out four principal sectors. These correspond to the arches supporting the dome, and each of them contains a distinct scene: Orpheus at one end answers to Homer at the other end of a diameter which they share, and at the two ends of the diameter at right angles to this the Greeks (including the pale Aspasia) grouped about Socrates 'in the shade of a clump of laurels and orange trees' counterbalance the Romans dominated by Cato of Utica, who is reading Plato. The axes between these diameters mark the cesuras between the four scenes and coincide with the axes between the rising of the arches: they are stressed by hexagonal pendentives, in which Saint Jerome, Cicero, Orpheus and the Muse of Aristotle represent Philosophy, Eloquence, Poetry and Science. XXXVII, page 371

In the hemicycle a sinuous line is superimposed upon the general curve which borders and underlines the shape of the arcature. This sinuous line, launched skywards by the flight of the victory who is holding out the crown to Alexander, pls 296, 297 is caught up by the branches of the palm trees and descends their trunks along the right-hand edge of the frame; at their feet it curves inwards, returning leftwards, then climbs again through the kneeling woman to Alexander's pedestal, carries its impulse on in the direction shown by his arm and crosses the central arch with its surmounting trophies; then, taking its direction from one of these and drawn onwards by the flowing flags, it completes the downward part of its trajectory at the bearers of the gold casket, particularly the kneeling one; reaching the ground, like a wave breaking against the frame, it gives a last leap upwards through the rider who has fallen from his chariot, and ends in the rearing movement of his horse.

## *The Galerie d'Apollon—The Salon de la Paix*

Master now of his new art, Delacroix thought only of pursuing it. In the spring of 1844, in seventeen days, he painted the wall in an aisle of the Church of Saint-Denis-du-Saint-Sacrement, the commission for which had first been given to Robert Fleury: it is 138 in. high and 197 in. wide, yet was barely sufficient for this *Pietà* (whose theme he had already laid down in a small picture painted in pl 269 1837). For this wall painting he was paid 6,000 francs.

In 1846 he was nearly commissioned to paint the dome of the cathedral of Arras, on the recommendation of Constant Dutilleux, who came from that city and was Robaut's father-in-law and a friend of Corot.[50] In 1847 the idea that he should decorate a staircase, also in the Luxembourg, aroused his enthusiasm. Here he proposed to treat modern subjects of heroic quality: they were to include *The Country rising to aid the Volunteers of '92, Bonaparte subjecting Egypt, Napoleon crowned by Glory* and even Marshal Bugeaud's recent victory (in 1844) over the Arabs at Isly. But nothing came of all this.

The Revolution had broken out in 1848. Delacroix showed little enthusiasm for the 'terrible June disturbances'. He took a gloomy view of the future, and wrote to his collaborator Lassalle-Bordes on 4 September 1848: 'When shall

XLV THE FANATICS OF TANGIER
*c. 1836-8 Oil on canvas. 39 x 52 (098 x 132)*
*Collection: Jerome Hill, New York*

we be together in front of a fine wall surface, brush in hand, with no thought except to do the best we can?'

And yet the new Director of the Beaux-Arts, Charles Blanc, still a young man and a critic favourable to Delacroix, saw to it that he was commissioned to paint a chapel in the Church of Saint-Sulpice—the Chapel of the Font at first, exchanged in the next year for the Chapel of the Holy Angels. He had hardly had time to think of this when, in March 1850, a new and vast task, which was to
pl 304 delay the other, was given to him—to finish the decoration of the Apollo Gallery in the Louvre, where Le Brun had left empty the central ceiling. Though the architect, Duban, was in favour of the choice of Delacroix, it was again Charles Blanc whose intervention was decisive. And so Delacroix found himself established 'in the finest place in the world, next to Le Brun's fine compositions'.

Contrary to the opinion of those (if there still are any) who persist in seeing Delacroix simply as a romantic and Le Brun as an academic, there was not such a distance between these two artists as to make it difficult for their work to harmonize. The work of Le Brun, who was brought up on the classical teaching of Poussin but shared the taste of Louis XVI for baroque pomp, is a mixture not altogether unrelated to that balance between energy and order, between passion and reason, at which Delacroix aimed. Only the distance of genius separates the two artists. And this essential difference made it possible for Delacroix's composition to blaze out with its full force in the centre of the other's total scheme without blowing it to pieces. It is a composition in which, to use Delacroix's own words, there is also present 'that indefinable power . . . which amazes us in Rubens, the element that his temperament—*vis poetica*—adds to a composition without seeming to change it.'[51]

pl 315 And indeed it was to Rubens that he went again in search of the shock that would set him in motion—this in the course of a second short visit to Brussels, on his way to Ems where he was to take the waters. As he tells Madame de Forget in a letter of 13 July 1850, 'The admirable paintings of Rubens have set me on fire.'

The ceiling was first shown to the public on 16-17 October[51] in the following year, and the payment for it was raised from 18,000 to 24,000 francs.

As in the Luxembourg dome, the composition, though here inscribed within a rectangle prolonged by two hemicycles, is based on a circular distribution of the figures at the edge: at the top of the picture there are the gods, either watching the fight (like Venus) or rushing to take part (like Minerva, Mercury and Hercules), surmounted by the flying Victory and the scarf of their messenger Iris. At the bottom, plunging into the darkness and waters of the Deluge, the serpent Python is surrounded by monsters and by the bodies of his victims. But the central part is no longer an empty space more or less occupied by secondary flying figures; now, at the centre and above it, in the heart of a solar blaze, there is
pl 305 Apollo, dashing forward in his chariot drawn by four headlong horses and letting

XLVI VIEW OF TANGIER FROM THE SEASHORE
*1858 Oil on canvas. 32 x 39 (081 x 100)*
*The Minneapolis Institute of Arts, Bequest of Mrs C.H. Lindley*

fly his victorious arrows. His movement carries him leftwards as he shoots at the serpent whose furiously twisting coils are retreating towards the right. Between these poles, a diagonal (which does not yet exist in the first sketch in the Hamburg Kunsthalle) strikes across, formed by the arrows shot downwards by the god, and by the black smoke rising from the mouth of Python in the direction indicated by the monster's raised claw. It is an admirable composition, which the sketch in the Musées Royaux des Beaux-Arts, Brussels, with its dizzying energy makes even more clear and legible.

Thus, bringing the varied resources of his art together and to their highest point, Delacroix imposed a firm order upon a space measuring 315 in. by 295 in., itself the centre of a ceiling which includes a great many painted surfaces and carved volumes. At the same time, through the subdivision of the main subject, the pronounced diagonal binding together the protagonists who are caught in movement, and the whirl of the surrounding figures, he imparted a thunderous animation to the whole; this indeed was necessary in order to compel attention in the midst of a decorative scheme that was already agitated—a complex of curves and divisions. The effect is as though, across the confused din of various wild beasts, there has come the roar of a lion. The feat required an authority, a dominating vigour of which only Michelangelo or Tintoretto could supply comparable examples. It required also a masterly application and hard work of which some idea may be gained from the hundreds of preparatory drawings Delacroix took the trouble to make of the general setting, using a mirror.

To sustain the impact of all the brilliance and grandiloquence accumulated by his illustrious predecessor, Delacroix needed the full resources of his palette. Andrieu, who worked as his assistant, reports[53] that 'nothing was intense or brilliant enough'. Delacroix got together his palette with very great application, thinking deeply about the properties of each colour, about the impression to which it was an answer and the effect he desired to get from it. Taking as key the scarf of Iris, which opens out at the top of the composition, he aimed at 'a marvellous mixture of all the colours . . . the colouring of nature allied to poetic magic.' He modelled Minerva, for instance, with Prussian blue and placed bright chrome in the highlights, with scumblings of crimson lake and cobalt over the whole. The palette prepared by him—and recorded by Andrieu—included twenty-eight pure tones and twenty-five made up of mixtures of them.[54]

The canvas, solidly mounted and attached to a perfectly dry vault, did not shift: only the war dangers of 1940 made it necessary to detach it, roll it up and place it in safety; and it was not restored to its position until the end of hostilities. I remember, not without emotion, these two extremely difficult operations, undertaken at my request and, fortunately, without damage to the work.

The new commission to which Delacroix harnessed himself almost at once—it dates from the end of 1851—was for work at the Hôtel de Ville, where indeed he sat, XLIII, page 395
from now onwards, as one of the municipal councillors: it was to paint, in the Salon de la Paix, a huge circular ceiling surrounded by eight coffers and a frieze with eleven subjects. The theme was similar in mood to the Apollo ceiling. In the centre was Cybele—that is, the Earth—asking help of the gods in order

to put an end to the ravages of conflict, bloodshed and conflagrations, the presence of which was no more than suggested in the lower part of the picture, like a lingering echo. This time 'the azure sky dusted with golden light', to quote Gautier's description (*Moniteur Universel*, 25 March 1854), with its light clouds bearing bright divinities as in a Tiepolo, filled the greater part of the surface.
pls 306, 307 Near the centre are Peace, Abundance, the Muses and Ceres 'crowned with ears of corn'. The coffers were divided between the gods of Olympus, and all round the room the exploits of Hercules gave the support of force used in a good cause to this repeated triumph of light.

At the beginning of 1852 Delacroix was already at work on it, again assisted by Andrieu; he worked at it constantly and was already, in October, beginning to prime the canvases. The whole was more or less finished by the middle of 1853—but not shown till March of the following year, for Delacroix was at first disappointed by its effect and insisted on revising it. Less than twenty years later these magnificent pictures were completely destroyed under the Commune in 1871, when the Hôtel de Ville was burnt. All that remains of them is a series of sketches: a number of these are magnificent, but the others owe more to the somewhat dull hand of Andrieu than to that of his master. According to Andrieu (whom Delacroix nicknamed *mon petit clerc*), the great painter returned in this work to the influence of Veronese, and was filled with 'an extreme love for vigorous effects'; he said, indeed, that 'this must be painted *à la* Veronese, brown figures against a clear background'. Delacroix carried out the whole in oils, but with a return to the mixture of virgin wax which he had given up in the Apollo ceiling.

## *The Chapel of the Holy Angels*

After 1856 Delacroix turned to another large-scale enterprise, which was to be his last: the paintings in Saint-Sulpice. He did not, in fact, set to work on these seriously until he had finished the Salon de la Paix, for various preliminary incidents delayed him. Delacroix explained this to Lassalle-Bordes in a letter of 22 January 1850:

'The chapel was the one containing the font; and the subjects arose naturally out of this: baptism, original sin, expiation, etc. . . . I obtained the curé's agreement and set to work on the composition of my pictures. At the end of three months I received a letter in the country, informing me that the baptismal chapel was under the church porch instead of being in the place I was to paint. . . . I was quite beside myself with justified anger.'

However, he had now 'practically decided' on the subjects, certainly on that of the ceiling, which would be 'the Archangel Michael overcoming the Devil'. Yet in the middle of 1855 he was still preparing the walls, and it was more than a year before he had passed the stage of sketches and went to the chapel itself 'to carry out the work so long delayed and ceaselessly interrupted.'[55] Many further interruptions were caused by his increasingly frequent and serious ill-health.

It was not till 1858, when he bought the house at Champrosay, that he really set to work at Saint-Sulpice. He then imposed on himself the discipline of commuting between his country home and Paris. As he wrote to Riesener on 7 October 1860, 'I take the train every morning, work at the chapel for four hours, and usually go home fairly early so as still to have time to enjoy the country.' At the end of 1857 he moved his Paris home to the Place Furstenberg, to be nearer this work. On the first day of 1861 he wrote in the *Journal*: 'What seemed to me at a distance easy to achieve presents horrible difficulties,' but he adds: 'What enchanting work it is,' and describes it as a 'happy compensation for what the good years have taken away with them; a noble use of the moments of that old age which now besieges me . . . yet leaves me still the strength to overcome the pains of the body and the griefs of the soul.' At the beginning of June 1861 he had at last finished, and on 21 July the public was allowed to see a work which may be considered as his last will and testament. Of the unveiling, he told Riesener that 'Neither the Minister nor the *Préfet* nor Nieuwerkerke nor anyone from the Court or from official circles turned up, in spite of my invitations . . . but, on the other hand, many artists.'

Each of the two great walls which Delacroix had to paint measures 281 in. by 191 in., and the ceiling is an oval surface whose diameters are 151 in. and 226 in. He was paid 20,000 francs.

Making full use of wax this time, he had obtained a mat surface that absorbed the paintings into the architectural whole; but he was not afraid, on the other hand, to fill the surface full of life by means of movement, to pierce it with the
suggestion of space, produced by the monumental perspective behind his *Helio-* pl 308
*dorus*, and behind his *Jacob* by the atmospheric perspective. The much debat- pl 311
ed question of decorative painting was resolved, for him, in the same way as the other problems that face an artist: one should not hesitate to go to the farthest limits of variety and richness, provided that the power of discipline masters the whole and raises it to unity; art, like life, must include as much as possible, but a strong central articulation must tie it all together. Delacroix's active and profound paintings bring life into the building, but they form part of it and complete it, as the flower completes its stalk.

Their centre of interest is man, in whom vital impulse and sculptural volume coexist. But he is prolonged and amplified by his setting. The inner life which makes him exist and pushes him forwards into the life of the world establishes its communion with this: it listens with enchantment or terror to its own limitless echoes in nature, which is the setting chosen by Delacroix for his *Jacob wrestling with the Angel.* Here he raises up titanic oaks, the idea of
which had come to him in the Forest of Senart but is now amplified to a Biblical pl 312
scale; these oaks become the patriarchs of the vegetable world, described by Barrès as 'the great oracular trees, garbed in eternity but a living eternity'. Yet on the left of the picture, counterbalancing the caravan that is passing by and

XLVII ARAB ON HORSEBACK ATTACKED BY A LION
*1849 Oil on canvas. 18 x 14 (046 x 036)*
*Potter-Palmer Collection, The Art Institute of Chicago*

moving away on the right, he puts a sparkling stream with little waterfalls and cool surfaces.

The redeeming power of thought enables us to rescue from the flux of things those abstract structures which can be embodied in stone: through it we build the absolute world of forms and ideas. On the walls of this chapel, which amount to a superb diptych, Delacroix instinctively gave to the *Heliodorus driven from the Temple* an architectural setting in contrast to the landscape setting of the *Jacob wrestling with the Angel.* Its firmly articulated verticals and horizontals are
fig 27 bound together by the strong diagonals of perspective and of shadows: only a curtain stirred by the wind reminds us of the animation of the air. There is a kind of antiphonal effect between the three oaks in the *Jacob*, whose bark and leaves descend in majestic sweeps towards the interlocked combatants, and the three columns of the Temple, whose rigid verticals fall, one of them on to the archangel's avenging arm, and the two others on to the central mêlée: even though it is the converging movement of the mounted angel and the flying angels that has borne the Emperor to the ground, where the horse is about to trample him, it is the heavy cylinder of the central column that is pinning him down.

For all the static quality produced by the pillars and the huge heavy lintels, the composition of the *Heliodorus* is chiefly governed by a single movement which binds its parts together. In this case it is a movement of convergence. The lines bear down upon the defeated man like arrows flying to their target—some of them by sheer weight, as for instance the central column, the downward movement of the staircase on the left and on the right the shape of the arcade, and others by being hurled forwards, as is the case with the bold trajectory made by the angel diving from above (Baudelaire remembered how, in this picture, 'a fury-angel sweeps from heaven like an eagle'[56]), or in that of the mounted angel's sceptre and the edge of his wing, the curve of which continues the verticals above it and is prolonged by a foreleg of the horse.

fig 28 In contrast, the unitary principle in the *Jacob*, though equally commanding, is based on divergence. The movement starts from the lower right-hand corner, going in a straight line along the javelin which lies on the ground; it is indicated with more suppleness by the caravan departing on the right, is taken up by the sinuous upward growth of the first oak and then by the second oak which diverges from it leftwards. The line of the javelin is continued by Jacob's tense right leg, by the butting movement of his left knee and by the axis of his body throwing all its weight forwards; it is endorsed by a play of parallels made up of the cord across his back and the arm and thigh of the angel bending under the assault. The thrust then loses itself in the depths of the green leaves and of the gorge. The last rib of this open fan is the bank of the little stream, very close to the horizontal of the frame base.

A further contrast is made by the ceiling: here, in the midst of clouds which amplify the curve of the overthrown bodies and produce an oval answering to the

XLVIII LION HUNT STUDY
*c. 1854 Oil on canvas. 34 x 45 (086 x 115)*
*Private collection, France*

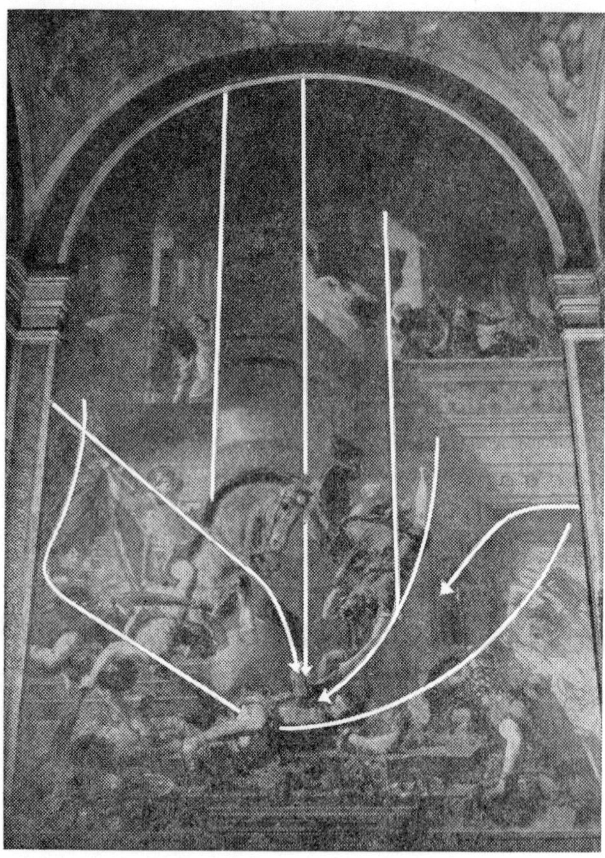

*Fig 27* HELIODORUS DRIVEN FROM THE TEMPLE
The vertical fall of the heavy column and the 'diving' attitude of the angels unite the fundamental ideas of baroque and classical painting, and seem to bear down upon the fallen Heliodorus.

*Fig 28* JACOB WRESTLING WITH THE ANGEL
All the expression here is in the straining figure of Jacob, leaping over the dagger as he tries to break the pliable resistance of the Angel, and is repeated in the ascending, tortuous lines of the trees.

shape of the area, the Archangel emerges from the luminous centre: his vertical movement indicated by the lance he is pointing downwards together with the almost perfect symmetry of his outstretched wings, symbolizes the post and beam of the spiritual scales from which the two opposing walls are suspended.

Thus the forms are arranged in accordance with overall schemes conceived by the artist's plastic imagination, but other, more subconscious, mechanisms have helped to govern this invention. Wide fields of the psychology of art remain to be explored. Take for instance, the landscape setting of the *Jacob wrestling with the Angel*, certainly one of the most astonishing in the history of art: how was it conceived? There is an element of realism, of borrowing from nature: it is even true that the oaks have their objective origin in the oaks of the Forest of Senart, of which several of Delacroix's many sketches have survived. But none of them is here reproduced exactly: they have all been caught up in the workings of a transforming sensibility. A breath from the world of legend seems to be shaping them afresh and changing them into creatures outside circumstance. They are, as Barrès put it, 'heroized', to fit in with the feelings of the combatants. We are outside time and in the world and the age where the pyre of Hercules was built up, where the vulture swooped on Prometheus,

LIII, page 465

where Venus emerged from the wave. We are in the land where myths form.

Not only are the trees, which Delacroix saw and retained in his memory, transmuted to fit the needs of his sensibility, but the knoll from which they are growing has also been subjected to what might be called a visual contagion, transferring it from the world of realism into the plastic world. Objective forms, when the artist takes hold of them, are indeed shaped afresh in two ways: to become valid, they must enter both the poetic and the plastic world. To enter
pl 313 the latter the knoll in the *Jacob wrestling with the Angel* has undergone contagion from a baroque masterpiece, the admirable holy water stoop situated close to Delacroix's chapel-studio, at the base of a nearby pillar. Its scalloped basin is supported by an imitation rock, and the twist of this has been imparted to the picture. If, forgetting what it represents, we compare this movement with the base of the principal oak, we at once recognize it: the ground on the right is hollowed in a similar way, to act as support for the steep slope which curves in response to the rugged roots, and these twist like the edge of the eighteenth-century basin. The interlacing vegetation about the knoll recurs in the holy water stoop, in the writhing tentacles of the marine animals. And in fact, if we compare the fresco with its preparatory drawing, we see that this movement imparted to the ground is a new development. Delacroix copies neither nature nor the masters: he nourishes himself from their substance, but assimilates it and takes it into his own world, where it is born again and is often unrecognizable.

When Delacroix's imagination had fashioned a form and marked it as his own, it was often retained and used again: thus the legs of the angel reappear, still the

*Fig 29* THE ABDUCTION OF REBECCA
Towards the end of his life, Delacroix developed the baroque diagonal in zig-zags like lightning flashes.

same, in the quite different movement of the Templar Bois-Guilbert carrying off Rebecca; the two pictures were painted at about the same time, around 1858. Even the root of the wings on the angel's back and the direction of their feathers recur, transmuted, in the knight's ample cloak swollen by the wind. pl 316

As for colour, it is worth while to go into some detail in order to see the pitch of technical and artistic subtlety to which Delacroix had now attained. Faithful to his method of starting from the local tones, that basic keyboard of his harmonies, and then working out the play of light, shadow and reflection upon them, he now indulged in the most novel and subtle combinations of colour. In the words of Andrieu, 'He always contrasted his light and shade, half-tone and reflection. Example: violet shadow, yellow light, local tone red, half-tone blue-green,' the local tone which he was using as a guide being placed 'between the half-tone and the bright colour; that local tone which, if not just right, would throw all the rest out of harmony. This is how Paolo Veronese proceeded. . . .'[57] In the *Jacob wrestling with the Angel* the masses of the foliage and the earth provide those 'neutral tones' obtained by the 'mixture of the neighbouring colours', tones 'on which the more lively colours converge and harmonize'. Emerald green is dominant; the blue by which it is broken eases the transition to the green leaves in the distance, azured as these are by the intervening air, but reinforces the contrast with the complementary ochres introduced by the russet tints of autumn that lead to the coppery reds of a sunset sky—while at the base of the trees there are twined branches that are almost pure rose-pink. The colours of the clothes enhance the chromatic violence: in the mass of people on the right, red and blue stand out against the white of the sheep and the reddish brown of the cattle; in the mass of the two wrestlers the salient points are offered by the red, which passes from vermilion through an intermediary mixture to the purple produced by madder lake; the carmine reflections which enliven the angel's dress serve as a transition to its broad area of violet. The eye is thus led towards the basic greys which attain metallic coldness in the angel's wings and the tree trunks.

Delacroix, with his passion for music, knew the nature of the fugue and was constantly transposing it into the field of colour: the grey of the wings combines with white to produce Jacob's garment. But this same grey, mixed with black, forms the main mass of the still-life in the foreground, and enables the straw yellow of the hat and the red to assert their tone beside the purest white in the composition.

In the *Heliodorus* the green-red-violet harmony of the *Jacob* is answered by a dominant harmony of yellows, oranges and turquoise. Here the feast for the eyes becomes intoxicating. And the fugue of colour equals, in its assurance and invention, the music of Bach. Over the area as a whole it allows of endless combinations, while in certain details, such as the overturned jewel casket, it is carried to the ultimate subtlety. The tones whose play is seen in the principal group are echoed in the group of watchers pressing about the High Priest on the balcony. The woman on the staircase, with her arms twisted in terror, is established in a harmony of blue and red; close by her, against a floor of golden light, the mounted archangel stands out, with his wings russet like a wild beast's pelt, his breastplate in which Naples yellow is dominant, and the fire colour of his garment in which cadmium and the vermilion mingle. In contrast the swooping angel is LIV, page 466 nocturnal and mysterious, answering the other with the great mass of violet, into which his fair hair imparts an echo of gold. Between them, forming the base of the curve that joins them, Heliodorus has collapsed upon a purple cloak, close to his helmet which is rolling away, the orange of its interior finding a subtle complementary in its exquisitely delicate turquoise blue plume. This harmony resumes and carries to extreme definition the gold and blue harmony which imbues the whole of the architectural setting with a series of surprising variations. On the extreme right the two warriors bring together wide areas of turquoise blue and of Prussian blue, and an orange red with an acid green, while on the extreme left the third avenging angel answers with a juxtaposition of bottle green and a violet-tinged red.

It is as though, to absorb his work more closely into the volume of the chapel, Delacroix laid hold of the daylight which falls from the wide lateral bay and introduced it into his compositions as one of their inherent parts. In the *Jacob wrestling with the Angel* the rays, falling at their normal angle, strike the bright plane formed by Jacob's back, and so seem to take part, with all their strength, in the weight of the attack, which is pushing one of the angel's wings backwards (while the other still resists like a strut) and seems to bend the line of the rock and stream behind them. In the *Heliodorus* the angle on which the light falls is materialized in the slope of the sceptre brandished by the riding angel and in that of the top edge of the staircase wall, seen in perspective, and the shadow cast by this wall against the background, prolonging the great fluttering curtain.

Further detailed description seems unnecessary: it would continue to reveal the same pure and inspired creative work reinforced by all the weight of accumulated technique and careful calculation. I cannot resist quoting the prophetic lines written by Delacroix himself, in August 1833, in his article on Sigalon's copy of Michelangelo's *Last Judgment*:

'One cannot help regretting the banal sentimentality which the moderns have introduced into the representation of sacred subjects, and the false style, which is hateful in the pretension it makes to rejuvenate the scenes of Scripture and the Gospel—scenes which are eternally beautiful and new, but only for those men who are really new and able to render them in all their simplicity.'

## *The Last Works*

Scarcely had Delacroix finished this masterpiece—which both by its scale and by its marvellous youthfulness seems beyond the strength of a dangerously ill man—before he had become impatient for a new task that would be worthy of him. Already on 17 October 1861 he was writing to Andrieu: 'I feel, as you do, that it is already a long time since our work was finished! I have forgotten the agonies it gave me: I am like the ant who is ready to start work again.' He had also resigned his position as municipal councillor. His time was free. And his health seemed to him, far from being exhausted by the enormous labour, to have improved—although it is clear that in fact, once the excitement had passed, his strength declined. Once again, and for the last time, he dreamed of travelling to Italy—with his old friend Schwiter. Once again he had to give up the idea. He wrote his article on Charlet and spent some months at Champrosay. Saint-Sulpice had in fact been the last of his 'great enterprises'—as we have said, a kind of testament.

In 1861 he set to work on a *Triumph of Bacchus* and a *Triumph of Amphitrite*;
but these were only two small works and he was never to finish the series of
four large pictures of the *Seasons*, commissioned from him in 1856 by the Alsa- pls 320, 321, 322
tian banker Frédéric Hartmann (who had also approached Millet). Hartmann
died in 1861 and the four unfinished panels—sold in 1864 with the contents of
Delacroix's studio and now in the Sao Paulo Museum—are merely sketches of
what would have been a world of enchantment: brilliant nudes, deep verdure,
limpid or stormy stretches of water, rocks, flowers, with Orpheus and Eurydice,
Diana and Actaeon, Bacchus and Ariadne and Juno and Aeolus each in turn LV, page 479
showing that Delacroix's imagination had never been closer to the myths of
Antiquity, or to Poussin. . . .

At this time, by a compensatory movement, his plastic invention seemed to incline towards a highly baroque type of composition—that of the S curve which, starting from one of the lower corners, impinges against the frame on the opposite side and swirls back till it does the same on the other side and resumes its original direction, ending at the upper corner opposite to its starting point. In the *Aeolus* it winds with the path (this is particularly evident in the Montpellier sketch). In the *Bacchus* it follows the chain of the figures: starting at the top with the streamer held by a Cupid, it swerves and then slopes down the joined arms of the god and Ariadne, until finally it follows the curve of her body.

The same arabesque dominates the design of his *Death of Lara*, painted in pl 318
1858. Indeed next year it recurred in that hard, rising road on which *Christ
Carrying the Cross* exhausts himself, in the picture in the Metz Museum: it was pl 314
exhibited at the 1859 Salon, together with the *Entombment*, in which the same
arrangement is reversed. (These two subjects were part of the Saint-Sulpice
plan at the time when it was still intended that Delacroix should decorate the
Baptismal Chapel.) In another picture exhibited at the same Salon, the *Abduc-* pl 316
*tion of Rebecca* (now in the Louvre), is to be found perhaps the most perfect
example of his use of this scheme: a slanting, broken piece of wood at the bottom fig 29
on the left starts if off; it is taken up by the horse, whose twisting movement
throws it back leftwards, while the watching soldier and the group formed by
Bois-Guilbert and Rebecca establish the slope which ends by impinging against
the support of the drawbridge; with it the line now moves upwards in the opposite direction; it has merely to follow the smoke from the fire pouring out through
the window to lose itself at the upper right-hand corner.

The 1862 *Medea* (now in the Louvre) is a reminder that this bold zig-zag
design had its origin a long way back, for it is there repeated from the 1838 picture on the same theme (in the Lille Museum). In 1863, Delacroix took it up pl 251
again and gave it even ampler treatment in the last important picture he painted,
the *Arabs skirmishing in the Mountains*; the line rises from right to left through the pl 319
fallen rider and turns the other way through his horse; it follows the slope of the
ground to a clump of trees from which, broken by a hill crowned by a castle, it
starts off again reversed; taken up afresh in the opposite direction by a final
mountain crest, it at last reaches the upper right-hand corner. Painted in the

*Fig 30* ARABS SKIRMISHING IN THE MOUNTAINS (COLLECTION OF THE ARAB TAXES) In the later works, the zig-zag (see fig. 29) became even more pronounced.

same year, his *Tobias and the Angel* makes use of the ground of the river-bank, the angel bending forwards and the outline of an overhanging rock, to create yet another version of the sinuous, alternating scheme. After this, Delacroix was to paint no more.

Indeed, the 1859 Salon had been the last at which he presented himself to the public. At this he showed eight magnificent pictures. Besides the works already
pl 237 mentioned, there was a *Saint Sebastian*, an *Ovid among the Scythians*, *Erminia*
pl 238 *and the Shepherds*, the *Banks of the River Sebou* and a final *Hamlet*—all of them canvases in which Delacroix resumed subjects that were dear to his heart, giving to them a solemn amplitude through the vastness of the landscape in which he set them. But critics and public were waiting for him, waiting to fall upon him: it might well be called his Waterloo. In any case he did not exhibit at the Salons of 1860 and 1861: he was too much absorbed by Saint-Sulpice, and perhaps discouraged. The reception of his work in the Chapel of the Holy Angels was also decidedly lukewarm. An increasingly sick man, Delacroix could only withdraw into his solitude. On 21 May 1863 he wrote sadly to Andrieu: 'I am not exactly happy about my health, and I have done practically nothing since I saw you!' He mentions a bad cold that has lasted three months, a fall against the corner of a piece of furniture, and trouble with his eyes from too much reading. Gloomily he leaves his pupil free to work for other people and confesses that he has little hope, 'at least for the moment', of launching out again into '*les grandes entre-*

*prises*', 'in spite of the passion I have for them'. Very soon he could not 'speak a word without coughing':[58] rest and absolute silence were prescribed. He had begun to spit blood. This increased and, as we have seen, after a last visit to Champrosay and a hurried return to Paris, he died on 13 August 1863. His remark to Jenny, a few days before his death, will be remembered: 'Oh, if I get well, as I think I shall, I shall do astonishing things; I can feel my brain seething. . . .'

And in fact what a number of pictures he managed to produce, even in the midst of the crushing labour of his great mural paintings! Pictures of Arabs, of wild beasts, of frantic lion hunts—but also flower paintings, landscape paintings, studies of sky and trees, and nudes such as the splendid *Turkish Women bathing*, pl 219 painted in 1854, in which the harmony between water, leaves and bodies is a prelude to the *Seasons* begun for Hartmann. In this period he was constantly taking up again those themes which, like obsessional dreams, had haunted him all through his life—themes from Shakespeare (Hamlet, Othello, Macbeth and Romeo and Juliet), from Byron (the Giaour or the Bride of Abydos), from Ariosto (Angelica, Marphisa, Olinda and Sophronia) and from Goethe (Goetz). He showed a growing inclination to take up again earlier compositions—in 1849 the *Women of Algiers*, in 1852 the *Crusaders* and the *Education of the Virgin*, in 1856 and again in 1862 the *Sultan of Morocco*, in 1857 the *Fanatics of Tangier* and in 1859 the *Demosthenes on the Seashore* from the Chambre des Députés together with the *Ovid among the Scythians*, which he resumed yet LVI, page 480 again in 1862 along with the *Education of Achilles* and the *Moroccan Caïd visiting a Tribe*.

As we have seen, while Delacroix reserved his power of construction and his classical resources for the wall paintings, he was more and more inclined to treat his easel paintings as the proper place in which to reveal his dreams. He constantly and with renewed joy returned to his most familiar and treasured themes, as though to favourite passages of books, or to beloved objects polished by the repeated touch of the hand. He returned most gladly to themes of romance and passion, to effects of atmosphere made musical by the vague expanse of the landscape and by the half-light and shadows. In them he satisfied his painterly sensuality, seeking the keen pleasures of the cunning hand excited by pattern or by touch and the voluptuous pleasures of the eye thrilled by colours as though by jewels—the contents of a secret casket, whose lid he always lifted with a tremor of delight. On the architectural surfaces which he was given to paint, he expended the appropriate resources upon the great themes of classical culture or of the Christian religion in order to enrich a crowd of onlookers: in small pictures he would reveal the secret of his desires and dreams (nourished by the works of the poets or opening out upon the spaces of the past and of the East) for the sake of some attentive individual who loved paintings: in both cases he was venturing deep into the solitude of the self in order to make contact with other people and set them vibrating in tune with him. Whether in public places or in privacy, he was always seeking to communicate—to communicate himself.

For this purpose it was necessary to use 'all the resources of art' in order that, by a combination of inspiration and the cunning hand, 'interest' might be awakened in other people; and 'the masters are practically the only ones who excite interest'. Both the origin and aim of this 'interest' can only be the revelation of the artist's soul to the soul of the spectator, provided that both of them are gifted with 'sensibility and imagination', faculties that are indispensable, though clearly in different degrees, to both. The means, Delacroix was aware, are different with different artists 'according to the individual leanings of their genius'.

What, then, is the deep motive that urges artists to 'exteriorize' themselves, to project their inner secret into their works and in the direction of other men? A passage published by Piron, but also written out again in a still unpublished notebook,[59] this second version being signed 'Moi', says: 'The love of glory is a sublime instinct granted only to those who are worthy of obtaining glory: the love of a vain reputation that merely flatters vanity is a quite different thing.'[60] For, in fact, the love of glory is a requirement of the self, while that of vain reputation is a sterile product of the desire to get on in society.

'Enthusiasm is self-nourishing. The approval of the crowd can certainly be flattering; but it does not give that divine intoxication which, in great souls, has its source in the feeling of their own strength.' Greed is replaced by a need for expansion, the generous need to give. The self, a source of egoism and rapacity, becomes transmuted into a source of spiritual munificence. Lavelle has made this question the theme of his *Erreur de Narcisse*, in which he says: 'It is the most personal and solitary type of man who is capable of the most disinterested and pure act of communion.' Delacroix, even as an adolescent, had seen this intuitively, 'What torments my soul is its loneliness.... But to live in the spirit of others is the intoxicating delight... and it can happen that all souls meet in our painting.'[61] The secret of the highest individualism is that it feeds itself only that it may thus feed others. And so, in the last resort and through his works, it is to the self of Delacroix that we must go now in search of his innermost secrets.

## NOTES ON THE PLATES TO CHAPTER VIII

*Delacroix embarks on mural painting*

The idea of classicism that was emerging in Delacroix's pictures was also finding its full expansion in his mural paintings. It was to make its appearance in the studies (pl 271) commonly dated 1821, for the dining-room of the great tragic actor Talma—whose official portrait (pl 272) Delacroix was to paint much later, in 1857. Like the Davidians, Delacroix first made studies of the figures naked, then draped. The paintings for the tops of doorways were a prelude to his 1834 frescoes at Valmont (pl 270).

270 *Leda and the Swan, 1834. Decorative painting at Valmont Abbey, near Fécamp.*

271 *Two Studies for 'The Seasons', decorative panels for Talma's dining room, 1821. Cabinet des Dessins, Louvre, Paris.*

272 *Talma in the role of Nero (Racine's 'Britannicus'), 1857. Comédie Française, Paris.*

*The study of the nude*

Mural painting demanded a deepening of his knowledge of the human body. Delacroix had already studied the human body from the life (pl 130) and even, after the invention of photography, from daguerrotypes (pl 274). But he also assiduously studied Greek and Roman sculpture, and made copies of the Parthenon metopes (pl 273).

273 *Theseus vanquishing the Centaur Eurytos, 1825. After a sculpture from the Parthenon in the British Museum. Lithograph.*

274 *Drawings of female nude after photographs. Cabinet des Dessins, Louvre, Paris.*

*Study of the classical painters*

Delacroix saturated himself in the classical painters: he took particular interest in the wall paintings at Fontainebleau, making copies of the frescoes in the Galerie Henri II (pl 276) when he was on his way to Morocco. Their disastrous restoration was then just beginning, and Primaticcio's drawings in the Louvre (pl 275) give us a truer idea of their style, which impressed Delacroix.

275 PRIMATICCIO: *Sketch for the fresco in the Galerie Henri II at Fontainebleau (executed by Niccolo dell'Abbate). Louvre, Paris.*

276 *The Poet Arion and the Philosopher Anaximander. After the frescoes at Fontainebleau. Louvre, Paris. (See pl 275.)*

*The Salon du Roi* In the first of his 'great enterprises', the Salon du Roi in the Palais-Bourbon, which was commissioned in 1833 and occupied him till 1838, Delacroix kept close to his memories of the classical painters: the elongated figures of the ceiling (pls 281, 282) continue those he had seen at Fontainebleau, while the standing figures (pls 279, 280), which are more supple, go back to solutions discovered by Jean Goujon (pl 278). The frieze (pl 277), in an effort towards a continuous movement, adopts an arrangement that is more free and animated. In the next enterprise, the Library, which he carried out from 1838 to 1847, the instances of recourse to the classical painters are still easy to pick out: the Wise Men who are being questioned by Herodotus (pl 283) have the monumental plasticity developed by Masaccio (pl 284).

277 *Justice, 1833-8. Frieze. Salon du Roi, Palais Bourbon, Paris.*

278 JEAN GOUJON: *Fontaine des Innocents: A Nymph. Louvre, Paris.*

279 *The River Seine, 1833-8. Pilaster. Salon du Roi, Palais Bourbon, Paris.*

280 *The River Rhône, 1833-8. Pilaster. Salon du Roi, Palais Bourbon, Paris.*

281 *Justice, 1833-8. Ceiling coffer. Salon du Roi, Palais Bourbon, Paris.*

282 *Agriculture. Sketch for a ceiling coffer. Salon du Roi, Palais Bourbon, Paris.*

283 *Herodotus questioning the Wise Men, 1838-47. 'Philosophy' cupola. Library of the Chambre des Députés, Palais Bourbon, Paris.*

284 MASACCIO: *The Sick Man healed by Saint Peter's Shadow. Fresco. Santa Maria di Carmine, Florence.*

*The cupolas of the Palais Bourbon Library* The decoration of these five cupolas shows how, starting from the human body, Delacroix contrived to find constantly fresh compositional schemes adapted to the unusual shape of the pendentives (pls XXXV, 285-290). Each of them was the result of long study, based largely on sources from Antiquity (pl 291), carried on through preparatory drawings (pl 285) and continued even during the actual painting, where these are further modified (pl 286).

285 *Sketch for the 'Education of Achilles', 1838-47. Louvre, Paris.*

286 *The Education of Achilles, 1844. Pendentive of 'Poetry' cupola. Library of the Palais Bourbon, Paris.*

287 *Study for the 'Captivity in Babylon' (for the 'Theology' cupola). Louvre, Paris.*

288 *Adam and Eve, 1838-47. Pendentive of 'Theology' cupola. Library of the Palais Bourbon, Paris.*

289 *Numa and the Nymph Egeria, 1838-47. Pendentive of 'Legislation' cupola. Library of the Palais Bourbon, Paris.*

290 *Pliny the Elder, 1838–47. Pendentive of 'Natural Sciences' cupola. Library of the Palais Bourbon, Paris.*

291 *Drawing after an engraving of a Pompeian fresco. Formerly Walter Pach Collection.*

292 *The Education of Achilles, 1862. Private collection.*

*The hemicycles of the Palais Bourbon Library*

The breadth of the space in the hemicycles suggested to Delacroix the idea of giving nature a large part in them, especially the *Orpheus* (pl XXXIV). In the *Attila* the movement of the deploying masses is associated with the elements (pl XXXIII), and here Delacroix returns to his romantic violence in all its frenzy (pl 293).

293 *Attila hemicycle, 1838–47 (detail). Library of the Palais Bourbon, Paris.*

*The Luxembourg Library*

Delacroix worked at the Luxembourg from 1840 to 1847. Here he amplified the sense of space begun in the *Orpheus* : the opening into heaven which the dome (pl 294) is, gains a gentle rhythm from its border of peaceful scenes taking place (pl XXXVIII) in the sacred wood where the poets reign with *Homer* as their chief (pls 295, XXXVII). In the hemicycle, after Alexander's victory, war is giving way to the triumphs of the spirit (pls 296, 297).

294 *The cupola (1845–7) of the Library of the Senate, Palais du Luxembourg, Paris.*

295 *Dante presented by Virgil to Homer. Sketch for the cupola of the Library of the Senate, Palais du Luxembourg, Paris. Private collection.*

296 *Alexander the Great causing the Poems of Homer to be placed in a Casket, 1845–7. Detail of the hemicycle of the Library of the Senate, Palais du Luxembourg, Paris.*

297 *Sketch for 'Alexander the Great' for the hemicycle of the Library of the Senate, Palais du Luxembourg. Cabinet des Dessins, Louvre, Paris.*

*Flowers*

The celestial meadows were depicted at the Luxembourg (pl XXXVIII); and Delacroix was now to pay fresh attention to flowers: he had taken to studying them in their native disorder (pl 299) at Nohant, before imposing on them the order of sumptuous bouquets (pl 298).

298 *Flower-painting. Musée des Beaux-Arts, Lille.*

299 *Peonies. National Gallery, Oslo.*

*Nature*

It was when he was about forty that Delacroix, till then obsessed by the human passions, began to enjoy the expansiveness and repose of nature. Skies (pl 302), wide spaces (pl 300) and craggy mountains (pl 301) alike attracted him, and in a landscape filled with a gleam of water which he had seen at Valmont (pl 303) he would find the inspiration for his *Ophelia* (pl XXXVI).

300 *Landscape. Cabinet des Dessins, Louvre, Paris.*

301 *Landscape in the Pyrenees, 1845. Louvre, Paris.*

302 *Sunset, from a window of Delacroix's house at Champrosay, 1849. Cabinet des Dessins, Louvre, Paris.*

303 *The grounds of Valmont Abbey, c. 1843. Study for the 'Death of Ophelia'. Private collection.*

*The triumph of 'Apollo'* In the ceiling of the Galerie d'Apollon in the Louvre, Delacroix faced the challenge of filling—in 1850 and 1851—the still vacant culminating part of a scheme of decoration by Le Brun (pl 304). His unbridled vigour (pl 305) moved easily within these limits, to render the victory of life and of the spirit.

304 *Apollo destroying the Serpent Python, 1850-1. Ceiling. Galerie d'Apollon, Louvre, Paris.*

305 *Study for Apollo's chariot, 1850-1. Cabinet des Dessins, Louvre, Paris.*

*The Salon de la Paix* Immediately after the Louvre, Delacroix turned to a hall in the Hôtel de Ville. The main part of the work was finished in 1852, but he kept on retouching it till 1854. This time it was the *Triumph of Peace.* The preparatory drawings (pl 307) again show evidence of classical sources; the sketch (pl XLIII) shows the rhythm carrying all before it; and the *maquette*, done with the help of pupils, exhibits the solidity of the composition (pl 306). The finished work was destroyed by fire in 1871.

306 *Peace recalling Abundance. A sketch for the ceiling of the Salon de la Paix, Hôtel de Ville, 1852. Musée Carnavalet, Paris.*

307 *Sketches for the ceiling of the Salon de la Paix, Hôtel de Ville, 1849. Cabinet des Dessins, Louvre, Paris.*

*Saint-Sulpice: 'Heliodorus'* Delacroix's last great effort, from 1850 to 1861, was the Chapel of the Holy Angels at Saint-Sulpice. In the *Heliodorus* the lightning flash of the drawing (pl 309) sets vibrating a composition streaked with bodies thrown forwards or backwards, with draperies fluttering in the wind (pl 308), in a strong and solid architectural framework (pl 310) over which plays a prodigious chromatic invention (pl LIV).

308 *Study for 'Heliodorus driven from the Temple', 1857.*

309 *Sketch for 'Heliodorus'. Cabinet des Dessins, Louvre, Paris.*

310 *Heliodorus driven from the Temple, 1856-61. Chapel of the Holy Angels, Church of Saint-Sulpice, Paris.*

*Saint-Sulpice: 'Jacob'* The same vehemence that was liberated in the *Heliodorus* hurls Jacob and the Angel at one another (pls LIII, 313). But this time, instead of the monumental architecture, there is the majesty of the oaks of the Forest of Senart, near Champrosay, to bring with it the power of the superhuman (pl 312).

311 *Study for 'Jacob wrestling with the Angel'. Claude Aubry Collection, Paris.*

312 *The Prieur Oak, c. 1850, one of a number of studies made in the Forest of Senart. Cabinet des Dessins, Louvre, Paris.*

313 *Jacob wrestling with the Angel, 1856-61. Chapel of the Holy Angels, Church of Saint-Sulpice, Paris.*

*The road to Calvary*

The themes which Delacroix at first envisaged for Saint-Sulpice have left us his *Christ Carrying the Cross*, which he finished in 1859 (pl 314). As in Rubens' great picture (pl 315), which he had in mind, Delacroix covers the surface of the picture with an all-embracing movement of brushwork which, more sinuous than in the Rubens, rises right to the top of the canvas.

314 *Christ Carrying the Cross, 1859. Musée de Metz.*

315 RUBENS: *The Ascent to Calvary. Musées Royaux des Beaux-Arts, Brussels.*

*Last works*

In his last pictures, Delacroix aimed at keeping up his vigour, indeed at making it more impulsive than ever (pl 317), and yet attaining the unity characteristic of great ordered designs. To this end he used an ascending composition that rebounds alternately to right and left: this zig-zag, which is to be found in the 1858 *Rebecca* (pl 316), reappears—likewise rising from left to right—in the *Death of Lara* (pl 318), painted in the same year, and again, more complicated, in the *Arabs skirmishing in the Mountains*, which he painted in 1863, the year of his death (pl 319).

316 *The Abduction of Rebecca, 1858. Louvre, Paris.*

317 *The Camp of Botzaris, c. 1862. Jacques Dupont Collection.*

318 *The Death of Lara, 1858. Bührle Collection, Zurich.*

319 *Arabs skirmishing in the Mountains (Collection of the Arab Taxes), 1863. Jerome Hill Collection, New York.*

*Final mural paintings*

The four canvases for the dining-room of the banker Hartmann, who died in 1862, were sketched out in 1861 and remained unfinished in Delacroix's studio. The sinuosities of the S-shaped composition (pl 321) support a final synthesis of human body an natural setting (pl 322), inspired by Antiquity and with a romantic freedom of gesture (pl 320).

320 *The Seasons. Spring: Orpheus and Eurydice, 1861. Museu de Arte de Sao Paulo, Brazil.*

321 *The Seasons. Summer: Diana and Actaeon, 1861. Museu de Arte de Sao Paulo, Brazil.*

322 *The Seasons. Autumn: Bacchus and Ariadne, 1861. Museu de Arte de Sao Paulo, Brazil.*

270

271

272

273

274

275

276

277

278

279

280

281

282

283

284

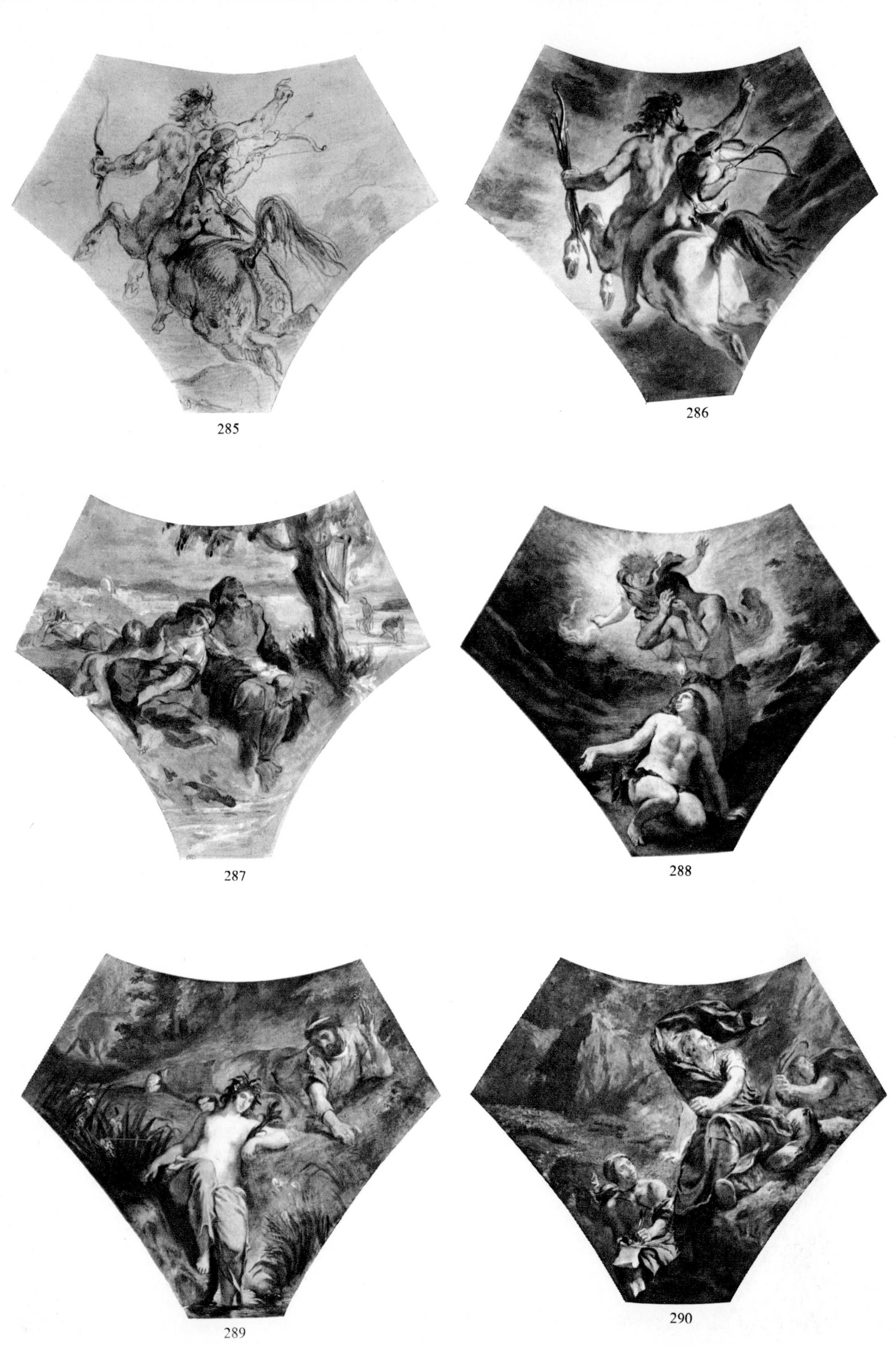

285

286

287

288

289

290

291

292

293

294

295

296

297

298

299

300

301

302

303

304

305

306

307

308

309

311

312

314

315

316

317

Delacroix.
1858.

320

321

322

# IX THE SECRETS OF THE SELF

*Mon esprit et l'histoire de mon âme . . .*[1]

*The reader may be surprised to find pictures, most of which have already been dealt with in earlier chapters, analyzed again in this one. The reason is that we have passed from external criticism, historical and descriptive, to a kind of criticism from within, an attempt to bring out the invisible reality—often obscure to the artist himself—that lies behind the visible. This attempt to explore the artist's work from the other side involves a fresh review of it as a whole, so as to reveal, connectedly, the* meaning *of the development that governed both his work and his life.*

ART HAS THE WONDERFUL PRIVILEGE of being able to translate into the visible not only what our minds can conceive and make clear, but also what our deeper life holds in its secret recesses—things that exert their pressure on our conduct and thinking, but still at the stage of crude vitality, in action, not yet elucidated by the intelligence.

Our inner being throws out, as it were, jets of vapour which, condensing, leave traces revealing their origin, direction and strength. Thus the collective soul of a people is made manifest through myths; and the artist's individual soul is no less surely revealed by his choice of subjects. He does choose them, whether from real life or from fiction: he takes those that he feels to be right for him—that is to say, capable of embodying the confused aspirations within him. A kind of *flair* makes him perceive in advance the theme that can embody what is tormenting him. Afterwards, when this lava has flowed and is cooling, he devotes his technique to the business of carving out of it images of himself.

This makes it possible to read a human being through his works—not for the sake of vain curiosity and in a quest for anecdote, but to find the very substance which his art endows with valid or breathtaking forms. This approach alone can produce in us that feeling of human brotherhood without which art would be merely a technical exercise or a jeweller's fancy. As Delacroix said when he was very young, 'All lies in the subject; the subject is yourself. . . .'

Delacroix, who copied out long passages from Senancour, might well have taken the following passage from *Obermann* (letter IV) as his own profession of faith:

'Whatever happens I must remain always the same and always myself—not as I am in certain habits that run counter to my needs, but as I feel I am, as I want to be, as I really am in that inner life which is the sole refuge of my sad affec-tions. . . . And this condition, once it is clearly known, I shall endeavour to keep, all my life long . . . convinced that one is never well, except when one is in harmony with one's nature.'

The themes chosen by an artist yield a visible embodiment—or one whose imminence we feel, even if we do not always recognize it—of the problems that make up the meaning of his life and personality. What is more, they evolve as he does. A work of art, at the moment when it breaks off from its author, reveals merely a cross-section of the growing stem: it cuts across the internal channels through which the sap is on the move towards its still unknown end. The governing design of a whole life is therefore made clear only from work to work, from cross-section to cross-section, through the development plotted by their succession.

This means that the choice of subjects is revealing both through its constants and through its gradual changes. These the historian of art can question, just as psychologists scrutinize that more amorphous mass, the dreams in which the cares of a human being and their gradual transformation are inscribed. From them there emerges what Jung has called the process of individuation—that is to say, the movement of a human being's inner life towards a realization (if only imaginary) of the balance proper to it, and of the deeper aim in which that life will feel itself fulfilled.[2]

## *Youth and the Power of the Instincts*

Adolescence is the time of appetite, of the search for intense experience, and Delacroix brought to this the quivering life of his over-acute nerves. He came upon something that was basic to him—the most animal part of him, which by sheer vitality made the instincts an exacting presence; and maturity was not yet there, to discipline it with the close mesh of reason. With the examples of Rubens, Gros and Géricault before him, he was attracted by the thoroughbred horse in all its impatience to leap forward. It is already rearing or darting ahead on the margins of his school notebooks, and in that precocious aquatint of *The Hunt*, which he did in 1816 after a picture by M. Auguste. One of his earliest canvases (1817) shows a horse carrying Nemesis along in much the same impetuous gallop that recurs in his *Abduction of Angelica* (1860), one of his last pictures. In the admirable water-colour in Budapest of 1824 it rises, white and pl 65
beside itself—*amens*—in the sudden lightning flash.

*Amens*: this was indeed the condition Delacroix expected of himself in the fire of inspiration—to be so tense, so carried away by one's inner forces as to lose control of them. It was a temptation that remained with him all his life. Even in 1850 he could still exclaim (21 July): 'One must be very bold. Therefore one must be beside oneself, *amens*, if one is to be all that one might be.' Yet at the same time this inner fury made him uneasy by its consequences, and already in 1824 (6 June) he made this plain: 'Do people know what it is to work under the dictation of inspiration? The terror, the ecstasy there is in awakening that sleeping lion, whose roarings shake your whole being?'

And indeed the lion and other wild beasts were to become as dear to him as the horse, though it was to be some years before he became familiar with them. They make their appearance already in 1827, sketched in the margin of one of his Faust lithographs (*Mephistopheles appearing to Martha*), and then in a picture and several studies in the following year. After this there were more and more of them, thanks to facilities for studying them given to Delacroix by Cuvier, whose *salon* he often visited. 'Tigers, panthers, jaguars, lions . . .—whence comes the movement caused in me by the sight of them?' he asked himself in one of his notebooks. But in his earliest years the horse was still the only embodiment of Delacroix's own moods of prancing impatience. Soon, fired by the news of the war in Greece, he began to depict horses in battle, excited by the smell of powder and the clash of arms. In 1821 there appeared the first picture in a long series which led to the *Massacre at Chios*: his *Turkish Horseman Firing*.

The rush of instincts and their gratification brought Delacroix up against
pl 329 humany destiny. He saw it, first, as carried away by them, like his *Mazeppa*, who rushes bound naked on the back of the steed with which he is now passively one, towards an unknown and limitless expanse. This theme, which he found in Byron and in Géricault, took hold of him as early as 1824 (if Robaut's dating of his No. 1493 is right), and he made it the subject of a painting in 1828. Géricault celebrated mainly human mastery in bringing the animal, whether horse or bull, to a standstill: this theme did not tempt Delacroix; what attracted him was the theme of *Mazeppa*, in which the life of the instincts irresistibly and without respite carries away with it the human will.

But into what does instinct hurl a man? The male creature, when given up to the greed of his body, cries out for an adversary—a man—and for a prey—a woman. The theme of woman brought Delacroix into the region of youthful voluptuous dreams. The half-naked captive in the *Massacre at Chios* is, as it were, the signal for these to go ahead: it starts the procession of his nudes. Some of them are realistic, like his pictures of *Mademoiselle Rose*; others, like his
pl 129 Odalisques, melt into the soft secrecy of a harem. For the most part the woman is the prey, caught and either submitting or still desperately struggling. She was to appear in the foreground of each of the great 'massacres'—fighting in the
III, page 67 bonds that tie her to the Turkish rider's saddle in the *Massacre at Chios* (1824),
XI, page 123 killed or offering herself to be so in the *Sardanapalus* (1827), collapsing under the
XXVII, page 283 feet of the horses of the *Crusaders* (1840). Much later even—in 1852—he com-
pl 355 posed his picture of the *Abduction of an Arab Woman by African Pirates*, in which the fair-haired captive's shrill and desperate cry is conveyed by a strident yellow (used already by Veronese to express the grief of the Virgin in the Louvre *Crucifixion*, a painting which Delacroix certainly knew well). And in the same year he took up the same theme again, even more cruelly, in the *Indian Woman carried off by a Tiger*: the beast has sprung upon her as she came down to the stream to drink, and is bearing her off in its maw. When Delacroix was at work preparing his *Massacre at Chios* he produced, already, a prelude to this associa-
pls 104, 105 tion of woman with pain, in his two pictures of an *Orphan Girl in a Graveyard*.

But side by side with the female prey, there was the male adversary. The *Massacre at Chios* was also a hymn to the unrestrained violence in which the human animal's hunger for power satiates itself: to rape were added fire and slaughter. And the burning Delacroix of his early youth could not resist celebrating the theme of savage anger, characteristic of the great wild beasts. Those who knew him by sight remarked, beneath his apparent impassiveness, the tension and the fire of the tiger. Several examples have already been quoted; here is one that is less well known. In his *Souvenirs littéraires* Maxime du Camp says that Delacroix's 'deep-set eyes and huge jaw-bones made one think of the muscles of leopards, and gave him a kind of energetic beauty.'[3] Gautier, it will be remembered, mentioned 'his wild beast eyes, his cat-like expression', and Dumas his 'dark, swarthy, mobile skin, rippling like a lion's'.

Delacroix was only too well aware of this shadowy, burning aspect of himself, and confessed that he had in him 'a dark element that has to be satisfied'—that *nescio quid horrendum* which Saint Augustine, likewise tormented in his youth by his instincts, had avowed. In a note that he made when he was about twenty,[4] Delacroix jotted down a theme which anticipates his *Attila* and even his *Apollo*—'The god Mars in his chariot, proud and indeed terrible. Fame is pl 328
fluttering about him, Fear and Death are striding ahead of his foam-flecked steeds. He is going into battle, and the dust of it begins to hide him from view.'[5] So indeed Delacroix flung himself into the battle that led to the *Massacre at Chios*.

Never had his inspiration been closer to Goya's—which, however, was still less balanced and more wild. On 20 June 1839 he wrote to 'M. Fr. Villot, philologue' to ask him for the historical data that would enable him to treat a subject he had been thrilled to find in Diderot—that of 'Commodus mauled to death by the fangs of the wild beasts. Please give me details. . . . It is a splendid theme for a man who chooses the society of bears and panthers, is it not?'

And in fact it was chiefly in wild beasts that he found the bold and fierce manifestations of the energy of which he dreamed. In 1853, in his *Journal* for 15 March, he copies out again (with the observation that 'I was more misanthropic then than I am now!') a note made in his youth, in which he described the passions, vices and crimes lying in wait under the surface of the sleeping city 'as though in a bottomless abyss' and says that 'Men are tigers and wolves, bent on destroying one another . . .', that 'These eager hands which shake you by the hand are sharpened claws ready to dig into your heart.' At the same time he was aware of a secret affinity that quivered in him at the sight of tigers and lions. In a note which he made in preparation for his 1829 article (and which evidently proved more useful still for that of 1854 entitled '*Questions sur le Beau*') he confessed: 'You have no less of it yourself, and you love the pictures which represent them to your view.' All this made him delight in the cruel impulses of the wild beast, whether he found these in animals or in men. His 1825 pictures of horses fighting show only the animals themselves, but the theme is taken up in other pictures of the same date, which depict horsemen fighting.[6] In the first version of the *Giaour and the Pasha* (1827) they recur, this time in oriental costume. pl 327
And the impulse renewed in Morocco issued in an *Encounter between Moorish*

XLIX SAINT GEORGE AND THE PRINCESS
*1854 Oil on canvas. 18 x 22 (046 x 055)*
*Musée de Peinture et de Sculpture, Grenoble*

*Horsemen*, painted in 1833 and engraved in 1834. Such fights are indeed one of Delacroix's basic themes, perhaps the principal one. In a lithograph of 1828, there is the *Wild Horse attacked by a Tiger*; another in 1829 shows the *Lion of Atlas* devouring a rabbit; and this is echoed, in 1844, by another depicting a *Lion devouring a Dead Horse*—in a welter of blood. Such examples among the canvases painted in 1847, 1848, etc., are legion: and the theme is extended to include wild beasts fighting wild beasts. The terrible clinch of two adversaries absorbed pl 326 into a single struggling mass, conceived by Delacroix in 1835 for another version of the *Giaour and the Pasha*, recurs in his 1856 drawings and water-colour of a fight between a lion and a tiger.

All these scattered elements were to be brought together in the whirlwinds of his *lion hunt* pictures. 'A terrifying confusion of lions, men and horses, a chaos of claws, fangs, cutlasses, lances, torsos and rumps, as Rubens loved to paint them', such is Gautier's description of the huge canvas (102 in. by 141 in.) pl 347 painted by Delacroix in 1855. A large part of it was destroyed by fire in 1870 at Bordeaux, but the sketch for it survives, and in it even the sparkling whirl of colour and the gasping, spasmodic drawing are scarcely quick enought to catch the XLVIII, page 410 leap of the lioness plunging her claws and teeth into the horse's bleeding rump, and the leap of the horseman as he transfixes the roaring lion which is already mauling another horseman who has fallen. In a variant painted in 1858 the wild knot of men and animals, clothes and fur, light, cries and blood, bristles in all directions with brandished weapons. In yet another, painted in the same year, it comes apart in a rush of fluttering clothes and dishevelled manes.

But the collisions between men are no less terrible. The Guillaume de la Marck who, in the 1829 picture, has the *Bishop of Liège* murdered in his presence is well named the Wild Boar of the Ardennes. We have seen to what a series of battle pictures this was the prelude—from the *Battle of Poitiers* (1830) and of *Nancy* (1831) throught the *Boissy d'Anglas* (with its bloodstained head of Feraud), to the *Battle of Taillebourg* (1837): soldiers locked in clinches, clawing, biting and tearing at one another like carnivores.

## *The Perpetual Struggle*

While Delacroix in his paintings gave to conflict the most physical expression possible, he also lived it on the plane of imagination and on that of morality. In the very first year of his *Journal*[7] he announces: 'I have struck out, or rather my energy has struck out, in another direction; I shall be the trumpet for those who will do great things.' He was already preparing to oppose those instincts which come from the most animal part of our nature and would carry us away helplessly if reason were absent. 'If only the soul had nothing to fight against but the body! But it too contains malignant leanings, and one part of it, the more

L AMADIS DE GAULE
*1860 Oil on canvas. 22 x 26 (055 x 065)*
*The Virginia Museum of Fine Arts*

slender and the more divine, should fight the other without respite. The physical passions are all vile. Those of the soul that are vile are real cancers, envy, etc.'

The course his destiny was to take was here laid down: the inner frenzies seething through his nervous system would be stealthily appeased in the rage and abandon of his pictures—a catharsis in the Aristotelian sense, an expansion, a relief, the elimination of a more or less physical excess of ardour. Yet at the same time the taste for conflict (of whose grandeur he was aware) would be retained—it would be diverted towards victories better worth winning: the victories that are won not merely over obstacles or over other people, but over the coarse facts of our nature. Like his war horses, Delacroix would respond to the clarion call: Dimicandum! Fight it out! '*Dimicandum*', he told Varcollier on 7 July 1825, 'is a motto I have made my own from necessity and, to some extent, from temperament', and he adds: 'To it I join this one: *Renovare animos*.' For him the conflict never ended—it was still with him less than ten years before his death. On 3 February 1853 he wrote to Mme. Lamey, wife of his 'dear and good cousin': 'In this world one is obliged to struggle in order to defend this miserable body, which is our tyrant, against accidents and, perhaps even more, against the temptations and the pleasures which this world offers so rarely.'

But the best weapon in this conflict was always hard work, a patient determination to overcome idleness or inertia. As we have seen, when he was working on the *Massacre at Chios*, he told himself that the life of the men who had risen above the common herd was 'a continual battle'[8]—and he added that it was first and foremost a 'struggle against idleness, and this is something the common man shares with them'.[9] And later, on 27 October 1838 when about to start work on the Library of the Chambre des Députés, he wrote to Thiers thanking him and saying: 'But indeed a mind like yours is familiar with the charm and the momentum of struggle, which doubles a man's strength and raises him above his usual self.' Not long before his death, when he was nearing the end of his overtaxing labours at Saint-Sulpice, he could still exclaim: 'I have been at work all day: a happy life. . . . Whence comes it that this perpetual fight, instead of exhausting me, raises me up, instead of discouraging me, consoles me and fills my time after I have left off?'

But the struggle was not only against the instincts and against idleness: it was also against 'the griefs of the soul'. As he wrote to Villot, at a time when both men were being sorely tried by the loss of dear friends, 'Some people push aside their sadness by means of physical enjoyments, others have to fall back on the quest for the beautiful, on contemplation and the passion for what is great.'

Here we come upon the principle of 'resistance' in which some thinkers have seen the definition of life: they point to an 'inner principle' which ceaselessly repulses the enemy forces besieging 'the human machine'.[10] This principle is to be found also in the life of the soul. And in the life of the soul, where does the real battle lie? It is everywhere, for our nature—in this, doubtless, resembling all life—is based on the principle of antagonism. First there is the antagonism between the soul and the body—of which Delacroix had been aware even in 1812, for in one of his school notebooks, on the inside of the cover, we find: 'The body and the soul are two friends who cannot part from one another and two enemies who cannot endure one another.' And there is the entry in the *Journal* for

4 June 1824: I live with a body, my silent companion, exacting and always present . . . my spirit has wings, but the brutal goaler is severe. . . . It glimpses only very rarely the azure of its celestial native land. . . . The unendurable weight of this living corpse!' We spend 'the greater part of our life' in 'suffering from it'. 'Through this ridiculous window . . . heaven has allowed us to witness the spectacle of the world. . . . O sad fate, to long unceasingly for my release. . .!' Prison is a recurring theme of his pictures: there are the heavy walls and bars of the prison in his *Tasso*, adding to the anguish of loneliness and of human ingratitude; there is the prison from which Faust cannot deliver *Marguerite*; there is the one that encloses the *Prisoner of Chillon* and his tragedy; and the one whose snare, in the 1849 picture, shuts down upon *Ugolino* and his terrible hunger. But there is also, from the same year, the picture of
pl 361 *Daniel in the Lions' Den*, where Daniel overcomes imprisonment and tames the wild beasts by his own light—and in the final version (1853) there is even an angel
pl 362 who comes, with outspread wings, to announce his deliverance.

Then there is the conflict of the soul with the soul. Lady Eglé Charlemont in her excellent article of 1867, saw clearly that this was one of the main motive forces in Delacroix's art. 'No one before', she suggested, 'went so deeply into . . . this duel of the soul with itself, this struggle between two contrary ideas, which clash deep down in the mind.' This division of a human being into two parts that draw him towards opposite slopes was very much a preoccupation of the romantic period. The classicist unifies the soul under the aegis of reason, and is anxious to ignore the forces rumbling beneath it. What, in fact, is romanticism if it is not the open rebellion of all that has been repressed by lucid and controlled thought—of that whole zone in us which remains in direct touch with our subconscious and escapes from the government of thought?

The nineteenth century stressed the existence of this obscure and disquieting zone, by insisting on the notion of 'the other', of 'the double'. This already found expression in the shadow of Pierre Schlemihl in Chamisso's book; it was the meaning of Musset's young man in black 'who resembled him like a brother'
pl 56 —and Delacroix's portrait of himself as Hamlet came close to being an image of it.[11] But it emerged chiefly in the rebirth of the old symbol of the Devil, which the classical centuries had fought, driven back and expunged. The romantics, with their determination to seek deep down in the self for the forces indispensable to the intensity at which they aimed, revived the image of the demon from among the remains of the Middle Ages, whose inheritors they wished to be. With the image of the demon, the subconscious acquired a face distinguishing it from that self of ours which we try to take as our one and only lucid personality. Even better than the shadow or the double, the demon embodies the unknown and the darkness in us. Baudelaire summed up this obsession, so characteristic of his time, in a line of his *Fleurs du Mal*: *'Sans cesse à mes côtés s'agite le Démon!'*[12]

The demon was, to begin with, the holder of those secret powers which are at the origin of all creative activity: as Delacroix himself put it, the artist is 'the man who lives with a demon who breathes into his ear his inspirations'[13]. He was also, and mainly, a 'local habitation' for all the dark desires which responsible consciousness refuses to recognize. When Faust, our brother, will not recognize in the shadow his own darkness, Mephistopheles takes it upon him. Good and Evil, light and shadow, God and the Devil—the eternal dualism again takes on consistency and presence.

Goethe, in one of his conversations with Eckermann, gave a good analysis of the fascination exercised upon Delacroix by this theme: '*Faust* is a work which pl 337
passes from heaven to earth, from the possible to the impossible, from the gross to the exquisite; all the antitheses which the play of bold imagination can create are there brought together; this is why Monsieur Delacroix felt at home in it . . . as though among his own family.' Faust was in tune with the anguish which Delacroix shared with the romantics, and of which he was looking for the key. The encounter between Faust and Mephistopheles fitted in with his pl 135
passionate interest in dualism and conflict too marvellously well for him not to be obsessed by it.

Faust and Mephistopheles were the embodiment of an eternal myth, which goes underground only in periods when the light of reason is determined to reign uncontested and refuses to recognize what Valéry called its 'melancholy shadow-half'. In the Middle Ages it manifested itself in the legend of Theophilus, and it re-emerged in the sixteenth century with the Faust legend. It may have been in Marlowe's version that Delacroix was so struck by it during his visit to England in 1825. At the end of the eighteenth century it was treated by Goethe on the grand scale. It enabled Delacroix to transfer to the moral plane the fight between man and beast—the beast being now within him.

In 1825 Delacroix met with the diabolical in Shakespeare also: in a lithograph and a painting he depicted the encounter between Macbeth and the Witches, pl 339
who gave shape to his repressed desires as Mephistopheles did for those of Faust:

*Double, double, toil and trouble,*
*Fire burn and cauldron bubble.*

Again in the same year Delacroix made use of a British source in his first picture of *Tam O'Shanter*, depicting the frantic but vain flight of the horseman through the Sabbath night from the witch whom he can never outdistance because she is holding on to the horse's tail. A sepia drawing done ten years later[14] returns to Goethe, this time to the *Erlkönig*, for another haunted rider: the horse, with its uncontrollable speed, becomes the instrument of an evil and irresistible fate. And indeed *Mazeppa* is only a variant of the same theme.

In 1826, after the visit to England, Delacroix was obsessed by Faust, and in the next year he exhibited a painting on this subject at the Salon and began the famous series of lithographs. In them he too is quite carried along in the hellish gallop to the Witches' Sabbath: he cannot part company with his obsessive companion, either when he is climbing the slopes of the Harz Mountains or when he pl 149
sees the shade of Gretchen rise before him; and Gretchen herself must listen to the voice of the Devil, heard by her alone, even in the church where she is trying

LI THE ABDUCTION OF REBECCA
*1846 Oil on canvas. 39 x 32 (100 x 082)*
*Metropolitan Museum of Art, New York*

to pray. In a much later work, *La Toilette*, the angel of darkness is still there, behind the mirror in which the fair-haired naked girl is admiring her own beauty. The same motif of the human being attentive to his hidden half, which separates itself from him to make itself heard more clearly, visited him again in 1835 when he read Ballanche's *Sac de Rome*. Again it took hold of him, and in one of his
pl 340 most impulsive drawings he shows the *Connétable de Bourbon* on horseback, pursued by a winged figure: this composition is almost the same as that of the *Erlkönig* (which is of the same date), but the meaning has been reversed, and instead of the man giving himself up to the blackness which is his own, Conscience has taken the place of the spirit of Evil.

## *The Angel makes his Appearance*

That other self which we hide sometimes awakens and may then carry us beyond our usual limits. The demon is then replaced by the angel, as in Rembrandt's *Saint Matthew*; or, if he remains the demon, it will be in the Greek sense, in Socrates' sense. When this happens Delacroix sees the demon as inspiration, as that other unknown force which rises out of our darkness, to dazzle us with its light and to oblige us to excel ourselves.

This change coincided in Delacroix with the waning of romanticism. It comes out in the great series of mural paintings, in which Delacroix attained classic equilibrium and in which, in consequence, his subconscious was more fully tamed and surmounted, or sublimated, than before. On the pendentives of the Library of the Chambre des Députés, the double is always the inspired soul. Delacroix's first thought had been to represent there *Socrates confronting his Judges*: in this he would have been faithful to his habit of taking some antithetical conflict as his subject. Other plans of the same sort included a *Moses before the Egyptian Magistrates*, a *Jesus among the Doctors*, a *Conversion of Saint Paul*. But the only ones he retained were his *Herodotus questioning the Wise Men* and his *Lycurgus before the Pythian Oracle*. As for *Socrates*, he chose finally to depict him in a halo of spiritual light, together with his daemon. Similarly his Numa goes in search of secrets to the nymph hidden in the heart of nature; and the dreamlike Muse, winged like the philosopher's daemon, visits the poet *Hesiod*.

The change had been indicated as early as 1826 when—for the huge composition destined for the Conseil d'État and destroyed in 1871—he had depicted
pl 341 *Justinian composing the Institutes* under the dictation of a great winged figure turning the pages of a book (like the angel appearing to Saint Matthew and inspiring him with his Gospel). Delacroix had also shown the angel appearing to *Christ in the Garden of Gethsemane*, though there unable to assuage the divine agony. He encountered the angel again towards the end of his life when in Saint-Sulpice he painted his supreme picture of conflict, that of *Jacob wrestling*.

LII HORSES COMING OUT OF THE SEA
*1860 Oil on canvas. 20 x 24 (050 x 061)*
*The Phillips Collection, Washington*

And in his last painting, once more, the angel is there by the side of *Tobias*. So, again and again, Delacroix perceived a presence by a man's side—sometimes the demon, but sometimes also the angel, in whom he sensed a principle of elevation. The struggle to achieve unity, to reach a balance between passion and reason, between romantic impulsiveness and classical discipline—a struggle which, as we have seen, was carried on in Delacroix's own life as well as in his art—was not enough: it led on to another struggle, for life is dynamic not static, and cannot be satisfied by any assured balance. A man struggles, not to reach a permanent state, but to progress without respite. He is committed to a movement of ascension. He must climb ceaselessly *per tenebras ad lucem* (to use the motto chosen by another passionate visionary, Van Gogh, whose life it explains). The wings of the angel must be outspread.

When he was about thirty, Delacroix's life changed signs: from the intoxication of the negative it gradually passed over to the exaltation of the positive, from the dark to the luminous. Although he was always anxious to be among 'those austere geniuses who fathom the depths of the soul and prefer to catch in their painting the terrible and pathetic side of human affairs,'[15] he always repudiated the bitterness for which he criticized Musset, who poured through 'incisions ... into the heart of man ... the corrosive acid of his own poisoned soul.' As Delacroix said to Philarète Chasles (who reported it in his *Mémoires*[16]): 'I prefer open wounds and the colour of blood!' Yet blood satisfied only a part of his ardour: he remained thirsty for something else. The journey to Morocco, with the sudden revelation it brought him, seems, if not a break, a hinge; but in reality the change had been preparing for a long time.

Its progress can be followed in the development of the theme of the massacres —in its gradual attenuation and dispersal. He himself has given us the hint by calling his *Sardanapalus* 'massacre number two'. In the first, that of *Chios*, the dying and the dead are simply the stinging foam of a magnificent wave—that formed by the rearing horse and the cruel, sumptuous rider; the wave curves through the splendid body of the captive woman, over the victims and out towards the breadth of the bright indifferent landscape. In that picture Delacroix gave himself up unreservedly to the intoxication of depicting action, passions and desire. This he shares with the romantics. Victor Hugo in *Légende des Siècles* seems to echo him:

*Et les coursiers fougueux ont traîné hors des tentes*
*Leurs corps vivants, de coups et de baisers meurtris ...*

while Baudelaire who, in *Le Voyage*, delights in evoking:

*Le bourreau qui jouit, le martyr qui sanglote,*
*La fête qu'assaisonne et parfume le sang ...*[17]

emphasizes how much what he called the 'molochist quality' was present in Delacroix.

At that stage, but only at that stage, 'everything in his work is merely desolation, massacres, fires; everything bears witness against the perpetual and incorrigible barbarousness of man. Blazing and smoking towns, slaughtered victims, raped women, the very children hurled under the feet of horses or stabbed by their own mother's dagger—everything in this picture, I say, is like some terrible hymn in honour of fate and irremediable misery.'[18]

But immediately after the *Massacre at Chios*, this cruel blaze began, almost insensibly, to decline. True, it was to flare up again terribly, from time to time, until the end: *Medea*, that most savage of all desperate mothers, painted by him in 1838, would still attract his brush in 1859 and 1862. But such cases must be regarded as repetitions. Till the end of his life, as we have seen, he liked to treat over again, in easel pictures, his well-tried themes, in order to give them, each time, a yet more precious and dazzling sparkle corresponding to the progress of his palette and his technique; but it is not in this that we should look for his line of development. This is only to be found validly in what were fresh leaps of his imagination, in those pictures in which he renewed himself, inventing new poems that answered to newborn needs in him. It is the line of these that we must follow to read his real trajectory.

xi, page 123 With his 'second massacre', *Sardanapalus* (1827), the development is decisive. At the first glance one sees only an orgy of wealth: everything—gleaming gold and precious stones, radiant bodies—is being thrown on to the pyre which the
pl 52 flame will soon devour. But whereas the Turk in the *Massacre at Chios* dominated the scene with his cruel pride and his appetite for bloodshed and for the flesh, Sardanapalus is very different. He is looking out beyond. He is letting go, dying to a certain kind of life. And already he is elsewhere, as Delacroix was elsewhere.

It was to this term, this indifference, that the theme of loneliness in the midst of human beings and of pleasures led. As we have seen, Delacroix had noted on 4 April 1824, three years before this, that the best moments of his life were flowing away amid distractions that brought him only boredom. For that the only cure he could find was creative work. And his Sardanapalus leans on his
pl 146 elbow in the same weary attitude already seen in his *Tasso*, disgusted with men and life—in the 1824 and 1825 versions as well as in the one painted in the same year as *Sardanapalus*. It was an attitude that answered to one of the lasting elements
pl 180 in Delacroix's art, and it reappears much later—in his *Michelangelo* (1850). Returning here, as he often did in his later years, to the dreams of his youth, Delacroix was simply taking up again the train of thought of his 1830 article on Michelangelo—of which indeed the picture is like a detailed illustration.

'I imagine him at a late hour of the night, seized with fear at the sight of his own creations, the first to savour that secret terror which he intended to awaken in men's souls through his terrible images of destruction and retribution. I like to imagine him also at those moments when, exhausted by having failed to reach in painting the sublimity of his ideas, he tried . . . to call poetry to his help. His expression then would be one of a deep melancholy, or else of his agitation and fear at the thought of the life to come. Regrets for youth, dread of the obscure and frightening future.'

When Delacroix re-read, after he was fifty, these lines written twenty years earlier, the impression they made on him must indeed have been poignant. At the moment when they were written they corresponded to the irremediable lassitude of Sardanapalus.

This lassitude finds its full expression in the last of Delacroix's great 'massacres', the *Entry of the Crusaders into Constantinople* (1840). Villehardouin had written: 'Night had almost come, the remnants of the army were weary of fighting and slaughter . . .' and Delacroix was indeed to make the theme his own. The trajectory is completed, and Delacroix is turning away from the mad, vain ardours of his past. He does not yet show to what unknown region he is going, yet it is now near. XXVII, page 283

## *The Boat on the Waves*

Another major picture belonging to the same year (1840), the *Shipwreck of Don Juan*, confirms the mood of the *Crusaders*, without as yet going beyond the expression of the anguish of men lost with no land in sight. This picture takes us from one of Delacroix's key themes, that of massacre, to another, that of the boat. This, of course, is one of the oldest human symbols—the passage across life, a human life as a small boat—and has been used and re-used to the point of banality.[19] Delacroix had it in mind when he copied out in his *Journal* (12 January 1824) these lines from Michelangelo: XXVI, page 274

*Giunto é già 'l corso della mia vita*
*Con tempestoso mar per fragil barca*
*Al commun porto . . .*[20]

As a subject for painting, it had obsessed him ever since Géricault had produced his *Radeau de la Méduse* in 1818. Already in 1821, as we have noted, he treated it in his *Castaways*.[21] And in 1822 it was given its full symbolic meaning, without anecdotal trimmings, in Delacroix's great picture, his *Dante and Virgil*. pl 81 II, page 58

Water and waves awaken deep, often unconscious associations in us, which have been studied by psychoanalysis. In this unstable, threatening element, refusing to be bound down, ceaselessly in movement like life itself but without life's *quasi*-logical organization, open indeed to devastating storms and furies, the imagination has perceived an equivalent to the seething instincts. But in addition, it is the subterranean sea, the sea of hell and the world of darkness, that Dante's boat is crossing. Dante—certainly a projection of Delacroix himself—looks as if he might at any moment cry out: 'In what darkness am I plunged . . . the future is all black. So is the past, which would not stay.' The words are those of Delacroix in his *Journal* of 7 April 1824.

The damned, in this picture, are the image of humanity at the mercy of the sea of the passions, carried along by it and able only to express despair. In painting them Delacroix was already filled with 'that solemn and funereal poetic feeling of the weakness of mankind, an inexhaustible source of the strongest emotions.'[22] He speaks of an allegory that might 'convey to the soul of others' what he had 'experienced' in his painting: 'Blind destiny hurrying away all those suppliants

LIII JACOB WRESTLING WITH THE ANGEL (detail)
*1856-61 Oil and wax. 281 x 191 (714 x 488)*
*Church of Saint-Sulpice, Paris*

who try in vain by their cries and prayers to arrest its inflexible arm'—a good description both of *Dante*, already painted, and of the *Massacre at Chios*.

In the fragile boat on the river of the dead, through the midst of the twitching damned in the subterranean night, Dante has beside him a companion, Virgil. Already, in this infernal setting, the Mantuan poet symbolizes the voice that counterbalances that of the demon, the voice of the spirit, the promise of a light in the midst of that physical darkness which, it seems, only the flames of conflagrations can ever illumine.

The picture on the theme of the boat of Delacroix's maturity was the *Shipwreck of Don Juan*. The same crushing horizon as in the *Crusaders* makes a stripe across the canvas, and, as Baudelaire noted, 'the low, heavy sky weighs down like a lid'.[23] The small boat is bounding forwards, but to the left, in the direction that is evil, sinister in its full sense.[24] Her movement is determined, obedient to the winds, but is in vain, for everywhere is the same emptiness. She is moving, but where? And what difference does it make? The oppressive expanse suggests Pascal, with his image of the sphere with centre everywhere and circumference nowhere. It suggests also Vigny's cry of anguish:

*Tout sera révélé dès que l'homme saura*
*De quel lieu il arrive et dans quel il ira.*

(All will have been revealed when man knows
From what place he has come and where he goes.)

And yet one presence is evident—that of Death. It alone stands waiting at the destination of that useless flight. Yet that last boat, that boat from anywhere or nowhere, is a fragment of the world and as such, though carried along at random, has a centre: all the passengers have turned away from the gunwale over which they might be contemplating the ocean and its enigma, to gaze with a fascination proportionate to the strength left to them at the drawing of the lots for the one who is to be eaten that the others may survive a little longer. The result is that the whole picture can be seen either as an arrow flying across space, or as a circle of human beings drawn inwards and hypnotized by a centre from which only death or its approach can detach them. And in fact it is both. In this lies the intensity of the tragedy.

At the 1847 Salon there appeared a weakened echo of this great master-
pl 343 piece, the *Castaways in a Ship's Boat*. Did this mean that for Delacroix the theme of the boat was exhausted? Certainly not. It was to have a surprising revival. In September 1852 Delacroix returned to Dieppe, which he had visited with Madame de Forget in the previous year, and wrote to her from there: 'You know my passion for the sea.' He had discovered the sea in his youth, at the time of the visits to Valmont; in 1834 he had even gone as far as Brittany; in 1838 he had visited Le Tréport with his cousin, and Trouville in 1841. His purpose

LIV HELIODORUS DRIVEN FROM THE TEMPLE (detail)
*1856-61 Oil and wax. 281 x 191 (714 x 488)*
*Church of Saint-Sulpice, Paris*

in going to Dieppe had been to recover from the extreme exhaustion caused by his work on the Apollo ceiling; but the impression made on him was so deep that he had to return. There is plenty of evidence in the *Journal*. 'This evening I enjoyed the sea for an hour and a half; I could not tear myself away.'[25] He could not get tired of 'the sea and its sublime effect'. When the sea rose, he rushed to the mole, to enjoy 'the fine spectacle for over four hours'. First and foremost, he found fresh enchantments of colour: one evening after a 'rather melancholy dinner' he found recompense, 'on the shore as the sun set through bands of sinisterly red and golden clouds which were reflected in the sea.'[26] Reading this, one cannot help thinking of the pastels and water-colours in which, before Boudin or the Impressionists, Delacroix managed to catch the intense and transient splendours of such skies.

But the rages of the sea awakened deeper responses in him. 'I stayed for more than half an hour in one place on the sand, at the edge of the waves, without ever wearying of their rage, of their return, the foam and the rolling pebbles. . . .' Sometimes, when darkness was added, it recalled visions from the time of the *Dante and Virgil*: 'In the evening, after a sleep, back to the mole. Beastly weather, only the moaning of the sea to enjoy, for nothing is visible but foam against a dark background.'[27] Sometimes, again, the *Shipwreck of Don Juan* is suggested: 'In the evening . . . to the mole. . . . The sea is raging; I can

*Fig 31* If one can find in Delacroix's ideas echoes of works which he had seen, it is equally possible to judge the influence which he himself exercized: this wood engraving after Gustave Doré, SHIPWRECKED MEN IN A BARQUE, clearly recalls the 'Shipwreck of Don Juan'.

*Fig 32* FISHING PORT. Sepia ink drawing. Cabinet des Dessins, Louvre, Paris.

hardly stand; I see two fishing-boats pass before me like arrows: the first one makes me shiver! They have lights on board. One could make something of these night effects.'[28] On the day before this last entry, he had reflected in more detail on what painting could make of such sights. 'But constantly seeing these seascapes, ships and interesting men, I am even more convinced than I was last year that the interest there is in all this has not yet been exploited.'

And in fact, in 1853, Delacroix had given prominence to the results of this sustained communion with the sea in a series of seven pictures of *Christ on the*
pls 117, 344 *Lake of Genesareth* in the storm. Some of these recall earlier shipwreck compositions: in one of them the enormous threatening wave from the 1821 picture, itself inspired by Géricault's wave, recurs. But the meaning has changed. Man is no longer left alone to face his terrible adventure and his fierce struggles. The grey and violent waves howling around the dismasted boat, and suggesting the raging of the blind forces of instinct are stronger and more active than ever; but the old theme has acquired a new stress: the sleeping Christ opposes his peace to this vast violence. It is the light, and against it the impetuosities of the physical are powerless because it does not belong to the same world as they. Taking fresh life from the artist's rediscovery of the sea, the old subject is transformed.

## *The Victory of Light*

For Delacroix the struggle was not ended, but it had now a new incidence. It became the struggle between light and darkness. One part of his nature was gradually freeing and asserting itself, throwing back into the shadows that part which would have liked to devour it entirely. In his painting, from now on, everything suggesting conflict between physical forces, whether animal or human, or even between the different passions, was only a reminiscence of his past, a resumption of his earlier works. The period of the fight against the passions, of the spirit's fight, was opening.

The date of the notes written by Delacroix in his heliotrope notebook is disputed, but many indications suggest that it was in 1845 or thereabouts. In it he copied out a passage from Custine:[29] 'Happiness is not the aim of man's mission here below.' Happiness is what the instincts and passions seek during a man's youth; but what is that real aim? Custine's answer is: 'That aim is entirely religious: it is the approach to moral perfection, struggle and victory.' The war-horse in Delacroix could still be roused by the trumpets calling to battle; but he was now ripe for the knowledge that the battle does not lie in a vain collision between attacks and resistance, but that what is necessary is to struggle in order to rise towards the worlds of the spirit.

The journey to Morocco and the crisis it had started in him had revealed to him an aspect of life and of art quite different from the clash between violent forces—the sunny aspect, where the vine of classicism, pruned and cared for, brings to ripeness the grapes of thought, and these dispense a different ecstasy, likewise intense, but serene, not convulsive. After Delacroix's death, Théophile Gautier, on the occasion of the 1864 Exhibition, observed with penetration: 'His journey to Morocco opened to him a whole world of light, serenity, azure.'[30] And after this first glimpse of them in Morocco Delacroix discovered what Vigny had called the '*paisibles joies*' for himself, with all the enchantment of surprise, in natural scenes, on visits to his friends and at Champrosay.

And now, to the wild beasts which he painted constantly as one might hum a military march, he began to add a counterpoise—flowers. Soon he was divided between these two recreations, which took it in turns to charm one side of his sensibility. George Sand stated that at Nohant she saw Delacroix 'trying for pl 267 the first time to paint flowers. . . . I came upon him in an ecstasy of enchantment before a yellow lily, of which he had just understood the beautiful 'architecture': that was the felicitous word he used.'[31] Here he found a fresh aspect of that life which delighted him so intensely in the movements of wild beasts. He painted at full speed, aware that 'at every moment his model, accomplishing in the water the full course of its flowering, was changing colour and attitude.' This was a less precipitate life; its rhythm was the vegetable and not the animal pls 298, 299 one, but still it was irrepressible life and just as overwhelming. Now came a whole series of flower paintings—a real sheaf of them in 1848, painted now at Champrosay, at a time when he was 'almost continually in the country'.[32] Another series followed in the next year at the same place, 'pieces of nature as they present themselves in gardens, where the greatest possible variety of flowers are brought together in the same setting': gladioli, stocks, China asters, anemones, foxgloves, roses, poppies, dahlias, hortensias, hollyhocks. He sent three pictures gleaming with blooms to the 1849 Salon. True, at the same time he painted a lion outside his cavern, exhibited in the 1848 Salon, and another devouring a corpse. The balance was about even.

*Fig 33* A LION. Pen drawing. Cabinet des Dessins, Louvre, Paris.

For the rest of his life Delacroix, for his recreation, was to oscillate, not perhaps with indifference but with equal passion, between his fierce wild beasts and his generous flowers. It might be thought that, having reached this stage, he had won his inner harmony by dividing his impatient forces between two diametrically opposed fronts. On the one hand, the theme of the carnivore took on a greater and greater amplitude till it reached his *Lion Hunts* and *Tiger
pl 349 *Hunts*, while on the other hand the compensating theme of flowers, starting from a few water-colours or pastels, expanded into pictures of great baskets of
xxx, page 292 blooms under arches thick with leaves and petals. One day the flowers became women. The swans, hornbeam hedges, hollyhocks and azure sky accompanying
pl 219 his *Turkish Women bathing* were painted in 1854, and the largest of his *Lion Hunts* in the year following.

But this peaceful co-existence of wild beasts and flowers happened only because the struggle had moved elsewhere. It had been changed into a conflict between the formidable weight of the physical instincts and the immaterial impulse of that which escapes them. It was enough that Delacroix should have found the way out into the air, the light and the sky, into the spiritual world.

The low and the high are the oldest of all symbols, and everyone finds them
pl 108 afresh by instinct. In the *Massacre at Chios* and in the *Crusaders*, the sky behind the protagonists had been a backcloth—at most a contrast; but in the great series of paintings in the Library of the Chambre des Députés the tumult and lassitude of those two pictures is replaced by an equilibrium between two poles.

At one end of the room there is *Orpheus* and the birth of poetry: here the hunters 'swathed in the spoils of lions and bears, approach enchanted by the new voice', and even Delacroix's wild beasts have come to roll on the ground at the hero's feet in catlike delight. But at the other end there is a hemicycle of equal importance: it shows the revenge of the sublimated instincts, and in it '*Attila* followed by his hordes of barbarians, tramples under his horse's feet an Italy in ruins'; the savage warriors 'descend from the mountains like a torrent' and in front of them there is the rising diagonal of a cloud of dark smoke and ash. The 'ferocious charger of the king of the Huns' is a brother to the one that carried Mephistopheles to the Witches' Sabbath. The forces of evil are always ready to reawaken. Evil and good answer one another, like Delacroix's wild beasts pl 354 and flowers. We are still, with this series of paintings, in the presence of a terrible and inconclusive collision.

The *Apollo* ceiling was a step forward from this. It was conceived in 1850, the Library of the Chambre in 1844: time had gone by and, although the basic element of conflict was still there (this time a conflict 'between the gods and the elements'), it had evolved. The eternal adversaries are once again face to face, now in a single composition; but the balance is now irrevocably tilted—Apollo will be the victor over the serpent Python. To Delacroix, as he himself announced, the composition was a 'symbol of the triumph of light over darkness and over the rebellion of the waters'. Some have wished to see in it a different symbol, that of glory triumphing over the envious. The property of the symbol is its multiplicity, its power to stir in our sensibility secret responses which may be various and associated; but certainly some are more important than others. It is impossible to lay too much stress on what Barrès wrote after studying Delacroix's paintings in Saint-Sulpice:

'We are never exaggerating when we attribute a limitless meaning to works of genius. These perpetual fighters have not an explicit knowledge of all the ideas that stir them; if they had they would die of it, they would be unable to carry all that. . . . But in any case, whether they are conscious of it or not, these beautiful forms and moving colours, the result of such profound study, have an intense spiritual meaning.'

Modern psychology has given us a better understanding of those images into which the deep preoccupations of our nature are directly transposed. The monster, the dragon and the serpent are, in the universal language of symbolism, the recurring image of the power of evil and its bestial qualities. If we look at the drawing made by Delacroix in 1828 for his lithograph of the ghost of *Marguerite appearing to Faust*, and then at the lithograph itself, we shall see that, in the former, there is a strange basilisk-like a lizard with claws crawling towards Faust and Mephistopheles with its head raised, while in the second its resemblance to a crocodile is increased by its being mingled with a sinister mass of toads, vipers and serpents. The serpent is opposed by Delacroix, again and again, to the solar strength of the lion; he even places it at the foot of the crucified Christ, in a pl 350 confrontation which is far more terrible than that between Apollo and the Python. In his first version of the *Crucifixion*, that of 1829, there was an all too human, fair-haired Magdalen *à la Rubens*. She later disappears and, in the 1847 pastel,[33] all that is left is the solitude of a vast mountainous landscape like those of

Morocco and in it the coiled serpent raising its head for a mute dialogue with the bent head of the dead Christ.

pl 357 Later Delacroix was to paint his *Perseus and Andromeda* and his *Roger and Angelica*, in which the symbolic serpent-dragon prepares the way for the battles of
pl 352 Saint George and—on the ceiling of the Saint-Sulpice Chapel—Saint Michel against the power of evil. And in 1863 the reptile which made its first appearance in the Faust picture of 1828 receives its last embodiment—crushed by the
pl 353 paw of a triumphant lion.

In the spontaneous language of the subconscious, the waters, with their blind rages, join easily with the serpent as images for the power of the inorganic elements. For Delacroix the 'rebellion of the waters' had been dominated, and soon—in 1853, two years after the *Apollo* ceiling had been unveiled—there came the pictures in which Christ, another symbol of light, sleeps peacefully in a boat which those waters toss in vain. The ideas which Delacroix disdains to make explicit yet expresses imaginatively form a connected progression. The balance in which the hordes of Attila and the songs of Orpheus were weighed had now come definitely down on one side.[34]

Thus in the *Apollo* ceiling the conflict, or rather victory, has become that of the high over the low: its axis is no longer within the plane of earthly life, but is vertical. In this transformation Delacroix was no doubt helped by the very conditions inherent in the kind of surfaces he had to paint—vaults and domes with their suggestion of openings in the ceiling that hangs between us and the sight of the celestial vault. Italian art, as we have already observed, had tended to make domes into openings upon the blue sky and the world of the immaterial. Yet this, for Delacroix, was at most one of those guiding touches that material circumstances often give to aspirations already in us.

Not long before the *Apollo* ceiling, Delacroix had painted the dome of the
XXXVII, page 371 Library in the Luxembourg, and here too he had made clear his ascending quest of light. The principal figure is that of *Dante*—so dear to Delacroix's imagination that his 'dear Chopin' appears with the features of Dante in a drawing of him done after his death. Dante, who had suggested to Delacroix his first great masterpiece in 1822, is now shown at a later stage in his journey through the Inferno: still guided by Virgil, he has left the dark and swirling waters of the damned and the conflagrations of the vices for regions in which earthly tumult is too distant to be heard—the Limbo described by Dante in his Fourth Canto: as Delacroix put it, 'It is a kind of Elysium.' Virgil is presenting his companion to the illustrious dead, and especially to Homer.

Dante, preceded by a guide, has only just climbed the slope, and still shows signs of the effort; and now a divine spring comes from the earth beneath his feet: he is about to see Orpheus, sitting, lyre in hand—Orpheus who also had renounced the world of human passions after trying to appease and sublimate it. Forgetting the Furies (whom Delacroix had at first thought of placing with him in one of the pendentives of the Chambre des Députés), he is giving himself up wholly 'to those varied melodies' which 'the Muse, fluttering at his side, seems to be dictating to him.' The panther has followed him, but is lying at his feet and is listening.

In 1852 Delacroix threw himself into the plans for the Salon de la Paix. In the lower part of the composition there were still, like a lingering memory, the corpses of men and animals which, in the *Apollo* ceiling, were seen deposited on the hill-tops by the ebbing of the Flood, but now, according to Théophile Gautier's description,[35] a few of them only lay close to the figure of Cybele, who represented 'the mourning earth, with her eyes raised to the sky in supplication for an ending to her miseries.' This ending was near—was indeed already being celebrated, for 'the time of ordeal is past'. There was a soldier extinguishing the torch of conflagration under his iron heel. 'Above, in the azure sky, in the light from which the clouds, those last vestiges of the storm now swept away by a powerful breeze, are fleeing, Peace appears, serene and radiant, bringing back Abundance and the sacred choir of the Muses who had fled.' Jupiter, enthroned in the height, was 'still threatening the maleficent divinities, the enemies of men's repose', with the same gesture that strikes down the Titans—but Mars, the Furies and Discord were in retreat. The rumblings of the storm were scarcely to be heard from the horizon, all was illumination and tranquillity.

Delacroix was now haunted by the theme of the defeated monster and of night in retreat. In 1855, as an entry in his *Journal* on 9 January shows, he was meditating on a 'magnificent subject: Noah with his family making sacrifice after the Deluge. . . . The monsters condemned by divine wisdom lie half-submerged in the mud'; and elsewhere[36] he adds: 'Trees still dripping with the waters of the Deluge raise themselves again towards the sky.' And again on 15 March 1860 he took up the project, repeating the description almost word for word but amplifying its symbolism: 'The clouds are rushing to the horizon; Eurus and Notus are dispersing them. The sun reappears, radiant: all seems reborn, singing a hymn to the Eternal.' But this project was not carried out.

At the Hôtel de Ville, on the supports of the ceiling, effort was still visible, embodied by Hercules, with a rippling of muscles, accomplishing labours and defeating adversaries. Hercules was shown overcoming wild animals too—the Nemean lion, the Erymanthean boar, 'straggling survivors of the monsters'; he crushed the Centaur with his club, he strangled Antaeus (who drew fresh life only from contact with the Earth); he bound Nereus, companion of the sea monsters, and by bringing Alcestis from Hades, he effected the same upwards movement that was achieved by Dante.

In these same years another significant theme, corollary to the development of the themes already mentioned, returns more than once—that of the ladder or stairway connecting with the light, to which it leads, the 'darkness of the abyss' into which (in the paintings of the Salon de la Paix) Discord fled 'like a night-bird caught by the day'.

In his youth Delacroix had treated the theme of prison—the dark and issueless prison of his *Tasso* and his *Marguerite*, or the shadowy lair of his *Alchemist*. He had shown a fondness for the diagonal composition so well suited, according to baroque canons, to express dramatic instability and *élan*—Mephistopheles' flight across the night sky, or Faust climbing with him the steep slopes of the Harz Mountains. In 1839 he had returned to the diagonal for the curse inflicted

on Desdemona by her father. In 1844, to express the menace of Attila, he had
marked out the diagonal by means of the terrible cloud which the horses in their
furious onset seem to be pushing before them as though to crush the victims
LI, page 459 with it. In 1846 he had recourse to it again for the *Abduction of Rebecca*—but
here it is used to express that effect of ascension, of movement upwards towards a
celestial issue, which now became the artist's preoccupation.

And in fact, in Delacroix's work from 1848 onwards, the prison has an issue:
the governing line of the composition tilts upwards and opens towards the height.
pl 367 In a picture whose theme he took from George Sand—that of *Lélia* bewailing the
suicide of her lover—the shut-in prison has become a dark cavern, whose jagged
background offers an opening towards the free air. In the following year the
dark and stifling pit into which *Daniel* has been thrown among the wild beasts
has an opening to the sky. And again in the year after that—1850—the theme
of a confrontation with death at the bottom of a rocky cavity returns: this time the
cavity is a tomb, and the dead man is *Lazarus*. One cannot help comparing this
picture with the *Lélia*: the setting is very similar. And yet everything has
changed: the body, which in the earlier picture lay back in an attitude of irre-
vocable abandon is here rising up; the draped woman, who had collapsed in her
grief, is here lifting her arms in surprise and hope; and the crouching witness is
replaced by a group of upright figures surrounding the slender figure of Christ.
Even the opening towards the light seems to undergo a stronger attraction up-
pl 365 wards and to spread out into the day. In the *Supper at Emmaus*, painted in
1853, Christ shines out his supernatural light before a hanging drapery that
prolongs his proud attitude of assurance and inspiration: he is at the foot of a
pl 364 stairway whose curve, like the one in Rembrandt's *Philosopher*, swirls up to
where the door giving on the free air can be discerned.

## *The Inspiration of Religious Themes*

When in 1849 Delacroix was commissioned to paint a chapel in Saint-Sulpice
and mistakenly believed that it was to be the Baptismal Chapel, his first plan was
to place on opposite walls a *Christ Carrying the Cross* and an *Entombment*. The
pl 366 two pictures exhibited at the 1859 Salon are clearly reflections of this earlier
idea, besides being related to the 1850 *Raising of Lazarus*. The Calvary is filled
with a movement of ascension, and in it the S-shaped road winds along the
flank of a rocky slope so that one cannot see where it comes from or where it is
going. The setting of rocks with a single strangled fissure through them recurs
in the *Entombment*; but here, of course, the movement is reversed, and the heavy,
inanimate body of the dead Christ is being carried down a curving stairway
away from the light of day into the interior of the rock. Smoky light from one
enormous torch is not enough to illumine the dark, threatening cavity. Inspired
by the same idea of a funereal engulfment, Delacroix painted also in 1859 a
new version of the *Saint Sebastian* theme, with the saint lying collapsed in a
hollow among rocks, painfully reached by the last evening glow.

This obsession with dark depth and luminous height and with the painful
path from the one to the other acquired, when thus applied by Delacroix to reli-

gious subjects, the full spiritual range which his intuition felt to be there. As we have seen, he was in the strict sense of the term an unbeliever: a Voltairean with the soul of a Pascal, he refused adherence to a faith, to dogmas and to ritual. Yet he was moved to the depths by all that gives nourishment to real religion. He, more than anyone, had the metaphysical uneasiness and, in the widest sense, a religious soul.

Being devoid of any intolerance (which is incompatible with a spirit as great and noble as his), he respected the devoutness of other people and their forms of worship: he had a lively sense of the fervour that could be expressed in these, especially when it came from simple and innocent hearts. 'I am very fond of churches', he noted on 20 August 1857, at the moment when he was leaving Plombières; 'I love to be in them, almost alone, and to sit in a pew, and there I stay in a meditation that does good. . . . It is age that makes them venerable. It is as though they are hung with a tapestry woven of all the prayers that suffering hearts have there breathed out to heaven. What can replace . . . those altars, those steps worn by the feet and knees of the generations who have brought their sufferings there, and over whom the ancient church has murmured the last prayers?' With all his humanity he shared the fervour of the simple before the figure of Christ and before his suffering and sacrifice.

And so he could not help being attracted to religious painting. In 1826, in his *Christ in the Garden of Gethsemane*—which still reflects the secular preoccupations expressed in his *Tasso* of about the same date—he felt and described chiefly the horror of the moral agony which Vigny, a little later, also expressed the loneliness:

*Il eut froid. Vainement il appela trois fois*
*'Mon Père!' Le vent, seul, répondit à sa voix.*
*Il tomba sur le sable assis et, dans sa peine,*
*Eut sur le monde et l'homme une pensée humaine.*

(He was cold. In vain he cried three times
'My Father!' The wind alone answered his voice.
He sat down on the sand, and in his grief,
Thought of the world and man a human thought.)

But *Christ in the Garden of Gethsemane*, like the other religious pictures painted by Delacroix up to that time, was a commissioned work. The *Mary Magdalene at the foot of the Cross* and the *Pietà* of 1829 deal with the tragic side of Christ's suffering and death in a manner still dominated by the influence of earlier masters, especially Rubens. It was not until 1834 that he first treated the theme of the Entombment, of the descent into the darkness—no doubt as a result of his grief at the death of his nephew (which also, as we have seen, inspired his *Prisoner of Chillon*). His 1835 *Christ Crucified between Thieves* pl 241
(now in the Museum at Vannes)—a sketch for the *Crucifixion* of 1837—does not go beyond emulation of Rubens. But from 1845 onwards a new feeling becomes apparent: the theme of the *Incredulity of Saint Thomas*, which he treated in 1846, still harks back to Rubens, but it indicates that a new significance is being attached to the life of Christ; and indeed it was soon followed by two other pictures of *Christ on the Cross* which show the line on which his

thinking was now firmly set. The tragedy is becoming more intense, less spectacular. 'The serious sadness of his talent', wrote Baudelaire, 'is perfectly suited to our religion, a religion that is profoundly sad, the religion of universal grief.'[37]

Thus Delacroix found in it something that answered to the change taking place within him. In 1854 in the article entitled '*Questions sur le Beau*', he raised the problem of religious painting, and stressed the beauty of those 'penetrating compositions, which take us into regions so different from what surrounds us that we are forced, in the midst of our sceptical life with its addiction to puerile distractions, to think of the mortification of the senses and the power of sacrifice and contemplation.'[38] Delacroix was developing: he was, as it were, raising his sights towards the sky and the light, and was beginning to see, through religion, a meaning other than the negative one he had hitherto attributed to death. Death had constantly obsessed him, as both his pictures and his notes show: it had been present everywhere in his 'massacres', in the victim and the wounded and the corpse. Yet sometimes the exciting din of horses' hooves and bloodshed in which it was drowned had fallen silent, and then, in that silence, there was room for nothing but a mute and heavy private dialogue—that between the orphan girl and the graves (in the 1823 pictures), that between Hamlet and the skull (in the 1828 version and in later ones), and that between Cromwell and the coffin of Charles I (1831), where everything is expressed by a simple juxtaposition of a vertical with a horizontal. His Hassan (1827) even rests alone in the midst of a space no longer troubled by any presence.

From the first *Entombment* (that of 1834) onwards, death becomes essentially the crucified Christ, who is taken down, lamented and placed in the tomb. In 1848, illustrating *Lélia*, Delacroix gave the collapsed and already stiff body of Stenio the same attitude which he was to repeat in his four pictures of the *Entombment* belonging to the same year; and indeed he used it again for the Arab whose corpse is being torn to pieces by a lion—another subject which he treated several times. Rarely has a more relentless attitude been imagined than this, in which the dead body, as though concentrated upon its own abolition, seems to sag in order to get under the earth where it would decompose.

Death—that emptiness which is merely the reverse of the carved surface of life—was a thought from which Delacroix constantly suffered, even from his early years. Warm-hearted beneath his cold manner, he received, as we have seen, incurable wounds from the deaths of his friends, one after another. 'Why are we still here?' he exlaimed to Soulier in 1843; 'Why are others not here any more? Inexplicable life, abyss of sadness and boredom when one looks out over the gunwhale at it.' And again: 'When one cannot sleep, when one is ill, when the end of it all is seen clearly in its nakedness, a man gifted with imagination needs a certain courage not to rush to meet the phantom and embrace the skeleton. . . .'[39]

This feeling had long been familiar to him. On the one hand he was haunted by the nothingness into which the past sinks, by oblivion—against which he fought with 'wretched fragile paper', with his *Journal*. 'My mind and the history of my soul—will all this, then, be annihilated? One must write, entrust it to 'these notes, the only memorial that remains to me.'

But there was also that other nothingness, the future. 'What shall we find beyond?' he asked George Sand on 4 December 1860; 'Night, fearful night. There is nothing better in store for us: that, at least, is what I sadly feel.' And on 23 November 1857: 'How can we justify the immortality of the soul when we look on all these souls filled with nothingness and with shadows? And they are more numerous than the leaves of the forest which the wind sweeps along to fatten the earth and make it bring forth new myriads of beings destined to the same annihilation.'

But in that case, what is to be done? Fight on. But the fight now has a new meaning: it is no longer the blind and unconsidered expending of defiant strength, but a man's own fight, the one which he alone knows—the fight against that inexorable nothingness which threatens us behind and before, and which we never escape except to remain suspended above its abyss for a short moment. How can it be overcome? Pascal said: 'A man is greater than that which kills him, because he knows that he is dying.' To overcome the nothingness means to rise up and to augment life and its meaning before these are wiped out. So it is possible for Christ to be placed in the tomb amid the human despair of those about him: he will rise again. Lazarus rose again: he was lying in the tomb, but at the voice which called to him he rose, stood up, and walked. Perhaps in the same way, beyond death, something of us will live, in our works, in the souls of others. . . .

The grave-clothes must be cast off: the soul—a new theme, this—must be awakened from its tomb of flesh; the princess, enchained by the body and at the mercy of the monster, of the new and covetous python, must be delivered. In Delacroix's art the time of the shuddering prey, the time of the Turkish horseman carrying off his captive to enjoy her, the time of Sardanapalus indifferent to the slaughter of those to whom he had owed his pleasure, and the time of the Crusaders, weighed down and weary and capable only of trampling yet other victims who merely encumber the way of disgust and dissolution—all these times were past.

The whole significance is now altered. The warrior still has his armour on, he is still mounted: fiery still, but with another fire, he still draws his sword for battle; but now he draws it to deliver the princess. The theme which Delacroix had now at last discovered is also one of universal application; but its meaning struck him with peculiar force, and he took it up again and again, with such indifference to the merely anecdotal side of it that the titles of the pictures might be interchanged. Perseus delivering Andromeda? Roger delivering Angelica? Saint George delivering his princess?—what matters, except the incantatory meaning? And what is this, constantly and essentially, except virile strength going out to meet the dragon and piercing it with lance or sword (as Apollo had done with his arrows) in order to liberate the enchained captive, the soul? To the soul, fainting with fear, it would then be possible to say: 'Rise and

XLIX, page 453

LV THE SEASONS. WINTER: JUNO AND AEOLUS
*1862 Oil on canvas. 78 x 68 (197 x 171)*
*Museo de Arte de Sao Paolo, Brazil*

walk.' Better still, on the horse (whether it be the hippogryph or Pegasus) that strikes the ground like a springboard in order to rise from it and leap forwards, it would be possible to realise that upward movement which becomes an obsessive appeal—as, for instance, in the upward jerk of the impatient head of one horse of Apollo's team of four (an expressive movement in which Redon was to recognize its full symbolic power). It is not without significance that the new theme comes into evidence at the moment when Delacroix was fully occupied with religious painting and was producing his pictures of the *Crucifixion* and the *Entombment*, of *Daniel*, of *Lazarus* (1850) and of the *Supper at Emmaus* (1853), the period also of his victorious Apollo.

In 1847 two versions of *Perseus and Andromache* and one of *Roger delivering Angelica* made their appearance almost simultaneously. Soon Delacroix would be at work on the Salon de la Paix and would there strike out a fresh variant of the theme in his *Hercules delivering Hesione:* she too is rivetted to a rock beside the waves and is threatened by a marine monster. In another panel Hercules was shown freeing another captive, Alcestis.

In 1853 there came another picture of *Daniel*, this time not alone in the pit with the wild beasts, but receiving the flying angel. A few months later, in 1854, he painted *Saint George*, in yet another fight against the hydra (which bears a singular resemblance, though on a greatly enlarged scale, to the small basilisk seen by Faust and Mephistopheles on the ground they are about to tread[40]). It may be thought that the *Lion Hunt* pictures which again formed part of Delacroix's output at this time have an obscure share in the new significance now given by him to wild beasts—as also those lions which in paintings dating from 1855 and 1856 are shown crushing reptiles with their paws. In any case there is a connection between all these and Delacroix's working out of the paintings in Saint-Sulpice (commissioned, it will be remembered, in 1849): they foreshadow the movement of Saint Michael stabbing the devil and that of the riding archangel who is about to trample the defeated Heliodorus.

The way of the soul, though its destination be the peaks of the spirit, passes throught the heart. Delacroix's absorption in his work and the disciplined coldness of his manner made many think that he was a stranger to tenderness; but, as we have seen, this was not the opinion of those who knew him best. As Baudelaire said of him: 'he could show himself helpful, courageous and warm-hearted when it was a question of something important,' and in friendship his sensibility was 'virile and deep.' And in fact affection for his intimate friends was one of the mainstays of his life. For instance, he wrote to George Sand on 10 April 1842:

'Cling firmly to those whom you love and who love you. It is a need one feels the more strongly the older one gets. I have had several more losses, and they have afflicted me keenly for some time now. When all those whom we love

LVI OVID AMONG THE SCYTHIANS
*1862 Oil on wood. 13 x 20 (032 x 050)*
*Private collection, Switzerland*

and beside whom we have browsed are under the earth, what remains above it to detain us? For me there will be nothing, and no doubt I shall pack up before that moment comes. Give me news of my Chopin.' On 20 November 1847, after the death of his aunt Riesener,[41] 'whom I loved like a mother', he wrote: '... I know already from experience that one's real life is in others.' And, intellectual as he was, he reveals a little-known aspect of himself in the following words of praise, which are about her: 'She was a woman in whom—a rare thing—the qualities of the soul came first: even if one had not loved her, one would have had to admire her.' Eight years later still, in a letter to his cousin Lamey, he wrote:[42] 'When a man has no more affection, he has nothing any more.' It was thus in goodness of heart that he looked for the narrow gate to the way he sought. And this comes out in his paintings. Already in 1836 he who had found such zest in the tragic spectacle of the violence of man or beast discovered the emotion of charity: in his *Saint Sebastian* the saint, bleeding from many arrow pl 248 wounds, forms part of the procession of victims which Delacroix painted with such bitter passion, but the holy women are there, bending over him; and with what care and gentleness the one nearest him is trying to pull one of the arrows out of its wound! Similar attitudes of compassion are assumed by the Bohemians who are lifting the wounded Goetz from his horse, in a work dating from that same year. But these were only preludes: it was not till nearly ten years later that he depicted *Romeo and Juliet*. 'In the cold light of morning', as XXXIX, page 381 they 'clasp one another religiously ... in the violent embrace of farewell'[43]—Baudelaire's description of the picture exhibited in the 1846 Salon, one of the rare songs of pure love that came from Delacroix's brush. In the next year there was Kaled, the girl disguised as a page, bending in a transport of grief over the body of the dying *Lara*; and again, four years later, *Juliet in the Tomb*, which seem open only to receive the lovers after their final embrace. These are moments of passion, full of pathos. In 1850 the deeper feeling found consistent expression. In three pictures painted in that year, a wounded man is being lifted with care on to a horse: they are the *Angelica and the Wounded* pl 370 *Medoro*, another *Goetz* and—in marked affinity with both of them—the *Good Samaritan*. In fact, the spirit of the Gospel had awakened in Delacroix, who till then had preferred to turn to the Old Testament. He was one of the few artists to come at all near to Rembrandt's depth and inwardness: although he had not Rembrandt's vocation for the New Testament, although his fibres responded more easily to heroism and violence than to compassion and love, he came close to Rembrandt in 1853 with his *Supper at Emmaus*, and with his *Good Samaritans* of 1850 and 1852.

In the 1850 version the man is all wounds and suffering: at the least movement one would hear him cry out, and his arm clings tightly about the helper's neck. And the helper, the Good Samaritan, is all effort—not now the effort of display and self-affirmation, but that of care and self-control, trying to slide the wounded man into the saddle without any jerk. The two men are locked together, not now like hand-to-hand fighters, nor like Romeo and Juliet, but as two human beings who are together only that they may be united in human brotherhood. The Samaritan's arm and leg are sharply bent, but in order to sustain with their soothing security the limbs of the man in pain. Even the horse,

by standing so still, seems to share in this solicitude. It is not surprising that Van Gogh, who was predestined to understand Delacroix both in his burning sense of life and in his magical power of rendering it in vibrant colour, should have recognized himself in this picture and painted a copy of it in Saint-Rémy in May 1890. Several months earlier he had transposed into his harsher style the
pl 368 *Pietà* which Delacroix had painted in the same year as the *Good Samaritan*—in which the Virgin holds out her arms, to tell how great is her grief, in a movement parallel to the attitude of her Son, whose inanimate limbs and collapsed body are pitiable like those of the man rescued by the Samaritan, but hopelessly so since this is death. In June 1890, a month before he killed himself, Van Gogh made another version of this *Pietà* for Dr Gachet. He told his brother Theo[44] that he had made the first copy when he was ill, and added that '. . . even when suffering, sometimes religious thoughts bring me great consolation.'

To these religious thoughts he had access through Delacroix. Delacroix had indeed not repudiated the hymn he had raised to universal suffering, but the contemplation of that suffering no longer produced in him a confusion and burning exaltation, it now stirred in him a compassion which was clearly of help to Van Gogh in his moral agony. It was now to find expression in many forms.

In 1852 came the second version of his *Crusaders*, that farewell to the splendours
pl 369 of cruelty, and of the *Good Samaritan*, representing him this time as he comes upon the wounded man and bends over him with sympathy, and the second version, too, of the *Education of the Virgin*, with its scene of tender affection bathed in the more ample range of colour of the trees and leaves. The same year brought his *Baptism of Christ* and his *Christ walking on the Waters*. In
XL, page 382 addition there was his *Marphisa*, from Ariosto: here the warrior maid, using the tip of her lance, forces the mistress of Pinabel to strip from her dazzling flesh its excessively rich adornments and give them to the old woman seated behind her. This gives Delacroix a pretext for one of his most sumptuous nudes, and yet it suggests Saint Martin or the opposition of Vice and Virtue rather than the warmth and langour of the harem.

In 1853 he painted the disciples and the holy women in the shadow of the city walls at twilight, raising up the body of Saint Stephen after the stoning:[45] in the foreground a young woman on her knees is staunching the blood shed by the first martyr for the new faith. The same year produced his *Scourging of Christ*,
pl 362 his *Christ on the Lake of Genesareth*, and a new version of his *Daniel*.

## *The Wrestling with the Angel*

Delacroix was at a turning-point in his life. On 27 October 1855 he was so struck by these lines from an article by Gautier on Robert-Fleury that he copied them out:

'When he reaches a certain point in his life, a painter must, on pain of repeating himself, change his point of view, and, having risen higher, embrace a wider horizon. It is, we recognize, a climacteric, a dangerous stage, the crossing of which is bound to be alarming.' And Delacroix now set himself to do this.

He was, indeed, changing: 'I am calmer,' he observed on 7 November, during a visit to Berryer at Augerville,'—but not colder!' He lived increasingly in himself. He was even coming to feel a certain reluctance to read during his leisure hours: 'Even in the past I could never understand the people who read when they are travelling. When are they ever with themselves? What do they do with their mind if they never look at it?' A year earlier, also at Augerville, he had been 'greatly struck by the Requiem Mass, by all that religion holds for the imagination, but at the same time by the way it speaks to a man's inmost feeling.' This inner feeling was now to be the fibre in himself that he would be the most concerned to set vibrating. He reached it by a new and indeed evangelical penetration, in which the last smoke of his youthful violence was dispersed. He had become sensitive to the spirit of goodness, and he responded to it: '*Beati mites, beati pacifici.* What doctrine has ever, like this, made gentleness, resignation and simple virtue the one and only object of man on earth?' Even genius bowed down and humbled itself. '*Beati pauperes spiritu*: Christ promises heaven to the poor in spirit: that is to say to the simple; this saying is not so much designed to abase the pride in which the human spirit delights when it considers itself, as to show that simplicity of heart prevails over reason.' Disciple of Voltaire and Byron as he was, Delacroix would never repudiate either the cold lucidity of the intelligence (which he had inherited from the former), or the ardours of sensibility (which he shared with the latter); but the third horse in Apollo's chariot team of four was the will, the cultivation of which Delacroix had found in himself and in the dignity of Dandyism; and now he had found the fourth, and this, which was indispensable to the others and, in a way, balanced them, was the simplicity of the heart obeying its vocation to love.

Thus his pictures of terrible hunting scenes cease after 1861, though the great wild beasts still make their hoarse roaring heard in his work until the end, until the *Lion with a Reptile* which he painted shortly before May 1863; but pl 353 there are no more Odalisques or voluptuous reveries. When, at Strasbourg, Delacroix gave the date, 27 August 1859, to a series of sketches of bathing women which are a prelude to Degas, he was signing a farewell. And indeed, during the visits he paid to Strasbourg almost every year between 1855 and 1859, to see not only his cousin Lamey but also the cathedral, his curiosity had taken a fresh course: his new inclinations towards the spiritual life had made him discover, beyond that outward roughness which repelled him, the beauty of Gothic. At the *Maison de l'Œuvre* he made drawings after 'models from a period considered as barbarous—and which I was the first to consider so—yet filled with what distinguishes the finest works of art.' This freed him from his 'last chains', and he saw that 'the beautiful is everywhere . . . not only does every man see it, but every man must absolutely render it in his own way.'

Delacroix was now to devote himself, as far as health allowed, to the Chapel of the Holy Angels, and he withdrew still more from social life. A note made in 1854 shows how much he was changing: 'Youth can disperse his energies among all the emotions: the treasure narrows with age.'

The Exposition Universelle, which opened in May 1855 and replaced the Salon of that year, enabled him to present to the public some forty pictures whose dates were spread out over his whole career. He received the Grande Médaille d'Honneur and was thus placed on the same level as Ingres, the two being recognized as the two masters of the French School. At last he was obtaining the acceptance of the public and of the critics, and the State joined in by making him a Commander of the Légion d'Honneur. Only the Académie des Beaux-Arts, tenacious and obstinate but exhausted in its resistance, still tried to ignore him: after another year's delay it elected him as a member, on 10 January 1857. Delacroix, it will be remembered, had stood for election eight times, and the Institut, with the conviction that would be proper to a wise discernment, had unfailingly passed over him in favour of men whose resounding names have since fallen into a complete and justified oblivion. 'The dust of the battle has settled,' wrote Gautier at the time of the Exposition Universelle, 'and the master, who has long been treated as a madman, appears in the brightness of a serene glory that is henceforth indisputable.'

The fight against men was over. (Though even at the beginning of 1853, Delacroix could still say—according to Silvestre, who was with him at the Duchess of Orleans' reception: 'For thirty years I have been delivered to the wild beasts.') The fight against the passions was also over, and Delacroix could put to himself the question: 'Ought this strange disharmony between the power of the mind, brought by age, and the weakening of the body, also resulting from age, be seen by us as a warning that it is chiefly towards the things of the mind that we must turn when the senses and the body fail us?'[46] One fight remained for him to face, the fight for which he had been for some time preparing instinctively and was now ready: the wrestling with the angel. This was the theme he was to develop in his paintings in Saint-Sulpice. The battles he had waged during his life are summed up in that between the Angel and *Heliodorus*, in which earthly appetites collapse, spilling their treasures and adornments, under the well-aimed and implacable blows of the celestial envoys. They are summed up also in the painting of *Saint Michael overthrowing the Devil* and his ally the serpent amid a profusion of victims and corpses. With the *Heliodorus* is fulfilled the renunciation adumbrated by the beaten Sardanapalus, and with the *Saint Michael* the rise of Apollo and his radiance dispersing the darkness.

There remains Jacob. He had set out with all his caravan on his earthly business, and was taking with him the presents with which he hoped to appease the anger of Esau. But there has appeared 'a man'; and Jacob, to meet him, has withdrawn from all his people, who are going on their way in the midst of dust, haste and agitation. He has gone into the forest, to a place where there is nothing but earth, trees and stream. In this solitude he has come face to face with the stranger, who 'begins an obstinate struggle with him'. With all his human strength Jacob has charged like a bull his unknown adversary, in the murmuring quiet spread by nature about him. All he has been able to do is to force him back one step.

What is the meaning of this mysterious struggle? In his note on the picture Delacroix merely says that it is 'regarded by the Scriptures as an emblem of the trials God sometimes sends to his elect'. Barrès felt that the perpetual combat which had been the motive power of Delacroix's life found its fulfilment and meaning in this picture: Jacob 'is battling as, in Delacroix's youth, his Saint Louis, his King John and his Count Baudoin had brandished their swords and raised their oriflammes. Charles the Bold, above all!' But it 'is not enough to enter Constantinople' with the *Crusaders*; 'it is necessary to set out for Jerusalem'. The 'world of sumptuous and romantic dreams' was past and done with: Sardanapalus had been aware of this already, but 'Jacob has passed over... youth, glory, love, temerity of heart, no longer count for him. . . . In this solitude, in this solemn Idumean night, he has cast away his cloak and is wrestling naked.' Yet Barrès still does not see far enough. The struggle Jacob is waging is not that of work and creation; nor is it now the struggle for glory: Delacroix was near his end, he was in search of something beyond celebrity and desired, as Goethe before him, to create works 'which take us a step forward, which make us greater and enrich us spiritually.'

All through his life Delacroix had moved forwards in the forest; through the thick undergrowth he had 'cut himself a path' (to quote Barrès again), and, as in the old legends, he had overcome the obstacle. At the end of the path he had found the gate, and when it shut behind him it shut off for ever the region in which his life had moved. On to what did it open? It was guarded by the angel, and it was 'the gate of the invisible'. Barrès touches upon the essential: 'The supreme greatness is to conquer the angel, to extract from him his secret.' But the angel will refuse even to tell his name. For the Bible says that when Jacob asked him: 'Tell me, I pray thee, thy name,' the angel replied: 'Wherefore is it that thou dost ask after my name?' And the Bible goes on: 'And he blessed him there.'

Human intelligence is there with Jacob, who with all his strength and in the pride of his muscles is rushing at the angel, hoping to force his way. But the angel, unmoved, will neither withdraw nor speak. The answer he gives is no doubt the one suggested by Delacroix in his *Journal* on 4 June 1824: 'Nature is an impenetrable veil'—and yet he blesses Jacob. They have left the road, they have gone apart into the solitude, in the midst of the enormous forces of nature ceaselessly begun again and wasted, indifferent to the transient form they take. And there Jacob has learnt that the object of the struggle is not to free the opening towards a secret, for to him this will remain unknowable; nor is it even to obtain the name of the intermediary whom he has seen face to face and fought hand to hand, for perhaps that intermediary has no name: the object of the struggle is to have tried to gain both these things. This passionate effort and this will and hope to surpass oneself were, by themselves, enough to make life worthwhile. They are the nobility and the greatness—that nobility which Delacroix had already been seeking in Dandyism, that greatness for whose sake, following Stendhal's unforgettable advice, he had 'neglected nothing'. For the angel has only recoiled one step, and even though behind him there is nothing to which he is defending the access, that one step will have been enough.

The rest of nature and the other living creatures are following the road marked out for them; they flow along it as a stream flows from its source to its mouth, where it loses itself and is ready to begin again, water's perpetual cycle. But man can do more—get out of the rut assigned to him and, having done so, attack the enigma in single combat and force it back one step, even though into emptiness. This step, even if useless, above all if useless, justifies the man who, outside the mechanical order of things and separate from the caravans hastening towards their own happiness, has striven to open up a direction that is his free choice, with what is perhaps an intuition of his true end.

Of this direction Delacroix had been aware ever since, renouncing the vain earthbound antagonisms of for and against, he had looked up towards the height —towards the opening of the underground caverns, towards the top of the staircase behind Christ at *Emmaus*, towards the uppermost branches pushed upwards by the ancient, twisted, patient oaks whose roots are in the same ground that the Angel and Jacob hammer with their feet as they measure their strength against each other.

On 31 January 1860 Delacroix returned to the problem of an after-life. He imagined some person who 'had difficulty in persuading himself that what is called soul . . . can continue to be that thing which he knows, whose existence he cannot doubt, when its dwelling-place, formed of bones and flesh, with the blood circulating in it and the nerves functioning, had ceased to be . . . that laboratory of life which sustains itself in the midst of contrary elements, through so many accidents and vicissitudes.' And so he 'wondered sadly where this immortal soul could have obtained the privilege of being alone immortal in the midst of everything that we see.'

Perhaps Delacroix had need of this supreme disinterestedness in order that the wrestling with the Angel should not have its origin merely in the desire to assure his immortality—that of his personal existence or that of his work; for he said, also, that the breath of inspiration, which gives life to a picture and makes it beautiful by bringing in to it 'a part of the genius of its author', is 'not able to preserve him from destruction.' Through Dandyism Delacroix had learnt that inner culture which was capable of carrying him to the full extent of himself. By the effort of his creative work, by that highest of struggles, he has made it possible for man to take a step forward in the direction he has chosen, and so to increase in the world the richness which his spirit introduces there.

Delacroix could now stop and wait for the death which was approaching. The angel was not again to recoil a step under his pressure. And yet he was to meet the angel once more—in 1863, in what was perhaps his last painting, his *Tobias*. In order to cure his father of blindness, Tobias has killed the monstrous fish which he has encountered in his journey and, following the advice of his travelling companion, a stranger, he has taken out its heart, gall and liver. These he is to keep, and it is by using them, and by continence and prayer, that he will escape unharmed from the demon who has killed all his wife's former husbands, and will restore his father's sight. Delacroix's imagination pondered over the mysterious story as his end drew near. He shows Tobias at the moment at which, bending over the fish and drawing out its entrails, he listens to the advice of his companion, who is touching him on the shoulder. Tobias is turning to look up at him. It is only when everything has been accomplished that he will know that this companion was the angel.

Angel with whom one wrestles, aiding and guardian angel, always refusing to tell his name—Rembrandt also knew him, and meditated many times over this story of Tobias.

And perhaps the truth is that Rembrandt and Delacroix are the two artists who have seen the angel most clearly, and can best help us to discover him with our inner gaze.

## NOTES ON THE PLATES TO CHAPTER IX

*Wild beasts*

There seems to have been something of the wild beast in Delacroix's deep, instinctive nature—a mixture of nervous quickness, feverishness and even a cruel greed, which was even noticeable in his facial expression and emerges in his passion for studying lions and tigers (pls 323, 324).

*323 Animal Studies. Private collection.*

*324 Study for the lithograph 'Royal Tiger', 1829 . Deroch Collection.*

*Fighting*

The theme of physical struggle, letting loose all the latent forces of the combatants, including the rage to kill, is a fundamental one with Delacroix. He shows the wild beast at grips with its prey (pls 333, 334), wild beast with wild beast (pl 332), wild beast with man (pl 330) and man with man. The horse adds its nervous energy to these frantic encounters (pls 326, 327, XLVII), which reached their climax in the whirlwind of the great *Hunts* (pl XLVIII). There is a spontaneous symbolism in the fact that the first of his teams of horses is the one that draws the chariot of Mars, the god of war (pl 328)—it came long before that of *Apollo* (pl 305). And human destiny is carried away by the blind fury of the passions, like *Mazeppa* bound to a wild horse's back (pl 329).

*325 Sketch for the 'Arab on Horseback attacked by a Lion'. The Fogg Art Museum, Cambridge, Mass.*

*326 Sketch or the 'Fight of the Gaiour and the Pasha' (1835 version). Louvre, Paris.*

*327 Sketch for the 'Fight of the Gaiour and the Pasha' (1827 version). Cabinet des Dessins, Louvre.*

*328 Study for the God Mars accompanied by Fame, Fear and Death, c. 1820-23 Cabinet des Dessins, Louvre, Paris.*

*329 Sketch for 'Mazeppa', 1828. Atheneum, Helsinki.*

*330 Lion attacking an Arab. G. Aubry Collection, Paris.*

*331 Lioness and Lion in a Cavern. The Montreal Museum of Fine Arts, Montreal.*

*332 Study for 'Fight between a Lion and a Tiger', 1856. Cabinet des Dessins, Louvre, Paris.*

*333 Lion devouring a Rabbit, 1856. Louvre, Paris.*

*334 Horse attacked by a Lioness, 1840. Louvre, Paris.*

*Despair with fate* Delacroix's spontaneous choice of subjects shows how he was haunted by the human predicament, in which the highest values are exposed to hatred and to madness, as in his *Tasso* (pl 335), or to neglect and desertion, as in his *Christ in the Garden of Gethsemane* (pls 181, 182, 336). His *Hamlet* (pl 242) and his *Faust* (pl 148) contemplate the mystery of the skull, and his *Michelangelo* (pl 180) meditates on the vanity of genius.

*335 Tasso in the Madhouse, 1824. Private collection.*

*336 Christ in the Garden of Gethsemane. Rijksmuseum, Amsterdam.*

*The spirit of evil* Preoccupied as he was by the negative presence of evil, Delacroix was fond, in accordance with romantic taste, of showing the Devil (pl 337) by the side of *Faust*, the Witches (pl 339) with *Macbeth*. And the harmless intoxication of the New Year's Eve celebrations of his youth (pl 338) awakened an obsession with vice and with the demonic.

*337 Sketch for the lithograph of Faust. Musée de Bayonne.*

*338 New Year's Eve, 1820-21. Louvre, Paris.*

*339 Macbeth and the Witches, 1825. Lithograph.*

*The double* By the side of his heroes Delacroix often depicts, as a counterpart to the demon, the apparition of the inspiring genius (pl 341) or conscience (pl 340). The Socratic *daemon* precedes the advent of the angel.

*340 The Connétable de Bourbon and his Conscience, 1835. G. Aubry Collection, Paris.*

*341 Sketch for the 'Emperor Justinian composing the Institutes', 1826. Musée des Arts Décoratifs, Paris.*

*The theme of the boat* Human fate at the mercy of elemental forces soon finds embodiment in the theme of the boat. The boat in the *Dante and Virgil* (1822, pl II) floats in the Inferno; later, in the 1839 *Don Juan*, the boat seems irretrievably lost in the infinite (pl XXVI), and yet the human being, blinded by his passions and his chains, does not suspect its presence, but goes on with his bitter struggle for life (pl 343), still depicted by Delacroix in 1847. But in 1853, in the midst of the tempest that menaces the boat, there arises divine calm and light, with

*Christ on the Lake of Genesareth* (pls 344 and XLI). In 1862 the boat appears once more: dismasted and broken, it runs upon an unknown shore (pl 345).

342 *Study for the 'Shipwreck of Don Juan', 1839. The Victoria and Albert Museum, London.*

343 *Castaways in a Ship's Boat, 1847. Pushkin Museum, Moscow.*

344 *Christ on the Lake of Genesareth, 1853. Private collection, Zurich.*

345 *Shipwreck on the Coast, 1862. Private collection, Zurich.*

*The wild beast hunts*

The theme is frequent in Delacroix's work. It allowed him to expand upon his memories of Rubens and of Morocco; and in it Delacroix, vibrating in unison with romanticism (pl 346), could express his appetite for extreme violence. It often leads him back (pls 348) to the whirling composition which he imagined for the great *Lion Hunt* in Bordeaux (pls 347, XLVIII), which has been partially destroyed by fire.

346 BOULANGER: *Attack by a Tiger. Lithograph.*

347 *Lion Hunt, 1855. Musée des Beaux-Arts, Bordeaux.*

348 *Lion Hunt, 1861. The Art Institute, Chicago.*

349 *Tiger Hunt (detail), 1854. Louvre, Paris.*

*The serpent*

Another immemorial symbol of evil, the serpent, recurs frequently in Delacroix's pictures: as he grew older and developed, he came to celebrate its extrusion. The Archangel nails it to the ground with Satan (pl 352). Already (pl 350) the dead Christ triumphed over it by simple confrontation. Apollo pierces it with his arrows (pl 304), and the royal and powerful lion (pl 351) crushed it. Sometimes, under the lion's claw (pl 353) or under Saint George's lance (pl 354), it changes into its other self, the dragon.

350 *Crucifixion. Private collection.*

351 *The Lion and the Serpent, 1856.*

352 *Saint Michael overthrowing the Devil, 1861. Ceiling. Chapel of the Holy Angels, Church of Saint-Sulpice, Paris.*

353 *Lion with a Reptile (detail), 1863. Kunsthalle, Hamburg.*

354 *Sketch of 'Saint George attacking the Serpent'. Below: a dragon. Cabinet des Dessins, Louvre.*

*Woman—victim*

All Delacroix's themes obey the same principle of development, thus showing that it is the artist's own. From the *Massacre at Chios* (pl III) to the *Crusaders* (pl 263), woman was the frail and pathetic victim of men (pls 355, LI) or of monstrous beasts (pl 356); but towards 1845 she becomes the Princess, who is freed by the Hero from the dragon (pls 357, XLIX) or from hell. Sometimes, as in the medieval miniatures, he breaks down the gates of the castle where she is shut up (pl L). Here again we have the triumph of the soul over chains and monsters.

355 *Abduction of Arab Woman by African Pirates, 1852. Louvre, Paris.*

356 *Study of woman and crocodiles. Cabinet des Dessins, Louvre, Paris.*

357 *Perseus and Andromeda, 1847. Collection Arthur Tooth & Sons, London.*

358 *Hercules and Alcestis, 1862. The Phillips Collection, Washington.*

*'Daniel in the Lions' Den'* In the 1849 picture (pl 361) Daniel, thrown into the pit with the wild beasts, makes them recoil by his divine light. In the 1853 picture (pl 362) the angel comes to his aid. While Delacroix drew from his instinctive poetic feeling the deep meaning of his chosen theme, he left his memory free to help him with its unconscious reminders of images seen by him, perhaps in books he had looked through as a child (pl 359), perhaps in the engravings of the masters which he loved to consult (pl 360).

359 N. DE LAUNAY: *The Fatal Revenge of Jealousy. Engraving after Marillier. (Illustration for the 'Romances', Berquin, 1776).*

360 RUBENS: *Daniel in the Lions' Den. Engraving by Weenix. Cabinet des Dessins, Louvre, Paris.*

361 *Daniel in the Lions' Den, 1849. Musée Fabre, Montpellier.*

362 *Daniel in the Lions' Den, 1853. Private collection.*

*The mysterious stairway* Delacroix's compositions came to make more and more of the high and low. In his *Pietà* of 1848 (pl 363) Christ lies rigid and horizontal at the bottom of the path that winds vertically towards Calvary; in 1859 the descent continues below the level of the earth, away from the light of day (pl 366); but in 1853 the stairway goes up towards that light of day, behind Christ who reveals his brightness at the *Supper at Emmaus* (pl 365). What happens above and below the mysterious staircase forming the background to the musings of Rembrandt's *Philosopher* (pl 364)?

363 *Pietà, 1848. Museum of Fine Arts, Boston.*

364 REMBRANDT: *The Philosopher. Louvre, Paris.*

365 *The Supper at Emmaus, 1853. Brooklyn Museum, Brooklyn.*

366 *The Entombment, 1859. Collection Antonio Santamarina, Buenos-Aires.*

*Charity* Over the death and suffering that dominated the earlier part of Delacroix's work, pity and love gradually cast their influence. This was hardly the case until 1848, when his Apollo triumphed over the Serpent and his Roger freed Angelica. After that, we have *Lélia* lamenting over the dead body of her lover in the cave (pl 367), the *Good Samaritan* of 1850 gently lifting the wounded man, and another version in 1852 (pl 369); and in 1850 there is Angelica tenderly supporting another wounded man, *Medoro* (pl 370). Van Gogh was not mistaken in his recognition of Delacroix's soul, and was led to copy both his 1850 *Good Samaritan* and the *Pietà* (pl 368), which was painted in the same year.

*367 Lélia, 1848. Musée Carnavalet, Paris.*

*368 Pietà, 1850.*

*369 The Good Samaritan, 1852. The Victoria and Albert Museum, London.*

*370 Study for 'Angelica and the Wounded Medoro', 1850. Formerly (1930) Frau Emil Staub Collection.*

*Wrestling with the angel*

In Delacroix's last works the angel becomes one of the protagonists: it is he that is subjected to *Jacob's* furious assault (pl 371), and it is he that, in the last picture Delacroix painted, guides *Tobias*, saving him from the demon and enabling him to catch the miraculous fish whose bile could make blind eyes again see the light.

*371 Jacob wrestling with the Angel, 1856-61 (detail). Chapel of the Holy Angels, Church of Saint-Sulpice, Paris.*

323

324

325

326

327

328

329

330

331

332

333

334

335

336

337

338

339

342

343

344

345

346

347

348

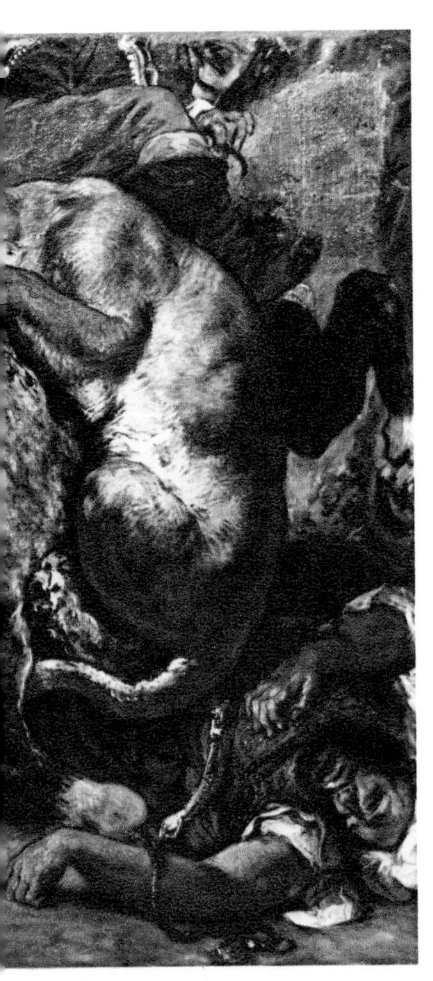

349

350

351

352

353

354

355

356

357

358

359

361

360

362

363

364

365

366

367

368

369

370

# NOTES ON THE TEXT

## I THIS WAS A MAN

1 Maxime du Camp, *Souvenirs littéraires.*

2 *L'Œuvre et la vie d'Eugène Delacroix* in Baudelaire: '*Curiosités esthétiques*', *Œuvres.* Ed. de la Pléiade, p. 866.

3 *Journal,* 20 February 1852. Delacroix's *Journal* has a secure place in French literature, in a line that runs from Montaigne to André Gide. Begun on 3 September 1822, it was unfortunately interrupted for twenty-three years, from 1824 to 1847, but was then resumed and continued almost to the painter's death. The many articles which he wrote on question of aesthetics and on individual artists also bear witness to his value as a writer.

4 Chapter XXV.

5 IV, p. 355.

6 Maxime du Camp, *Souvenirs littéraires,* XII, *Ateliers de peintres.* (The chapter on Delacroix appeared in the *Revue des Deux Mondes* for 15 July, 1882.)

7 Baudelaire, '*Curiosités esthétiques*', *Œuvres.* Ed. de la Pléiade, p. 860.

8 The studio was in fact rented from the end of October 1844, but the redecoration and removals delayed occupation for several months. Meanwhile Delacroix put up at 29 rue de La Rochefoucauld. In April 1847 Madame de Forget went to live in this same street, at no 19.

9 Baudelaire, *op. cit.,* p. 864.

10 *Histoire du Romantisme,* p. 203.

11 Published in 1929, long after his death, by Joubin.

12 The first part of this letter has been found by M. Alfred Dupont.

13 These letters were published in 1954 by their discoverer, M. Alfred Dupont, to whom I am indebted for allowing me to read them prior to publication. See *Eugène Delacroix, Lettres intimes,* Gallimard, 1954.

14 Despite Raymond Escholier's valuable *Delacroix et les Femmes* much still remains to be discovered and much needs correction concerning Delacroix's relationships with women. To undertake such a study here would lead us too far from the man whom we seek through his work. The unpublished material collected by M. Roger Leybold and M. Camille Bernard deserves to be given book form, and we look forward to such an enterprise.
It seems certain, as M. Roger Leybold has shown, that '*la Cara*' was the wife of the '*bon général*', Count de Coëtlosquet. Delacroix mentions him in his *Journal,* and when in his *Correspondence* he speaks of the 'inhabitants of the rue Saint Dominique', or the 'Dominicans', he is referring to their household. The General was fifteen years older than Delacroix, and died in 1836. He was Director of Staff at the Ministry of War, and knew Delacroix through Soulier. He commissioned *Still Life with Lobsters* and the question of the weapons in the picture is raised on several occasions. In one of these unpublished letters, *la Cara* writes in formal tones that 'the General wishes you to return his firearms'.

15 It has always been said that Madame Dalton disappeared from Delacroix's life after she went to Algeria in 1839, but M. Roger Leybold has a letter from Delacroix dated 8th March 1840 which proves that he was still in touch with her. At this time she had returned to Paris and was living at the 'Hotel Voltaire, quai Voltaire, 17', which was close to Delacroix's studio and lodgings of some ten years later, at no. 15. George Sand lived nearby at no. 19.

16 We know that in 1839, when Mme Dalton left for Algeria, Delacroix went in September to Belgium with Elisabeth Boulanger, and much has been written of their flight together, and of the abrupt departure of this lady, supposedly leaving him angry and distressed. The facts are otherwise. M. Camille Bernard has a brief diary of the journey kept by Delacroix: he left on 4 September and was joined by Elisa two days later. Their sudden departure together is pure fiction. The presence of a third person, a woman, shows that the lovers had provided themselves with a chaperone as protection against accusations of indiscretion. It was doubtless on this same account that on 20 September, after accompanying Delacroix to the

seaside, to Bruges and Antwerp, Elisa left him to continue his journey to The Hague and Rotterdam without her. Letters in the possession of M. Leybold show that two months later, on 26 November, Elisa wrote to Delacroix in the most affectionate terms. This letter, among others, deserves to be quoted.

It is addressed to Delacroix at 17 rue des Marais-Saint-Germain, and is postmarked 26 November 1839.

'Friend and confidant of my soul, why may I not spend these evenings with you when the heart, spirit, mind, and even more, our silences contribute everything. What joy there is in the repose of two beings who have filled their day well, who are physically tired but whose spirits are exalted by what they have created. What happiness there is in being able to tell each other: I am contented, or not contented, with my day, and even greater happiness in our being able to understand one another.

Yesterday I missed one of these delightful evenings and I can't forgive myself for it. I returned at nine o'clock. I could have come back sooner, you could have come, and we would have been peaceful. I am furious with myself for only thinking of it when I was returning. I threw myself back upon my sketchbook, on my love and on the blue bed of delight. I thought of what I had been speaking of all evening. I had hung a very pretty cross from my chatelaine and everyone commented on it, and I played with the word and thought of the object, for the meaning is you, the object that occupies me, that vexes me, that makes me happy, that makes me sad, that fills me, makes me brim over with happiness. Someone is ringing. I leave you with my love...

If tomorrow I am not with you at 5 o'clock, it's understood you will be at the School of Medicine office at 5.30.'

An unpublished letter from Delacroix of 10 July 1846 (from Champrosay) to M. Cavé is extremely interesting: it says, in effect, that Delacroix owed the rosette of the Légion d'Honneur to him—and to Mme Cavé.

17 It seems necessary to re-clarify the relationship between Jenny Le Guillou and Delacroix, since the centenary of Delacroix's death has provided an opportunity for the revival of a legend long ago discredited.

Jenny was born in 1801 and was of humble Breton stock. It was Madame Pierret who found her for Delacroix (in about 1835-7), wishing to help her husband's friend with the management of his bachelor household. Jenny gradually came to reign supreme over it, with the other servants under her authority. As Léon Riesener has remarked, she was as fiercely devoted to Delacroix—to his work, his health—as she was jealous of outside influences on him. For one reason or another she tried to ward off intruders—and also too-engrossing friends. The Pierrets, with whom Delacroix had for long been in the habit of spending his free evenings, were the first victims of this exclusion. To Delacroix's intimates, this peasant woman with her unprepossessing person never appeared to be more than a sort of housekeeper-governess, whose absolute devotion to him touched Delacroix, winning his increasing trust and friendship. The absurd story that Jenny was Delacroix's mistress arose from a piece of malicious gossip by Gustave Lassalle-Bordes, his pupil and collaborator, dismissed by him after 1847. (Lassalle-Bordes posed as the principal author of the decorative painting in the library of the Chambre, with which he had assisted.) But Jenny must not be confused with Delacroix's sister's maid, Caroline, with whom he had been in love in 1819. This girl had been dismissed after their love affair and subsequently found refuge with the Pierret family. It would be strange had Pierret kept her with them from his youth and after his marriage for more than a quarter of a century, only to give her up to Delacroix at the end. Besides, Jenny had never been called Caroline, but was Jeanne-Marie in full. And finally, of course, one cannot see Delacroix renewing the liaison after a lapse of twenty-six years or more.

Raymond Escholier deals in his *Delacroix* (1927, Vol. II, p. 211 f.) with this malicious story, which went so far as to see in Delacroix's portrait of Jenny's daughter a picture of his own child. (Escholier even casts doubt on the attribution of this picture to Delacroix, but it is nevertheless by his hand, although he was obviously not greatly inspired by the uncomely face.) It is only necessary to turn to Escholier to discredit the whole tale.

18 Baudelaire, *'Curiosités esthétiques'*, *Œuvres*. Ed. de la Pléiade, p. 865.

19 Baudelaire, *L'Œuvre et la vie d'Eugène Delacroix*, *Œuvres*. Ed. de la Pléiade, p. 869.

20 Delacroix, *Œuvres littéraires*. Ed. Crès, Book II, p. 134.

21 *Journal*, 9 June 1823.

22 Raymond Escholier, *Eugène Delacroix et sa 'consolatrice'*. Ed. Colin, 1932.

23 It was long thought that Madame de Forget's letters in reply to Delacroix had disappeared. They had in fact been preserved: some were given by Count Bernard de Féligonde to M. Raymond Escholier, who published them in an Appendix to his *Delacroix et les femmes* (Arthème Fayard, 1963); others are in the hands of M. Leybold, a noted collector, to whom I am most grateful for having allowed me to study them and to publish two of them. See Appendix, p. 528 *f*.

24 In an article in *Figaro* for 16 September 1932.

25 Book III, p. 440.

26 *Œuvres littéraires*. Ed. Crès, Book I, p. 124.

27 Book IV, p. 356.

28 'The day before yesterday was the anniversary of my beloved mother's death. On that day I began to keep

my diary. May her shade be present when I write, and may nothing in this diary make her blush for her son!'

29 How much I regret not having persuaded the Louvre to buy this portrait, nearly fifteen years ago, in spite of my urgent representation before the Conseil des Musées!

30 The whole passage (*Journal*, 16 May 1853) is well worth reading.

31 Baudelaire, '*Curiosités esthétiques*', *Œuvres*. Ed. de la Pléiade, p. 861.

32 Letter to Varcollier, 7 July 1852.

33 To George Sand, 25 November 1860.

34 It is as if Delacroix, in some strange way, opened the path which French spiritual philosophy was soon to follow: in particular that of Jules Lagneau (1851-1894), who defined God as an inner force, which we perceive in our demand for 'values', or again that of Léon Brunschvicq (1869-1944), which identifies God with our conscience and spirit.

35 Letter to Theo, Cuesmes, July 1880 (no. 133). *The Complete Letters of Vincent van Gogh*, Thames and Hudson, London; New York Graphic Society, 1958.

36 Newgate, London, 1871.

37 Baudelaire, *Journaux intimes*, *Fusées* I, *Œuvres*. Ed. de la Pléiade, p. 1181.

38 Baudelaire, '*Mon cœur mis à nu*', XLVI, p. 1212.

39 *Œuvres littéraires*, Ed. Crès, Book I, p. 119.

40 *Journal*, 1 July 1854.

41 *Journal*, 5 September 1847.

42 Piron, *Eugène Delacroix, sa vie et ses œuvres*. Ed. Jules Claye, 1865, p. 469.

43 Delacroix, *Œuvres littéraires*. Ed. Crès, Book I, p. 119.

44 *Journal*, 25 February 1857.

45 To Soulier, 14 [December 1858?].

## II STARTING POINTS

1 *Journal*, 22 May 1854.

2 Still unpublished.

3 The operation took place on 14 September 1797. The information in the brochure was repeated in the *Moniteur Universel* of 13 April 1798. Eugène was born on 26 April.

4 The date of Eugène's conception was in July, at the beginning of August or later, and even if Charles Delacroix was in Paris at that time he was clearly impotent then.

5 M. Paul Loppin, honorary Councillor to the Cour de Cassation and author of an article on Charles Delacroix has also compiled an interesting study on the riddle of the birth of Eugène Delacroix, in which he resolutely sides with those opposed to the view that the birth was illegitimate. I am grateful to him for having let me read it. Although he succeeds in correcting certain mis-statements or instances of loose thinking that have helped to gain credence for the Talleyrand hypothesis, he is forced to suppose that Delacroix was conceived a very short time after the operation on his father and was born prematurely, after barely seven months: this new hypothesis is at least as arbitrary as the other and has no factual or documentary support. Nonetheless M. Loppin adduces one argument of some weight in favour of his conviction: how, he asks, is it conceivable that Charles Delacroix, whose firm moral principles were recognised by his contemporaries and praised by Eugène, could have accepted in his home, and brought up with a kindness that is well attested, a child known by him to be the offspring of adultery? or that he should not have cast off his wife if her infidelity to him was notorious? To this it might be objected that, given the importance of the social proprieties to a man holding high official posts, such conduct might seem the best way of scotching the rumours about his wife; also that, to him, she could plead extenuating circumstances.
Forgiveness of his wife would be in keeping with his generosity of spirit. Why, if M. Loppin's arguments are valid, did not Madame Delacroix bring them forward herself? This might explain the existence—until recently unknown, apart from an allusion by M. Jullian at the sale at the Hôtel Drouot in 1962—of a certain proclamation by Charles Delacroix, signed by himself, his wife and other witnesses (some of their servants) dated 12 November 1797 (19 Brumaire, year VI). This proclamation, on which its owner M. Roger Leybold has prepared a study, records the operation, describes the tumour which was preserved in a specimen jar, and announces the return of the patient to complete health. Perhaps Madame Delacroix thought by this means to forearm herself against possible gossip, and had advised her husband for both their sakes to establish a term which, though short, would not rule out the hypothesis that the coming birth was simply premature. The problem remains obscure.
In the course of his article (see Bibliography p. 542, '*Charles et Eugène Delacroix*', *les grandes figures champenoises*, Pierre Béarn, Paris, 1963), M. Loppin establishes some useful incidental points. Givry-en-Argonne, from which the Delacroix family came, is in Champagne, not (as is sometimes stated) in the Meuse; under the *Ancien Régime* it was a dependency of Sainte-Menehould. Claude Delacroix, Eugène's grandfather, was factor to Louis-Guy Guérapin de Vauréal, Count de Belval, who was Bishop of Rennes and a member of the Académie Française. His son Charles went to Holland about the New Year of 1798 and returned to Paris on 25 May, one month after the birth of Eugène.

6 Letter to Pierret, 20 October 1820.

7 Book III, p. 402.

8 The expression used by Mme Jaubert in her *Souvenirs*.

9 Roger Lacroix was born in 1728, collaborated with the younger Boulle and his brother Simon; he died the year after his great-grandson Eugène was born.

10 Piron, *Eugène Delacroix, sa vie et ses œuvres*, p. 37.

11 *Ibid.*, p. 79.

12 Delacroix's earlier schooling (from 1805) was as a boarder at the lycée at Bordeaux. 'M. Eugène de Lacroix,' then aged seven and in the 'First class', showed his gift for penmanship by gaining an award (4th) for handwriting at the school prize day on 17 September (30 Fructidor, year XIII). This information appears in the city records.

Three years later he entered the lycée in Paris. M. Raymond Schiltz, the headmaster of the Lycée Louis-le-Grand (called the Lycée Impérial when Delacroix was a pupil there) has given me the following information—all, it appears, that is available—from the Lycée archives, and I gratefully acknowledge his kindness.

*Extract from the 'Register of Entries of Pupils: 1 August 1807 to 1 October 1813'.*

DELACROIX Ferdinand, Victor, Eugène,
born 26 April 1798 at Charenton,
entered on 3 October 1806
c/o Mme. his mother, rue de l'Université, no. 114, at the corner of the rue de Bourgogne.
Left on 30 September 1814,
took courses in Humanities, second year, and in Arithmetic (M. Bordière).
Note — Pupil Delacroix, who had notified his intention to leave on 30 September 1814, remained at the Lycée till 30 June 1815.

Awards

| | | |
|---|---|---|
| 1807 | Seventh Class | 4th in Latin Composition<br>4th in Grammar |
| 1808 | Sixth Class | 1st in French Grammar |
| 1810 | Cours Supplémentaire (equivalent to the Fifth at present) | 4th in Greek Translation |
| 1811 | Second Grammar Class (equivalent to the Fourth at present) | 4th in History and Geography |
| 1812 | The Lycée records show nothing for this year; the class notebooks show that in October 1811 he entered on the First Course in Humanities, and spent a second year in this class from 1812-13, which explains the absence of any mention of Delacroix in the awards of 1812. | |
| 1813 | First Course in Humanities (equivalent to the Third at present) | 5th in Latin Translation<br>6th in Greek Translation<br>4th in Drawing |
| 1814 | Second Course in Humanities (equivalent to present Second) | 4th in Greek Translation<br>1st in Drawing |

13 Particularly in *Art and the Spirit of Man*, Book III, p. 386 *f*.

14 Delacroix entered the École des Beaux-Arts in his studio, on 16 March 1816.

15 R. Regamey, *Géricault*, p. 14.

16 This little picture is dated 1821 by Robaut as no. 40 (see note 20 below, concerning Robaut), but this seems impossible to reconcile with its already bold and developed technique. Moreover, Delacroix's face at that time was broader, and more massive, as may be seen from his 1819 self-portrait, engraved by Villot, and from Géricault's portrait of him. The thinner face in the picture under discussion is much more like the pencil drawing by Alexandre Colin from the pastel by Riesener, both of which were done in 1824 when Delacroix had been emaciated by his first attacks of fever. There has been much argument about the identity of the imaginary character whom Delacroix is impersonating. A name 'Raveswood' pencilled on the stretcher was at first thought to mean Ravenswood, the lover of Lucy of Lammermoor; but it was the nickname given to Hippolyte Carrier, the miniaturist to whom Delacroix gave the picture and whom he made one of his executors. Later the costume was thought to indicate Hamlet. It is directly descended from the one in the Spanish portrait, and even the long-hilted sword reappears; but this costume may also well have given Delacroix the idea for the one in which he represented the Prince of Elsinore.

17 Delacroix emphasized: 'When David expressed his great admiration for Rubens' *Crucifixion*, and generally, for his most spirited paintings, was it not because of the resemblance these pictures bore to the antique which he idolized?' (*Œuvres littéraires*. Ed. Crès, Book I, p. 27.)

18 Delestre, *Gros, sa vie et ses ouvrages*, p. 107.

19 *Œuvres littéraires*. Ed. Crès, Book II, p. 230.

20 Alfred Robaut came from Douai. He was the son of a lithographer, Félix Robaut, who was a contemporary of Delacroix, being born in 1799 (a year later). He married the daughter of Constant Dutilleux (1817-1865), a landscape painter who had left Douai for Arras, where he set up business as a printer-lithographer and founded, in 1855, the Société des Amis des Arts. Delacroix became honorary president of this Society at Dutilleux's request in 1861. Dutilleux's other daughter was married

to Charles Desavary, a painter, who took over the business in Arras from his father-in-law in 1860, when the latter went to live in Paris. Dutilleux was exceptionally clear-sighted in artistic matters; he was a fervent admirer of Delacroix, with whom he became friendly in 1839, and of Corot, whom he met in 1847 and of whom he was soon an intimate friend. On 14 February 1863 Delacroix wrote to Desavary asking him to express his gratitude to Dutilleux 'of whom I am very fond, for whom I have the highest possible consideration, and who has given me countless proofs of his affection.' It was in this way that it came about that, for a while in 1846, there was a question of Delacroix being commissioned to paint the dome of Arras cathedral, which had been finished in 1834. In 1859 Dutilleux again intervened to persuade the Arras Museum to buy Delacroix's *Saint Stephen*.

Alfred Robaut inherited his father-in-law's admirations and friendships, and produced two books that were epoch-making in the history of art: these were attempts at a complete inventory, in chronological order, of the works, first of Delacroix, then of Corot. Each picture was represented by a drawing on a reduced scale, made with the *camera obscura*. The *Delacroix* appeared in 1885 and the *Corot* in 1905 (two years before Robaut died). To carry out the second enterprise, he even went to live in Paris in 1870, to be near the aged Corot, and in 1872 transported the painter's studio to Arras, in order to have it photographed by Desavary. The Cabinet des Estampes of the Bibliothèque Nationale contains notes and other material by Robaut on both Delacroix and Corot. On Robaut's *L'Œuvre complet d'Eugène Delacroix*, see Bibliography, p. 539.

21 Delacroix, *Œuvres littéraires*, Book I, p. 65.

22 Supplement to *Journal*, Book III, p. 405.

23 Delacroix, *Œuvres littéraires*, Book I, p. 114.

24 'esthetica': the realm of feeling as opposed to that of intellect.

## III BEGINNING OF A CAREER

1 A man of fashion at the time of the Directoire.

2 Michel Florisoone, '*Comment Delacroix a-t-il connu les "Caprices" de Goya?*' *Bulletin de la Société de l'Histoire de l'Art français*, 1958, pp. 131-144.

3 It will be remembered that the notes in Robaut, *L'Œuvre complet d'Eugène Delacroix*, are by Ernest Chesnau, art critic.

4 Piron, *Eugène Delacroix, sa vie et ses œuvres*, p. 61.

5 This detail seems to be a slip of the memory, for Delacroix did not leave the rue de l'Université for the rue de la Planche until April 1820, and the *Radeau de la Médus* was sent to the 1819 Salon.

6 Piron, *op. cit.*, p. 55.

7 Piron, *op. cit.*, p. 61.

8 *Journal*, 5 March 1857.

9 *Journal*, 5 March 1857.

10 *Journal*, 11 April 1824.

11 Piron, *op. cit.*, p. 57.

12 Delestre, *Gros*, p. 356.

13 Piron, *op. cit.*, p. 63.

14 Robaut no. 3.

15 The exhibition was held in the Orangerie of the Louvre.

16 'The entry in the *Journal* for 15 December 1847 reports an example. There is also a letter from Auguste addressed, in about 1830-35 to: 'Monsieur E. La Croix, quay Voltaire, No. 15', which says: 'Please be so kind, Monsieur, as to lend me a sketch by Bonnington, I will give it back to you almost at once. *Recevez, je vous prie, l'expression du plus sincère attachement.*' Delacroix, who was Carle Vernet's successor at the Quai Voltaire studio, and who, along with Auguste and Géricault, shared Vernet's passion for horses, drew a sketch of one in lithograph chalk on the back of this letter: it was found among his papers at his death.

17 I myself remember pointing out one of them to that great collector, Doctor Viau, who possessed a *Negress mounting a Horse* from the Chéramy Collection, attributed to Delacroix—a picture which even Raymond Escholier has reproduced with its false attribution (Volume II, p. 129). He has done the same (Volume II, p. 60) with two profiles of Arabs. And again, quite recently I tried without success to rectify the same error in the case of a picture acquired by a museum in Great Britain under the name of Delacroix.

18 Joubin believes that Robaut's dating of this picture in 1860 (no. 1407) is wrong. In fact the sketch for the composition and the detail of the bottom right hand corner, both in the collection of M. Jacques Dupont, seem to be a later version of an idea of Delacroix's from before the *Massacres at Chios*.

19 Louvre, R.F. 9219.

20 Louvre, R.F. 9203.

21 Baudelaire, '*Curiosités esthétiques*', *Œuvres*. Ed. de la Pléiade, p. 852.

22 *Burlington Magazine*, LXII. Jan.-June, 1933, pp. 285 *f.*

23 *Journal of the Warburg and Courtauld Institutes*, 1957, Volume XX, Nos. 1-2.

24 The lesson of the Dutch painters had already been brought back to France by certain landscape artists, such as Georges Michel who passed it on to Rousseau and the Fontainebleau School. But Delacroix seems not to have known the work of this painter, who was a more or less solitary bohemian.

25 Supplement to the *Journal*, 23 September [1846?], p. 451.

26 Delacroix, *Œuvres littéraires*, Book I, p. 64.

27 *Journal*, 11 December 1855.

28 This subject is discussed more fully in Chapter VIII, p. 393 *f*.

## IV IMPETUS AND RELAPSE

1 *Journal*, 12 October 1854.

2 *Journal*, 8 October 1822.

3 *Journal*, 26 January 1824.

4 Chapter VIII.

5 Piron, *Eugène Delacroix, sa vie et ses œuvres*, p. 70.

6 Piron, *op. cit.*, p. 71.

7 1826. Robaut no. 193.

8 I have had an opportunity to study this picture at the 1963 Delacroix Exhibition at Bordeaux, and in my opinion the attribution to Bonington is incorrect. Although it shows his direct influence, it appears to be the work of a French artist, and one thinks of a painter such as Baron Schwiter, who was a friend of both Delacroix and Bonington and who had been to Venice. However we know little of Schwiter's work.

9 *Journal*, 15 March 1858.

10 Henry de La Madelène, article in the *Nouvelle Revue de Paris*, 1 September 1864.

11 Delacroix adds: 'He has a magnificent Watteau.' Joubin (in his note in the *Journal*, 3 April 1847) says the picture in question is certainly '*Plaisirs du Bal* . . . now in the Wallace Collection, London.' The matter is less simple: the picture known by that title is in the Dulwich College Art Gallery, to which it was presented in 1811 by Sir Francis Bourgeois; there was an engraving of it by Scotin, as Joubin says. The Wallace Collection has a copy of it by Pater which was in fact bought from Morny. But it is more likely that the picture acclaimed by Delacroix was one of the two Watteau masterpieces that went from the Morny Collection to the Marquess of Hertford's collection, which he passed on to Wallace. These were the *Divertissements champêtres* and *Les Champs-Élysées*, which at the Morny sale in London in 1848 fetched the sums of £1,050 and £945 respectively, enormous at the time. Morny had, however, other pictures by Watteau, which came up at later sales, in 1852 and 1865; at the 1865 sale Wallace bought for 31,000 francs the *Rendez-vous de Chasse*, which had been included in the 1852 sale and then withdrawn.

12 *Journal*, 11 January 1857.

13 *Journal*, 26 April 1824.

14 In the second edition of the *Journal* the editor André Joubin added the notes made by Delacroix during his Moroccan journey (January to June 1832).

15 He is alluding to the small picture in the manner of Bonington which he painted for his amusement at about the same time.

16 Vincent van Gogh, letter to Theo [Cuesmes] July 1880 (no. 133). *The Complete Letters of Vincent Van Gogh*, 3 vols. Thames and Hudson, London; New York Graphic Society, 1958.

17 Baudelaire, *Fleurs du Mal, Œuvres*. Ed. de la Pléiade, p. 84.

18 The picture has the same title as Byron's tragedy, published in 1821 and dedicated to Goethe.

19 He was the brother-in-law of a descendent of Claude Delacroix, the painter's uncle, whose great-grand daughter was the celebrated Baroness Vaughan whose destiny was linked with that of King Leopold I of the Belgians.

20 Robaut states that Delacroix's *Death of Cato* (pl 113) was inspired by David's '*Patroclus*'; but the latter picture (in the Cherbourg Museum) is quite different from *Cato*, and shows a figure seen from behind. The inspiration was in fact provided by David's *Death of Hector* (Musée Fabre, Montpellier) of which there is a replica in the Louvre (Cat. Brière 195). David made use of this picture for his *Funeral of Patroclus*; hence, no doubt, the confusion.

21 Published posthumously in 1927.

22 Alfred de Vigny, *Les Destinées, Œuvres complètes*. Ed. de la Pléiade. Vol. I, p. 204.

23 Piron, *op. cit.*, p. 78.

24 Introduction to Robaut, p. XXI.

25 'Delacroix considered that the *Bishop of Liège* should preferably be seen by lamplight, with the beam concentrated by a reflector.' (Villot, preface to the catalogue of his sale of 11 February 1865, p. 2.)
Delacroix himself—and later his friend Villot when he owned this picture, and again when he sold it—tried this several times; it has also, as is known, been tried with paintings by Rembrandt.

26 Villot, catalogue to his sale of 1865, p. 1.

Mlle Michèle Toupet, in her study of the *Murder of the Bishop of Liège* which appeared in the *Revue du Louvre* for 1962-3, rightly points out that while the setting of *Melmoth* is directly suggested by the Salle des Pas-perdus of the Palais de Justice at Rouen, the roof of the hall where the *Murder of the Bishop* takes place has a different source.
This roof is closely similar—as Germain Bazin has also noted—to that of Saint Stephen's Hall, Westminster. Delacroix may well have been impressed by this roof and have studied it during his visit to London in 1825, not many years earlier.

27 See letter to Pierret dated 30 September 1831.

28 A much more detailed analysis of this picture may be found on pages 229 *f.* of my *Discovery of Art* (Thames and Hudson, London; Abrams, New York, 1959).

29 *Journal*, 20 May 1853.

30 It is well worth while to consult on this subject '*Delacroix et la musique*' by Q.J. Aubry (*Revue musicale*, 1 April 1920), and R.O. Evans, *Les romantiques français et la musique* (thesis published by Champion, 1934).

31 Introduction to Robaut, p. xv.

32 Ibid.

33 Robaut's description.

34 Baudelaire, *Curiosités esthétiques, Œuvres*. Ed. de la Pléiade, pp. 883 *f*.

35 Dated 1830 by Robaut, but in the summer of 1821 by Lee Johnson: 'Delacroix's decorations for Talma's dining-room' in the *Burlington Magazine*, March 1957 (pp. 78 *f*.).

## V DANDYISM IN FRANCE

1 Baudelaire: *Le peintre de la vie moderne, Curiosités esthétiques, Œuvres*. Ed. de la Pléiade, p. 899.

2 *Victor Hugo par un témoin de sa vie*, Chapter XLIX.

3 Piron, *Eugène Delacroix, sa vie et ses œuvres*, p. 67.

4 In a letter to his friend Trébutien on 25 September 1844.

5 In 1911 Gustave Koehler published *Der Dandyismus im französischen, Roman des neunzehnten Jahrhunderts*. In 1938 Elisabeth Creed made *Le Dandysme de Jules Barbey d'Aurevilly* the subject of her thesis. Before this, in his remarkable *Esthétique de Baudelaire*, published in 1933, André Ferran had devoted the second chapter to *Le Dandy intérieur*. Otto Mann has stressed the wide implications of the problem in his *Der moderne Dandy: ein Kulturproblem der XIX Jahrhunderts*, Berlin, 1925.

6 Baudelaire, *Curiosités esthétiques, Œuvres*. Ed. de la Pléiade, p. 899.

7 Baudelaire, '*Les Phares*', *Fleurs du Mal, Œuvres*. Ed. de la Pléiade, p. 88.

8 *Journal*, 4 October 1854.

9 *Journal*, 15 November 1853.

10 Alfred de Vigny, *Journal d'un poète*, 1826.

11 Baudelaire, '*Les Sept Vieillards*', *Fleurs du Mal, Œuvres*. Ed. de la Pléiade, p. 158.

12 *Journal*, 29 March 1857.

13 Baudelaire, '*Le Voyage*', *Fleurs du Mal, Œuvres*. Ed. de la Pléiade, p. 201.

14 Translation by Robert Lowell, in his *Imitations*.

15 *Journal*, 14 May 1824.

16 *Journal*, 4 October 1854.

17 Supplement to *Journal*, Book III, p. 399.

18 Paul Valéry, *Œuvres*. N. R. F., Book III, p. 1933.

19 *Journal*, 10 February 1850.

20 Born Dublin c. 1786, Sidney Owenson became the wife of a doctor, Sir Thomas Charles Morgan, and made her name as a writer. Among her works (novels, travel books, etc.) Lady Morgan published a 4 volume work on *France*, where she had spent three years under the Restauration. This was followed by another visit and book: *France in 1829 and 1830*. (Translated into French in 1817 and 1830.) Despite their weaknesses these works provide a valuable source of information.

21 Baudelaire, *Curiosités esthétiques, Œuvres*. Ed. de la Pléiade, p. 862.

22 Ibid., p. 861.

23 Ibid., p. 862.

24 Barbey d'Aurevilly, article on Walpole, *Le Constitutionnel* of 21 September 1874.

25 Philarète Chasles, *Études sur les hommes et les mœurs du XIX^e siècle*, 1850.

26 Baudelaire, study of Gautier, *Œuvres*. Ed. de la Pléiade, p. 1036.

27 Mme Ancelot, *Un Salon de Paris*, Dentu, 1866.

28 *Journal*, 10 October 1854.

29 Baudelaire, *Œuvres posthumes*, N. R. F., II, p. 180.

30 Baudelaire, *Le Spleen de Paris, Œuvres*, Ed. de la Pléiade, p. 330.

31 *Journal*, supplement, Book III, p. 444. See also *Journal*, 21 July and 6 August 1850.

32 *Journal*, 25 January 1857. Book III, p. 40.

33 Mérimée, article on Byron in *Le National*, 7 March and 3 June 1830; quoted by Estève.

34 See Baudelaire, *Curiosités esthétiques, Œuvres*. Ed. de la Pléiade, p. 860. In all the adherents of Dandyism in France the cult of this dualism is to be found. While Baudelaire recognized in Delacroix 'a great deal of the man of the world', but also 'a great deal of the savage', and made use of his famous image, 'a volcano artistically concealed beneath bouquets of flowers', Mérimée in *Le Vase étrusque* depicts his Sainte Clair as gifted with 'a too-expansive sensibility' yet 'sedulously hiding all outward sign of it'. Vigny, in 1832, in his *Journal d'un poète* (p. 61), speaks of his own 'extreme sensibility. . . . shut up in the most secret corner of the heart'. Baudelaire sums up (in *Le peintre de la vie moderne*) by saying that the Dandy possesses an 'ardent need' of 'an originality' but also an ability to remain 'content within the exterior limits of the conventions'. (See also *Curiosités esthétiques, Œuvres*. Ed. de la Pléiade, p. 899.)

35 Baudelaire, *Curiosités esthétiques, Œuvres*. Ed. de la Pléiade, p. 880.

36 See the quotation from the *Journal* for 9 October 1849 on page 239 above.

37 Baudelaire, *Curiosités esthétiques, Œuvres*. Ed. de la Pléiade, p. 850.

38 In her book, *Un Salon de Paris*, she confirms that 'Mérimée was, with Beyle, Eugène Delacroix and the delightful Baron de Mareste, the chief adornment of my parties and of Gérard's.'

39 Baudelaire, *Curiosités esthétiques, Œuvres*. Ed. de la Pléiade, p. 860.

40 Ibid.

41 Estève's celebrated thesis on *Byron et son influence en France* has brought out a number of these resemblances.

42 *Journal*, 14 May 1824.

43 *Journal*, Ems, 1 August 1850.

44 Delacroix, *Œuvres littéraires*. Ed. Crès, Book I, p. 117.

45 Ibid., p. 118.

46 *Journal*, 30 April 1850.

47 *Journal*, 23 November 1857.

48 Delacroix, *Œuvres littéraires*. Ed. Crès, Book I, p. 118.

49 Byron, *Manfred*, III, 1.

50 On the relations between Delacroix and Baudelaire and the influence of the former upon the beliefs and thinking of the latter, I may perhaps be allowed to refer readers to the chapter I have written, under the title '*Le poète à l'école du peintre*' in the *Baudelaire* of the series *Génies et Réalités*, Hachette, 1961, Chapter VIII, pp. 207-224.

51 Baudelaire, '*Mon cœur mis à nu*', LXXXIX, *Œuvres*. Ed. de la Pléiade, p. 1226.

52 Baudelaire, '*Mon cœur mis à nu*', LXXIX, *Œuvres*. Ed. de la Pléiade, p. 1222.

## VI BLAZE OF NOON

1 Eugène Delacroix, *Lettres intimes*, p. 193, note 1.

2 Letter of 6 November 1818, to Pierret.

3 *Journal*, 12 October 1853.

4 Letter to Pierret, 8 February.

5 Louvre, Cabinet des Dessins.

6 Robaut nos. 130 and 131.

7 Letter to Armand Bertin, 2 April.

8 Ibid.

9 Where Villot later drew Delacroix to follow him.

10 On this point Baudelaire was to part company with Delacroix. At the end of his *Salon de 1845* he wrote: 'The *painter*, the real one, will be the man who manages to bring out the epic side of present-day life, and to make us see and understand, by means of colour and design, how great and poetic we are in our neck-ties and our polished boots.' In his *Salon de 1846*, where he shows himself so deeply impressed by Delacroix, Baudelaire again refers, in conclusion, to 'the heroism of modern life', and asks: 'Does not the much ridiculed tail coat have its own beauty and its native charm? In 'the black tail coat and the frock coat' he points not only to 'political beauty, which is the expression of the equality of all' but even to 'poetic beauty, which is the expression of the soul of the people' (*Curiosités esthétiques, Œuvres*. Ed. de la Pléiade, p. 670).
A new side of modern art was about to come into being. Professor Y. Abé, of Chuo University, Japan, pointed out in December 1962 (in '*Un enterrement à Ornans*' *and Baudelaire's tail coat*) that Courbet's *Après-dîner à Ornans* was not painted till 1849, his *Casseurs de pierres* and his *Enterrement* not till 1850, the latter being significantly entitled 'a historical picture'. He finds in this the first conscious application of Baudelaire's doctrine; and in so doing he is at one with Champfleury himself, who in an article published in *L'Ordre* on 21 September 1850 (just before the opening of the Salon) wrote: 'The painter from Ornans has fully understood the ideas of a rare and strange book (*Le Salon de 1846* by M. Baudelaire).' And on 25 December 1861 Courbet stated the doctrine in a 'letter to his pupils' (published in 1864 in Castagnary's *Libres Propos*, pp. 179 ff.): 'I repudiate historical art as applied to the past. Historical art is essentially contemporary.' Here, then, is the gulf that separated Delacroix from naturalism and from one whole side of Impressionism: the quest for 'modernity' remained foreign to him.

11 Baudelaire, *Curiosités esthétiques, Œuvres*. Ed. de la Pléiade, p. 883.

12 Ibid., p. 886.

13 Ibid., p. 884.

14 Letter to Baron Theodore Gudin, 23 February 1832.

15 *Journal*, 28 April 1832.

16 But Delacroix, that subtle humanist, did make one reservation in a letter of 2 April to Armand Bertin: 'One thinks oneself in Rome or Athens, minus the atticism.'

17 Auguste Jal, born in Lyons in 1795, was art critic to the principal reviews of his day. He exhibited at the Salons of 1819, 1824, 1827 and 1831; in 1864 he published his *Dictionnaire critique de Biographie et d'Histoire*. He died in 1873.

18 Robaut no. 469.

19 Robaut no. 130.

20 Frankfurt, Städelsches Kunstinstitut. Robaut no. 468.

21 Montpellier, Musée Fabre. Robaut no. 408.

22 The original sources, the accounts by Charles de Mornay and Charles Cournault, were given by Burty in '*Eugène Delacroix à Alger*', in *L'Art*, 1883, no. 1. But the most complete study of the question is that of Elie Lambert, *Delacroix et les 'Femmes d'Alger'*, Laurens, 1937.

23 Thus I was able to show the fichu of the Algerian woman in the centre, which was loaned by André Joubin, in the retrospective exhibition of 1930. More recently, in the 1963 exhibition 'Delacroix, Citizen of Paris', Raymond

Escholier was able to assemble a whole display case of such clothing, remarkably well preserved.

24 Robaut no. 479, dated 1833.

25 Claudel, *Introduction à la peinture hollandaise*, Ist edn., p. 86.

26 According to Robaut, but the date seems more likely to have been about 1823.

27 The physical resemblance between these three models has led to confusion between them (Escholier, plate facing p. 104, incorrectly gives the title *Aspasie* to the first model). The first model, whose name is not known, was an image dear to Delacroix to the end of his days. In his *Journal* (28 May 1824) Delacroix confesses (in Italian) that the coloured girl 'Nera' who posed for the *Massacre* became his mistress. At this time the *Journal* tells us that though Delacroix admired '*Les grandes vertus*', he himself was 'not strong enough' to be 'truly virtuous'. This first model is a prelude to the bared breast of one of the *Women of Algiers* in the lithograph dated 1833 by Robaut. She is later combined with the Algerian model —an excellent example of the way in which Delacroix stored and mingled his memories and impressions.

28 *Journal*, 9 October 1822.

29 *Les Épaves*, III, *Femmes damnées*, *Œuvres*. Ed. de la Pléiade, p. 210. (The title suggests the pastels of M. Auguste rather than Delacroix's *Women of Algiers*.)

30 *Fleurs du Mal*, LIII, *Invitation au Voyage*, *Œuvres*. Ed. de la Pléiade, p. 125.

31 Louvre, R. F. 4185.

32 *Les Épaves*, *Pièces diverses*, XVII, *Œuvres*. Ed. de la Pléiade, p. 227.

33 Elie Lambert, however, connects this picture with a sentence in the *Journal*—as late as 1854—in which Delacroix says he has made progress with 'the small Woman of Algiers with a greyhound.'

34 *Curiosités esthétiques*, *Œuvres*. Ed. de la Pléiade, p. 852. See above, chapter III, p. 126, for the complementary idea: the 'key tone' of a painting.

35 Robaut no. 1515.

36 *Fleurs du Mal*, LIII, *Œuvres*. Ed. de la Pléiade, p. 125.

37 Left to the Louvre by Moreau-Nélaton. No. 9291. 1854.

38 Water-colour, Robaut no. 484.

39 Robaut no. 829.

40 Robaut no. 406.

41 Elie Lambert, in his *Histoire d'un tableau, l'Abd-er-Rahman, sultan du Maroc, de Delacroix* (Collection Hespérus, Institut des Hautes Études marocaines, 1953), has explained this cut by the fact that, by 1844, Mornay's embassy was no longer topical.

42 *Journal*, 20 November 1857.

43 Robaut no. 611.

44 *Revue des Deux Mondes*, 15 July 1854.

## VII THE SEARCH FOR BALANCE

1 The fact that the theme of Hamlet held a particular attraction, almost amounting to an obsession, for Delacroix may be explained by a personal preoccupation: he is known to have been familiar with the reports of the operation on his legal father, and to have been aware that his father was impotent at the time of his conception. He had been forced to face the fact that he was not the son of the man he had deeply loved and admired as a child, and to recognize the misconduct of his mother, also deeply loved, who had sent him, after his father's death, as a boarder to the Lycée Louis-le-Grand, and had herself gone to live in Marseilles with General Cervoni, to look after that gentleman's daughter.
Delacroix must have suffered keenly, and regarded Hamlet with particular feeling as a representation of his sufferings.
Baudelaire, while he lived at the Hôtel Pimodan, from 1843 onwards, had on his walls Delacroix's *Hamlet* series, which had been published in that year. He, too, felt himself to be the victim of maternal treachery, since after her widowhood his mother had replaced Baudelaire's father by General Aupick, whom he violently detested; and he too must have found in Hamlet's plight an echo of his own feelings. It is a fresh point in common with Delacroix, whom he was to come to know well in about the middle of 1845.

2 The analogy is even clearer if one compares the preparatory drawings: see my *Discovery of Art*, pages 246 and 247.

3 Elie Lambert, *Gazette des Beaux-Arts*, 1932, II, pp. 245 *ff.* and 317 *ff.*

4 *Journal*, 21 October 1860; 12 and 20 October 1853.

5 On this problem of composition Baudelaire has once again expressed Delacroix's thought : 'There is no such thing as chance in art, any more than in mechanics. A picture is a 'machine' in which all the systems are intelligible to the trained eye, where everything has its reason—if it is a good picture. . . .' *Salon de 1846*.

6 Villot's description of this will be found above, Chapter III, p. 129.

7 Chapter IV, p. 164.

8 *Curiosités esthétiques*, *Œuvres*. Ed. de la Pléiade, p. 697.

9 In 1834 he wrote from Nohant: 'I have endless talks alone with Chopin, of whom I am very fond, and who is a man of rare distinction. He is the most genuine artist I have ever met.'

10 Those who wish to go further into the strange processes of imaginative thought as it takes up forms again and treats them afresh may compare the composition of this *Pietà* with the version of the *Bride of Abydos* treated in breadth (Robaut no. 773)—a picture very different in mood but painted by Delacroix at much the same time on a theme he had already treated. It will be seen how, starting from the same *datum* (a central group to be

balanced laterally), he reversed the problem: the group, instead of being made to stand out against the sky, is set in front of the plane of the rock and the openings through this to right and left cut out related bays. So this composition becomes, as it were, the 'negative' of the preceding one, since in it the voids take the place of the solids and *vice versa*. I wrote of this parallel in '*Universalité de Delacroix*', *Formes*, June 1930. No. 6, pp. 10-13. Twelve years later Lucien Rudrauf repeated the observation in his *Delacroix*.

11 I drew attention to this correspondence in '*Universalité de Delacroix*', *Formes*, June 1930, no. 6, pp. 10-13. Eight years later Lucien Rudrauf repeated my observations in *Delacroix et le Rosso*. (See Bibliography p. 543.)

## VIII THE GREAT ENTERPRISES

1 Baudelaire, *Curiosités esthétiques*, *Œuvres*. Ed. de la Pléiade, p. 609.

2 Théophile Silvestre, *Histoire des artistes vivants*, p. 75.

3 Robaut no. 702: Robaut dated this water-colour 1839 without good reason. In the proofs he corrected in the possession of the Bibliothèque Nationale, he has altered this date to *c.* 1833. 1832 would appear to be more exact.

4 It was not a momentary aberration which led Delecluze to say in 1831 that the *Liberty* recalled the style of Jouvenet. He repeated this view in 1847, speaking of *Marcus Aurelius*, and went on to express adverse criticism of the painting.

5 *Journal*, 22 February 1860.

6 Commissioned in April 1833, but not finished until October 1836.

7 While Robaut dates the preparatory sketches (nos. 332 to 335) 1830, Lee Johnson places them (it would seem correctly) in 1821 (see Bibliography, p. 544).

8 These are to be found chiefly in the Moreau-Nélaton collection in the Louvre.

9 On this question see Mesuret, *Pierre Lacour*, p. 71.

10 See the letter of 27 December 1836 to the Minister of the Interior.

11 See Maurice Tourneux, *Eugène Delacroix devant ses contemporains*.

12 *Œuvres littéraires*. Ed. Crès, Book III, p. 138.

13 Ibid., Book II, p. 42.

14 *Journal*, 7 May 1824.

15 *Journal*, 8 May 1824.

16 *Journal*, 15 January 1857.

17 Supplement to *Journal*, undated [? 1840], Book III, p. 427.

18 *Journal*, 25 January 1847.

19 *Œuvres littéraires*. Ed. Crès, Book I, p. 76.

20 *Journal*, 13 January 1857.

21 *Journal*, 22 March 1857.

22 *Œuvres littéraires*. Ed. Crès, Book I, p. 110. (Champrosay, 17 April 1846.)

23 *Journal*, 25 January 1857.

24 In notes preserved by his family and made available to Mlle Vieillefond for her 1952 thesis.

25 *Journal*, 6 June 1851.

26 Odilon Redon, *A soi-même*, p. 166.

27 *Journal*, 15 January 1857.

28 *Journal*, 13 January 1857.

29 *Journal*, 21 October 1860.

30 Planet, *Souvenirs* (published by Joubin), p. 33.

31 In Robaut, discussing no. 971, p. 254.

32 *Journal*, 29 April 1854.

33 *Journal*, 5 May 1852.

34 *Journal*, 10 July 1847.

35 *Journal*, 11 January 1857.

36 On his conception of the technique of painting the most precious evidence is still *Les palettes de Delacroix*, published in 1931 by René Piot, a pupil of Andrieu who was the direct heir of the master's tradition.

37 *Journal*, 14 May 1830.

38 *Journal*, 25 January, 1857.

39 *Œuvres littéraires*. Ed. Crès, Book I, p. 73.

40 Ibid., p. 71.

41 *Journal*, 11 January 1857.

42 *Journal*, 11 January 1857.

43 *Œuvres littéraires*. Ed. Crès, Book I, p. 63.

44 Baudelaire, *Curiosités esthétiques*, *Œuvres*. Ed. de la Pléiade, p. 699.

45 *Journal*, 2 January 1853.

46 The most important of these are quoted in my *Discovery of Art*, p. 207.

47 Kindly placed at my disposal by Maître Ribault Ménetière.

48 '*Mémoires de Delacroix*' in *L'Artiste*, 4 October 1846.

49 Letter to Villot, 16 September 1840.

50 See his letter of 27 May 1846. *Correspondance*, Book II, p. 272 and note 1.

51 *Journal*, 8 June 1850.

52 The inauguation of the newly decorated Apollo Gallery took place in June, but the ceiling was still unfinished, and so was not unveiled until four months later.

53 See the account contributed by him to the book on the *Galerie Bruyas*, Paris, 1876.

54 See page 390 above for Redon's description.

55 Letter to Dutilleux, 24 August 1856.

56 Baudelaire, *Nouvelles Fleurs du Mal*, *Œuvres*. Ed. de la Pléiade, p. 240.

57 René Piot, *Les palettes de Delacroix*, p. 98.

58 Letter to Guillemardet, 3 June, 1863.

59 Kindly made available by its owner, M. Camille Bernard.

60 Delacroix corrects the judgement by which he had confused love of glory and vanity in a letter to Soulier of 26 April 1828 (also quoted above Chapter IV, p. 184).

61 *Journal*, 14 May 1824.

## IX THE SECRETS OF THE SELF

1 *Journal*, 7 April 1824.

2 For a more detailed study of this question, I may perhaps be permitted to refer the reader to my *Discovery of Art*, in particular to chapters V, VI and VII.

3 *Revue des Deux Mondes*, 15 July 1882, p. 250.

4 *Journal*, Book III, p. 342.

5 A drawing in the Louvre seems to be a first idea for Apollo's chariot—it already has its triumphant movement.

6 E. g. *Horsemen Fighting on the Plain* in the Moreau-Nélaton collection in the Louvre. Ch. Sterling in his catalogue of the *Peinture au Musée du Louvre, Nineteenth-century French School*, II, No. 670, suggests a later date for this picture: c. 1830. I prefer the traditional dating.

7 *Journal*, 8 October 1822.

8 *Journal*, 6 June 1824.

9 In one of his unpublished school notebooks, dated 1814, there is this jingle:

*C'est un péché que la paresse;*
*Mes amis, travaillons sans cesse.*

10 26 [September 1840].

11 On this question of the other and the double Otto Rank's book on *Don Juan* is illuminating.

12 Baudelaire, '*La Destruction*', *Fleurs du Mal*, *Œuvres*. Ed. de la Pléiade, p. 179.

13 Delacroix, article on Michelangelo, *Revue de Paris*, 1830.

14 Robaut no. 619.

15 Delacroix, article on Prud'hon, *Œuvres littéraires*. Ed. Crès Book II, p. 153.

16 Paris, 1876.

17 Baudelaire, *Fleurs du Mal*, *Œuvres*. Ed. de la Pléiade, p. 199.

18 Baudelaire, *Curiosités esthétiques*, *Œuvres*. Ed. de la Pléiade, p. 863.

19 See Aeppli, *Le Rêve*, in particular p. 77.

20 'Already arrived, the course of this my life
Across tempestuous sea in a frail bark,
Before the common port . . .'

21 Robaut no. 1473.

22 *Journal*, 25 April 1824.

23 Baudelaire, *Fleurs du Mal*, LXXVIII, *Œuvres*. Ed. de la Pléiade, p. 144.

24 On this symbolism of space, see my *Discovery of Art*, p. 278.

25 *Journal*, 9 September 1852.

26 *Journal*, 17 September 1854.

27 *Journal*, 12 October 1855.

28 *Journal*, 11 October 1855.

29 Supplement to the *Journal*, Book III, p. 407.

30 Théophile Gautier, *Moniteur Universel*, article dated 18 November 1864.

31 There is, however, a flower painting dating from 1833, which belonged to Villot. (Robaut mentions another which he assigns to 1834, after Delacroix returned from Africa; but this date contradicts the categorical statement of George Sand, who was the owner of the picture.)

32 Letter to Lassalle-Bordes, 4 September 1848.

33 Robaut no. 997.

34 There was already, among his early projects for the Chambre des Députés, a representation of the sun rising —in the background of the *Contest of Young Spartan Girls*.

35 In *Moniteur Universel*, 25 March 1854.

36 *Journal*, 7 December 1856.

37 Baudelaire, *Curiosités esthétiques*, *Œuvres*. Ed. de la Pléiade, p. 617.

38 Delacroix, *Œuvres littéraires*. Ed. Crès, I, p. 33.

39 Letter to Soulier, 14 [December] 1858. *Correspondance*, IV, p. 63.

40 This refers to the version in the Grenoble Museum.

41 In May 1963 André Gavoty published an extremely full biographical study of Delacroix's 'good aunt' Riesener (see Bibliography, p. 542) who married the son of the second marriage of Delacroix's grandmother. Madame Riesener, *née* Félicité Longrois, was the grand-daughter of Pierre Longrois, 'keeper' of the furniture in the château de la Muette, who was guillotined at the age of eighty-four. An uncle who became tapestry-maker to the Tuileries helped her to obtain an appointment in the Imperial service as Woman of the Bed-chamber, and her father shortly afterwards became a 'Gentleman usher'. Mlle Longrois was soon promoted '*dame d'annonce*', and in 1805 she attracted the attention of Napleon—indeed became his mistress in that year. The liaison lasted until the beginning of 1806. During the summer she married the painter Henri Riesener, who was then nearly forty years of age, while she was no more than twenty. The Empress Josephine signed the prenuptial contract. Reisener painted his bride with her sister, and the portrait was a great success at the Salon of 1808. It was shown again in 1814 before going to the Musée de Peinture at Orleans.

42 Letter to Madame Auguste Lamey, 15 October 1855. *Correspondance*, Book III, p. 295.

43 Baudelaire, *Curiosités esthétiques*, *Œuvres*. Ed. de la Pléiade, p. 620.

44 Letter 605. (*The Complete Letters of Vincent van Gogh*, Thames and Hudson, London; New York Graphic Society, 1958.)

45 Arras Museum.

46 *Journal*, 18 January 1856.

# APPENDIX

THESE TWO LONG LETTERS from Mme de Forget to Delacroix, written on notepaper with the letter-heading JF and a coronet, will be enough to convey the tone of the relationship between the painter and his cousin. There is in them a feeling of melancholy, sometimes turning to bitterness, caused by the painter's evasiveness—his decision to stay in the country, for which Mme de Forget cared very little, and to seek there the happiness she would have preferred him to find, as she did, in the social life of Paris. It was essentially the evasiveness of a creative artist anxious not to become absorbed and deflected from his task, of which the woman whom he clearly loved most betrays a certain jealousy.

In 1844 their liaison had been going on for ten years. In June of that year Delacroix had just set up house at Champrosay, where he was to spend more and more time: this set a distance between him and Paris—and his mistress. In the same month he wrote to George Sand of 'the life I am leading and the obligations that keep me here . . . all the weight of my chain' (he was at work on the decoration of the Palais Bourbon and the Luxembourg, had just finished the *Pietà* for Saint-Denis-du-Saint-Sacrement, was about to begin restoring Le Sueur's paintings in the Hôtel Lambert, and was longing for the country). He adds: 'You know how I love gardens and flowers. I think this is why I am so fond of you. No-one has depicted the divine beauty of nature as you have.'

On 1 July he wrote to Mme de Forget, describing his new home at Champrosay: 'You will see how happy one can be in a modest retreat.' Yet he hastens to assure her: 'If it weren't for the need to restore my health a little, I would come back at once to take you in my arms.' After a brief return to Paris he wrote again from Champrosay on 8 July, promising to invite her there when the Villots had gone away—apparently wishing to keep the secret of their liaison. It was a mistake to mention the presence of Mme Villot and her sister-in-law, Mme Barbier, for this, as will be seen, gave Mme de Forget a twinge of jealousy. On Thursday, 11 July, he wrote again to thank her for sending some flowers and to say that he was looking forward to receiving her portrait in daguerreotype—but also to put off her visit again, since there was still a '*maudite ouvrière*' in the house; he added, however: 'I long to see you again and to hold you close to me.'

Two days later Mme de Forget replied:

*Saturday morning* [13-7-1844]

Well, my dear friend, I learned yesterday evening that you are neither drowned nor lost; it was a great relief to me to hear from you, for I was beginning to be anxious and wonder why you did not return. The little letter you sent two days ago spoke of no other plan, so I thought you would be coming back as you assured me when you left—that is why I did not write again. I was counting on your coming on Monday or Tuesday, especially as the weather is so dreadful. I confess I didn't think about the woman, the dust-covers, your supply of paper, the agreeableness of the neighbourhood, and the hundred and one other things that hinder you from returning to Paris, and remembering you have a friend there who is all alone and made most sad by your long absence. It would have been kind at least to have written sooner, to let her know you meant to stay longer in the country, and to calm her anxieties and console her a little for not being with you. But then, you have so many other things to think about!!! *All the same*, you know my tender feelings for you and also that I cannot resist the smallest signs of affection from you. So now, my resentment over, I am delighted that you are pleased with your house, and that you are so well and making such good use of your time. I do not only consider myself, dear friend, and if you are content, then so am I. Only my heart is still wounded and sad that I wasn't first in your thoughts. Didn't you know, then, that I needed your thoughts and comfort? I still don't know which day you will come, but you are waiting for *the counsel of your womenfolk* to decide, and when the work is finally finished you will come back to me, and I need not say how happy I will be to see you again. I hope I shall be the first to congratulate you on your new good health and handsomeness. I shall have so much to tell you, and you will have so many *pardons* to beg of me. Write to me immediately if there is anything you want.

M. Gaultron told me last Thursday that he had written to you in Paris, not knowing your address in the country. It is about a studio he knows of that is to let and he needs to have a prompt reply. The poor boy is quite changed; I don't know how an indisposition could put him in such a state. I suspect (between ourselves) that his new lodgings have put him in temptation's way, and he has succumbed. That is what is in store for people who go to live in the place of perdition!!! [Delacroix was going to live in the rue Notre-Dame-de-Lorette in October.]

If I had had an opportunity—and I am sorry I haven't—I would have sent you the new daguerreotype of your lady friend. It seems that you need it to remind you that she is still among the living! I don't know whether you will like it better. The face seems to me brighter and younger but, alas, as ugly as ever?

I am cross that you did not leave your watch-stand with me; it would have been repaired and you would have found another on your return. Do send it as soon as you arrive and I will bring it straight back, so you can leave the other one in the country.

If you can bring back the small basket I last sent you flowers in (and if you think it worth the trouble) I can use it to send some more later on. I hope the plants are climbing well and growing beautiful. Surely you wouldn't deny me the pleasure of making you so small a gift? Don't depend on it, and if you are not more agreeable another time I shall send you so many you will be ruined with baskets sent 'carriage forward'.

I have news of Hortense [Mme de Querelles, Mme de Forget's aunt. Delacroix had enquired about her in his letter of 8 July] from Ostend where she is established. She is delighted with her new house, but must be greatly disappointed by this weather, which prevents her from taking up her sea-bathing. Her husband has sent off some drawings and articles for *L'Illustration*; I expect they will appear soon.

You will tell me, will you not, when you are going to appear in that journal, for I mean to take it. You can imagine how interested I am in it now.

The weather here is wretched. Each day it rains. Truly I feel sorry for dwellers in the country, always excepting those who can bear its discomforts! I am very well, although I sleep badly. The workmen wake me up as early as five in the morning with their infernal noise and then I am devoured by ennui. I was at the theatre yesterday, the only time since our visit to the Français.

Adieu, dear friend, I wish you good health, amusements, and for my own part an early return. I shall be very happy to see you again, my dear; we lead a strange life, surely, for people who love one another? Ah well, one must be philosophical in this life, and I certainly need to be. Awaiting what fate brings, I love you and my sad heart embraces you.

*Consuelo*

*On Monday 15 July Delacroix wrote again to apologize for 'the peevish mood' in which he had parted from Mme de Forget. 'You are so good I take advantage of you', he wrote, 'Scold me, treat me as I deserve!' He promised to come to dinner that very Tuesday and begged 'forgiveness with heart and soul'. He spoke of fits of pessimism, when he lay awake at night reviling himself as 'the greatest blockhead born'. 'Consuelo's' reply on the following Sunday indicates that he did not carry out his promise but remained in the country. It also allows her resentment, and her jealousy of the painting he prefers to her company to appear more clearly.*

I quite thought that *the charms* of the country would detain you some days more. I am sensible of your kind thoughts. I am persuaded that this little stay in the country will do you good, my friend, since your health needs rest from time to time. You can see that you are mistaken to curse the necessity that compels you to work, since the idleness you so often wish for bores you to death; so there is another reason to be content with your lot. What do you complain of then, my poor friend? You are a *privileged* artist, since you devote yourself entirely to your painting. It is your strongest passion, your ruling one, and nothing and no-one can replace it.

How fortunate an artist is—and even if life centred on a single preoccupation and with a single aim has its chagrins, it has its compensations too. I have come to realize that you have no need of the comforts and solaces which serve for so many people; I have gone about it in a thousand ways and have not succeeded. So I am convinced now that the consolations of tender and devoted affection are swallowed up in your imagination, which is so vital, so impressionable, so changeable and at times so unhappy! My dear friend, the remedy for your ills lies in yourself. First you need the strength to repel all gloomy thoughts whenever they enter your mind, and then while taking care for your health and husbanding it, you must avoid worrying yourself as you do; seek all diversions and pleasures that do not lead to fatigue, for the sake of your work, and why regret the anxieties that this brings? It is a real friend to you, a comfort and a resource, and the passion it arouses in you cannot be luckless, you will agree? And it will protect your heart from many disappointments and discouragements, which you will never know. And how happy one must be to have a talent which occupies one constantly, and to have inside oneself all that is needed for happiness.

As for me, you ask if I am sufficiently amused and what I am doing; I am so far convinced that a good understanding is the main constituent of happiness that I can hardly wish to tell you all my woes, which are tedious and without end. I pass my days like an *oyster*; a trifle monotonous perhaps, but since the winter I have met with so many disappointments, so many hurts that my heart has grown a *shell*; lately I have started to go out a great deal, the use of my limbs and fresh scenes before my eyes do me good. I try to avoid thinking. The past has only bitter memories, the future seems sorrowful and the present is slipping away. It is all very vexing, and you will see that your existence is to be preferred to mine; when one's heart is not tied one has many more resources with which to deal with one's fate, and particularly with ills of the imagination like yours. With your nature you must seek diversion and amusements wherever they are to be found—but for this you must not be too *settled*. If you were able to travel now I am sure it would do you a great deal of good. But I realize that this is impossible just now. Why not put the plan into action in a few months, in the spring, as I have already suggested? Until then give yourself *body and soul* to painting and the time will pass quickly.

M. de Bercagny came to see me yesterday and we philosophized together; he believes there is only one way to be happy, and that is to have a constant preoccupation, whatever it may be. For you it is painting; you have not chosen an unrewarding one; your friends come second. Don't think, my dear, that I seek to annoy you by speaking so frankly about your nature; heavens! I know it so well and bear it not the least ill will in the world. I am not reproaching you, we cannot change our natures—they remain as God made them. What we need is a willingness to accept our fate. This is necessary for you too, and you must not say 'that you are unable to enjoy life as others do, and that heaven formed you in a moment of spleen'. The accusation is not just, heaven has been generous to you.

As for *all your little afflictions*, they are not sent by heaven but are of your own making and you must have strength to bear them.

I must seem to wish to be another Saint-Simon, a reformer. I do not want to change anything, reform anything, I just run on and chatter to you. Forgive my speaking of my own troubles. As for yours, I can always listen to them, I promise you, and I rely ever on your unchanging friendship.

*Joséphine*

Do forgive my long letter. If you return to Paris next week come and ask me to dine with you next Tuesday, without my saying anything further.

*Sunday, half past eleven*

Fig 34 SIGNATURES OF EUGÈNE DELACROIX 1819-1863

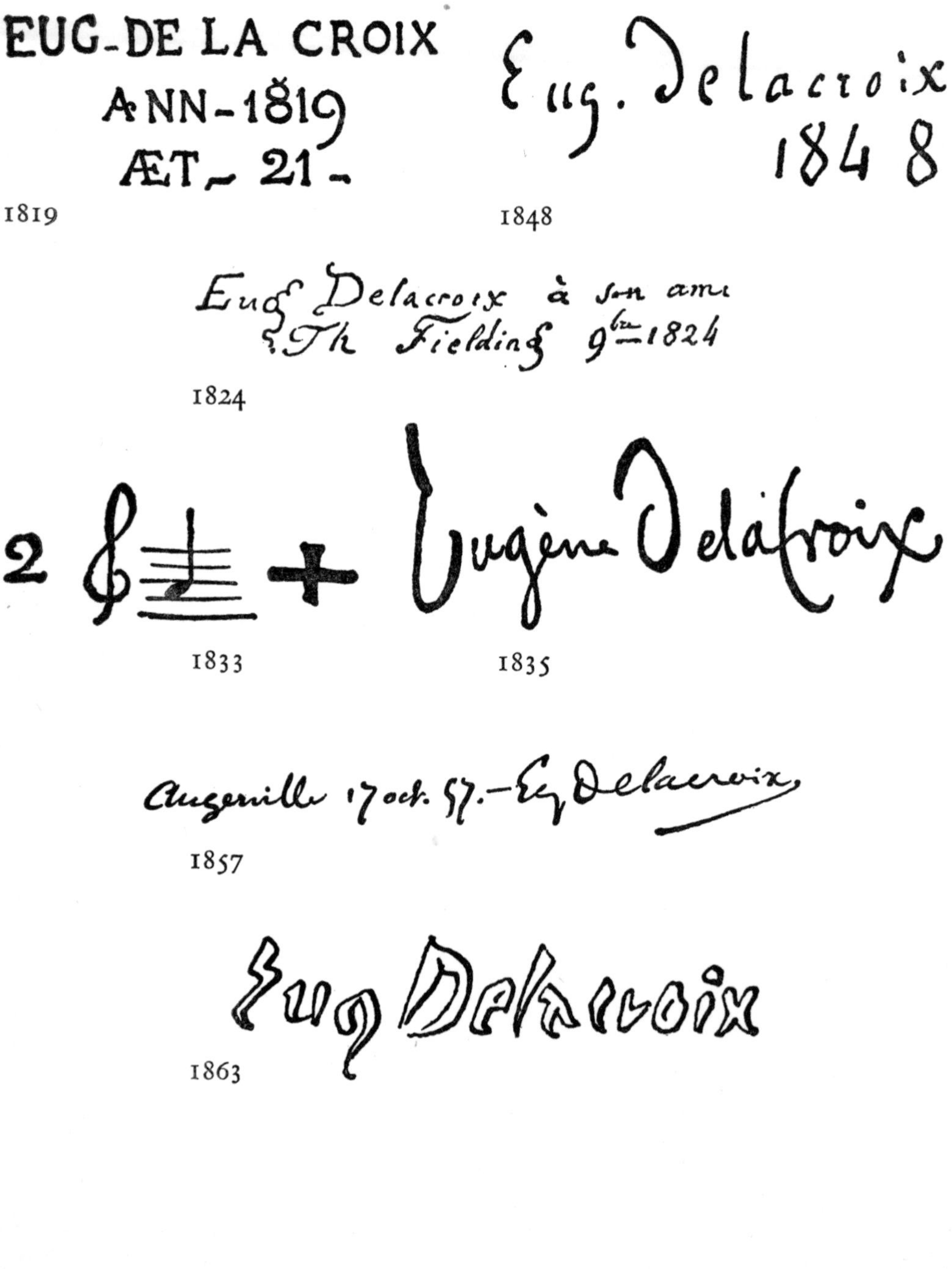

EUG-DE LA CROIX
ANN-1819
ÆT-21-

1819

Eug. Delacroix
1848

1848

Eug Delacroix à son ami
Th Fielding 9bre 1824

1824

1833

Eugène Delacroix

1835

Augerville 17 oct. 57.—Eug Delacroix

1857

Eug Delacroix

1863

# CHRONOLOGY

1798
26 April: Birth at Charenton-Saint-Maurice (Seine) of Ferdinand Victor Eugène Delacroix, son of Charles Delacroix, a former Minister under the Directoire and future *Préfet* under the Empire, and of Victoire Oeben, whose father had been cabinet-maker to Louis XVI.

1805
26 August: Death of Charles Delacroix, then *Préfet* of the Gironde, at the age of sixty-four.

1806
At the beginning of the year Mme Delacroix returns to Paris, living at 50 rue de Grenelle, the home of her daughter Henriette de Verninac. In October Eugène Delacroix becomes a boarder at the Lycée Imperial (later Lycée Louis-le-Grand), where he gets a sound classical education. Throughout his life he will remain so indelibly marked by his classical studies that he will be the most cultivated of the romantic artists, protected against all excess by the harmonious intellectual balance he had already acquired as an adolescent.

1813
Wins school awards for drawing in this and the following year. First stay at Valmont, near Fécamp, at the home of his cousin Nicolas-Auguste Bataille.

1814
Visits Rouen from Valmont and is greatly impressed by Gothic architecture.

1815
Leaves school in June. His mother having died the year before, Delacroix lives with his sister Henriette and her husband Verninac at 114 rue de l'Université. Recommended by his uncle, the painter Henri Riesener, on 1 October he enters the studio of Pierre-Narcisse Guérin (1774-1833), an accomplished David follower and former Director of the Villa Medici. There he finds instruction from the classical well-springs and fellow-students enthusiastic about a more modern art, among them Géricault and Bonington, who become his friends. He publishes his first engravings and lithographs in *Le Miroir.*

1816
16 March: Enters the École des Beaux-Arts. He forms lifelong friendships with Leblond, Pierret, and Guillemardet. Copies after the masters at the Louvre.

1817
Falls in love for the first time, with an English girl, Elisabeth Salter, who is in service with his sister, and paints her portrait.

1818
Stays on the family estate of La Boixe (Charente) from August to December.

1819
Paints the *Virgin* for the church at Orcemont (Seine-et-Oise), his first commission. Is influenced by Géricault's unfinished *Radeau de la Méduse.* Stays at La Boixe from August to November.

1820
His family is ruined by unfortunate lawsuits concerning the La Boixe property. April: Delacroix finds accommodation at 22 rue de la Planche (now rue de Varenne). In September he falls ill. Stays at Le Louroux (Indre-et-Loire), at the home of his brother Charles in August-September, at La Boixe in September-October, and at Souillac in October-November.

1821
Delacroix, in financial straits, is helped by a commission handed over to him by Géricault for a *Virgin of the Sacred Heart.* Paints *La Favorite.*

1822
Exhibits a picture at the Salon for the first time: *Dante and Virgil in the Inferno.* A great sensation, the work is bought

by the State. On 3 September he begins to keep his *Journal.* Stays at Le Louroux with his brother Charles from July to September. Death in this year of his brother-in-law Verninac.

1823
Lives at 118 rue de Grenelle Saint-Germain, and has a studio at 16 rue des Gris. October: Moves to 20 (now 52) rue Jacob with his friend the English watercolourist Thalès Fielding.

1824
Géricault's death on 27 January affects him greatly. Copies from the Venetian masters. Is influenced by the English painter Constable. He exhibits at the Salon: *The Massacre at Chios,* bought by the State; *Tasso in the Madhouse, The Death of Cato, Orphan Girl in the Graveyard.* 5 October: discontinues his *Journal,* to be resumed in 1847.

1825
New studio at 14 rue d'Assas. Lives at 46 rue de l'Université, with Pierret. A stay in England from the end of May to August is particularly beneficial. He visits the museums, meets Sir Thomas Lawrence and Sir David Wilkie, and is impressed by performances of Shakespeare. His liaison with Mme Dalton begins in this year.

1826
Associates with the romantic circle, gets to know Victor Hugo, etc. Commissioned to paint a big picture for the Conseil d'Etat: *The Emperor Justinian composing the Institutes,* exhibited in 1827. In June stays with General de Coëtlosquet at La Charité-sur-Loire.

1827
Death of his sister Henriette de Verninac. During May he shows, 'in aid of the Greeks', *Greece Expiring on the Ruins of Missolonghi.* At the Salon he exhibits twelve important pictures bearing witness to the freedom and technical skill acquired in contact with the works he admired in London. Among the most important: *The Death of Sardanapalus,* unfavourably criticized; *Still Life with Lobsters; Count Palatiano; Christ in the Garden of Gethsemane* for the church of Saint-Paul-and-Saint-Louis in Paris; *The Execution of the Doge Marino Faliero,* one of his favourite works, which was successfully shown in London the same year; *Scenes from the Present War between the Greeks and Turks.* During September he sees performances of Shakespeare in Paris. In October he takes up residence at 15 rue de Choiseul and stays with the Rivets at Mantes.

1828
Studio at 9, Passage Saulnier. Completes *Cardinal Richelieu celebrating Mass* for the Duke of Orleans. Sosthène de La Rochefoucauld commissions a *Battle of Nancy.* Stays at Mantes with the Rivets in September and at Tours with his brother Charles in November.

1829
January: moves to 15 Quai Voltaire (where Vernet has lived previously, and Corot was to live later). In spite of financial difficulties, due to the ruin of his family, which compel him to turn out 'pot-boilers' (portraits of the young prize-winners at his friend Goubaux's boarding-school), Delacroix, does a lot of work: lithographs of animals, which he studies with the sculptor Barye, and a series of nineteen lithographs inspired by Goethe's *Faust.* Through meticulous research in libraries he prepares the history pictures that have been commissioned from him (such as a *Battle of Poitiers* commissioned by the Duchess of Berry). Yet he does not neglect society, and goes out a great deal, frequenting Gérard's salon where he meets Stendhal and Mérimée, and that of Mme Ancelot, which is often attended by Victor Hugo, with whom he becomes friendly. Makes the acquaintance of Alexandre Dumas, for one of whose receptions he will paint the *King Rodrigues.* Publishes his first articles on aesthetics in the *Revue de Paris.* Stays with his cousins at Valmont during October and November.

1830
Finishes *The Battle of Poitiers.* The 'three glorious days' of July and the Revolution heighten a sense of freedom that he asserts chiefly in art. They inspire him to paint *Liberty Leading the People,* which will appear at the Salon of 1831 and be purchased by the State. Article on Raphael for the *Revue de Paris.*

1831
January: Joins the Société Libre de Peinture et de Sculpture. March: the new government honours Delacroix with the Légion d'Honneur. Open competition for paintings for the debating chamber of the Chambre des Députés. This Salon sees some of his best canvases, including: *Liberty Leading the People, Cardinal Richelieu celebrating Mass* (burned in 1848); *Young Tiger playing* and *The Murder of the Bishop of Liège,* inspired by the episode in Sir Walter Scott's *Quentin Durward.* Stays at Valmont at the end of September.

1832
11 January: Embarks at Toulon for Morocco, accompanying Louis-Philippe's ambassador to the Sultan's Court, Count Charles de Mornay, whose friend he will remain. On 24 January they are at Tangier, and stay there till 5 March. Then the mission leaves for Meknes, arriving 15 March, where it meets the Sultan Abd-er-Rhaman (22 March), who receives it with great pomp and has it conducted round his palace and gardens. Delacroix explores the town but has difficulty in making sketches because of the hostility of the local inhabitants. 12 April: Back at Tangier, awaiting the diplomatic papers required for the Chancery, he finds native models. Then, allured by Spain, he goes to Cadiz

and Seville from 16 May to 28 May. 10 June: Leaves Tangier with Count de Mornay, calling at Oran (18 June) and Algiers (25-28 June), and arriving at Toulon on 5 July. Here he remains during a quarantine period, which seems to have lasted at least until 20 July, making sketches and the water-colours for the Mornay Album. Delacroix then returns to Paris. During his absence the gallery of the Musée Colbert has organized an exhibition on behalf of the Paris victims of the cholera epidemic, in which five of his small pictures appear, including: *Woman with a Parrot*, now at the Musée des Beaux-Arts, Lyons; *Charles VI and Odette*, and *Leda*. From this year date various portraits, among them those of Villot and Paganini.

1833
On becoming Minister of Trade and Public Works, Adolphe Thiers obtains large grants for the purpose of embellishing Paris. He starts the work of painting the Chambre des Députés by commissioning Delacroix in April to decorate the Salon du Roi in the Palais Bourbon. At the Salon: *The Rooms of the Count de Mornay*, *Portrait of M. D.* (Dr Desmaisons), *Portrait of M. de B.*

1834
The death of his nephew Charles de Verninac at New York in July is a great shock to Delacroix during this period of intense creation, in which he amasses portraits, official commissions, and souvenirs of Africa, as well as carrying out methodical research on composition and technique for the Chambre des Députés decoration. A need to console himself prompts him to go back, during September, to his beloved Valmont in Normandy, the home of his Bornot cousins. There he works on an interesting series of frescos that still decorate a gallery in the building *(Anachreon, Leda, Bacchus)*. The Salon, at which two of his works are rejected, witnesses the blossoming of his art in: *The Battle of Nancy*, *Melmoth* (sometimes wrongly called *L'Amende Honorable*), inspired by Charles Robert Maturin's novel; *Street in Meknes*, *Women of Algiers*, and a *Portrait of Rabelais* commissioned for Chinon. Lithographs illustrating *Hamlet*, a series he will not finish until 1843, and a subject borrowed from Byron's poem: *The Prisoner of Chillon*—which he will exhibit at the Salon of 1835—show the continuity of his literary enthusiasms. His cousin Mme de Forget becomes his mistress. Paints a portrait of Georges Sand.

1835
The laryngitis whose malignant development is eventually to prove fatal assails Delacroix in January. He works at speed to complete the Salon du Roi, where only the big *grisaille* figures of the rivers are still unfinished when the King comes to inaugurate it on 18 December. The public opening will take place in October 1836. Besides *The Prisoner of Chillon* for the Duke of Orleans, Delacroix shows at the Salon: *Christ Crucified between Thieves*, *The Natchez*, *The Arabs of Oran*, *Portrait of Guillemardet*. Various portraits, including those of his cousin Henri Hugues and of Mme Riesener, and *The Fight of the Giaour and the Pasha* are important. Paints the *Portrait of Tourville*. Stays with the Rieseners at Frépillon in February. In October Delacroix leaves 15 Quai Voltaire, where he has lived since 1829, and moves to 17 rue des Marais-Saint-Germain (now rue Visconti).

1836
Only one picture at the Salon: *Saint Sebastian rescued by the Holy Women*. Embarks on the series of lithographs for *Goetz von Berlichingen*, which will be completed in 1843. October: public opening of the Salon du Roi.

1837
First unsuccessful candidature for the Institut (Baron Gérard's seat). Works on the big picture commissioned for the Galerie des Batailles at Versailles, which Louis-Philippe has turned into a museum of history: *The Battle of Taillebourg*. Only this canvas appears at the Salon. At about this time (1834-7), Jenny Le Guillou (1801-1869) becomes his housekeeper, found for him by his friends the Pierrets.

1838
A new set-back at the Institut (Thévenin's seat) does not prevent him from getting the commission to decorate the Library of the Chambre des Députés and, a few months later, to paint for Versailles *The Entry of the Crusaders into Constantinople*, which he will exhibit at the Salon of 1841. At the Salon he shows: *Medea*, *The Fanatics of Tangier*, *Moroccan Caïd visiting a Tribe*, *Interior of a Moroccan Courtyard*, *Don Juan*. During November he sets up a studio in the rue Neuve-Guillemin to train the team of assistants which will work with him at the Palais Bourbon. A holiday at Le Tréport with Mme de Forget in August and a visit to Valmont in September are his only periods of relaxation from intensive work.

1839
Takes in hand the pendentives for the Library of the Chambre, painting them at the studio. Sends to the Salon: *Cleopatra and the Countryman*, *Hamlet in the Graveyard*, *Tasso in the Madhouse* (painted 1824). In September he makes a trip with Elisabeth Boulanger to Holland and then to Belgium in order to see the Rubens paintings (where Elisabeth left him).

1840
The death of his childhood friend Félix Guillemardet affects him greatly. April: entrusted with the decoration of the cupola and hemicycle of the Luxembourg. As the academic artist Robert-Fleury has been unable to paint the Chapel of the Virgin in Saint-Denis-du-Saint-Sacrement, the *Préfet* of the Seine gives this commission to Delacroix. At the Salon he shows *The Justice of Trajan*, a huge canvas inspired

by a passage from Dante, and bought by the State for the Musée des Beaux-Arts at Rouen. During his stay at Valmont the stormy sea suggests to him with what will become *The Shipwreck of Don Juan*, exhibited at the Salon of 1841.

1841
Suffers continual ill-health, but works strenuously at the sketches for the Chambre pendentives and their execution. At the end of the year the theme for the Luxembourg dome is chosen and the design roughed out. At the Salon: *The Entry of the Crusaders into Constantinople, The Shipwreck of Don Juan, Jewish Wedding in Morocco.*

1842
Suffers another attack of the laryngitis that will give him pain until his death. To take a rest he stays in March with his Riesener cousins at Frépillon and then in June with George Sand at Nohant, where he enjoys a period of happiness in the beauty and calm of the Berry countryside and the friendship of Chopin. Paints *The Education of the Virgin.*

1843
Prepares the great *Pietà* for Saint-Denis-du-Saint-Sacrement, does the 'Theology' and 'Legislation' cupolas at the Chambre, returns to the 'Orpheus' hemicycle, and designs that of 'Attila'. The lithographs for *Hamlet* and for *Goetz von Berlichingen* provide a rest from his toil on the large decorative paintings. A trip to Vichy in June, a visit to Nohant in July.

1844
Completes the 'Legislation' and 'Poetry' cupolas. A mishap with the 'Orpheus' hemicycle, whose canvas becomes detached, forces him to begin everything again straight on the walls. He executes the *Pietà* for Saint-Denis-du-Saint-Sacrement, where the lighting is unsatisfactory, and restores the paintings by Le Sueur at the Hôtel Lambert. Pierre Andrieu, who will be his most faithful follower, enters his studio. In June he installs himself at Champrosay near his friends the Villots. During October he leaves his studio in the rue des Marais-Saint-Germain. He has rented another in the rue Notre-Dame-de-Lorette (No. 54, now 58), but occupation is delayed by redecoration and he puts up temporarily at 29 rue de La Rochefoucauld, moving to the rue Notre-Dame-de-Lorette in 1845.

1845
Completes and sets in place the decorations for the Palais Bourbon pendentives and those for the Luxembourg dome. The classical preoccupations that haunt him in connexion with his decorative works are clearly apparent in the subjects and compositions of his pictures at the Salon: *The Death of Marcus Aurelius, The Sibyl with the Golden Bough*; there is also the painting of *The Sultan of Morocco surrounded by his Court.* Delacroix is delighted by some Iowa Indians brought to Paris by the American painter Georges Catlin, and makes numerous sketches of them from life. A spell of treatment for his throat in the Pyrenees at Les Eaux-Bonnes, by way of Bordeaux, during July-August, brings him an imposing vision of the mountains (drawings, water-colours, and pastels from nature). He is struck by the oddity of Pyrenean types and costumes. Henceforth the landscapes in his big compositions will recall the epic quality of the storms and peaks of the Ossau region. On 30 December his brother General Charles Delacroix dies.

1846
February: article on Prud'hon in the *Revue des Deux Mondes.* Delacroix is made an officer of the Légion d'Honneur. His efforts to finish the *Alexander* hemicycle at the Luxembourg and to hurry on the *Orpheus* and *Attila* for the Chambre des Députés completely engross him in spite of his exhausting illness. The Library of the Luxembourg is opened to the public in December. At the Salon: *The Abduction of Rebecca* inspired by Scott's *Ivanhoe*; *Romeo and Juliet, Marguerite in Church.* A stay at Bordeaux, for the settlement of his brother's estate, and another at Nohant in July.

1847
In January he resumes his *Journal.* From now on he will jot down recollections, quotations from his reading and his thoughts. Completes the two hemicycles and the 'Philosophy' cupola of the Library of the Chambre, which is inaugurated in December. At the Salon: *Crucifixion, Moroccan Military Exercises, Jewish Musicians of Mogador, Castaways in a Ship's Boat, Odalisque, Corps de Garde at Meknes.*

1848
The February Revolution does not arouse Delacroix's enthusiasm. His *Richelieu celebrating Mass* disappears in the burning of the Palais Royal. During September he writes an article on Gros for the *Revue des Deux Mondes.* In December the election of Napoleon to the Presidency of the Second Republic gives him hopes—thanks to the Bonapartist friendships of his cousin Josephine de Forget, *née* Lavalette, and to his family connexions—of an official career. At the Salon: *Pietá, Death of Valentine, Death of Lara, Arab Actors and Clowns, Lion devouring a Goat.* In June and July he is at Champrosay, in August at the home of his friend Count de Mornay, and in September at Champrosay again.

1849
May: a member of the Fine-Arts Commission and the Salon hanging committee, he receives a commission to decorate a chapel in the Church of Saint-Sulpice. Stands a fourth time for election to the Institut, only to see Léon Cogniet preferred. Offers himself a fifth time, then withdraws his candidature. Prepares four flower-paintings for the Salon, but only shows two of them, plus one from the preceding year, with a second version of the *Women of Algiers, Othello and Desdemona, Syrian Arab and his Horse.* In May and September he is at Champrosay. During October he stays at Valmont and is

enchanted by the beauties of the old abbey and the sea. On his return he learns of the death of his great friend Chopin.

1850
March: Thanks to Charles Blanc is commissioned to decorate the ceiling of the Galerie d'Apollon in the Louvre. Taking as his subject *Apollo destroying the Serpent Python*, he works out the composition very quickly. He will execute it on a canvas to be glued to the ceiling. Andrieu assists him in this enormous task. At the Salon: *The Raising of Lazarus, Le Lever, The Giaour, Lady Macbeth, The Good Samaritan*. During May he rests in the calm countryside of Champrosay. In July he leaves for a cure at Ems, travelling via Brussels and Antwerp to see the Rubens paintings again, and then goes on to Cologne. Death in this year of his friend Jules-Robert Auguste, whose paintings of horses and collection of Eastern costumes had influenced and helped Delacroix.

1851
Offers himself as a candidate for Drolling's seat, and once again the Institut rejects him. The Galerie d'Apollon is opened in June even though the ceiling not yet finished. This is completed in October. Appointed a City Councillor, Delacroix is charged with the responsibility of giving advice on the restoration of certain churches. The *coup d'état* of 2 December, re-establishing the Empire, does not cause him any grief. December: commissioned to decorate the ceiling of the Salon de la Paix in the Hôtel de Ville. Stays at Champrosay, and from August to September at Dieppe.

1852
During the intervals in his work for the Hôtel de Ville, where he is aided by Andrieu, he rests at Champrosay and in September at Dieppe.

1853
Becomes acquainted with one of his admirers, Alfred Bruyas, of whom he paints what is probably his finest portrait. Seventh candidature for the Institut. At Champrosay he prepares an article on Poussin for the *Moniteur Universel*. At the Salon: *Disciples and Holy Women raising the Body of Saint Stephen, The Supper at Emmaus, Abduction of an Arab Woman by African Pirates*. Seven versions of *Christ on the Lake of Genesareth*. Stays at Champrosay in May.

1854
July: For the *Revue des Deux Mondes* he writes '*Questions sur le Beau*'. Finishes the Salon de la Paix ceiling and the 'Labours of Hercules' frieze at the Hôtel de Ville. These decorations were destroyed by fire during the Commune in 1871. Stays at Champrosay in March, at Dieppe in August, and at Augerville with Antoine Berryer from October to November.

1855
During intervals in his work of preparation for Saint-Sulpice, the organizing of the Exposition Universelle, at which he shows forty-two canvases, and his social life, he goes to Champrosay in June and then to Augerville in July. In September, with the Verninacs at Croze in the Lot region, reecovers treasured memories of his sister and nephew. After a brief stay with his Lamey cousins at Strasbourg, where the Gothic enchants him, he is at Dieppe in October. Stays at Augerville in November. He receives the Grande Médaille d'Honneur and was made a commander of the Légion d'Honneur.

1856
The work for Saint-Sulpice is interrupted at the end of the year by his illness. A journey through the Argonne (Ante, Givry) in September introduces him to the region of origin of his father's family. In November he offers himself as a candidate for the seat of Paul Delaroche. Four large pictures of *The Seasons* commissioned but never completed.

1857
10 January: He is finally elected to the Institut. His illness prostrates him and makes him unable to continue the Saint-Sulpice work for three months. Recuperating at Champrosay, he plans a Dictionary of the Fine Arts. A brief stay at Strasbourg followed by a cure at Plombières in August, and then a spell at Augerville in October, are his only other visits. On 28 December he takes up residence at 6 Place Furstenberg. '*Des Variations du Beau*' published in the *Revue des Deux Mondes*.

1858
A fresh bout of his illness forces him to spend long periods at Champrosay, where in August he buys the house he had previously rented. A cure at Plombières during July restores him to health, and he resumes work on the Chapel of the Holy Angels in Saint-Sulpice. Paints *The Death of Lara*.

1859
At the Salon, the last to which he sends exhibits: *Christ Carrying the Cross, The Entombment of Christ, Saint Sebastian, Ovid among the Scythians, Erminia and the Shepherds, The Abduction of Rebecca, Hamlet, The Banks of the River Sebou*. Saint-Sulpice is his great anxiety, work there being scarcely interrupted in August by a trip to Strasbourg and Ante, and in October by the necessary recuperation in the country at Champrosay and Augerville.

1860
Ill again, he once more finds himself compelled to break off work on the Chapel of the Holy Angels, and only resumes it in the spring. Husbanding his strength he installs himself at Champrosay until November, but travels to and fro all through the summer in order to finish his work: on the ceiling,

*Saint Michael overthrowing the Devil*; on the right wall, *Heliodorus driven from the Temple*; on the left wall, *Jacob wrestling with the Angel*. An exhibition at the Galerie Martinet in the Boulevard des Italiens brings together sixteen of his pictures. He spends a fortnight at Dieppe in July.

1861
Sees the completion of his masterpiece in Saint-Sulpice. The lack of official interest at the inauguration of the chapel on 21 July distresses him. From August on he is back at Champrosay. Sketches out the *Seasons*.

1862
The winter exacerbates his laryngitis. While ill he writes an article on Charlet. Exhibits again at the Galerie Petit. In September he makes a trip to Ante, returns to Champrosay and then goes in October to Augerville.

1863
During January his illness becomes acute; he spends most of the time in the country. He paints his last important pictures: *Arabs skirmishing in the Mountains (The Collection of the Arab Taxes)* and *Tobias and the Angel*. On 13 August he dies at his apartment in the Place Furstenberg.

# BIBLIOGRAPHY

*A complete chronological bibliography would run the risk of bewildering the reader. It seemed preferable to classify the most useful publications and to guide the reader's investigation of them.*

## I BASIC WORKS


Essential reading, despite its considerable age, remains:
*L'Œuvre complet d'Eugène Delacroix, peintures, dessins, gravures, lithographies,* catalogued and reproduced by ALFRED ROBAUT, with a commentary by ERNEST CHESNEAU, Charavay Frères, Paris, 1885.

This catalogue includes no less than 1,968 items, and for the majority gives a diagrammatic sketch done with the camera obscura and representing the composition. Robaut was the son of Félix Robaut, a lithographer from Douai whom Delacroix mentions several times in his *Journal,* and the son-in-law of the Arras painter Constant Dutilleux, a friend of Corot and Delacroix, and so was in a good position to prepare this enormous list. At the Bibliothèque Nationale there is a copy with his corrections and additions.

The Arras collector C. LE GENTIL, a friend of Dutilleux, published: *M. Alfred Robaut et l'œuvre de Delacroix (Salon de 1879)* (a lecture given at the Académie d'Arras), Arras, 1879.

Two monumental biographies have been devoted to Delacroix:

ÉTIENNE MOREAU-NÉLATON, *Eugène Delacroix raconté par lui-même,* 2 vols, Henri Laurens, Paris, 1916.

This work is largely made up of the numerous documents, comprising in particular a great many letters, that the author assembled and left to the Louvre and the Bibliothèque Nationale.

RAYMOND ESCHOLIER, *Delacroix, peintre, graveur, écrivain,* 3 vols (I 1798-1833, II 1832-48, III 1848-63), Floury, Paris, 1926, 1927, 1929.

Embodying as it does all the data published by Moreau-Nélaton and adding a considerable amount of often fresh information, this is the fundamental work. In 1963 its author published a new, more limited version, which constitutes the rounding off of his thought: *Eugène Delacroix,* Editions Cercle d'Art, Paris.


## II LITERARY WORKS OF DELACROIX


The literary production of Delacroix, who is entitled to a place among the great writers of the nineteenth century, comprises:

I Youthful works: a play, *Victoria,* soon to be published, and two short stories. One of the stories, *Les Dangers de la Cour,* was published in 1960 by JEAN MARCHAND, Aubanel ed., Avignon; the other, *Alfred,* was introduced by JEAN MARCHAND in *Les Nouvelles Littéraires,* 14 August 1952, under the heading *'Delacroix fut écrivain avant d'être peintre'.*

II Articles that appeared during his lifetime in the *Revue de Paris, Revue des Deux Mondes, Moniteur Universel,* and *Plutarque français.* Some deal with aesthetics (*'Des critiques en matière d'art', 'De l'enseignement du dessin', 'Questions sur le Beau', 'Des variations du Beau',* etc.); others with the great artists (Raphael, Michelangelo, Poussin, Puget, Prud'hon, Lawrence, Gros, Charlet, etc.).

The painter's executor PIRON produced the first compilation of them, adding some extracts from the notebooks and sketchbooks, in an edition limited to 300 copies: *Eugène Delacroix, sa vie et ses œuvres,* Imprimerie Jules Claye, Paris, 1865. G. DARGENTY, in his *Eugène Delacroix par lui-même,* J. Rouan, Paris, 1885, attempted a biography based mainly on extracts from the painter's own writings.

The great critic ELIE FAURE produced a new edition of the articles: *Œuvres littéraires* in 2 vols: I *Études esthétiques (doctrines, impressions et méditations),* II *Essais sur les artistes célèbres,* G. Crès (Bibliothèque Dionysienne), Paris, 1923. It contains many additions.

The *'Questions sur le Beau'* was published in an edition of 275 copies by F. Billerey, Montbéliard, 1955.

*'Des critiques en matière d'art'* has been translated into English

by WALTER PACH as *On Art Criticism*, Curt Valentin, New York, 1946; Wittenborn, New York.

III Notes made by Delacroix in his sketch-books, in his notebooks, and on loose sheets.

The first edition of these was compiled by PAUL FLAT, with an introduction: *Journal d'Eugène Delacroix*, 3 vols, Plon et Nourrit, Paris, 1893-5. ANDRÉ JOUBIN was responsible for the second edition, carefully revised after the original manuscript and including an introduction and notes: 3 vols (I 1822-52, II 1853-6, III 1857-63), Plon, Paris, 1932. The same publisher brought out a new edition in 1960, more copiously illustrated and preceded by an important preface by Jean-Louis Vaudoyer, of the Académie Française.

In English there is a selection from the *Journal* translated by WALTER PACH, published by Covici, Friede, New York, 1937; Cape, London, 1938; Crown, New York, 1948; Grove Press (Evergreen Books), New York, 1961. HUBERT WELLINGTON has edited and LUCY NORTON translated another selection, Phaidon, London, 1951.

IV An extremely important correspondence. After J.-J. GUIFFREY had collected and published the *Lettres inédites*, Imprimerie Rillet et Dumoulin, Paris, 1877, PHILIPPE BURTY assembled for the first time the *Lettres d'Eugène Delacroix*, Quantin, Paris, 1877. A second edition, revised and enlarged (2 vols), was issued by Charpentier, Paris, 1880.

The publication of these earliest collections was followed by that of many more volumes of *Lettres inédites*, brought together by CHARLES DE LACOMBE (with Berryer, 1885), ALFRED ROBAUT (with Constant Dutilleux), AURORE SAND (with George Sand, 1930), TOURNEUX (to his sister, 1937), etc.

A new, more complete edition became necessary: this was the *Correspondance générale d'Eugène Delacroix*, 5 vols (I 1804-37, II 1838-49, III 1850-57, IV 1858-63, V supplement and tables), Plon, Paris, 1936.

ALFRED DUPONT has assembled the *Lettres intimes* (to Piron Guillemardet, Soulier, Charles Delacroix), *correspondance inédite*, preserved in his collection of original manuscripts: Gallimard, Paris, 1954. In the same year, CAMILLE BERNARD included in the *Mercure de France* of 1 May, a youthful letter, part of which had not previously been published, and in *Les Nouvelles Littéraires*, 9 May 1963, he brought out part of the unpublished correspondence with Madame Dalton under the title '*Une Liaison orageuse*'. Certain unpublished letters from George Sand to Delacroix were collected and introduced by ALFRED DUPONT and published by Blanchard, Paris 1953 in conjunction with André Maurois' *Lelia* in their series "Club du Meilleur Livre". RAYMOND ESCHOLIER, in the appendix of his book *Delacroix et les Femmes*, has assembled numerous unpublished letters written to Delacroix by Madame de Forget, Madame Dalton, and Elisa Boulanger.

Among the incomplete editions may be mentioned: *Écrits d'Eugène Delacroix, extraits du Journal, des lettres et des œuvres littéraires*, 2 vols, Plon, Paris [1942].

## III STUDIES BY CONTEMPORARIES

Among the famous authors or critics who devoted studies to Delacroix the following must be noted:

CHARLES BAUDELAIRE wrote substantially on him in hi analyses of the Salons and exhibitions, united in the *Curiosités esthétiques (Salon de 1845, Salon de 1846, Exposition universelle de 1855)*, Michel Lévy, Paris, 1868. In the same publisher's *l'Art romantique*, 1868, have been grouped: *L'Œuvre et la vie d'Eugène Delacroix, au rédacteur de l'Opinion Nationale* and *Peintures murales d'Eugène Delacroix à Saint-Sulpice*. Later on were published: *Eugène Delacroix par Charles Baudelaire*, Crès, Paris, 1927; and *Charles Baudelaire. La vie et l'œuvre d'Eugène Delacroix*, preface by JACQUES CREPET, R. Kieffer, Paris, 1928.

J. M BERNSTEIN has translated *L'Œuvre et la vie* into English as *Eugène Delacroix, his Life and Work*, Lear, New York, 1947. It is also included in *The Mirror of Art, Critical Studies by Charles Baudelaire*, translated and edited by JONATHAN MAYNE, Phaidon, London, 1955; Doubleday, New York, 1956.

Finally, ELIE FAURE re-edited the *Curiosités esthétiques*, with the various texts on Delacroix, in the Bibliothèque Dionysienne published by Crès.

PHILIPPE BURTY included Eugène Delacroix in his *Maîtres et petits maîtres* (p. 51 ff.), Paris, 1877.

ERNEST CHESNEAU discussed him in *La Peinture française au XIXe siècle*, Dentu, Paris, 1862; in *L'Art et les artistes modernes*, Didier, Paris, 1864; and in *Peintres et statuaires romantiques*, Charavay Frères, Paris, 1880.

Likewise, AMÉDÉE CANTALOUBE in *Eugène Delacroix, l'homme et l'art, ses amis et ses critiques*, Dentu, Paris, 1864; HENRI DELABORDE in *Mélange sur l'art contemporain* (p. 72 ff.), Paris 1866; ALEXANDRE DUMAS in *L'Art et les artistes contemporains du Salon de 1859* (p. 9 ff.).

THÉOPHILE GAUTIER wrote on him in *Les Beaux-Arts en Europe*, 2 vols, Paris, 1852, and in *Eugène Delacroix*, Paris, 1855. Jointly with ARSÈNE HOUSSAYE and PAUL DE SAINT-VICTOR, he published *Dieux et demi-dieux de la peinture*, Morizot, Paris, 1864, which includes Delacroix.

HENRY DE LA MADELÈNE, '*Eugène Delacroix*', *Nouvelle Revue de Paris*, 1 September 1864, and *Eugène Delacroix à l'exposition du boulevard des Italiens*, Paris, 1864.

PAUL MANTZ in '*Artistes contemporains*', *Revue française* (p. 250 ff.), Paris, 1864.

THÉOPHILE SILVESTRE in *Histoire des artistes vivants*, Blanchard, Paris, 1855; in *Les Artistes français, études d'après nature*, Brussels and Leipzig, 1861 (re-edited by ELIE FAURE in the Bibliothèque Dionysienne, Crès, Paris, 1926); and lastly in *Eugène Delacroix, documents nouveaux*, Michel Lévy, Paris, 1864.

M. A. STEVENS in *Salon de 1863*, followed by an essay on '*Eugène Delacroix*', Paris, 1866.

THÉOPHILE THORÉ-BÜRGER in *Les Salons (1844-1868), études de critique d'esthétique*, Paris, 1893.

Among the painters who have referred to Delacroix must be noted THOMAS COUTURE in *Méthodes et entretiens d'atelier* (p. 194 ff.), Paris, 1867; ODILON REDON in *A soi-même*, Paris, 1878. THÉODORE ROUSSEAU in *Lettres sur Ingres et Delacroix*, Paris, 1859, and *Souvenirs sur Théodore Rousseau* (p. 242 ff.), by ALFRED SENSIER, Paris, 1872. Slightly later one finds references by SEURAT, in F. FÉNEON *'Notes inédites. . .'*, *Bulletin de la Vie artistique*, 1 and 15 April 1922, and by VAN GOGH in his letters to his brother Théo. *The Complete Letters of Vincent Van Gogh*, 3 vols, Thames and Hudson, London, 1958; New York Graphic Society, 1958. Among more recent writers, one should consult MAURICE BARRÈS, *'Le Testament d'Eugène Delacroix'*, *Revue hebdomadaire*, 18 June 1921, and OCTAVE MIRBEAU, *Des artistes. Première série*, Flammarion, Paris, 1922.

## IV COMPREHENSIVE STUDIES

There is a comparatively large number of these. Among the earlier ones, ADOLPHE MOREAU'S *Eugène Delacroix et son œuvre*, Librairie des Bibliophiles, Paris, 1873, is the first essay provided with a catalogue.

At the beginning of our century, MAURICE TOURNEUX, who as early as 1886 had summarized prior opinions on the artist in *Eugène Delacroix devant ses contemporains, ses écrits, ses biographes, ses critiques*, wrote a general study published by Henri Laurens, Paris, 1902. In 1871 EUGÈNE VÉRON produced an *Eugène Delacroix* for the Artistes Célèbres series, Librairie de l'Art, J. Rouan, Paris, and Gilbert Wood, London, 1887. Of the most important works, the next was the German biography by JULIUS MEIER-GRAEFE, *Eugène Delacroix Beiträge zu einer Analyse*, R. Piper, Munich, 1913.

As the centenary of romanticism approached and at the time of the exhibition organized on this occasion at the Louvre, these studies became more numerous. PAUL JAMOT produced his *Eugène Delacroix*, Henri Laurens, Paris, 1928. It was included in *Le Romantisme et l'art* (p. 93 ff.), a joint work, same publisher, 1928. In 1930 LOUIS HOURTICQ'S *Eugène Delacroix, l'œuvre du maître* came out in the 'Classiques de l'Art' series, Hachette, Paris. Also see the special number of the *Revue de l'Art ancien et moderne*, for January 1930, and that of the *Bulletin des Musées de France*, for June, by RENÉ HUYGHE, completed by the same author's *Après l'exposition Delacroix* (p. 238 ff.) of the same year. PAUL JAMOT comments on the same exhibition in *Documents* (p. 249 ff.), Paris, 1930. PIERRE COURTHION, whose *Vie de Delacroix* had been published in 1928 by Gallimard, Paris, wrote the text for an album of colour reproductions brought out by Skira, Geneva, in 1939. There is an English language version, issued by Zwemmer, London.

Apart from the very beautiful picture-book in the 'Demi-Dieux' series, Éditions du Dimanche, Paris, 1947, in which magnificent photographs, particularly of details, are accompanied by a historical summary and an essay by JEAN CASSOU, one finds henceforward mainly small popular works, such as that of MICHEL FLORISOONE in the 'Maîtres' series (60 pl.), Braun, Paris-Mulhouse, 1938, or those of JEAN PELLOTIER, for Hyperion, and JACQUES LASSAIGNE, for Flammarion. The first includes an English version of the text, the second was translated for Hyperion by LUCY NORTON (1951), and the third has been published in a translation made by D. I. WILTON (Longmans, London, and Harper, New York, 1950).

The year of Delacroix's centenary, 1963, has been the occasion of many new publications of this kind, for example *Delacroix, a pictorial biography* by YVONNE DESLANDRES, Thames and Hudson, London, 1963, and Viking Press, New York, 1963. In connection with this occasion, one might also refer to the many special numbers of various reviews: *Apollo*, January; *Europe*, April; *Jardin des Arts*, June; *La Revue du Louvre*, 1963, No. 2; *Les Nouvelles Littéraires*, 9 May; *Arts*; *Le Figaro*, etc.

A few works adopt a more specific point of view, such as FERNAND VALLON, *Au Louvre avec Delacroix*, preface by ELIE FAURE, Arthaud, Grenoble, 1930; or ANNE FONTAINE, *Delacroix poète*, Grasset, Paris, 1953, or *'Delacroix, homme de lettres d'après trois œuvres de jeunesse'* in *le Livre et l'Estampe*, the review of the Société des Bibliophiles Iconographes de Belgique (p. 173 ff.) No. 9 (3rd in 1959).

Several writers have turned their attention more particularly to Delacroix's philosophy: MICHEL FLORISOONE in *'A la recherche de Delacroix homme et âme'*, *Les Études*, July 1963; MADELEINE OCHSÉ in *'Delacroix et le drame chrétien'*, *Ecclesia*, August 1963.

On Delacroix's aesthetic position and its importance, see LIONELLO VENTURI, the great Italian critic, who enters upon this in his *Peintres modernes*, Albin Michel, Paris, 1941 (translated by HENRY FURST as *Modern Painters*, Charles Scribner's Sons, New York and London, 1947). LUCIEN RUDRAUF has devoted a monumental work to *Eugène Delacroix et le problème du romantisme artistique*, Henri Laurens, Paris, 1942, in which the extremely thorough study is accompanied by a very full bibliography. In 1928 HUBERT GUILLOT produced his *Eugène Delacroix, l'homme, ses idées, son œuvre*, les Belles-Lettres, Paris, in which Delacroix's views on life, literature, and art are analysed at the same time as his creative position, both ideological and in the works. RENÉ HUYGHE discusses *l'Universalité de Delacroix* in *Formes*', no VI, June 1930. The same author made a study of *'L'Éthique de Delacroix'* and drew attention to Delacroix's dandyism in his course at the Collège de France (a resumé appears in the yearbook of the Collège for 1953), and he has dealt with *'Delacroix peintre du combat de l'homme'* in *Historia* (p. 59 ff.), No. 200. CHARLES LALO has already concerned himself with the psychological aspect in *'Eugène Delacroix, esquisse d'un type psycho-esthétique'*, *Journal de Psychologie normale et pathologique*, April and June, 1940-41. BLANCHE REY'S approach is that of the graphologist in *'Eugène Delacroix d'après son écriture'*, *La Thesbaine*, May-June, 1927.

## V BIOGRAPHICAL PARTICULARS

On Delacroix's parentage: ANDRÉ GIRODIE, '*Delacroix est-il le fils de Talleyrand?*', *L'Art vivant* (p. 681 ff.), 1926. DR BENASSIS, same title, *Revue thérapeutique*, January 1932. E. GRAVE, '*Le Père de Delacroix*', *Intermédiaire des Chercheurs et des Curieux*, 10 September 1911. DR MAURICE GENTY, '*Le Chirurgien Ange Imbert Delonnes et l'opération de Charles Delacroix*', *Le Progrès médical*, illustrated supplement (p. 25 ff.), April 1932. ANDRÉ JOUBIN, '*Documents nouveaux sur Eugène Delacroix et sa famille*', *Gazette des Beaux-Arts* (p. 173 ff.)., January 1933. PAUL LOPPIN, '*Un ministre calomnié, Charles Delacroix*', *Revue des Deux Mondes*, 1 January 1955. This same study was published in conjunction with '*L'Énigme de la naissance d'Eugène Delacroix*' under the title *Charles et Eugène Delacroix: les grandes figures champenoises*, Pierre Béarn, Paris, 1963. ANDRÉ GAVOTY has supplied complete biographical information about Félicité Riesener in '*La "Bonne Tante" de Delacroix*', *Revue des Deux Mondes* (p. 248 ff.), 15 May 1963.

On the details of his life, it is again ANDRÉ JOUBIN who has provided the largest number of partial studies: '*Logis et atelier d'Eugène Delacroix*', *Bulletin de la Société de l'Histoire de l'Art français* (p. 60 ff.), 1938; '*Les Modèles d'Eugène Delacroix*', ibid. (p. 135 ff.), 1936; same title, *Gazette des Beaux-Arts*, June 1936; '*Mr Haro entre Ingres et Delacroix*', *L'Amour de l'Art* (p. 85 ff.), 1936; '*Un sosie de Delacroix*', *Bulletin de la Société de l'Histoire de l'Art français* (p. 42 ff.), 1934; '*La Candidature de Delacroix à l'Institut*', ibid. (p. 5 ff.), 1935, etc. About Delacroix's attachment to Madame de Forget, RAYMOND ESCHOLIER has written *Eugène Delacroix et sa 'consolatrice'*, Armand Colin, Paris, 1932. He enlarges on the subject in *Delacroix et les femmes*, Fayard, Paris, 1963.

On the company Delacroix kept and on the idea that may have been formed of him by contemporaries who associated with him, one may read LÉON SECHÉ's *Le Cénacle de Joseph Delorme* (1827-1830), Paris, 1911, and also recollections of the period: those of artists, like *Paul Huet d'après ses notes et sa correspondance*, edited by RENÉ-PAUL HUET, Henri Laurens, Paris, 1913; and those of writers, like MAXIME DU CAMP's, *Souvenirs littéraires*, first in the *Revue des Deux Mondes*, 1882, then in two volumes, Hachette, Paris, 1882-3; new edition 1963 of ALEXANDRE DUMAS the elder's *Mes Mémoires* is obtainable in the 'Livres de Poche' series (Union générale d'Édition, Paris). Both the latter works have been translated into English: the first as *Maxime Du Camp's Literary Recollections*, 2 vols, Remington, London and Sydney, 1893; the second as *My Memoirs*, translated by E. M. WALLER and introduced by ANDREW LANG, 6 vols, Methuen, London, 1907-9. One may consult in addition PHILARÈTE CHASLES, *Mémoires*, Charpentier, Paris, 1876; or GEORGE SAND, *Journal intime*, edited by Aurore Sand, Calmann Lévy, Paris, 1926 (published in English as *The Intimate Journal of George Sand*, translation and notes by MARIE JENNEY HOWE, Williams and Norgate, London, 1929).

Society women have also left interesting documents, such as MADAME JAUBERT (Caroline d'Alton), *Souvenirs*, Paris, 1881, or Lady EGLÉ CHARLEMONT, '*Eugène Delacroix*', *Revue de Paris*, 20 January 1867.

The journey to Morocco is an episode in Delacroix's life that has given rise to many publications. First of all, the sketchbooks in which he fixed with pen and brush his impressions and his memories were reproduced with commentaries: JEAN GUIFFREY, *Le Voyage d'Eugène Delacroix au Maroc*, a facsimile of the Louvre sketchbook (106 pp.), with a description of the Musée Condé sketchbooks from the MOREAU-NÉLATON and MORNAY collections, 2 vols, André Marty, Paris, 1909; and, with the same title, a facsimile of the sketchbook preserved at the Château de Chantilly (66 pp.), 2 vols, J. Terquem et P. Lemar, Paris, 1913. Much precise detail has been provided by ANDRÉ JOUBIN in *Voyage au Maroc, 1832*, Les Beaux-Arts, Paris, 1930, which contains letters, water-colours, and drawings, with an introduction and notes; and by ELIE LAMBERT in his article '*Un nouveau Document sur le séjour de Delacroix à Tanger*', *Gazette des Beaux-Arts*, 1939 (p. 119 ff.). One may also refer to the catalogue of the *Vente du Comte de M*[ornay], comprising two oil-paintings and eight watercolours, Hôtel Drouot, Paris, 1877; to M. REGARD, '*Eugène Delacroix et le Comte de Mornay au Maroc, documents inédits*', *Études d'Art* (p. 31 pp.), 1952; to M. SERULLAZ, *Delacroix, Watercolours of Morocco*, Zwemmer, London, and Hazan, Paris, 1952; and to M. HOSOTTE-REYNAUD, '*Un Ami méconnu et deux œuvres inédites d'Eugène Delacroix*', Hespéris, vol. 40 (p. 534 ff.), 1953. (This concerns works offered by the painter to the consul Delaporte.)

To Delacroix's interest in other regions, we owe: LYDIE BOUTHET, '*Delacroix et l'Angleterre*', *Musées de France* (p. 139 ff.), July, 1948; '*Delacroix et l'Espagne*' seen by ELIE LAMBERT, *Revue des Arts* (p. 159 ff.), 1951 and by ESTHER VAN LOO in *La Revue Française* (p. 15 ff.), 1955, no. 65; '*Delacroix et l'Abbaye de Valmont*' by ANNIE CONAN, *Art de France* (p. 271 ff.), III, P. Bérès, Paris 1963; '*Delacroix et les Charentes*' by B. LOISY, *Le Pays d'Ouest* (p. 2 ff.), 1946, no. 5.

On Delacroix and his connections with music there are several articles, including G. J. AUBRY, '*Delacroix et la musique*', *Revue musicale*, 1 April 1920, and the study by R. O. EVANS, *Les Romantiques et la musique*, Champion, Paris, 1934. See also J.-L. VAUDOYER's important introduction to the latest edition of the *Journal* and his study '*Chopin et son ami Eugène Delacroix*', *Revue française*, no. 18, 1948. Also JULIUS STARZYNSKI, '*Delacroix et Chopin*', section 34 of the proceedings of the Conférences de l'Académie polonaise des Sciences.

## VI INFLUENCES AND RELATIONS

The admiration of Eugène Delacroix for Antiquity, paradoxical in a romantic, has often been stressed: WALTER PACH demonstrated '*Le Classicisme de Delacroix*' in the *Revue des Arts*, vol. 2 (p. 109 ff.), 1952, by basing himself on a drawing copied from a Pompeian fresco. B. POLAK extended the study of these connections in *'De invloed van enige monumenten der Oudheid op het classicisme van David, Ingres en Delacroix'*, *Nederlandsch Kunsthistorisch Jaarboek*, 1948-9, and CHARLES PICARD showed *'Les Emprunts antiques de David, Ingres et Delacroix'* in the *Revue d'Archéologie*, vol. 40 (p. 105 ff.), 1952.

From a more philosophical standpoint, GERMAIN BAZIN has related *'Delacroix et Marc Aurèle'* in *Formes* (p. 14 ff.), 1 September 1930.

Among earlier painters, Rubens has been particularly considered: LOUIS HOURTICQ, *'Rubens et Delacroix'*, *Revue de l'Art ancien et moderne*, 10 September 1909; ELIE LAMBERT, *'Delacroix et Rubens'*, especially with regard to Delacroix's *The Justice of Trajan*, *Gazette des Beaux-Arts*, 1932, II (pp. 245 ff. and 317 ff.); LUCIEN RUDRAUF, *'Imitation et invention: Delacroix et Rubens'*, chiefly in connection with *Christ carrying the Cross*, *Mélanges Georges Jamati* (p. 277 ff.), Paris, 1956.

On Rembrandt: HERTA WEGENER: *'The Disciples at Emmaus by Eugène Delacroix'*, *Brooklyn Museum Bulletin*, vol. 15, no. 3 (p. 2 ff.), 1954. OTTO BENESCH, *'Rembrandt's artistic heritage: From Goya to Cézanne'*, *Gazette des Beaux-Arts* (p. 101 ff.), 1962, II.

On Goya: M. FLORISOONE, *'Delacroix et Goya'*, *Bulletin de la Société de l'Histoire de l'Art français* (p. 131 ff.), 1958.

On Rosso: LUCIEN RUDRAUF, *Imitation et Invention dans l'Art d'Eugène Delacroix: Delacroix et le Rosso*, Tartu, C. Mattiesen, 1938.

As regards contemporary painters, most attention has been given to Monsieur Auguste (CHARLES SAUNIER, *'Un Artiste romantique oublié, Monsieur Auguste'*, *Gazette des Beaux-Arts*, 1910, especially in the chapter published in July, and the same artist's retrospective exhibition, at the end of the catalogue of the *Delacroix au Maroc* exhibition at the Orangerie, Paris, 1933); to Bonington (DOUGLAS COOPER, *'Bonington and Quentin Durward'*, *Burlington Magazine* 1946, p. 112 ff.); to Constable (ANDREW SHIRLEY, *'Paintings by John Constable in Paris'*, *Gazette des Beaux-Arts*, p. 173 ff., 1943, I); to Etty (DENNIS FAR, *'Delacroix and Etty'* *Burlington Magazine*, p. 80, March 1952); and to Géricault (CLAUDE ROGER-MARX, *'Géricault, Delacroix et l'Angleterre'*, *L'Art vivant*, p. 245, 1932; LUCIEN RUDRAUF, *'Une Variation de Delacroix sur le thème du Radeau de la Méduse'*, Deuxième Congrès international d'Esthétique, II, p. 500 ff., Paris, 1937). On Huet, who read the eulogy at Delacroix's funeral on behalf of his friends, there is the extremely well-documented book by PIERRE MIQUEL, *Paul Huet, de l'aube romantique à l'aube impressionniste*, Ed. de la Martinelle, 1962. One might also refer to RENÉ HUYGHE's preface to the catalogue of the exhibition in Bordeaux, *Delacroix maître parmi les maîtres*.

Among writers, interest has been focused mainly on Byron (EDMOND ESTEVE, *Byron et le romantisme français*, an essay on the success and influence of Byron's work in France from 1812 to 1850, Hachette, Paris 1907; ANDREW SHIRLEY in *Gazette des Beaux-Arts*, 1943; GEORGE HEARD HAMILTON, *'Eugène Delacroix and Lord Byron*, op. cit., 1943, I, p. 99 ff. and *'Hamlet or Childe Harold'*, op. cit., 1943, II, p. 365 ff.; by the same author, *'Delacroix, Byron and the English Illustrators'*, op. cit., 1950, XXVI, p. 261 ff.; JACK LINDSAY, *'Death of the Hero'*, *Burlington Magazine*, 1958); and on Goethe (P. JAMOT, *'Goethe et Delacroix'*, ibid., vol. 2, 1932). M. FLORISOONE investigated a Spanish source in *'Moratin, Inspirer of Géricault and Delacroix'*, *Burlington Magazine*, p. 303 ff., September 1957. GABRIEL ROUCHÈS examined *Eugène Delacroix et la littérature italienne'*, as a whole in *Mélanges H. Hauvette*, les Presses françaises, Paris, 1934. ELIE LAMBERT devoted an article to a painting inspired by Tasso: *'Une Scène du Roland Furieux'*, *Bulletin de la Société d'Histoire de l'Art français*, p. 146 ff., 1936.

Among contemporary writers, attention must be called above all to Baudelaire (ANDRÉ FERRAN'S thesis, *l'Esthétique de Baudelaire*, Hachette, Paris, 1933, gives the matter much space, even devoting a whole chapter to it; RENÉ HUYGHE's course of lectures on these relations at the Collège de France has not been published, but summaries of the lectures will be found in the *Annuaire du Collège de France* for the years 1951 to 1959, while the conclusions reached are set out in *L'Esthétique d'individualisme à travers Delacroix et Baudelaire*, Clarendon Press, Oxford, 1955, and *'Le Poète à l'école du peintre'*, chapter 8 of the *Baudelaire* in the 'Génies et Réalités' series, Hachette, Paris, 1959, and also in *'Delacroix and Baudelaire, A New Epoch in Art and Poetry'*, *Arts Yearbook 2, Romantic Art*, p. 26 ff., The Art Digest, New York, 1958; see also RENÉ JULLIAN, *'Delacroix et Baudelaire'*, *Gazette des Beaux-Arts*, p. 311 ff., 1956 and WOLFGANG DROST, *'Baudelaire et le néo-baroque'* in *Gazette des Beaux-Arts*, p. 115 ff., 1950, II); attention is also called to Musset (ÉMILE DACIER, *'A propos d'un portrait d'Alfred de Musset par Eugène Delacroix'*, *Gazette des Beaux-Arts*, 1911); and to George Sand (ANDRÉ JOUBIN, *'L'Amitié de George Sand et d'Eugène Delacroix'*, *Revue des Deux Mondes*, p. 833 ff., 1934; in the July 1926 number of the same review A. DE ROTHMALLER had considered *'Les Portraits de George Sand par Delacroix'*). MICHEL FLORISOONE wrote on *'La Mort d'une amitié: Delacroix et Villot'*, in the *Bulletin de la Société d'Histoire de l'Art français* (p. 383 ff.), 1959.

The pupils of Delacroix have been the subject of several studies: Madame ELISABETH BOULANGER-CAVÉ, known to have had an amorous escapade with Delacroix in Belgium, was honoured with an article by her master, published in the *Revue des Deux Mondes*, 15 September 1859, regarding her book *Le Dessin sans maître*, Suisse Frères, Paris, 1836, completed by a second part entitled *La Couleur*. ANDRÉ JOUBIN wrote about her in *'Deux amies de Delacroix. Madame Elisabeth Boulanger-Cavé et Madame Rang-Babut'*, *Revue de l'Art ancien et moderne*, January 1930. MME RANG-BABUT, also a pupil, has been presented in several articles: *'Une Élève de Delacroix'*, *Le Temps*, 4 August 1913; W. ROUMIEUX, same title, *Mercure de France*, 1 August 1913. PIERRE DU COLOMBIER revealed *'Un Élève inconnu d'Eugène Delacroix:* ÉMILE

KNOEPFLER' in *L'Amour de l'Art*, February 1937; and ANDRÉ JOUBIN introduced Louis de Planet, whose *'Souvenirs'* he published in the *Bulletin de la Société d'Histoire de l'Art français* (p. 368 ff.), 1928, and under the Armand Colin imprint, Paris, 1929. JOUBIN also wrote *'Les Conversations d'Eugène Delacroix avec M. de Planet'*, *L'Amour de l'Art* (p. 18 ff.), January 1928. Under the title *'Sténio'*, the *'journal intime d'un futur élève d'Eugène Delacroix durant les vacances de 1863, illustré par lui-même et commenté par Étienne de Planet'* had appeared in *L'Art méridional*, no. 46 ff., Toulouse, 1939.

On the influence of photography: BEAUMONT MEWHALL, *'Delacroix and Photography'*, *Magazine of Art* (p. 300 ff.), 1952.

## VII TECHNIQUE AND WORKS

RENÉ PIOT has passed on the information he obtained from his master Andrieu, who had worked with Delacroix, in *Les Palettes de Delacroix*, Librairie de France, Paris, 1931. PAUL SIGNAC considered mainly the teachings: *D'Eugène Delacroix au néo-impressionnisme*, Éditions de la Revue Blanche, Paris, 1899, republished by Floury, Paris, 1939 (4th edit.). Finally, FRITZ GYSIN, curator of the Historisches Museum at Basel, set about defining the successive styles in *Eugène Delacroix, Studien zu seiner künstlerischen Entwicklung*, Herz, Strasbourg, 1926.

Some studies have concentrated on Delacroix's themes: *'Eugène Delacroix et le thème de l'Odalisque'* by JACQUES MATHEY, *Gazette des Beaux-Arts* (p. 51 ff.), 1933, I; *'Delacroix et le thème de la Barque'* by RENÉ HUYGHE, *Revue du Louvre et des Musées de France* (p. 65 ff.), 1963, no. 2.

Delacroix's principal works have been the subject of many separate essays, among them: *Dante and Virgil in the Inferno* (1922): LEE JOHNSON, *'The formal Sources of Delacroix's Barque du Dante'*, *Burlington Magazine* (p. 228 ff.), July 1958. The same writer, who during recent years has contributed considerably to our knowledge of Delacroix, places the *Seasons*, done for Talma's dining-room, in the early years: see *'Delacroix's decorations for Talma's dining-room'*, ibid. (p. 78 ff.), March 1957. *The Massacre at Chios* (1924): JOACHIM GASQUET, *'Delacroix et les Massacres de Scio'*, *L'Amour de l'Art*, May 1921; ANDRÉ JOUBIN, *'Les Sources du Massacre de Scio'*, *Bulletin de la Société d'Histoire de l'Art français* (p. 40 ff.), 1935; MICHEL FLORISOONE, *'Constable and the Massacres de Scio by Delacroix'*, *Journal of the Warburg and Courtauld Institutes*, vol. 20, nos. 1 and 2, 1957. PAUL-HENRI MICHEL devoted to this work one of the 'Musée des Chefs-d'Œuvres' series, Paris, 1947. As *Delacroix: The Massacre of Chios*, it was published in an English translation by Max Parrish, London, 1947. Lastly, MARIE-THÉRÈSE COULLERY MIRA, in *'Delacroix et le Massacre de Scio'*, *Geneva*, new series, vol. 3 (p. 73 ff.), 1955, studied the preparatory sketches for the picture in connection with the one at the Musée d'Art et d'Histoire, Geneva, which it entered in 1888. Unfortunately, we do not think it is genuine.

*Tasso in the Madhouse* (1924 and 1927): ANDRÉ JOUBIN, *'A propos du Tasse'*, *Gazette des Beaux-Arts*, 1934, I (p. 247 ff.).

*Greece Expiring on the Ruins of Missolonghi* (1827): GEORGE H. HAMILTON, *'Delacroix's Memorial to Byron'*, *Burlington Magazine* (p. 257 ff.), 1952.

*The Death of Sardanapalus* (1827): JEAN GUIFFREY, *'La Mort de Sardanapal'*, *Gazette des Beaux-Arts* (p. 193 ff.), October 1921. The same writer examined the sketch for this picture in *Beaux-Arts*, 1 May 1925. LEE JOHNSON has shown *'The Etruscan Sources of Delacroix's Death of Sardanapalus'* in the *Art Bulletin*, vol. 42, Art Association of America, December 1960. BEATRICE FARWELL discusses the influence of India in *Art Bulletin*, 1958.

*The Murder of the Bishop of Liège* (1829): MICHÈLE TOUPET, *Revue du Louvre* (p. 83 ff.), 1963, no. 2.

*Liberty leading the People* (1830): HÉLÈNE ADHEMAR, *'La Liberté sur les barricades de Delacroix étudiées d'après des document inédits'*, *Gazette des Beaux-Arts* (p. 83 ff.), 1954. G. HEARD HAMILTON, *'La Liberté et Childe Harold'*, *Studies of Art and Literature*, 1954.

*The Battle of Nancy* (1831): GASTON SAVE, *'La Mort du Téméraire'*, *Bulletin de la Société artistique de l'Est*, Imprimerie coopérative de l'Est, Nancy, 1899. Returning to the conclusions of an article he had published in Switzerland during 1942, RENÉ HUYGHE followed the birth of the composition in *Dialogue avec le Visible* (p. 226 ff.), 1955. (Translated into English by Norbert Guterman as *Discovery of Art*, Thames and Hudson London 1959; Abrams, New York). See also *'A propos de la Bataille de Nancy par Eugène Delacroix'* by THÉRÈSE CHARPENTIER, *Revue du Louvre*, 1963, II.

*King Rodrigue* (1831): EMIL WALDMANN, *'Le Roi Rodrigue'*, *Documents* (p. 145 ff.), Paris, 1929. At the end of 1833 Delacroix embarked on his decorative paintings, to which MAURICE SERULLAZ has devoted a study: *Les Peintures murales de Delacroix*, Éd. du Temps, Paris, 1963. On the frescoes painted at Valmont in 1834 he has published *'Les premières Décorations murales de Delacroix'*, in *Arts de France*, III (p. 265 ff.) Pierre Bérès, Paris 1963.

*Encounter between Moorish Horsemen* (1833): LEE JOHNSON, *'Delacroix's Rencontre de cavaliers Maures'*, *Burlington Magazine* (p. 417 ff.), October 1961.

*Women of Algiers* (1834): ELIE LAMBERT, *Delacroix et les Femmes d'Alger*, Henri Laurens, Paris, 1937.

Salon du Roi decorations: JEAN GUIFFREY, *'Le Salon du Roi à la Chambre des Députés'*, *L'Art*, vol. 13 (p. 257 ff.); and, with regard to one of the scuncheons of the Library, THÉOPHILE HOMOLLE, *'Pline commenté par Eugène Delacroix'*, *Comptes rendus de l'Académie des Inscriptions et Belles-Lettres*, 7-10, 1921.

*The Entry of the Crusaders into Constantinople* (1840): ANDRÉ LINZELER, *'Une Source d'inspiration inconnue d'Eugène Delacroix'*, *Bulletin de la Société d'Histoire de l'Art français* (p. 47 ff.), 1932.

*The Justice of Trajan* (1840): M. ALLINNE, *La Genèse d'un chef-d'œuvre: la Justice de Trajan*, Rouen, 1930. ELIE LAMBERT looked for the source of the composition in Rubens' *The Elevation of the Cross*, *Gazette des Beaux-Arts* (p. 245 ff.), November 1932.

*Pietà* (1843): JULIEN STIRLING, *A propos d'un tableau d'Eugène Delacroix*, I-IV, la Cité, Paris, 1920.

*The Sultan of Morocco* (1845): ELIE LAMBERT, *Histoire d'un tableau, l'Abd-er-Rahman . . .*, Institut des Hautes Études marocaines, no. 14, Larose, Paris, 1953. LEE JOHNSON examined '*Une Source possible de l'Abd-er-Rahman*' (Lebrun's *Chancelier Séguier*) in the *Revue des Arts* (p. 249 ff.), November-December 1957.

Decoration for the Chambre des Députés (1845-7): A. HUSTIN, '*Peintures d'Eugène Delacroix au Sénat*', *Les Arts*, no. 191, 1920; on '*La pensée Orphique du plafond d'Homère de Delacroix*' see JULIUS STARZYNSKI in *Revue du Louvre* (p. 73 ff.), 1963, no. 2.

*Apollo vanquishing the Serpent Python* (1850): MME J. BOUCHOT-SAUPIQUE published a preparatory drawing, given to the Louvre by Count Doria, in *Musée de France*, 1948; and JENNIFER MONTAGUE has made a study of '*Le Brun et Delacroix dans La Galerie d'Apollon*' in *Revue du Louvre* (p. 233 ff.), 1962.

*Michelangelo* (1850): CH. DE TOLNAY published a study of this work in the *Gazette des Beaux-Arts*, February 1962.

Saint-Sulpice, chapel of the Holy Angels: F. GRUBAR studied drawings for the *Heliodorus* in '*Two Drawings by Delacroix*', *News*, Baltimore Museum of Art, vol. 17 no. 1 (p. 1 ff.), 1953. The preparatory drawings at the Albertina, Vienna, have been examined by ALFRED STIX in '*Studien Delacroix' zu seinem Wandgemälde Jakob . . .*', *Belvedere*, vol. 7 (p. 63 ff.), Vienna (1925). LUCIEN RUDRAUF compared *Jacob wrestling with the Angel* to Salvator Rosa's *Temptation* at the Musée Condé, Chantilly in *Apollo*, no. 23 (p. 11 ff.), 1951. It is primarily to the period of Saint-Sulpice that RAYMOND REGAMEY devoted his extremely important book, *Eugène Delacroix, époque de la chapelle des Saints-Anges (1847-63)*, Renaissance du Livre, Paris, 1931. In fact this work has a wider scope, and is among the most profound studies of the thought and soul of Delacroix.

## VIII THE DRAWINGS

We owe a general study to GUILLAUME JANNEAU: *Le Dessin de Delacroix*, Paris, 1921. RENÉ HUYGHE published an article with the same title in the review *L'Art à Saint-Étienne et en Forez*, Bulletin de l'Association des Amis du Musée, no. 2, n.d. One should also refer to the introductions by CLAUDE ROGER-MARX to the exhibitions of drawings held at the Galerie Dru, Paris, in April-May 1925 and at the Kunsthaus, Zurich, from January to April 1939.

Several publications offer a selection of reproductions. As early as 1864, there is ALFRED ROBAUT, *Fac-similés de dessins et de croquis originaux*, Paris. More recently, CHARLES MARTINE, *Eugène Delacroix, soixante-dix dessins, croquis . . .*, Helleu et Sergent, Paris, 1928. In the following year, the review *Documents* (p. 255 ff.) published '*Un album de dessins de Delacroix*' (then in the David-Weill collection). In 1933 appeared CLAUDE ROGER-MARX's *Choix de cinquante dessins de Delacroix*, in the *Dessins et Peintures des Maîtres du XIX^e siècle à nos Jours* collection, 2nd series, Braun, Paris-Mulhouse; and in 1938 PIERRE LAVALLÉE's *Eugène Delacroix, quatorze dessins*, Éditions des Musées nationaux, Paris, 1938. In 1946 there was KURT BADT, *Eugène Delacroix, Drawings*, 2nd. Edn. Cassirer, Oxford, 1946.

On particular periods: LEE JOHNSON, '*The early drawings of Delacroix*', *Burlington Magazine* (p. 22 ff.), January 1956. MAURICE SERULLAZ has published with detailed commentaries: *Les Dessins de Delacroix au Musée du Louvre (1817-27)*, Albert Morancé, Paris, [1952]. One can only hope that this enterprise will be continued. In 1928 Le Garrec brought out *Trente et un dessins et aquarelles du Maroc*, as facsimile reproductions. For the works of Delacroix's last years: MAURICE SERULLAZ, *Album de croquis* (1855-59), one volume of facsimiles and one of text, Quatre Chemins-Editart, Paris, 1961. MICHEL BUNDORFF selected several unpublished drawings from the Louvre and published them under the title '*Delacroix un siècle après sa mort*', *Médecine de France* (p. 17 ff.), no. 145, August 1963.

## IX THE PRINTS

For the prints as a whole, see LOYS DELTEIL, *Le Peintre-graveur illustré*, vol. 3, Paris, 1908 (the most complete); and the same author's *Manuel de l'amateur d'estampes des XIX^e et XX^e siècles*, with catalogue, vol. 1, Paris, 1925. A small book containing a selection of twenty-eight reproductions appeared as no. 2 in the 'Graveurs Français Nouveaux' series, Gallimard, Paris, 1929, under the title *L'Œuvre gravé d'Eugène Delacroix*, with a preface by CLAUDE ROGER-MARX. See also the same writer's article of the same title in *L'Amour de l'Art* (p. 182 ff.), 1929.

The special studies include: GERMAIN HEDIARD, '*Les Lithographies de Delacroix*', *L'Artiste*, August, September, and October 1889; JEAN LARAN, '*Péchés de jeunesse d'Eugène Delacroix (1815-20)*', *Gazette des Beaux-Arts*, 1930, 1 (p. 55 ff.); and GABRIEL ROUCHES, '*La Suite lithographique d'Eugène Delacroix pour Goetz de Berlichingen*', *Estampes* (p. 33 ff.), 1927.

## X EXHIBITIONS

Immediately after Delacroix's death there was an exhibition of his work (1864) at the Société Nationale des Beaux-Arts, Boulevard des Italiens, following the posthumous sale. The catalogue, Clay, Paris, 1864, has a preface by d'Arpentigny. In 1878 Delacroix was represented in the retrospective exhibition of paintings and drawings by modern masters, organized by the Galerie Durand-Ruel in Paris.

About seven years later, during March and April 1885, a big show was held at the École des Beaux-Arts in aid of the subscription for the monument subsequently raised in the Jardin du Luxembourg. AUGUSTE VACQUERIE and PAUL MANTZ introduced the catalogue. Not until the centenary of romanticism in 1930 was there a large retrospective exhibition (342 items), held during June and July at the Louvre. The catalogue, of which a second, corrected edition appeared, was prefaced by PAUL JAMOT and completed by an album of 137 reproductions, Éditions des Musées Nationaux, Paris, 1930.

From then on up to the Delacroix centenary year, 1963, one can only point to exhibitions of limited scope.

First must be mentioned those organized almost yearly by the Société des Amis de Delacroix at the appartments and studio in the Place Furstenberg, which were rescued by the society and then acquired by the Musées Nationaux. These exhibitions have had varied themes: '*Delacroix and his Times*' in 1946, '*Delacroix and the Companions of his Youth*' in 1947, '*Delacroix and England*' in 1948, '*Delacroix and Romantic Portraiture*', '*Delacroix and the Orientalism of his Times*', and finally, in 1963, '*Delacroix, Citizen of Paris*'. The society also put on exhibitions of drawings to mark the occasion of the opening (for which it was responsible) of the rooms decorated by Delacroix at the Chambre des Députés and the Senate. All these shows have been accompanied by small catalogues: that of the drawings for Delacroix's decorations at the Chambre des Députés includes a schematic plan of the compositions and their distribution. Besides an official one devoted to Delacroix's journey to Morocco at the Orangerie in 1933, some exhibitions held at dealers' galleries should be noted, such as those of the Galerie Paul Rosenberg (January-February 1928), the Galerie Maurice Gobin (November-December 1937), and the Galerie Daber, which showed several little-known pictures in its 'Paintings, 1830-1940' exhibition during May 1962. Watercolours and drawings have been assembled by the Galerie Dru (April-May 1925) and the Galerie Nina Dausset (May-June 1953). In the provinces, the Palais des Arts at Nice presented during 1930 the works that belonged then to the Baron Vitta collection.

In 1963, the Delacroix centenary year, there was another great retrospective exhibition at the Louvre in May. The catalogue contained a preface by RENE HUYGHE, and MAURICE SERULLAZ reviewed the Centenary Exhibition in *Revue du Louvre*, 1963, no. 2 (p. 49 ff.). At the same time the Galerie des Beaux-Arts in Bordeaux organized an exhibition entitled *Delacroix, his masters, his friends, his pupils;* the Bibliothèque Nationale mounted an exhibition on the theme: *Delacroix and the Romantic Print;* the Cabinet des Dessins in the Louvre showed Delacroix's drawings, and a travelling exhibition was set up entitled *The role of drawing in the work of Delacroix.* Abroad, the most important exhibitions have been, in England, the one put on by Wildenstein and Co. at their London gallery (June-July 1952), to which must be added the 'Romantic Movement' exhibition at the Tate Gallery (July to September 1959), as it included a number of works by Delacroix; in Italy, the retrospective held at the Museo Civico Correr, Venice, during June to October on the occasion of the 1956 Biennale; and in Switzerland, the exhibition of 1939, open at the Kunsthaus, Zurich, from January till April, then at the Kunsthalle, Basle, in April and May.

In 1889-90 The American Art Galleries of New York mounted an exhibition devoted to Barye and including paintings of other nineteenth-century artists. Of recent years, America has become more and more interested in Delacroix. Let us cite the exhibitions held at the Art Institute of Chicago (March-April 1930); at Knoedler and Co.'s galleries in New York and Chicago (November and December 1938), which grouped Gros and Géricault with Delacroix; at the San Francisco Museum of Art, with the same grouping (April-May 1939); at the Phillips Memorial Gallery, Washington, D.C. (January-February 1945); at the Smith College Museum of Art, Northampton, Mass., on the theme 'Ariosto and Tasso' (1946); and at the Fogg Art Museum, Cambridge, Mass., on 'Delacroix in New England Collections' (October-November 1955). In 1962 Canada organized an exhibition of works from American collections, which opened at the Art Gallery of Toronto in December and closed at the National Art Gallery of Canada, Ottawa, in February 1963.

## XI COLLECTIONS AND SALES

The collections that contained works by Delacroix are without number. It is hard to make a selection from them, so I will confine myself to mentioning two. First: that of the Montpellier collector Alfred Bruyas, whose portrait Delacroix painted, is the subject of a publication dating from 1859: *Explication des ouvrages de peinture du cabinet de Monsieur Alfred Bruyas* (p. 270-415 on Delacroix). Second: *La collection Cheramy, description d'environ soixante-dix tableaux, aquarelles . . . d'Eugène Delacroix* (edited by Julius Meier-Graefe and Klossowoski, Munich, 1908).

A few sale-catalogues are particularly important, such as that of the sale held after the painter's death, with a preface by PHILIPPE BURTY. The auction took place from 16 to 29 February 1864 after an exhibition on 10, 11, and 12 February at the rue Furstenberg residence and on 16 February at the Hôtel Drouot. It met with a success as great as it was unforeseen, reflected in the contemporary press. An unpublished note from the copy of the catalogue in my possession gives some amusing details: 'Auctioning went on all day and every night up to eleven o'clock. On Thursday 25 the valuer [Petit], ill with fatigue, could not continue in the evening. It was Tedesco who replaced him, getting by with all the comicalness of which an Italian Jew is capable. On Friday, Petit having resumed, lions, tigers, and animals were sold; Maine bought the lot, even those copied by Maurice Sand and other weak hands.' On 23 April of the same year, again at the Hôtel Drouot, a sale of pictures including many by Delacroix took place; it involved George Sand's collection. A hand-written commentary on my copy of the catalogue runs: 'Delacroix had long been the admirer and friend of George Sand. He went several times to Nohant, where he painted and left Madame Sand a number of pictures: *The Education of the Virgin* among others is a study of Berry peasants. . . . Scarcely a month after the Delacroix sale, M. Maurice Sand sent to Petit all the pictures from Nohant, just when his mother had gained twenty thousand francs by the success of *Le Marquis de Villemer:* Delacroix dead—dead the friendship!' The opponents of Delacroix had not yet laid down their arms. The success of Delacroix's posthumous sale made them angry, and Edmond About sourly commented in the *Nouvelle Revue de Paris*, 1864, part 4: 'How is one to explain the raving madness of a public that has paid twenty-seven thousand francs for four pictures of flowers fit to be thrown out of the window, and covered with gold the most trivial sweepings from the studio, ill-formed sketches that look like the work of some schoolboy in detention, or even the glazier across the way. I saw a man not well off, almost poor, carry home triumphantly a formless daub, without top or bottom, in which the Devil himself would have been unable to discover where the screw-ring went. It cost him five hundred francs, the poor wretch! Didn't he deserve to be declared unfit to manage his own affairs? His charming purchase will be worth a hundred francs in three months time. I hope that in three years one will be able to have it for forty sous.' It is right that these lines by a once-famous writer be remembered. The Bibliothèque Nationale has a copy of the Delacroix sale catalogue giving the buyers and their bids.

In 1865 two important sales took place at the Hôtel Drouot: on 11 February that of the *cabinet* of 'Monsieur F. V.' [Villot] and on 21 April that of the collection of 'Monsieur . . ., general legatee of Monsieur Eugène Delacroix' [Piron]. A few comparatively recent sales may be recorded: at the Galerie Petit in 1911 that of '130 drawings by Eugène Delacroix forming the collection of Monsieur Jean Psichari'; and at the Hôtel Drouot on 11 March 1933 that of the Georges Aubry collection; and again, on 8 December 1948 that of the former Verninac collection.

# LIST OF ILLUSTRATIONS

*Measurements given are for the whole picture, not details. Inches precede centimetres and height precedes width.*

## COLOUR PLATES

## BLACK AND WHITE PLATES

*Chapter I* *Plates 1-34 between pages 32 and 49*



*Chapter II* *Plates 35-67 between pages 88 and 105*

*Plate*

50 THÉODORE GÉRICAULT: *Portrait of Eugène Delacroix* *c.* 1818 Oil on canvas. 24 x 19 (051 x 039)
51 FRANÇOIS GÉRARD: *Portrait of Madame Le Cerf* 1794 Oil on canvas. 22 x 18 (056 x 047)
52 *The Massacre at Chios* 1824 (detail)
53 THÉODORE GÉRICAULT: *Five Horses in a Stable* 1817 Chalk and water-colour. 15 x 18 (038 x 046)
54 GÉRICAULT: *Officier de Chasseurs.* Study for painting exhibited at 1812 Salon Oil on canvas. 20 x 11 (052 x 040)
55 *Charles II of Spain, after Carreño da Miranda* 1824 Oil on canvas
56 *Self-portrait in the costume of Hamlet* 1821 Oil on canvas. 16 x 12 (040 x 031)
57 *Frightened Horse emerging from the Water* 1828 Lithograph. 9 x 9 1/2 (023 x 024)
58 *Study of Horses.* Water-colour. 7 1/2 x 10 (019 x 025)
59-60 JACQUES-LOUIS DAVID: *The Rape of the Sabine Women* 1799 (details) Oil on canvas. 152 x 205 (386 x 520)
61 DAVID: *Bonaparte crossing the Saint Bernard Pass* 1800 Oil on canvas. 97 x 91 (246 x 231)
62 ANTOINE-JEAN GROS: *Murat at the Battle of Aboukir* Oil sketch for painting now at Versailles 1805 34 x 55 (087 x 140)
63 THÉODORE GÉRICAULT: *The Race of Riderless Horses on the Corso in Rome* 1817 Oil on canvas. 18 x 24 (045 x 060)
64 *The Battle of Taillebourg* 1837 (detail) Oil on canvas. 191 x 216 (485 x 555)
65 *White Horse frightened by a Storm* 1824 Water-colour. 9 1/2 x 13 (024 x 032)
66 *Portrait of Elisabeth Salter c.* 1817 Oil on paper mounted on canvas. 9 1/2 x 7 1/2 (024 x 019)
67 Letter to Elisabeth Salter from one of Delacroix's note-books (Carnet 9156, *pp* 22, 23)

*Chapter III Plates 68-111 between pages 136 and 161*

68 *Roman Matrons giving up their Jewels for their Country* 1818 Pencil and water-colour. 6 x 8 (016 x 020)
69 Studies for the '*Virgin of the Harvest*' 1819 Pen, pencil and wash. 7 1/2 x 10 (019 x 025)
70 RAPHAEL: *La Belle Jardinière.* 48 x 31 (122 x 080)
71 *Virgin of the Harvest* 1819 Oil on canvas. 49 x 29 (125 x 074)
72 *Virgin of the Sacred Heart c.* 1821 Oil on canvas. 102 x 60 (258 x 152)
73 Study for the '*Virgin of the Sacred Heart*' 1821 Pencil, gouache and water-colour. 9 x 7 (022 x 017)
74 Engraving on the bottom of a copper saucepan 1814 2 x 3 1/4 (005 x 009)
75 '*The Ridiculous Kiss*' *c.* 1818-20 Sketch after Rowlandson. 11 x 28 (027 x 070)
76 *Studies of heads after Rowlandson c.* 1818-20 Ink and pencil
77 FRANCISCO GOYA: *Que se la llevaron!* (And so they kidnapped her!) *Caprichos.* First edition 1799
78 *Sketch by Delacroix after Goya's engraving: 'Que se la llevaron!' c.* 1818-24 Pen and wash

*Plate*

79 THÉODORE GÉRICAULT: Study for '*Le Radeau de la Méduse*' 1818. 26 x 33 (065 x 083)
80 A.-L. GIRODET: *Scene from the Deluge* (detail), Salon of 1806
81 THÉODORE GÉRICAULT: '*Le Radeau de la Méduse*' 1818 Oil on canvas. 192 x 282 (491 x 716)
82 GÉRICAULT: *The Wounded Cuirassier* 1814 Oil on canvas. 115 x 89 (292 x 227)
83 *Two sketches after Géricault's 'Radeau de la Méduse' c.* 1820 Black chalk
84 *Studies of heads after a hunting picture by Rubens* Black chalk
85 Preliminary sketch for '*Dante and Virgil in the Inferno*' *c.* 1821 Pencil, pen and indian ink. 9 1/2 x 7. (024 x 018)
86 *Dante and Virgil in the Inferno* 1822 Oil on canvas. 74 x 97 (189 x 246)
87 Study of a boatman for '*Dante and Virgil in the Inferno*' *c.* 1821 Pen and ink on tracing paper. 5 x 3 1/2 (012 x 009)
88 Studies of the damned for '*Dante and Virgil in the Inferno*' 1822 Chalk on tinted paper. 11 x 16 (027 x 041)
89 *Study for Dante c.* 1821 Pencil
90 *The Infernal City in Flames* 1822 Water-colour. 5 1/2 x 7 1/2 (014 x 019)
91 *Heads of Dante and Virgil* 1822 Pastel, pencil. 8 x 12 (020 x 031)
92 ANTOINE-JEAN GROS: Sketch for '*Bucephalus vanquished by Alexander*' 1798. Brush drawing
93 *Horse attacked by a Tiger c.* 1825. Water-colour. 7 x 10 (018 x 025)
94 *Delacroix and his friends on New Year's Eve* 1817 Indian ink wash and pencil. 10 x 8 (025 x 020)
95 *Head of a Man c.* 1818 Black chalk
96 *Self-portrait at about twenty years of age c.* 1818 Pencil
97 *Study of a horse* Pencil
98 JULES-ROBERT AUGUSTE: *Eastern Woman crouching on a Rush Mat* Pastel. 11 x 9 (028 x 022)
99 AUGUSTE: *Study of Arab Horses* Water-colour. 8 x 10 (20 x 25)
100 *Study after Persian miniatures,* with colour notes *c.* 1825 Pencil and water-colour
101 *Study after Persian miniatures,* with colour notes *c.* 1825 Pencil and water-colour
102 Sketch for '*Count Palatiano*' Pencil
103 *Studies of Egyptian Art c.* 1825 Pencil
104 *Orphan Girl in the Graveyard* 1823 Oil on canvas. 26 x 21 (065 x 054)
105 *Orphan Girl weeping in the Graveyard* 1823 Oil on canvas. 16 x 14 (041 x 037)
106-106a Preliminary drawings for the '*Massacre at Chios*' 1824 Pencil. 8 x 12 (020 x 031) 10 x 8 (025 x 020)
107 Preliminary drawing for the '*Massacre at Chios*' 1824 Pen and pencil. 7 1/2 x 9 1/2 (019 x 024)
108 *The Massacre at Chios* 1824 (detail) Oil on canvas. 164 x 139 (417 x 354)
109 JOHN CONSTABLE: *View of the Stour near Dedham* 1822 Oil on canvas. 51 x 74 (130 x 188)
110 CONSTABLE: *The Hay Wain* 1821 (detail) Oil on canvas. 51 x 73 (130 x 185)
111 *The Massacre at Chios* 1824 (detail) Oil on canvas.

*Chapter IV* *Plates 112-171 between pages 208 and 233*

112 *Landscape near London* 1825 Water-colour. 6 x 9 (015 x 023)
113 *English Landscape* 1825 Water-colour. 10 x 12 (025 x 030)
114 *'A Doctor of Civil Law' at Oxford c.* 1825 Pencil
115 *Studies of horses c.* 1825-30 Pen and wash. 10 x 7 (025 x 017)
116 *Studies of horses c.* 1824-5 Water-colour and pencil. 5 1/2 x 9 (014 x 023)
117 *Christ on the Lake of Genesareth* 1853 Canvas. 23 x 29 (059 x 073)
118 William Etty: *The Storm* 1829-30 Oil on canvas. 36 x 42 (091 x 106)
119 Richard Parkes Bonington (School of): *The Doges' Palace* 1826 Oil on canvas. 31 1/2 x 26 (080 x 065)
120 *The Execution of the Doge Marino Faliero* 1827 Oil on canvas. 57 x 45 (145 x 115)
121 First sketches for *'Marino Faliero' c.* 1827 Water-colour. 11 x 14 (028 x 035)
122 *François I and his Mistress* 1826-7 Water-colour, gouache, varnish. 9 x 6 1/2 (022 x 016)
123 Richard Parkes Bonington: *François I and Marguerite of Navarre* 1827 Oil on canvas. 18 x 13 (046 x 034)
124 *View from the studio of Thalès Fielding, 20 rue Jacob* Water-colour. 9 1/2 x 7 1/2 (024 x 019)
125 J. D. Harding: *Portrait of Bonington* Lithograph after a picture by Margaret Carpenter
126 *Bonington c.* 1825 Chalk and sepia wash. 10 x 13 (025 x 022)
127 *Interior of a Farmhouse* Water-colour. 3 1/2 x 6 (009 x 015)
128 *Seated Woman reading* Gouache. 4 x 6 (011 x 015)
129 *Odalisque* 1825 Oil on canvas. 15 x 18 (037 x 045)
130 Drawing for *'Woman with a Parrot'* 1827 Black chalk. 9 x 12 (023 x 031)
131 *Baroilhet the Singer in Turkish Costume* 1825 Oil on canvas. 18 x 15 (045 x 037)
132 *Pierret in Turkish Costume* 1825 Oil on canvas. 13 x 9 1/2 (032 x 024)
133 *The Flight of the Smuggler* 1826 Lithograph, 3rd state. 3 1/2 x 6 (009 x 015)
134 Théodore Géricault: *The Derby at Epsom* 1821 Oil on canvas. 36 x 48 (091 x 122)
135 *Faust and Mephistopheles* 1828 Lithograph. 8 1/4 x 11 (021 x 028)
136 *Scenes from the Present War between the Turks and Greeks* 1827 Oil on canvas. (065 x 080)
137 *Young Turk fondling his Horse* 1825-6 Oil on canvas. 12 x 16 (031 x 040)
138 *Scenes from the War between the Turks and Greeks* 1856 Oil on canvas. 26 x 31 1/2 (065 x 080)
139 *Moorish Horseman.* Water-colour. 7 x 8 (017 x 020)
140 *The Death of Sardanapalus* 1827 (detail) Oil on canvas. 145 x 195 (395 x 495)
141 Studies for the *'Death of Sardanapalus'* Pen drawing
142 Study of still-life for the *'Death of Sardanapalus'* Pen drawing. 10 x 13 (025 x 033)
143 Two nude studies for the *'Death of Sardanapalus' c.* 1827 Sepia wash. 7 1/2 x 6 (019 x 015)

*Plate*
144 *Death of Cato* 1824 Oil on canvas. 24 x 18 (060 x 044)
145 Jacques-Louis David: *The Death of Hector.* Engraving by Jules David
146 *Tasso in the Madhouse* 1827 Oil on canvas. 24 x 20 (060 x 050)
147 *Study for Tasso* 1824 Pencil
148 *Faust in his Study* 1827 Lithograph, 4th state. 10 x 7 (025 x 017)
149 *Faust and Mephistopheles in the Harz Mountains* 1827 Lithograph, 3rd state. 9 1/2 x 8 (024 x 021)
150 *M. Bruyas in his Study* Chalk and wash
151 *Renaissance Scene* Oil on canvas. 23 x 30 (057 x 077)
152 *Ruins of the Abbey of Valmont* 1831 Water-colour. 7 1/2 x 6 (019 x 016)
153 *Delacroix painting the Ruins of Valmont c.* 1831 Oil on canvas. 18 1/2 x 15 (047 x 038)
154 *Study of stained glass windows* Pencil. 3 1/2 x 6 (009 x 015)
155 *Studies of Gothic sculpture* Brush drawing
156 *Medieval staircase c.* 1831 Black chalk
157 *The Two Foscari* 1855 Oil on canvas. 37 x 52 (093 x 132)
158 *The Great Hall in the Palais de Justice at Rouen* Nineteenth-century lithograph
159 *Faust and Marguerite in Prison* 1827 Lithograph. 10 x 9 (025 x 022)
160 *Front de Bœuf and the Witch* 1829 Lithograph. 8 x 7 1/2 (021 x 020)
161 *Marguerite at the Spinning Wheel* 1827 Lithograph. 9 x 7 (022 x 018)
162 *Louis XI* 1829. Illustration for Béranger's 'Chansons'. Engraving by Pourvoyer. 3 x 2 1/2 (008 x 006)
163 Study for *'Cardinal Richelieu celebrating Mass'* 1828 Oil on canvas. 16 x 13 (040 x 032)
164 Sketches of Louis XIII costumes for *'Cardinal Richelieu' c.* 1828 Pencil
165 *The Death of Charles the Bold at the Battle of Nancy* 1831 Oil on canvas. 93 x 140 (237 x 356)
166 Sketch for the *'Battle of Nancy'* 1828 Oil on canvas. 19 x 28 (049 x 070)
167 *L'amoureuse au piano* 1843 Pen and sepia wash. 9 x 10 1/2 (022 x 017)
168 *Portrait of Paganini* 1832 Oil on cardboard panel. 17 x 11 (043 x 028)
169 *Gluck at the Piano c.* 1830 Engraving by Villot after Delacroix. 9 x 10 1/2 (022 x 017)
170 Study for *'Liberty Leading the People'* 1830 Pencil and chalk. 13 x 9 (032 x 023)
171 Study for *'Liberty' c.* 1830 Pencil and chalk. 12 x 8 (029 x 020)

*Chapter V* *Plates 172-184 between pages 256 and 265*

172 *Frédéric Chopin* 1838 Oil on canvas. 18 x 15 (045 x 037)
173 *Baron Schwiter c.* 1827 (detail) Oil on canvas. 86 x 56 (218 x 143)
174 *Self-portrait* 1842 (detail) Oil on canvas. 26 x 21 (066 x 054)
175 S. J. Rochard: *Prosper Mérimée* 1853
176 Charles Baudelaire. Photograph by É. Carjat, *c.* 1863

*Plate*

177 Stendhal (Henri Beyle). Contemporary engraving
178 Eugène Delacroix. Daguerreotype, 1842
179 Eugène Delacroix. Photograph by Nadar, 1861
180 *Michelangelo in his Studio* 1850 Oil on canvas. 24 x 16 (060 x 040)
181 Study for '*Christ in the Garden of Gethsemane*' 1826-7 Water-colour and pencil. 10 x 8 (025 x 021)
182 Sketch for '*Christ in the Garden of Gethsemane*' Pencil and wash
183 *Mirabeau and the Marquis of Dreux-Brézé* 1831 Oil on canvas. 31 x 36 (078 x 092)
184 Sketches for *Mirabeau c.* 1831 Pencil drawing

*Chapter VI* *Plates 185-238 between pages 304 and 329*

185 *Prince Anatole Demidoff in the Rooms of the Count de Mornay* 1833 Oil on canvas. 31 x 26 (078 x 065)
186 FRANÇOIS GÉRARD: *Portrait of Mademoiselle Mars* Lithograph by Grevedon
187 *The Count de Mornay*, from the Moroccan sketchbook 1832 Black chalk. 7 1/2 x 5 (019 x 013)
188 *Self-portrait in travelling costume* 1832 Black chalk. 7 1/2 x 5 (019 x 013)
189 *The Straits of Gibraltar* 1832 Water-colour. 6 x 9 (016 x 024)
190 *The Algerian Coast* 1832 Pencil. 5 x 7 1/2 (012 x 019)
191 *View of Tangier* 1832 Water-colour. 5 x 7 1/2 (012 x 019)
192 *Page from the Moroccan sketchbook* Tleta dei Rissana 1832. 7 1/2 x 5 (019 x 012)
193 *Page from the Moroccan sketchbook*, Sidi Kassem, Zar Hone 1832. 7 1/2 x 5 (019 x 012)
194 *Delacroix's room at Meknes* 1832 Water-colour. 5 x 7 1/2 (012 x 019)
195 *Arrival at Meknes* 1832. 7 1/2 x 5 (019 x 012)
196 *Meknes* 1832. Pencil and wash. 7 1/2 x 5 (019 x 012)
197 *Young Moroccan dancing* 1832 Ink and wash
198 *Arab in a Turban* 1832 Water-colour. 12 x 8 (030 x 021)
199 *Page from the Moroccan sketchbook* 1832 Chalk and wash
200 *Street in Seville* 1832 Water-colour. 4 x 6 (010 x 015)
201 *Page from the Moroccan sketchbook:* Alcassar-el-Kebir, 1832 Pen and pencil. 7 1/2 x 5 (019 x 012)
202 *Cadiz: Spaniards, a moonlit street* 1832 Water-colour. 7 1/2 x 5 (019 x 012).
203 *Horsemen fighting on the Plain* 1825 Oil on canvas. 32 x 41 (081 x 105)
204 *Combat of the Giaour and the Pasha* 1827 Oil on canvas. 23 x 28 (058 x 072)
205 *Encounter between Moorish Horsemen c.* 1843-46 Oil on canvas. 32 x 39 (081 x 098)
206 *Combat of the Giaour and the Pasha* 1835 Oil on canvas. 29 x 24 (073 x 060)
207 *Arab Fantasia* ('*Military Exercises*') 1832 Oil on canvas. 23 x 28 (059 x 072)
208 *Arab Fantasia* ('*Courses de Poudre*') 1833 Oil on canvas. 24 x 29 (060 x 073)
209 *The Jewish Bride* 1832 Water-colour. 11 x 9 (028 x 023)
210 *Moroccan Woman* 1832 Water-colour. 7 1/2 x 5 (019 x 012)

*Plate*

211 *Three sketches of Arab women* 1835. 5 x 7 1/2 (012 x 019)
212 *Women of Algiers* 1834 (detail) Oil on canvas
213 *The Massacre at Chios* 1824 (detail) Oil on canvas
214 *Greece Expiring on the Ruins of Missolonghi* 1827 (detail) Oil on canvas. 82 x 58 (209 x 147)
215 *Liberty Leading the People* 1830 (detail) Oil on canvas. 102 x 128 (260 x 325)
216 *The Natchez* 1824 (detail) Oil on canvas. 35 x 46 (089 x 117)
217 Study for the '*Women of Algiers*' 1833. Pastel 11 x 16 (029 x 042)
218 *Interior of a Harem at Oran* 1847 Oil on canvas. 16 x 12 (040 x 032)
219 *Turkish Women bathing* 1854 Oil on canvas. 36 x 31 (092 x 078)
220 *Woman of Algiers in her Apartment (Odalisque)* 1857 Oil on canvas. 15 x 11 (037 x 028)
221 *Du Guesclin at the Château de Pontorson* 1829 Sepia. 10 x 8 (026 x 020)
222 *Moroccan Caïd visiting a Tribe* 1837 Oil on canvas. 39 x 50 (098 x 126)
223 *The Sultan of Morocco surrounded by his Court* 1845 Oil on canvas. 148 x 134 (377 x 340)
224 *Sultan of Morocco* 1862 Oil on canvas. 26 x 22 (066 x 056)
225 *The Martyrdom of Saint Stephen* 1862 Oil on canvas. 19 x 15 (047 x 038)
226 *Disciples and Holy Women raising the Body of Saint Stephen* 1853 Oil on canvas. 58 x 45 (148 x 115)
227 *The Fanatics of Tangier* 1857 Oil on canvas. 18 x 22 (046 x 056)
228 *The Fanatics of Tangier* 1836-8 (detail) Oil on canvas. 39 x 52 (098 x 132)
229 *Columbus on his Return from the New World* 1839 Oil on canvas. 36 x 46 (090 x 116)
230 TITIAN: *Presentation of the Virgin in the Temple*
231 *Chess-players in Jerusalem* 1835 Oil on canvas. 18 x 22 (046 x 055)
232 *Arab Women at a Fountain* 1832 Pencil and water-colour. 10 x 7 1/2 (026 x 019)
233 *Horses at the Fountain* 1862 Oil on canvas. 30 x 36 (076 x 091)
234 *Head of an Arab woman* Pencil
235 *Arab Actors and Clowns* 1848 Oil on canvas. 36 x 51 (093 x 130)
236 *Arab Actors and Clowns* 1836 Water-colour. 16 x 23 (042 x 058)
237 *Ovid among the Scythians* 1859 Oil on canvas. 34 x 51 (088 x 130)
238 *Erminia and the Shepherds* 1859 Oil on canvas. 32 x 39 (081 x 100)

*Chapter VII* *Plates 239-269 between pages 350 and 367*

239 *The Prisoner of Chillon* 1834 Oil on canvas. 29 x 36 (073 x 092)
240 *Clifford finding the Corpse of his Father on the Battlefield* 1834 Lithograph. 6 x 9 (016 x 022)
241 *Christ Crucified between Thieves* 1835 Oil on canvas. 72 x 53 (182 x 135)

Plate

242 *Hamlet and Horatio in the Graveyard* 1839 Oil on canvas. 31 1/2 x 26 (080 x 065)

243 *The Battle of Taillebourg* Sketch for a stained glass window Water-colour. 17 x 9 (044 x 023)

244 Sketch after an engraving (reversed) of the right half of Rubens' '*Battle of the Amazons*' Pencil.

245 *The Battle of Taillebourg* 1837 Oil on canvas. 183 x 214 (465 x 544)

246 PETER PAUL RUBENS: *The Battle of the Amazons* 1618 Oil on canvas

247 RUBENS: *The Deposition*

248 *Saint Sebastian rescued by the Holy Women* 1836 Oil on canvas. 85 x 97 (215 x 246)

249 ANDREA DEL SARTO: *Charity* 1518 Oil on panel. 73 x 54 (185 x 137)

250 Sketch for '*Medea*' 1838 Pencil. 9 x 5 (022 x 012)

251 *Medea* 1838 Oil on canvas. 30 x 65 (260 x 165)

252 *Medea* 1859 Oil on canvas. 51 x 39 (130 x 099)

253 *The Death of Marcus Aurelius* 1845 Oil on canvas. 118 x 146 (300 x 370)

254 NICHOLAS POUSSIN: *Death of Germanicus* Oil on canvas. 58 x 77 (148 x 196)

255 POUSSIN: *Testament of Eudamidas*

256 *The Sibyl with the Golden Bough* 1845 Oil on canvas. 51 x 38 (130 x 097)

257 *Cleopatra and the Countryman* 1838 Oil on canvas. 39 x 50 (098 x 127)

258 Sketches for the '*Justice of Trajan*' 1839 Pencil.

259 PETER PAUL RUBENS: *Crowning of Marie de Medici at Saint Denis*

260 *The Justice of Trajan* 1840 Oil on canvas. 193 x 106 (490 x 390)

261 *The Entry of the Crusaders into Constantinople* 1852 Oil on canvas. 32 x 39 (080 x 100)

262 Sketches for the '*Crusaders*' 1840 Pencil

263 *The Entry of the Crusaders* 1840 (detail) Oil on canvas. 161 x 196 (410 x 498)

264 *Sketch for the double portrait of Chopin and George Sand* 1838 Pencil. 5 x 5 1/2 (012 x 014)

265 *Portrait of George Sand* 1838 Oil on canvas. 32 x 22 1/2 (080 x 057)

266 *Mother and Child* 1842 Pencil and wash. 9 x 6 (022 x 016)

267 *George Sand's garden at Nohant* 1842 Oil an canvas. 18 x 22 (044 x 056)

268 Study for the '*Pietà*' 1830 Pencil

269 *Pietà* 1844 Church of Saint-Denis-du-Saint-Sacrement. 140 x 187 (356 x 475)

*Chapter VIII Plates 270-371 between pages 424 and 448*

270 *Leda and the Swan* 1834 Valmont fresco. 26x35 (067x088)

271 Two studies for '*The Seasons*' 1821 Pencil

272 *Talma in the role of Nero* 1857 Oil on canvas. 35 1/2x28 (090 x 071)

273 *Theseus vanquishing the Centaur Eurytos* 1825 Lithograph. 5 1/2 x 7 (014 x 017)

274 *Female nude studies* Pen and ink

275 PRIMATICCIO Sketch for the frescos in the Galerie Henri II at Fontainebleau

Plate

276 *The Poet Arion and the Philosopher Anaximander* 1833 Water-colour. 3 1/2x5 (008 x 012)

277 *Justice* 1833-38 Oil and wax on plaster. Frieze. Salon du Roi, Palais Bourbon. 102 x 459 (260 x 1100)

278 JEAN GOUJON: *Fontaine des Innocents: A Nymph* 1546

279 *The River Seine* 1833-38 Grisaille. Pilaster. Salon du Roi, Palais Bourbon. 117 x 39 (300 x 100)

280 *The River Rhône* 1833-38 Grisaille. Pilaster. Salon du Roi, Palais Bourbon. 117 x 39 (300 x 100)

281 *Justice* 1833-38 Oil on canvas. Ceiling coffer. Salon du Roi, Palais Bourbon. 55 x 150 (140 x 380)

282 *Agriculture* Black chalk. Sketch for a ceiling coffer. Salon du Roi, Palais Bourbon

283 *Herodotus questioning the Wise Men* 1838-47 Oil on canvas. 'Philosophy' cupola. Library of the Chambre des Députés, Palais Bourbon. 87 x 115 (221 x 291)

284 MASACCIO: *The Sick Man healed by Saint Peter's Shadow* 1427-28 Fresco.

285 Sketch for the '*Education of Achilles*' 1838-47 Pencil. 9 x 12 (023 x 030)

286 *The Education of Achilles c.* 1844 Oil on canvas. Pendentive of 'Poetry' cupola. Library of the Chambre des Députés, Palais Bourbon. 87 x 115 (221 x 291)

287 Study for the '*Captivity in Babylon*' Water-colour, gouache and pencil on brown paper. 10 x 12 (025 x 031)

288 *Adam and Eve* 1838-47 Oil on canvas. Pendentive of 'Theology' cupola. Library of the Palais Bourbon. 87 x 115 (221 x 291)

289 *Numa and the Nymph Egeria* 1838-47 Oil on canvas. Pendentive of 'Legislation' cupola. Library of the Palais Bourbon. 87 x 115 (221 x 291)

290 *Pliny the Elder* 1838-47 Oil on canvas. Pendentive of 'Natural Sciences' cupola. Library of the Palais Bourbon. 87 x 115 (221 x 291)

291 Drawing after an engraving of a Pompeian fresco Pencil

292 *The Education of Achilles* 1862 Oil on canvas. 15 x 18 (038 x 046)

293 *Attila hemicycle* 1838-47 (detail). Library of the Palais Bourbon. Oil and wax. 289 dia. (735)

294 The cupola (1845-47) of the Library of the Senate, Palais du Luxembourg. Oil on canvas. 276 dia. (701)

295 *Dante presented by Virgil to Homer.* Sketch for the cupola of the Library of the Senate, Palais du Luxembourg. Paper on canvas. 19 x 23 (049 x 058)

296 *Alexander the Great* 1845-47 Detail of the hemicycle of the Library of the Senate, Palais du Luxembourg. Oil on canvas. 268 dia. (680)

297 Sketch for '*Alexander the Great*' for the hemicycle ol the Library of the Senate, Palais du Luxembourg. Pencif

298 *Flower-painting* Oil on canvas

299 *Peonies* Oil on canvas

300 *Landscape* Water-colour

301 *Landscape in the Pyrenees* 1845 Water-colour

302 *Sunset, from a window of Delacroix's house at Champrosay* 1849 Pastel on grey paper. 7 x 9 1/2 (018 x 024)

303 *The grounds of Valmont Abbey c.* 1843 Water-colour and gouache. 11 x 9 (028 x 023)

304 *Apollo destroying the Serpent Python* 1850-51 Oil on canvas. Ceiling. Galerie d'Apollon, Louvre. 315 x 295 (800 x 750)

*Plate*

305 *Study for Apollo's chariot* 1850-51 Pencil. 11 x 18 (028 x 045)
306 *Peace recalling Abundance.* Sketch for the ceiling of the Salon de la Paix, Hôtel de Ville. 1852 Oil on canvas. 31 dia. (078)
307 *Sketches for the ceiling of the Salon de la Paix*, Hôtel de Ville 1849 Pen and ink
308 Study for '*Heliodorus driven from the Temple*' 1857 Oil on canvas. 10 x 4 (055 x 039)
309 Sketch for '*Heliodorus*' Pencil. 11 x 12 (027 x 031)
310 *Heliodorus driven from the Temple* 1856-61 Oil and wax on plaster. Chapel of the Holy Angels, Church of Saint-Sulpice. 281 x 191 (714 x 488)
311 Study for '*Jacob wrestling with the Angel*'
312 *The Prieur Oak c.* 1850 Pencil
313 *Jacob wrestling with the Angel* 1856-61 Oil and wax on plaster. Chapel of the Holy Angels, Church of Saint-Sulpice. 281 x 191 (714 x 488)
314 *Christ Carrying the Cross* 1859 Oil on wood. 20 x 18 (052 x 046)
315 PETER PAUL RUBENS: *The Ascent to Calvary*
316 *The Abduction of Rebecca* 1858 Oil on canvas. 39 x 32 (100 x 081)
317 *The Camp of Botzaris c.* 1862 Oil on canvas. 22 x 36 (055 x 092)
318 *The Death of Lara* 1858 Oil on canvas. 24 x 20 (062 x 050)
319 *Arabs skirmishing in the Mountains (Collection of the Arab Taxes)* 1863 Oil on canvas. 36 x 29 (092 x 074)
320 *The Seasons. Spring: Orpheus and Eurydice* 1861 77 x 67 (195 x 171)
321 *The Seasons. Summer: Diana and Actaeon* 1861. 77 x 67 (195 x 171)
322 *The Seasons. Autumn: Bacchus and Ariadne* 1861. 77 x 67 (195 x 171)

*Chapter IX Plates 323-371 between pages 492 and 517*

323 *Animal Studies* Sepia ink. 9 1/2 x 13 (024 x 032)
324 Study for the lithograph '*Royal Tiger*' 1929 Sepia. 3 x 7 1/2 (008 x 019)
325 Sketch for '*Arab on Horseback attacked by a Lion*' 1849 Pencil. 17 x 12 (044 x 031)
326 Sketch for the '*Fight of the Giaour and the Pasha*' (1835 version).
327 Sketch for the '*Fight of the Giaour and the Pasha*' 1827
328 *Study for the God Mars accompanied by Fame, Fear and Death c.* 1820-23 Pen and ink. 9 x 16 (022 x 041)
329 Sketch for '*Mazeppa*' 1828 Water-colour
330 *Lion attacking an Arab* Pencil
331 *Lioness and Lion in a Cavern* 1856 Oil on canvas. 15 x 18 (037 x 045)
332 Study for '*Fight between a Lion and a Tiger*' 1856 Pencil. 7 1/2 x 9 (019 x 022)
333 *Lion devouring a Rabbit* 1856 Oil on canvas. 18 x 22 (046 x 056)
334 *Horse attacked by a Lioness* 1840 Oil on canvas. 13 x 17 (033 x 042)
335 *Tasso in the Madhouse* 1824 Oil on canvas. 19 x 24 (049 x 060)

*Plate*

336 *Christ in the Garden of Gethsemane* 1851 Oil on canvas. 13 x 17 (033 x 042)
337 *Sketch for the lithograph of Faust c.* 1828
338 *New Year's Eve* 1820-21 Pen and pencil on mauve paper. 10 x 8 (025 x 020)
339 *Macbeth and the Witches* 1825 Lithograph. 13 x 10 (032 x 025)
340 *The Connétable de Bourbon and his Conscience* 1835 Sepia wash. 12 x 8 (024 x 020)
341 Sketch for the '*Emperor Justinian composing the Institutes*' 1826 Oil on canvas. 22 x 18 (055 x 047)
342 Study for the '*Shipwreck of Don Juan*' 1839 Oil sketch. 32 x 39 1/2 (081 x 099)
343 *Castaways in a Ship's Boat* 1847 Oil on canvas. 14 x 23 (036 x 057)
344 *Christ on the Lake of Genesareth* 1853 Oil on canvas. 20 x 24 (050 x 060)
345 *Shipwreck on the Coast* 1862 Oil on canvas. 18 x 21 (046 x 054)
346 LOUIS BOULANGER: *Attack by a Tiger* Lithograph
347 *Lion Hunt* 1855 Oil on canvas. 102 x 141 (260 x 359)
348 *Lion Hunt* 1861 Oil on canvas. 30 x 39 (076 x 098)
349 *Tiger Hunt* (detail) 1854 Oil on canvas. 29 x 37 (074 x 093)
350 *Crucifixion* Pastel. 10 x 7 (025 x 017)
351 *The Lion and the Serpent* 1856 Oil on canvas. 20 x 24 (051 x 061)
352 *Saint Michael overthrowing the Devil* 1861 Ceiling. Chapel of the Holy Angels, Church of Saint-Sulpice. 151 x 226 (384 x 575)
353 *Lion with a Reptile* (detail) 1863 Oil on canvas.
354 Sketch of '*Saint George attacking the Serpent*'. Below: a dragon. Pencil and wash
355 *Abduction of Arab Woman by African Pirates* 1852 Oil on canvas. 25 x 31 1/2 (064 x 080)
356 *Study of woman and crocodiles* Pencil
357 *Perseus and Andromeda* 1847 Canvas on panel. 16 1/2 x 19 1/2 (042 x 050)
358 *Hercules and Alcestis* 1862 Oil on canvas mounted on panel. 12 x 19 (031 x 049)
359 N. DE LAUNAY: *The Fatal Revenge of Jealousy c.* 1776 Engraving after Marillier
360 RUBENS: *Daniel in the Lions' Den* Engraving by Weenix
361 *Daniel in the Lions' Den* 1849 Oil on canvas. 27 x 19 (067 x 048)
362 *Daniel in the Lions' Den* 1853 Oil on canvas. 29 x 24 (074 x 060)
363 *Pietà* 1848 Oil on canvas. 63 x 51 (160 x 130)
364 REMBRANDT: *The Philosopher* 1633 Oil on canvas. 12 x 13 (029 x 033)
365 *The Supper at Emmaus* 1853 Oil on canvas. 22 x 18 (056 x 046)
366 *The Entombment* 1859 Oil on canvas. 22 x 18 (056 x 046)
367 *Lélia* 1848 Pastel
368 *Pietà* 1850 Oil on canvas. 14 x 11 (036 x 028)
369 *The Good Samaritan* 1852 Oil on canvas. 14 x 17 (036 x 043)
370 Study for '*Angelica and the Wounded Medoro*' 1850 Oil on canvas. 32 x 26 (081 x 065)
371 *Jacob wrestling with the Angel* 1856-61 (detail)

## FIGURES IN THE TEXT



## SOURCES OF PHOTOGRAPHS

### *Colour Plates*

Brompton Studio I, II, III, IV, VI, VII, X, XII, XIV, XV, XVII, XVIII, XIX, XX, XXIV, XXV, XXVI, XXVII, XXVIII, XXIX, XXXI, XXXII, XXXIII, XXXIV, XXXV, XXXVI, XXXVII, XXXVIII, XLIII, XLVIII: Henri Bron, Montpellier XXII, XLII: J. Camponogara, Lyons IX: Walter Drayer, Zurich LVI: Giraudon LIII, LIV: Hans Hinz, Basle XXXIX: Johnson Collection, Philadelphia XXX: Philadelphia Museum of Art XXIII: Studio Piccardy, Grenoble XLIX: Studio Puytorac, Bordeaux V, XVI: Thames and Hudson Archives VIII, XI, XIII, XXI, XLVII, LI, LII: Armand Tornow, Sao Paolo LV: Art Gallery of Toronto XLV, XLVI: Virginia Museum of Fine Arts L: Walters Art Gallery, Baltimore XL, XLI.

### *Black and white illustrations*

ACL, Brussels 315 Alinari-Giraudon 64, 174, 316 Anderson 230 Annan, Glasgow 231 Archives Photographiques *Fig.* 17 Pls 3, 6, 8, 10, 14, 16, 22, 23, 27, 30, 32, 41, 51, 54, 57, 65, 66, 71, 72, 80, 85, 94, 98, 102, 105, 107, 126, 130, 131, 132, 139, 142, 151, 152, 153, 163, 167, 175, 179, 183, 185, 187, 188, 189, 190, 194, 200, 209, 210, 219, 224, 229, 232, 238, 241, 245, 248, 252, 257, 264, 267, 269, 292, 295, 298, 301, 303, 304, 341, 349, 350, 362, 363 Musée Municipal, Arras 226 Art de France 270 Art Gallery of Toronto 227 Art Institute of Chicago 348 Aubert, Bayonne 337 Author's Archives *Figs.* 7, *12, 22, 25, 26, 31, 33* Pls 39, 40, 42, 44, 82, 117, 122, 133, 136, 138, 144, 180, 181, 198, 208, 220, 228, 233, 236, 242, 247, 266, 268, 282, 291, 293, 308, 323, 324, 330, 340, 344, 349, 351, 355, 368, 370 Sophus Bengtsson, Copenhagen 166 Bibliothèque Nationale, Paris 5, 13, 33, 38, 74, 161, 169, 176, 178, 273, 339 Boymans van-Beuningen Museum, Rotterdam 179 Bulloz 20, 29, 50, 56, 63, 75, 81, 92, 111, 141, 150, 165, 172, 199, 204, 206, 215, 221, 235, 260, 263, 265, 272, 306, 347, 352, 360 Camponogara Industrie, Lyons 253 Robert David 7 Fogg Art Museum, Cambridge, Mass. 122 Foto-Commercial, Helsinki 329 Vladimir Fyman, Prague 15 Giraudon 4, 9, 12, 21, 26, 28, 35, 36, 37, 48, 49, 52, 53, 61, 62, 70, 79, 86, 104, 108, 129, 134, 135, 140, 157, 203, 207, 211, 212, 213, 214, 217, 239, 243, 249, 259, 274, 278, 286, 294, 310, 320, 321, 322, 333, 334, 336, 345, 364, 367, 371 Huntington Library and Art Gallery 109 Jacqueline Hyde, Paris 1, 2, 34, 145 H.-G. Joli, Paris 277, 280, 281, 283, 288, 289, 290 Lefevre Gallery, London 216 Librairie Larousse 24, 25 Lavaud, Paris 17, 18, 19 Studio Gerondal, Lille 250, 251 Musée de la Ville, Luxembourg 137 Madec, Nantes 222 City Art Gallery, Manchester 118 Mansell Collection 230, 284 Minneapolis Institute of Arts 254 The Montreal Museum of Fine Arts 331 Moreno 366 Dr Peter Nathan, Zurich 124 The National Gallery, London 110, 173, 237, 318 National Gallery of Art, Washington 319 The National Gallery of Canada 119 Publications Filmées d'Art et d'Histoire 279, 285, 287, 313 The Phillips Collection, Washington 168, 358 Prillot, Metz 314 Radio Times Hulton Picture Library 177 Musée des Beaux-Arts, Rouen 218 Service de Documentation Photographique de la Réunion des Musées Nationaux 58, 68, 73, 87, 88, 302, 338, 343, 365 Statens Museum for Kunst, Copenhagen 255 Strack, Hamburg 353 Henri Tabah, Paris 311 Thames & Hudson Archives *Figs. 1, 2, 3, 4, 11, 13, 16, 24, 32* Pls 11, 43, 45, 46, 47, 59, 60, 67, 69, 76, 77, 78, 83, 84, 89, 90, 91, 93, 95, 96, 97, 99, 100, 101, 103, 106, 106a, 112, 113, 114, 115, 116, 121, 125, 127, 128, 143, 147, 148, 149, 154, 155, 156, 158, 159, 160, 162, 164, 170, 171, 182, 184, 186, 191, 192, 193, 195, 196, 201, 202, 234, 240, 244, 246, 258, 261, 262, 271, 275, 276, 297, 300, 305, 307, 309, 312, 313, 325, 326, 327, 328, 332, 346, 354, 356, 359, 361 Arthur Tooth and Sons, London 357 Musée des Augustins, Toulouse 223 Musée des Beaux-Arts, Toulouse 226 Vaering, Oslo 299 Victoria and Albert Museum, London 342, 369 The Wallace Collection, London 120, 123 The Walters Art Gallery, Baltimore 205 Widmer, Basle 44 Wildenstein & Co., London 31, 225 Wildenstein Gallery, New York 256

# INDEX

*Italicized numbers refer to black and white plates, roman numbers to colour plates, and figure numbers to illustrations in the text.*